Civil Litigation

THIRD EDITION

Laurence M. Olivo

Mary Ann Kelly

2014
Emond Montgomery Publications
Toronto, Canada

Emond Montgomery Publications Limited
60 Shaftesbury Avenue
Toronto ON M4T 1A3
http://www.emp.ca/highered

Printed in Canada.

We acknowledge the financial support of the Government of Canada through the Canada Book Fund for our publishing activities.

The events and characters depicted in this book are fictitious. Any similarity to actual persons, living or dead, is purely coincidental.

Publisher, higher education: Mike Thompson
Senior developmental editor: Sarah Gleadow
Director, editorial and production: Jim Lyons
Copy editor: Cindy Fujimoto
Production editor: Andrew Gordon
Proofreader: David Handelsman
Indexer: Paula Pike
Cover and text designer: Tara Wells
Cover image: wickedberlin / iStockphoto.com

Library and Archives Canada Cataloguing in Publication

Olivo, Laurence M., 1946-, author
    Civil litigation / Laurence Olivo and Mary Ann Kelly.—Third edition.

Includes index.
ISBN 978-1-55239-557-8 (pbk.)

    1. Civil procedure—Ontario—Textbooks. 2. Actions and defenses—Ontario—Textbooks. 3. Civil procedure—Ontario—Forms. 4. Actions and defenses—Ontario—Forms. I. Kelly, Mary Ann, 1948-, author II. Title.

KEO1119.O45 2014   347.713'05   C2013-906164-9
KF8840.ZB3O45 2014

Contents

PART I

AN OVERVIEW OF THE CIVIL LITIGATION PROCESS

PART II

FROM COMMENCEMENT OF PROCEEDINGS TO CLOSE OF PROCEEDINGS

PART III

FROM DISCOVERY TO TRIAL

List of Figures

Preface to the First Edition

In the past, when we taught civil litigation subjects to students in law clerk programs, we both noticed that students were able to master individual rules of procedure but were often unable to see how these rules fit into the process of getting a case to trial. In short, students were unable to see the forest for the trees. To solve this problem, members of faculty contributed to a collection of materials that supplemented the commercially published annual edition of the *Rules of Civil Procedure*. When the supplemental materials grew to the size and weight of the Toronto telephone book, but with much less coherence, we realized that we had better do something.

This book is our solution. Using a case study, which involves the misadventures of the fictional Abigail Boar, you will follow the process of a typical civil action, looking at both the forest and the trees, and using exercises at the back of each chapter to practise analytic and drafting skills. We hope that you will gain an understanding of the process as a whole, as well as a grasp of specific procedures.

This book would probably not have appeared without our students' helpful comments on what was lacking in our teaching materials and the encouragement of our colleagues in the School of Legal and Public Administration and the School of Office Administration at Seneca College. The suggestions of students and colleagues, both solicited and otherwise, were welcome even if the proffered advice was not always followed. Any errors or omissions can be sent to the attention of the publisher.

The text reflects the law generally and the *Rules of Civil Procedure* in particular as of February 2003. The Rules Committee of the Superior Court is not inactive. Changes to the rules are to be expected from time to time, and care must be taken to see that your knowledge remains current. This text is designed to be used in conjunction with one of the commercially published annual versions of the *Rules of Civil Procedure*, and you should always refer to the text of the rules when examining a particular procedure or step in the process.

Laurence Olivo
Mary Ann Kelly
Toronto, February 2003

Preface to the Second Edition

Law texts are not like fine wines. Fine wines improve with age. Law books become obsolete and are soon fit only to be used as doorstops. Thus it is with the first edition of *Civil Litigation*. While the format and approach to the subject developed in the first edition continues to meet the test of time, the content is now in need of revision and a new edition is necessary.

The Rules Committee of the Superior Court has continued to be active in refining and revising the rules of procedure and the associated forms, and this edition keeps pace with those changes. In this connection, as we were going to press in early 2009, the government announced that it would proceed with a number of reforms to the civil court system, to take effect in January 2010. Because many of these changes will not come into effect until a year after publication, we have created new sections in relevant chapters, noting what the changes are generally, and what their intended effect is, when that can be discerned. The devil is, as usual, in the details, and the details are in O. Reg. 438/08 (amendments to the *Rules of Civil Procedure*) and in O. Reg. 439/09 (increase of the Small Claims Court monetary jurisdiction from $10,000 to $25,000 as of January 1, 2010).

These new amendments to the superior court rules introduce a new concept, the principle of proportionality, in which the complexity and cost of proceedings must be in proportion to the value to the client. This has led to a more complex simplified procedure, the introduction of a form of case management to the discovery process, new controls and requirements for pretrials, details on when and how case management is to be used, new restrictions on the use of expert reports, and, generally, the introduction of more conferencing, timetabling, and compulsory cooperating. Good lawyers have been doing most of this already; whether those who did not will be made to "behave" by the rule changes remains to be seen. One suspects that the process has simply been made more complicated, and the extra complexities will make things no quicker or cheaper for litigants. Time will tell us whether we have turned a corner in the struggle with cost and delay, or whether we have been tinkering and making matters worse.

One of the more noticeable changes we made in this edition, as a result of changes to the law in Ontario, was the decision to omit Chapter 25, "Motor Vehicle Insurance Claims in Ontario." There were several reasons for this. First, in a text designed for basic litigation courses in a law clerk diploma program, this topic seemed too broad, complex, and specialized for basic litigation courses. It really deserves a book of its own. Second, the establishment of licensing regulations for paralegals has, in our view, taken this practice area away from law clerks (the majority of our readers) and given it over to paralegals—law clerks will no longer have the right of audience before adjudicative bodies of the Financial Services Commission of Ontario. In the circumstances, it seemed sensible to delete a chapter that was of marginal use.

And, of course, we listened to the feedback we received from instructors and our students, and made corrections and provided clarification where necessary.

Laurence M. Olivo
Mary Ann Kelly
Toronto, January 2009

Preface to the Third Edition

Just as we were finishing the second edition of *Civil Litigation*, the Ontario government announced a series of reforms to the civil justice system in the province, based on recommendations in the *Civil Justice Reform Project* (sometimes referred to as the Osborne Report, named after its principal author, former Superior Court Justice Coulter Osborne, QC).

While the principal recommendations were clear enough, aimed at reducing cost and delay in the civil court system, it was less clear how they would be implemented or what the impact of those changes would be, because changes to the *Rules of Civil Procedure* were not to come into force until January 1, 2010. In the end, we highlighted proposed changes as they appeared to affect topics throughout the text, to alert our readers to what was coming.

Since that time, what was coming has arrived. Not all of the recommendations were implemented, but many were, and by 2013, the revised system was in place. A number of important and significant changes were made to the *Rules of Civil Procedure* that resulted in changes in the way a civil court action is conducted. In addition to those changes, new practice directions were introduced and old ones were amended, and court forms were changed. The profession responded as well—for example, by tackling growing problems in keeping e-discovery under control. Whether all these changes would reduce cost and delay in civil matters is far from clear, but the civil process that we described in 2009 was sufficiently transformed so that a new edition was required to accurately analyze and explain how the process now works.

In this book, where a reference also includes a URL for web access to information, we have included the URL as of the date of publication. But URLs change with some frequency, so if a URL doesn't work, try searching for the site name or reference given to find the current website.

The reader will find discussion of the impact of the proportionality rule that governs proceedings generally, and discovery in particular. There have been great changes in how discovery is conducted, largely driven by technological changes that affect how information is handled. Changes in motion procedure, particularly in Toronto, are described. Mandatory mediation has undergone changes, and the latest version of case management bears little resemblance to the original version. Summary judgment has been made much more accessible, greatly assisted by decisions of the Supreme Court of Canada that came out in early 2014. There have been a variety of minor changes to the process of listing for trial, and expanded use of pretrial conferences, with greater powers vested in judges presiding at pretrial to give directions with respect to a case going to trial. The use of expert evidence is subject to new procedures, and simplified procedure has been modified, hopefully making it more efficient and more useful.

The 2010 changes described here have indeed had a major impact on the civil process. It is our hope that we have been successful in accurately describing and analyzing them.

Laurence M. Olivo
Mary Ann Kelly
Toronto, March 2014

About the Authors

Laurence M. Olivo

Laurence M. Olivo, BA, MA, JD is a lawyer and professor in the Faculty of Business, Seneca College, with over 30 years' experience in post-secondary teaching in a variety of college programs. His legal practice experience includes civil litigation and family law, as well as policy development work with the Ontario Ministry of the Attorney General. He is the author of more than 15 texts in various areas of law and has developed specialized online courses for use by post-secondary institutions. In the absence of any mandatory retirement requirements, he intends to keep on doing all this for the foreseeable future.

Mary Ann Kelly

Mary Ann Kelly retired after having taught for 14 years in Seneca College's School of Legal and Public Administration in Toronto. She is a lawyer and a member in good standing of the Law Society of Upper Canada, holding a BA from the University of Toronto and a JD from Osgoode Hall Law School. She has also studied international law at The Hague Academy at the International Court of Justice in the Netherlands.

Mary Ann practised law as a partner in a small law firm before moving to the Ontario Ministry of the Attorney General, where she acted as Reciprocity Counsel from 1990 to 1997. In that role she managed the ministry's obligations under the *Hague Convention on the Civil Aspects of International Child Abduction* and the *Reciprocity Act*. From 1997 to 2000 Mary Ann acted as a legal policy consultant to the federal Department of Justice, working on drafting and implementing policy and legislation. She has also taught in the faculties of Business and Continuing Education at Ryerson University.

PART I

An Overview of the Civil Litigation Process

CHAPTER 1 Overview of a Civil Lawsuit

Overview of a Civil Lawsuit

1

Introduction

This chapter presents the "big picture" of how a civil proceeding unfolds. The balance of the book fills in the details. In order to help you see both the big picture and later the details, we start by setting out a fact situation involving Abigail Boar and her various difficulties. Using Abigail's story, we demonstrate how a civil case progresses from the initial stage of hiring a lawyer to the final stage of appealing a trial judgment.

Fact Situation: The Sad Tale of Abigail Boar

Introduction

It is now time to introduce you to the unfortunate Abigail Boar, who set out to buy a sports car and ended up with serious injuries resulting from the apparent negligence of others involved in what lawyers usually refer to as a "slip and fall case." We will follow Abigail's case from the time Abigail consults a lawyer, through the various pretrial stages, to trial in the Ontario Superior Court.[1] As we proceed, we will discuss the steps that are taken, including the preparation of many of the documents that are required in a civil action. The facts set out here present a broad outline of what occurred. As we proceed we will add more detail where it is required.

Facts

Abigail Boar is a 28-year-old securities analyst employed by Megadoon Investments Ltd. She is earning more money than she ever thought she would and decides the time has come to do some conspicuous consuming, so she buys her first car. After talking to friends, she decides that the right kind of car for her is a two-seater sports coupe. On September 14, year 0, she decides to go after dinner to look at the hot new line of sports coupes manufactured by the Skunk Motorcar Company Ltd., which are being sold at Rattle Motors Ltd. After work, she stops at Barbeerian's, a trendy bar frequented by financial types, where she has a quick dinner and two glasses of wine. She then walks over to Rattle Motors Ltd. at 1240 Bay Street, Toronto.

At about 6 p.m., Fred Flogem, a salesperson employed by Rattle Motors Ltd., notices that there is some oil on the floor next to the Super Coupe model. He peers underneath the car and discovers oil leaking from underneath the engine. Because this is hardly good advertising for a new car, Fred does not want to draw customers' attention to the problem by cleaning up the mess immediately. Instead, he shuts off two of the four spotlights that illuminate the Super Coupe, hoping that no one looking at the car will notice the mess on the floor. Fred intends to clean up the mess when there are no customers in the showroom, or when the showroom closes for the day.

Abigail walks in the front door of the showroom at about 7:30 p.m. There are several sports cars on display. On seeing her come in, two salespersons get up from their desks and make a beeline for Abigail. Linda Lucre gets there first, so the second salesperson, Fred Flogem, sits down again and busies himself with some paperwork. Abigail tells Linda what she is looking for, and Linda shows her the floor models. Abigail looks at one car and then walks over, with Linda behind her, to look at another. The second car is in an area of the showroom where two of the four spotlights meant to illuminate the car are off so that the side of the car nearest to the wall is in relative darkness. As Abigail walks around to the darker side of the car, she steps into some oil, slips, loses her balance, and falls, striking the left side of her head against the side of the car. Abigail is knocked unconscious. Her body twists as she falls heavily to the floor, with the result that she fractures her right wrist and several bones in her right arm.

Linda goes to her office and phones for an ambulance. Abigail is taken to Toronto Hospital, where she is treated. The broken bones in her wrist and right arm are set in a cast. Because of the head injury, Abigail remains for neurological observation and after four days, she is sent home, where she remains for six weeks until the cast is taken off her arm. After that, she goes to physiotherapy once a week for 10 weeks.

After her release from the hospital, Abigail had no memory of slipping and falling. She continues to have chronic lower back pain and headaches. She is unable to walk long distances or sit at her desk at work for prolonged periods. Abigail, who is right-handed, has limited mobility in her right arm and is unable to work at her computer for more than 10 minutes at a time without experiencing pain.

She returns to work on March 1, year 1 for a month. However, because of chronic pain and her difficulty using a computer, which is essential for her job, she is unable to continue working so she then goes on long-term disability.

Before her accident, Abigail was an avid tennis player and a good amateur violinist. After her accident, she is unable to enjoy these activities and is far less active, both physically and socially, than she had been. She used to be a lively individual: cheerful, with a good sense of humour. She has, since the fall, become quieter and more withdrawn and has difficulty sleeping. Her family physician has begun treating her for depression, prescribing an antidepressant and painkillers.

At the time of the accident, Abigail was earning $80,000 gross per year. Her employer does not have a short-term sick leave plan but does have a long-term disability plan that pays Abigail 60 percent of basic monthly earnings after four months' absence from work resulting from illness or injury.

Abigail has consulted I.M. Just, a lawyer, and intends to sue Rattle Motors Ltd. and Fred Flogem because she believes they are responsible for the injuries she sustained.

An Overview of the Civil Litigation Process

Now that you have met Abigail and read about her situation, we can consider some preliminary matters and turn to a general description of what happens after she decides to sue.

What Is Civil Litigation?

By consulting and retaining a lawyer, Abigail is about to involve herself in what is called civil litigation. Civil litigation describes the court process that is used to resolve disputes and conflicts where one person claims that the acts of another have caused harm. If the harm is of a type that the law recognizes, then the party who caused the harm will be ordered by the court to compensate the party who was harmed, usually by paying money to the injured party. The general goal of civil litigation is to compensate a person for his or her injuries or losses—to restore a person to the position that he or she was in prior to harm being done—to the extent that the payment of money damages can accomplish this.

Civil litigation cases can take various forms. Debt collection cases, personal injury claims, wrongful dismissal, shareholder disputes, and disputes over property use or ownership are all examples of civil litigation cases. These disputes usually involve private rights and obligations, as opposed to public ones, although there may be public interest and public policy aspects to civil cases. In this context, the government can be a party to a civil litigation case. Consider, for example, a recent case in which several parents of autistic children sued the Ontario Government for failure to pay for a specific and expensive educational program. On the surface this was a private dispute where one party said the other was legally obliged to compensate it, but the outcome would also determine health and education funding obligations of the Crown, generally.

People are often more familiar with criminal litigation than they are with civil litigation. They often assume that what goes on in one process goes on in the other, but in fact they are very different. Criminal litigation involves the prosecution by the Crown of actions that have been legally defined as criminal and harmful to the public in general, so that the object of criminal law is to protect the public generally, rather than to protect the rights of those individuals who may have been harmed by criminal acts. While in some cases the criminal accused may be ordered to pay restitution, which is like paying civil damages, that is not the primary purpose of the criminal law. The goal of criminal law is to punish wrongdoing and maintain public order, usually by the imposition of fines payable to the Crown (and not the person harmed) or by the imposition of terms of imprisonment.

There are also vast differences between civil and criminal procedure. In a civil case, the plaintiff is obliged to make out a case and prove each factual and legal element on the balance of probabilities. This means that if the plaintiff is successful, his or her version is, more likely than not, the correct version. If the plaintiff fails to show this, the defendant wins, and the case is dismissed. In criminal cases, the accused is presumed to be innocent, unless the Crown can prove its case beyond a reasonable doubt, a much higher standard of proof and a much greater burden for the Crown than the one a plaintiff bears in a civil case. These differences also explain some of the differences in civil and criminal procedure. For example, because a criminally accused person is presumed to be innocent, he or she can sit back and say nothing and provide no information to the court. The Crown is obliged to prove its case on its own, and is not permitted to extract information from the accused. In civil cases, both parties are obliged to make full disclosure of everything that is relevant to the issues in dispute, both helpful and harmful. So if you have some familiarity with criminal law and procedure, you may find civil litigation to be quite different, driven by quite different purposes and goals.

What Happens When Abigail Decides to Sue?

Generally, a civil proceeding can be divided into the following stages:

1. hiring of a lawyer,
2. preliminary investigations and research,
3. commencement of proceedings,
4. exchange of pleadings (statement of claim and statement of defence),
5. examinations for discovery of the parties, discovery of documents and, where relevant, other forms of discovery
6. motions to determine pretrial issues,
7. pretrial conference and trial preparation,
8. trial, and
9. appeals.

Figure 1.1 lists the principal rules in the *Rules of Civil Procedure* ("the Rules") that relate to these steps.

The Hiring of a Lawyer

Unless she is suing in Small Claims Court, where people often represent themselves or hire paralegals to do so, as a practical matter Abigail needs to hire a lawyer either to negotiate a settlement or to take her case to trial. Rattle Motors Ltd. and Fred Flogem, the likely defendants in a personal injury case, are probably covered by insurance taken out by Rattle Motors Ltd. to cover its own torts and those of its employees. If so, Rattle Motors Ltd.'s obligation is to notify the insurer immediately of a potential claim. The insurance company will then hire and direct lawyers to act for Rattle Motors Ltd. and Fred because it is the insurance company that will have to pay Abigail if the case settles or if she wins at trial. For that reason, the insurance company controls the conduct of the case and instructs the lawyers even though Rattle Motors Ltd. and Fred are the defendants. If Rattle Motors Ltd. is not insured, it must hire and instruct its own lawyer to represent it and Fred. If there is a conflict between Fred and Rattle Motors Ltd. concerning any issue in dispute, Fred must be separately represented. If not, one lawyer may act for both.

Figure 1.1 Steps in an Action

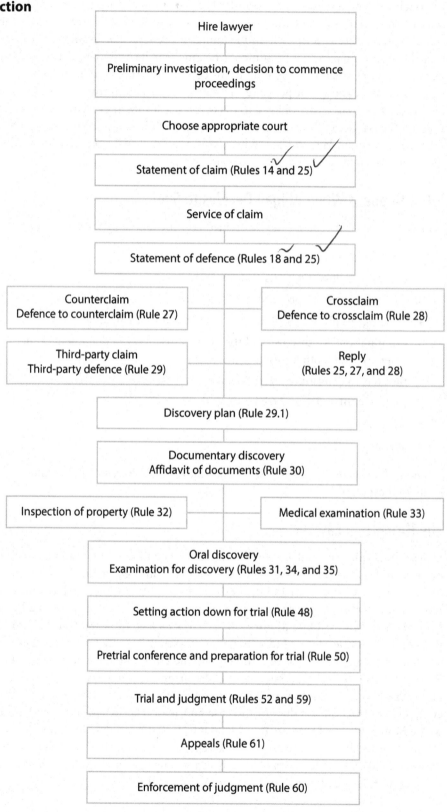

How does Abigail go about choosing a lawyer? She could seek a recommendation from friends or relatives, call the lawyer referral service at the Law Society of Upper Canada, or look in the Yellow Pages. Any lawyer can take her case, but she would be wise to choose one who practises personal injury law. Because many people are injured in circumstances that give rise to legal remedies, personal injury law is a high-volume area with many lawyers to choose from.

Once Abigail has made a choice, she should formally engage the lawyer's services by signing a retainer. A retainer is a contract between a lawyer and a client that sets out a description of the work to be done by the lawyer and the terms and conditions for the payment of **fees** and **disbursements** by the client. The lawyer may also ask Abigail to pay a deposit to be applied to future fees and disbursements. This deposit is also called a retainer.[2] Abigail and her lawyer may make other arrangements for the paying of legal fees. It is not uncommon for personal injury lawyers to take no fees or disbursements at the beginning of a case; instead, they are often paid what they are owed out of the trial judgment or settlement. A lawyer who loses a case is still entitled to be paid for services rendered. However, collecting fees from clients in these circumstances is not easy, particularly if clients do not have the resources to pay and feel that the lawyer's services have produced nothing of value. Note that a **contingency fee**, where a lawyer is paid a percentage of the judgment *only* if he or she wins the case, has been permitted in Ontario since 2003.[3] Contingency fees have long been permitted in most other Canadian provinces and in the United States.

In deciding what to charge Abigail, the lawyer may consider several factors:

- the amount of money at stake in the action,
- Abigail's ability to pay,
- the amount of time the lawyer will spend on the pretrial stage and the trial,
- the degree of complexity of the legal and/or factual issues, and
- the degree of success the lawyer is able to achieve.

Once Abigail has retained a lawyer, she will be interviewed at some length by the lawyer or the law clerk to determine the facts of the case, who the witnesses are, and who the other parties are. From this information, the lawyer has to decide whether Abigail has a good **cause of action** or not.

Preliminary Investigations and Research

Determining the Cause of Action

In order for the lawyer to decide if there is a good cause of action, the lawyer has to ask whether the facts, as related by the client, identify a legal right or issue that gives rise to a legal remedy for the client. If there is a cause of action, the lawyer must then consider whether there is sufficient evidence to prove the facts. In the end, the evidence must lead the **trier of fact** to conclude that it is more probable than not that the facts set out by the client are correct. To put it another way, facts are conclusions that can be drawn by assessing the evidence.

If there is not enough evidence to prove the facts, the lawyer may have to advise the client to not continue with the case. The facts as Abigail relates them disclose

fees
payment to lawyers for services rendered

disbursements
amounts lawyers pay on behalf of clients to third parties that lawyers can recover from clients

contingency fee
fee payable to a lawyer only if he or she wins the case for a client

cause of action
legal right to sue to obtain a legal remedy

trier of fact
judge or jury whose job is to determine the facts of the case from the evidence

that there is probably negligence on the part of Fred Flogem, for which Fred's employer, Rattle Motors Ltd., is vicariously liable and perhaps directly liable. Negligence is Abigail's cause of action.

Relationship Between Proof and Evidence

In a civil case, the burden of proof is on the plaintiff, who is obliged to prove her case on the balance of probabilities—that is, the plaintiff must show the court that it is more likely than not that her version of the case is true. The plaintiff establishes her version of the facts through the evidence of witnesses and other types of evidence. The facts, and the evidence that proves those facts, focus on two issues: who is liable or at fault and how much is to be paid to compensate the plaintiff for the damage done.

There are four main types of evidence:

1. *Testimonial evidence.* The lawyer will determine from Abigail who the likely witnesses are and will interview any witness who is willing to talk to him or her. It is unlikely that the defendants, Fred and Rattle Motors Ltd., would be willing to talk to Abigail's lawyer, and they certainly would be advised by their lawyer not to. If the lawyer can discover the identity of any bystanders who saw the accident, the lawyer will want to interview them. Abigail's doctors will be interviewed about the injuries she sustained. Any witness interviewed should be asked to sign a statement setting out what they said in the interview. This statement can be used by the lawyer as a reference and in notes used to refresh the memory of a witness at trial. If a witness says that he or she saw nothing, a signed statement to that effect will prevent the witness from surfacing later with damaging information.

2. *Documentary and demonstrative evidence.* Any document, diagram, photograph, video, or audio recording may contain relevant evidence. In Abigail's case, there may be accident reports written by Fred or Linda, medical emergency admission reports, and reports and emails from Abigail's physician, the rehabilitation staff, and Abigail's employer concerning her return to work. Tweets and entries from Abigail's Facebook page may also contain relevant information about the nature and extent of her injuries. Demonstrative evidence, such as a diagram of the car showroom, photographs of the showroom taken with the floodlights around the car turned on and off, and photographs of Abigail in her cast and showing her injuries can also be included. All of these documents are admissible in evidence once the person who made the record proves their authenticity. In some cases, such as a doctor's report or other expert reports, a document may be admissible without having its maker give oral evidence.

3. *Physical evidence.* This evidence consists of physical objects, such as the car's leaking engine or oil pan.

4. *Expert evidence.* This evidence usually consists of the reports and testimony of experts asked to comment on some aspect of the case where specialized knowledge and interpretation of evidence is required. Normally, a witness is

restricted to evidence about what they actually observed. An expert can go beyond that and give opinions and offer speculation. The report of a lighting engineer on the lights in the showroom might constitute expert evidence.

Close of the Preliminary Investigation: Consideration of Whether and How to Proceed

At this point, Abigail has retained I.M. Just as her lawyer and he has found out the basic facts and made some preliminary investigations from which he can give Abigail advice on how to proceed. Abigail finds out that if she is successful in her action, she will obtain a judgment in her favour in which she will receive monetary compensation called **damages**. As a successful litigant, Abigail will also recover some of her legal fees and disbursements from the defendants because a judgment usually gives a successful litigant an order for payment of some legal costs (called an "award of costs"). However, if Abigail loses, she will not recover any money for her injuries, and she will have to pay some of the legal costs incurred by the successful defendant. She will also have to pay her own legal fees and disbursements in full. (In some cases, a lawyer might accept a case on a contingency-fee basis. *If the plaintiff wins, the lawyer is paid a percentage of the judgment; if the plaintiff loses, the lawyer is paid nothing.*)

It is important that Abigail consider her options carefully. The outcome of her case may be uncertain for a variety of reasons. The legal issues involved may not be clearly resolved. There may be conflicting decisions on the point in issue. More usually, the problem lies with the facts: Is there convincing evidence that will prove the facts of Abigail's case? If, on the lawyer's advice, Abigail thinks she has a good case, she may elect to start a legal proceeding to recover the remedy she seeks.

The Concern with Cost and Delay

An additional concern for Abigail is how much this might cost her, and how long it will take to bring the case to a conclusion. Over the past 20 years, there has been increasing concern that civil litigation in the Superior Court has become slow and expensive. Civil case management (discussed in Chapter 21) and simplified procedure (discussed in Chapter 23) are two attempts to control cost and delay that have not been entirely successful. The Civil Justice Reform Project made further recommendations, some of which were adopted by the Civil Rules Committee and that took effect on January 1, 2010.[4] It will be interesting to see whether these changes are any more effective than earlier reforms in reducing cost and delay, and making the courts more accessible to the public. So far, there is little sign of this.

The civil court rules now contain a general **principle of proportionality** to guide lawyers and the courts in applying the Rules, generally. The time and expense devoted to any step in a proceeding, and to the proceeding generally, now have to reflect what is at stake for the parties. Cases that are legally and factually straightforward and of lower value should not take as long or cost as much as large, complex cases or cases where much is at stake. While this has always been a rule of thumb, the principle of proportionality is now incorporated in the Rules (Rule 1.04(1.1)). For

damages
compensation awarded by a court for harm done

principle of proportionality
requires that the time spent on and the expense of a lawsuit be in proportion to the value of the case that is at stake for the parties

Abigail, this would mean that if her case were worth $250,000 rather than $50,000, her lawyer might hold more extensive and lengthy discoveries and bring motions that he otherwise might not bring.

Commencement of Proceedings

Court Jurisdiction

As a plaintiff in a civil proceeding, Abigail must choose between two possible courts: the Small Claims Court and the Ontario Superior Court of Justice. In order to decide which court Abigail should sue in, it is necessary to understand the basis for a court's jurisdiction—its power to hear a case and grant remedies.

There are three types of jurisdiction:

1. *Jurisdiction over the subject matter of the lawsuit.* Does the court have the power to hear this type of case and provide the remedies Abigail seeks? For example, if the court has jurisdiction over criminal law matters only, it does not have jurisdiction to hear Abigail's lawsuit. Similarly, if Abigail were seeking an injunction as a remedy, she could not do so in Small Claims Court because this court has no authority to grant this remedy. In Ontario, the Superior Court of Justice can hear civil cases dealing with any subject other than a subject over which Canada's Federal Court has exclusive jurisdiction or a subject that has been allocated by statute to a particular court. It can also grant any civil remedy known to law: injunctions, declarations of rights, orders for the return of property, and monetary damages. The Small Claims Court, by contrast, is restricted to making orders for the return of personal property and the payment of money.

2. *Jurisdiction over the monetary amount claimed in the lawsuit.* The issue here is whether a court has the power to order payment of the amount of money being claimed. The Small Claims Court's monetary jurisdiction as of 2010 is $25,000. This means that the court may grant a judgment for the payment of money for any amount up to and including $25,000 exclusive of interest and costs. However, it has no authority to give judgment for more than that amount. The Superior Court, on the other hand, has an unlimited monetary jurisdiction. It can grant judgment for any amount of money, including an amount within the jurisdiction of the Small Claims Court.[5] Abigail's injuries are serious, so she will choose the Superior Court because her damages are likely to greatly exceed $25,000. The lawsuit will be more expensive to conduct than it would be in Small Claims Court, where proceedings are simpler and less formal.

3. *Territorial jurisdiction.* Does the court have the power to hear a case where the events that the case is based on took place outside its territorial jurisdiction or the parties' residence is outside its geographical jurisdiction? In general, courts in Ontario have territorial jurisdiction over cases where the event giving rise to the lawsuit took place in Ontario, the parties are in Ontario, or the parties agreed to give Ontario jurisdiction as a term of a

Figure 1.2   Ontario Court System Structure

Supreme Court of Canada

Ontario Court of Appeal

The highest court in Ontario; it hears appeals from the lower courts of the province.

Ontario Superior Court of Justice

- The Divisional Court
- The Small Claims Court
- The Unified Family Court (UFC)

The highest level of trial court in Ontario; it deals with civil and criminal trials (with or without a jury).

Ontario Court of Justice
- Criminal law
- Family law

Administrative Tribunals

WEBLINK

The Ontario Courts website provides information about court services, jurisdiction, court locations, rules of procedure, and court forms, as well as other useful information: http://www.ontariocourts.on.ca.

contract. But questions will arise if some of the events took place in another jurisdiction or if one or more of the parties resides outside Ontario. For example, if Abigail had gone to Buffalo, New York to buy her car and had been injured there, if events leading up to the injury occurred in Buffalo, or if the defendants resided there, could Abigail or should Abigail sue in Ontario or New York? The answers to questions of this type are often complicated. As issues of private international law, they are often determined on a case-by-case basis on a test of the balance of convenience to the parties.[6]

Even within Ontario, there can be issues of territorial jurisdiction that may arise as a result of the plaintiff's choice of place to sue, also referred to as the choice of forum. Abigail, as plaintiff, has the right to commence her proceeding in the Superior Court office in any county or region in Ontario, unless a statute requires that it be commenced in a particular county or region. However, if her choice is much more inconvenient to other parties than to her, or it is impossible to get a fair trial in the chosen county, any party may apply to the court to have the case transferred to another county or region. For example, if she and the defendants were all in Toronto and she chose to start her proceeding in Thunder Bay, it is likely that the defendants would bring a motion to move the trial to Toronto on the balance of convenience. Note that her case will be tried in the county or region where it was commenced, unless the court orders otherwise.

Rules of Civil Procedure

In commencing proceedings, Abigail must use the appropriate court forms and follow the procedural rules for conducting a civil case. These rules are set out in the Ontario *Rules of Civil Procedure*. (We will refer to these henceforth as "the Rules," as lawyers do.) The rules are actually regulations made pursuant to the *Courts of Justice Act*. The power to make the Rules is vested in the Civil Rules Committee, consisting of staff from the Ministry of the Attorney General, members of the judiciary, and lawyers. Supplementing the Rules are practice directions. Rule 1.07 provides a procedure for creating practice directions. The purpose of a practice direction is to allow the senior judge in a judicial region to customize the Rules and create additional procedures to deal with problems that are specific to that region and are not covered by existing rules. For example, because of difficulties in scheduling trials in the Toronto region, there is a practice direction that requires counsel to attend trial scheduling courts, and that trials are scheduled year round. The additional procedures in this practice direction are presumably not necessary for the administration of justice in other judicial regions, where they do not apply. It is now clear that a practice direction carries the force of law and must be followed. Previously, the status and validity of practice directions were questioned because there was no clear authority for creating them, but now Rule 1.07 sets out a procedure for creating them. To bring some consistency and uniformity to practice directions, the power to authorize and approve a practice direction is vested in the Chief Justice of the Superior Court.

You should become familiar with the practice directions that operate in the judicial region where cases you work on are heard. When practice directions are created, they are posted both online (http://www.ontariocourts.ca/scj/en/notices) and in regional courthouses. They are also published in the *Ontario Reports*, the Law Society's publication of Ontario cases, which all lawyers receive. The *Ontario Annual Practice* reproduces practice directions next to the rules to which they apply. It also contains an index of published practice directions, so you can easily locate the one you are looking for. Other commercially published versions of Superior Court practice materials also contain this information.

Motions

At first glance, it seems that all you need to do is read a rule and follow it. The rules appear to be clear but, like all legal rules, they require interpretation. Because the parties are in an adversarial position, both Abigail's lawyer and the defendants' lawyers may use the Rules to attempt to gain the upper hand or assert a position that will be helpful to them. Where one party seeks to use a rule against another party that is allegedly violating the rule, there is a procedural dispute that the court must sort out at the pretrial stage. This is done when one party brings a motion. A motion is a proceeding brought within the main action to settle a procedural issue that has arisen at the pretrial stage. A judge, or in some cases a junior judicial official called a master, will hear submissions from counsel on a motion, read submitted material, and decide the issue by making an order. An order on a motion usually does not dispose of a case on its merits, although this can happen. For example, if Abigail had made a claim not recognized by the law, the defendants could bring a motion to strike out her statement of claim and dismiss her action. If the court was persuaded by the defendants that Abigail did not have a legal reason for suing, the court could strike out her statement of claim, and that would be the end of her case. But this is most unusual. Motions are discussed in more detail later in this chapter and in Chapter 9.

Actions and Applications

Abigail's lawyer is now ready to start the case or, in the language of the Rules, to "commence proceedings." In Ontario, there are two ways for a plaintiff to commence proceedings. Abigail can start an **action** by issuing a statement of claim, or she can start an **application** by issuing a notice of application. Usually a party commences an action. Applications are used when a statute or the Rules require them, or when it is unlikely that there will be any material facts in dispute and the matter turns on an interpretation of law. Otherwise, a plaintiff must proceed by way of an action. An action has a much longer and more complex pretrial procedure than an application. It is largely devoted to giving the parties the opportunity to review evidence and determine facts before trial. In an application, where there is usually little in the way of factual disputes, we have a much simpler and less time-consuming pretrial procedure. There is no need to conduct discovery or otherwise investigate the facts exhaustively. The trial is more like a hearing with no oral evidence. Each party's lawyer spends most of the hearing time on legal arguments, with the evidence introduced through the use of sworn written statements called affidavits.

The facts and issues in Abigail's case are complex and crucial to her proving negligence against the defendants. It is appropriate that her case proceed as an action rather than as an application.

action
one of the two procedures by which a civil matter is commenced in the Superior Court; the other such procedure is an application

application
one of the two procedures by which a civil matter is commenced in the Superior Court; the other such procedure is an action

Exchange of Pleadings: Statement of Claim and Statement of Defence

Statement of Claim

I.M. Just is now ready to commence proceedings by starting an action with a statement of claim. He prepares this document, which sets out

- the remedies Abigail is asking for, referred to as the "claim for relief";
- the identification of the parties in terms of their legal status—for example, Abigail and Fred are individuals, and Rattle Motors Ltd. is a corporation; and
- the facts on which Abigail relies, as well as statements of the laws that entitle her to a remedy.

With the statement of claim, he also files a form called "Information for Court Use," which provides the court with information about the causes of action and whether the case is using any special procedure. Once prepared, the documents are taken by a law clerk or office courier to the local office of the Superior Court to be issued. After the law office courier pays the prescribed fee for issuing a claim, the registrar opens a court file, assigns the case a court file number, which is placed on the document, and issues the statement of claim by sealing and signing the document on behalf of the registrar of the court. As the registrar is doing this to the original, the lawyer's clerk makes a **true copy** of the statement of claim. The lawyer's clerk does this by copying on a copy of the statement of claim the information the court clerk has put on the original. The true copy goes into the court file, and the lawyer's clerk brings the original back to the law office. The lawyer pays the prescribed fee of $181.00[7] to the court on Abigail's behalf. If Abigail's case were urgent and I.M. Just did not have time to draft a statement of claim, I.M. Just could issue a **notice of action**, and file the statement of claim later. This might happen if Abigail had not sued until the limitation period for her cause of action had almost run out. To preserve a client's rights before the limitation period expires, a lawyer can use a notice of action to start the lawsuit and "stop the clock" on the soon-to-expire limitation period.

Once the statement of claim is issued, all further filed documents must bear the appropriate **general heading** identifying the court, the court file number, and the names of the parties. The names of the parties and the status in which they are suing or being sued that appears within the general heading is referred to as the **title of proceedings**. If there are many defendants or plaintiffs, the case is generally referred to by the short title of proceedings, used on the **backsheet** of the court forms. In Abigail's case, the short form is *Boar v. Rattle Motors Ltd. et al.* Figure 1.3 shows the general heading of the statement of claim, including the title of proceedings, where Abigail sues Rattle Motors Ltd. and Fred Flogem in the Superior Court.

Figure 1.4 shows the backsheet for this statement.

true copy
copy of an original document that is like the original in every particular, including copies of alterations, signatures, and court file numbers; signatures or other handwritten parts of the original are usually inside quotation marks on the copy

notice of action
document informing defendants that they have been sued

general heading
heading on all court documents that identifies the court, the parties, and the status of the parties

title of proceedings
part of the general heading that identifies the parties and their status in a lawsuit

backsheet
part of every court document, it contains the name, LSUC number, address, and telephone and fax numbers of the lawyer who prepared the document, the short title of proceedings, the court and court file number, the fax number of the person to be served (if known), and a large space reserved for court officials to make entries on

Figure 1.3 General Heading of Statement of Claim (Form 4A)

Court file no. 01-CV-1234

ONTARIO
SUPERIOR COURT OF JUSTICE

BETWEEN:

ABIGAIL BOAR

Plaintiff

and

RATTLE MOTORS LTD. and FRED FLOGEM

Defendants

Figure 1.4   Backsheet (Form 4C)

ABIGAIL BOAR
Plaintiff(s)

and

RATTLE MOTORS LTD. ET AL.
Defendant(s)

(Short title of proceeding)

Court file no. 01-CV-1234

ONTARIO
SUPERIOR COURT OF JUSTICE

Proceeding commenced at Toronto

STATEMENT OF CLAIM

Name, address and telephone number of plaintiff's lawyer or plaintiff:

I.M. Just
LSUC #12345R

Just & Coping
Barristers and Solicitors
365 Bay Street – 8701
Toronto, Ontario, M3J 4A9

tel. 416-762-1342
fax 416-762-2300

Lawyers for the Plaintiff

Now that I.M. Just has issued the statement of claim, he must serve a copy of it on the defendants within six months from the date on which the claim was issued. Because defendants may not know they have been sued until they are served with the first document in the lawsuit against them, the Rules are strict about ensuring that they are properly served with the first or originating document.

Serving the Statement of Claim

The statement of claim, the originating document in this case, must be served personally on the defendants or must be served by a permitted alternative to personal service. Personal service means that the statement of claim must be handed directly to the defendant if the defendant is an individual. Service is effective even if the defendant refuses to take the document, tears it up, or throws it away. Therefore, a process server can simply hand a copy of the document to Fred. But what about serving Rattle Motors Ltd.? There are special rules for serving individuals on behalf of a corporation. Here, a process server can serve the corporate defendant by handing a copy of Abigail's statement of claim to the manager of Rattle Motors Ltd., or to a director or officer.

It is also possible to use one of the three alternatives to personal service to serve an originating document.

1. If I.M. Just knows that Rattle Motors Ltd. and Fred have lawyers acting for them in this lawsuit, he can serve the lawyers' office. This is valid service, provided that the lawyers sign a document stating that they accept service on behalf of the defendants. To do that, the lawyers should have instructions from the clients to accept service on their behalf.

2. I.M. Just can send a copy of the claim to the defendants' last known addresses by ordinary mail with an acknowledgment of receipt form, prescribed under the *Rules of Civil Procedure*. Service is valid as of the date of service, if the form is returned by the recipient. But if the recipient does not return it, he or she will have to be served by another means.

3. If he has first attempted personal service, I.M. Just can deliver the statement of claim in an envelope to the defendant's residence and leave it with an apparently adult person who appears to be a member of the household. He can then mail a copy of the claim to the defendant the next day. This mode of service applies only when serving an individual, such as Fred Flogem.

Substituted Service

All of the methods of service that we have discussed so far assume that I.M. Just knows or can find out the defendants' last known addresses and that the defendants are actually there. But what if Fred has moved and no longer works at Rattle Motors Ltd.? Or what if he is evading service? I.M. Just may have tried personal service and the alternatives to personal service and failed to serve him. If I.M. Just does not know exactly where Fred is, the other modes of service will be ineffective. In these situations, plaintiffs can ask the court to permit them to use substituted service. I.M.

Just must suggest a method of service that satisfies the court that there is a reasonable probability that Abigail's statement of claim will come to Fred's attention. Depending on what seems likely to be most effective, the court may order service by registered mail, or service on a close relative or friend with whom the defendant appears to be in touch, or service by an announcement in the newspaper. Whatever method is ordered by the court, once I.M. Just does what the order says, Fred is presumed to be served, even if he did not actually receive a copy of the statement of claim. Abigail can continue with her lawsuit. If substituted service will not be effective, a court may order that service be dispensed with altogether, although this is a rare occurrence.

Other Forms of Service

There are special rules for personally serving corporations and other legal entities, such as estate executors, trustees, mentally incompetent persons, and children. There is another set of rules for serving a party who does not reside or carry on business in Ontario. There are often special procedural rules that must be followed when serving someone who lives in a foreign country. Those who reside outside Ontario are given more time to respond to a lawsuit.

Once the originating document is served, the rules for service are relaxed, as those parties with an interest in the lawsuit are now presumed to know about it and about their obligations to respond. Subsequent documents may be served in a variety of ways:

- by mailing a copy to the opposite party's lawyer's office (this document is deemed to be served on the fifth day after it is mailed);
- by physically delivering a copy to the lawyer's office and leaving it with an employee, usually a receptionist;
- by depositing a copy at a document exchange of which the lawyer is a member if the copy is date-stamped as received by the document exchange (this document is deemed to be served on the day after the document exchange receives it);
- by faxing a copy to the lawyer's office, including a cover sheet setting out information that the document is being served by fax and showing who served it (some documents may not be served this way);
- by sending a copy to the lawyer's office by courier (this document is deemed to be served two days later); and
- by emailing a document to the lawyer's office, provided that the sender indicates in the email message who he or she is and provided that the lawyer served in this way emails back an acceptance of the document served (this document is deemed to be served on the day following the day the message is sent).

Proof of Service

Someone who is served with a document, whether originating or not and whatever the mode of service, may deny that he or she was served. If so, that person claims to have no notice of the lawsuit. This can be problematic. A defendant who does not respond to a claim will find that the plaintiff may still proceed in that defendant's absence.

A defendant who claims that he or she was not served, and finds that he or she has been sued or that a judgment has been obtained, may move to set aside the proceedings or set aside the judgment. If the defendant is successful, the plaintiff may have to start all over from the beginning with added expense and delay. It is therefore important that I.M. Just is careful to ensure that he serves the defendants and can prove it. This is particularly important for originating documents, such as a statement of claim, which give notice to the defendant that he or she has been sued. It is less crucial with subsequent documents because a misadventure of service does not mean the action has to be restarted.

Proof usually consists of an affidavit of service, in which the person who served the document swears that he or she did so and describes the method of service, the date, and other details. The rules permit the affidavit of service to be written right on the backsheet of the originating or subsequent document. Where a lawyer accepts service, his or her endorsement is proof of service. Where service is through a document exchange, the document exchange's date stamp is sufficient evidence to prove service. No additional affidavit is required.

Statement of Defence

Now that I.M. Just has served Fred and Rattle Motors Ltd. with Abigail's statement of claim by personally serving the defendants or by using an alternative to personal service, the defendants must respond to the statement of claim by serving and filing a statement of defence. If they are served in Ontario, they have 20 days to serve and file a statement of defence. If they are served elsewhere in Canada or in the continental United States, they have 40 days. If they are served anywhere else on the planet, they have 60 days to serve and file a defence. If time is running out before they have finished preparing a defence, they may file a notice of intent to defend. This extends the time for filing the statement of defence for a further 10 days.

Generally, plaintiffs in the same proceeding do not have conflicts of interest and are represented by the same lawyers. A plaintiff cannot be forced to have others join him or her as plaintiff. One lawyer may also represent multiple defendants, provided that their defences do not conflict. For example, if one defendant says the plaintiff's injuries were caused by the acts of the other defendant, there is a clear conflict if the other defendant denies liability. Fred and the manager of Rattle Motors Ltd. will have to decide whether one lawyer can represent both of them. In this case, Rattle Motors Ltd. will be vicariously liable for the acts of its employee even if it did not itself commit separate acts of negligence. In cases like this, where both the employer and employee are sued, they are usually represented by one lawyer because it is likely that the employer or its insurer will end up paying any damages. If a conflict develops between the defendants, however, a lawyer is obliged to tell both defendants that he or she can no longer act for either of them and to help arrange for separate representation.

Let us assume that one lawyer represents both defendants. This lawyer reviews Abigail's claim, which sets out a concise statement of the facts but not the evidence by which these facts are to be proven. The claim should also identify the cause of action and set out the legal principles that Abigail relies on. Finally, the claim should set out the remedies sought. After reviewing this document the lawyer may advise one of three possible responses to the claim:

1. *Do nothing.* In this case, Abigail will obtain a default judgment, after noting that the defendants have defaulted on their defence.

2. *Bring a motion to dismiss on the ground that the claim discloses no known cause of action.* This type of motion is rare and unlikely in our case because Abigail's claim is not unusual.

3. *Serve and file a statement of defence.* In this statement, a lawyer sets out defences that, if proved, will result in Abigail's claim being dismissed. The defendants must admit those paragraphs in Abigail's claim with which they agree. They must then deny those paragraphs that contain statements with which they disagree. Then, if applicable, they must identify those paragraphs in the claim about which they have no knowledge. They must also set out their own version of the facts and the law they rely on. This last requirement is sometimes referred to as an affirmative defence because it consists of more than denials of the plaintiff's claim. The paragraphs in Abigail's claim that the defendants admit are deemed to be proved and need not be proved at trial. This is one of the ways in which the pleadings serve to narrow the issues before trial.

After the statement of defence has been served on Abigail's lawyer and filed in court, I.M. Just reviews it. If he finds that the statement of defence has raised an issue or facts related to that issue that were not dealt with in the statement of claim, Abigail may serve and file a reply to the statement of defence. For example, if the defence states that Abigail showed up at the showroom in an intoxicated state, the defendants may argue that there was contributory negligence on Abigail's part. Abigail may need to serve and file a reply denying that she was intoxicated if those facts and issues were not covered in the statement of claim. If the plaintiff simply wishes to deny the defendant's defence generally, there is no need to serve and file a formal reply.

Other Pleadings

In some cases, there are other types of legal issues that may result in other pleadings. Suppose Abigail sues Fred and Rattle Motors Ltd. but not Skunk Motorcar Company Ltd., the manufacturer of the Super Coupe. If the two defendants think that it was not their negligence but the negligent manufacturing of the Super Coupe that caused Abigail's damages, they may issue a third-party notice to add Skunk Motorcar

Company Ltd. to the proceedings. This is a notice to the manufacturer that says that the defendants hold Skunk Motorcar Company Ltd. wholly or partly responsible for Abigail's damages, so that if they are found liable, they will argue to have that liability transferred to the manufacturer, which they are adding as a third party. They must send Skunk Motorcar Company Ltd. all the pleadings to date, and Skunk Motorcar Company Ltd. may serve and file a defence against the claim made by the defendants against it. Skunk Motorcar Company Ltd. is also entitled to raise any defence against the plaintiff's claim in the main action that the other defendants did not raise but could have raised. Thereafter, Skunk Motorcar Company Ltd. is treated as a defendant in the main proceeding, and the third-party issues are part of the trial of the main action, although in some cases they may be tried separately. It is also possible for a third party to deny liability and claim that the fault, if any, is that of a fourth party. This would result in the issuing of a fourth-party notice with the fourth party having the same rights vis-à-vis other parties as the third party.

If one defendant has a claim against the other defendant that is related to events or transactions in the main action, the defendant with the claim should file a cross-claim against the other defendant. In a case like Abigail's, this is most likely to occur with respect to a claim for contribution by one defendant against the other under the *Negligence Act*. That Act permits one defendant to have the degree of liability between the defendants assessed to determine how much each should pay, and it allows a defendant that settles the action to claim financial contributions from other defendants. In our case, Fred may wish to argue that if the defendants are liable to Abigail, Rattle Motors Ltd. is 90 percent responsible for Abigail's injuries. If Fred seeks to pin most of the responsibility on Rattle Motors Ltd., he needs to do it by crossclaim against Rattle Motors Ltd. The recipient of a crossclaim may counterclaim against the crossclaimant or serve and file a defence to the crossclaim. A crossclaim is not dependent on the main action but is usually tried with it.

If either defendant can argue that Abigail acted in some way to cause them a legally recognized injury (unlikely in this case), the defendant can file a counterclaim with the statement of defence. Abigail would then have to respond with her own defence to counterclaim.

Once a reply has been made to every defence filed, or the time for replying has expired, the pleading stage is complete. Facts that are admitted do not have to be proved at trial. Facts that are not admitted must be proved. For example, if Rattle Motors Ltd. and Fred admit that Abigail sustained the injuries and suffered the damages she claims but deny that the damages resulted from their negligence, damages are admitted and need not be proven at trial. However, Abigail will still have to prove negligence because liability is not admitted. Both parties will have to advance evidence to prove facts on the issue of negligence.

Because a party can only introduce evidence relevant to the facts as pleaded, evidence relating to facts that were not pleaded but should have been pleaded cannot be admitted. This happens rarely, but when it does happen it can be fatal to the party who forgot to plead a necessary fact to support his or her case. Sometimes the party can ask the judge to let the party amend the pleadings, but the other party will object, and the judge may decide that it is too late to permit amendments and re-open the pretrial stage for discovery on these "new" facts if the case is already at trial. This is one of the reasons it is necessary to read statements of claim and defence carefully to ensure that the pleadings fit the theory of your case.

A Variation: Mandatory Mediation

If Abigail brings her case in Toronto, Ottawa, or the County of Essex (Windsor), unless a court orders otherwise, in most cases the parties are required under Rule 24.1 to participate in mandatory mediation in order to attempt a settlement. The first mediation session must be held within 180 days of the filing of the first defence. The purpose is to have the parties focus on trying to settle their case at a relatively early stage in the proceedings. Mandatory mediation is discussed in Chapter 22.

Examinations for Discovery of Parties and Discovery of Documents

The pleadings should set out the case from each party's point of view. You should now know the basic facts in dispute, the legal issues, the case your law firm has to prove, and the case it has to meet. The pleadings are a concise statement of material facts—a lot of the details are missing. For this reason each party is entitled to have discovery of the other party's case to obtain more information about the supporting evidence and details. There are a number of different types of discovery available, including medical examinations and inspections of places or property. For example, with regard to Abigail's neurological problems, Fred and Rattle Motors Ltd. may request that she submit to a medical or psychological examination by a medical professional of their choice. The evidence from that examination can be received in the form of the doctor's **viva voce evidence** or the doctor's report. Abigail, on the other hand, may wish to have a lighting expert and an expert on flooring examine Rattle Motors Ltd.'s showroom. Discovery in the form of inspection of property is available to her because she does not have possession of the property or a right to enter it for the purposes of inspecting it. These types of discovery are used only in actions where they are helpful. The main types of discovery used in almost every civil case are discovery of documents and oral examination for discovery.

viva voce **evidence**
oral evidence

Discovery of Documents

The rules require that all parties meet and confer at the earliest opportunity to discuss the nature and extent of discovery. They are expected to consider and apply the concept of proportionality to the discovery process as a control on the process becoming more complicated and expensive than is warranted by the nature of the case and what is at stake for the parties. I.M. Just and the defendants' lawyer are expected to draw up a written discovery plan dealing with the range of discovery and the steps the parties are to take in order to complete the process and follow the expected schedule. If the parties cannot come to an agreement on a discovery plan, the court may impose a plan on them. Following the creation of a discovery plan, each party is to prepare an affidavit of documents in which each party discloses under oath the identity and nature of every document they now have or had previously that might be relevant to the action. Documents also include information stored electronically. In recent years, issues have arisen over how extensive a search of electronic files must be to discover relevant documents. Because of the great number and possible long length of electronic files on disks and hard drives, on networks, and on the Internet, a search can be daunting, particularly given the time, money, and effort required to conduct one. Fortunately, in Abigail's case there are unlikely to be voluminous electronic records to review. Abigail, for example, must disclose all of the subsequent medical records that underlie her claim that she suffered specific serious injuries. Rattle Motors Ltd. must disclose any reports it has concerning leaking oil pans on the Super Coupe. Documents are given a broad interpretation and may include computer disks, audio and video tapes, photographs, and other media of communication. All documents that a party has or had must be listed. If the document is still in existence and obtainable, it must be produced for inspection by the other side. Usually, each side provides the other with copies of its own documents.

An exception to the disclosure rule exists with respect to documents for which a party claims legal privilege. For example, lawyer–client correspondence is routinely claimed as privileged based on lawyer–client privilege: the right to keep lawyer-client communications confidential. Similarly, documents or reports prepared specifically because of the litigation are also privileged and need not be produced. If privilege is claimed for a document, it must be listed but does not have to be produced at trial. If a party decides to waive the privilege and rely on the document for the party's own case at trial, then the privilege is lost, and the document must be disclosed. However, where a document is not privileged it must be listed in the affidavit of documents and produced.

Examination for Discovery

Once documentary discovery has taken place, the parties, following the discovery plan, usually arrange for an oral examination for discovery. Here, each party's lawyer is entitled to up to seven hours to question the other parties, under oath, about the case, the statement of claim or defence, and the documents disclosed in the discovery of documents process. Questions can be wide ranging. If a party does not know the answer to a question, he or she may be asked to undertake to provide an answer or produce a document later. On a lawyer's advice, the party either accepts or rejects the undertaking. If the undertaking is rejected, the party asking the question may bring a motion to compel the other party to re-attend at his or her own expense to answer the question, provided that the judge on the motion agrees that the question is a proper question.

These examinations are held outside court, usually in an office rented for the purpose. Abigail would be present with her lawyer to answer questions put to her by the lawyer for Rattle Motors Ltd. and Fred. Fred and a representative of Rattle Motors Ltd. may attend to observe and to advise their lawyer. Abigail may also be present when her lawyer questions the defendants in their lawyer's presence. Also present is a court reporter or stenographer to take down a record of the proceedings. This record can be used both in preparing for cross-examination of a party and for preparing a client for examination-in-chief at trial. Where a party gives different answers or tells a different story from the one given at discovery, the discovery transcript can be used to challenge the credibility of the evidence given by the party at trial. The transcript can also be used to "read in" admissions by the opposite party on issues and facts in the case, although this is more likely to be done on a "request to admit" before trial. We discuss "requests to admit" later in this chapter and in Chapter 15.

Motions

Thus far, we have been describing how a civil action proceeds. It appears to be orderly and without any procedural disputes. On occasion, we have made reference to one or the other of the parties applying to the court for an order concerning the conduct of the action. For example, if a lawyer omits an essential fact or legal issue from a statement of claim, he or she can ask the court for permission to amend the claim to add the missing information. But how do you ask the court? The answer is that you bring a motion to obtain the relief or remedy you request. Motions are generally proceedings within an action and may be brought at any time during the proceedings, including at trial. Their purpose is to settle a dispute about some procedural point that the parties are unable to resolve themselves. On a motion, the court hears argument by the parties and then issues an order that resolves the problem. Such orders rarely decide the case on the merits and bring it to an end. Instead, the parties usually do as the order directs and get on with the case. Appeals from orders made on motions are rare. The right to appeal this kind of order is restricted, and it is usually too expensive and time-consuming since the issues are often procedural and not crucial to ultimate success. Examples of procedural motions include motions to extend the time for filing pleadings, motions for particulars (details) of allegations in a statement of claim or defence, and motions to compel a party to produce documents or attend discovery. Occasionally, a motion may decide the case without a trial: A motion for default judgment will do this where a defendant has failed to file a defence. A motion to strike out a statement of claim as disclosing no cause of action may do this as well.

Motions are usually made on notice to the other party. The party who brings the motion, called "the moving party" whether plaintiff or defendant, serves "the responding party" with a notice of motion. The notice of motion tells the responding party what the moving party wants the court to do and provides a brief statement of the reasons why the moving party is entitled to the order. The notice of motion also sets out the documents or sources of information relied on. Evidence on the motion is usually given by affidavit rather than orally. The affidavit sets out the facts that entitle the moving party to the relief claimed in the notice of motion. The responding party may also file an affidavit or other documents to support its case and may bring a cross-motion if it also has related issues that it wishes to resolve. Counsel then appears before a judge or master of the Superior Court and presents the motion orally. The judge or master decides the issues raised in the motion and issues an **order**. If a motion is made at trial, it is not necessary to use formal notices of motions because the parties are already before the court. While motions are generally made on notice, some motions may be made without notice to the other side. An

order
generic term used in the *Rules of Civil Procedure* to describe commands issued by courts on motions and at trials

example is a motion for substituted service of a claim when the other party cannot be located for service.

One motion that might occur when pleadings have been exchanged is a motion for summary judgment. While a default judgment may be obtained if the defendant files no statement of defence, a summary judgment is obtained when a party argues that the other party's pleadings disclose no genuine issue requiring a trial. If the motion is successful, a judgment should be issued—to dismiss the action if a defendant brings the motion, or to grant judgment if a plaintiff brings the motion. If the issue is one of law alone, the judge may decide it. If it involves questions of credibility or facts that are in dispute, the judge is more likely to use the motion to narrow the issues, establish facts, and order a speedy trial. If, for example, the defendants bring a motion for summary judgment to dismiss Abigail's action on the basis that the limitation period for tort actions has expired, they must file affidavits as to when the accident occurred and when the action was commenced, with reference to the pleadings and perhaps discovery transcripts. On a motion for summary judgment, the facts of a case must be simple and unambiguous. There are heavy cost penalties for a party that brings a futile and unnecessary motion.

Pretrial Conference and Trial Preparation

The parties have now exchanged pleadings, discoveries have been completed, and, usually, any motions necessary to ensure compliance with the Rules have been brought, heard, and determined. The parties need no more information before trial. At this point, lawyers and their clients often assess their chances for success at trial, weighing the pros and cons of their case. Most cases get this far because there is a dispute about the facts. No lawyer will tell a client with certainty that he or she will win or lose; when facts are disputed, much will depend on the credibility of witnesses, which is hard to assess.

In this atmosphere and at this stage, either side or both sides may attempt to settle the case. If the parties reach a settlement, they file a consent to dismiss the action on the basis of the terms of the settlement. If the settlement involves payments by one side to the other, the action is not dismissed until the payment is made in order to prevent the payer from reneging on the promise. The parties may pursue informal discussions, or they may make formal written offers—the latter have some important consequences if they are rejected. Briefly, if a formal offer to settle is made, it is made in writing to the other side, and a sealed copy is filed with the court. If the other side accepts the offer on its terms and within the time during which the offer is open for acceptance, the case is over. But if the offer is rejected and the party who rejected the offer does not do as well at trial as he or she would have done had he or she accepted the offer, there are negative cost consequences.

For example, if Abigail is offered $300,000 to settle but thinks she can get $500,000 at trial, she may reject the offer. However, if she recovers only $200,000, she will receive costs only to the date the offer was made, and she will be deprived of costs thereafter. Further, the defendant is entitled to the usual costs from the date the offer was made to the date of judgment. If Abigail made an offer to Fred and Rattle Motors

Ltd. and they rejected it, and if Abigail received a judgment that was equal to or better than the offer she made, Abigail will receive costs to the date the offer was made and a higher cost award from the day the offer was made to the date of judgment. In a long and complex lawsuit, legal costs can reach a significant amount. When they realize that a large part of the judgment will be eaten up by their obligations to pay their own and part of their opponent's legal costs, litigants may think twice about continuing on with a lawsuit.

Setting the Case Down for Trial

If the case does not settle on the close of discoveries, either party may signal that he or she has completed all necessary information-gathering steps and all motions, and is ready to go to trial. This is done by filing a trial record after serving it on the other party. Sixty days after that is done, the court registrar will put the action on the trial list by setting the case down for trial. If no party sets the matter down for trial, there are provisions for the registrar to force the action on for trial, or to dismiss the action for want of prosecution after giving notice to the parties. Cases are tried in the order in which they are placed on the trial list. There are three separate lists: one for jury trials, one for non-jury trials, and one for speedy trials.

Trial Record

The trial record is a booklet with grey cardboard covers. It is prepared for the use of the trial judge by the party who sets the action down for trial. It contains a table of contents, a copy of each of the pleadings filed, and a copy of any orders made at the pretrial stage as a result of motions. The back cover of the record is set up as a backsheet, with a large blank space in which the judge is to write his or her **endorsement**. An endorsement is a handwritten note that records the judge's decision, although not usually the judge's reasons for his or her decision.

endorsement
judge's handwritten order or judgment from which a successful party is expected to prepare a formal draft of the order or judgment

Pretrial Conference

After the matter has been set down for trial, either party may request a pretrial conference within the next 180 days. A pretrial conference is mandatory under the Rules, and if the parties do not schedule one within 180 days after the matter in action is set down, the registrar will schedule one for them. Each party serves on the other and files with the court a pretrial conference brief that sets out the issues between the parties. The lawyers, with the parties, appear before a pretrial conference judge. The role of the judge is to listen to the lawyers, review the issues with them, and give a frank assessment of the case. What may happen at this point is that an impartial judge may inject a dose of reality into the proceedings that could facilitate settlement, particularly where the parties are being obstinate. The judge's goal is to promote settlement and, failing that, to narrow the issues in order to speed up and simplify the trial. Unless the parties consent, the judge who conducts the pretrial conference does not preside at the trial of the matter.

Requests to Admit

As a means of speeding up the proof of facts at a trial, either party at any time may serve on the other a **request to admit**. The party served with a request to admit is being asked to admit the truth of a fact or the authenticity of a document. The party receiving the request must admit, deny, or refuse to admit, and explain any refusal to admit. Failure to respond leads to a finding that the fact is deemed to be admitted, or the document is deemed to be authentic. An admission, as noted earlier, eliminates the need to prove that fact at trial and can reduce the time it takes to try the case.

Assignment Court

After the pretrial conference, the action is placed on a controlled list for trial. As the case gets closer to the top of the list, it goes to a weekly assignment court, where the lawyers appear and, with the judge, set a specific date for trial. However, if cases ahead of it on the list settle on the eve of trial, the list may collapse, and the parties may find that their trial date has suddenly moved up. Similarly, another trial may take longer than estimated, and the parties' case may be delayed. Note that the procedures for trial lists vary from one judicial region to another.

Pretrial Preparation

Once you know your client is going to trial, there is much to do. I.M. Just needs to decide what witnesses he will call to provide the evidence that will prove the facts alleged. Abigail will obviously give evidence of what happened to her. In addition, I.M. Just will have to issue and serve a **summons to a witness** on each of the other witnesses to ensure that they will attend trial and give evidence. If a witness has relevant documents that he or she can speak about, the summons should direct the witness to bring those documents to court. Because Abigail's medical reports are important evidence on the issue of damages, I.M. Just must give notice of his intent to produce these records at trial. The records will be admitted in evidence unless the opposite party wishes to cross-examine the doctor or maker of the report. There are other notices that might have to be served, though perhaps not in this case; for example, one of the parties might serve a notice to introduce business records, such as invoices or an account record. As with medical reports, business records may be admissible without the maker of the record having to prove their validity and authenticity. I.M. Just and the defendants' lawyer may wish to prepare a trial brief. This brief includes a list of witnesses, what they will say, and what opposing witnesses are likely to say, and contains points about cross-examining witnesses. It may also include matters for opening and closing arguments and a guide for proving each fact necessary to the case.

Time must then be spent preparing witnesses for their examinations-in-chief and cross-examinations and preparing demonstrative and other physical and documentary evidence for trial.

Variations on the Civil Process: Simplified Procedure, Case Management, and the Commercial List

If Abigail were claiming less than $100,000, her case would proceed under the mandatory Rule 76 simplified procedure. Oral discovery is limited, notice periods for steps are shorter, and there is provision for a summary trial that permits trials to be considerably shorter than usual. Simplified procedure is discussed in Chapter 23.

In the County of Essex (Windsor), Ottawa, and Toronto, if the case is very complex and the parties are having difficulty in scheduling and cooperating on moving the case forward, a party or the court itself can intervene and place the action under case management under Rule 77. Under case management, a judge or master may impose a timetable for completing all pretrial procedures and take other steps to reduce cost and delay. Case management is discussed in Chapter 21.

If this were a case involving certain commercial law issues, in Toronto the case might be commenced in the Commercial List Office where it would follow the usual pretrial procedures but would be tried by a Commercial List judge who has expertise in commercial law. The Commercial List is discussed in Chapter 24.

Note that other types of civil cases, such as estate disputes and family law disputes, may proceed under specialized rules and follow specialized procedures. These matters are not covered in this text.

Trial

Because Abigail is the plaintiff, her lawyer opens the case, perhaps with an opening statement to explain what it is about. The statement may be brief because it is presumed that the trial judge has read the trial record and knows that this is a "slip and fall" negligence case with issues concerning both liability and damages; however, if this were a jury trial it would be necessary to have a detailed opening statement because jurors know nothing about a case until they hear about it in an opening statement. I.M. Just then calls his witnesses, probably starting with Abigail. He examines Abigail in chief, and the defendants' counsel cross-examines her. The same sequence is followed with the plaintiff's other witnesses. When I.M. Just has finished presenting Abigail's case through the testimony of witnesses, he closes the case. At this time, the defendants open their case. If their lawyers think that the evidence adduced from the plaintiff's witnesses does not prove the facts alleged by the plaintiff, they may move that the action be dismissed and elect not to call evidence. But it is more likely that they will not run this risk, and that they will call the first witness. The case then proceeds with examination and cross-examination of the defence witnesses. When the defendants close their case, each side sums up, the plaintiff going first.

Having heard the evidence, read the documents, and heard counsel, the trial judge may then decide the case on the spot. But if the judge needs to think about the issues, he or she reserves judgment and gives judgment on a later date. If the judge reserves judgment, he or she may also issue written or oral reasons for judgment. These reasons may be reported in the law reports or be available through an online service such as Quicklaw.

Jury Trials

If Abigail had wanted a jury trial, she would have been required to issue a jury notice before the close of pleadings and discovery. The defendants could then have moved to have the jury notice struck out on the ground that the case was not appropriate for a jury. This usually happens when the evidence is technical or complex, although it is now harder to strike out a jury notice on these grounds than it once was.

If the matter proceeds before a jury, the trial takes longer than it does before a judge sitting alone. This is because juries are not experienced in trying cases, nor are they knowledgeable about the law. Lawyers may have to move more slowly in questioning witnesses and be more thorough in their summing up and in their opening remarks. At the end of the trial, the judge charges the jury, giving a neutral summing up of the evidence and explaining how the law is to be applied to whatever facts the jury finds. The judge carefully drafts the charge, bearing in mind suggestions made by the lawyers. It is up to the jury to assess the evidence to determine what facts have been proven from the evidence it has heard. The judge instructs the jury on what the law is in the charge to the jury that he or she has drafted. Unlike the situation in the United States, civil juries are relatively rare in Canada.

Judgment

At the end of the trial, the judge gives judgment. If there is a jury, it gives a verdict on which the judgment is based.[8] If Abigail is successful, she will be given a judgment requiring Fred and Rattle Motors Ltd. to pay damages to her for her injuries. Each defendant may be ordered to pay a specific share if the judge assesses liability for each of them, or they may be jointly and severally liable to pay. Abigail is likely to receive general damages for her pain and suffering, and special damages for her out-of-pocket expenses, which cover her actual out-of-pocket expenses and other **pecuniary** losses caused by the defendants' negligence. She will receive prejudgment interest from the date that she was injured to the date of judgment, and she will also be awarded postjudgment interest on the amount of the judgment from the day of judgment to the day of payment of that judgment. If Abigail wins her case, she is likely to be awarded partial indemnity costs that amount to approximately one-third to two-thirds of her actual legal costs. If Abigail is not successful, her claim will be dismissed. She will not receive anything. The successful defendants will receive their partial indemnity costs, which Abigail will have to pay.

A judgment in Abigail's favour does not mean that she will simply receive a cheque. A judgment is a command to pay, but if the defendants choose not to pay up voluntarily, Abigail will have to take steps to enforce her judgment. Abigail can file **writs of seizure and sale** against Fred and Rattle Motors Ltd. She can then direct the sheriff of Toronto, or the sheriff of any county in which she has filed a writ and the defendants have property, to seize and sell the property under the authority of the writ. Abigail then satisfies her judgment from the proceeds of the sale. For example, the sheriff could seize Fred's bank account or sell his car or house. The sheriff could also seize the property on which Rattle Motors Ltd. has its building, as well as its inventory of cars. Alternatively, Abigail could garnish Fred's wages or any amounts due to either defendant from third parties. A notice of

pecuniary
of monetary value

writ of seizure and sale
order from a court to a sheriff to enforce the court's order by seizing and selling the defendant's property and holding the proceeds to satisfy the judgment debt to the plaintiff; also known as a writ of execution

garnishment is sent to third parties who owe money to either defendant, telling them to pay the funds due to the defendant to the sheriff to be held to satisfy the judgment.

garnishment
notice directed to a third party who owes money to a defendant as a means of enforcing a judgment

Effect of the Judgment

Once a judgment is given, it is final and may not be challenged unless it is appealed. The matter is then said to be *res judicata*, which means that any issue tried and decided in a court proceeding cannot be relitigated in a subsequent proceeding.

res judicata
Latin phrase meaning that a matter decided by a court is final and incapable of being relitigated in a subsequent proceeding

Appeals

The rules and the *Courts of Justice Act* provide for an appeal from almost any trial court's decision. In some circumstances, appeals are heard by the Divisional Court, a branch of the Superior Court. In Abigail's case, which originated in the Superior Court, the appeal (if the damages are substantiated) would be heard in the Ontario Court of Appeal, the highest court in the province. If, for example, the defendants felt that the damage award for Abigail's pain and suffering was excessive and not supported by legal principle or the evidence, they could appeal by filing a notice of appeal in which they set out the grounds on which the appeal is based. Here the defendants are called the "appellants" in the title of proceedings because they are appealing the trial decision. Abigail will be called the "respondent" on the appeal.

The appellants are required to file with the court a statement of fact and law, which sets out the facts of the case, the legal issues raised on appeal, and a brief resumé of the law on which they rely. I.M. Just will file a statement of fact and law in reply. The appellants will also order those parts of the trial transcript that are required to support their factual and legal arguments. The transcripts and documents that were exhibits at trial are the only evidence. No witnesses are heard on an appeal.

The Court of Appeal has very broad powers, but it exercises them sparingly and with discretion. The court may affirm the trial decision, reverse it, or vary it. It may substitute its own decision for that of the trial judge, although this is unusual. More often, a new trial is ordered. In most cases, the appeal is dismissed and the trial decision affirmed. The major reason why most appeals fail is because the appeal court will not interfere with the findings of fact made by the trial court, even if the appellate judges would have come to a different conclusion if they had been adjudicating at trial. Appellate judges will not substitute their findings of fact for those of the trial judge if there was any reasonable basis for the trial judge's having drawn the conclusions that he or she did from the evidence at trial. The reasoning is that the trial judge saw and heard the witnesses and, from personal observation, was able to draw conclusions about credibility that the Court of Appeal, having only the transcripts of evidence, is not in a position to do. Therefore, errors of fact rarely give rise to a successful appeal, leaving major errors of law as the main basis of a successful appeal. If the trial judge misapplied the law, the appellate court can identify the error and vary the judgment without a new trial. If a jury was improperly charged on the law and reached an erroneous verdict, a new trial will be ordered because a jury's reasoning process is unknown.

If appealing to the Ontario Court of Appeal is difficult, appealing from that court to the Supreme Court of Canada is even more so. Anyone who can pay for it can appeal from a Superior Court trial judgment. You do not need the appellate court's permission. While your chances for success on appeal from a lower court decision may be poor, they worsen at the Supreme Court of Canada. In order to appeal from the provincial appellate court to this court, you need the Supreme Court's permission, which is called "leave to appeal." To get leave to appeal, you need to show that there are conflicting lines of case authority in different provinces or that the matter you are raising is a public policy issue of great importance.

You have had a broad overview of how a civil action proceeds through to trial and appeal. We will examine the process in more detail in subsequent chapters.

CHAPTER SUMMARY

In this chapter, using Abigail Boar's claim for negligence against the defendants Rattle Motors Ltd. and Fred Flogem, we have followed the conduct of a civil action through the Ontario Superior Court of Justice to the Court of Appeal. The procedure began when Abigail hired I.M. Just to sue on her behalf. I.M. Just conducted preliminary investigations to determine whether there was a good cause of action against the defendants. Once the decision to sue was made, proceedings were commenced with the issuing of a statement of claim. The defendants answered with a statement of defence. When both sides exchanged pleadings, the pleading stage closed, and the parties proceeded to oral examinations for discovery and discovery of each other's documents. Until the end of discovery, the parties could bring motions to resolve disputes concerning the application of procedural rules in this case. Once discovery ended, the matter was set down for trial by filing a trial record, and a pretrial conference was held. The parties then proceeded to prepare for trial. At the end of the case, the judge gave judgment, and the parties considered their options on appeal.

KEY TERMS

action, 15

application, 15

backsheet, 16

cause of action, 9

contingency fee, 9

damages, 11

disbursements, 9

endorsement, 27

fees, 9

garnishment, 31

general heading, 16

notice of action, 16

order, 25

pecuniary, 30

principle of proportionality, 11

request to admit, 28

res judicata, 31

summons to a witness, 28

title of proceedings, 16

trier of fact, 9

true copy, 16

viva voce evidence, 23

writ of seizure and sale, 30

NOTES

1. Civil cases where the remedy sought is $25,000 or less may be tried in Small Claims Court. This court has its own rules of procedure, which are less formal and complex than those used in the Superior Court. This text is about the civil process in the Superior Court. For a discussion of the rules of procedure in Small Claims Court, see Laurence Olivo and DeeAnn Gonsalves, *Debtor–Creditor Law and Procedure*, 4th ed. (Toronto: Emond Montgomery, 2012).

2. The use of the word "retainer" to describe both the contract for services and the deposit paid by a client for services to be rendered is confusing. The reason for this usage is that the payment of a deposit serves to retain the services of a lawyer, even if there is no written contract of retainer. Hence, the deposit is often described as "the retainer" even where a separate "contract of retainer" is signed. To further the confusion, some retainers are not deposits to be set off against future accounts rendered by a lawyer, but are payments made directly to a lawyer for agreeing to be available to provide unspecified services for a given period of time. This practice is common in commercial law, where a company may have a law firm on an annual retainer.

3. For example, a contingency fee is permitted in a class action under the *Class Proceedings Act, 1992*, SO 1992, c. 6, as well as in other civil actions.

4. Some of the amendments came into force immediately, in December 2008. These amendments generally extended the revocation dates of pilot projects involving general case management (Rule 77), case management in Toronto (Rule 78), and mandatory mediation (Rule 24.1) from various dates in 2009 to January 1, 2010. Since 2010, the old versions of Rules 77 and 78 have been repealed and replaced with new Rule 77, which creates a form of discretionary

case management in Toronto, Ottawa, and the County of Essex (Windsor). Rule 24.1 was also revised as of 2010 and covers most proceedings in Toronto, Ottawa, and the County of Essex (Windsor), and also applies in some other circumstances.

5. A claim within the monetary jurisdiction of the Small Claims Court usually goes there, and there can be cost penalties for suing in the Superior Court for a small amount of money. However, there are reasons for suing for small sums in Superior Court that the court will recognize as appropriate: a test case on which many other similar cases depend or a novel cause of action should be brought in the higher court.

6. "Balance of convenience" is a practical, fact-based test in which the court examines how difficult, expensive, or time-consuming it is for the parties to try a case in one location rather than another. If the plaintiff has chosen a location, a defendant who wishes to change the location needs to show that he or she is at a great disadvantage because of where the witnesses live, travel costs, and similar matters.

7. $181.00 is the fee as of the time of writing; fees increase from time to time.

8. The jury will give a verdict on which the judgment is based unless the verdict is completely against the weight of the evidence, in which case the judge will set the jury's verdict aside and substitute the verdict that should have been given. This is, however, an unusual occurrence.

REFERENCES

Carthy, James J., W.A. Derry Millar, and Jeffrey G. Cowan, *Ontario Annual Practice* (Aurora, ON: Canada Law Book, published annually).

Class Proceedings Act, 1992, SO 1992, c. 6.

Courts of Justice Act, RSO 1990, c. C.43.

Guide to Ontario Courts at http://www.ontariocourts.on.ca.

Negligence Act, RSO 1990, c. N.1.

Olivo, Laurence M. and DeeAnn Gonsalves, *Debtor–Creditor Law and Procedure*, 4th ed. (Toronto: Emond Montgomery, 2012).

Ontario Reports.

Rules of Civil Procedure, RRO 1990, reg. 194.

REVIEW QUESTIONS

1. What are the principal steps in a civil lawsuit?

2. How does Abigail Boar go about retaining a lawyer?

3. What is a retainer?

4. What are the usual terms of a retainer?

5. What is a contingency fee? Can a lawyer in a civil action accept a contingency fee?

6. How are legal fees determined?

7. What does it mean to have a good cause of action?

8. What is the standard of proof in a civil matter, and what kinds of evidence meet this standard?

9. Give examples of the kinds of evidence in question 8 that may arise in Abigail's case.

10. What matters are considered in determining a court's jurisdiction? Which court should Abigail sue in?

11. What is the relationship between a practice direction and the *Rules of Civil Procedure*?

12. What are the two main types of civil procedure, and how do they differ?

13. How does an action commence, and what is the function of the first document?

14. How is a statement of claim issued?

15. What are originating documents and how are they served?

16. What happens if you cannot find a defendant for service because he or she has moved or gone on vacation?

17. What might happen if the defendant never saw the statement of claim and the plaintiff signed default judgment when no defence was filed?

18. What choices do Fred and Rattle Motors Ltd. have when served with a statement of claim?

19. What other pleadings might one find in a civil case, and what is their function?

20. What is mandatory mediation?

21. What is discovery?

22. What is a motion, and what is its purpose?

23. When the parties have completed pleadings and discovery, how do they get on the list for trial?

24. What happens if both parties file pleadings but do not proceed with the case?

25. What is case management?

26. Could Abigail's case be tried as a Commercial List case?

27. If Abigail obtains a judgment in her favour, does she sit back and wait for the defendants to send her a cheque?

28. What does it mean when we say that the issue of liability in Abigail's case is *res judicata*?

29. Why would an appeal from a decision in Abigail's case based on an error of fact be unlikely to succeed?

DISCUSSION QUESTIONS

1. The primary purpose of the *Rules of Civil Procedure* is to reduce cost and delay. Discuss.

2. Suppose Abigail arrived drunk at the showroom and was staggering when she slipped on the oil. Suppose that she took a fancy to Fred and made unwelcome physical advances. Suppose Fred felt he had not been negligent in any way. And suppose that Rattle Motors Ltd. discovered that there had been numerous incidents of leaking oil pans on the Super Coupe. How might these situations change the type of pleadings used?

3. Identify three pretrial procedures that appear to be designed to reduce cost and delay in the civil process, and explain how these procedures might have that effect.

PART II

From Commencement of Proceedings to Close of Pleadings

Procedure Before Commencement of Proceedings

2

Introduction

When a client brings a civil litigation matter to the law office, there are a number of steps that both the lawyer and the legal staff must complete before going to the court office to issue the statement of claim. Before the claim issues, the apparent facts must be assessed to figure out what the cause of action is. Is the lawyer commencing the action in time or has the limitation period passed? You will have to perform a number of checks: Is the defendant solvent and worth suing? Have you named the defendant correctly for the purposes of the suit? Is any of the claim covered by insurance? You must prepare a retainer for the client to sign if he or she is to retain your firm's services. Then you will have to set up a client account or have the firm's accounts office or bookkeeper do it. Finally, you will open and set up an office file.

Determining the Cause of Action and Other Preliminary Steps

Is There a Good Cause of Action?

After Abigail tells I.M. Just the story of her misfortune, I.M. Just must decide whether the facts as related by Abigail amount to the breach of a legal right that gives rise to a remedy. In Abigail's case, that is not difficult. The facts as disclosed indicate that some acts of Fred Flogem, Rattle Motors Ltd., and Skunk Motorcar Company Ltd. caused or contributed to her injuries and may amount to negligence. Therefore, in Abigail's case, the breach of the duty of care that caused her injuries amounts to a breach of a legal right and gives rise to the remedy of monetary damages. This breach is her legal reason for suing, or her cause of action.

Although this is a straightforward situation where the cause of action is easy to identify, it is not always so simple to determine the cause of action from the facts. For example, in what is now a landmark case,[1] a woman (known by the name Jane Doe to preserve her privacy) sued the Toronto Police and various individual officers in tort for failing to warn her of the danger of sexual assault she faced from a serial rapist. This man sexually assaulted Doe. Her argument was that the police had a duty to warn her, given their knowledge of the case, particularly because she alleged that the police used her as bait to catch the perpetrator. When she commenced her proceeding, the defendants brought a motion to dismiss her statement of claim on the ground that it disclosed no reasonable cause of action. Their argument was that the police had by statute and at common law a general duty to the public, but that they had no specific duty to an individual in Doe's situation. To hold otherwise, they argued, would put them in the position of being an insurer of everyone's safety and liable to everyone who was a victim of crime. On the face of things they had a good argument, and the decision on the motion went through several stages of appeal.

Many lawyers would have told Doe that while she may have been treated badly, she had no reasonable cause of action because the duty owed by the police had never been extended as far as Doe was claiming it should be extended. However, she persevered and eventually won her case. While Doe faced an uphill fight on this issue, the common law does evolve; old principles and established causes of action are refined and extended. The courts are aware of this and they will scrutinize a novel cause of action carefully. Just because courts have not previously granted remedies, there is no reason why they cannot extend the law. In *Doe*, the court held that if the claim discloses a cause of action—a tort—the fact that it is novel is of no concern. For the purpose of assessing a case of this type, the facts in the pleadings are presumed to be true. If they disclose a cause of action with some chance of success, though novel, the action should proceed to trial.[2]

Not every claimed cause of action will succeed, even if the facts are proved. For example, if I invite you to dinner, and you promise to come but do not show up, I may be mortified, humiliated, and have my feelings hurt, but the law of contract does not enforce this type of promise. Neither will the tort of deceit be applicable in this situation. The courts are not ready to extend legal rights and remedies to take into account what the law currently regards as a trifling matter or bad manners—although that could change.

You need to be aware that even if there is a good cause of action, the client might be advised not to sue. Suppose Abigail were fired by her employer without just cause. She could then sue for salary in lieu of having been given reasonable notice.[3] If, however, the day after she was fired, she landed another job that paid more than the job she had been dismissed from, Abigail would not have suffered any damages. Instead, her position would have improved. Although she had a good cause of action in that her contract of employment was breached, she suffered no damages and would receive no remedy. There would be no rational basis for her to continue with the suit.

Correctly Naming Individual Defendants

Suing in the wrong name can result in an unenforceable judgment. For example, if you are suing Fred Flogem and obtain a judgment in that name, the judgment is useless if it turns out that Fred's real first name is Frederico, but that he informally changed it to Fred. Legally, Frederico Flogem exists, but Fred Flogem does not, at least for the purposes of enforcing a judgment if all of Fred's assets are in his formal name, Frederico Flogem. Therefore, getting the proposed defendant's name right is important both to enforcing the judgment and conducting searches to determine whether the defendant is worth suing.

Verifying a Name

Name Search: Individuals

If you are suing an individual rather than a business, you should verify the legal name of the defendant. There are several ways in which you can verify a defendant's correct name.

WEBLINK

The Service Ontario website provides access to several government search sites that you can use to conduct name verification and other searches discussed here: http://www.ontario.ca or http://www.ontario.ca/government/services.

STATEMENT OF DRIVING RECORD

If you have the individual's driver's licence number, you can request a 3-Year Uncertified Driver's Record (also called an abstract), which provides a three-year history of the driver, including the name of the driver, licence status information (including a physical description and date of birth), and a record of driving offence convictions. The person's driving record can help you verify the name of the individual and verify that you have the right person. In this connection, the information about height, gender, and date of birth might be useful in performing other searches. For example, having the date of birth makes it easier to verify who an individual is on a *Personal Property Security Act* (PPSA) search. A driving record search may be especially useful with someone who has a common last name, like Smith or Wong. Note, however, that this search will not provide an address for the licence holder—privacy restrictions keep addresses out of the public record. An authorized requester may obtain the driver's address. You may become an "authorized" requester if

1. you apply for authorization and enter into an agreement with the Ministry of Transportation, and

2. your search is conducted for one of the purposes for which authorization will be granted, such as debt collection, litigation, claims, and accidents. Authorized investigators may include private investigators, security guards, lawyers, and others acting for these purposes.

For further information about authorization to obtain personal information, including addresses, contact:

> Ministry of Transportation
> Supervisor
> Special Enquiry Unit, Licensing Administration and Support Office
> Main Floor, Room 178, Building A
> 2680 Keele Street
> Downsview, ON M3M 3E6
>
> Tel. 416-235-2999 or toll free at 1-800-387-3445

You may conduct your search online, paying by credit card or debit card, to receive a driver's record (also called an abstract). The search site for this record and other driver and automobile-related searches described here is the Service Ontario site on the Ontario Government website, which can be found at http://www.ontario .ca/government/services#Important.[4]

Figure 2.1 shows a sample 3-Year Uncertified Driver's Record.

PLATE HISTORY AND VEHICLE HISTORY ABSTRACTS

If you have the vehicle identification number (VIN) or the licence plate number for a vehicle that you think is owned by the defendant, you can use either number to do a plate or VIN search, either of which will provide the name of the owner, his or her driver's licence, the date the vehicle was registered, and whether it has changed owners recently.

Figure 2.1   3-Year Uncertified Driver's Record

Ontario

Ministry
of
Transportation

Ministère
des
Transports

Ministry No./No. du ministère

Search Date/Date de recherche (Y/A M D/J)
2012/07/13

```
3 YEAR DRIVER RECORD SEARCH                                            PAGE   1
RECHERCHE DANS LE DOSSIER DU CONDUCTEUR DES 3 DERNIÈRES ANNÉES
. . . . . . . . . . . . . . . . . . . . . . . . . . . . . . . . . . . . . . . .

DRIVER INFORMATION/RENSEIGNEMENTS SUR LE CONDUCTEUR

Name/Nom . . . . . . . . . . . . . . .
Address/Adresse  . . . . . . . . . . . . .


Reference No.  or Driver's Licence No./
No de référence ou du permis de conduire  . . . . . . .
Date of Birth/Date de naissance (Y/A M D/J). . . . . . .
Sex / Sexe  . . . . . . . . . . . . . . .
Height / Taille  . . . . . . . . . . . . .
Class / Catégorie  . . . . . . . . . . . .
Condition / Restriction. . . . . . . . . . . . . .
Earliest Licence Date Available /
Date d'obtention du premier de conduire . . . . . . . . 2008/03/05
Expiry Date / Date d'expiration (Y/A M D/J). . . . . . . . 2013/11/16
Status / Statut . . . . . . . . . . . . . . .   LICENCED/TITULAIRE D'UN PERMIS DE CONDUIRE
. . . . . . . . . . . . . . . . . . . . . . . . . . . . . . . . . . . . . . . .

DATE       CONVICTIONS, DISCHARGES AND OTHER ACTIONS
Y/A M D/J  CONDAMNATIONS, LIBÉRATIONS ET AUTRES ACTIONS
. . . . . . . . . . . . . . . . . . . . . . . . . . . . . . . . . . . . . . . .
           CATEGORY S IS FOR INTERNAL TEST USE ONLY
           CATÉGORIE S RÉSERVÉE POUR ÉVALUATION INTERNE

           NO PUBLIC RECORD / AUCUN DOSSIER PUBLIC
```

Again, the address of the owner will not be provided unless you have obtained the authorization described in the previous section, 3-Year Uncertified Driver's Record. You may also do these searches online using the web address provided in the previous section.

You can see what a Certified Plate Search—Recent Owner looks like in Figure 2.2. The VIN search record is similar.

ONLINE SEARCHES

In the last several years, various search engines and other online sources have been expanded and refined to allow you to submit the name of an individual to obtain addresses, telephone numbers, and other information about an individual that can help you verify a name, obtain other identifying information, and locate the person. These searches can be used to find both individuals and other legal entities, such as businesses operating under a business name. You may also do a **reverse search** on many of these sites by submitting a telephone number, address, email address, or other information that will help you to obtain the correct name of a defendant, as well as other details about that person. Reverse searches of phone numbers will often identify subscribers of unlisted landlines and cellphones. Many sites are free, but some charge for information, in which case you can pay by credit card. The websites in the Internet Searches for People, Addresses, and Phone Numbers table were useful at the time of publication.

reverse search
a reverse search allows you to submit an address, telephone number, or email address to obtain the name of a resident or subscriber

Correctly Naming Businesses

To get the name of a business right you must know the form of business entity used by the proposed defendant. If the business is a sole proprietorship—that is, a business carried on by an individual using the individual's name—then searching the individual's name may be sufficient.

However, suppose that the proposed defendant carries on business using a business or trade name:

- If the business is incorporated, you must sue the corporation in its legal corporate name and not in the trade name it uses to carry on business.
- If the business is a sole proprietorship, you may sue the individual sole proprietor in his or her own name, or sue the sole proprietorship in the business name. Note that Rule 8 of the *Rules of Civil Procedure* makes it easy to sue in the business name, and then expand enforcement rights later against a sole proprietor in his or her own name.
- If the business is a partnership, you may sue in the partnership name or sue the partners individually in their own names. Again, Rule 8 makes it easy to sue in the name of the partnership and then expand enforcement rights later against individual partners.

Identifying the business name and the business entity correctly is very important. For example, if the plaintiff wants to sue Mary Chen's Golf Driving Range, the

Internet Searches for People, Addresses, and Phone Numbers

Canada411	http://www.canada411.ca	Submitting a name to this site can turn up a telephone number. Reverse searching is also available.
WhitePages.ca	http://www.whitepages.ca	This site allows you to look up names to obtain addresses and phone numbers and also allows you to do reverse directory searches of addresses and phone numbers to identify and locate individuals.
Yellow Pages	http://www.yellowpages.ca	Can be used to find the telephone number of a business along with their address. Reverse searches are possible.
Yahoo People Finder Canada	http://yahoo.Canada411.ca	You may search by name, with or without the city or state. This may turn up addresses and other miscellaneous information, some of which could be useful. Offers reverse address and phone searches as well as a proximity search.
Yahoo People Search United States	http://search.yahoo.com/people/email.html	You may search for a phone number and address by name, with or without the city or state. Also offers email and reverse phone number searches.
Pipl	http://www.pipl.com	This site searches the "deep web," including online databases, to find references to any name you submit. It accesses databases in many countries.
NetTrace	http://www.nettrace.com.au/resource/search/people.html	This Australian site is a gateway to a variety of search sites that allow you to search in various countries, including Canada, by inputting phone numbers, addresses, email addresses, names, and other data. Many of the sites will search various public and private databases, including many in Canada. Some charge fees.
Telus	http://www.mytelus.com/phonebook	This site allows you to submit names to obtain addresses and phone numbers, including unlisted cellphone numbers. You may also do reverse searches on phone numbers and addresses to identify and locate individuals.
Reverse Phone Lookup	http://www.reversephonelookup.com	This site allows you to search by phone number and will turn up account holder names and addresses, including those for unlisted landlines and cellphones.

Figure 2.2   Certified Plate Search—Recent Owner

Ontario   Ministry   Ministère
of   des
Transportation Transports

```
MINISTRY CONTROL NO./NO. DE CONTRÔLE DU MINISTÈRE   SEARCH DATE/DATE DE RECHERCHE

                                                    12/07/13

SEARCH TYPE/TYPE DE RECHERCHE                       INQUIRY KEY/CRITÈRE DE RECHERCHE

PLATE                                               PLATE/PLAQUE·.
PLAQUE
========================================================================================
REGISTRANT/CONDUCTEUR
NAME/NOM·
                                                        STAGGER/ÉCHELONNER·0930
· · · · · · · · · · · · · · · · · · · · · · · · · · · · · · · · · · · · · · · · · · · · ·
VEHICLE/VÉHICULE
VEHICLE IDENTIFICATION NO./NO L'IDENTIFICATION DU VÉHICULE·
CLASS/CATÉGORIE· PASSENGER/VOITURE PARTICULIÈRE              MAKE/MARQUE· FORD
MODEL/MODÈLE· YYY
BODY TYPE/TYPE DE CARROSSERIE· 2 DOOR SEDAN/COUPÉ
NO. OF CYLINDERS/NO DE CYLINDRÉE· 04
MOTIVE POWER/FORCE MOTRICE· GASOLINE/ESSENCE
COLOUR/COULEUR· RED/ROUGE                                   YEAR/ANNÉE· 82
STATUS/STATUT· FIT/EN ÉTAT DE MARCHE          WEIGHT EMPTY/POIDS À VIDE·
BRAND/BRAND· REBUILT/RECONSTRUIT              NO. OF AXLES/NO D'ESSIEUX·
ODOMETER ON (YYMMDD)/COMPETUER KILOMÉTRIQUE LE (AAMMJJ)· 00125000 KM 10/01/27
· · · · · · · · · · · · · · · · · · · · · · · · · · · · · · · · · · · · · · · · · · · · ·
PLATE/PLAQUE
PLATE/PLAQUE·                                               YEAR/ANNÉE·
SERIES/SÉRIE· PASSENGER/VOITURE PARTICULIÈRE
STATUS/STATUT· ATTACHED/FIXÉE
FORMAT·           PLATE REGISTRATION DATE/DATE D'ENREGISTREMENT DES PLAQUES·
· · · · · · · · · · · · · · · · · · · · · · · · · · · · · · · · · · · · · · · · · · · · ·
VALTAG NO./NO DE VIGNETTE·             REGISTERED WEIGHT/POIDS ENREGISTRÉ·
DECLARATION/DÉCLARATION·
START/DÉPART· 11/10/01                 EXPIRY/EXPIRATION· 12/09/30
PERMIT NO./NO DE CERTIFICAT·           DATE ISSUED/DATE DE DÉLIVRANCE·  12/06/25
· · · · · · · · · · · · · · · · · · · · · · · · · · · · · · · · · · · · · · · · · · · · ·
```

business name known to the plaintiff, and the business is incorporated as Chengolf Ltd., the plaintiff must sue in the correct corporate name. If you sue Mary Chen personally or sue in the name of Mary Chen's Golf Driving Range, you are likely to meet a defence that these persons had no liability because it was the corporation that was legally liable, not Mary Chen as an individual or Mary Chen carrying on business as Mary Chen's Golf Driving Range. So identifying a business by its correct legal name is important, and you will avoid wasting your client's time and money if you correctly name the business you are suing.

Naming the proper parties to a lawsuit will be discussed in more detail in Chapter 5. For now, we will concentrate on verifying the names of proposed defendants that are businesses.

Unless a business is carried on in the owner's name, it must register its business name with the Companies and Personal Property Security Branch, Ministry of Government Services (the Companies Branch). If you submit a business name on a search, it will result in the identification of the individual person if the business is a sole proprietorship. If the business is a partnership, submission of the business name will result in identification of the partners registered at the time of the search. Similarly, if the business is a corporation, submission of the business name will get you the correct legal corporate name. Remember that when you sue a corporation, you have no choice concerning how to name the company: you must use its proper legal name. Do not be surprised if the corporate name that turns up has no relation to the business name used. If Rattle Motors was simply a name used to carry on business as a trade name, it could turn out to be a "numbered company"; for example, its corporate name could be 1234 Ontario Ltd. There is nothing sinister about this. If the company intends to use, in its day-to-day operations, the business name that it used before its incorporation, it does not matter what the limited company is called, and the number initially assigned to a new corporation by the Companies and Personal Property Security Branch of the Ministry of Government Services will do as well as anything else as a company name, because the company will use the name under which it was carrying on business and not the numbered company name assigned by the province.

A business name search can be done in two ways. You can attend in person at the public search office of the Companies and Personal Property Security Branch, Ministry of Government Services, Service Ontario at 375 University Avenue, 2nd floor, Toronto, Ontario, M5G 2M2 where there are computers on which you can conduct a search, or you can conduct an online search on the Ministry of Government Services Service Ontario website at https://www.services.gov.on.ca/locations/start.do?.

A business names report will identify persons using a business name and will show their address. If the business name is not registered, you can obtain a certificate of non-registration showing that a business name that may be in use has not been registered. There are penalties for failing to register a business under the *Business Names Act*, although this will not directly affect a plaintiff suing an unregistered defendant. However, if a plaintiff is suing in an unregistered name, his or her action will be **stayed**.

stayed
a legal proceeding may be stopped from proceeding further, or stayed by a judge, until one of the parties does something they are obliged to do; for example, a plaintiff who is suing using an unregistered business name will have the proceeding stayed until he or she proves that the name has been registered as legally required

An online search can be inexpensively done, provided that the name you are searching has been registered with the Companies and Personal Property Securities Branch. At the Service Ontario website, http://www.ontario.ca/serviceontario, follow the Business link to Featured Online Services where you will see the "Search, register, renew your business and get a Master Business Licence" link. This link will take you to the Business Name Search, Registration, and Renewal page where you can follow the links to perform an Enhanced Business Name Search. You can see a sample Enhanced Business Name Search—Search Criteria online form in Figure 2.3. You can search the exact business name, words within the name, or use the Ontario Business Identification Number (if you have it) that all businesses are given when their names are registered. You can pay for the search online by credit card. Searching can also be done, for a fee, through Cyberbahn & Marque d'or (Cyberbahn) and Corporate Searchers (Centro Legal Works) or through OnCorp; they are recognized Ontario government providers. You can access their search services online and also view samples of documents such as a Corporation Profile Report (which contains a corporation's address and the names of its directors).There is a sample of a Corporation Profile Report at http://www.oncorp.com/home/services_onbis_corp.asp, and you can also see a sample Corporation Profile Report in Figure 2.4. This report is useful because it sets out the corporation's legal name and the names of the directors. The Law Society's By-Law 7.1 requires lawyers to verify a client's identity to prevent clients engaged in fraud from using false names. You can use the Corporation Profile Report to verify a corporate client's identity in order to meet the requirements of By-Law 7.1, and do so at the client's expense, if you are not sure of the client's identity.

If you require a document that is not available through the government website or you do not have the time to search on your own, there are companies that will conduct searches for you for a fee. You may also do your own online searches by using private search and registration services such as those previously mentioned: OnCorp (http://www.oncorp.com) or Cyberbahn (http://www.cybermarque.com). To use these sites, start at the homepage and follow the directions and links. These search sites will also allow you to conduct a variety of other searches of public business records maintained by the federal and provincial governments. Search costs can be passed on as disbursements to the clients that required the searches. Note that if a corporation is carrying on business in Ontario but is incorporated in another province, or is federally incorporated, an Ontario corporate search will not be useful. However, any of these search sites can be used to obtain information about companies that are incorporated federally or in other provinces.

Because detailed web addresses (URLs) often change, another way to conduct a search when a precise URL does not work is to do a broad search. Start with http://www.gov.on.ca, and on the homepage do a search using the name of the form or the name of the procedure you want to use. If you are successful, that will take you to the URL you need.

Figure 2.3   Enhanced Business Name Search—Search Criteria

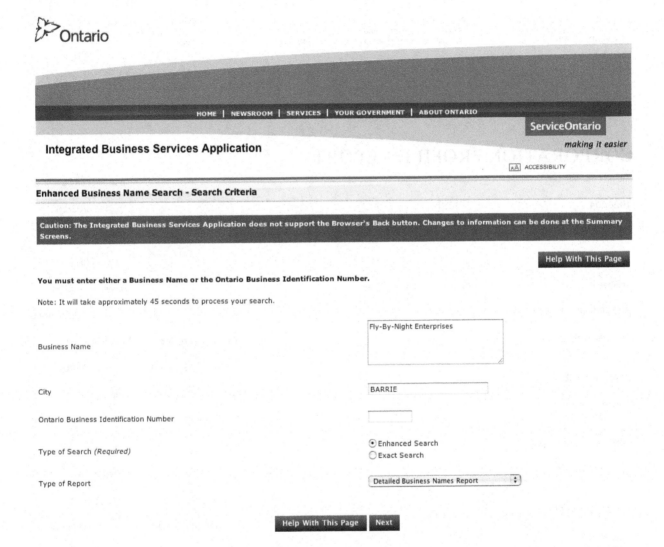

Figure 2.4   Corporation Profile Report

Request ID:	000177620	Province of Ontario	Date Report Produced:	2005/10/21
Transaction ID:	12871109	Ministry of Consumer and Business Services	Time Report Produced:	14:38:07
Category ID:	UN/E	Companies and Personal Property Security Branch	Page:	1

CORPORATION PROFILE REPORT

Ontario Corp Number	Corporation Name		Incorporation Date
1990004	TEST		1993/02/25

Jurisdiction

ONTARIO

Corporation Type	Corporation Status		Former Jurisdiction
ONTARIO BUSINESS CORP.	ACTIVE		NOT APPLICABLE

Registered Office Address		Date Amalgamated	Amalgamation Ind.
		NOT APPLICABLE	NOT APPLICABLE
2 QUEEN STREET			
		New Amal. Number	Notice Date
Suite # 222			
TORONTO		NOT APPLICABLE	NOT APPLICABLE
ONTARIO			
CANADA M6M 6M6			Letter Date

Mailing Address

NOT APPLICABLE

		Revival Date	Continuation Date
2 QUEEN STREET		NOT APPLICABLE	NOT APPLICABLE
Suite # 222			
TORONTO		Transferred Out Date	Cancel/Inactive Date
ONTARIO			
CANADA M6M 6M6		NOT APPLICABLE	NOT APPLICABLE

	EP Licence Eff.Date	EP Licence Term.Date
	NOT APPLICABLE	NOT APPLICABLE

	Number of Directors Minimum Maximum	Date Commenced in Ontario	Date Ceased in Ontario
	UNKNOWN UNKNOWN	NOT APPLICABLE	NOT APPLICABLE

Activity Classification

NOT AVAILABLE

Figure 2.4   Continued

Request ID: 000177620
Transaction ID: 12871109
Category ID: UN/E

Province of Ontario
Ministry of Consumer and Business Services
Companies and Personal Property Security Branch

Date Report Produced: 2005/10/21
Time Report Produced: 14:38:07
Page: 2

CORPORATION PROFILE REPORT

Ontario Corp Number	Corporation Name
1990004	TEST

Corporate Name History	Effective Date
TEST	1993/02/25

Current Business Name(s) Exist: YES

Expired Business Name(s) Exist: YES - SEARCH REQUIRED FOR DETAILS

Administrator:
Name (Individual / Corporation)   Address

ADAM

EVE   77 5TH STREET

                                                        KINGSTON
                                                        ONTARIO
                                                        CANADA   N5N 5N5

Date Began	First Director	
2004/07/01	NOT APPLICABLE	
Designation	Officer Type	Resident Canadian
DIRECTOR		Y

Figure 2.4   Continued

Request ID: 000177620
Transaction ID: 12871109
Category ID: UN/E

Province of Ontario
Ministry of Consumer and Business Services
Companies and Personal Property Security Branch

Date Report Produced: 2005/10/21
Time Report Produced: 14:38:07
Page: 3

CORPORATION PROFILE REPORT

Ontario Corp Number

1990004

Corporation Name

TEST

Administrator:
Name (Individual / Corporation)

ADAM

EVE

Address

77 5TH STREET

KINGSTON
ONTARIO
CANADA   N5N 5N5

Date Began

2004/07/01

First Director

NOT APPLICABLE

Designation

OFFICER

Officer Type

GENERAL MANAGER

Resident Canadian

Y

Administrator:
Name (Individual / Corporation)

JANE

JANENE

Address

99 15TH AVENUE

OTTAWA
ONTARIO
CANADA   L7L 6K5

Date Began

2003/02/28

First Director

NOT APPLICABLE

Designation

DIRECTOR

Officer Type

Resident Canadian

Y

Figure 2.4 Continued

Request ID: 000177620
Transaction ID: 12871109
Category ID: UN/E

Province of Ontario
Ministry of Consumer and Business Services
Companies and Personal Property Security Branch

Date Report Produced: 2005/10/21
Time Report Produced: 14:38:07
Page: 4

CORPORATION PROFILE REPORT

Ontario Corp Number

1990004

Corporation Name

TEST

Administrator:
Name (Individual / Corporation)

JANE

JANENE

Address

99 15TH AVENUE

OTTAWA
ONTARIO
CANADA   L7L 6K5

Date Began

2003/02/28

First Director

NOT APPLICABLE

Designation

OFFICER

Officer Type

PRESIDENT

Resident Canadian

Y

Administrator:
Name (Individual / Corporation)

JAMES

JONES

Address

2 KING STREET WEST

TORONTO
ONTARIO
CANADA   M7M 7M7

Date Began

1999/05/05

First Director

NOT APPLICABLE

Designation

DIRECTOR

Officer Type

Resident Canadian

Y

Figure 2.4   Continued

Request ID: 000177620 Transaction ID: 12871109 Category ID: UN/E	Province of Ontario Ministry of Consumer and Business Services Companies and Personal Property Security Branch	Date Report Produced: 2005/10/21 Time Report Produced: 14:38:07 Page: 5

CORPORATION PROFILE REPORT

Ontario Corp Number

1990004

Corporation Name

TEST

Administrator:
Name (Individual / Corporation)

JOHN
P.
SMITHEX

Address

88 QUEEN STREET NORTH

TORONTO
ONTARIO
CANADA   L7L 5M5

Date Began

2004/07/01

First Director

NOT APPLICABLE

Designation

DIRECTOR

Officer Type

Resident Canadian

Y

Administrator:
Name (Individual / Corporation)

JOHN
P.
SMITHEX

Address

88 QUEEN STREET NORTH

TORONTO
ONTARIO
CANADA   L7L 5M5

Date Began

2004/07/01

First Director

NOT APPLICABLE

Designation

OFFICER

Officer Type

SECRETARY

Resident Canadian

Y

Figure 2.4   Concluded

Request ID: 000177620
Transaction ID: 12871109
Category ID: UN/E

Province of Ontario
Ministry of Consumer and Business Services
Companies and Personal Property Security Branch

Date Report Produced: 2005/10/21
Time Report Produced: 14:38:07
Page: 6

CORPORATION PROFILE REPORT

Ontario Corp Number

1990004

Corporation Name

TEST

Last Document Recorded

Act/Code	Description	Form	Date
CIA	CHANGE NOTICE	1	2005/08/30 (ELECTRONIC FILING)

THIS CORPORATION HAS RECEIVED A NOTICE OF INTENTION TO DISSOLVE ON THE DATE INDICATED IN THE "NOTICE DATE" FIELD
AND IS SUBJECT TO CANCELLATION.

THIS REPORT SETS OUT THE MOST RECENT INFORMATION FILED BY THE CORPORATION ON OR AFTER JUNE 27, 1992, AND RECORDED
IN THE ONTARIO BUSINESS INFORMATION SYSTEM AS AT THE DATE AND TIME OF PRINTING. ALL PERSONS WHO ARE RECORDED AS
CURRENT DIRECTORS OR OFFICERS ARE INCLUDED IN THE LIST OF ADMINISTRATORS.

ADDITIONAL HISTORICAL INFORMATION MAY EXIST ON THE COMPANIES AND PERSONAL PROPERTY SECURITY BRANCH MICROFICHE.

The issuance of this report in electronic form is authorized by the Director of Companies and Personal Property Security Branch

Impecunious Clients and Opponents

Cost is a factor in determining whether to sue or not. The probable costs should be discussed candidly with the client in relation to the probable relief to be obtained. If Abigail's chances of establishing liability are good, she is likely to be awarded substantial damages. Because the corporate defendant is likely to carry insurance, the chances of being paid those damages are very good. Consequently, even if Abigail does not have a lot of spare cash, I.M. Just may be prepared to take his payment at the end of the case, as is common in many personal injury actions. Her lawyer may also take the case on a contingency-fee basis, which is now permissible in Ontario. In this case, Abigail would pay nothing, but if she won, I.M. Just would be paid by taking 20 to 30 percent of the damage award as his fee.

In more speculative or uncertain cases, the client can be billed on a periodic basis. Payment by installments that the client can manage is common in litigation cases. A client who cannot pay at all may have to go without a remedy unless the lawyer is prepared to act on a **pro bono** basis. Legal aid is virtually unobtainable in civil cases. "Justice," as an English appeals judge once observed, "is like the Ritz Hotel. Anyone who has the price of a room may stay there."

If your opponent is **impecunious**, there is another set of problems to consider. If you get a judgment against the defendant, will he or she be able to pay it? If Rattle Motors Ltd. has no assets and is teetering on the edge of bankruptcy, it may be better not to sue, but to make a claim in the ensuing bankruptcy instead. Otherwise, you might spend both money and effort to win a case and then be left with a paper judgment—that is, a judgment that is of no more value than the paper it is written on because the client has no money or assets to pay it.

Determining Solvency

If the solvency of the potential defendant is at issue, there are some searches that can be done to determine whether it would be worthwhile to sue the defendant.

If the defendant has been successfully sued before, but the judgment has never been paid, there is likely to be a writ of seizure and sale (also called a "writ of execution") on file in the sheriff's office in the county or judicial district where the defendant resides or carries on business. If the writ has been unsatisfied for some time, this tells you that a previous judgment creditor has sued and been unsuccessful in recovering anything on the judgment debt. In addition to providing information about the likelihood of the judgment being paid, the writ of execution can confirm the proper name or spelling of the name of the defendant so that he, she, or it will be correctly named in the statement of claim if you do proceed.

A number of outstanding writs of execution indicate that the proposed defendant has generally been defaulting on claims. They may also indicate that the proposed defendant is adept at hiding assets.

If the writs are all recently filed, it can mean that judgment creditors are closing in and that bankruptcy may be imminent. Suing is a waste of time if the proposed defendant is **judgment-proof**. If the proposed defendant goes bankrupt, the plaintiff may obtain more by making a claim as an unsecured creditor in the bankruptcy proceedings.

pro bono
abbreviation of the Latin term *pro bono publico*, meaning "for the public good," used where a lawyer takes on a case without charging a fee as part of a duty to see that justice is done

impecunious
insolvent

judgment-proof
unlikely to be able to pay any amount of a judgment

Illustration of a Pro Rata Distribution of the Proceeds of Execution

Amount owing to execution creditor A	$500
Amount owing to execution creditor B	$200
Amount owing to execution creditor C	$100
Total	$800

Execution creditor C levies execution and recovers $300 as a net amount after the costs of execution have been deducted from the gross amount.

Formula:

$$\text{amount recovered on levy} \times \frac{\text{amount owing to creditor}}{\text{amount owing to all creditors}} = \text{share paid to creditor}$$

A will receive $300   × $500/800$ = $187.50
B will receive $300   × $200/800$ = $75.00
C will receive $300   × $100/800$ = $37.50

Finding no writs of execution on file may indicate that the proposed defendant is solvent, but it may also indicate that you have not searched the counties or districts where the writs are lodged. The problem with searching writs of execution is that there is no province-wide online system that can be searched. You need to search the files in each county or judicial region where the proposed defendant has or is likely to have had assets.

Even if there are writs on file, if the proposed defendant has not gone bankrupt, it may be useful to sue anyway and obtain judgment. The reason for taking this approach is that the *Creditors' Relief Act, 2010* requires that execution creditors (all those who have filed writs of execution) share on a pro rata basis if any execution creditor succeeds in seizing and selling assets. When assets are seized and sold, the sheriff is obliged to distribute a share of the money to each of the execution creditors in proportion to what they are owed. This means that execution creditors with large judgments receive a larger share of the money than those who have judgments for smaller amounts. There are some exceptions: family support creditors and tax authorities take precedence over other creditors.

How to Conduct a Search of Executions

To conduct a search of executions against the name of a defendant, at the sheriff's office, request a certificate indicating whether there are writs of seizure and sale on file in that office. The sheriff's office is usually located in the local Superior Court of Justice courthouse. The local court office and the sheriff's office are listed in the blue government pages of the local telephone directory.

In Toronto, execution searches at the sheriff's office are done online after payment of the prescribed fee. Key in the same kind of information you would provide for the certificate and the system will produce an on-screen response and, if desired, a printout of that response. In time, this system will extend to other parts of Ontario, and may one day be available online from your office computer.

Give the full name of the defendant; if the defendant is an individual, give middle names as well as the first name, if possible. If the defendant is a business, be sure to give the business's proper legal name. With sole proprietorships and partnerships, it may be wise in most cases to list the name of the individual who is the sole proprietor or the names of the partners. File the certificate in the sheriff's office for the county or district where the defendant is likely to have assets, lived, or carried on business. As mentioned above, in Toronto it is possible to use a computer to do your own search, which will give you immediate information on writs on file. Once you have results, you can ask for copies of the writs to find out the particulars, such as the name of the judgment creditor, the amount owing, and the length of time the debt has been unsatisfied. You can also call the judgment creditor's lawyer whose name appears on the writ to find out about any attempts to collect that have been made.

You can pay to have an online writ of execution search carried out by using the writs search service provided by Teranet. An Ontario-wide search (OWL—Ontario Writs Locator) can be ordered through Teranet. To access this service you need to register as a member at https://www.teranetexpress.ca/csp. Membership is free. You can also perform execution searches at Cyberbahn at http://www.cybermarque .com. Corporate Searchers (Centro Legal Works) also provides this service at http:// www.centrolegalworks.com/realestate-search.html.

Bankruptcy and Insolvency Act Search

A bankruptcy search is useful to determine whether the defendant has gone bankrupt or is about to go bankrupt. There is no point in suing a bankrupt defendant because any action would be automatically stayed. Instead, the creditor should file a proof of debt claim with the defendant's trustee in bankruptcy. The trustee will review the claim and, if it is in order, the creditor may recover some of the money owing, but is unlikely to ever see all of it. Secured creditors are entitled to seize their secured property to satisfy the debt owing to them and to do so ahead of the claims and rights of unsecured creditors claiming through the trustee. Unsecured creditors, which include ordinary judgment creditors, get what is left over. After all of the bankrupt's creditors, both secured and unsecured, have had their interests attended to, the defendant is usually discharged from bankruptcy, free and clear of the debts incurred before bankruptcy, with some exceptions.[5]

As a result of the bankruptcy rules, there is often little of value left for unsecured creditors of the bankrupt. For this reason, unsecured creditors may recover no more than 10 or 20 cents on each dollar owed to them because the secured creditors have already taken all the major assets.

There are two ways to go bankrupt: (1) in certain circumstances, an unpaid creditor can put a debtor into bankruptcy using a petition for bankruptcy, or (2) the debtor can make an assignment in bankruptcy. As an alternative to bankruptcy, a debtor who owes up to $250,000 (excluding a mortgage) may make a consumer proposal to his creditors through a trustee in bankruptcy. All bankruptcy searches are done through the Office of the Superintendent of Bankruptcy. All bankruptcies and proposals filed in Canada since 1978 are on file. The Office of the Superintendent of Bankruptcy is represented in each province by its offices of the Official Receiver. Official Receivers are individuals authorized to handle various functions under the *Bankruptcy and Insolvency Act*.[6] There are four offices of the Official Receiver in Ontario. Their locations and telephone numbers are as follows:

- 55 Bay Street North, 9th Floor, Hamilton, Ontario, L9R 3P7, 905-572-2847
- 451 Talbot Street, Suite 303, London, Ontario, N6A 5C9, 519-645-4034
- 160 Elgin Street, 11th Floor, Suite B-100, Ottawa, Ontario, K2P 2P7, 613-995-2994
- 25 St. Clair Avenue East, 6th Floor, Toronto, Ontario, M4T 1M2, 416-973-6486.

The toll-free number for all offices is 1-800-376-9902.

The bankruptcy and insolvency database, which includes information on bankruptcies, proposals, and receiverships, may be searched online through the Office of the Superintendent of Bankruptcy at http://www.ic.gc.ca/app/scr/bsf-osb/ins/login .html or by calling 1-877-376-9902 (toll free) instead. In order to conduct searches you must open an account with the Office of the Superintendent of Bankruptcy. First you must set up an account with Industry Canada. You can do this online at https://www.ic.gc.ca/cgi-bin/allsites/registration-inscription/home.html?lang=eng.

A bankruptcy search will also reveal if the defendant is in receivership. This may happen when a business debtor has defaulted on a loan, which gives the creditor the right, on default, to appoint a receiver to run the debtor's business or take it over to liquidate assets. Unless your client has some priority right over the secured lender in this situation, he or she is unlikely to recover any money, because the secured lender will dispose of virtually all of the assets free of any claim by your client. The Office of the Superintendent of Bankruptcy maintains online records of receiverships nationwide since 1993.

Insurance

Always review a client's insurance policies. Rattle Motors Ltd. is likely to have occupier's insurance covering precisely the kind of situation that arises in Abigail's case. Subject to a deductible, damage awards must be paid by the insurance company. If you have a claim, you should advise the insurer immediately. Insurance companies usually have their own lawyers and prefer to have them defend the case. Your firm should not be taking steps to defend unless the insurer instructs you to do so or unless it is necessary in order to preserve a defendant's rights.

The insurer may resist providing coverage on the ground that the client has failed to comply with the terms of the policy or on the ground that the claim falls outside the terms of the policy. The lawyer for Rattle Motors Ltd. should try to persuade the insurer to defend on a non-waiver basis. This means that the insurer defends, but it reserves the right to make a claim against the insured for any amount the insurer has to pay out on the insured's behalf. If this happens, Rattle's lawyer may still act for its client, not just to defend against Abigail, but against Rattle's insurers on the issue of whether the insurance company is obliged to cover the claim. If the insurance company refuses to honour a claim, Rattle's lawyer should proceed to defend and serve a third-party notice on the insurer.

I.M. Just should check to see whether Abigail's homeowner's insurance, workplace health insurance, or any other policy of insurance provides any coverage. Sometimes homeowner's policies are very broad and may provide full or partial coverage for her losses. If so, this may eliminate some issues and remedies in the case, or it may make it unnecessary to sue if the loss is completely covered by the insurer. Abigail must be assisted in making a claim as quickly as possible, and I.M. Just's office should take steps to see that she fully complies with the terms of the policy. If Abigail's insurance company seeks to recover from the defendants what it paid to Abigail, you may need to take initial steps to safeguard Abigail's right to sue until the insurance company takes control of the litigation.

Conflicts of Interest

Your law firm will need to ensure that in representing a client it does not have a conflict of interest. The rules about conflicts of interest have become more complicated as large law firms merge, join international networks, and acquire partners from professions other than law. Rule 2 of the Law Society's *Rules of Professional Conduct* make several things clear:

- A lawyer cannot act against a former client on the same or a similar matter on which he or she acted for that client previously.

- When one lawyer in a firm acted for a former client, his or her partners cannot later act against that client unless the former client consents or the interests of justice demand it.

- A lawyer can act for two clients on the same matter on a joint retainer; however, if a conflict develops, the lawyer must cease acting for both clients. Further, there is no confidentiality between the two clients so that information given to one client cannot be withheld from the other. If a lawyer is acting for both Fred and Rattle Motors Ltd. and the lawyer has a continuous and on-going professional relationship with Rattle Motors Ltd., Fred must be advised of that fact.

- When a lawyer transfers from firm A to firm B and discovers that firm B is acting against firm A's client *and* the lawyer has actual knowledge of confidential matters about firm A's client, firm B must transfer the case to another firm, unless firm A's client consents to firm B's staying on the case. The former client may consent if the transferring lawyer agrees not to communicate with the lawyers handling the case against firm A's client.

Fortunately, our case is simpler. I.M. Just is practising with one salaried lawyer employed as an associate and can easily tell whether a conflict of interest will arise.

If a conflict did arise, he would be obliged to tell Abigail at once and help her find another lawyer.

When a case comes into the office, the names of the defendants and the client should be cross-checked against names on closed files, using either client cards or computerized client lists. There is software available that is designed to run conflict checks of this sort. However, this may not catch all conflicts.

An example case is where lawyer A, an associate in a firm, sued a charitable organization on behalf of an employee. The organization was headed by B, and the lawsuit turned on B's conduct toward the employee. There was no apparent conflict between the parties because lawyer A and the firm had never acted for either party before. However, a chance remark by a partner led to the discovery by lawyer A that the partner had acted for B in another matter and knew a great deal about B. At that point, there was a conflict of interest, although the case was well under way. The parties agreed that the partner with knowledge of B's affairs would not discuss any aspect of the case with A.

Limitation Periods

Care should be taken to determine when the cause of action is complete. In Abigail's case, this occurs at the moment she comes to rest in a pool of oil on Rattle Motors' showroom floor. All the acts that caused her damages have occurred, so an action may now be commenced against the defendants, although the extent of those damages may not be known for some time. Lawyers sometimes say at this point that "the cause of action has accrued." From this moment, the clock begins to tick and the limitation period begins to run.

Negligence is a tort. Under the Ontario *Limitations Act, 2002* the basic limitation period for almost all causes of action, including Abigail's, will be two years from the time the events occurred (s. 4) or could reasonably be discovered (s. 5).

Sometimes it is difficult to tell when the cause of action is complete. For example, if you are negligently exposed to excessive radiation that might cause cancer, you may not be able to sue because the cause of action does not accrue until you are actually diagnosed with cancer. If you never get cancer, you cannot sue because the cause of action did not accrue.

There are other issues concerning the discovery of the cause of action. Usually, time begins to run when the act or omission occurs. But, as noted above, s. 5 of the *Limitations Act, 2002* sets out situations where time does not begin to run when the act or omission occurs. Rather, it begins to run when the plaintiff can show that a reasonable person knew or ought reasonably to have known that the act occurred and they could move to obtain a legal remedy.

When a client has given you the basic facts, you then have to determine the specific cause of action and the applicable limitation period. Under the *Limitations Act, 2002*, the period is almost always two years from the time the cause of action arose, or from when it could reasonably be discovered.

However, there are exceptions. Some of the more notable exceptions are:

- Minors and persons under disability: limitation periods are generally suspended until a litigation guardian is appointed; at that point the limitation period begins to run (ss. 6 to 9).

- Where the cause of action involves assault or sexual assault, limitation periods are suspended while the plaintiff is physically, mentally, or psychologically unable to act. The plaintiff in such a case is presumed to be unable to act. If the defendant thinks the limitation period should be running, he or she must present evidence to rebut the presumption (s. 10).

- In some circumstances, where a limitation period is suspended, the limitation period runs for a maximum of 15 years, with some exceptions. Where a person is mentally, physically, or psychologically incapable of starting proceedings, or where a person is a minor and not represented by a litigation guardian, the limitation-period suspension might exceed 15 years (s. 15).

- For some causes of action there is no limitation period: proceedings for a declaration of a right where there is no damage claim and some proceedings involving claims by Aboriginal peoples against the Crown (s. 2(1)).

- If a limitation period is set out in another act, it does not apply unless it is set out as an exception in the schedule at the back of the act (s. 19).

There is also a transition rule to cover transitions between the old limitation rules and those under the current Act.

Note that the *Limitations Act, 2002* only affects causes of action arising under Ontario law. If a lawsuit involves a federal statute, you need to look at the limitation periods set by federal statutes.

Retainers

Once Abigail has decided to retain I.M. Just to represent her, and I.M. Just has agreed to act, their agreement should be incorporated into a contract of **retainer**. See Figure 2.5 for an example of a retainer. The retainer should be more than just a brief notation of a contractual relationship. It should at least cover the basics—scope of legal services and costs—but preferably it will set out all of the major terms governing the relationship. Because the lawyer is an expert in these matters, and the client is dependent on the lawyer for sound and honest advice, there is said to be a **fiduciary relationship**: the lawyer is obliged to ensure that the client is treated fairly and scrupulously. One of the ways to ensure this is to explain the terms of the retainer and spell out the corresponding duties and obligations of both lawyer and client.

As a result of the Supreme Court of Canada's decision in *Canadian National Railway Co. v. McKercher LLP*,[7] it is now clear that the definition of what constitutes a conflict of interest for lawyers is stricter than it previously was. Law firms must conduct a careful check of their client databases to see that a new client's matter does not result in a conflict of interest with a current or past client of the firm. For example, if the new client is proposing to sue a former client of the firm, even on an unrelated matter, that is an obvious conflict of interest for the law firm, and the retainer cannot be accepted unless the former client agrees.

retainer
contract between a lawyer and client describing the services to be provided by the lawyer and the terms of payment by the client; also refers to a cash deposit to be used by a lawyer to pay future fees and disbursements as they are incurred

fiduciary relationship
one-sided relationship where one party relies on the other party's honesty and advice given in the reliant party's best interests

Figure 2.5   Retainer

DATE: Sept. 16, year 0

CONTRACT OF RETAINER

BETWEEN:

JUST & COPING, BARRISTERS AND SOLICITORS

and

ABIGAIL BOAR

1. I, Abigail Boar, retain you as my lawyers to commence proceedings against Fred Flogem and Rattle Motors Ltd. in respect of injuries sustained by me in an accident on September 14, year 0.
2. I understand that I have retained the firm, and not just an individual lawyer, and that other lawyers and staff may work on my case.
3. I understand that the hourly rates of those who may work on my file are as follows:

    I.M. Just, lawyer: $250/hour
    N.O.T. Coping, lawyer: $200/hour
    Edward Egregious, law clerk: $75/hour

4. I understand that the hourly rates of office staff may increase by no more than 5 percent on the first day of March, year 1, and on the first day of March in subsequent years. I agree to pay the increased amount for work done after the date on which the rates change.
5. I understand that if I am dissatisfied with the amount of the account, I have the right to have that account assessed by the court.[*]
6. I understand that before work begins under this retainer, I am required to pay a deposit of $3,000 to be credited against accounts when rendered. I understand that I may be required to furnish future deposits from time to time to cover future fees and disbursements.
7. I understand that I must pay accounts promptly when they are rendered and that interest is chargeable on overdue accounts at the rate of 18 percent per year.
8. In the event settlement funds are received, I direct that they be paid to I.M. Just in trust, and that you may deduct any fees or disbursements owing at the time settlement funds are received, on rendering an account to me, and that the balance of the settlement funds will then be paid to me.
9. I understand that it is my obligation, on receiving advice and being asked for instructions, to provide you with instructions as requested.

Signed: *Abigail Boar*   *September 16, year 0*

---

[*] We have yet to see this in a retainer or hear of a lawyer who conveys this information as a matter of course to clients; but in our view, given the fiduciary nature of the relationship, this information should be in the retainer.

The retainer must:

- identify the names of the parties (law firm and client);
- identify the work to be done (in Abigail's case, "to commence proceedings against Rattle Motors Ltd. for personal injuries arising out of an incident"); and
- be signed by the client to indicate that she has agreed to retain the firm.

The retainer should:

- make clear that other members of the law firm, such as other lawyers, clerks, and staff, may work on the file;
- set out the hourly rate for these individuals;
- indicate that the rate changes periodically, and the client is obliged to pay at the new rate for work done after the date on which the rate changes;
- indicate that if the client is dissatisfied with an account, he or she has the right to have the account assessed by the court;
- indicate the amount of the deposit required before work under the retainer begins;
- indicate that the client will be billed at stated intervals, that the client will be required to pay further deposits, and that interest will be charged on overdue accounts;
- make clear that deposits will be used to pay accounts when rendered;
- make clear that any settlement funds are to be paid to the law firm, from which accounts will be paid before the balance is paid to the client; and
- indicate that the lawyer will advise the client and that it is the client's obligation, on being given advice, to give the lawyer instructions when asked to do so.[8]

In addition to the retainer form used in Figure 2.5, the lawyer's malpractice insurer, the Lawyers' Professional Indemnity Company (usually referred to as LawPro), provides a variety of precedent documents and retainer forms that may be adapted for use by most law practices and which represent professional best practices. These files may be found at http://www.practicepro.ca/Practice/financesbookletprecedents.asp.

In some cases, clients concerned about the affordability of legal services may wish to consider a **limited scope retainer** rather than the traditional retainer we have just described, where the lawyer provides all legal services. A limited scope retainer is now permitted by the Law Society.[9] The lawyer should candidly discuss the services to be provided and, where appropriate, whether the services can be provided within the financial means of the client. The lawyer should confirm which services he or she will be providing, and which are not being provided, all of which should be set out clearly in writing. In Abigail's case, for example, she might wish to try negotiating with the defendant's insurers, and retain I.M. Just to conduct proceedings if negotiations are not successful. Abigail might also wish to consider having I.M. Just represent her on a contingency-fee basis, where the lawyer is paid a percentage of the damages awarded.

limited scope retainer
a retainer where a lawyer performs some but not all legal services for a client

Personal Injury Actions: The Ghost Client

In a case like Abigail's where the client has been injured as the result of the negligence, wrongful act, or omission of another, you may have a ghost client—the Ontario Health Insurance Plan. Under the provisions of the *Health Insurance Act* (ss. 30 and 31 and s. 39(2) of O. Reg. 552) and the *Home Care and Community Services Act* (ss. 59(2) and 59(7)) you may be required to take steps to protect the health plan's **subrogated right** to recover health care costs incurred as a result of Abigail's injuries from the person who caused those injuries. This right will clearly arise when you act for someone in a slip and fall case, like Abigail's, or in car, boat, rail, and air accident claims, or in incidents involving the malfunction of equipment, and so on. While we mostly think in terms of physical injury, psychological stress resulting from the act of another may also be included, if it caused the health care plan to incur expense.

If you believe that the client's injuries will result in health care costs, you are obliged to notify the health care plan's general manager. For this, you will require Abigail to give you the insurance number on her health card. The plan will send you statements showing costs incurred in respect of Abigail's injuries. The list can be useful to provide supporting evidence of the nature and extent of injuries in the context of treatment provided.

Subrogation inquiries to the Ministry may be made to:

> Ministry of Health and Long-Term Care
> Corporate Services Division
> Supply Chain and Facilities Branch
> Macdonald-Cartier Bldg., 2nd Floor
> 49 Place d'Armes
> Kingston, ON K7L 5J3
>
> Telephone: 613-548-6663, Fax: 613-548-6763

subrogated right
the legal right that a person (or corporation) has when he or she pays someone's debt to recover that money from the debtor

There have been a number of incidents where lawyers have found themselves acting for clients who were using false identities to engage in mortgage fraud or other criminal activity. As noted on page 48, Law Society By-Law 7.1 requires lawyers and paralegals to verify the identification of clients, both individuals and organizations. In particular, this is required whenever a lawyer or paralegal transfers funds on behalf of a client, with some exceptions if the money is transferred to a public body, public company, or financial institution, or when it is transferred to or from another licensee's trust account.

When your office agrees to be retained, you will need to obtain identity information from the client, which you must then verify. For individuals, you inspect the original and make a copy of a birth certificate, driver's licence, health card, or passport. You must retain copies of these documents in your records. If the client is a business, obtain copies of the articles of incorporation or partnership agreement, as the case may be.

Rules Governing Lawyers' Conduct Toward Clients and Others

As is the case with other professions, there is a code of professional conduct that applies to lawyers and bylaws that lay out standards of professional and general conduct for lawyers vis-à-vis their interactions with others. In particular, the *Rules of Professional Conduct* specify the following:

- Rule 5 sets out clear descriptions of what constitutes sexual harassment and discrimination on the basis of the prohibited grounds in the *Human Rights Code,* such as race, religion, and gender. The rule is quite clear that lawyers may not engage in any sexual harassment or discrimination in employment of staff or in the provision of services to the public. In particular, a sexual relationship between a lawyer and a client is looked upon with suspicion by the Law Society because of the unequal power relationship between a lawyer and most clients. Other professions have also adopted similar professional standards.

- Rule 6 addresses the responsibility of lawyers to the Law Society and other lawyers. Of growing concern in recent years has been what appears to be a lack of civility by some lawyers toward other professionals. Litigation is by nature adversarial and, for some lawyers, it may be easy to slip into incivility. However, the Law Society is clear that lawyers are expected to be courteous to their opponents and to act in good faith and not to engage in sharp practice. In recent years, the Law Society has been offering courses on the issue of civility as part of its professional continuing education programs. Civility is not the only responsibility of a lawyer toward others; if a lawyer finds that another legal professional has behaved dishonestly, the lawyer is expected to report the matter to the Law Society. If a lawyer is contacted by the Law Society about a professional conduct matter, he or she is expected to reply promptly. A frequent reason for lawyers being disciplined is because they fail to respond in a timely manner to communications from the Law Society about possible misconduct.

Client Accounts

Once the client has retained the firm, a client account must be opened. This can be done by a bookkeeper or bookkeeping department, but you or another staff member may do it. The Law Society has strict rules about keeping a lawyer's own money separate from money the lawyer holds on behalf of clients. Clients' money is to be kept in a separate trust account or accounts. A lawyer's own money is kept in a general account. If a large sum is being held for a client for more than a few days, the lawyer may open a separate trust account; otherwise trust funds are deposited into one trust account for all clients.

Funds held in trust include settlement payments and retainer deposits made by clients. Abigail's $3,000 deposit, for example, does not go into I.M. Just's general account but into the firm's trust account. Part of it can be transferred from the trust to the general account when I.M. Just renders his account. If there is any of the deposit left, it remains in trust as a credit on any amount the client may owe in future.

In order to accurately record client money transactions, the firm sets up a client ledger card or a computer version of one. On this card, all moneys received on behalf of the client and all debits for expenses chargeable to the client are recorded. Each firm has a method of tracking client expenses so that they eventually can be billed to the client ledger card: petty cash vouchers are used for cash transactions on behalf of the client, and cheque requisitions are used for cheques for the client's case (for example, to pay the court fee to issue the claim). These forms authorize a withdrawal from the firm's general account and allow the expense to be tracked so that it can be debited to the client on the ledger statement. In addition, there is a disbursement journal in which all in-office expenses are recorded so that they can be charged to the client's account. Included, for example, are charges for photocopying, long-distance telephone calls, and document deliveries.

Chapter 18 examines how this information is used to assess or fix costs if a party has been awarded costs. Chapter 19 shows how the information is used to prepare a client's account.

Docketing

While actual disbursements incurred on the client's behalf can be tracked and recorded from cheque requisitions, petty cash vouchers, and disbursement journal entries, all of which are recorded on the client's file in the office electronic accounts system, we still need to record the fees to be charged. Lawyers and law clerks charge an hourly rate. In order to determine how many hours they put in on Abigail's file, they need to keep track of their time. This is done by lawyers and law clerks when they electronically docket time spent on a client's file in the electronic accounts system. Units of time are broken down into tenths of an hour, each tenth being a six-minute block of time. On a docket, the time and the nature of the work are recorded. When a client account is billed, the dockets are referred to and the total time is calculated. See Figure 2.6 for a sample docket from a computerized accounts system.

Everyone who works on the file should be able to docket their time, so that when the account is sent to the client, all of the docket information can be assembled to show the work that has been done and the time it took to do it. It is important that this information be backed up on the system and retained. Should the client move to assess the account, the burden is on the lawyer to justify the amount of time spent on the case. That is a lot easier to do, and the lawyer's statements will be much more believable, if the lawyer can produce docketing information from the office software accounting system to show the work that was done and time that was taken to do it. It is easy to forget to enter docketing information on the software system, and, interestingly, when dockets are not kept carefully, many lawyers tend to underestimate the time spent on a case and will undercharge clients on the matter.

Electronic Docket Slip

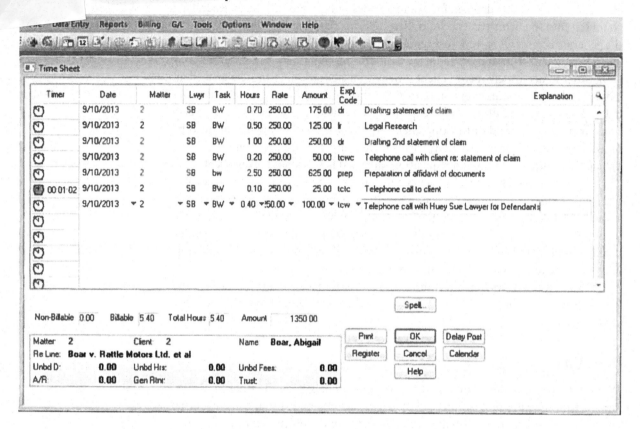

It is important for law clerks to document their time. For one thing, it can be charged to clients on an account. For another, docketed proof of work done can make the case for a raise in pay because it shows the chargeable value of that work.

File Organization

A file must be opened for Abigail's case. In a small firm, this may be an informal process, done by the lawyer, law clerk, or office assistant. In a larger firm, a central file office may do it. However it is done, there are certain practices that, with variations, are usually followed.

The case must be assigned a file number and case name. This may be as simple as the name of the client, "A. Boar," or the name followed by further information. In this case, it might be "Boar v. Rattle et al.," using a short form of the title of the proceedings. This will be useful if Abigail has several files dealing with different legal matters with this law firm. If Abigail were the defendant, the name on her file might read "Boar ats Rattle." The letters "ats" mean "at the suit of" and indicate that the client is being sued by Rattle. After the case name is established, a file number is assigned. It may be as simple as a sequential number, followed by the year the file was opened. For example, "231/13" indicates the 231st file opened in 2013. In larger firms, the system may also record the category or subject matter, state the identity of the lawyer opening the file, and provide other such information. For example, "231/13-FL-IMJ" indicates that this is the 231st file opened in 2013, that this file is a family law file, and that it was opened by I.M. Just.

Because it is difficult to work on the case if the file or part of it goes missing, a law firm may have rules about how files are stored. In a small firm, the lawyer who has carriage of the file may simply store it in his or her filing cabinet, where anyone who is working on it can find it. In larger firms, where there are more people working on a case and centralized filing is used, the centralized filing office may control the file. This means files must be checked in and out like library books. It may also mean that files cannot remain out overnight or leave the office unless special procedures are followed. This prevents inadvertent loss or the misplacing of files and is also a security measure. Files contain original documents, some of which may be valuable, and are full of confidential and privileged information. Access to them needs to be controlled.

Once opened, the file must be set up and organized. The main file is a large file folder with the case name and file number on the outside. Inside the main folder are subfiles with differently coloured subfolders to identify them at a glance. The office should have a system for maintaining a consistent colour code for subfiles. Otherwise, confusion will reign.

The main file should include a file management checklist, such as the one shown in Figure 2.7, for noting when necessary steps have been taken or are to be taken. Anyone in the office who picks up the file will know at a glance what the status is and what has to be done next. You will also find the file management checklist useful as a study guide for your course because it provides a practical step-by-step overview of the litigation process.

Subfiles

The following list describes the subfiles usually used in a litigation case and their contents. The contents of subfiles vary from law firm to law firm:

- correspondence: includes all correspondence sent and received in sequential order, with the oldest correspondence on the bottom of the pile;
- pleadings: includes copies of all pleadings, including motions;
- evidence: includes witness statements, factual memos, expert reports, photographs, and other demonstrative evidence;
- discovery: includes a copy of the discovery plan, all discovery transcripts, documents produced with the affidavit of documents, and discovery exhibits in sequential order;
- law: includes research memoranda, copies of relevant cases, and research notes;
- client documents: includes all original client documents;

- opponent documents: includes all originals and copies not in other subfiles; and

- accounts: includes all statements of account, dockets, and disbursement records.

Tickler Systems

A file management checklist is not a substitute for an automatic reminder of crucial deadlines. The Law Society and the Lawyers' Professional Indemnity Company (the Law Society's malpractice insurance body) require all lawyers to maintain a reminder system as a form of protection against professional negligence claims by clients that arise from missed deadlines, especially missed limitation periods.

The reminder system may take the form of a desk calendar or daybook, or it may be a computerized reminder system. It should give several reminders before the crucial date for taking action arrives: 30 days, 1 week, 3 days before the date, and then the date itself. Lawyers, clerks, and office assistants must take responsibility for checking the tickler system daily. At the time a file is opened, the law clerk should note the expiry date of the limitation period, as well as the dates for serving and receiving pleadings and taking other steps in the proceeding. If the file falls under the case management system, it will also be necessary to enter the dates of the mandatory timetable for steps in the proceeding. Failure to set up, maintain, and check a tickler system may amount to professional misconduct and can lead to malpractice claims and higher insurance premiums for the lawyer.

Figure 2.7 File Management Checklist

Court file no.: _____   Lawyer: _____

Reference: _____   File no.: _____

Document	Date served	Date filed	Document	Date served	Date filed
Notice of action			Client's answers to undertakings		
Statement of claim			Request for other side's answers to undertakings		
Notice of intent to defend			Answers to undertakings received		
Statement of defence			Security for costs		
Reply			Motions		
Defence and counterclaim			Trial record and setting down for trial		
Defence and crossclaim			Waiver of privilege (10 days) (Rules 30.09, 31.07)		
Third-party claim			Notice of expert witness (10 days) (Rule 53.03)		
Third-party defence			Notice for business records (7 days) (Rule 35)		
Offer to settle			Notice for medical reports (7 days) (Rule 52)		
Discovery plan			Trial brief		
Affidavit of documents (plaintiff)			Book of authorities		
Affidavit of documents (defendant)			Summons		
Notice to admit					
Notice of examination					
Examination for discovery					
List of undertakings					

CHAPTER SUMMARY

In this chapter, we discussed some of the steps taken by a law firm when it accepts a client's case. We began by assessing the facts as related by the client to determine if there was a good cause of action based on whether rights of the client had been breached and whether damages arose from the breach. We then conducted various searches to identify and name the right individuals or businesses as parties so that the correct person is sued on behalf of the client. We then determined whether the potential party was solvent and able to pay a judgment or was "judgment-proof" and not worth suing. Various searches were identified to determine whether the proposed defendant was insolvent. We also determined whether the client could afford to pay for a lawsuit, noting that civil litigation is rarely funded by legal aid. The issue of insurance coverage was explored with the client because insurance may cover the claim and make a lawsuit unnecessary for a plaintiff. If acting for an insured defendant, proper notice of a claim must be given to the insurer.

We explored whether a conflict of interest arose for the lawyer with the new or a former client. If so, the lawyer might need to turn the case over to someone else. Next, limitation periods were checked to see whether the lawsuit was timely. We observed that once a firm decides to act for a client, the client needs to sign a formal retainer that sets out the contractual relationship between the lawyer and the client. The lawyer must also verify the identity of the client on being retained. Office systems were activated for the client. A client ledger card was set up to record receipts and disbursements on the client's behalf, and methods of tracking the client's costs and expenses were identified. We noted that of particular importance is the need to docket all work done so that fees can be charged accurately. Suggestions were made about how a litigation file should be organized and maintained, and how time limits in the file can be kept track of.

KEY TERMS

fiduciary relationship, 62

impecunious, 56

judgment-proof, 56

limited scope retainer, 64

pro bono, 56

retainer, 62

reverse search, 44

stayed, 47

subrogated right, 65

NOTES

1. *Doe v. Metropolitan Toronto (Municipality) Commissioners of Police* (1990), 74 OR (2d) 225 (Gen. Div.).

2. New causes of action arise infrequently, but they do arise. In a recent case, the Ontario Court of Appeal recognized "intrusion upon seclusion," a new tort that occurs when

   a. there is an unauthorized intrusion into an individual's private life,

   b. the intrusion is highly offensive to a reasonable person,

   c. the matter intruded upon is private, and

   d. the intrusion causes mental anguish and suffering to the individual.

   See *Jones v. Tsige*, 2012 ONCA 32.

3. An employer can terminate an employee if the employee's services are no longer necessary or desired but must pay an amount equal to the salary for the period that would have been required had notice been properly given. If an employer has just cause to dismiss an employee, however, no notice need be given.

4. Because online sites are relatively easy and inexpensive to update compared with paper systems, we have found that websites are often altered, usually for the better, to facilitate searches, and that among commercial and private search sites there is much competition, so sites are frequently transformed with the result that URLs come and go with some frequency. You may have to search and play with links

or use Google or another search engine to find a site that seems to have disappeared or is not where you saw it last. This may be frustrating, but that is the way the Internet is these days.

5. Although most debts are extinguished on the discharge of the bankrupt, some, like child support debts, are not.

6. This Act and other federal legislation are available online at http://laws.justice.gc.ca.

7. *Canadian National Railway Co. v. McKercher LLP*, 2013 SCC 39.

8. In addition to the sample of a simple retainer in Figure 2.5, you will find other useful precedent retainers on the website of the Law Society's professional malpractice insurer, the Lawyers' Professional Indemnity Company (LawPro), at http://www.practicepro.ca/practice/financesbookletprecedents.asp.

9. *Rules of Professional Conduct*, Rules 2.02(6.1) to (6.3).

REFERENCES

Bankruptcy and Insolvency Act, RSC 1985, c. B-3, as amended.

Business Names Act, RSO 1990, c. B.17.

Creditors' Relief Act, 2010, SO 2010, c. 16, sch. 4.

Doe v. Metropolitan Toronto (Municipality) Commissioners of Police (1990), 74 OR (2d) 225 (Gen. Div.).

Execution Act, RSO 1990, c. E.24.

Health Insurance Act, RSO 1990, c. H.6.

Home Care and Community Services Act, 1994, SO 1994, c. 26.

Human Rights Code, RSO 1990, c. H.19.

Jones v. Tsige, 2012 ONCA 32.

Law Society of Upper Canada, *Rules of Professional Conduct* (Toronto: LSUC, 2000, as amended) (also available at http://www.lsuc.on.ca).

Limitations Act, 2002, SO 2002, c. 24, sch. B.

Ontario Limitations Manual, 3rd ed. (Toronto: LexisNexis Canada, 2006).

Personal Property Security Act, RSO 1990, c. P.10.

Rules of Civil Procedure, RRO 1990, reg. 194.

REVIEW QUESTIONS

1. Roger Redoubt was hit by a car while walking along the left side of a road. Roger has always been tone deaf. As a result of the accident, he suffered some painful injuries to his legs, which have now healed, and a concussion. However, since the accident, he is no longer tone deaf and is able to play the violin like a maestro. Does Roger have a good cause of action?

2. If a client is advancing a cause of action that has not been previously recognized, should a lawyer tell him or her to sue anyway?

3. Why is it important to be accurate about the names of the parties you are suing or on whose behalf you are suing?

4. Why does a plaintiff need to know if a defendant has judgment creditors or is bankrupt?

5. What searches should a law clerk make in the ordinary course of preparing to commence proceedings?

6. Does it matter whether the defendant went into bankruptcy voluntarily or was petitioned?

7. What insurance issues should be covered with the client?

8. Describe two situations that might give rise to conflicts of interest in a law office.

9. What steps do you need to take to safeguard a client from the expiry of limitation periods?

10. What should be included in a retainer?

11. What needs to be done to set up and maintain a client's account?

12. Describe how a client file is organized.

DISCUSSION QUESTIONS

1. Read the following memorandum and follow the requests outlined in it.

> To: Edward Egregious, law clerk
>
> From: I.M. Just, lawyer
>
> Re: Boar v. Rattle Motors et al.
>
> We have been retained by Abigail Boar. I wish you to conduct the usual searches to verify the name of the individual defendant, known to us as Fred Flogem, and to make sure we have the correct business name for Rattle Motors. I suspect that Rattle is a limited company. Please prepare the necessary search forms in draft.
>
> I have heard rumours that Rattle is in financial difficulty and want to ensure it is solvent before suing it. Please prepare the documentation to search executions, and tell me what I need to do for a bankruptcy search.

2. Using your own name or that of a friend, business, or parent, find out as much information as you can from one or more of the "people searches" search sites.

Client Management and Interviewing

3

Introduction

In many law offices, it is the law clerk who has the most ongoing contact with the client as the case proceeds. It is often the law clerk who is involved in preliminary interviewing of the client and who speaks to him or her on the telephone. Therefore, it is important that the law clerk have some basic interviewing and some effective client management skills. It is important to remember that client contact is not just about getting information. It is also about conveying information to the client.

Obtaining Information from the Client

Much of the initial and ongoing contact with the client involves information gathering. A lawyer needs to know as much about the facts of the case as possible in order to plan the case.

When clients come to the office for a meeting, make certain they are seen in private. They should also have an appointment time that is uninterrupted by telephone calls. A law office may be very busy but clients need to know that the office will not be so busy that staff cannot spend time on their case. The best way to convey this is to give clients undivided attention during their arranged appointments. Be alert, make eye contact, and listen to what they are telling you.

Interviewing is a skill, and there are many books written on the subject. Here is a short overview of some techniques that may be helpful.

Ask the client **open-ended questions**. Questions such as "What would you like to tell me about the case?" or "Is there something more I should know about the facts?" are open-ended questions. They do not box clients in. Open-ended questions encourage clients to tell the story in their own way and to convey information that is important to them. Sometimes clients may talk too much about matters that are of no consequence to the case. It is a good idea to try to redirect clients back to the issues by asking short clarifying questions to help them focus. A question that starts with, "So, what you're saying is" may be enough to turn their minds back to their narrative.

Once clients have finished relaying their story, you can then ask questions that tend to narrow the issues and focus on matters that require more elaboration. While the client has been talking, you have been deciding what parts of the story are more important or what further information you may need about certain points. **Narrow questions** tend to direct the conversation. By asking narrow questions, the questioner can get at specific points. For instance, Abigail Boar may have related her story to you about the slip and fall in the Rattle Motors Ltd. showroom. You may want to ask some details about the lighting or how many drinks she had before ambling over to look at cars.

Listen carefully to what the client is saying. Taking notes is a good idea, but try to do so unobtrusively. You can encourage a client to continue by nodding or making small verbal responses such as "uh-huh." If clients are upset or expressing their feelings, you can show empathy by saying things like, "So, you are frustrated and

open-ended questions
questions that allow the persons interviewed to choose what they want to talk about to the interviewer

narrow questions
questions in which the interviewer tries to elicit specific information

angry." Litigation is often a very emotional experience for clients, and it is perfectly acceptable to acknowledge your clients' feelings if they are raising them.

There are some common mistakes made by many people who are "listening." Some of these are:

- jumping in to add comments when clients are telling their stories;
- fidgeting with paper or tapping a pencil or pen;
- answering a question with a question;
- pretending to understand a situation when they do not understand it; and
- using clichés, such as "I hear you."

Communicating with the Client

Taking a case through the litigation process can take a long time. You know what has happened on the file, but the client does not. One of the major complaints that clients have about litigation is that their lawyer's office does not keep them informed of the progress of the case or that no one returns their telephone calls. Therefore, it is important to establish, right at the beginning, when and how their lawyer or you will be communicating with them.

There are several issues in establishing proper communications with clients. It is wise at the outset to advise clients how often during the litigation process you will be providing them with updates. Tell clients how the office will keep them informed. The method of communication must fit a client's understanding and ability to understand. It is useless to tell a client that you will fax or email information if the client has no equipment for receiving fax or email messages. It is not safe to assume that all clients have access to a computer.

Ask clients how they wish to receive communications. Do they prefer telephone contact or written communications? If they prefer to speak to someone on the telephone, it is a good idea to send a confirming letter to ensure that there is no misunderstanding about what was said.

Ensure that all the client contact information is correct. Do you have the correct mailing address and postal code, the correct email address, the correct telephone or fax number? If your clients have both a home and a business telephone number, find out which number is the most convenient for them. Do not call clients at their place of business unless they indicate that that is the best manner of communicating with them. If you telephone, ensure that you do not leave too much information with whoever answers the telephone. Clients may not have advised people that they are involved in litigation and may not be happy to have it revealed to a co-worker in a message from the lawyer's office. It should be sufficient to say no more than, "This is Joe Clerk calling from Susie Seneca's office. Would you please ask Ms. Client to call me?" There is no need to say that Susie Seneca is a lawyer or that you are her law clerk.

Once the method of communication has been settled, it is a good idea to determine how often clients can expect to hear from the law office. Will you update them once a month? Will you contact them only at certain milestones in the process? If so, determine what the milestones are and approximately when they will occur. Let clients know whether to expect a formal written report or an informal telephone chat.

One effective method for communicating with clients is sending them copies of relevant documents as they come into or leave the office. In this way, clients are kept abreast of developments as they occur. Some documents that may be sent to clients are:

- copies of all correspondence the office sends or receives on the matter,
- pleadings and court documents, and
- memoranda to file confirming communications or meetings.

Find out if your law office has a standard maximum length of time that it takes to return a client's telephone call. If such a standard exists, make sure you adhere to it. Often the standard is one business day. Whether there is an office standard or not, it may be a good personal policy to try to return client calls within 24 hours. If a lawyer is tied up in court and unable to return the call, make certain that this information is conveyed to the client.

It is also important to establish how clients will keep the office informed of developments in the case or new information pertaining to the litigation. They should be advised if there are certain things they should be watching for in terms of facts or situations.

When a practical and effective method and time frame of communication with the client is set up, the client has more confidence in the process and is less likely to inundate the office with telephone calls that interrupt work and create stress for all involved.

CHAPTER SUMMARY

This chapter introduced some general techniques and practices used in dealing with clients in a law office. It set out practical suggestions to guide you in interviewing clients and witnesses, including the appropriate use of open-ended and narrow questions to elicit information relevant to a case. The chapter also discussed appropriate techniques for maintaining communication with clients to ensure that the client receives necessary information in a timely fashion.

KEY TERMS

narrow questions, 76
open-ended questions, 76

REVIEW QUESTIONS

1. Give three examples of open-ended questions.

2. Considering the Boar case, give three examples of narrow questions you might ask Abigail.

3. What should you not do while interviewing a client or a witness?

4. Why is it important to maintain communication with the client as the case progresses?

5. What sort of information should clients receive from a law firm?

DISCUSSION QUESTION

1. Work in pairs for the following listening exercise. Look at the list of comment starters below. One student chooses any of the statements listed and uses it to begin speaking for a few minutes.

   When the first student is finished, the second student paraphrases the first student's comments. Take turns speaking and listening.

   - I would like to take a trip to … because …
   - One thing that I feel strongly about is …
   - I am taking this course in college because …
   - My favourite television show is … because …
   - When I go to a party …
   - This college is …
   - When I graduate, I would like to …
   - My ideal job is …

Introduction to the Rules of Civil Procedure and the Courts of Justice Act

4

Introduction

The Courts of Justice Act and the Law of Equity

The *Courts of Justice Act* sets out the jurisdiction of the Ontario courts, the way those courts function, and other matters related to the makeup and operation of the courts. For instance, the Act tells you the route from court to court that must be followed on an appeal, it provides for the use of French and English as the official languages of the court, it spells out the names of the courts and their jurisdiction, and it requires that court hearings be open to the public except in special circumstances. It even tells you how to address judges in the courtroom.

Until the late 19th century, there were two types of courts: the common law courts and the courts of equity. The common law courts applied **common law** principles, and the courts of equity dealt with the **law of equity**. These two separate sets of legal rules created a complicated and sometimes rigid system that made it difficult for litigants and lawyers. A major court reform about a hundred years ago merged the two courts. The statute that joined the courts was a predecessor to the *Courts of Justice Act*. Now any Superior Court in Ontario can apply both the common law and the law of equity. Superior Court judges have the power to give an equitable remedy to a party in a proceeding. They can grant injunctions and specific performance of contracts.

common law
law that is made by judges following precedents set by higher courts; often called "case law"

law of equity
a type of law developed several hundred years ago in England wherein judges, rather than following precedents, look at the issues in a case and apply certain principles to ensure a fair outcome

The Rules of Civil Procedure

The *Courts of Justice Act* requires that a Civil Rules Committee be set up. This committee has the responsibility for making the rules of practice for the Superior Court of Justice and the Court of Appeal. The *Rules of Civil Procedure* ("the Rules") are actually regulations to the *Courts of Justice Act*.

Under s. 66(1) of this Act, the rules committee may make rules for the Superior Court of Justice and the Court of Appeal in relation to the practice and procedure of those courts in all civil proceedings. Other committees set the rules for family law matters and criminal matters. The Small Claims Court also has its own rules; therefore the rules made by the Civil Rules Committee do not apply in that court.

It is the Civil Rules Committee that makes and amends the *Rules of Civil Procedure*. Because the committee is made up of judges, lawyers, representatives of the provincial attorney general and court administrators, its members are familiar with the manner in which courts operate from a number of different perspectives.

Working with the Rules

The Rules tell you everything you need to know about preparing a civil case for court. Your first task is therefore to learn how to use them.

Structure of the Rules

Rule 1 tells us how to cite the Rules, that is, as the *Rules of Civil Procedure*. In addition, this rule provides an explanation as to how the Rules are numbered and subdivided.

All of the rules with the same starting number comprise a rule. For instance, Rules 1.01, 1.02, 1.03, etc., are all part of Rule 1. However, all of these subdivisions are themselves rules. The subdivision of a rule uses the main number and a decimal point, followed by the number of the subdivision of the rule, starting with .01; for example, Rules 1.01, 1.02, and 1.03, and so on.

As well, each major subdivision may be subdivided into

- subrules, indicated by a number in parentheses (for example, subrule 1.01(2));
- clauses, indicated by a lowercase letter in parentheses (for example, clause 1.01(2)(c) or 2.02(a));
- subclauses, indicated by a lowercase Roman numeral in parentheses (for example, subclause 1.01(2)(c)(iii) or 7.01(c)(i));
- paragraphs (for example, paragraph 1 of subrule 52.07(1)), and
- definitions (for example, the definition of "originating process" in Rule 1.03).

The layout of the Rules generally follows the steps that are taken in a court case from start to finish. In addition, lawyers, law clerks, judges, court officers, and court staff become familiar with the Rules and come to know very quickly that Rule 37 deals with motions and Rule 56 with costs. However, from time to time, the Rules are amended to add new rules or subrules, or to revoke existing ones.

To avoid creating confusion by changing all the numbers or by putting a rule out of the order in which it applies to a proceeding, the Rules use a numbering system that allows the insertion of new rules in the appropriate order without having to renumber those that follow. For example, in 2004, a new rule was created to deal with how to determine the proper place for commencement of a hearing or trial. Because the Rules, as we have mentioned, are set up in order to follow a case throughout the entire court process, the appropriate place for this rule to fall was right before existing Rule 14, which deals with the documents necessary for the commencement of proceedings, because, obviously, you must determine the proper place to start your proceeding before preparing the necessary starting or originating documents. Therefore, this new rule is best placed in the Rules between Rules 13 and 14.

As with all new rules, the newly inserted rule is designated by the major rule number followed by a decimal point. A further decimal point then indicates any major subdivision of the rule. Therefore, the new rule's number looks like this: Rule 13.1, and its subdivisions look like this: subrule 13.1.01(1). The number following the first decimal point is crucial to designating the rule and distinguishing it from the original, existing Rule 13.

In another example, a new rule governing the use of information obtained from discovery, "the deemed undertaking" rule, was added to the Rules by amendment. It was placed after the rule it was most closely associated with, Rule 30, and was numbered Rule 30.1.

The same numbering principle is followed when a new subrule or subsection of a rule is added. In Rule 24, a subrule was inserted between Rules 24.05 and 24.06. The number for the subrule is 24.05.1. In Rule 24.04, a subsection has been added between subsection 24.04(1) and (2). It is designated as Rule 24.04(1.1).

While this manner of numbering rules may seem unduly complicated when we first look at it, keep in mind that it was devised in order to avoid renumbering all the existing rules that follow when a new rule that adds a new step in a proceeding is placed in the order in which that step is to be taken.

Using the Ontario Annual Practice

As discussed above, the *Rules of Civil Procedure* are a regulation to the *Courts of Justice Act*. Like most Ontario legislation, this regulation can be found on the Ontario government's e-Laws website. The *Ontario Annual Practice* is a two-volume publication that contains the *Rules of Civil Procedure* along with additional material that is helpful to litigators, law clerks, court officials, and court staff when they are working in a litigation environment. It is helpful to have related legislation, practice directions given by the court to lawyers, and the various procedural charts prepared by the editors of the publication collected in one volume, and the court forms in a second, related volume; this facilitates easier access to the material. In addition to the published volumes in book and CD form, the *Ontario Annual Practice* is also available in a mobile version.

The Procedural Charts

There is a Procedural Guide in the *Ontario Annual Practice* that offers a number of procedural charts that take you through the various steps for several types of proceedings under the Rules. Included in the guide are charts for steps in actions, actions under the simplified procedure, applications, motions, and various types of appeals, among other proceedings. Until you become familiar with the steps to be taken in a specific type of proceeding, these charts can be invaluable because they tell you the nature of the step required, when it must be taken, and who must take it.

Synopsis, Comment, and Advocacy Notes

In the *Ontario Annual Practice* there is an introduction to each rule, provided by the editors. A synopsis summarizes the content of the rule in easy-to-read language. In addition to the synopsis of the rule, there may also be a comment by the editor and/

or advocacy notes. A comment draws attention to any recent changes in that rule and provides additional helpful information about the change. Advocacy notes offer useful tips to lawyers in relation to proceedings in the court. You should not overlook these valuable tools while working with the Rules.

Annotations

Annotations are the short summaries of cases that follow most rules in the *Ontario Annual Practice*. These cases provide court interpretations and applications of the rule.

Finding Rules

The index at the back of the main volume of the *Ontario Annual Practice* can lead to a long, roundabout search if you do not know what you want to find. A preferable way to find a rule, particularly for those who are working with them for the first time, may be to use the following three-step technique:

1. Look at the "summary of contents" at the beginning of the Rules, and choose a rule that looks relevant to the information you are seeking.
2. Go to the "table of contents," which follows the summary of contents; look at the outline of what is covered in that rule, and choose a section.
3. Turn to the rule, and look through the section to find the information that is required.

The summary of contents provides a general overview of the Rules. The table of contents breaks the summary into smaller components according to the various subsections of the rule. Because the summary allows a "big picture" overview of the Rules, it also assists you in seeing where the particular component for which you are searching fits into the entire scheme.

Some rules are much easier to find and read than others and do not require all three steps, but until you are familiar with the Rules, it may be best to use this technique.

Definitions and Application of the Rules: Rules 1 and 2

A court case runs in a fairly predictable manner from start to finish. The Rules, for the most part, as was previously indicated, are set out in the same chronological order that a court case follows. The first steps you must take are set out in the first rules. In fact, the very first rules tell you the basic things that you need to know.

Rules 1.01 and 1.02 tell you how to cite the Rules and where and how they are to be applied.

Rule 1.03 is one of the most important rules because it is the definition rule. There are many words and terms that are used continually throughout the Rules, and this rule defines many of them. You must be careful when reading the Rules that you do not automatically apply everyday interpretations to the words used in them.

An ordinary English word may have a different meaning in the context of the *Rules of Civil Procedure* than it has in general usage. For instance, in the Rules, the word "holiday" means not only statutory holidays, as you might expect, but also any Saturday or Sunday (Rule 1.03). In the ordinary, general use of the word "holiday" we would not normally refer to regular weekend days as "holidays."

Over time, you will become familiar with the list of words that are defined in Rule 1.03, but until you do, every time you read a new rule, you should go back to Rule 1.03 to check that there are no words in the rule you are reading that have a special definition.

Rule 2 spells out the consequences of not following the Rules properly. The Rules do not set up a system of proceeding that is so rigid that parties lose the right to continue with their case if they do not comply with them. On the contrary, the court usually allows parties to correct their mistakes or to bring their documents or steps into compliance. However, mistakes or failures in compliance will cost your client money and time, and it is therefore essential that you always make every effort to comply with the requirements of the Rules.

Practice Directions

The Rules are applied in the same manner in every courtroom of the Ontario Superior Court of Justice throughout the province. However, some rules may need to have additional administrative details added in order to assist lawyers and court staff in their proper application.

Also, because there are courts all over Ontario, and the administrative needs of one court may be quite different from those of another, there may be a need to put a specific administrative practice in place in one or more courts, but not in all courts in the province. For instance, regions with a high volume of cases, such as Toronto, Ottawa, and the County of Essex (Windsor) may require special procedures to facilitate the management and organization of courts in those regions. These special procedures would make no sense in smaller courts with fewer cases.

practice direction
instructions set out by a chief justice to inform lawyers about special procedures that must be followed in particular courts as a result of administrative needs

In either instance, Rule 1.07 provides that the Chief Justice of the Ontario Superior Court or a senior regional judge may give a **practice direction** to other judges and to lawyers. The Chief Justice of the Superior Court, who is the leading judge of the court, signs practice directions that apply in the Superior Court throughout Ontario, while the regional senior judge for a particular region signs practice directions that apply only in that region, and the Chief Justice countersigns.

A practice direction is like a memorandum that outlines how a particular court operates in specified areas. The practice directions are signed or countersigned by the chief justice of the appropriate court, filed with the secretary of the Civil Rules Committee, published in the *Ontario Reports*, and posted on the website for the court: http://www.ontariocourts.on.ca. If the practice direction is only operable in specific regions, the regions where it applies are named in the direction.

You must always check to find out whether there is a practice direction that relates to the litigation step you wish to take in a proceeding. The court may refuse to file your documents if you do not comply with a related practice direction.

In the *Ontario Annual Practice*, practice directions precede the rule to which they relate. As an example, there are a number of different practice directions that apply to the procedure for bringing motions in various judicial regions in the province, particularly in Toronto: the practice directions for Rule 37: Motions—Jurisdiction and Procedure precede that rule.

The Difference Between "Shall" and "May"

The words "shall" and "may" are used throughout the Rules. In traditional legal interpretation, the word "shall" is an imperative. This means that when the word "shall" is used, the procedure must be followed. For example, Rule 20.04 deals with a motion for summary judgment. (The procedure for summary judgment is dealt with in depth in Chapter 11.) Rule 20.04(2) uses the word "shall," and the court is therefore required to grant summary judgment if it is satisfied that there is no genuine issue for trial or the parties consent to the procedure.

In legal interpretation, the word "may" is permissive. This means that the procedure can be used or not—it is discretionary. Rule 20.04(3) uses the word "may," and the court therefore has discretion as to whether or not it will order summary judgment if the only genuine matter at issue is the amount of money to be paid.

Until relatively recently, these interpretations of the words "shall" and "may" were set out in the Ontario *Interpretation Act*. However, that statute has now been repealed in favour of allowing judges a fair, large, and liberal interpretation that fits with the objects or purposes of a particular statute or regulation. See s. 64 of the *Legislation Act, 2006*.

Despite the repeal of the Ontario *Interpretation Act* and the more liberal interpretation approach in the *Legislation Act*, courts will still have a tendency to interpret "shall" and "may" in the traditional manner unless it would lead to an injustice. In relation to the Rules, denying a party the ability to proceed with their case for a breach of a minor procedural step would likely be seen as an injustice, but every effort should always be made to comply with the requirements set out in the Rules.

Computation of Time: Rule 3

The Rules require that many steps in a court proceeding be taken within certain time limits. For instance, there are time limits for the service and the filing of documents. Rule 3 tells you how to compute time. You might ask why there needs to be a special rule to tell you how to count days when it is something everyone knows how to do. Counting time during a court proceeding, according to the Rules, is different from counting time in ordinary life. For instance, if someone told you on Thursday that you had three days to do something, you would probably think that meant you had until Sunday. However, if you were counting in the time prescribed by the Rules, your answer would be different.

Under Rule 3.01(1)(a), when you count days, do not count the first day, but do count the last day. For example, Rule 34.05 requires you to give a party who lives in Ontario not less than two days' notice of the time and place for examinations for discovery. If you give notice on Monday, you do not count Monday as the first day. Tuesday is the first day, and Wednesday is the second. Since you count the last day as a full day, the earliest you can require the party to attend for examination is Wednesday.

Where the Rules have a time limit of seven days or *less*, holidays are not counted as days (Rule 3.01(1)(b)). If the time limit required by the rule is more than seven days, you do count the holidays. Under Rule 1.03, "holiday" includes Saturdays and Sundays. This means that if a rule requires three days to do something, you do not count Saturdays, Sundays, or other holidays listed under the definition of "holiday" in Rule 1.03.

When the last day for taking a step in the court proceeding falls on a holiday, the step may be taken on the first day afterward that is not a holiday (Rule 3.01(1)(c)). Therefore, our example above about being given, on a Thursday, two days to do something doesn't mean that you have until Saturday. Because the second day falls on a Saturday, which is a holiday under the Rules, and Sunday is also a holiday, the deadline is extended until Monday, assuming that Monday is not a holiday. If Monday is a holiday, then the next day that is not a holiday after Saturday is the following Tuesday.

If you serve a document other than an originating process after 4 p.m. or on a holiday, the document is regarded as having been served on the next day that is not a holiday (Rule 3.01(1)(d)). This means that if you served a document on Friday afternoon at 4:15 p.m. and the following Monday is Labour Day, the Rules regard the document as being served on the Tuesday after Labour Day.

Although Rule 3.02(1) permits the court to extend or shorten the time, you must bring a motion to ask the court to do this unless you can obtain the written consent of the opposing party or parties. You cannot rely on the other party's consent, and it will cost the client more money and result in delay if you must bring a motion to extend time. Therefore, it is important to keep to the time limits required by the Rules.

Rule 3.04 permits the parties to change a timetable made by a judge or master for taking certain steps if the agreement is in writing, unless the order clearly prohibits them from doing so. However, parties may not amend the date before which the action shall be set down for trial or restored to a trial list.

Adhering to timetables is also very important. In the event that a party fails to comply with a timetable on a motion brought by any other party, a judge or case master may stay or dismiss the proceeding if the offending party is the plaintiff, strike out the defence if the offending party is the defendant, or make any other order that is just.

Format for Court Documents

The Rules tell you what a court document should look like. Rule 4 prescribes in specific detail the format and content of court documents, provides for the use of electronic documents, tells you how to issue and bind documents, and gives all the other information you need to make your documents easy to read. Although instructions on how to prepare documents might seem far removed from conducting a court hearing, the documents are an integral part of the proceeding. The first impression a judge has of your client's case arises when he or she reads your documents in preparation for a hearing or a trial.

In addition, during the court proceeding, it is necessary for the lawyers to refer the judge to parts of the documents that have been filed. It can be very irritating to a judge to try to find his or her way around a set of court documents that are not properly formatted or are badly written or poorly put together. Make your court documents as professional as possible; they should reflect the seriousness of your client's case. The presentation of court documents reflects directly on the lawyer and the law firm.

Format of Documents: Rule 4.01

Rule 4.01 gives specific requirements for the set-up of documents to be filed in any court proceeding. Documents are to be typewritten and double spaced with a margin of approximately 40 mm on the left side of the text. The font must be at least 12 point or 10 pitch size. Remember that fonts that are too small are difficult to read. White paper must be used and the pages must be 216 mm by 279 mm. This is the measurement for standard 8.5 × 11-inch stationery. Do not be tempted to use legal-sized paper. It is not acceptable in part because it is difficult to fit into the court files. Documents can be printed on one side or both sides of pages.

Contents of Documents: Rule 4.02

Every document in a court proceeding must have both a general heading and a backsheet. In addition, there are requirements for the contents of the body of the particular document.

General Heading: Rule 4.02(1)

The general heading is a standard beginning for every document. There is a precedent for the set-up of the general heading in the forms that are attached to the Rules. The general heading for an action is in Form 4A and for an application it is in Form 4B. Note that the form number is the same as the rule number related to it. Each general heading must contain:

- the name of the court;
- the court file number, if one has been issued by the court (if you are preparing the first document in the case and it has not yet been served or filed, there will be no court file number, but if you are preparing documents in an ongoing case, you must make sure that the correct file number is put on the document so that it will make its way to the proper court file); and
- the title of the proceeding (this is a fancy way of saying "the name of the case"). The title of the proceeding is sometimes called the "style of cause," but this is an old-fashioned term. What is the title of the proceeding? If Abigail Boar is suing Rattle Motors Ltd., the title of the proceeding is *Abigail Boar v. Rattle Motors Ltd.*

If there are more than two parties on documents that are not originating process (a statement of claim or notice of application), or a court order, report, or record, you can use the name of one plaintiff and one defendant. For example, *Boar v. Rattle Motors Ltd. and others* is the short title of proceedings where Abigail Boar sues Fred Flogem and Rattle Motors. However, on originating process, and court orders, reports, and records, all of the parties must be named in full.

Body of the Document: Rule 4.02(2)

The body of each document must contain:

- the title of the document (is it a notice of motion, an affidavit?);
- the date the document was prepared;
- the name, address, and telephone number of the person filing the document; and
- the address of the court.

If the person having the document filed is a lawyer, the lawyer's name, address, and telephone number are to appear on the document. If a party has no lawyer and is representing himself or herself, the party's name, address, and telephone number are to appear on the document. It is a good idea to put a fax number on the document as well since some documents can be served by fax.

Backsheet: Rules 4.02(3) and 4.07

Every court document must have a backsheet. The prescribed form for a backsheet is Form 4C. Judges usually write their endorsements on the backsheet, so it is an important part of the document. Figure 1.4 in Chapter 1 shows an example of a backsheet. An endorsement is a short summary of the order that the court has made.

The backsheet must contain:

- the short title of the proceeding;
- the name of the court and the court file number;
- the location of the court office where the proceeding is commenced;
- the title of the document (is it a notice of motion, an affidavit?);
- the name, address, telephone, and fax number of the lawyer serving or filing the document;
- if the person filing is a lawyer, the lawyer's Law Society registration number; and
- the fax number, if possible, of the person being served.

In addition, if the document is an affidavit, the backsheet must also contain the name of the deponent and the date when he or she swore that the document was true.

There are usually many types of documents filed in a court proceeding. In a long case with many parties, the documents are often brought into the court on trolleys. The Rules prescribe a method for telling the documents apart. They are given different coloured backsheets. Being able to tell the documents apart is very useful in a proceeding because it makes for easier access: the judge and lawyers do not need to search through a stack of documents that all look the same.

Records for motions, applications, trials, and appeals must have a light blue backsheet. Transcripts of evidence must have a light grey backsheet, except for transcripts that are to be used on an appeal. Those must have a red front and back binding (Rule 4.07(4)). Although not all court documents require a special colour for the binding, you should check Rule 4.07 to make certain that the document you are preparing does not require a special colour. If it does not, you can use white, $176g/m^2$ cover stock (Rule 4.07(6)).

CHAPTER SUMMARY

In this chapter, we looked at the *Courts of Justice Act*, and you were introduced to the *Rules of Civil Procedure*. These rules provide a detailed set of directions as to how a court proceeding is conducted in the Ontario Superior Court of Justice and the Ontario Court of Appeal. For the most part, the Rules are laid out in the same order as the chronological progress of a court case. It is essential to learn how to find the correct rule and use it properly. Until you are familiar with the Rules, we suggest that you use the "three-step" approach to finding the appropriate rule that is described in this chapter.

Rule 1 tells you how to cite the Rules and where and how they are to be applied. It also contains a list of definitions that are crucial to your understanding of the rest of the Rules. Rule 1 also provides that the chief justice may give practice directions about certain court procedures to the judges and lawyers in a particular court region. These directions must be followed.

Rule 2 spells out the consequences of not complying with the *Rules of Civil Procedure*. Although every effort must be made to follow the Rules properly, the court has the ability to dispense with compliance if the interests of justice make it appropriate to do so. However, seeking the court's permission to dispense with compliance after a mistake has been made is costly to a client and should be avoided.

Many steps in the litigation process involve time limits. Rule 3 tells you how to count time when the Rules prescribe a time limit. You must be able to use this rule in reference to the definitions section in Rule 1.03 to ensure that you are applying the correct usage of the terms and mechanisms contained in Rule 3.

Rule 4 prescribes the format and general content of all court documents. It also tells you the size, colour, and type of paper that is required for each type of court document. Your documents provide the material for a judge's first impression of your client's case, and it is therefore essential that the documents be presented correctly and in a professional manner.

KEY TERMS

common law, 82

law of equity, 82

practice direction, 86

REFERENCES

Carthy, James J., W.A. Derry Millar, and Jeffrey G. Cowan. *Ontario Annual Practice* (Aurora, ON: Canada Law Book, published annually).

Courts of Justice Act, RSO 1990, c. C.43.

Legislation Act, 2006, SO 2006, c. 21, sch. F.

Rules of Civil Procedure, RRO 1990, reg. 194.

REVIEW QUESTIONS

1. Using the three-step process outlined in this chapter, find the rule (or rules) that:

   a. provides for service of a document on a corporation,

   b. permits the amendment of pleadings,

   c. prescribes how to commence a proceeding in the Ontario Superior Court of Justice,

   d. requires a title of proceedings on all court documents,

   e. requires that service of originating process must be personal,

   f. permits service of court documents on a party's lawyer,

   g. tells when an appointment for an examination for discovery can first be served,

   h. determines the contents of a motion record, and

   i. determines the contents of a trial record.

2. To what courts do the *Rules of Civil Procedure* apply? Name the rule that tells you that.

3. What rules apply in Small Claims Court? How do you know?

4. What is the definition of "judgment" in the Rules?

5. Are there special forms that you must use under the Rules? If so, where do you find them?

6. What form gives you a precedent for a backsheet?

7. Must you include a fax number in your documents?

8. What rule applies to the contents of an affidavit?

9. What colour backsheet belongs on an application? What rule applies?

10. What rule tells you who should make an affidavit for a corporate party?

11. How and where do you issue and file a document?

12. Who must sign a practice direction for the Superior Court of Justice?

DISCUSSION QUESTIONS

1. A motion record is served on Brad Pout on Friday, May 10 at 4:25 p.m. It is returnable—that is, it is to come to court—on May 20. However, Brad is entitled to six days' notice of the return date. Was he served in time?

2. Your firm wants to have a motion in court on Tuesday, July 3 and must give three days' notice. What is the last possible day you can serve the opposite party with the motion record?

Identification of Parties, Joinder of Claims and Parties

5

Introduction

We know that the parties to an action are called "plaintiff" and "defendant." But it is not always clear who the plaintiff or defendant is, or who should be included as a party. Can Abigail's boyfriend be a plaintiff because he has lost the pleasure of the company of the pre-accident Abigail? Can Skunk Motorcar Company Ltd. be a party defendant? Can you **join** Barbeerian's, where Abigail had two glasses of wine before going to the car showroom? How about Abigail's employer: Haven't Abigail's injuries cost Megadoon Investments something? Would it make a difference procedurally if Abigail were under 18 or mentally disabled? If any of the defendants were partnerships, are there things you would need to do?

In this chapter, we examine the relevant rules in the *Rules of Civil Procedure* to determine the answers to some of these questions. Set out below are the rules we examine and the issues they address:

- Rule 5: who should be included as a party to a lawsuit;
- Rule 5: which claims can be included together in one lawsuit;
- Rule 6: how separate proceedings may be joined together into one proceeding;
- Rule 7: how parties who are under a disability are represented in proceedings;
- Rule 8: how partnerships and sole proprietorships are named as parties;
- Rule 9: how estates and trusts sue and defend civil suits;
- Rule 10: how unidentified persons with an interest in the issues are joined to civil suits;
- Rule 11: how an interest in a lawsuit may be transferred by a party to a non-party, who then joins the proceeding;
- Rule 12: how many persons who have the same interest in a lawsuit may be joined together to be represented by one plaintiff or defendant; and
- Rule 15: whether a party to a lawsuit must be represented by a lawyer.

join (a party or claim)
add a party to an existing proceeding

joinder
describes the process of adding a party or claim to an existing proceeding

Our primary focus is on **joinder** of claims and parties (Rule 5), consolidation of claims (Rule 6), parties under disability (Rule 7), and proceedings on behalf of and against sole proprietorships and partnerships (Rule 8). You will encounter these basic rules for procedural matters often. The other rules and procedures are encountered less often unless you work in specialized areas of practice, such as estate litigation. We nevertheless include a general discussion so that if you find yourself working in these areas, you will have some familiarity with the procedural requirements.

Joinder of Claims and Parties: Rule 5

Abigail is suing Rattle Motors Ltd. and Fred Flogem for negligence concerning the failure to clean up the oil spill. But she may also have a claim against Skunk Motorcar Company Ltd. arising from the defective design or manufacture of the oil pan on the Super Coupe. Should Skunk Motorcar Company Ltd. and Abigail's claim against it be joined to a lawsuit against Flogem and Rattle Motors Ltd. that is, in some respects, about something else? Must all defendants be involved with all issues in the main lawsuit, whether their personal interest in them is minor or major? Rule 5 provides guidance in answering these questions.

Remember the basic principle in Rule 1.04(1): the aim of the Rules is to reduce cost and delay in the process of resolving disputes. Rule 5 is a more specific version of that general principle tied to the issues of what claims can be joined together in a lawsuit and what parties can be included as either plaintiffs or defendants. The thrust of Rule 5 is that all parties with an interest in an issue in the litigation should be before the court in one hearing, so that all persons with an interest have a chance to be heard and are bound by a single judgment. Generally, the Rules frown on multiple proceedings involving common events, transactions, or factual issues. However, where inclusion of several parties in one proceeding would be prejudicial to the rights of a party, issues may be tried separately.

Joining Claims

There are three procedural guidelines for joining claims set out in Rule 5.01:

1. If a plaintiff has several claims against one party, he or she may join those claims together in one proceeding.

2. If a plaintiff has different claims against different defendants, he or she may include all of the claims against the defendants in one proceeding, even if some defendants have no interest in some claims made against other defendants.

3. A plaintiff may sue in more than one capacity. For example, a party may have been injured and sue for his or her own injuries, but that party may also be the litigation guardian for a child injured in the same accident. In that case, in the capacity of litigation guardian, the party makes claims for the child's injuries, and in a personal capacity, the party makes claims on his or her own behalf.

For example, if Abigail sued Fred and Rattle Motors Ltd. for negligence, she might also sue Barbeerian's for continuing to serve her alcohol when she was intoxicated. These are separate incidents of negligence involving different parties. The only link the defendants have to each other is Abigail. But indirectly the issues involving the separate defendants are linked because they are part of the same transaction, event, or series of events. If Abigail were partly intoxicated, some of the liability for her injuries may lie with Barbeerian's, so she would include all claims she may have against any defendant. This is particularly important since the court might have to apportion liability among all defendants who were causally linked to Abigail's injuries.

However, the rule is flexible, and the court may refuse to join all of the plaintiff's claims together if some of the claims are disconnected from the others. For example, after the accident, Abigail's change in personality may have had a negative impact on her relationship with her boyfriend, to whom she had just become engaged. Suppose he breaks off the engagement? If she has a claim against him for engagement gifts she gave him, demanding their return, should she join that claim to her negligence action against the other defendants? There is some link between the claims. But for the accident, the relationship would likely have continued. The fact that the claim against the boyfriend might be in contract rather than in tort is not important. But a causal link such as this may be so remote that a court would hold it to be prejudicial to the other defendants to require them to spend time and money on a contractual issue in which they have no interest, direct or indirect, and that does not affect their cases. In this situation, the court might order that the contractual issue be severed from the negligence issues, and that the action against the boyfriend be tried separately. This means that if Abigail pursues both claims, she must do so in two separate lawsuits, which may raise costs and result in more stress for her. In considering whether to join claims or sever them, a court must balance the prejudice and relative inconvenience to all parties.

Joinder of Parties

At least initially, the plaintiff can decide what claims to include in a lawsuit, with the understanding that where it is both fair and possible, all claims that are logically related should be disposed of in one proceeding. We now turn to Rule 5.02 and the issue of when parties can join or be joined in a lawsuit.

Plaintiffs

To be joined as plaintiffs in the same proceeding, the plaintiffs or applicants must have the same lawyer of record and must assert claims arising out of the same event, series of transactions, or occurrence where a common question of law or fact may arise or where joining the parties may "promote the convenient administration of justice." There are two essential requirements. First, the same lawyer must represent all plaintiffs in the proceeding. This means that while the plaintiffs may advance different claims, there are no conflicts of interest among them with respect to those claims. Second, the claims must be related because they arise out of the same events where either it is convenient in terms of cost and delay to join the plaintiffs or there is a common question of fact and/or law that links the plaintiffs, even if some of the claims are different.

For example, suppose that Abigail were a key employee so that her injuries caused loss of profits to her employer because she was unable to work. Abigail might sue for her injuries, and the employer might sue for its profit loss. The claims are different, but there is no conflict of interest between the plaintiffs. There is a common question of fact or law (whether the defendants were negligent), and the claims arise out of the same occurrence (the accident). This case might well proceed with the two plaintiffs, represented by one lawyer, making claims in one proceeding. Otherwise, each plaintiff would need to sue separately. They would also have to sue separately if any conflict between them made them adverse in interest to each other. Lawyers must be alert to this and warn multiple plaintiffs that if a conflict develops, other lawyers must represent them both separately, and their cases must be divided and tried separately.

Defendants

While plaintiffs must be united and not in conflict to proceed together, this is not the case for defendants. Defendants may have little interest in each other, be at each other's throats, and be separately represented. If defendants are in agreement on their defence, are united against the plaintiff's claim, and have no conflict of interest with each other, they may be represented by the same lawyer, subject to the development of a conflict of interest. But it is the plaintiff who decides who the defendants are, simply because it is the plaintiff who decides whom to sue. Most lawyers follow the "sue everybody in sight" approach, particularly in the early stages of a case. Everyone who might be liable or who should be bound by the judgment is included initially. Later, often after discovery when the plaintiff has more information, the plaintiff may discontinue proceedings against some of the defendants, though he or she may have to pay some costs to do so.

Guidelines as to who may be added as defendants are set out in Rule 5.02(2)(a) to (e).

1. *Persons against whom the plaintiff makes claims arising out of "the same transaction or occurrence, or series of transactions or occurrences" may be joined as defendants.* These claims may be made against defendants who acted together or who acted separately from each other. If a claim against one defendant fails, it can be made alternatively against another defendant. The uniting factor is not the relationship between the defendants or between the defendants and the plaintiff; it is the relationship of all to an occurrence or transaction. For example, Abigail may sue Barbeerian's, Fred, Rattle Motors Ltd., and Skunk Motorcar Company Ltd. Her reason for suing each is different, but they are each connected to an occurrence: the accident that gave rise to damages for which they are allegedly liable in various ways.

2. *Persons who are linked together by a common fact or issue of law may be joined as defendants.* For example, if a plaintiff seeks to determine who among several people share an interest in property, all of those people may be made defendants because of their link to and interest in an issue of law (the ownership of property). In this case, the plaintiff may seek a declaration as to who is entitled to the property rather than damages. Note that the plaintiff here may not be making allegations that a particular defendant has done anything wrong.

3. *All potential defendants may be joined in the proceeding when the plaintiff is not sure who is liable and from whom a remedy can be obtained.* This is the basis for the "sue everybody in sight" rule. In medical malpractice there may be several medical practitioners who are responsible for the plaintiff's injury, but because of the nature of treatment or the patient's state, or both, the patient may not know who among all the doctors, nurses, and other medical professionals caused the damage. The plaintiff therefore sues them all.

4. *All potential defendants may be joined when the plaintiff has sustained a loss caused by more than one defendant, even where there is no factual connection between the potential defendants and there is doubt as to which defendant caused what damage.* This rule applies to a situation where, for example, a plaintiff was physically injured in an accident and then taken to a hospital where negligent medical staff caused further physical damage. The nature of the physical damage may prevent the plaintiff from knowing which potential defendant caused what part of the damage. In this case, this rule permits the plaintiff to sue everyone involved. This situation differs from that contemplated by the previous subrule. Here, we think various defendants each did some damage. In the previous situation, we think that one or more defendants did all the damage, but we do not know which one was responsible. While the Rules seem to contemplate distinct situations giving rise to joinder of defendants, you will find that often several of the subrules can apply to a case.

5. *Notwithstanding the failure of a case to come within the first four rules, defendants may be joined if joinder promotes the convenient administration of justice.* The term "convenient" incorporates the concept of "balance of convenience." The court, in examining balance of convenience, looks to see whether joinder will cause the proceeding to be less expensive and less time-consuming for the parties, on the whole, without prejudicing a party's right to a fair trial.

Joinder and Misjoinder of Necessary Parties: Rules 5.03 and 5.04

As a general rule, the court has the power to join in a proceeding any person whose presence is necessary to decide the issues in the case. This means, for example, that if a person who is not a party to the proceeding will be affected by a decision, that person should have standing as a party in the proceeding.

If a plaintiff claims a remedy to which another person is also entitled, the plaintiff is obliged to join the other person to the proceeding. If there is no conflict of interest and if the "add-on" agrees by filing a consent under Rule 5.04(3), the add-on is joined as a plaintiff. If the add-on does not consent or objects, he or she is added as a defendant so as to be bound by the decision, even though no claim is made against the add-on. While the add-on cannot be compelled to be a plaintiff, he or she cannot easily prevent being made a defendant. In general, if a person who is not a party to the proceeding could be affected by the decision, he or she should be added as a defendant. As a general rule, if a plaintiff is in doubt, the plaintiff should add the person as a defendant, even if there is no claim made against that defendant, so that the defendant is bound by the judgment. This is important because a **judgment *in personam*** is more common than a **judgment *in rem***. A judgment *in personam* arising, for example, from a negligence action is binding only on the parties; a judgment *in rem* arising, for example, from a declaration of land ownership binds the parties, but it also binds non-parties. If you are declared the owner of Pink Acre, then you have an interest superior to the whole world, even though the whole world was not a party to the proceeding.

judgment *in personam*
judgment that is binding only on the parties to the proceeding

judgment *in rem*
judgment that is binding on everyone, whether a party to the proceeding in which the judgment is pronounced or not

In the event that a plaintiff fails to include a necessary party, any person can apply to the court to be made a party, or the court can add a party on its own motion. The ground for such addition brings us back to the main principle: a party is added where his or her presence is necessary for the court to completely determine the issues in the proceeding. Similarly, under Rule 5.03(6) the court may also permit someone who ought to be joined to be relieved of that obligation. Remember that being joined to a lawsuit is expensive and time-consuming. Rule 5.04(1) confronts this issue as well.

Rule 5.04 generally recognizes that the naming of parties to a lawsuit is primarily left to the plaintiff, not to the court. Plaintiffs can make errors in including people who should have been left out and in omitting people who should have been included. Rule 5.04 gives the court broad powers to correct the errors of litigants. It does not require the dismissal of a case where persons have been wrongfully included or omitted. It allows the court to determine the dispute without the presence of a person who should have been added, but without prejudice to that person's rights, which may be litigated in a subsequent proceeding. The court may also add, substitute, or drop parties, or correct the name of a party who was incorrectly named in the lawsuit, without the lawsuit having to be dismissed and restarted against the correct parties. This power is consistent with Rule 2.01, which treats procedural errors as irregularities rather than nullities. However, if the failure to include a party is so prejudicial that it cannot be compensated for by costs and an adjournment, then the failure may result in a nullity notwithstanding Rule 2.01. For example, if a party was omitted and the limitation period has expired, it may be prejudicial to add the party at that time.

Claim by an Assignee of a Chose in Action

Rule 5.03(3) contains specific provisions about assignments of the right to sue. An **assignee** is a person to whom a right, usually a contractual right, has been transferred. A **chose in action** is a type of property that is intangible—that is, its value does not lie in its physical properties but in what it represents. For example, a cheque is a chose in action; its value lies not in the printed piece of paper that it physically is, but in what it represents: the promise to pay the sum written on it.

Where an **assignor** has assigned his or her right to collect a debt or other chose in action, the assignee acquires all the rights the assignor had, including the right to sue to collect the debt or the value of a chose in action. However, Rule 5.03 requires that the assignor be added as a party. If Henry had assigned his right to Herbert to collect on a loan that Henry had made to Stanislaus, including giving Herbert the right to sue Stanislaus for nonpayment, and Stanislaus did not pay, Herbert can sue Stanislaus, but Henry must be added as a party to the action, even though he no longer has a claim for repayment. However, there is one common circumstance where the assignor need not be added: if the assignment was absolute, so that the assignor retains no further rights in the asset *and* notice in writing of the assignment has been given to the person obliged to pay the debt or deliver up the chose in action. For example, if Anil lent money to Gregor on a promissory note signed by Gregor where Gregor promised to repay Anil with interest, and Anil sold all interest

assignee
person to whom rights, usually contract benefits, are granted by an assignor

chose in action
intangible personal property whose value lies in what it represents

assignor
person who grants contract rights to an assignee

in the promissory note to Fly-By-Night Finance Ltd. and gave notice to Gregor that the promissory note had been sold to Fly-By-Night, then Anil does not have to be added as a party to any lawsuit between Gregor and Fly-By-Night.

Relief Against Joinder

We have already noted how, under Rule 5.04, a court has the power to correct joinder errors without making the lawsuit a nullity. But sometimes, the correct joinder of parties results in a cumbersome proceeding that causes judges and lawyers to flee in horror. Relief from this situation is available under Rule 5.05. Where a case is unduly complicated or will be delayed or prejudice a party because of joinder of multiple claims or parties, the court may take a number of procedural steps. It can order separate hearings. For example, if Abigail sued Fred, Rattle Motors Ltd., and Skunk Motorcar Company Ltd. for negligence, and her employer for wrongful dismissal all in one proceeding, the court could break the matter into two separate proceedings: negligence and wrongful dismissal. It could also order claims in one proceeding to be transferred to another proceeding or allow costs to a party compelled to attend part of a proceeding in which it has no interest. It can also **stay proceedings** against one defendant while a proceeding against another defendant is completed and bind the party against whom proceedings are stayed by the findings of fact and law made in the previous proceeding. This rule may be invoked when the same issues affect both defendants, so that trying both is repetitious, and the decision in the first case is justly binding on the defendant in the stayed proceeding.

stay proceedings
stop proceedings for a given or indefinite period, pending the fulfillment of a condition, without dismissing the proceedings

Consolidation or Hearing Together: Rule 6

Just as the court may order parties or issues to be severed from a proceeding and tried separately when convenient, so may the court order the consolidation of separate proceedings. As a means of reducing cost and delay, the court will combine separate proceedings, where possible, rather than have several related proceedings continue separately. An additional reason for consolidation is that the courts wish to avoid two or more decisions on an issue or fact that is common to both proceedings. Inconsistent decisions are to be avoided because they lead to instability, uncertainty, and further proceedings by way of appeal—all things that the common law tries to eliminate.

Under Rule 6.01(1)(a) to (c), proceedings may be consolidated when:

- there is a common question of law or fact (not just common issues or questions raised by litigants);
- the relief claimed arises out of the same fact situation; or
- there is some other good reason for consolidation, leaving the court broad discretion to deal with each case on its facts within the confines of the principles stated above.

Rule 6.01 also goes on to give the court broad powers to direct how a consolidated proceeding is to be conducted justly in relation to the parties with minimal cost and delay. The two proceedings can be consolidated to be heard together as one proceeding, with the plaintiff presenting all its issues and evidence and the defendants following. However, if it is logical to have one issue or set of issues heard first because this is necessary in order to render a decision on a second set of issues, the court may order the cases to be consolidated but tried one after the other.

For example, if Abigail sues Fred in one proceeding and Rattle Motors Ltd. in another, it may make sense to consolidate the two into one proceeding but to try the case against Fred first. If Fred turns out not to be liable for failing to mop up the oil, there may be no case against Rattle Motors Ltd. to answer. If Rattle is allegedly liable for failing to direct Fred and Fred is not liable, neither logically is Rattle Motors Ltd. If the plaintiff's first case fails, her second case can be dismissed without further evidence being heard, saving time and money for all of the parties.

The court also has the power to stay one proceeding until the other is heard or asserted as a counterclaim by the defendant in the plaintiff's action. In practical terms, the court is free under Rule 6.01(1)(d) and (e) to control its own process and customize consolidation orders to save time and money and to yield a just result. In Rule 6.01(2), the court is given the power to make an order for directions that may dispense with service of a notice of listing for trial and abridge the waiting time for placing a case on the trial list. In fact, the court can order the matter to proceed immediately and fix a date for trial. Note the use of the motion for directions to break procedural logjams and clean up procedural messes. Lawyers generally have carriage of how an action proceeds, who gets sued, and what issues are included. Each lawyer is focused on his or her client's needs, and if there are multiple issues and parties, there needs to be some objective supervision. If a case is going from a straightforward matter to chaos with multiple parties, proceedings, and issues, a party may use a motion for directions to sort out the mess. In Toronto, Ottawa, and the County of Essex (Windsor), where proceedings may be subject to case management under Rule 77, the kind of litigation chaos described here may result in the case coming under case management, where a case management judge or master can take the initiative to untangle procedural knots, set out a timetable, and even fix a date for trial. Alternatively, the kind of chaos described here might be sorted out by a case conference judge under Rule 50.

In 2010, Rule 6.1 was added to permit parties, on consent, to have separate hearings on one or more issues in a proceeding. This can include hearings on liability and damages, for example, or separate hearings on several legal issues, with further provision that the outcome on one issue may determine whether some of the other issues need to be heard or decided.

Parties Under a Disability: Rule 7

The common law has long barred parties who are not of "full age and capacity" from initiating and defending lawsuits on their own. The reasoning here is that children and mentally ill adults do not have the judgment, experience, or resources to engage in litigation on their own, just as they may not contract on their own in some cases. They are not barred from suing and being sued, however, since access to the courts is a fundamental right. Instead, they may exercise rights as litigants but must have a mentally competent adult or a public body assist them in the enterprise. The rules governing the duties and procedures to be followed by a **litigation guardian** are set out in Rule 7.

litigation guardian
competent adult who directs and takes responsibility for the litigation of a legally disabled party, such as a minor, an absentee, or a mentally disabled person

Minors and mentally incapacitated persons are generally referred to in Rule 7 as "persons under disability"; this term replaces the now-derogatory terms "infant," "imbecile," or "lunatic" previously used at common law and under older statutes. Persons under disability must have a litigation guardian. Such people include:

- a minor;
- a person who is mentally incapable of understanding proceedings and instructing counsel on an issue in those proceedings, whether the person has a guardian or not;[1] and
- an **absentee** under the *Absentees Act*.

absentee
person whose rights or interests are being determined in a proceeding and whose whereabouts are unknown

The court can dispense with litigation guardians in an appropriate case. A sophisticated minor, almost 18 years of age, may be allowed to proceed without a litigation guardian if the court thinks this is appropriate. The other instance where a litigation guardian is not needed involves an application for a declaration that a person is incompetent. Where a litigant seeks to declare someone mentally incompetent so as to appoint a guardian to make decisions about the alleged incompetent's property and person under the *Substitute Decisions Act, 1992*, the alleged incompetent need not have a litigation guardian appointed under Rule 7 unless the court requires it.

To make some sense of the law in this area, you need to understand that, under legislation, if a person is unable to manage his or her own assets because of mental illness or another infirmity, the law provides for a procedure to have the person declared mentally incompetent. Such a declaration means that the person could not manage day-to-day life decisions, especially concerning his or her money and assets. Note that not all mental illness is equivalent to legal mental incapacity. A person may be a schizophrenic and suffer specific delusions but be able to manage his or her own business affairs. If so, the court does not often intervene to appoint a guardian. But if the person cannot manage his or her business affairs, to prevent waste to the person's estate or harm to him or her physically, the court can order one or more people to act as the committee of the incompetent person, after making a finding of mental incompetence. This is the route that is often followed if someone suffers from Alzheimer's disease or some other form of dementia.

In addition, a person who recognizes that he or she can no longer handle his or her own affairs or who wishes to provide for that situation when it occurs may voluntarily, without a finding of mental incompetence, make his or her own arrangements for someone to manage his or her estate. This is done by appointing a person to take on this task under a power of attorney. No court order is or was required for this. The person granted power of attorney has the power to enter into contracts and generally deal with the assets of the person who made the appointment. In addition, the law also provides for a power of attorney for personal care, in which an individual may appoint a person to make decisions about personal care, including medical decisions, when and if the person making the appointment is no longer able to do so. Again, no court order is required. It is not uncommon for an elderly person to grant a younger, trustworthy relative both a power of attorney regarding property and a power of attorney for personal care to make decisions about health care.

Rule 7.01(3) is a transition section that takes into account new legislation in the mental health area introduced between 1990 and 1995. A person who was named as the committee of a mental incompetent in the older legislation, to represent the incompetent in proceedings, continues as a litigation guardian. Where there was no individual to do this and the public trustee was appointed to act for the mental incompetent under the *Mental Health Act*, the Public Guardian and Trustee continues to act as litigation guardian. You should note that the Rules generally are littered with such transition provisions when older legislation is amended or repealed and replaced. Often only the terminology is changed, but read the relevant rule and the legislation referred to carefully because there may be substantive changes as well.

Litigation Guardians for Plaintiffs

Rules 7.02(1) and (2) lay out a complete code governing litigation guardians for a plaintiff or applicant. Any person who is not under a disability may act as the litigation guardian of a person under a disability. No court order is required. The assumption is that a person under a disability who has a cause of action also has friends or relatives who will step in. This is almost always the case for minors. Where a person is mentally incapable, it may be more complicated, especially if the mental incapacity is connected to homelessness or substance abuse and the individual has become disconnected from friends and family. If Abigail were a minor, she would be identified in the title of proceedings as "Abigail Boar, a minor, by her litigation guardian, Henrietta Boar, Plaintiff." If she were mentally incapacitated, she would be identified in the proceedings as "Abigail Boar, a mentally incapable person, by her litigation guardian, Henrietta Boar, Plaintiff." See Figure 5.1.

If Henrietta were suing for her own damages as well as acting as litigation guardian for Abigail, the title of proceedings would read "Abigail Boar, by her litigation guardian, Henrietta Boar, and Henrietta Boar personally." The same formats would be used if Abigail and Henrietta were defendants instead of plaintiffs.

Mentally incapable persons may have existing representatives act as litigation guardians without a court order unless the court orders otherwise. If a mentally incapable person has a guardian, or had a committee under older legislation, or voluntarily appointed an attorney[2] to manage his or her affairs under a power of attorney, that person may act as litigation guardian. However, in the case of a power of attorney, the power to act as a litigation guardian must have been included as one of the powers under the power of attorney appointing him or her. If the Public Guardian and Trustee acted for an incompetent, as would be the case where there was no relative to appoint as committee or attorney under a power of attorney, and the person was sued, the Public Guardian and Trustee would act as litigation guardian.

Figure 5.1   Affidavit Filed Pursuant to Rule 7.02(2) (Form 4D)

Court file no. 01-CV-5678

ONTARIO
SUPERIOR COURT OF JUSTICE

BETWEEN:

ABIGAIL BOAR, A MENTALLY INCAPABLE PERSON,
BY HER LITIGATION GUARDIAN,
HENRIETTA BOAR

Plaintiff

and

RATTLE MOTORS LTD. and FRED FLOGEM

Defendants

AFFIDAVIT OF HENRIETTA BOAR

I, Henrietta Boar, of the City of Toronto, in the Province of Ontario, MAKE OATH AND SAY:

1. I consent to act as litigation guardian for Abigail Boar, the plaintiff in this action.
2. I have given written authority by way of a retainer signed on September 16, year 0 to I.M. Just to act as lawyer in this proceeding.
3. The plaintiff, as a result of her injuries, is unable to concentrate, understand complex concepts, or take any interest in her surroundings. She is depressed and passive. Dr. Alice Wunderkind, a psychologist who has examined the plaintiff, advises me that the plaintiff is unable to instruct her lawyer in this proceeding. Now marked exhibit A to my affidavit is a copy of the medical report of Dr. Wunderkind dated September 29, year 0, when this assessment was made.
4. Both the plaintiff and I are ordinarily resident in Ontario.
5. I am the mother of the plaintiff.
6. I have no interest in the proceeding adverse to that of the plaintiff.
7. I acknowledge that I have been informed by my lawyer that I may be liable to personally pay any costs awarded against me or against the plaintiff.

SWORN before me at the)	
City of Toronto,)	*Henrietta Boar*
in the Province of Ontario,)	Henrietta Boar
on October 16, year 0.)	
I.M. Just)	
I.M. Just)	
Commissioner for Taking Affidavits)	

RCP-E 4D (July 1, 2007)

While no court order is required to appoint a plaintiff's litigation guardian, an individual who seeks such an appointment must file a certificate or a sworn affidavit setting out the nature of the disability. The **affiant** must also generally show that he or she is a proper person to act as litigation guardian and that there is no conflict of interest. The affiant must also agree to pay any costs awarded against him or her or against the plaintiff. If neither the affiant nor the plaintiff resides in Ontario, they may be asked to provide security for costs as well (Rule 7.02(2)).[3]

affiant
person who swears an affidavit

The body of a sample affidavit to be filed with the court pursuant to Rule 7.02(2) is set out in Figure 5.1.

This affidavit uses the provisions of Rule 7.02(2) as an outline to set out the information required. The affidavit also uses the language and vocabulary of the rule with simple modifications. Why make the job of drafting harder than it is?

Litigation Guardians for Defendants

Rule 7.03 provides a detailed code governing the appointment of litigation guardians for defendants or respondents. A defendant's litigation guardian must be an appropriate person: someone willing and able to act on behalf of the defendant. There must be no conflict of interest with the defendant, and the person cannot be under disability. As with plaintiffs, if the defendant is a minor, parent, guardian, or other close relative, he or she will likely be approved as litigation guardian. If the defendant is mentally incapable, a close friend or relative is likely to be approved to act as litigation guardian. Unlike the case with plaintiffs under disability, a defendant's litigation guardian must apply to the court by motion to be approved as litigation guardian. However, a court appointment is not necessary if:

- the defendant is a minor with an interest in an estate or trust (in which case he or she is represented by the **Children's Lawyer**);
- the defendant is mentally incapable or an absentee and either has a guardian, an attorney under a power of attorney, or a committee, all with authority to act as litigation guardian; or
- the defendant is mentally disabled, in which case he or she is represented by the Public Guardian and Trustee.

Children's Lawyer
official of the Ontario Ministry of the Attorney General whose office oversees the rights of some minors involved in civil litigation and custody disputes

A person who is to act as a litigation guardian for a mentally incapable defendant must file a certificate or affidavit under Rule 7.03(10) signifying his or her ability and willingness to act. If the litigation guardian is the Public Guardian and Trustee or the Children's Lawyer, the affidavit is abbreviated and omits material dealing with potential conflict of interest between the guardian and the disabled party.

A person who seeks to act as a litigation guardian must file a notice of motion asking to be appointed before acting for the disabled defendant, and must support the motion with the affidavit or certificate referred to in Rule 7.03(10). If a litigation guardian is already acting for a plaintiff, he or she may defend a counterclaim without bringing a motion (Rule 7.03(3)).

A sample affidavit to be filed pursuant to Rule 7.03(10) is set out in Figure 5.2.

Figure 5.2   Affidavit Filed Pursuant to Rule 7.03(10) (Form 4D)

Court file no. 01-CV-7890

ONTARIO
SUPERIOR COURT OF JUSTICE

BETWEEN:

HENRY SMOKE

Plaintiff

and

ABIGAIL BOAR

Defendant

AFFIDAVIT OF HENRIETTA BOAR

I, Henrietta Boar, of the City of Toronto, in the Province of Ontario, MAKE OATH AND SAY:

1.   This is an action for breach of contract brought against the defendant.

2.   The cause of action arose on or about April 10, year 0, and the action was commenced on July 19, year 0.

3.   The defendant was served with a statement of claim and a notice requesting appointment of a litigation guardian on July 24, year 0.

4.   The defendant suffers from Alzheimer's disease. As a result, she often behaves impulsively, suffers from delusions, and is unable to understand the issues in this lawsuit or give instructions to counsel.

5.   The defendant ordinarily resides in Ontario.

6.   I, the proposed litigation guardian, am the daughter of the defendant.

7.   I am ordinarily resident in Ontario.

8.   I consent to act as litigation guardian in this proceeding. I am a proper person to be appointed as litigation guardian. I have no interest in the proceeding that is adverse to that of the defendant. I understand that I may incur costs that may not be recovered from the other party.

SWORN before me at the	)
City of Toronto,	) *Henrietta Boar*
in the Province of Ontario,	) Henrietta Boar
on November 24, year 0.	)
I.M. Just	)
I.M. Just	)
Commissioner for Taking Affidavits	)

RCP-E 4D (July 1, 2007)

If no one moves to become litigation guardian for a defendant, the plaintiff may move for the appointment of a litigation guardian for the defendant. The moving party must also serve a request to appoint a litigation guardian on the defendant, personally or by an alternative to personal service. This notice may be served with the originating documents, but must be served at least 10 days before the **return date** of the motion. The motion may be made without notice to a defendant, but it is necessary to move to dispense with notice in the notice of motion to appoint a litigation guardian. This may be done as part of the motion to appoint by asking for leave to proceed without serving the disabled defendant and, if leave is granted, for an order appointing a litigation guardian. This eliminates the need for bringing a motion to dispense with service separately. If the goal is to appoint the Children's Lawyer or the Public Guardian and Trustee as the defendant's litigation guardian, those bodies must be served with the motion (Rule 7.03(4) to (9)).

return date
the date on which the motion will be heard by the court

Figure 5.3 sets out Form 7A, the notice to appoint a litigation guardian for a defendant. With modifications, it can be used to appoint a litigation guardian for the plaintiff.

Representation of a Party Under Disability When No One Volunteers to Be Litigation Guardian

Being a litigation guardian is not considered one of life's joys. There are disabled plaintiffs and defendants with no relatives, no friends, and no one to step in and help. Where no one comes forward for the plaintiff or defendant, and where a plaintiff moves to have someone appointed as a litigation guardian for a defendant where there is no likely person available, the court may appoint:

- the Children's Lawyer to represent a minor, or
- the Public Guardian and Trustee to represent a person who is mentally incapable and has no guardian or attorney under a power of attorney.

If the disabled party is both a minor and mentally incapable, the court may appoint either the Public Guardian and Trustee or the Children's Lawyer (Rule 7.04(1)). Where a disabled person is not a party and the court deems that he or she should be, then the party must be added. The Children's Lawyer or the Public Guardian and Trustee, as the case may be, is appointed as litigation guardian.

The Children's Lawyer and the Public Guardian and Trustee are government officials. Their departments operate with high caseloads and limited resources. This is particularly true for the Public Guardian and Trustee, where staff have very heavy workloads. In dealing with people's property, they also often have contentious and adverse relationships with the relatives of mentally disabled persons.

Powers of the Litigation Guardian

Once appointed, a litigation guardian may make any decision and take any step a litigant of full capacity can make. This includes retaining and dismissing counsel and being advised by and instructing counsel. A litigation guardian may take further

Figure 5.3   Request for Appointment of Litigation Guardian (Form 7A)

Court file no. 01-CV-1011

ONTARIO
SUPERIOR COURT OF JUSTICE

BETWEEN:

ABIGAIL BOAR

Plaintiff

and

MAXIM FURTWANGLER

Defendant

REQUEST FOR APPOINTMENT OF LITIGATION GUARDIAN

THE PLAINTIFF BELIEVES THAT YOU ARE UNDER A LEGAL DISABILITY. As a party under disability, you must have a litigation guardian appointed by the court to act on your behalf in defending this proceeding.

YOU ARE REQUIRED to have some proper person make a motion to this court forthwith to be appointed as your litigation guardian.

IF YOU FAIL TO DO SO WITHIN TEN DAYS after service of this request, the plaintiff may move without further notice to have the court appoint a litigation guardian to act on your behalf.

July 14, year 0

Just & Coping
Barristers and Solicitors
365 Bay Street – 8701
Toronto, Ontario, M3J 4A9

I.M. Just
LSUC #12345R
tel. 416-762-1342
fax 416-762-2300

Lawyers for the Plaintiff

TO: Maxim Furtwangler
       123 DeCory Street
       Toronto, Ontario, M4R 1Z6

RCP-E 7A (July 1, 2007)

proceedings, such as counterclaims, crossclaims, and third-party claims. A litigation guardian, other than the Children's Lawyer and the Public Guardian and Trustee, cannot act on his or her own. He or she must retain a lawyer to represent the disabled party in court (Rule 7.05).

Removing a Litigation Guardian

Being a family member or friend of a person under disability does not necessarily make a person capable as a litigation guardian. There are provisions to remove a litigation guardian where the court thinks it is appropriate or it is otherwise required. If a minor reaches the age of majority, the litigation guardian may file an affidavit setting out that fact, and the registrar will grant an order authorizing the action to continue without the litigation guardian. The order will be served on all other parties.

An order in Form 7B to continue a proceeding where a party has reached the age of majority is set out in Figure 5.4. It can be modified for a party whose incapacity has ended.

Note that this is one of the few instances where the title of proceedings changes after litigation commences. Similarly, if a person is under disability for other reasons—mental incapacity, for example—and the incapacity ends, the litigation guardian or the party may move to continue the proceeding without the litigation guardian. This order is served on all other parties.

If the court is of the opinion that the litigation guardian is not acting in the best interest of the party under disability, the court may remove the litigation guardian and substitute the Children's Lawyer, the Public Guardian and Trustee, or any other person (Rule 7.06).

Protection Against Default Judgment

When a defendant fails to defend an action, the plaintiff can note the defendant in default and move without notice for default judgment. If the claim is for a liquidated amount that is easily calculated by objective standards—such as a debt and interest on it—the clerk may sign immediate judgment. Because a litigation guardian may inadequately represent a disabled party or there may be difficulty in finding a litigation guardian or getting him or her to respond, it is easy for a plaintiff to move quickly for a default judgment. However, if a plaintiff moves for default judgment and the responding party is under disability, the defendant may not be noted in default without leave of a judge of the court. If the plaintiff knows of the disability, he or she is obliged to serve a motion to note (the defendant) in default on the litigation guardian of a person under disability, and on the Children's Lawyer if the defendant is a minor, unless the Public Guardian and Trustee is the litigation guardian (Rule 7.07).

Often, however, a defendant who is a minor or who is mentally incapable may not appreciate or understand the need to file a defence and, by doing nothing, defaults. The plaintiff may be unaware that the defendant is under disability until he or she attempts to enforce the judgment. At that point, a family member or friend of

Figure 5.4   Order to Continue (Form 7B)

Court file no. 01-CV-1415

ONTARIO
SUPERIOR COURT OF JUSTICE

BETWEEN:

EMILY BOAR, A MINOR, BY HER
LITIGATION GUARDIAN, ABIGAIL BOAR

Plaintiff

and

J.S. BACH LTD.

Defendant

ORDER TO CONTINUE

On the requisition of the plaintiff, Abigail Boar, and on reading the affidavit of Abigail Boar, filed, which states that the minor, Emily Boar, has reached the age of majority on August 14, year 0,

IT IS ORDERED that this proceeding continue by Emily Boar, without a litigation guardian and that the title of the proceeding be amended accordingly in all documents issued, served, or filed after the date of this order.

Date: August 17, year 0

Signed by: _____
                    Local registrar

Address of
court office: Courthouse
                   393 University Avenue
                   Toronto, Ontario, M5G 1E6

RCP-E 7B (November 1, 2005)

the defendant may become involved, leading to the appointment of a litigation guardian who has a right to move to set the default judgment aside on the ground of the incapacity of the defendant, with leave to defend.

Approval of Settlements for Parties Under Disability

Neither a party under a disability nor a litigation guardian has the power to settle a proceeding on behalf of a disabled party or make a settlement before proceedings are commenced without the approval of the court. This reflects a long-standing common law rule that the courts must oversee and supervise settlements made by parties under disability to ensure that those parties are not taken advantage of. An unapproved settlement is not binding on the disabled party, who may have up to six years after the disability ends to sue again. For example, a minor who is injured at age 4 by a defendant's negligence can, after turning 18, sue the defendant and may have as long as six years from the time he or she turns 18 to do so before the limitation period expires.

Rule 7.08 sets out a procedural code for obtaining approval of a settlement for a disabled party. If a claim is settled before proceedings are commenced, the parties must, by application to a judge, ask for approval of the settlement by the court. If proceedings have been commenced, approval of the court must be obtained on a motion within the proceedings. The application or motion for approval must be accompanied by an affidavit of the litigation guardian that sets out the facts, the reasons for settling, and the opinion of the litigation guardian as to the proposed settlement. The lawyer acting for the litigation guardian must, by affidavit, set out his or her position on the proposed settlement. This requirement is intended as a safeguard against an improvident agreement by a litigation guardian who ignores a lawyer's advice. It puts the court on notice to examine the matter further. If the litigation guardian is acting on a lawyer's advice, the lawyer's affidavit will usually mirror the litigation guardian's.

If the person under disability is a minor over the age of 16, the consent of the minor should be filed unless the court orders otherwise.

If a judge has any qualms or questions about the propriety of the settlement, he or she may direct the material to be served by the moving party on the Public Guardian and Trustee or on the Children's Lawyer, depending on the circumstances. The official served must report back to the court orally on the return date of the motion or in writing with recommendations. Reasons for recommendations in connection with the proposed settlement must also be provided.[4]

Partnerships and Sole Proprietorships: Rule 8

There are special rules for suing sole proprietorships and partnerships. These two forms of business organizations share an important legal characteristic. The individuals who own the businesses are personally liable for the business debts, and the general liabilities of the business. The business, regardless of its name, is not a separate entity from the individuals who own it. By contrast, the liability of shareholders as the owners of a corporation for the corporation's acts is limited; the corporation is a legal person separate from its owners, so that only the corporation is liable for its actions.[5]

Suing Partnerships

If your law firm is going to sue a partnership, the suit is usually brought in the partnership's name, which you verify through a business name search. If the suit is brought in the partnership's name, the judgment may be enforced only against the partnership's assets. If Rattle Motors Ltd. were a partnership, you could seize its property—for example, its land and showroom, office furniture and equipment, bank account, income from sales, automobiles, and other inventory. But you could not seize the personal assets of partner A, B, or C. If partner A had a house, bank account, and car, none of which was used in the partnership business, this property could not be seized to enforce the judgment against the partnership (Rule 8.06(1)).

However, a plaintiff may be interested in seizing partnership assets *and* personal assets of the partners to enforce and satisfy a judgment. After all, partners are liable at common law for the debts and liabilities of the partnership, and the rules of procedure do not change the substantive law. Rule 8 makes provision for a plaintiff to claim against partnership assets and a partner's personal assets. If your law firm wishes to enforce a judgment against an individual partner, when it serves originating process against a partnership on the partner, it must also serve on the partner a notice to an alleged partner, in Form 8A, stating that the individual partner was a partner at the time stated in the notice (usually when the cause of action arose). The person is then deemed to be a partner unless he or she files a statement of defence in his or her own name, denying that he or she was a partner at the relevant time. An example of a notice to an alleged partner is set out in Figure 5.5.

When suing partnerships, how the parties are named in the title of proceedings depends on whether you wish to enforce a judgment against partnership assets alone, or against partnership assets and the assets of individual partners. It also depends on whether you use the procedure in Rule 8 or not, when claiming against individual partners.

- Assuming for the moment that Rattle Motors is a partnership, if you are claiming against the partnership and intend to enforce a judgment only against the partnership, name the parties as follows: ABIGAIL BOAR, Plaintiff v. RATTLE MOTORS, Defendant.

- Under Rule 8, if you are claiming against the partnership and the partners and intend to enforce a judgment against the assets of the partnership *and* the personal assets of the individual partners, name the parties in the same way as in the preceding example, but remember to serve a notice in Form 8A on the individual partners you seek to enforce against at the same time you serve an originating process on them.

Figure 5.5   Notice to Alleged Partner (Form 8A)

Court file no. 01-CV-1516

ONTARIO
SUPERIOR COURT OF JUSTICE

BETWEEN:

ABIGAIL BOAR

Plaintiff

and

RATTLE MOTORS

Defendant

NOTICE TO ALLEGED PARTNER

YOU ARE ALLEGED TO HAVE BEEN A PARTNER on Sept. 14, year 0 in the partnership of Rattle Motors, named as a party to this proceeding.

IF YOU WISH TO DENY THAT YOU WERE A PARTNER at any material time, you must defend this proceeding separately from the partnership, denying that you were a partner at the material time. If you fail to do so, you will be deemed to have been a partner on the date set out above.

AN ORDER AGAINST THE PARTNERSHIP MAY BE ENFORCED AGAINST YOU PERSONALLY if you are deemed to have been a partner, if you admit that you were a partner or if the court finds that you were a partner, at the material time.

October 4, year 0

I.M. Just
LSUC #12345R
Just & Coping
Barristers and Solicitors
365 Bay Street – 8701
Toronto, Ontario, M3J 4A9

tel. 416-762-1342
fax 416-762-2300

Lawyers for the Plaintiff

TO: Adolphus Ambrose
123 Elm Street
Scarborough, Ontario, M8Y 2Z8

RCP-E 8A (July 1, 2007)

- If you wish to claim against the individual partners only, simply sue the individuals: ABIGAIL BOAR v. SAM SLIPP and BOB CHATTERJEE.
- If you are not using Rule 8, but wish to claim against both the partnership and the individual partners on distinctly different bases of liability for the partnership and the individual partners, then name each party you seek to enforce the judgment against: ABIGAIL BOAR v. SAM SLIPP and BOB CHATTERJEE and RATTLE MOTORS. Usually, however, you will sue in the business name and use Rule 8 to expand enforcement rights against the individual partner's assets.

If you seek to fix personal liability on partners by giving them notice under Form 8A, you need to know who they are. Think about a large law firm. Of the 200 lawyers, perhaps 150 may be partners. Further, as lawyers pursue career opportunities, several lawyers may become partners and several may leave the partnership in a given year. The firm name may not be any help. Most large firms use the names of just one or two partners, and other types of businesses may use commercial names that do not include the names of any partners. If you wish to know who the partners were five or six years ago, the business records of the Companies and Personal Property Security Branch will not be helpful because they contain mostly current records. Rule 8.05 provides the answer to a plaintiff's problem. Where there is a proceeding brought by or against a partnership, Rule 8.05 entitles any party to serve a notice on the partnership requiring the partnership to set out the names and addresses of partners for the time period or date specified in the notice. In this way, a party can find out who the partners are, and then serve partners individually with the notice in Form 8A, provided that this is done within 15 days of receiving the information. If the partnership wants to stall and prevent liability from resting on the individual partners by not providing the information, the rule provides a solution: The action will be stayed if the partnership is a plaintiff, and the defence will be struck out if it is a defendant.

Suppose a claim against a partnership gives rise to crossclaims between partners, where one partner, for example, claims that the other promised to indemnify him or her from suits by the plaintiff, or claims that he or she was not a partner when the plaintiff's cause of action arose. If one partner's defence is different from or adverse to the positions of other partners or the partnership, that partner may apply to the court on motion for leave under Rule 8.02 to file a separate defence. If the partner denies being a partner at the relevant time, he or she may file a separate defence pursuant to Rule 8.03(2) and Rule 8.04(a).

Once the plaintiff has a judgment in a proceeding against a partnership, he or she may enforce it against partnership assets. If a partner was named individually, the plaintiff may also enforce against that person's personal property, provided that the procedure for giving the individual partner notice under Rule 8.03 was followed. Rule 8.06(3) provides further relief for a plaintiff who failed to name an individual under Rule 8.03. Here, if the plaintiff obtains judgment against the partnership and then seeks to enforce it against an individual defendant not previously named, the plaintiff must apply to a judge on a motion for leave to enforce against a named individual. The order is granted if the individual admits or is found to be a partner at the relevant time.

Sole Proprietorships

Sole proprietorships are treated in the same way as partnerships, as if the sole proprietor were a partner. Rule 8.07(1) indicates that you can sue a person carrying on a sole proprietorship in the business name, and that is the approach usually taken. Rule 8.07(2) then tells you that the rules for giving notice to individual partners and demanding the identity of partners at the relevant time apply to sole proprietorships. This will allow you to pursue the individual's personal assets as well as their business assets, as was the case for partnerships. However, the details for dealing with sole proprietors are not spelled out, so you have to use Rules 8.01 to 8.06 as models and guidelines for procedures; similarly, you have to adapt and modify the forms used for partnerships for use in dealing with a sole proprietorship. So, if you wish to expand enforcement rights by giving notice to the individual sole proprietor that he or she was the sole proprietor at the relevant time, you have to edit the partnership version of the form. And the sole proprietor could answer by claiming not to have been the sole proprietor at the relevant time. Similarly, you can demand that a sole proprietorship reveal who the sole proprietor was at the relevant time, and the sole proprietor must respond in the same way that a partner would. While this might sound strange, if the plaintiff is dealing with a business entity that uses a business or trade name, the plaintiff might be uncertain as to who the actual sole proprietor is, especially if the cause of action arose in the past, and the business was sold to someone else as an ongoing business operation, including its business name. At the time the lawsuit begins, the new owner may have no personal liability, and finding the previous owner may be required in order to expand liability to include enforcement of a judgment against the previous owner's assets.

Suing Corporations

A corporation is required by law to include in its name some indication that it is a corporation with limited liability. It does this by having the words "Limited," "Incorporated," "Ltd.," or "Inc."[6] following its name or as part of its name. However, your client may have dealt with what he or she thought was a business called "Prissy's Plants." You will need to search that name, which will tell you whether you are dealing with a sole proprietorship, partnership, or corporation, and who its principals are. If the defendant turns out to be a corporation, the plaintiff *cannot* sue in the business name. He or she must sue in the proper corporate name as revealed in your search.

Estates and Trusts as Parties: Rule 9

We now turn to some rules governing the naming, joining, and severing of parties and issues in litigation involving trusts and estates. A trust is a means of holding property where the legal owner is acting not for the benefit of himself or herself, but for the benefit of beneficiaries of the trust, who are also the beneficial owners of the trust assets. If a grandmother wants to give a minor grandchild the benefit of a large capital fund, she may, as the grantor, set up a trust, where the person she names as trustee is the legal owner and controls the assets for the benefit of the minor, who cannot directly get at the capital and waste the assets. An estate is similarly structured, although the grantor who creates the trust through a will is deceased. The **executor** or **estate administrator** acts in the interest of the estate beneficiaries. The same is true for trusts, where the trustee acts for the benefit of beneficiaries.

Rule 9 sets out procedural rules for naming parties. The general rule is that an estate or trust may sue or be sued by naming the administrator, executor, or trustee as the estate representative, without naming the beneficiaries specifically because they are deemed to be included. There are some exceptions where beneficiaries must be named:

executor
person appointed by the maker of a will to administer an estate under the provisions of the will; a female executor is sometimes called an executrix

estate administrator
person appointed by a court to administer an estate where there is no will or where the appointment of an executor is ineffective

- a suit to contest the validity of a will;
- a suit brought to interpret a will;
- a suit to remove the personal administrator of an estate;
- a suit alleging fraud against a personal representative of an estate, or a trustee; and
- a suit to force the administration of an estate or the carrying out of the terms of a trust where the trustee, executor, or administrator has failed to or refused to act (Rule 9.01(1), (2)).

Where there is more than one executor, administrator, or trustee, what happens if one does not agree to join the others as plaintiff? Because they may have some liabilities and an interest in the outcome, they are joined as respondents or defendants even though no claim is made against them. This is done so that they will be in the lawsuit and bound by the judgment. In addition, the court may order any creditor or beneficiary to be added as a separate party (Rule 9.01(3), (4)).

If an estate has no personal representative, your law firm will sue the estate in its own name and apply to the court for the appointment of a litigation administrator (Rule 9.02). The proceeding can then continue, and any order will be binding on the estate and its beneficiaries. A litigation administrator can be an estate creditor with an interest in defending the plaintiff's lawsuit, a relative or business partner of the deceased, or a trust company that will accept the appointment. Estate departments of trust companies routinely administer estates under wills and charge a fee for doing so. The appointment of a litigation administrator will depend on the facts and circumstances of the case and whether there are estate assets that make the effort worthwhile.

Rule 9.03 is a child of Rule 2.01 in that it prevents accidental slips, omissions, and errors from derailing a lawsuit by making it a nullity. An error is treated as an irregularity that can be cured by the court, subject to costs or an adjournment to compensate the other side from being unduly disadvantaged.

If a personal representative commences proceedings on behalf of an estate before the grant of probate has confirmed the appointment, the proceeding is deemed to be properly constituted, provided that the administrative grant is approved. The title of proceedings for an action commenced by or against an estate by naming the estate as a party—for example, the Estate of Abigail Boar—results in an irregularity, and the court may simply order that the action continue against the personal representative of the estate, with the title of proceedings being amended accordingly. If your law firm sues a deceased person in his or her own name, or if a party it has sued dies before it starts the suit, the court can order that the title of proceedings be amended so that the personal representative of the estate is the named party. If the court appoints a litigation administrator and then finds that there was a personal representative already appointed under a will or otherwise, the action continues against the previously appointed personal representative.

In the event that an action is not properly constituted, as noted in the situations above, the court may order that the case be properly constituted and continue, but the proceeding is stayed until the errors are corrected. If the corrections are not made—for example, by applying for a litigation administrator—the proceeding can be dismissed. The court may also order that a personal representative of an estate be relieved of personal liability if he or she paid money out of an estate to beneficiaries before becoming aware of a proceeding against the estate, provided that he or she acted in good faith (Rule 9.03).

Unidentified and Unascertained Parties and Representation Orders: Rule 10

In cases like Abigail's, there is no difficulty in determining who the parties are or might be. Abigail's claim against Barbeerian's or Skunk Motorcar Company Ltd. may be more speculative and uncertain than the one against Fred Flogem and Rattle Motors Ltd. However, you can identify these entities as parties, and define and describe the claim against them, including the damages for which they may be responsible.

But consider, for example, an estate where the beneficiaries include grandchildren and great-grandchildren of specific persons named in a will. If someone challenges the validity of the will, Rule 9.01(2)(a) requires that the beneficiaries be made parties to the proceeding. The persons named in the will can easily be added, but what about the class of grandchildren? It is possible that we may not know at the time who all of the individuals in the class are. Some of these persons are not yet born but may have a future interest. Rule 10 provides a procedure for representing those who have an interest in the outcome of a proceeding where either the interest or the person cannot be ascertained at the time of the suit, or the person cannot otherwise be represented.

The provisions of the rule apply to certain types of proceedings:

- the interpretation of documents, such as contracts and wills, that create rights and interests, and proceedings that interpret the legislation that affects rights and interests;
- the interpretation of a question or issue that has arisen in the administration of an estate or trust;
- the approval of a sale, purchase, settlement, or other transaction involving interests that cannot be ascertained or where the members of a class of persons are not known;

- the variation of the terms of a trust because the provisions did not take into account some state of affairs that prevents the trust's objects from being carried out (for example, if the trust authorizes payments to a class of beneficiaries to "advance their station in life," does this authorize flying lessons for one of the beneficiaries?);
- the administration of an estate where a question about its administration arises; and
- any other matter where it appears necessary to make a representation order.

Rule 10.01(1) gives the court considerable leeway in deciding when to make such an order. Generally, when there appears to be a present, future, or even a contingent interest (an interest contingent on the fulfillment of a condition precedent) of persons who are unborn or not yet ascertained, a representation order can be made. An order may also be made if a person is a member of a class whose interests may be affected even if the identity of the individual is not yet known. Where a large number of people are affected by the interpretation of a government regulation or a provision of a pension fund, for example, you may not know whether the class member is still alive or whether he or she still qualifies as having an interest. You may know who the persons in the class are but may not be able to find them or serve them all. In these cases, the procedural shortcut is to have one person represent the interests of all. Rule 10 governs situations similar to class proceedings, which are covered by Rule 12, but Rule 10 is a broader provision.

Once a representation order is made, the person named in it becomes a party, representing the class of persons identified in the order—the unborn grandchildren of Fred Flogem, for example. The person or class of persons named in the order as being represented is bound by any judgment or order made in the proceeding. This means that one of Fred's grandchildren cannot come forward and say that he or she was not consulted, had no notice, and is therefore not bound. If a settlement offer is made to, and accepted by, the representative of the class, the members of the class are bound by the settlement. An individual class member may escape from the settlement in some circumstances, although the test for doing so is a difficult one to meet (see Rule 10.03).

If an estate of a deceased person has an interest in an issue in a case and there is no executor or administrator, the judge may order the proceeding to continue in the absence of an estate representative. The judge may also name a representative for the purpose of the proceeding, in which case the estate of the deceased person is bound by the outcome (Rule 10.02).

Although a judge may make a representation order in an appropriate case, the judge in the case or in a subsequent case can order the person or estate not to be bound, provided that

- the order was obtained by fraud,
- the interests of the person appointed and the estate or person represented were in conflict, or
- there is a good reason to set the representation order aside (Rule 10.03).

Because a court's discretion under Rule 10 is broad, case law needs to be consulted. The purpose of Rule 10 is to encourage a quick means of resolving contentious proceedings without having to resort to the more cumbersome class proceeding procedure covered by Rule 12. The test that should be applied by the court in considering whether or not to make a representation order is not whether the members of the group can be found or ascertained, but whether it is more convenient to issue a representation order than to insist that each member of the class be served and allowed to participate. The court must also check to see that there is no conflict between the members of the class and the representative (Rule 10.03).[7] In fact, the representative of the class should have all of the crucial characteristics of the class members. In a pension case, for example, the representative of the class of retirees must have the same characteristics as the retirees in the class who are affected by the issue in question: The representative must be a retiree, from the same occupation, with a right to the same types of benefits.

Transfer or Transmission of Interest: Rule 11

Rule 11 gives you directions about what to do if the legal status of a party changes in the course of an ongoing proceeding. For example, if Abigail Boar starts an action as a plaintiff in her own name and then dies, her legal status changes. The lawsuit must be continued in the name of her estate's personal representative. Another example occurs where the rights being litigated are transferred by assignment from one person to another. For example, a person becoming bankrupt transfers his or her property to a trustee in bankruptcy for the general benefit of creditors. Whatever the reason, Rule 11.01 requires a proceeding to be stayed until the court makes an order to continue the proceeding by or against the "new" litigant—for example, the estate's personal representative or the trustee in bankruptcy. The new litigant is not usually personally liable: The estate is the focus of the judgment, not the estate's personal representative who is the "new" party.

The order is obtained on requisition from the registrar, on the filing of an affidavit by any party setting out the fact that the interest or liability of a party has been transferred. A formal motion is not necessary because the matter is usually a procedural formality. If, however, the transmission is contested, the requisition may be challenged by bringing a motion to set aside the order to continue. An example of the registrar's order to continue, Form 11A, is set out in Figure 5.6.

Class Proceedings: Rule 12

While Rule 11 gives the court general powers to make one person the representative of a class in ordinary litigation, it is also available for the less complex representative or class proceeding. Rule 12 contains specific procedures that apply to actions certified as class proceedings under the *Class Proceedings Act, 1992*. The Act and Rule 12 are designed to deal with proceedings more complex than those to which Rule 11 applies. It is necessary to know something about the Act before we examine Rule 12.

Figure 5.6   Order to Continue (Form 11A)

Court file no. 01-CV-1234

ONTARIO
SUPERIOR COURT OF JUSTICE

BETWEEN:

ABIGAIL BOAR

Plaintiff

and

RATTLE MOTORS LTD. and FRED FLOGEM

Defendants

ORDER TO CONTINUE

On the requisition of Henrietta Boar and on reading the affidavit of Henrietta Boar, filed, which indicates that on July 24, year 1, Abigail Boar, the plaintiff in this action, died, and her right of action was transferred to her estate, of which Henrietta Boar is the representative, as the executrix of the estate of Abigail Boar,

IT IS ORDERED that this proceeding continue and that the title of the proceeding in all documents issued, served, or filed after the date of this order be as follows:

Henrietta Boar, Estate Trustee, With a Will of the Estate of Abigail Boar

Date: February 6, year 3

Signed by: _____
Local registrar

Address of
court office: Courthouse
393 University Avenue
Toronto, Ontario, M5G 1E6

A party who wishes to set aside or vary this order must make a motion to do so forthwith after the order comes to the party's attention.

Where a transmission of interest occurs by reason of bankruptcy, leave of the bankruptcy court may be required under section 69.4 of the *Bankruptcy and Insolvency Act* (Canada) before the proceeding may continue.

RCP-E 11A (November 1, 2005)

What follows is an overview of the highlights that make a class proceeding or class action different from other types of civil proceedings. If you are involved in a class proceeding, there are other resources you should use that provide detailed procedural guides.[8]

Overview of the Class Proceedings Act

Suppose Abigail Boar, along with several thousand other people, bought a Super Coupe in its first model year. Within the first year the car was on the market, there were frequent reports of sudden engine failure. In about 30 percent of the cases, the engine failure also led to car fires, which caused serious injuries. Approximately 10 percent of the engine failures involved serious accidents, with injuries, but no car fires. In Abigail's case, let us suppose that the engine failed, but Abigail was able to steer her car off the road, so that she was uninjured. When she consulted I.M. Just, she discovered that there had been a number of incidents involving the Super Coupe.

The purpose of the *Class Proceedings Act, 1992* is to allow numerous potential plaintiffs or defendants to have their claims considered as members of a class represented by one plaintiff or defendant. This allows justice to be done by allowing many small claims to be considered. Otherwise, no claim might ever have been made because of the expense. The Act also eliminates the possibility of the courts having to deal with a torrent of separate lawsuits.

I.M. Just, or the lawyer of any claimant, can apply to certify a proceeding as a class proceeding, in which case Abigail and all others with claims against the defendant, Skunk Motorcar Company Ltd., may be separated into classes and subclasses. Here all would be included in the class claiming for product failure, but there would also be subclasses for those who were injured in car fires and for those who were otherwise injured. Because Abigail suffered only from product failure, she is a member of the main class but not the subclasses. The purpose of this arrangement is to require class members to incur expense only on issues that affect them. Each class or subclass would have a representative plaintiff. The representative must have all the relevant attributes or qualities of the class on the issues that concern the class. Often the court will have to sort out competing class action claims by a variety of plaintiffs.

The lawyers for the plaintiff whose action is certified by the court face problems and opportunities. The firm will require staff and resources to administer the proceeding, identify the members of the class, and process their claims. At the same time, if the suit is successful, the fees, which are payable on a contingency basis, will be lucrative for the firm.[9]

Under the *Class Proceedings Act, 1992*, a potential plaintiff cannot be involuntarily joined to another plaintiff's proceeding and can opt out of a class proceeding (s. 9). If Abigail wants to go it alone, she may apply to the court to do so.

Once a proceeding is certified, potential plaintiffs need to know about it so that they can contact the lawyer for the class representative and have their claims included. To facilitate the process, the court requires that a public notice be prepared, approved by the courts, and published as a legal notice, or sent by mail or by any other means (ss. 17 to 22). In Abigail's case, the court may require the defendant to furnish a list of all purchasers, in which case Abigail may receive a registered letter or a couriered letter giving her notice of the proceeding.

Individual legal or factual issues involving a class or subclass may be tried separately. Thus, one class proceeding may give rise to several subproceedings (see s. 27). Abigail, for example, may be included in the class that suffered property damage but not in the classes that sustained personal injuries.

If the representative party agrees to settlement, the court must approve the settlement because it affects other class members (s. 29). Abigail will receive notice of the settlement and be entitled to voice objections as a class member.

Because running a representative proceeding is speculative and expensive, s. 33 of the Act permits lawyers for a class to be paid their costs on a contingency-fee basis. And of course, this is now generally permitted in civil proceedings.

Because the costs incurred before trial by a law firm are high, the Act permits the law firm for a class representative to apply for funding for disbursements at various points in the class proceeding from the **class proceedings fund**. This fund, which is administered by the Law Society of Upper Canada, was set up to provide funding for class proceedings, especially where there are many individual class members with small claims.

If the plaintiff receives assistance from the class proceedings fund, a successful defendant in the proceeding is entitled to claim payment of costs awarded by the court from the fund.

Application of Rule 12 to Class Proceedings

Rule 12 deals with certain procedural requirements of class proceedings. After the names of the parties and as part of the title of proceedings, there must appear the words "Proceeding under the *Class Proceedings Act, 1992*." These words must be included in all court documents, commencing with the notice of motion to certify the proceeding as a class proceeding (Rule 12.02). An example is set out in Figure 5.7.

A class member as well as the class representative may be examined for discovery. Only parties are usually subject to examination for discovery. Admissions in the class member's discovery transcript can be read into the record at trial (Rule 12.03(1)). Parts of Rule 31, setting out the basis for examining non-parties, do not apply because that matter is covered in Rule 12. Similarly, the sanctions under Rule 34 for a class member who does not cooperate in the discovery process do not apply because they include dismissal of the proceeding. If Abigail were summoned as a class member and refused to cooperate in the discovery process, the proceeding should not be dismissed against the class representative, who is the actual party, because of Abigail's misconduct.

If the plaintiff has received financial support from the class proceedings fund, the Law Foundation of Ontario is entitled to notice of any motion or request for an order for costs or an assessment of costs after costs have been awarded. The fund's representative is entitled to make submissions, cross-examine witnesses, and present evidence on the issue of costs, including appeals on the issue of costs (Rule

class proceedings fund
public fund of the Law Foundation of Ontario, administered by the Law Society of Upper Canada, to provide funding for the costs of class actions that otherwise might be beyond the financial reach of the parties

Figure 5.7   General Heading Under the Class Proceedings Act, 1992

Court file no. 00-XX-0000

ONTARIO
SUPERIOR COURT OF JUSTICE

BETWEEN:

ABIGAIL BOAR

Plaintiff

and

SKUNK MOTORCAR COMPANY LTD.

Defendants

Proceeding under the *Class Proceedings Act, 1992*

12.04). This makes sense because the fund may well be paying the costs that are being disputed.

Judgments and orders made in a class proceeding, including an order approving a settlement, must contain provisions that

- detail how the award will be distributed to class members and how the costs of making the distribution will be paid,
- outline the payments owing on a contingency agreement between the lawyer and a representative party,
- detail the payment of costs of the proceeding, and
- detail payments of any levy to the fund (Rule 12.05).

Defendants with the same interest may defend a proceeding on behalf of or for the benefit of all defendants and may be authorized as a class in a class proceeding for that purpose (Rule 12.07).

Where there are many members of an **unincorporated association** or a trade union and it would be unduly expensive and complicated to apply to certify a class proceeding, one or more of the members may be authorized to commence a proceeding on behalf of and for the benefit of all (Rule 12.08). Note that this rule is restricted to unincorporated associations and trade unions, so that a mass of individuals with a common interest is not able to use this rule. Rule 12.08 is also only available to plaintiffs. A plaintiff suing a voluntary association or trade union would have to name all the members of the association as defendants or commence a class proceeding.

unincorporated association association of persons formed to carry out a specific purpose and not formally incorporated

Representation by a Lawyer: Rule 15

As a general rule, an individual is entitled to represent himself or herself in every court in Canada, including the Supreme Court of Canada. This does not mean it is a good idea. There is a saying among lawyers that "a lawyer who represents himself has a fool for a client." As you already can see, knowledge of and experience with both substantive law and procedure are necessary to conduct a case, as is detachment and objectivity. Advocacy skills are also necessary. Most non-lawyers lack these skills and experiences. If you are dealing with a party who is acting in person, be prepared for the proceeding to go more slowly and for there to be numerous irregularities as parties stumble through the pretrial stages. Abigail could represent herself, and might do so if she cannot afford to hire a lawyer. Legal aid is very difficult to obtain in civil proceedings.

There are some parties that *must* be represented by a lawyer in proceedings in the Superior Court,[10] and they include parties who are acting in a representative capacity, parties under a disability, and parties that are corporations unless the court grants leave for someone else to represent the corporation. Where, for example, an individual is sued along with a corporation that he or she controls, the individual has a right to represent himself or herself and may be granted the right to represent the corporation as well.

Once Abigail has retained I.M. Just and instructed him to commence proceedings, I.M. Just and his firm have the authority to proceed. I.M. Just's name, address, telephone number, fax number, and Law Society registration number appear on the backsheet of every court document, starting with the originating process. Since I.M. Just is a member of a firm, both his name and the firm's name must be disclosed, along with his individual phone number or extension. Once the proceeding is commenced, the court will note and record I.M. Just's name and the firm name from the backsheet, making I.M. Just the **lawyer of record**. I.M. Just or a member of his firm is then obliged to appear for Abigail unless she fires him or he obtains the court's permission to be removed from the record.

lawyer of record
lawyer recognized by the court as the legal representative of a party in a proceeding

Requiring a Lawyer to Prove Authority to Act

Anyone may require a lawyer of record to state in writing whether he, she, or the client authorized the commencement of proceedings. If there is no authority to proceed, the court may stay or dismiss the proceeding (Rule 15.02). This rule is not often used, but it may be resorted to, for example, where there are warring factions in a privately held company or association and one such faction questions the company's proceedings.

Changing Lawyers

What happens if Abigail is unhappy with I.M. Just and wishes to fire him and hire Brenda Smart to carry on the case? What usually happens is that once Brenda Smart agrees to take the case, she prepares a notice of change of lawyer (Form 15A), indicating that Abigail has changed lawyers, and serves it on I.M. Just and every other party or the lawyer for every other party, if the other party is represented by counsel (Rule 15.03(1)). Then, with an affidavit of service or other proof of service, the notice is filed in the court office. The court amends its records to show who the new lawyer of record is. A notice of change of lawyer in Abigail's case is set out in Figure 5.8.

Similarly, a party who has been representing himself or herself must also give notice through, and serve on all other parties and file with the court, a notice of appointment of lawyer in Form 15B, with proof of service (Rule 15.03(2)). An example of the notice is set out in Figure 5.9.

A party who has a lawyer but who wishes to dispense with the lawyer's services and represent himself or herself may do so by serving his or her lawyer and all other parties with a notice of intention to act in person in Form 15C (Rule 15.03(3)). The notice should be filed in court with proof of service. An example of the notice is set out in Figure 5.10.

Lawyer's Lien

When a client changes lawyers, the former lawyer is entitled to a lien on the client's documents in the former lawyer's possession until the client has paid his or her account with the law firm. A party may bring a motion for an order to determine what, if any, right the former lawyer has to maintain and enforce the lien (Rule 15.03(4)).

Lawyer's Request to Be Removed as Lawyer of Record

A client is free to change or remove a lawyer at will, but how does a lawyer get rid of a client? Once the lawyer is "on the record" as lawyer of record, he or she is expected to represent and protect the client's interest until the matter is concluded, the client serves a notice under Rule 15.03, or the court makes an order relieving the lawyer of the responsibilities as lawyer of record. The lawyer cannot "fire" a client just because the client is difficult or obnoxious.

There are two primary reasons for a court to grant an order relieving a lawyer of the obligation to act for a party: the client has refused to pay the lawyer's account or the client refuses to give the lawyer instructions when asked for them. Refusal to give instructions also includes giving instructions that are unlawful and that would require the lawyer to breach the *Rules of Professional Conduct* or his or her duties as an officer of the court. In this case, because of rules requiring the lawyer to keep the client's confidence, the lawyer cannot usually reveal what the client has requested. Instead, the lawyer states that he or she is unable to obtain instructions.

To do this, a lawyer must serve the client with a notice of motion for an order to be removed as lawyer of record. The client must be served personally, by an alternative to personal service, or by mailing the motion to the client's last known address. There are special rules for serving parties under a disability: The litigation guardian must be served along with the Children's Lawyer if the party is a minor, and the Public Guardian and Trustee must be served in every other case. Corporations are

Figure 5.8   Notice of Change of Lawyer (Form 15A)

Court file no. 01-CV-1234

ONTARIO
SUPERIOR COURT OF JUSTICE

BETWEEN:

ABIGAIL BOAR

Plaintiff

and

RATTLE MOTORS LTD. and FRED FLOGEM

Defendants

NOTICE OF CHANGE OF LAWYER

The plaintiff, formerly represented by I.M. Just of Just & Coping, Barristers and Solicitors, has appointed Brenda Smart as lawyer of record.

July 25, year 1

> Brenda Smart
> LSUC #45678L
> Barrister and Solicitor
> 1201 Bay Street – 458
> Toronto, Ontario, M1P 2B9
>
> tel. 416-203-7798
> fax 416-203-7797
>
> Lawyer for the Plaintiff

TO: I.M. Just
> LSUC #12345R
> Just & Coping
> Barristers and Solicitors
> 365 Bay Street – 8701
> Toronto, Ontario, M3J 4A9
>
> tel. 416-762-1342
> fax 416-762-2300
>
> Former Lawyers for the Plaintiff

AND TO: Huey Sue
> LSUC #23456T
> Barrister and Solicitor
> 65 False Trail
> Toronto, Ontario, M6Y 1Z6
>
> tel. 416-485-6891
> fax 416-485-6892
>
> Lawyer for the Defendants

RCP-E 15A (July 1, 2007)

Figure 5.9   Notice of Appointment of Lawyer (Form 15B)

Court file no. 01-CV-1234

ONTARIO
SUPERIOR COURT OF JUSTICE

BETWEEN:

ABIGAIL BOAR

Plaintiff

and

RATTLE MOTORS LTD. and FRED FLOGEM

Defendants

NOTICE OF APPOINTMENT OF LAWYER

The plaintiff, Abigail Boar, formerly acting in person, has appointed I.M. Just of Just &
Coping, Barristers and Solicitors, as lawyer of record.

July 25, year 1

Just & Coping
Barristers and Solicitors
365 Bay Street – 8701
Toronto, Ontario, M3J 4A9

I.M. Just
LSUC #12345R
tel. 416-762-1342
fax 416-762-2300

Lawyers for the Plaintiff

TO:
Huey Sue
LSUC #23456T
Barrister and Solicitor
65 False Trail
Toronto, Ontario, M6Y 1Z6

tel. 416-485-6891
fax 416-485-6892

Lawyer for the Defendants

RCP-E 15B (July 1, 2007)

Figure 5.10   Notice of Intention to Act in Person (Form 15C)

Court file no. 01-CV-1234

ONTARIO
SUPERIOR COURT OF JUSTICE

BETWEEN:

ABIGAIL BOAR

Plaintiff

and

RATTLE MOTORS LTD. and FRED FLOGEM

Defendants

NOTICE OF INTENTION TO ACT IN PERSON

The plaintiff, Abigail Boar, formerly represented by I.M. Just as lawyer of record, intends to act in person.

Date: July 26, year 1

Signed by: Abigail Boar
72 Sumach Street
Toronto, Ontario, M4R 1Z5

tel. 416-928-0001
fax 416-928-0002

TO: Just & Coping
Barristers and Solicitors
365 Bay Street – 8701
Toronto, Ontario, M3J 4A9

I.M. Just
LSUC #12345R
tel. 416-762-1342
fax 416-762-2300

Former Lawyers for the Plaintiff

AND TO: Huey Sue
LSUC #23456T
Barrister and Solicitor
65 False Trail
Toronto, Ontario, M6Y 1Z6

tel. 416-485-6891
fax 416-485-6892

Lawyer for the Defendants

RCP-E 15C (July 1, 2007)

also given notice in the motion to remove the lawyer from the record that they must retain new counsel or other suitable representation within 30 days after being served with the order removing the lawyer. The notice must inform the corporation that failure to obtain new representation may result in the case being dismissed, or the corporation's defence being struck out. For parties other than corporations, an order removing a lawyer must include the client's last known address and any other address where service might be effective. Also, the client must be warned that a new lawyer must be retained within 30 days of the order being served or the claim may be struck out, or the defence dismissed, as required under Rule 15.04(8) and (9).

The affidavit to support the motion must give the court some reason to take the lawyer off the record because leaving a client unrepresented can have serious consequences for the client. The affidavit need not give details and should not violate lawyer–client privilege by revealing the contents of any disagreement on strategy or tactics between the lawyer and the client. A sample affidavit is set out in Figure 5.11.

While Rule 15.05 does not explicitly provide for other parties to apply to remove one party's lawyer of record, other parties may do this if there is a conflict of interest, using the Rule 15 procedure with necessary modifications. For example, if I.M. Just had previously acted for Fred Flogem or Rattle Motors Ltd., the defendants could bring a motion to have I.M. Just removed as lawyer for Abigail on the grounds of there being a conflict of interest.[11]

Figure 5.11   Affidavit in Support of Motion for Removal as Lawyer of Record (Form 4D)

Court file no. 01-CV-1234

ONTARIO
SUPERIOR COURT OF JUSTICE

BETWEEN:

ABIGAIL BOAR

Plaintiff

and

RATTLE MOTORS LTD. and FRED FLOGEM

Defendants

AFFIDAVIT

I, I.M. Just, lawyer in the law firm of Just & Coping, of the City of Toronto, in the Province of Ontario, MAKE OATH AND SAY:

1. I am the lawyer of record for Abigail Boar, the plaintiff in this proceeding and, as such, have knowledge of the matters deposed to in this affidavit.

2. I commenced proceedings on behalf of the plaintiff with a statement of claim and have received the statement of defence filed by the defendants. The defendants have served a notice for examination for discovery to be held on February 10, year 1. I have repeatedly called and left messages for the plaintiff, and have written to advise her of the date for discovery and the need to prepare for it. She has not answered my letters, nor has she returned my calls or otherwise contacted me or given me instructions.

3. I am unable to act on behalf of the plaintiff without instructions from her.

4. The plaintiff's last known address is 72 Sumach Street, Toronto, Ontario, M4R 1Z5.

5. I make this affidavit for an order to be removed as lawyer of record for the plaintiff.

SWORN before me at the	)
City of Toronto,	) *I.M. Just*
in the Province of Ontario,	) I.M. Just
on February 1, year 1.	)
U.R. Merely	)
U.R. Merely	)
Commissioner for Taking Affidavits	)

RCP-E 4D (July 1, 2007)

CHAPTER SUMMARY

This chapter was primarily concerned with joinder and severance of parties and issues from one proceeding into other proceedings. We began by examining the rules for determining who can be a party to a lawsuit and which claims can be included in a lawsuit. We noted that, where possible, unless it is prejudicial or inconvenient, all proper parties and claims should be included in one proceeding rather than several because this usually reduces cost and delay. We then turned to special rules governing lawsuits for and against parties under disability. We noted that minors and those with a mental incapacity must be represented by litigation guardians. If none can be found, the parties must be represented by the Children's Lawyer and Public Guardian and Trustee, respectively.

Partnerships and sole proprietorships can sue or be sued in their business name or in the name of the owners. There are special provisions to assist you in finding out who the owners are or were at the relevant time. There are also provisions to include individual owners as parties, particularly if you want their individual as well as their business assets available to satisfy a judgment.

Estates and trusts, unascertained persons, and the transmission by assignment of an interest in a lawsuit from a party to a non-party were also examined with respect to who is, or who represents, a party in proceedings. For more complex representative actions, we set out the highlights of the *Class Proceedings Act, 1992* and examined the specific procedural rules governing some aspects of class proceedings. Finally, we examined the circumstances in which a party can represent himself or herself as well as the circumstances in which a party must have a lawyer. We also examined the procedure for both lawyers and clients where someone wished to change lawyers once proceedings had started.

KEY TERMS

absentee, 104

affiant, 107

assignee, 101

assignor, 101

Children's Lawyer, 107

chose in action, 101

class proceedings fund, 124

estate administrator, 118

executor, 118

join (a party or claim), 96

joinder, 96

judgment *in personam*, 100

judgment *in rem*, 100

lawyer of record, 126

litigation guardian, 104

return date, 109

stay proceedings, 102

unincorporated association, 125

NOTES

1. See ss. 6 and 45 of the *Substitute Decisions Act, 1992,* SO 1992, c. 30, as amended.

2. "Attorney" as used here does not mean lawyer; it means a person who is authorized to act as an agent for another person.

3. If a person does not reside in Ontario, he or she probably has no assets in Ontario against which to enforce an order to pay costs. For that reason, a non-resident may be asked to post security for costs by depositing an asset or title to an asset with the court.

4. The Children's Lawyer has issued a memorandum setting out the information it requires and how it should be contacted. This document is reproduced in most commercially published versions of the Rules.

5. There are some narrow exceptions. A shareholder may be liable for a corporate act in some circumstances for an amount equal to the value of his or her shares. Where the owner of all shares is also the directing mind of the corporation and uses it to shield himself or herself from liability, the court may "lift the corporate veil" and allow a plaintiff to sue the owner directly. But this is very unusual.

6. Or the French equivalent of these words.

7. See *Police Retirees of Ontario Inc. v. Ontario Municipal Employees' Retirement Board* (1997), 35 OR (3d) 177 (Gen. Div.); *Township of Bruce v. Thornburn* (1986), 57 OR (2d) 77 (Div. Ct.).

8. W. Branch, *Class Actions in Canada* (Toronto: Canada Law Book, 2000) (loose-leaf updates).

9. See s. 5 of the *Class Proceedings Act, 1992*.

10. A party is free to represent himself or herself or use a lawyer or paralegal in Small Claims Court.

11. See, for example, *Harding v. Fraser* (2006), 81 OR (3d) 708, 23 MPIR (4th) 288 (SCJ).

REFERENCES

Absentees Act, RSO 1990, c. A.3.

Bankruptcy and Insolvency Act, RSC 1985, c. B-3, as amended.

Branch, W., *Class Actions in Canada* (Toronto: Canada Law Book, 2000) (loose-leaf updates).

Bruce (Township) v. Thornburn (1986), 57 OR (2d) 77 (Div. Ct.).

Class Proceedings Act, 1992, SO 1992, c. 6.

Estates Administration Act, RSO 1990, c. E.22; 2006, c. 19, sch. C, s. 1.

Law Society of Upper Canada, *Rules of Professional Conduct* (Toronto: LSUC, 2000, as amended) (also available at http://www.lsuc.on.ca).

Mental Health Act, RSO 1990, c. M.7.

Police Retirees of Ontario Inc. v. Ontario Municipal Employees' Retirement Board (1997), 35 OR (3d) 177 (Gen. Div.).

Rules of Civil Procedure, RRO 1990, reg. 194.

Substitute Decisions Act, 1992, SO 1992, c. 30.

REVIEW QUESTIONS

1. Abigail Boar would like to sue Fred Flogem for negligence in one proceeding, Rattle Motors Ltd. for negligence in another, and Skunk Motorcar Company Ltd. for negligence in a third. Can she do this?

2. Can Abigail force defendants into the same lawsuit when the defendants have claims against each other?

3. In deciding to join or sever parties or issues, the court uses the balance of convenience test. Explain what this test is.

4. What are judgments *in personam* and *in rem*?

5. Can a party avoid joinder?

6. Can the court order two or more proceedings to be consolidated?

7. Can the court order separate hearings on issues in the same proceeding?

8. Suppose that Abigail is 6 years old instead of 26 years old and wants to sue. Can she?

9. Why might a litigation guardian have to post security for costs?

10. How is a litigation guardian for a defendant appointed?

11. Who acts as litigation guardian if no one comes forward on behalf of the party under disability?

12. What obligations does a litigation guardian have toward a party under disability and toward the opposite party?

13. What happens if no one comes forward to act as litigation guardian for a defendant?

14. What happens if the court is not satisfied that there is an appropriate person to appoint as litigation guardian?

15. Can a litigation guardian be removed?

16. Suppose Fred Flogem is a party under disability and fails to file a statement of defence. Can Abigail sign default judgment?

17. Can a litigation guardian settle a case on behalf of the party under disability?

18. If Rattle Motors is a sole proprietorship owned by Fred Flogem, whom should Abigail sue?

19. Should Abigail sue Rattle Motors if Regina Rattle and Fred Flogem own Rattle Motors as partners?

20. When does a partner file a separate statement of defence from that of the partnership?

21. Suppose you do a name search of Rattle Motors and discover that Rattle Motors is a trade name. The business is owned by 1234 Ontario Ltd. What party do you sue?

22. Whom does I.M. Just sue if he discovers that Abigail's estate has no personal representative?

23. If your law firm sues Abigail and she dies after the action is commenced, can you continue to sue her?

24. How does a class proceeding differ from other types of representative proceedings?

25. What must be done to turn a lawsuit into a class proceeding?

26. May any litigant represent himself or herself in a proceeding?

27. What does the phrase "on the record" mean?

28. What does Abigail need to do if she wishes to change lawyers or remove her lawyer and represent herself?

DISCUSSION QUESTIONS

1. Herkimer Spittoon, aged 26, is an electrical engineer and brother of Sam Spittoon. On August 4, year –2, Herkimer suffered brain injuries when he was involved in an automobile collision. As a result of the injuries, he suffers from mood swings and impulsive behaviour, when he goes on wild spending sprees. He has little sense of financial reality, and does not understand that he is living on a small disability allowance and does not have the income he once had. He also does not understand or accept advice on the management of his financial affairs. A creditor has sued him for purchases he made on April 4, year 0. The claim was issued on June 4, year 0 and served on June 6, year 0. Both Sam and Herkimer live in Toronto. Sam has just become aware that Herkimer has been sued. Sam has come to the law office you work in for some advice because Herkimer is ignoring the whole situation.

    a. Explain to Sam why Herkimer cannot defend this action by himself, and explain what must be done.

    b. Explain to Sam what his duties are as litigation guardian.

    c. Draft the body of Sam's affidavit, assuming that he is moving to be appointed litigation guardian.

2. Johnson Eversharp retained Huey Sue to act for him in a complicated piece of commercial litigation. The pleading stage has closed, and the opposition has served Huey with a notice of examination for discovery of Johnson to be held on August 14, year 0. On August 3, year 0, Huey's law clerk phoned Johnson but got the answering machine. This happened on four subsequent days. Phone calls and emails to Johnson's home got no better results. The date of discovery is rapidly approaching. Huey decides that this client is not cooperating and wants to get off the record before there are further difficulties. The client still has $1,000 to his credit in the law office trust account, which will cover services to date. Draft the body of Huey's affidavit.

Commencing Proceedings

Important to go back to formst procedure to commence a proceeding + chptr. 7 "Pleadings"

6

Introduction

In Ontario, court cases proceed in one of two ways, by action or by application. The steps to be taken and the pleadings are generally different if you are proceeding by action rather than by application, and in this chapter we will look at each of these ways of proceeding.

Rule 14.02 requires that a matter proceed by action unless a specific rule or statute requires otherwise. Rules 7.08(3), 65, 67, and 68, for example, provide that proceedings commenced under those rules are to be by application. Rule 66 allows that the proceeding under that rule may be either by action or by application. However, the vast majority of proceedings are by action.

Rule 14.01 requires that all proceedings, whether actions or applications, are to be commenced by the **issuing** of an originating process. The only exceptions are a counterclaim against persons who are already parties to the main action, a cross-claim, and an application for a certificate of appointment by an estate trustee. Rules 14.01(2) and 14.01(2.1) provide that these documents need not be issued before being delivered to the parties requiring notice.

issuing
official commencement of court proceedings whereby documents that are originating processes are signed by the registrar, dated, sealed with a court seal, and given a file number

Issuing and Filing

The pleadings that are originating processes are listed in the definition of originating process in Rule 1.03. Generally, an originating process can be described as the first document or pleading in a court case. Although the parties in a proceeding may have had extensive contact and been involved in lengthy negotiations before the first steps were taken to bring the matter to court, the court has no knowledge of a case until it receives the first court document or pleading. The step that notifies the court that a proceeding is being commenced is called "issuing."

The process of issuing is dealt with in Rule 4.05. The originating process is drafted in the law office and is then taken to the court office to have the registrar sign, date, and put a seal on it. It is the court seal that lets the other side know that the court proceeding is genuine. During issuing, the registrar also assigns a court file number to the proceeding and it is at this point that the court opens a file, which will later hold other court documents relating to the case. Until the registrar assigns a court file number, the space on the originating process for the number remains blank. Once a number is assigned, this number must appear on every other pleading in the case when it is prepared in the law office.

It is only in very small court offices that the registrar personally signs each originating process. In big court offices, such as Toronto, numerous court staff who work in the issuing office are designated by the registrar to sign the documents on his or her behalf.

Issuing the document also normally requires the payment of a fee.[1] The person from the law office who takes the document to the court to be issued must also bring a cheque from the law firm made out to the Minister of Finance in the required amount. The fees charged by the Superior Court of Justice for the processing of documents are set out in a regulation to the *Administration of Justice Act*, O. Reg. 293/92.

The current fee for various court functions can be obtained by referring to this regulation on the e-Laws website at http://www.e-laws.gov.on.ca, by calling the court office, or by checking on the Ontario government's website under the Ministry of the Attorney General, Court Services, which can be found at http://www .attorneygeneral.jus.gov.on.ca/english/courts. You should take two copies of your document with you. Only one copy will be signed and sealed. The original signed and sealed document will be returned to you and the court will keep a copy in its file.

While the court clerk is signing and preparing the original, you need to create a true copy for the court to keep in its file. This is done by copying by hand everything that the clerk is writing on the original. You put the signature of the registrar in quotation marks to indicate that it is a copy of the signature and not the original. On your copy, put a circle on the document in the same place that the clerk affixes the court seal. Inside the circle, write the word "seal." This process of making a true copy at the court counter, while your document is being issued, is called "**truing up**" the document. Once the original has been issued, the clerk will give it back to you and take your trued-up copy for the court file. The original, sealed document is kept in the client's file in the law office. You can then make copies of it on a photocopier for serving on the other side.

Once the originating process has been issued, only then can it be served on the other parties in the case. "Serving" a document, in very general terms, involves giving a copy to the other party or parties. Service must be done according to the Rules, and this process is dealt with in detail in Chapter 8.

Only an originating process need go through the process of issuing. All the other documents in the proceeding may be served on the other parties and then filed with the court office. Filing involves merely taking a document to the court, with the appropriate fee, and having the court staff place a copy on the court file. The document may also be filed by mailing it to the court office along with the required fee, but the document is not regarded as filed until it is received by the court and stamped with the court filing stamp, unless the court orders otherwise.

The Rules also provide for the electronic filing of documents if the authorized software is used, but to date the courts are not set up to receive electronic filings, so with the exception of some Court of Appeal and Divisional Court documents and documents for the Commercial List (which is dealt with in Chapter 24), it is not possible to file electronically.

Rule 4.05(2) sets out in which court the documents are to be filed, and that is usually the court office in which the proceeding was commenced or to which the proceeding has been transferred unless a motion or application is to be heard in some other place. A motion to transfer a proceeding to another court must be filed in the court to which the transfer is sought.

truing up

making a handmade copy of a document at the court counter, usually by adding a seal and the registrar's signature inside quotation marks, by hand, to a photocopy of the original document

Proceedings by Way of Action

Generally, the originating process that starts an action is a statement of claim, the precedent for which can be found in Form 14A (general actions) or Form 14B (mortgage actions). Some exceptions to this can be found in Rule 14.03(1)(a) to (e).

Abigail Boar's case does not fit into the exceptions under Rule 14.02 or 14.03, so it will proceed by way of action and the originating process will likely be a statement of claim. But perhaps Abigail has been uncertain about whether she wants to sue the defendants. She spends so much time thinking about what she is going to do that the limitation period for starting an action against Rattle Motors and Fred Flogem may be running out.

It takes time to properly draft a statement of claim and perhaps Abigail only goes to see a lawyer three days before the limitation period on her case is about to expire. This is a relatively common situation because most people without any legal training do not realize that limitation periods exist.

limitation period
specified time within which court proceedings must be commenced

A **limitation period** is the time in which a plaintiff may sue another person who he or she believes may be legally responsible for causing him or her damage. The limitation period in most cases is two years, but once the limitation period has passed, a plaintiff loses forever his or her right to sue. It is therefore very important that the court proceeding be started before the limitation period expires. It is important to note that a limitation period is not the same as a time period set out in the Rules. Limitation periods are set out in the *Limitations Act, 2002*, an Ontario statute. They are absolute and cannot be changed by the court. Time periods set out in the Rules are to be followed, but as we have discussed, the court may shorten (legally this is called abridging) or extend a time period set out in the Rules if it is fair and just to do so.

If I.M. Just, Abigail's lawyer, does not have enough time to draft a lengthy and detailed statement of claim before the limitation period expires, he can instead issue a notice of action under Rule 14.03(2). Figure 6.1 sets out a notice of action for Abigail's case.

The issuing of a notice of action stops the limitation period and gives Abigail 30 more days from the date the notice of action is issued to serve and file the statement of claim. If a notice of action is used, the form for the statement of claim changes a bit. Instead of using the general Form 14A, the plaintiff who files a notice of action first must file a statement of claim using the prescribed Form 14D. The claim made by the plaintiff in the notice of action is usually the same as the claim that is later made in the statement of claim. But sometimes more information about the plaintiff's claim comes to light after the notice of action has been filed. In that case, Rule 14.03(5) allows the plaintiff to alter or extend the claim stated in the notice of action.

If you start your action with a notice of action instead of a statement of claim, it is only the notice of action that is issued. The statement of claim is filed with the court when it is ready. This means that the court seal is on the notice of action and not on the statement of claim.

Whether the action is started by a statement of claim or a notice of application, you must also file Information for Court Use, Form 14F (see Figure 6.2).

Figure 6.1   Notice of Action (Form 14C)

Court file no. 01-CV-1234

ONTARIO
SUPERIOR COURT OF JUSTICE

BETWEEN:

ABIGAIL BOAR

Plaintiff

and

RATTLE MOTORS LTD. and FRED FLOGEM

Defendants

NOTICE OF ACTION

TO THE DEFENDANT

A LEGAL PROCEEDING HAS BEEN COMMENCED AGAINST YOU by the plaintiff. The claim made against you is set out in the statement of claim served with this notice of action.

IF YOU WISH TO DEFEND THIS PROCEEDING, you or an Ontario lawyer acting for you must prepare a statement of defence in Form 18A prescribed by the Rules of Civil Procedure, serve it on the plaintiff's lawyer or, where the plaintiff does not have a lawyer, serve it on the plaintiff, and file it, with proof of service, in this court office, WITHIN TWENTY DAYS after this notice of action is served on you, if you are served in Ontario.

If you are served in another province or territory of Canada or in the United States of America, the period for serving and filing your statement of defence is forty days. If you are served outside Canada and the United States of America, the period is sixty days.

Instead of serving and filing a statement of defence, you may serve and file a notice of intent to defend in Form 18B prescribed by the Rules of Civil Procedure. This will entitle you to ten more days within which to serve and file your statement of defence.

IF YOU FAIL TO DEFEND THIS PROCEEDING, JUDGMENT MAY BE GIVEN AGAINST YOU IN YOUR ABSENCE AND WITHOUT FURTHER NOTICE TO YOU. IF YOU WISH TO DEFEND THIS PROCEEDING BUT ARE UNABLE TO PAY LEGAL FEES, LEGAL AID MAY BE AVAILABLE TO YOU BY CONTACTING A LOCAL LEGAL AID OFFICE.

IF YOU PAY THE PLAINTIFF'S CLAIM, and $750.00 for costs, within the time for serving and filing your statement of defence, you may move to have this proceeding dismissed by the court. If you believe the amount claimed for

Figure 6.1   Concluded

costs is excessive, you may pay the plaintiff's claim and $400.00 for costs and have the costs assessed by the court.

Date: January 4, year 1   Issued by: _____
                                                          Local registrar

                                           Address of
                                           court office: Courthouse
                                                            393 University Avenue
                                                            Toronto, Ontario, M5G 1E6

TO: Rattle Motors Ltd.
       1240 Bay Street
       Toronto, Ontario, M8H 0K8

AND TO: Fred Flogem
           21 Cypress Boulevard
           Scarborough, Ontario, M8Q 1P3

CLAIM

1.   The plaintiff claims against both defendants:

      a.   General damages in the amount of $200,000.00;

      b.   Special damages in the amount of $3,649.00 to the date of this pleading;

      c.   Prejudgment and postjudgment interest pursuant to the *Courts of Justice Act*,
            RSO 1990, c. C.43;

      d.   Costs of this action;

      e.   Such further relief as seems just to this court.

2.   The plaintiff's claim is a result of a slip and fall that occurred on September 14,
      year 0.

Date of Issue: _____   Just & Coping
                                        Barristers and Solicitors
                                        365 Bay Street, Suite 8701
                                        Toronto, Ontario, M3J 4A9

                                        I.M. Just
                                        LSUC #12345R
                                        tel.: 416-762-1342
                                        fax: 416-762-2300

                                        Lawyers for the Plaintiff

                                                   RCP-E 14C (July 1, 2007)

Figure 6.2 Information for Court Use (Form 14F)

ONTARIO
SUPERIOR COURT OF JUSTICE

BETWEEN:

ABIGAIL BOAR

Plaintiff

and

RATTLE MOTORS LTD. AND FRED FLOGEM

Defendants

INFORMATION FOR COURT USE

1. This proceeding is an: [x] action [ ] application

2. Has it been commenced under the *Class Proceedings Act, 1992*? [ ] yes [x] no

3. If the proceeding is an action, does Rule 76 (Simplified Procedure) apply? [ ] yes [x] no

Note: *Subject to the exceptions found in subrule 76.01(1), it is MANDATORY to proceed under Rule 76 for all cases in which the money amount claimed or the value of real or personal property claimed is $100,000 or less.*

4. The claim in this proceeding (action or application) is in respect of:

*(Select the **one** item that **best** describes the nature of the main claim in the proceeding.)*

Bankruptcy or insolvency law	[ ]	Motor vehicle accident	[ ]
Collection of liquidated debt	[ ]	Municipal law	[ ]
Constitutional law	[ ]	Partnership law	[ ]
Construction law (other than construction lien)	[ ]	Personal property security	[ ]
Construction lien	[ ]	Product liability	[ ]
Contract law	[ ]	Professional malpractice (other than medical)	[ ]
Corporate law	[ ]	Real property (including leases; excluding mortgage or charge)	[ ]
Defamation	[ ]	Tort: economic injury (other than from medical or professional malpractice)	[ ]
Employment or labour law	[ ]		
Intellectual property law	[ ]	Tort: personal injury (other than from motor vehicle accident)	[x]
Judicial review	[ ]	Trusts, fiduciary duty	[ ]
Medical malpractice	[ ]	Wills, estates	[ ]
Mortgage or charge	[ ]		

CERTIFICATION

I certify that the above information is correct, to the best of my knowledge.

Date: _____ January 4, year 1 _____

_____
I.M. Just
Signature of lawyer
(if no lawyer, party must sign)

RCP-E 14F (November 1, 2008)

Time Limits for Serving the Statement of Claim

Once the statement of claim is issued, you can serve it on the other side. Chapter 8 deals with the specific steps required to serve a court document. Very simply, service of a document means giving a copy of the document to the other side. Abigail's lawyer will have to ensure that both Rattle Motors Ltd. and Fred Flogem are given copies of the claim according to the methods prescribed in the Rules.

Rule 14.08(1) requires that the statement of claim be served within six months after it is issued. This means that you want to be certain of the defendant's location before you issue the statement of claim. Otherwise, you may spend more than six months looking for him or her. If your statement of claim cannot be served within six months, you will have to bring a motion before the court to extend the six-month time period. Usually, if there is a good reason why the statement of claim could not be served within the time period, an extension of time will be granted. In Abigail's case, we know the location of Rattle Motors and Fred Flogem.

If Abigail's lawyer must start the proceeding with a notice of action because a limitation period is about to expire, the notice of action is not served separately on the defendant. Both the notice of action and the statement of claim in Form 14D are served on the defendant together. You have six months to serve the documents together, but the six months starts running as soon as the notice of action is issued, not when the statement of claim is filed later with the court.

Proceedings Commenced by Application

A court proceeding in the Ontario Superior Court of Justice may also be by application instead of action. Although proceeding by application is much faster and more expeditious than proceeding by action, the use of applications is limited. A proceeding must be by action unless a statute or the Rules say it is to be commenced in some other manner (Rule 14.02).

There are a number of rules that require a proceeding by application instead of by action.[2] In addition, Rule 14.05(3) provides a list of types of situations where plaintiffs can proceed by application. Therefore, the first step is to decide whether the case you are commencing is one that can proceed by application. If it does not fit into one of the categories provided by the Rules and there is no statute that authorizes you to proceed by application, then you must proceed by action and follow the steps outlined above in relation to actions.

It is important to note, however, that Rule 14.05(3)(h) permits an application to be brought on any matter where it is unlikely that there will be any material facts in dispute. Material facts are those central to the case. If no such facts are in dispute, the most expeditious way to deal with a case may be by way of application.

If you can commence the action by application, you use a different originating process than you do with an action. In an application, you start the proceedings with a notice of application. The general form for a notice of application is Form 14E, but there is a special notice of application if your application is for judicial review under Rule 68 or is a proceeding to register an order from the United Kingdom for enforcement by the Ontario court under Rule 73. For judicial review, you

Figure 6.3   Notice of Application (Form 14E)

Court file no. 03-CL-8926

ONTARIO
SUPERIOR COURT OF JUSTICE

BETWEEN:

DINGLEHOOFER OFFICE SUPPLIES LTD.

Applicant

and

DONALDSON PRINTING CORPORATION

Respondent

APPLICATION UNDER the *Business Corporations Act*, RSO 1990, c. B.16, ss. 207-18 and s. 248, as amended.

NOTICE OF APPLICATION

TO THE RESPONDENT

A LEGAL PROCEEDING HAS BEEN COMMENCED by the applicant. The claim made by the applicant appears on the following page.

THIS APPLICATION will come on for a hearing on March 10, year 2, at 10:00 a.m., at Osgoode Hall, 130 Queen Street West, Toronto, Ontario, M5H 2N5.

IF YOU WISH TO OPPOSE THIS APPLICATION, to receive notice of any step in the application or to be served with any documents in the application you or an Ontario lawyer acting for you must forthwith prepare a notice of appearance in Form 38A prescribed by the Rules of Civil Procedure, serve it on the applicant's lawyer or, where the applicant does not have a lawyer, serve it on the applicant, and file it, with proof of service, in this court office, and you or your lawyer must appear at the hearing.

IF YOU WISH TO PRESENT AFFIDAVIT OR OTHER DOCUMENTARY EVIDENCE TO THE COURT OR TO EXAMINE OR CROSS-EXAMINE WITNESSES ON THE APPLICATION, you or your lawyer must, in addition to serving your notice of appearance, serve a copy of the evidence on the applicant's lawyer or, where the applicant does not have a lawyer, serve it on the applicant, and file it, with proof of service, in the court office where the application is to be heard as soon as possible, but at least four days before the hearing.

IF YOU FAIL TO APPEAR AT THE HEARING, JUDGMENT MAY BE GIVEN IN YOUR ABSENCE AND WITHOUT FURTHER NOTICE TO YOU. IF YOU

Figure 6.3   Continued

WISH TO OPPOSE THIS APPLICATION BUT ARE UNABLE TO PAY LEGAL
FEES, LEGAL AID MAY BE AVAILABLE TO YOU BY CONTACTING A LOCAL
LEGAL AID OFFICE.

Date: February 26, year 2   Issued by: _____

                                                         Local registrar

                                         Address of
                                         court office: Courthouse
                                                        393 University Ave.
                                                        Toronto, Ontario, M5G 1E6

TO: Donaldson Printing Corporation
      3276 College Street North
      Toronto, Ontario, M7Y 4F7

APPLICATION

1. The applicant makes application pursuant to the Ontario *Business Corporations
    Act*, RSO 1990, c. B.16, s. 207, for:

    a. an order that the voluntary winding up of the respondent corporation be
        continued under supervision of the court;

    b. the costs of the application; and

    c. such other order as seems just to this court.

2. The grounds for the application are:

    a. the applicant is a creditor of the respondent corporation, which is currently in
        the process of being voluntarily wound up;

    b. the respondent corporation owes the applicant a debt for supplies in the
        amount of $5,000;

    c. it is not in the interests of the contributories and creditors that the proceedings
        should be continued under the supervision of the court for the following
        reasons:

        i. (*here set out reasons*);

    d. the applicant relies on the provisions of the *Business Corporations Act*, RSO
        1990, c. B.16, ss. 207-218 and s. 248.

Figure 6.3   Concluded

3. The following documentary evidence will be used at the hearing of the application:

Affidavit of Bradley Pittbottom, president of the applicant corporation, dated February 20, year 2 and the exhibit referred to therein.

Date of issue: February 26, year 2

Fair and Duguid
Barristers and Solicitors
50 Justice Way
Suite 1000
Toronto, Ontario, M9V 6J2

Bonnie Fair
LSUC #98765D
tel. 416-555-1225
fax 416-555-1226

Lawyers for the Applicant

RCP-E 14E (March 31, 2010)

commence the application with a notice of application for judicial review using Form 68A. For the registration of an order from the United Kingdom, you must use Form 73A. An example of the general notice of application, Form 14E, is set out in Figure 6.3. In addition to the notice of application, Information for Court Use, Form 14F, must also be filed (see Figure 6.2).

In addition to Rule 14, Rules 38 and 39 spell out the procedure and the evidence to be used on applications.

In an application, the parties are not called the plaintiff and the defendant. Instead, they are the applicant and the respondent. The application must state the rule or statute under which it is commenced and set out the precise relief sought and the grounds for the relief. It should list the documentary evidence that will be used in the hearing of the application. All applications are brought before a judge. A master has no jurisdiction to hear an application (Rule 38.02).

Because a notice of application is an originating process, the court must issue it before it is served on the other side. It must then be served on all parties at least 10 days before the date of the hearing unless it is served outside Ontario. Then it must be served at least 20 days in advance.

One of the reasons that an application is a much faster procedure than an action is that it relies mostly on **affidavit** evidence. The affidavit is usually served on the respondent along with the notice of application. An affidavit is a sworn document that lays out the facts that a party is relying on. It is evidence in the proceeding. It must be clear, precise, and based on the knowledge or belief of the person who is swearing that the facts in the affidavit are true. See Chapter 9 for more information on drafting affidavits.

affidavit
written statement setting out the evidence of the person who swears or affirms its contents are true

A respondent who has been served with a notice of application serves and files a notice of appearance in Form 38A. An example of a notice of appearance is set out in Figure 6.4. A respondent who does not serve and file a notice of appearance cannot file material, examine a witness, or take other steps in the proceeding, and is not entitled to any further notice of other steps in the application.

Place and Date of Hearing of the Application

The applicant names the place of hearing, which is usually the court nearest the place where the applicant resides, unless a statute or rule requires that the application be brought in a specific location.

You may pick any date for the hearing of the application when a judge is scheduled to hear applications as long as the hearing is estimated, by the lawyer, to take less than two hours. You need not obtain the date from the court before you complete and serve the notice of application (Rule 38.03(2)). However, if the hearing is to take longer than two hours, a date must be obtained from the court office first unless it is an urgent case (Rule 38.03(3)). An urgent matter may be scheduled for any day that applications are being heard in the court, even if it is going to take more than two hours to argue. In some courts, practice directions apply to the scheduling of applications, and you must therefore check whether a practice direction exists for the court in which you wish to bring an application.

Figure 6.3 sets out a notice of application in Form 14E.

Material for Use on the Application

factum
document that sets out the facts, statutes, and cases that a party relies on to obtain a favourable decision

The applicant is required to serve and file an application record and a **factum**, along with proof of service, at least four days before the hearing of the application. A factum is a document that sets out the facts and the law on which the party relies. Rule 38.09 provides that an application record must contain the following information:

- a table of contents describing each document by its nature, date, and, if it is an exhibit, its exhibit number;
- a copy of the notice of application;
- a copy of all affidavits and other material served by any party for use on the application;
- a list of all relevant transcripts of evidence in chronological order, but not necessarily the transcripts themselves; and
- a copy of any other material in the court file that is necessary for the hearing of the application.

All of the above must be bound together in consecutively numbered pages and be in the order specified above. The application record will have a light blue backsheet and the applicant's factum will be bound, front and back, with white covers.

The respondent must serve and file his or her factum, stating the facts and the law on which the respondent relies, at least two days before the hearing. The respondent's factum must be bound both front and back with green cover stock paper. For more information about factums, refer to Chapter 20 on appeals.

Figure 6.4   Notice of Appearance (Form 38A)

Court file no. 03-CL-8926

ONTARIO
SUPERIOR COURT OF JUSTICE

BETWEEN:

DINGLEHOOFER OFFICE SUPPLIES LTD.

Applicant

and

DONALDSON PRINTING CORPORATION

Respondent

APPLICATION UNDER the *Business Corporations Act*, RSO 1990, c. B.16, ss. 207-18 and s. 248, as amended.

NOTICE OF APPEARANCE

The respondent intends to respond to this application.

March 10, year 2

Tilley Townsend
LSUC #76543U
Barrister and Solicitor
10 Winding Road
Newmarket, Ontario, N0M 1D0

tel. 905-666-1010
fax 905-666-1011

Lawyer for the Respondent

TO: Fair and Duguid
Barristers and Solicitors
50 Justice Way
Suite 1000
Toronto, Ontario, M9V 6J2

Bonnie Fair
LSUC #98765D
tel. 416-555-1225
fax 416-555-1226

Lawyers for the Applicant

RCP-E 38A (July 1, 2007)

If the respondent believes that the applicant's record is incomplete, he or she may serve and file his or her own application record. The respondent's application record must contain a table of contents, the exhibits relied on, and copies of any other material that the respondent intends to rely on at the hearing.

If for any reason either or both parties believe that an application record or a factum is not necessary for the hearing of the case, they may bring a motion before a judge, asking for an order dispensing with the application record and factum.

A party who wishes to rely on a transcript of evidence must file a copy of the transcript in accordance with Rule 34.18. It must be filed at least four days before the hearing of the application.

Confirmation of an Application

An applicant who brings an application on notice must confer or attempt to confer or discuss the application with the respondent no later than 2 p.m. two days before the date for the hearing. The purpose of this discussion is for the parties to determine whether the application will proceed as scheduled, whether an adjournment is being sought, or whether the parties can settle the matter completely or in part. Then the applicant must send a confirmation of application, Form 38B, to the registrar of the court, confirming that the application will be proceeding as scheduled, or advising whether an adjournment, or another type of order listed on the form, is being sought. Form 38B may be sent to the court in person, by fax, or by email (if the court has an available email address). A copy must also be sent to the respondent by fax or email.

If the confirmation is not sent as required, the application will not be heard on the date originally scheduled, unless the court orders otherwise. The applicant must also ensure that if the situation changes after the confirmation is sent, the court is provided with updated information.

Disposition of an Application

After the judge has heard the application, he or she may grant the relief the applicant is seeking, dismiss the application, adjourn the application, or direct that the matter go to trial. If the application is ordered to trial, it is turned into an action.

Evidence on an Application

Evidence on an application is presented in an affidavit, which is a sworn document laying out the facts in the case. It must be based on the personal knowledge or belief of the person who makes it and swears it to be true. The person who makes the affidavit is called the **deponent**. Although the evidence is written down and not given in court through witnesses, the opposite party has a right to cross-examine the deponent on the facts he or she claims to be true. On cross-examination, a lawyer for the opposite party asks questions to test the credibility of the deponent. The cross-examination takes place in the office of an official examiner or a reporting service (Rule 34.02(1)). The evidence is recorded word-for-word, and a transcript is pre-

deponent
person who makes an affidavit

pared. If a party wishes to present the cross-examination at the hearing, it does so by filing a copy of the transcript.

A lawyer who wants to cross-examine a witness on an affidavit must serve and file all the affidavits he or she intends to rely on in the hearing of the application. It is only then that he or she may cross-examine a deponent for the other side. Once a lawyer has conducted a cross-examination, he or she cannot file any more affidavits for his or her client without permission from the court.

For more information on affidavits and cross-examinations, you may refer to Chapter 9 on motions and Chapter 14 on discovery.

CHAPTER SUMMARY

We have seen that all civil proceedings in Ontario are commenced by application or by action. The Rules require a proceeding to be commenced by action unless a statute or the Rules require that it should be commenced by way of application.

The document that starts a court proceeding is called an originating process. There are different types of originating processes, depending on the type of court proceeding that is being started. All of the originating processes are listed under the definition in Rule 1.03. Generally, the originating process that starts an action is a statement of claim. All originating processes, including a statement of claim, must be issued by the registrar of the court. A statement of claim must be served on the defendant within six months after it is issued. If the action is commenced by a notice of action, it is served along with the statement of claim.

If the case is one that is proceeding by application, the originating process is a notice of application. We noted that it must also be issued before it is served, and it must be served at least 10 days before the hearing of the application. Once the application has been commenced, Rule 38 dictates how the application proceeds through the court process. Rule 39 specifies what evidence can be brought. An application record and a factum must be filed in all applications.

After the parties have presented their cases at the hearing of the application, the judge may dismiss the application, grant the relief the applicant is seeking, or adjourn the matter. These resolutions are similar in any other type of hearing. However, the judge has an additional option on an application: he or she may order that the application be turned into an action. If this occurs, any further steps in the case must follow the procedural requirements for an action.

KEY TERMS

affidavit, 147

deponent, 150

factum, 148

issuing, 138

limitation period, 140

truing up, 139

NOTES

1. In certain instances where a person cannot afford the fee and would otherwise be unable to access justice, the *Administration of Justice Act*, ss. 4.1 to 4.5 and 4.7, and O. Reg. 2/05, Fee Waiver provide the authority and the process for obtaining a waiver of fees. This information can also be found at the Ministry of the Attorney General, Court Services website at http://www.attorneygeneral.jus.gov.on.ca/english/courts under Court Fees.

2. See Rules 65.01, 66.01, 67.01, and 68.01.

REFERENCES

Administration of Justice Act, RSO 1990, c. A.6.

Superior Court of Justice and Court of Appeal—Fees, O. Reg. 293/92.

Limitations Act, 2002, SO 2002, c. 24, sch. B.

Partnerships Act, RSO 1990, c. P.5.

Rules of Civil Procedure, RRO 1990, reg. 194.

REVIEW QUESTIONS

1. What are the two ways that a court case may be commenced in Ontario?

2. What is the originating process that usually commences an action? Can another originating process be used to start an action?

3. What is an issued document?

4. What do you have to do to "true up" an issued document, and when do you do it?

5. Why is it important to get as much information about the location of the defendant as possible before you issue the statement of claim?

6. Your client was one week away from the expiry of the limitation period under the *Limitations Act, 2002* when she contacted your office. You did not have time to prepare a statement of claim so you filed a notice of action to stop the limitation period from running out. Twenty-nine days after you issued the notice of action, you filed your statement of claim. How much time do you have left to serve the statement of claim?

7. Must you serve the notice of action on the other side?

8. Will Abigail Boar commence her court case by way of application or by way of action?

9. What is the procedure for obtaining a hearing date for an application?

10. What are the contents of an application record?

11. Under what circumstances would a respondent file an application record?

DISCUSSION QUESTION

1. Brad Pout, an avid horse enthusiast, met an experienced horse trader, Tom Craze. They discussed their mutual interests over lunch on several occasions and decided to go into partnership to carry on the business of buying horses. Brad contributed $100,000 to the partnership and Tom was to buy the horses, but he contributed no money. They did buy and sell many horses and made a big profit but they eventually had a falling out. Tom now wants to dissolve the partnership. There is $300,000 in the partnership bank account. Tom wants his half of the $300,000 because he says that he contributed all the work. Brad says Tom is only entitled to $100,000, which amounts to 50 percent of the profit after Brad deducts the money he put into the partnership in the beginning. Tom is relying on s. 5 of the *Partnerships Act*, which allows a partner to make an application to the court for a dissolution of the partnership when circumstances have arisen that make it fair for the partnership to be dissolved. He wants the court to order that he receive $150,000 from the partnership's remaining assets. Draft a notice of application for Tom.

Drafting Pleadings

7

Introduction

In this chapter, we turn to some of the matters you must consider in drafting statements of claim and defence as well as replies to statements of defence. Drafting issues that involve notices of application are dealt with in Chapter 9 because procedurally and in terms of format, notices of application have more in common with motions than they have with statements of claim. The procedural aspects of commencing an action are discussed in Chapter 6.

General Drafting Considerations

Getting Organized

Before you start to draft a statement of claim or other pleading, you need to think about what you wish to say and organize your material. As a law clerk, you will usually be working under the supervision of a lawyer. Speak to him or her to be sure that you understand your instructions and the theory of the case. The theory of the case is the focus or basis of liability on which you organize the facts and decide which facts are relevant. For example, if I.M. Just's theory is that Abigail Boar was injured solely because of the negligence of Fred Flogem, you include only allegations about what Fred did or did not do properly. You do not include statements to show that Rattle Motors Ltd. or Skunk Motorcar Company Ltd. is liable. If, on the other hand, I.M. Just's theory is that Fred was negligent, Rattle Motors Ltd. is responsible for Fred's acts, and Skunk Motorcar Company Ltd. negligently manufactured the car that caused the oil leak, you will include allegations about Skunk Motorcar Company Ltd. and statements of law that Rattle Motors Ltd. is responsible for the negligent acts of its employees. What you plead depends on the theory of the case.

Assemble and review the interview notes from meetings with the client and with any witnesses. Also review client documents, expert reports, or any other evidentiary material that you have. Summarize the evidence on the facts that you will plead. If there is no hope of proving a fact because there is no evidence to support it, the fact should not be pleaded, and the supervising lawyer may need to revise his or her theory of the case.

Peruse precedents for other statements of claim in the firm's files. Most firms keep precedent binders, and you should too, starting with the forms and documents you create in this course and other courses as assignments and projects. A precedent can show you the proper format, act as a guide for drafting an outline, and sometimes give you the language to express a certain claim or principle of law. But precedents should be used with caution. You are unlikely to find a statement of claim into which you can simply plug in Abigail's name. You need to look at precedents critically, being prepared to use your own language to express your meaning and purpose. Be aware that many precedents, particularly older ones, use what is called the common law drafting style—an archaic legal style that is repetitious and full of jargon. Mercifully, it is fast disappearing as young lawyers in Ontario are trained to use plain language drafting techniques. Plain language has been part of the bar admission curriculum since 1990 and has had some impact on drafting. This style, also referred to as the Citibank style, originated with loan agreements used by the First National City Bank of New York, a major American commercial bank. The simpler and clearer documents used by the bank have been credited with reducing the volume of the bank's litigation by reducing the ambiguity of the documents. Plain language drafting has since spread throughout the common law world. This plain language style is also used in modern Ontario statute drafting, and the contrast with older statutes is startling. Do not be afraid to use simple language to express your meaning. Cut to the chase. Avoid legal jargon such as "the plaintiff states and the fact is" or "the defendant alleges." Instead, say "the plaintiff states" or "the defendant states."

Prepare an outline. The format of the statements of claim and defence as outlined in Forms 14A and 18A sets this out in part, but you still need to outline the facts and law that you rely on.

Type out or dictate a first draft. With minimal polishing, this can be forwarded to a client for comment and feedback. A client will often have important corrections to make to basic facts as pleaded. As you revise and go to later drafts, be sure to label the draft with the date so you do not mistakenly rely on an earlier imperfect draft.

Revise and polish the draft after getting client and lawyer feedback. A law clerk should forward what he or she thinks is the final draft to the lawyer for approval before serving and filing the pleading in question.

Check for internal consistency. If you make a cross-reference to another paragraph in the claim or to a fact alleged elsewhere in the claim, be sure your reference is in the right place.

Give the document a fast read to see that it flows logically and that the facts and law as pleaded support the theory of the case.

Language and Tone

You already know that you should avoid jargon and legalese. Most commentators think that it is best to use simple language in pleadings. Facts should be simply stated as facts. You need not search the thesaurus for a string of colourful adjectives to describe Abigail's pain. It is sufficient to describe it as "chronic and severe pain in the neck and back," for example. Use relatively short, blunt sentences that are devoid of flowery language. If a fact is material, it should be stated positively, and if possible, in a separate sentence. Tell the story in a logical way so that the reader can follow it. Usually, telling a story chronologically works well. Use an outline to be sure that you have included everything that is material and so that the story flows logically.

Drafting Statements of Claim

Format

The format of a claim is in part prescribed by Rule 14 and Form 14A.[1] It consists of the following, discussed in sequential order:

General Heading and Title of Proceedings

The format for this is prescribed by Form 4A. It must head every court document, including a statement of claim.

Prescribed Text

boilerplate
standard wording that
is part of every copy of a
particular type of document

Generally referred to as **boilerplate**, this is the part of the statement of claim that follows the general heading and title of proceedings. It begins with the words "TO THE DEFENDANT." The language here is prescribed by the Rules, and the wording must appear in every claim. Fortunately, there is litigation software available that reproduces this and eliminates the need for copy typing and pre-printed forms. The boilerplate for the generic statement of claim, Form 14A, is reproduced in Figure 7.1 at the end of the chapter.

The only information you need to add to the boilerplate section of the statement of claim is an amount for costs, the date that the claim is issued, the address of the court office, the name and address of the defendant, and the name, address, and telephone number of the plaintiff's lawyer. The amount for costs should not be an astronomical sum and should reflect the cost of an uncontested action where the claim is paid right after it issues. An amount between $700 and $900 should be sufficient.

You will also need to prepare Form 14F: Information for Court Use. This form indicates whether the proceeding is an action or an application, whether it is a class proceeding, and whether Rule 76 (simplified procedure) applies. It also requires you to indicate what the cause of action is. Form 14F must be filed with every statement of claim. Figure 6.2 in Chapter 6 sets out a completed Form 14F.

Format of Pleadings: Rule 25.02

The body of the pleadings following the boilerplate is set out in consecutively numbered paragraphs. As far as possible, each allegation should be set out in a separate paragraph. This may make for some two- or three-sentence paragraphs, which may seem short to you, but they are appropriate for pleadings.

Claim for Relief: Rule 25.09

The claim for relief, which is paragraph 1, begins with the words "The plaintiff claims." In the claim, you set out each head of damage together with an amount, where that amount is known, in separate subparagraphs. Other relief claimed, such as an injunction or a declaratory judgment, must be specified as well. If there is more than one plaintiff, the claims for each plaintiff must be set out separately. If there is more than one defendant, you are obliged to set out how much you claim from each defendant for each claim you make unless the claim is made against all defendants jointly. Remember that each defendant is entitled to know the details of the claim made against him or her by each plaintiff.

Abigail is likely to claim **general damages** and **special damages**. It is not always possible at the beginning of a lawsuit to determine what special damages will be at trial. For example, Abigail has become depressed and antidepressants may be prescribed for her to take. At the time the claim issues, she may have spent $300 for these, but she does not know how much she will have spent by the time of trial. Rule 25.06(9) provides a solution. The plaintiff is permitted to claim special damages calculated to the date of pleading and can undertake to deliver particulars of further claims when they are known and, in any event, within 10 days of the start of the trial.

You should always claim prejudgment and postjudgment interest, which are available under ss. 127 to 130 of the *Courts of Justice Act*—they will not be awarded unless they are specifically claimed. Prejudgment interest runs from the date the cause of action arises until judgment or payment, so you need to set out the date the cause of action arose in the pleadings. In this case, the cause of action arose on September 14, year 0, when Abigail was injured. Postjudgment interest runs from the date of judgment until payment. Because you do not know these dates, a bare claim for postjudgment interest is sufficient.

You must also claim costs: Failure to claim them means they may not be awarded. The practice has developed among some lawyers of claiming costs on a substantial indemnity basis. This is a punitive costs award, and judges award it when one party has behaved badly or improperly in the course of the litigation. In our view, you should simply claim costs without elaborating unless you believe this is a case for a punitive costs award—for example, where one side has tried to hide evidence or has behaved maliciously. In that case, a claim for substantial indemnity costs is appropriate, and you may also wish to claim punitive or aggravated damages in respect of particularly outrageous or high-handed behaviour by a defendant. Otherwise, you should refrain from overstating your claim. When you do that, you raise your client's expectations, which cannot be fulfilled, and you fool neither your opponent nor the trial judge.

Most lawyers include a final claim for "such further relief as seems just to this court." This is probably unnecessary, but nearly all lawyers do it. It amounts to a security blanket to cover claims you should have made but did not. In fact, if you seek specific relief, you must state it in your claim, or the court cannot grant the relief at trial. This is because your opponent will say, with justification, that he or she is prejudiced in his or her defence because if the defendants had been aware of the claim at the beginning of the case, they would have prepared to defend it and presented their case differently. In a situation like this, the security blanket in the claim for relief will not help you. If there is a variation on a claim that is made within the scope of the pleadings, the security blanket is probably unnecessary. But most lawyers continue to put it in as if it were some kind of legal rabbit's foot or lucky charm. So, with misgivings, we include it too.

general damages
monetary damages for pain and suffering that cannot be determined on the basis of a formula

special damages
monetary damages that are specific, ascertainable, and measured on an objective basis; sometimes referred to as out-of-pocket expenses

Abigail Boar's claim for relief against Fred Flogem and Rattle Motors Ltd. is set out in paragraph 1 of her statement of claim, which appears in Figure 7.2 at the end of the chapter.

Cast of Characters

After the claim for relief, which is set out in paragraph 1, you identify in subsequent numbered paragraphs each plaintiff and each defendant. If a party is an individual, you say so. If it is relevant, you may wish to add a party's occupation, and you should add a general address, consisting of a town or city and province or state. Street addresses are not used as a matter of custom. The purpose of setting out the residence of an individual, or in the case of a party that is not an individual, the place where it carries on business, is to identify whether a party is a non-resident for purposes of service, determine whether the party should post security for costs, and identify other territorial jurisdiction issues. If the party is not an individual, its status should be set out: corporation, non-profit corporation, Crown corporation, or government agency, for example. This paragraph may also briefly describe the party's involvement in the case. An example of a cast of characters appears in paragraphs 2 to 4 of Abigail Boar's statement of claim, which is set out in Figure 7.2.

Facts and Law Underlying the Claim

In the subsequent paragraphs, you tell Abigail's story. Before doing this, however, we need to discuss a number of basic rules of pleading that apply to the drafting of claims and defences. There are also some rules that apply only to the drafting of defences, which we will discuss later in this chapter.

Plead Material Facts but Not Evidence: Rule 25.06(1)

You must plead a concise statement of material facts on which the party relies, but not the evidence that will be used to prove the facts of your case. There are three elements to this rule:

- Be concise.
- Plead material facts.
- Do not plead evidence.

"Be concise" means that you should not use 15 words when 5 will do. Avoid flowery language and excessive use of adjectives. Keep sentences and paragraphs reasonably short, confining a material fact to a single sentence where possible. Don't be surprised to find yourself writing paragraphs of two to three sentences. This is probably not what you learned in English class, but then you weren't being asked to do this kind of specialized writing.

"Material facts" are the facts that are necessary to prove or defend the claim based on your theory of the case. Before you can know what the material facts are, you must be familiar with both the events involved in the case and the law that applies to the situation. For example, in Abigail's case, the material facts concern her slipping and falling on the oil on the floor. Because the law involved is the law of negligence, material facts will be those that show negligence by the defendants. Here your facts include the lawful entry of Abigail into the area where the oil spill was, the lack of lighting, the fact that Fred knew about the spill, the fact that he did nothing to clean it up, the fact that Abigail was not warned or protected, the fact that she fell, and the fact that she was injured. What may not be relevant in this instance, though it may be interesting, are the facts that Fred is married with five children, that Abigail is very fond of the colour red, and that she had a happy childhood. Similarly, it is of no relevance to Abigail's claim that Rattle Motors Ltd. has sold far fewer cars this year than last and is teetering on bankruptcy. This last fact may be relevant in enforcing a judgment against Rattle Motors Ltd., but it is irrelevant to making a claim for negligence against it. Some of these facts may be relevant in some situations but not others. For example, if Abigail were going to participate in a psychological study relating colour preference to personality, then her preference for the colour red would be relevant indeed.

"Not pleading evidence" is the last element of this rule. Evidence of a material fact is information from which a material fact may be proven or deduced. For example, to state that "the plaintiff fell because there was oil on the floor" is to state a material fact. But to go on to say that "Abigail knew Fred was negligent because Fred admitted to Abigail that he knew about the spill and had not cleaned it up" is to set out the evidence (the admission) used to prove the material fact.

Pleading Points of Law: Rule 25.06(2)

Rule 25.06(2) permits you to plead any point of law in a claim or defence that is relevant to your case. If you are drawing a legal conclusion, the rule requires you to set out the facts on which that conclusion is based. For example, suppose Abigail wishes to claim against Rattle Motors Ltd. by raising the issue that it is vicariously liable for the acts of its employees. To plead this principle of law, she needs to set out the material facts that underlie it: that Fred is an employee of Rattle Motors Ltd. and that the acts of negligence complained of were done by Fred in the course of his employment. If you are pleading a statute or regulation as part of a point of law, be sure to give the full citation.

Pleading Conditions Precedent: Rule 25.06(3)

A condition precedent is something that must be done before one is legally entitled to do something else. For example, if one party refuses to close a real estate transaction, the other party may tender on the party refusing to close. In order to successfully tender, the tendering party must have met the conditions precedent for tendering by showing that he or she was ready, willing, and able to close the transaction before tendering. In an action, if one party alleges that he or she tendered on the other, this rule says that the allegation alone is sufficient, and that it is not necessary to also plead that the party was ready, willing, and able to close the transaction. In other words, you need not plead the performance of the conditions precedent to tendering by setting out all of the elements of the conditions precedent. The performance of the conditions precedent is presumed without your having to state them. If the opposing party believes that the tendering process was defective because you had not fulfilled the conditions precedent, that party must say so in his or her response to your pleading, specifying the nature of the defect.

Inconsistent Pleadings: Rule 25.06(4)

It is considered appropriate to plead inconsistent or apparently contradictory allegations in a claim or defence, provided that it is clear that the statements are made in the alternative. For example, in a negligence action involving a car accident, it is not always clear to the plaintiff, especially in the early stages of an action, exactly what acts of the defendant constitute negligence. The other driver may have failed to apply the brakes in time, or he may have been talking on his cellphone and not paying proper attention, or his car may have been poorly maintained. In this situation, it is permissible to plead as follows: "the defendant failed to keep a proper lookout; or in the alternative, he failed to apply his brakes; or in the further alternative, his brakes malfunctioned because he had not properly maintained and serviced his vehicle." In this case, evidence on discovery or at trial may show that one or the other of these facts is correct.

The important thing is that the evidence at trial has to correspond to the case as pleaded. If the evidence shows that the negligence of the defendant was different from what the plaintiff said it was in his or her claim, the plaintiff may have his or her case dismissed for failing to prove the claim as pleaded. You are therefore encouraged to plead broadly and in the alternative where there is factual uncertainty of the type described here so that the range of possibilities pleaded will cover what is revealed at trial to have occurred.

The rule about pleading alternative versions presumes that of five versions pleaded in the alternative, one will be factually correct. But go back to our example of a motor vehicle collision: What if it turns out that the car had malfunctioning brakes *and* the driver was talking on his cellphone and was not paying attention to the road? If this is the case, your pleading will catch the problem because you have covered both causes of the collision. However, if you suspect that there is more than one cause but you are not sure what they are at the time of pleading, it is permissible to plead "the defendant failed to keep a proper lookout. *Further or in the alternative,* he failed to properly maintain his brakes so that they functioned properly."

No Contradicting an Allegation in a Previous Pleading: Rule 25.06(5)

Rule 25.06(5) identifies a situation where inconsistent or alternative pleading is not permitted. You may not in your reply to the statement of defence plead facts that contradict the facts in your statement of claim or raise a new cause of action. If you wish to do so, you must move to amend your earlier pleading to include the new cause of action or to amend the facts in your previous pleading so that the facts in the claim are consistent with those in the reply. If you were allowed to plead different versions of the facts in the claim and the reply, you can see what the problem would be for the defence. The defendants have no procedural vehicle to counter the contradictory allegation (there is no defendant's reply to a plaintiff's reply) nor do they know the case they have to meet, which is the prime purpose of pleadings. The purpose of a reply is not to permit the plaintiff to split her case, but to allow her to reply to issues raised in the statement of defence that were not covered in the claim.

At the same time, you do sometimes have to deal with a fact that is relevant but occurred after the statement of claim was issued. For example, if Abigail Boar recited her injuries as the basis for her damages in her claim, and then later on more symptoms developed that indicated more serious injuries, she can get the new facts before the court. Rule 14.01(4) allows a party to rely on a fact that occurs after a proceeding commences, even though it is not specifically pleaded. However, the party relying on a new fact that is not connected to a fact previously pleaded should move to amend pleadings to include it. The purpose of this rule is to allow a party who has sustained damage to include damage discovered after pleadings where there is some relationship between the facts as pleaded and the facts as discovered later.

Pleading Notice: Rule 25.06(6)

You can usually plead that notice was given by simply saying so: "The plaintiff gave the defendant notice to quit the premises." However, if the form of notice is material, you need to go into more detail. For example, if notice to a tenant to quit commercial premises must be given by registered mail, it is appropriate to plead it: "The plaintiff gave the defendant notice to quit the leased premises by giving notice in writing sent by registered mail to the defendant."

Pleading Documents or Conversations: Rule 25.06(7)

This rule echoes the requirement in Rule 25.06(1) that pleadings be concise. If you are pleading the contents of a conversation, you need merely state the effect or purpose of a conversation or a document without repeating the precise conversation or document in its entirety. The exception to this rule occurs where the exact language is material; for example, in a libel action, in which case the precise wording should be set out and surrounded by quotation marks.

Pleading the Nature of an Act or a State of Mind: Rule 25.06(8)

This rule states that where the intentional torts of fraud, misrepresentation, or breach of trust are pleaded, the full facts underlying these allegations must be pleaded with more particularity or detail than pleading usually requires. The second branch of the rule says that if you are pleading a mental element such as malice, intent, or acting knowingly, it is permissible to state that the party acted with malice, or acted knowingly, or with intent without explicitly connecting the relevant allegations to specific factual events. The reason for this is that there is rarely a smoking gun when an allegation of malice is made—that is, the allegedly malicious party is unlikely to say, "I am motivated by my malice to act in this way." Instead, malice must be inferred from surrounding circumstances, which may be pleaded in some detail, as noted above, as facts. It is then up to counsel, in his or her submissions at trial, to use the facts as pleaded to make the appropriate inferences and draw the appropriate conclusions.

Body of a Statement of Claim

The narrative part of Abigail Boar's claim begins at paragraph 5 and continues to the end of Figure 7.2. Paragraphs 5 to 9 take you chronologically and sequentially through the events immediately leading up to the accident. They omit a lot from the original summary of Abigail's story as immaterial and irrelevant to the cause of action. It does not matter, for example, what Abigail's motivations were in deciding to buy the Super Coupe, nor whom she worked for, nor what her age was. These matters are not material to the issue of negligence.

At paragraph 10, we switch to describing Abigail's injuries and their effects. We provide the particulars of the damages, both general and special, that are described briefly in the claim for relief in paragraph 1. Paragraphs 10 to 11 describe the injuries themselves in a crisp, matter-of-fact way, and paragraphs 12 to 15 describe the consequences for Abigail. The consequences are described chronologically in the sense that the earliest known consequences are described first, but information is also grouped by its effect on Abigail's lifestyle—an important factor in determining the extent of general damages. We do not connect specific injuries to special or general damages. That will be done in submissions later in the proceedings, although some lawyers do plead by identifying special and general damages. There is nothing wrong with that approach; it is simply a style preference. There is lots of room for good pleading in a variety of styles.

Drafting Statements of Defence

A statement of defence must follow the format prescribed by Form 18A. It begins with the same general heading (the court file number, court name, and title of proceedings) as used in the statement of claim. It then sets out the title, "STATEMENT OF DEFENCE." Paragraph 1 sets out admissions of allegations in the statement of claim, paragraph 2 sets out denials of allegations in the statement of claim, and paragraph 3 sets out allegations in the claim of which the defendants have no knowledge. After that, defendants set out in consecutively numbered paragraphs each allegation on which they rely for their defence, containing their version of the facts. All of the general rules of pleading in Rule 25.06 apply to drafting statements of defence. Also applicable are some specific rules in Rule 25.07.

Pleading Admissions: Rule 25.07(1)

The defendant must admit every allegation of fact in the statement of claim that he or she deems to be correct by admitting that the paragraph containing it is accurate. For example, Fred and Rattle Motors Ltd. will probably admit the allegations in paragraphs 1, 2, 3, and 4 of Abigail Boar's statement of claim, set out in Figure 7.2, because these paragraphs accurately describe the legal status of the parties. But they probably will not admit much else. Many of the allegations that they may admit are in paragraphs that have allegations that they will not admit because their admission would hamper the defence. For example, look at paragraph 8: "The Super Coupe model was in an open area of the showroom, where two of the four spotlights trained on the car were off, so that one side of the car was well illuminated while the other was not well illuminated."

The defendants may wish to admit that the car was in an open area and that some of the lights were off. But they may hotly deny that the area was not well illuminated. They may allege, for example, that there was other perfectly adequate lighting. If so, their best bet is to deny the allegation in the paragraph altogether and plead their own version later in the statement of defence. This gives them more control as to how they present their defence in terms of both substance and content, and it prevents them from inadvertently admitting something while trying to admit part of a paragraph. Rule 25.02 asks that you confine each allegation to one paragraph so that a paragraph can be admitted if the allegation is true. But often, as in our case, a paragraph will contain an allegation that cannot be admitted in its entirety. In that case, deny it and proceed.

Figure 7.3 (at the end of the chapter) presents the joint statement of defence of Rattle Motors Ltd. and Fred Flogem. In it, Fred and Rattle Motors Ltd. admit Abigail's allegations in paragraph 1. We are assuming there is no conflict between the defendants on any issue.

Pleading Denials and Pleading "No Knowledge": Rule 25.07(2)

If there are allegations that the defendant denies are true, he or she must deny the allegations by identifying the paragraph in the claim that contains them. Again, if some of the contents of the paragraph are to be admitted and some denied, then it is best to deny the whole paragraph and plead your version later in the defence. If you are silent on the allegations in a paragraph, they are deemed to be admitted. Each paragraph of the claim must be scrutinized carefully and critically. When in doubt, deny. Most lawyers follow this practice with the result that after admitting the paragraphs identifying the parties, they deny most, and often all, of the other paragraphs in the claim. You will note below that the defendants have neither admitted nor denied paragraph 1, the claim for relief, and paragraphs 5 and 6, which are non-controversial facts that may be omitted from the list of denials, can be admitted. It follows logically, and also according to the rule, that an allegation that is not denied or admitted is deemed to be admitted. But what happens when a defendant comes across an allegation that he or she cannot deny or admit because he or she knows nothing of it? In that case, it is permissible for the defendant to state that he or she has no knowledge of the allegation, in which case the plaintiff must prove it. It is not necessary for the defendant to deny the claim for relief if damages are claimed because damages are deemed to be in issue unless the defendant admits them (Rule 25.07(6)).

Paragraph 2 of Fred and Rattle Motors Ltd.'s statement of defence, set out in Figure 7.3, contains their denial of Abigail's allegations.

Different Version of the Facts Must Be Pleaded: Rule 25.07(3)

It is not sufficient for the defendant merely to deny the plaintiff's version of the facts. If the defendant has a different view of the facts, he or she is obliged to set it out in consecutively numbered paragraphs after having dealt with admissions and denials in paragraphs 1 and 2 of the statement of defence.

This is an appropriate place to deal with paragraphs in the statement of claim where the defendant wishes to deny some and admit other allegations: "The defendants admit that two of the four spotlights were off but deny that the area was not well illuminated." The rule explicitly prohibits a bare denial without an explanation. Before the creation of this rule, you might have seen statements of defence which simply denied the plaintiff's allegations: "The defendants deny every allegation in the statement of claim and put the plaintiff to the strict proof of them." This rule eliminates that approach.

Plead Affirmative Defences: Rule 25.07(4)

If a defence is more than a denial of the legal basis for the plaintiff's claim—for instance, a denial by the defendants that they were negligent—it is necessary to set out further defences and the facts on which they rest. For example, Abigail did not mention that she had two glasses of wine before coming to the defendants' premises. But if the defendants know of it, they may want to plead contributory negligence specifically. In the alternative, they may want to claim that Abigail became the sole author of her own misfortunes when she voluntarily put herself into an intoxicated state and, for that reason, fell and injured herself. If the defendants take this route, they are introducing a new issue, with new facts to support their position on that issue. As we will see, the plaintiff is entitled to deal with it in her reply to the statement of defence.

Effect of Denying the Existence of an Agreement: Rule 25.07(5)

Where an agreement is alleged in a statement of claim, a denial of it in the statement of defence is deemed to be no more than a denial of the making of the agreement or a denial of facts from which an agreement can be implied by law. It is not to be construed as a denial that the alleged agreement was legal or sufficient in law to have an effect. If the defendant wishes to deny the legality or legal sufficiency of an agreement, he or she must set out the particulars on which he or she relies. For example, if a defendant denies entering into a lease with a plaintiff, it is sufficient to deny that there is a lease between the parties. If, however, the defendant wishes to allege that the lease is invalid, he or she must state that the lease is invalid and give particulars—for example, it was not signed by the parties or a copy was not delivered to the defendant as required under its terms.

Drafting Replies

A reply to a statement of defence is necessary only when the defendant has pleaded a version of the facts or raised issues in the statement of defence that are different from the facts pleaded in the claim. A reply should be used in the following two situations:

1. Where a plaintiff contests the version of the facts as pleaded in the statement of defence, he or she should deliver a reply to the statement of defence, setting out his or her version of the facts unless this has been covered in the claim (Rule 25.08(1)).

2. Where a defendant raises a defence with which the statement of claim does not deal, the plaintiff should respond to this defence in a reply.

Other than in these two situations, no reply should be issued. If no reply is issued, the plaintiff is deemed to have denied the allegations in the statement of defence. In dealing with the version of facts set out in the defence, the plaintiff should admit any allegation of fact in the defence that is correct. If the defence alleges an agreement, the reply may deny it, in which case the denial is a denial of the making of an agreement or of the facts from which an agreement may be implied by law. It is not to be construed as a denial of the legality or legal sufficiency of the agreement (Rule 25.09(2)). This must be pleaded specifically, as is the case under Rule 25.07(5).

Figure 7.4 (at the end of the chapter) sets out Abigail Boar's reply to the statement of defence. You will notice in this example that the plaintiff does not bother to deny allegations that she has already dealt with in the claim, but she denies those new allegations that allege intoxication, contributory negligence, exaggeration of damages, malingering, and failure to mitigate. None of these issues were raised in the claim, but having been raised in the defence, they must be answered if there is a version of these allegations by the defendant that the plaintiff wishes to advance—as is the case here, where Abigail states that her drinking did not contribute to her injuries. She also deals with the defendant's allegations about malingering, exaggerating her injuries, and failing to take steps to mitigate her damages. Remember that allegations in the reply cannot be inconsistent with or contradict statements in the claim. The defendant has to know which version of the facts the plaintiff is relying on. Where a reply is inconsistent with the claim, it is likely that the claim needs to be amended.

Demand for Particulars

While a pleading must be a concise statement of material facts, it must not be so skimpy that it is impossible to respond to. While the modern version of the Rules emphasizes the need to give full disclosure before trial to promote settlements, lawyers, for strategic reasons, often try to hold back as much information as possible. One of the ways of doing this is to plead enough to cover an issue without revealing important factual details. Those adopting this strategy hope that the lack of specificity will not be noticed and that the opponent can then be taken by surprise. This is a risky approach because a court may conclude that this kind of strategy amounts to trial by ambush. Penalties may await those who pursue this strategy. One should not assume that the other side is stupid. Other lawyers also know these strategies, and your opponent has a remedy when facing a pleading that is too general. Rule 25.10 permits a party to request particulars. If you receive such a request, you must supply the details requested. The initial request and the response to it may be made by letter between law offices. But if the request is not answered within 10 days or if a party refuses to comply because he or she believes the request is unwarranted, the party making the request may ask the court on a notice of motion to order particulars. In considering the motion, the court asks itself whether the pleading is clear enough so that the opposite party can frame an answer to the issues raised and will not be surprised at trial. The additional information provided should constitute further detail of material facts, but not be so detailed as to amount to evidence.

Suppose Abigail had pleaded that as a result of her fall, she suffered "severe and catastrophic injuries that prevented her from working." This does not indicate what the injuries were or how they prevented Abigail from working, so the defendants cannot determine whether the damages claimed have any basis in fact. The defendants might then write to I.M. Just and ask him to provide details. They will likely be interested in knowing what specific injuries she sustained, the treatment for those injuries, the specific activities that the injuries prevent her from engaging in, the prognosis, her attempt to mitigate her damages, and whether she attempted to return to work.

Striking Out Pleadings

Occasionally a pleading is so defective in failing to follow Rule 25 that, on a motion by the other side, the court may strike out all or part of the pleading (Rule 25.11). Usually the court gives leave to amend the pleading, but on occasion it strikes out a wholly unmeritorious pleading without leave to amend, in which case plaintiffs may have their claim dismissed or defendants may have judgment signed against them.

There are three general grounds for the court to strike all or part of a pleading or other document under Rule 25.11:

- the contents of the pleading "may prejudice or delay the fair trial of the action";
- the contents are "scandalous, frivolous or vexatious"; and
- the contents constitute an "abuse of the process of the court."

A pleading may be defective because it violates all or one of these grounds. Generally, allegations that cannot be proven are deemed to be prejudicial because the opponent is being asked to respond to allegations or issues on which no proof can or will be offered. For example, if Abigail pleads the contents of documents that are not admissible in court, she cannot prove the allegations because she cannot present admissible evidence on them.[2] Therefore, the defendants should not have to respond to those allegations: it would not be fair, and that is what "prejudicial" really means. Similarly, allegations that stray well beyond the issue involved in the lawsuit may simply lengthen the pretrial and trial without being relevant to the matter being decided. A barrage of allegations only tenuously connected may be deemed to be improperly delaying proceedings if the issue being litigated involves only one allegation in the barrage of allegations.

A pleading is scandalous, frivolous, or vexatious when a fact is set out that could be proved but that would not be allowed to be proved. For example, if Fred and Rattle Motors Ltd. wanted to undermine Abigail's credibility by showing her to be a person of low character, they might make various allegations about her general dishonesty. If these allegations are not relevant to the issues raised in the proceeding, then while they may be true and could be proved, they would likely not be allowed to be proved. This is not because they are scandalous[3] or shocking in the ordinary sense, but because they are irrelevant and immaterial to the issues being tried and are introduced solely to add "atmosphere." Some courts have asked whether the allegation can have any effect on the outcome. If not, it is probably scandalous, frivolous, or vexatious. If the issue in the lawsuit concerned Abigail's allegedly fraudulent behaviour, allegations about her general honesty, no matter how embarrassing or scandalous in the ordinary sense, are relevant and ought not to be struck out.

Any of the "bad" pleading behaviour described in the preceding paragraphs may also constitute an abuse of process, particularly when it is done knowingly or intentionally.

With the increase in the number of self-represented litigants, there is an increase in defective pleadings as the self-represented are unlikely to be familiar with the requirements of Rule 25. The resulting increase in motions to deal with defective pleadings is one of the examples of how self-represented litigants can make an action much more difficult, slow, and expensive than it otherwise would be.

Where a pleading is attacked on an issue that goes to the court's jurisdiction or otherwise might lead to a final order disposing of the case in its entirety—either through dismissal of the action, or granting of judgment on the motion to strike a pleading—the motion should be brought before a judge, not a master. Masters have the jurisdiction to deal with procedural matters, but they do not usually have the power to make orders that finally dispose of the rights of the parties.

CHAPTER SUMMARY

In this chapter, you were introduced to the rules and conventions that govern the drafting of claims, defences, and replies. We examined some of the steps that must be taken to organize material and information, develop a theory of the case, prepare outlines, and use sample precedents before drafting the document. When drafting you should try to use simple language that is clear and direct.

We then examined specific rules in Rule 25 of the *Rules of Civil Procedure*. Rule 25 governs all pleadings, as well as specific rules governing defences and replies. We illustrated how these rules work by setting out a claim, defence, and reply in Abigail Boar's case. Finally, we looked at what can be done if pleadings are inadequate, examining demands for particulars as well as motions to strike out pleadings that are manifestly defective.

KEY TERMS

boilerplate, 158

general damages, 159

special damages, 159

NOTES

1. Form 14A is the generic version of a statement of claim. The subsequent versions of Form 14 deal with various specialized types of claims.

2. *F. (M.) v. Sutherland* (July 5, 2000), doc. CA C32601 (Ont. CA).

3. Some cases use the word "embarrassing" in the same way that the word "scandalous" is used. The words have roughly the same meaning in this context: immaterial, irrelevant, and introduced to create an atmosphere so as to make the other side look bad. Similarly, the terms "scandalous," "frivolous," and "vexatious" tend to be used synonymously in cases.

REFERENCES

Courts of Justice Act, RSO 1990, c. C.43.

F. (M.) v. Sutherland (July 5, 2000), doc. CA C32601 (Ont. CA).

Occupiers' Liability Act, RSO 1990, c. O.2.

Rules of Civil Procedure, RRO 1990, reg. 194.

REVIEW QUESTIONS

1. Edward Egregious, I.M. Just's law clerk, has just interviewed a client and intends to transcribe his notes into a statement of claim and issue it. Have you any advice for him?

2. Can Edward claim $15,000 for costs in the space provided on the boilerplate for costs?

3. Edward thinks that the paragraphs in a pleading should be lengthy and detailed. Is he correct?

4. Edward wants to know the order in which information is to be presented in a statement of claim. Tell him what that order is.

5. In the following paragraphs, indicate which parts are material facts and which parts are evidence.

   a. The plaintiff states that the area was not properly lit. A lighting expert who examined the site confirmed this.

   b. The plaintiff states that the area was not properly illuminated. The defendant admitted this to the plaintiff at the time of the accident.

   c. The standard of care exercised by the defendant was well below the standard followed by other engineers. One engineer referred to the standard as "antique," claiming no one she knew used it.

   d. The defendant drove her car down Mill Lane at an excessive rate of speed for the road conditions. The speed was in excess of the stated speed limit.

   e. In borrowing from the plaintiff, the defendant failed to disclose that he was about to be petitioned into bankruptcy. The defendant knew this because he had received a letter from another creditor advising him that he would be petitioned into bankruptcy if he did not pay what was owing.

6. In drafting Abigail's claim, suppose Edward set out the facts leading to Abigail's fall, the damages sustained, and then followed with a statement that the defendant Fred was negligent and caused harm to the plaintiff, for which the corporate defendant is legally responsible. How would you advise him in improving his efforts?

7. Suppose Elizabeth Egret placed an order to buy some Framitses. The contract requires a 10 percent deposit before Egmont Pigeon will ship the goods. In her claim for delivery of the goods, Elizabeth states that she demanded delivery in accordance with the terms of the contract but that the defendant neglected or refused to deliver the goods. Is that a sufficient statement of her right to delivery?

8. Edward wants to plead that Fred was negligent in turning off the spotlights or in the alternative that he did it knowingly or with reckless intent. Can he do this?

9. Is it permissible for Edward to plead negligence in the claim and to state in the reply to the statement of defence that the defendants conspired to injure Abigail intentionally?

10. If Abigail has a claim that rests on the contents of a 10-page contract, does she need to quote the whole contract in the statement of claim?

11. If Abigail wants to claim that Fred attempted to defraud her, is it sufficient for her to state that Fred acted fraudulently?

12. If Abigail commences the proceeding in Brampton but wishes to have it tried in Toronto, what does she do?

13. Fiona Flapdoodle must prepare the defendant's statement of defence. She wants to know what she needs to include and in what order.

14. If a defendant wishes to deny that he or she entered into an agreement, how does the defendant do this?

15. When should a reply be delivered?

16. In what situations should you demand particulars?

17. When might a lawyer move to strike all or part of a pleading?

DISCUSSION QUESTIONS

1. Sarah Jacobs, her husband Jack Jacobs, and her 15-year-old daughter Mary kept their boat at Tom's Marina near their cottage. Since summer was approaching, they wanted to arrange to get their boat ready for the season. The Jacobses went to Tom Shanks's marina on May 24, 1999. When they arrived at the marina, Tom Shanks, the owner and sole proprietor, was not there, but his long-time employee Kevin Coaster was in the main office. Kevin said that he would take them down the dock to their boat. He knew a shortcut along a dock at the side of the marina office. The Jacobses followed Kevin. As they were walking along the dock, several planks gave way because they were rotten. Sarah fell against a support beam, hitting the lower part of her face and then her arm as she fell backward into the water. Mary injured her ribs when she also fell against the support beam. The Jacobses have come to your law firm. They want to sue for their injuries. Draft a statement of claim.

2. Your law firm is acting for Tom Shanks. He is very annoyed with Kevin Coaster because he had told Kevin repeatedly that Kevin was not to take the shortcut because the dock is a mess and there are a lot of rotten boards. He also says Kevin was not supposed to be at work that day and that the marina was to be shut and locked until he arrived later. Tom wants you to draft his defence.

Figure 7.1   Statement of Claim (General) (Form 14A)

(General heading)

STATEMENT OF CLAIM

TO THE DEFENDANT

A LEGAL PROCEEDING HAS BEEN COMMENCED AGAINST YOU by the plaintiff. The claim made against you is set out in the following pages.

IF YOU WISH TO DEFEND THIS PROCEEDING, you or an Ontario lawyer acting for you must prepare a statement of defence in Form 18A prescribed by the Rules of Civil Procedure, serve it on the plaintiff's lawyer or, where the plaintiff does not have a lawyer, serve it on the plaintiff, and file it, with proof of service in this court office, WITHIN TWENTY DAYS after this statement of claim is served on you, if you are served in Ontario.

If you are served in another province or territory of Canada or in the United States of America, the period for serving and filing your statement of defence is forty days. If you are served outside Canada and the United States of America, the period is sixty days.

Instead of serving and filing a statement of defence, you may serve and file a notice of intent to defend in Form 18B prescribed by the Rules of Civil Procedure. This will entitle you to ten more days within which to serve and file your statement of defence.

IF YOU FAIL TO DEFEND THIS PROCEEDING, JUDGMENT MAY BE GIVEN AGAINST YOU IN YOUR ABSENCE AND WITHOUT FURTHER NOTICE TO YOU. IF YOU WISH TO DEFEND THIS PROCEEDING BUT ARE UNABLE TO PAY LEGAL FEES, LEGAL AID MAY BE AVAILABLE TO YOU BY CONTACTING A LOCAL LEGAL AID OFFICE.

(Where the claim made is for money only, include the following:)

IF YOU PAY THE PLAINTIFF'S CLAIM, and $_____ for costs, within the time for serving and filing your statement of defence, you may move to have this proceeding dismissed by the court. If you believe the amount claimed for costs is excessive, you may pay the plaintiff's claim and $400.00 for costs and have the costs assessed by the court.

Date: _____   Issued by: _____

                                                    Local registrar

                                    Address of
                                    court office: _____

                                                    _____

TO: *(Name and address of each defendant)*

RCP-E 14A (July 1, 2007)

Figure 7.2 Statement of Claim of Abigail Boar (Form 14A)

Court file no.

ONTARIO
SUPERIOR COURT OF JUSTICE

BETWEEN:

ABIGAIL BOAR

Plaintiff

and

RATTLE MOTORS LTD. and FRED FLOGEM

Defendants

STATEMENT OF CLAIM

TO THE DEFENDANTS

A LEGAL PROCEEDING HAS BEEN COMMENCED AGAINST YOU by the plaintiff. The claim made against you is set out in the following pages.

IF YOU WISH TO DEFEND THIS PROCEEDING, you or an Ontario lawyer acting for you must prepare a statement of defence in Form 18A prescribed by the Rules of Civil Procedure, serve it on the plaintiff's lawyer or, where the plaintiff does not have a lawyer, serve it on the plaintiff, and file it, with proof of service, in this court office, WITHIN TWENTY DAYS after this statement of claim is served on you, if you are served in Ontario.

If you are served in another province or territory of Canada or in the United States of America, the period for serving and filing your statement of defence is forty days. If you are served outside Canada and the United States of America, the period is sixty days.

Instead of serving and filing a statement of defence, you may serve and file a notice of intent to defend in Form 18B prescribed by the Rules of Civil Procedure. This will entitle you to ten more days within which to serve and file your statement of defence.

IF YOU FAIL TO DEFEND THIS PROCEEDING, JUDGMENT MAY BE GIVEN AGAINST YOU IN YOUR ABSENCE AND WITHOUT FURTHER NOTICE TO YOU. IF YOU WISH TO DEFEND THIS PROCEEDING BUT ARE UNABLE TO PAY LEGAL FEES, LEGAL AID MAY BE AVAILABLE TO YOU BY CONTACTING A LOCAL LEGAL AID OFFICE.

Figure 7.2   Continued

IF YOU PAY THE PLAINTIFF'S CLAIM, and $500.00 for costs, within the time for serving and filing your statement of defence, you may move to have this proceeding dismissed by the court. If you believe the amount claimed for costs is excessive, you may pay the plaintiff's claim and $400.00 for costs and have the costs assessed by the court.

Date: January 4, year 1

Issued by: _____
            Local registrar

Address of
court office: Courthouse
                 393 University Avenue
                 Toronto, Ontario, M5G 1E6

TO: Rattle Motors Ltd.
       1240 Bay Street
       Toronto, Ontario, M8H 0K8

AND TO: Fred Flogem
           21 Cypress Boulevard
           Scarborough, Ontario, M8Q 1P3

CLAIM

1. The plaintiff claims, against both defendants:

    a. general damages in the amount of $200,000;

    b. special damages in the amount of $3,649 to the date of this pleading. The full extent of special damages is not yet known, but full particulars will be furnished before the date of trial.

    c. prejudgment interest from September 14, year 0 to the date of payment or judgment pursuant to the *Courts of Justice Act*, RSO 1990, c. C.43;

    d. postjudgment interest from the date of judgment to the date of payment pursuant to the *Courts of Justice Act*, RSO 1990, c. C.43;

    e. costs of this action; and

    f. such further relief as seems just to this court.

2. The plaintiff is an individual who resides in the City of Toronto, in the Province of Ontario, and at the relevant time was a customer lawfully on the premises of the corporate defendant.

Figure 7.2   Continued

3. The defendant Fred Flogem is an individual who resides in the City of Toronto, in the Province of Ontario, and at the relevant time was an employee of the corporate defendant.

4. The defendant Rattle Motors Ltd. is a business corporation, incorporated under the laws of Ontario with business premises in the City of Toronto, in the Province of Ontario.

5. On September 14, year 0, at about 7:30 p.m., the plaintiff entered the retail automobile premises owned and operated by the defendant Rattle Motors Ltd. at 1240 Bay Street, in the City of Toronto, in the Province of Ontario, in order to view a Super Coupe, which she was thinking of purchasing, in the showroom.

6. She was met at the door by Linda Lucre, a salesperson employed by the corporate defendant, who showed her some of the automobiles displayed on the showroom floor.

7. The plaintiff saw a Super Coupe model on the showroom floor and walked over to have a better look at it.

8. The Super Coupe model was in an open area of the showroom, where two of the four spotlights trained on the car were off, so that one side of the car was well illuminated while the other was not well illuminated.

9. The plaintiff walked around to the side of the car near the wall, which was in relative darkness. She walked onto a part of the floor that was covered with oil. Because of the restricted lighting, she did not see the oil, slipped on it, lost her footing, and fell.

10. As a result of the fall, she struck her head, suffered a concussion, and lost consciousness. She also fractured her right wrist and several bones in her right arm.

11. Following the fall, the plaintiff was hospitalized for 4 days and the plaintiff's arm was in a cast for 6 weeks; she suffered much pain and discomfort. In addition, she was required to attend for physiotherapy for 10 weeks after her cast was removed.

12. As a result of these injuries, the plaintiff suffers from pain in her arm and head as well as chronic lower back pain, and is unable to walk long distances or sit at a desk for long periods. She has limited mobility in her right arm and is unable to work at a computer keyboard for more than 10 minutes without experiencing pain. The plaintiff is right-handed and severely disadvantaged by these injuries.

13. Since she sustained these injuries, and as a result of them, the plaintiff has become far less active physically than she had been before the accident, and she is far less

Figure 7.2 Continued

cheerful and gregarious than she had been. She is now quieter, more withdrawn, and has difficulty sleeping. She also suffers from depression. Before being injured, the plaintiff was an avid tennis player and a competent amateur violinist. Since sustaining the injuries, and as a result of them, she is unable to engage in either activity. She also has suffered some memory loss. In particular, she has no memory of sustaining the injuries complained of.

14. Since the plaintiff sustained these injuries, she has been unable to return to her work as a securities analyst. She returned to work for the month of March, year 1, but because of chronic pain, and difficulty using a computer which is essential to her work, she was unable to continue. She has been off work since April 1, year 1, and on long-term disability, where she remains at the time of pleading.

15. The plaintiff has suffered catastrophic and permanent injuries, and it is unlikely that she will ever be able to return to work as a securities analyst. At the time of injury, she earned $80,000 per year in this occupation. She would likely have had a lengthy career with a high level of income, had she not been injured.

16. The defendant Fred Flogem, a salesperson employed by the corporate defendant, caused the plaintiff's injuries through his negligence, for which the corporate defendant is at law responsible. The particulars of negligence are as follows:

a. He was aware that there was oil on the floor and knew or ought to have known that the oil constituted a danger to the safety of persons such as the plaintiff.

b. He knew or ought to have known that he had a duty to see that persons such as the plaintiff did not come to harm while on the premises.

c. He failed to clean up or remove the spill expeditiously, although he had the opportunity and the means to do so.

d. He turned off lighting that illuminated the area where the plaintiff fell, with the intention of making the oil spill less visible or noticeable to persons such as the plaintiff. By so doing, he negligently, or in the alternative knowingly, created a situation of danger for the plaintiff.

e. He knowingly created a situation of danger for the plaintiff by deliberately not taking steps to clean up the spill so as to hide a defect in the automobile from the plaintiff and other customers.

17. The defendant Flogem was an employee of the corporate defendant, for whose acts of negligence the corporate defendant is vicariously liable.

Figure 7.2   Concluded

18. The corporate defendant is also directly responsible for the injuries sustained by the plaintiff as a result of its negligence, the particulars of which are as follows:

a. It failed to take such care as was reasonable to see that the plaintiff entering the corporate defendant's showroom would be reasonably safe while on the property. The plaintiff pleads and relies on the *Occupiers' Liability Act*, RSO 1990, c. O.2.

b. It failed to instruct its employees, including the individual defendant, in maintaining safe premises.

c. It knew or ought to have known that the floor area where the plaintiff fell was unsafe for the plaintiff.

d. It failed to maintain a system of inspection to ensure that the showroom was safe for persons on the premises, including the plaintiff.

e. In the alternative, it knowingly permitted the area where the plaintiff fell to remain in an unsafe condition so as not to attract customer attention to a defect in the car it was selling.

Date of issue: January 4, year 1

Just & Coping
Barristers and Solicitors
365 Bay Street – 8701
Toronto, Ontario, M3J 4A9

I.M. Just
LSUC #12345R
tel. 416-762-1342
fax 416-762-2300

Lawyers for the Plaintiff

RCP-E 14A (July 1, 2007)

Figure 7.3   Statement of Defence (Form 18A)

Court file no. 01-CV-1234

ONTARIO
SUPERIOR COURT OF JUSTICE

BETWEEN:

ABIGAIL BOAR

Plaintiff

and

RATTLE MOTORS LTD. and FRED FLOGEM

Defendants

STATEMENT OF DEFENCE

1. The defendants admit the allegations contained in paragraphs 1, 2, 3, and 4 of the statement of claim.

2. The defendants deny the allegations contained in paragraphs 5, 6, 7, 8, 9, 10, 11, 12, 13, 14, 15, 16, 17, and 18 of the statement of claim.

3. The plaintiff entered the corporate defendant's premises at about 7:30 p.m. on September 14, year 0. She indicated to Linda Lucre, a salesperson on the showroom floor at that time, that she was interested in purchasing a Super Coupe.

4. Lucre showed the plaintiff several automobile models. Then the plaintiff walked over, on her own, to look at another model. She walked around the car and fell.

5. The defendants admit that there was a small pool of oil on one side of the car but claim that it was easily visible to any reasonably prudent person who could have avoided it without difficulty.

6. The defendants admit that two of the four spotlights were off but deny that the area was not well illuminated. The defendants state that the area was well and clearly illuminated. Any hazard, if there was one, which is specifically denied, could easily be seen and avoided.

7. The defendants admit that the plaintiff fell and appeared to lose consciousness momentarily. She also appeared to injure her lower right arm in the fall.

8. The defendants state that the plaintiff, before coming to the corporate defendant's place of business, had consumed two glasses of wine and that she was intoxicated when she entered the defendant's premises.

Figure 7.3   Concluded

9.   The plaintiff fell solely as a result of her intoxication. Any injuries she sustained were solely the result of her own intoxicated state and not the result of any acts of the defendants.

10.   With respect to paragraphs 10, 11, 12, 13, 14, and 15 of the statement of claim, the defendants deny that the plaintiff suffered such injuries as described. Further or in the alternative, the defendants state that the plaintiff has exaggerated both the extent of her injuries and the consequences of them.

11.   With respect to the plaintiff's allegation that she cannot return to work, the defendants state that the plaintiff is exaggerating her injuries and that she is a malingerer. In the alternative, the defendants state that the plaintiff has failed to mitigate her damages.

12.   With respect to the allegations of negligence in paragraph 16, the defendant Flogem states that he knew there was oil on the floor but that it was contained and did not constitute a danger to any reasonably prudent person. The defendant Flogem admits that he turned off two of the four spotlights, but he specifically denies that he created a situation of danger for the plaintiff because the area in question remained well illuminated and safe for a reasonably prudent person.

13.   The defendants therefore request that this action be dismissed with costs.

January 12, year 1

Huey Sue
LSUC #23456T
Barrister and Solicitor
65 False Trail
Toronto, Ontario, M6Y 1Z6

tel. 416-485-6891
fax 416-485-6892

Lawyer for the Defendants

TO: Just & Coping
Barristers and Solicitors
365 Bay Street – 8701
Toronto, Ontario, M3J 4A9

I.M. Just
LSUC #12345R
tel. 416-762-1342
fax 416-762-2300

Lawyers for the Plaintiff

RCP-E 18A (July 1, 2007)

Figure 7.4   Reply to Statement of Defence

Court file no. 01-CV-1234

ONTARIO
SUPERIOR COURT OF JUSTICE

BETWEEN:

ABIGAIL BOAR

Plaintiff

and

RATTLE MOTORS LTD. and FRED FLOGEM

Defendants

REPLY

1. The plaintiff admits to the allegations in paragraphs 1, 3, and 4 of the statement of defence.

2. The plaintiff denies the allegations in paragraphs 2, 5, 6, 7, 8, 9, 10, 11, 12, and 13 of the statement of defence.

3. The plaintiff admits that she had two glasses of wine at dinner, well before she entered the corporate defendant's premises, and she denies that she was intoxicated. She neither contributed to nor solely caused her fall and subsequent injuries.

4. The plaintiff states that she has made every effort to fully regain the good health she enjoyed before being injured, following medical advice and undertaking therapy and treatment as advised. Further, she was eager to return to work and did so for a period of one month but was unable to carry out her duties, which required extensive use of a computer, solely because of her injuries. The plaintiff specifically denies that she has exaggerated the extent and consequences of her injuries and denies that she has been malingering or has failed to mitigate her damages.

Date: February 2, year 1

Just & Coping
Barristers and Solicitors
365 Bay Street – 8701
Toronto, Ontario, M3J 4A9

I.M. Just
LSUC #12345R
tel. 416-762-1342; fax 416-762-2300
Lawyers for the Plaintiff

TO: Huey Sue
LSUC #23456T
Barrister and Solicitor
65 False Trail
Toronto, Ontario, M6Y 1Z6

tel. 416-485-6891; fax 416-485-6892

Lawyer for the Defendants

Service of Court Documents

8

Introduction

Once the initiating documents have been prepared, Abigail, as plaintiff, must let the court know that she wants to begin a court case, and she must let the defendants know about the details of the case that she is bringing against them. The process in which the plaintiff lets the court know about the case is called "issuing." We looked at issuing documents in Chapter 6. The process in which Abigail gives a copy of her pleadings or documents to the defendants is called "**service**."

service
process by which documents are brought to the attention of a party in accordance with the Rules or a court order

As soon as the defendants know about Abigail's case against them, they will have a chance to prepare their defence to the allegations that Abigail is making. The defendants must give Abigail a copy of any documents they prepare in the case. (All the documents that are prepared in a court proceeding must be given to the other side.) It is through service of the documents that the parties exchange formal information about the court case. When service of the documents has been completed according to the Rules, we say that service has been "effected."

Not only must the defendants know the details of the case that is brought against them, the court must also be satisfied that each side has provided the other side with their pleadings. Therefore, when pleadings are served, an additional document, proving service according to the Rules, must be filed in the court along with the documents. This process is called providing "proof of service." Service is proven by way of affidavit. The person who served the document must, in writing, provide the details of how the document was served and swear that the details are true. The affidavit is called an affidavit of service, which appears as Form 16B. If service is performed by the sheriff's office, the sheriff's officer provides a certificate of service by sheriff, Form 16C.

Rule 16 tells you how documents are to be served within Ontario. Rule 17 tells you how they are to be served if the other party is not in the Province of Ontario. Rule 4.05 tells you how documents are to be issued and filed in the court.

Although all documents in the court proceeding must be served on the other side, the Rules require different methods of serving the document depending on the type of document. If a document is an originating process, it must be served in a different manner from other pleadings.

Service of an Originating Process

originating process
first document in a lawsuit that tells parties that they are being sued

A document that is an **originating process** must be served either personally or by an alternative to personal service (Rule 16.01(1)). If you are not certain whether the document with which you are working is an originating process, you must look at the definition of originating process in Rule 1.03. If a pleading is an originating process, it will be listed there. Any document not listed there is not an originating process and therefore does not need to be served using personal service or an alternative to personal service.

Personal Service

According to Rule 16.02(1)(a), personal service on an individual can be made by leaving a copy of the document with the person that you wish to serve. But if the individual is a person under a disability, there are special provisions as to how they are to be served personally (Rule 16.02(1)(j) and (k)). For instance, if a party is a minor, the document is served on the minor's litigation guardian or, if there is no litigation guardian, on the minor *and* a parent who has custody of the child. Leaving the document with either the parent or the litigation guardian of the minor qualifies as personal service on the minor.

There are also specific provisions in Rule 16.02 governing personal service on a corporation, a municipality, a partnership, a sole proprietorship, and other entities. When you are serving a document that requires personal service under the Rules and the party is not a competent adult individual, refer to Rule 16.02 to determine the manner in which you are required to serve your document.

Service by Way of Alternative Service

If an originating process is not specifically required by the Rules to be served personally, it can be served by means of an alternative to personal service. When a rule says a particular document can be served either personally or by an alternative to personal service and you decide to serve it by an alternative to personal service, you must look at Rule 16.03, which lists the only alternatives to personal service permitted by the Rules. There are three general alternatives to personal service and a fourth special provision for alternative service that relates only to corporations in Rule 16.03.

1. *Acceptance of service by a lawyer: Rule 16.03(2).* If the party to the proceeding has a lawyer, you may serve the lawyer with the document. However, this type of alternative to personal service is valid only if the lawyer agrees to accept the service on behalf of his or her client and signs a copy of the document acknowledging that he or she has accepted service. Most lawyers are not willing to do this unless they have specific permission from their client because by accepting service for their client, they are representing to the court that they have the authority to do so.

2. *Service by mail to the last known address: Rule 16.03(4).* Service by mail is an effective alternative to personal service only if the person who is being served signs and returns the acknowledgment of receipt card, Form 16A, which is sent along with the document that is being served.[1] Form 16A appears in the exhibit attached to Figure 8.5. If the party fails to return the card, service is not valid. Do not use this method unless you know beforehand that the party you are serving is cooperative and will return the card.

3. *Service at place of residence: Rule 16.03(5).* You may use this alternative method of service only if you have attempted, at least once, to serve the document personally. Then you may leave the document, in a sealed envelope, at the residence with a person who appears to be an adult. However, the same day or the day after you leave the document with someone at the

residence, you must also send another copy of the document by mail to the person to be served.

4. *Service on a corporation: Rule 16.03(6).* This rule applies only when you wish to serve a corporation by an alternative to personal service. You may use this alternative method only after you have tried to effect personal service on the corporation and you find that the corporation is not at its last address registered with the Ministry of Government Services, Companies and Personal Property Security Branch. In that case, you may mail the document to the last registered address. It is quite possible that the corporation will not receive the document. However, because a corporation is required by statute to keep its records with the Ministry up to date, the corporation's own failure to comply with legal requirements is the cause of this situation.

For example, if Abigail Boar tried to serve Rattle Motors Ltd. and found that it was no longer at its last known address, her lawyer's clerk would do a search for the corporation's records with the Ministry of Government Services. If the corporation had registered a new address with the Ministry, Abigail would need to effect service at the new address. However, if Rattle Motors Ltd. had failed to notify the Ministry of its new address, Abigail's lawyer could simply have mailed the documents to that address and service would have been effected in accordance with the Rules.

Documents That Can Be Served on a Party's Lawyer of Record

Although a document that is an originating process can only be served personally or by an alternative to personal service, there is an additional service option available for a document that is not an originating process. A document that is not an originating process can usually be served on a lawyer of record for the party. This means that there are three options for the service of a document that is not an originating process:

1. it can be served personally,
2. it can be served by an alternative to personal service listed in the Rules, or
3. it can be served on a party's lawyer of record.

Service can only be on a lawyer of record, not on a lawyer that the party may have consulted or retained in the past for a case. A lawyer becomes a lawyer of record only if he or she has either filed documents in a particular proceeding on behalf of the party or appeared in court in this proceeding for the party.

Rule 16.05(1)(a) to (f) sets out how a lawyer of record may be served with documents that would otherwise require personal service or an alternative to personal service. These methods are:

- mailing a copy of the document to the lawyer's office,
- leaving a copy of the document with the lawyer or an employee in the lawyer's office,

- faxing a copy to the lawyer's office,
- emailing a copy of the document to the lawyer's office,
- sending a copy to the lawyer's office by courier, or
- depositing a copy of the document at a document exchange of which the lawyer is a member.

Service by Fax on a Lawyer of Record

If you serve a lawyer of record by fax, there are special conditions under Rule 16.05 to make this method of service effective.

- You must attach a cover page that includes all of the information required in Rule 16.05(3).
- If a document is longer than 16 pages, you may serve it by fax only between 4 p.m. and 8 a.m. unless the party gives prior consent for you to serve it during another time period (Rule 16.05(3.1)).
- If you serve by fax between 4 p.m. and midnight, service is not effective until the next day (Rule 16.05(1)(d)).
- You may not serve a motion record, application record, trial record, appeal book and compendium, or book of authorities by fax unless the party being served gives prior permission for you to do so (Rule 16.05(3.2)).

Service by Email on a Lawyer of Record

To effect valid service on a lawyer of record by email under Rule 16.05(1)(f), the following conditions must be met:

- The message to which the court document is attached must contain all the information required by Rule 16.05(4), including the name of the person transmitting the message and his or her address, telephone number, fax number, and email address; the date and time of the message; and the name and telephone number of a contact should there be transmission problems.
- The lawyer of record who is being served must provide an email response saying that he or she is accepting service and giving the date of the acceptance.
- If the email acceptance of service by the lawyer of record is received between 4 p.m. and midnight, service is deemed to have occurred the next day.

Service on a Lawyer of Record by Courier

Since someone must sign for a courier delivery, there is an independent record of receipt of the document in the lawyer of record's office, but it is important to note that service is effective on the second day following the day the courier was given the document to serve unless the second day is a holiday. In this case, service is deemed to have occurred on the next day that is not a holiday (Rule 16.05(2.1)).

Service on a Lawyer of Record Through a Document Exchange

A document exchange is a centralized service that has been formally set up by lawyers to send and receive court documents. At one time it was a common method of serving documents, but with service by fax and email now permitted, these exchanges are not as widely used as they once were. Many law firms still use them, however. For service on a lawyer of record through a document exchange to be valid, the lawyer of record must be a member of that document exchange, and a copy of the document being served must be date-stamped by the document exchange in front of the person who is depositing the copy for service (Rule 16.05(1)(c)). Service then becomes effective on the first day that is not a holiday after the document has been deposited and date-stamped.

Substituted Service and Dispensing with Service

Sometimes it is extremely difficult to effect service according to the Rules. It may be that parties cannot be located despite the best of efforts, or it may be that parties are doing everything they can to avoid service. The fact that you have not been able to serve the opposite side does not mean that you cannot proceed with a lawsuit. If every effort has been made to serve a party and service has not been possible, the lawyer for the party trying to serve the documents may bring a motion for an order for substituted service or for an order dispensing with service.

A party that obtains an order dispensing with service has the court's permission to proceed with its case without serving the other side. It is only in the most exceptional circumstances that a party is granted an order dispensing with service. The reason is that the other side would have no notice of the party's court proceeding and therefore no opportunity to answer the allegations made against it.

However, an order for substituted service is relatively common in litigation. Such an order permits a party to use a method of service not prescribed by the Rules. When the court makes an order for substituted service, it will also make an order specifying exactly what method of service may be substituted for the method required by the Rules. Often this means that the party requesting substituted service may place a notice in a newspaper or serve by ordinary mail. An order for substituted service specifies when the service becomes effective (Rule 16.04(2)). For example, the order might say that service is effective on the 10th day following the publishing of the notice in the newspaper.

Proof of Service

Once you have served the document according to the Rules, you must prepare another document that proves to the court that you have served your document on the other parties. The court requires this proof because if parties fail to file documents or fail to appear in court, and if it can be proven that they had proper service of all necessary documents, the court can make a decision about the case in their absence.

The court will not accept any document for filing unless you file proof of service at the same time.

There are three methods of proving service:

1. affidavit of service,
2. certificate of service by the sheriff, or
3. proof of acceptance or admitting of service by the other side.

Affidavit of Service

Documents are usually served by a person hired specifically to effect service or by a member of the law firm, usually the law clerk who is dealing with the file. The server must provide evidence to the court that the party whom they served was served according to the Rules. The server does this by way of an affidavit of service. An affidavit is a document sworn under oath or affirmed that can constitute evidence in a court proceeding. The person who serves the document must give details of the steps that he or she took to effect service.

An affidavit of service is set out in Form 16B. Figures 8.1 to 8.5 provide precedents for affidavits of service in various circumstances. The affidavit of service need not be a separate document. Many law offices use a stamp that is put on the backsheet of the copy of the document that is to be filed with the court. When documents must be served in a hurry, these stamps are often used. The stamp is completed when the document is served, and it can be signed and commissioned at the court office.

Certificate of Service by Sheriff

Each judicial area in the province has a **sheriff**. He or she is a judicial official who is appointed under the *Public Service Act* and who has certain duties that involve the courts and the judicial system. Each sheriff has numerous people who work under his or her supervision.

At one time, one of the duties of the sheriff was to serve court documents. The party serving the document would be charged a fee to have a sheriff's officer go out and serve the documents. Now the sheriff's duties have been changed, and sheriffs only serve documents that involve the enforcement of judgments and orders. This means that if you have documents that involve enforcement—for example, a writ of seizure and sale or a garnishment—you may have them served by either a private process server or the sheriff.

When a document is served through the sheriff's office, the sheriff's officer prepares a certificate of service by sheriff. This precedent is Form 16C, which appears as Figure 8.6. It contains much of the same information that an affidavit of service contains. All the details concerning the steps taken to effect service are included in the document. The certificate is often put right on the copy of the served document that is filed with the court.

If you use the sheriff to serve the enforcement documents, the sheriff's office will provide you with a completed certificate. Although you will not need to prepare the document itself, you should know what it looks like.

sheriff
official appointed by the provincial government to assist in various court-related functions, such as the enforcement of orders and judgments

Figure 8.1   Affidavit of Service by Leaving Copy with Adult at Residence (Form 16B)

Court file no. 01-CV-1234

ONTARIO
SUPERIOR COURT OF JUSTICE

BETWEEN:

ABIGAIL BOAR

Plaintiff

and

RATTLE MOTORS LTD. and FRED FLOGEM

Defendants

AFFIDAVIT OF SERVICE

I, Joe Splitz, of the City of Toronto, in the Province of Ontario, MAKE OATH AND SAY:

1.   I am the process server for the law firm of Just & Coping, Barristers and Solicitors, and as such have knowledge of the matters to which I herein depose.

2.   I served Fred Flogem with the statement of claim by leaving a copy on January 6, year 1, at 2:30 p.m., with Belinda Flogem, who appeared to be an adult member of the same household in which Fred Flogem is residing, at 21 Cypress Blvd., Scarborough, Ontario, M8Q 1P3 and by sending a copy by regular lettermail on January 6, year 1 to Fred Flogem at the same address.

3.   I ascertained that the person was an adult member of the household by means of the fact that she identified herself as Fred Flogem's wife and confirmed that she was over 18 years of age.

4.   Before serving the documents in this way, I made an unsuccessful attempt to serve Fred Flogem personally at the same address on January 5, year 1.

SWORN before me at the)	
City of Toronto,)	*Joe Splitz*
in the Province of Ontario,)	Joe Splitz
on January 6, year 1.)	
I.M. Just)	
I.M. Just)	
Commissioner for Taking Affidavits)	

RCP-E 16B (January 1, 2008)

Figure 8.2   Affidavit of Service on Lawyer of Record (Form 16B)

Court file no. 01-CV-1234

ONTARIO
SUPERIOR COURT OF JUSTICE

BETWEEN:

ABIGAIL BOAR

Plaintiff

and

RATTLE MOTORS LTD. and FRED FLOGEM

Defendants

AFFIDAVIT OF SERVICE

I, Cynthia Patel, of the City of Toronto, in the Province of Ontario, law clerk for Huey Sue, lawyer for the Defendant, MAKE OATH AND SAY:*

1. I served Abigail Boar, the plaintiff, with the statement of defence, dated January 12, year 1, by sending a copy by fax to 416-762-2300 on January 14, year 1 to I.M. Just, Just & Coping, Barristers and Solicitors, the lawyers for the plaintiff.

SWORN before me at the)	
City of Toronto,)	*Cynthia Patel*
in the Province of Ontario,)	Cynthia Patel
on January 15, year 1.)	
Huey Sue)	
Huey Sue)	
Commissioner for Taking Affidavits)	

RCP-E 16B (January 1, 2008)

---

* *When serving a lawyer by mail, substitute the following:*

1. I served Abigail Boar, the plaintiff, with the statement of defence, dated January 12, year 1, by sending a copy by regular lettermail on January 14, year 1 to I.M. Just, Just & Coping, Barristers and Solicitors, the lawyers for the plaintiff, at 365 Bay Street – 8701, Toronto, Ontario, M3J 4A9.

When serving a lawyer by courier, substitute the following:

1. I served Abigail Boar, the plaintiff, with the statement of defence, dated January 12, year 1, by sending a copy by UPS to I.M. Just, Just & Coping, Barristers and Solicitors, the lawyers for the plaintiff, at 365 Bay Street – 8701, Toronto, Ontario, M3J 4A9.

2. The copy was given to the courier on January 12, year 1.

Figure 8.3   Affidavit of Personal Service on Corporation (Form 16B)

Court file no. 01-CV-1234

ONTARIO
SUPERIOR COURT OF JUSTICE

BETWEEN:

ABIGAIL BOAR

Plaintiff

and

RATTLE MOTORS LTD. and FRED FLOGEM

Defendants

AFFIDAVIT OF SERVICE

I, Joe Splitz, of the City of Toronto, in the Province of Ontario, MAKE OATH AND SAY:

1. I am the process server for the law firm of Just & Coping, Barristers and Solicitors, and as such have knowledge of the matters to which I herein depose.

2. On January 5, year 1 at 2:35 p.m., I served Rattle Motors Ltd. with the statement of claim by leaving a copy with Sunil Tharper, president and general manager, at the corporation's place of business at 1240 Bay Street, Toronto, Ontario, M8H 0K8.

3. I was able to identify the person by means of him providing me with his name and confirming that he was the president and general manager of the corporation.

SWORN before me at the) City of Toronto,) in the Province of Ontario,) on January 6, year 1.) _I.M. Just_) I.M. Just) Commissioner for Taking Affidavits)	_Joe Splitz_ Joe Splitz

Figure 8.4   Affidavit of Personal Service on Individual (Form 16B)

Court file no. 01-CV-1234

ONTARIO
SUPERIOR COURT OF JUSTICE

BETWEEN:

ABIGAIL BOAR

Plaintiff

and

RATTLE MOTORS LTD. and FRED FLOGEM

Defendants

AFFIDAVIT OF SERVICE

I, Joe Splitz, of the City of Toronto, in the Province of Ontario, MAKE OATH AND SAY:

1. I am the process server for the law firm of Just & Coping, Barristers and Solicitors, and as such have knowledge of the matters to which I herein depose.

2. On January 5, year 1, at 2:35 p.m., I served Fred Flogem with the statement of claim by leaving a copy with him at 21 Cypress Boulevard, Scarborough, Ontario, M8Q 1P3.

3. I was able to identify the person by means of his confirmation that he was Fred Flogem.

SWORN before me at the)	
City of Toronto,)	*Joe Splitz*
in the Province of Ontario,)	Joe Splitz
on January 6, year 1.)	
I.M. Just)	
I.M. Just)	
Commissioner for Taking Affidavits)	

RCP-E 16B (January 1, 2008)

**Figure 8.5   Affidavit of Service on Defendant by Mail (Form 16B)
with Acknowledgment of Receipt Card (Form 16A) Attached as Exhibit**

Court file no. 01-CV-1234

ONTARIO
SUPERIOR COURT OF JUSTICE

BETWEEN:

ABIGAIL BOAR

Plaintiff

and

RATTLE MOTORS LTD. and FRED FLOGEM

Defendants

AFFIDAVIT OF SERVICE

I, Edward Egregious, of the City of Toronto, in the Province of Ontario, MAKE OATH
AND SAY:

1. I am a law clerk for the firm of Just & Coping, Barristers and Solicitors, lawyers for
    the plaintiff, and as such have knowledge of the matters to which I herein depose.
2. On January 5, year 1, I sent to the defendant Fred Flogem by regular lettermail a copy
    of the statement of claim.
3. On January 12, year 1, I received the acknowledgment of receipt card, attached here as
    exhibit A, bearing a signature that purports to be the signature of Fred Flogem.

SWORN before me at the	)
City of Toronto,	)
in the Province of Ontario,	)
on January 12, year 1.	)
I.M. Just	)
I.M. Just	)
Commissioner for Taking Affidavits	)

Edward Egregious
Edward Egregious

RCP-E 16B (January 1, 2008)

Figure 8.5   Concluded

Court file no. 01-CV-1234

ONTARIO
SUPERIOR COURT OF JUSTICE

BETWEEN:

ABIGAIL BOAR

Plaintiff

and

RATTLE MOTORS LTD. and FRED FLOGEM

Defendants

TO: Fred Flogem

You are served by mail with the documents enclosed with this card in accordance with the Rules of Civil Procedure.

You are requested to sign the acknowledgment below and mail this card immediately after you receive it. If you fail to do so, the documents may be served on you in another manner and you may have to pay the costs of service.

ACKNOWLEDGMENT OF RECEIPT

I ACKNOWLEDGE that I have received a copy of the following documents:

Statement of claim of Abigail Boar, issued January 4, year 1

Fred Flogem
_____
Fred Flogem

(The reverse side of this card must bear the name and address of the sender and the required postage.)

THIS IS EXHIBIT A REFERRED
TO IN THE AFFIDAVIT OF
EDWARD EGREGIOUS,
SWORN BEFORE ME ON
January 12, year 1

I.M. Just
_____
Commissioner for Taking Affidavits

RCP-E 16A (November 1, 2005)

Figure 8.6 Certificate of Service by Sheriff (Form 16C)

CERTIFICATE OF SERVICE BY SHERIFF

I, Joe Shmoe, sheriff's officer of the Township of Vaughan, certify that on March 1, year 2, at 10 a.m., I served Donald Donaldson with a writ of seizure and sale by leaving a copy with him at 400 Starry Lane, Woodbridge, Ontario, L4V 9V6.

I was able to identify the person by means of his confirmation that he was Donald Donaldson.

Date: March 1, year 2

Joe Shmoe
Joe Shmoe

RCP-E 16C (January 1, 2008)

Proof of Acceptance or Admitting of Service by the Other Side

When you are serving a document, very often the lawyer for the other side will admit service. It is a good idea to put the following wording on the backsheet of the document to be filed with the court:

Service of a copy of this
document admitted on

[date]

[signature]
Lawyers for *[party being served]*

The lawyer for the party being served, or one of the staff in his or her office, may be willing to fill in the date and sign for the document. This signature tells the court that the other side agrees that it has been properly served according to the Rules. There is no need to prepare an affidavit of service. The copy of the document on which service has been admitted can be filed with the court without any further proof of service being required.

It is not always possible to use this method of proof because the lawyer for the opposite side may not be in the office when the document is served and may not have left instructions with a staff member to admit service. *It is very important that you never admit service of any document unless you have been given specific instructions by the lawyer you work for to do so.* If there is a problem with the service—for example, if it is not in keeping with the Rules—and service has been admitted, the service cannot usually be challenged later.

Acceptance of service works the same way as admitting service, but the wording that is put on the backsheet of the document being served is slightly different.

> Service of a copy of this
> document accepted on
>
> ____[date]_____
>
> ____[signature]_____
>
> Lawyers for [party being served]

The acceptance wording is used when you are serving a lawyer with an originating process under Rule 16.03(2) as an alternative to personal service. Remember, if the lawyer does not accept service by signing the document, service has not been effected. Under Rule 16.05, if you are serving a lawyer of record with a document that is not an originating process, you are to use the admittance of service wording. A lawyer of record is a lawyer for another party in the case who has already filed documents for his client in the proceeding. He or she is now in the records of the court as the party's lawyer.

Service Outside the Province

Sometimes one of the parties to a proceeding lives or is located outside Ontario. When serving a party outside the province, in addition to following Rule 16, you must also follow any additional procedures prescribed by Rule 17. This means that an originating process served outside the province must still be served personally or by an alternative to personal service under Rule 16. However, you must also look at Rule 17 to see if there are additional steps that must be taken or additional procedures that must be followed.

Rule 17.01 changes the definition of originating process by adding an additional document to the list contained in Rule 1.03. Counterclaims against parties to the main action and crossclaims are also included as originating processes for the purpose of serving someone outside the province.

Not all documents served outside the province can be served without a court order, although many can. To determine whether your case is one in which you can serve outside the province without a court order, you must first look at Rule 17.02. If your case is one of the types of cases listed under this rule, you may serve outside the province without leave, or permission, from the court. If your case is not one of the types listed under Rule 17.02, you must first bring a motion to get leave from the court to serve the party who is outside the province (Rule 17.03). The motion is usually a motion without notice. Notice is usually not required in these circumstances because you are trying to get permission to serve the originating process on someone outside the province. The court grants leave for a type of case not listed in Rule 17.02 only if it can be satisfied that the courts in Ontario are the appropriate courts to hear the case.

Where an originating process is being served outside the province without leave under Rule 17.02, you must state in the document which part of the rule you are relying on to serve without leave (Rule 17.04(1)). For instance, if you are serving someone in Manitoba with a statement of claim in a case that involves the breach of a contract made in Ontario, your statement of claim must contain a paragraph that states that fact and mentions Rule 17.02(f)(i). Rule 17.02(f)(i) says that you do not need leave from the court to serve a document on a party when the case involves a claim relating to a contract made in Ontario.

If you are dealing with a claim that requires leave to serve outside the province, the order that grants leave must also be served along with the originating process (Rule 17.04(2)).

Rule 17.05 deals with the method of service you must use when serving documents outside Ontario. Basically, when you want to serve an originating process outside the province, you may do so by having the document personally served or served by an alternative to personal service as described in Rule 16. In addition, you may also serve by whatever method of service is permissible in the other jurisdiction as long as that method of service is likely to bring the document to the attention of the person being served.

However, if you want to serve an originating process in a foreign country, you must first find out if that country is a **contracting state** to the Hague *Convention on the Service Abroad of Judicial and Extrajudicial Documents in Civil or Commercial Matters*. This is the international convention, or agreement, that Canada has entered into with many other countries. All the countries that have signed the convention are called "contracting states." They have agreed that they will help litigants from the other countries serve documents. If you are dealing with a country that is part of the convention, you must send your documents to the central authority in Ontario. That central authority then sends the documents to the central authority in the other country. The central authorities are government offices in each country that has signed the convention. The central authority in the other country takes care of serving the documents and preparing the proof of service, which it will send back to you. A country that is a convention state will provide whatever proof of service is legal in that country, and it will be acceptable as good proof in an Ontario court (Rule 17.05(4)).

To find out whether a country is a contracting state to the convention, you may look at the website for the Hague Conference on Private International Law at http://www.hcch.net/index_en.php?act=conventions.status&cid=17. You may also telephone Foreign Affairs and International Trade Canada, Criminal, Security and Diplomatic Law Division in Ottawa at 613-995-1135. That office will also be able to give you advice on the procedure for serving Ontario court documents in a signatory country.

A party that has been served outside Ontario can bring a motion, in an Ontario court, to set aside service of an originating process or to stay or stop the proceeding as long as the party commences the motion before filing any documents. When dealing with such a motion, the judge looks at whether the documents have been properly served under the Rules and whether the Ontario court is the proper court in which to hear the proceeding. When you wish to serve a document in a contracting state, you must complete Forms 17A, 17B, and 17C. You are usually required to provide a translation of the document as well.

contracting state
country that is a signatory to a contract or convention

CHAPTER SUMMARY

This chapter introduced the various methods that must be used to serve a document under the Rules. Generally, there are specific methods set out for the service of a document that is an originating process and other methods set out for documents that are not.

You must first look to see if there is a specific rule relating to the document you want to serve that requires a specific method of service. If not, an originating process may be served either by personal service through one of the methods listed in Rule 16.02 or by an alternative to personal service listed in Rule 16.03. Only the alternatives to personal service listed in that rule may be substituted for personal service.

If a document is not an originating process and the party is represented by a lawyer of record, it is possible to serve the document on the lawyer by one of the methods provided in Rule 16.05. If the party is representing himself or herself in the proceeding, a document that is not an originating process may be served by mail to the address provided by the party on the originating process or by personal or alternative service.

If it is impossible to serve a person because the person is avoiding service or cannot be found, the party wishing to serve the document may bring a motion to ask for an order of substituted service or an order dispensing with service. It is only in the most extraordinary circumstances that a court will make an order dispensing with service.

Once service has been effected according to the Rules or a court order, the person who served the document must make an affidavit that provides evidence of the steps that he or she took to serve the document. However, it is not necessary to prepare an affidavit of service if the lawyer for the opposite party admits or accepts service and certifies that he or she has done so on the backsheet of the served document. Likewise, no affidavit is necessary where the document has been left in a document exchange. The stamp of the document exchange on the document is sufficient service.

A document may be served outside Ontario without leave of the court if the type of proceeding is listed in Rule 17.02. If the proceeding is of any other type, the party wishing to serve the document must obtain a court order first. If you wish to serve a document on a person who is in a contracting state to the Hague *Convention on the Service Abroad of Judicial and Extrajudicial Documents in Civil or Commercial Matters*, the person must be served, in accordance with Rule 17.05(3), by a central authority in the country where the party is located.

KEY TERMS

contracting state, 196
originating process, 182
service, 182
sheriff, 187

NOTE

1. This is not the same as registered mail. Form 16A must be used.

REFERENCES

Hague Conference on Private International Law, *Convention on the Service Abroad of Judicial and Extrajudicial Documents in Civil or Commercial Matters*, November 15, 1965: http://www.hcch.net/index_en.php?act=conventions.text&cid=17.

Public Service Act, RSO 1990, c. P.47.

Rules of Civil Procedure, RRO 1990, reg. 194.

REVIEW QUESTIONS

1. How do you effect service on a partnership?

2. When can you serve a motion record on a lawyer by fax?

3. Julie Giudice served the defendant's lawyer of record by mail with a document that was not an originating process. The document was mailed on Friday, September 23. What date will service be effective?

4. A process server wants to serve Frasier Croon with a statement of claim. He goes to Frasier's house and finds the cleaning woman there alone. The process server leaves a copy of the statement of claim with the cleaning woman and mails a copy to Frasier at the same address on the same day. Is this good service? Explain your answer.

5. Jaspal wants to serve a 15-page statement of defence on the lawyer of record for the plaintiff. He is running out of time and decides to serve the document by fax at 9:30 a.m. Is this good service?

6. You are a law clerk for Seneca and Associates, Barristers and Solicitors, 1750 Finch Avenue East, Toronto, Ontario, M2J 2X5. Your client is John Ahab, who is suing Moby's Whale of a Time Inc., a chain of restaurants, for negligently leaving a bone in his sushi. You have just served Moby's Whale of a Time Inc. with a statement of claim. You went to the restaurant closest to the law office, at 5910 Yonge Street, North York, Ontario, M7U 4T8 and left a copy with the manager of the restaurant, Ishmael Bosun. Draft an affidavit of service. If there is any necessary information that you think is missing, make it up.

7. You sent the process server out to serve a sole proprietorship personally. When the process server came back, he produced an affidavit that said he left a copy of the statement of claim with Ginny, the assistant cashier at the place of business. Is this service adequate?

8. In the following situations, will it be necessary to seek leave of the court to serve a party with an originating process outside Ontario?

   a. Joe died in Ontario. His heirs want to sue his nurse, Betty, who they believe removed some of Joe's property from his home after he died, and they want the property to be returned.

   b. Stacey lives in Toronto. She was in a car accident in New York State. She wants to sue the owner of the car that hit her car. He lives in New York State.

   c. The parties made a contract in Manitoba, but since they knew that one of the parties was moving his business to Toronto the next month, they agreed to a term in the contract that the law of Ontario should govern.

9. You are a law clerk with the firm of MacDonald, Reed, and Buss. Your supervising lawyer is Jacqueline Reed. The address of the firm is:

   MacDonald, Reed, and Buss
   Barristers and Solicitors
   200 Bay Street, Suite 1100
   Toronto, Ontario, M5V 3T3
   Tel.:   416-595-5000
   Fax: 416-595-5050
   Email: MDRB@sympatico.ca

   Your law firm acts for the plaintiffs, Yorkful Developers Inc. The defendant is Louis LaFrance. The process server is Jacky Dillhopper. Jacky phones and tells you he has effected service on Louis LaFrance by attending at his residence at 100 Bloor Street North, Toronto, Ontario, M6Y 4R7. He left a copy with Louis's wife, Celine, after she identified herself as Louis's wife. Draft an affidavit of service for Jacky to sign when he gets back to the office.

Motions

9

Introduction

This chapter is about motions procedure and the preparation of **motion** documents. It includes Appendix I: Motion and Application Procedure in Toronto, which refers to the special motion procedure used in Toronto, Appendix II: Special Motions, which provides examples of special motions you are likely to encounter in practice, and Appendix III: Complete Motion Record, which shows an example of what is contained in a motion record.

You will notice that both the procedure and the documents for motions are very similar to those used in applications. This is not accidental. Documents and procedures in motions and applications are designed to be dispatched in a summary fashion, with a short timeline between raising a legal issue and obtaining an answer from the court.

Purpose of Motions

The purpose of a motion is to settle issues that arise in the course of civil litigation, usually before trial.[1] We have already identified some circumstances where motions are required to resolve a problem prior to trial: a motion to join parties to a lawsuit, a motion to strike out pleadings, and a motion to demand particulars. It used to be the case, and sometimes still is, that a party with money to spend would try to delay proceedings by bringing one motion after another, thereby driving up the legal costs at the pretrial stage. The opposing party, if more financially limited, would soon be forced to drop the lawsuit or settle on disadvantageous terms. This practice was sometimes referred to as "motioning the other side to death." The Rules discourage this kind of litigation strategy, and the courts have the power to award punitive costs against parties who resort to it. In some cases, the courts award costs against lawyers who engage in these dark arts (Rule 57.07). A court may also bar a party from bringing further motions unless the court's permission is first obtained (Rule 37.16).

But there are often good reasons to bring motions. Suppose that I.M. Just, Abigail Boar's lawyer, has read the statement of defence stating that the area around the Super Coupe was properly illuminated and therefore safe. That matter is now an issue between the parties. To help settle it, I.M. Just asks Huey Sue, the defendants' lawyer, to permit a lighting engineer to come to the showroom and examine the lighting. Huey refuses to permit this. So I.M. Just decides to bring a motion to ask the court to order an examination of the premises by the lighting engineer.

Motions With Notice: Overview of Procedure

While we will look at various aspects of motion procedure in detail, here we set out a general overview of the process of bringing a motion with notice.

The moving party prepares a notice of motion and a supporting affidavit and serves it on the responding party at least seven days before the motion is to be heard and files it at least seven days before the hearing (Rules 37.07(6) and 37.08(1)).

The day picked for the **return of the motion** depends on the practices in the court where the motion is returnable. In Toronto, an appointment for a motion before a judge or a master must be obtained *before* serving the responding party. This is discussed in more detail in Appendix I to this chapter.

Motions shall be brought and heard where the proceeding was commenced, unless otherwise ordered (Rule 37.03(1)). This is consistent with Rule 13.1, governing the place of trial. However, if the motion is a motion to change the venue (place of trial), the motion may be brought in the county where the party is seeking to move the proceeding (Rule 13.1.02(3.1)).

The responding party may serve an affidavit or other evidentiary material or a cross-motion and supporting documents on the moving party up to four days before the hearing.

A motion record must be prepared, usually by the moving party, and should contain a table of contents, the notice of motion, affidavits, and any other documents the parties intend to refer to on the motion. It is then filed in the court where the motion is to be heard, seven days before the hearing. In the event that the responding party is not satisfied with the motion record filed by the moving party, the responding party can file a separate motion record four days before the date of the hearing. See Appendix III for an example of what a motion record looks like.

You will notice that if you read these rules, the parties will have to serve all materials for use on the motion well in advance of the hearing date, as it all must be filed with the court at least seven days prior to the hearing (except if the responding party decides to file his or her own motion record, in which case it can be filed four days before the hearing). This requires the parties to observe time limits for serving each other and allow each other enough time for all documents to be served and a motion record to be assembled—this requires cooperation. For this reason, the Rules now require a party who brings a motion to confer with the other party to ensure that all necessary steps can be taken, all documents can be filed on time, and the hearing date confirmed. A confirmation of motion in Form 37B (see Figure 9.7) must be given to the court office, and a copy sent to the other party.[2] Failure to confirm may mean that the motion will not be heard. Further, if the information on which a confirmation was given is incorrect, a party must deliver a corrected confirmation of motion form to the court and send a copy to the other party (Rules 37.10.1(1) and (2)).

Either party may ask to cross-examine the maker of an affidavit that is filed on the motion. This is done out of court before a court reporter or **official examiner**, and the transcript, or a part of it, may be used at the hearing. If the parties have not allowed enough time for cross-examination between the date the motion is served and its return date (the hearing date), the request to cross-examine is made on the return date of the motion; if the request is granted, the motion is adjourned pending completion of cross-examination. The Rules require that a party who seeks to cross-examine should move to do so "with reasonable diligence." Because cross-examination causes delay, its misuse may lead to an imposition of cost penalties on the party that improperly resorts to it or the court may deny permission for cross-examination altogether (Rule 39.02(3)). A party who cross-examines on an affidavit may not file supplementary affidavits responding to what was said in cross-examination without the court's consent. This puts an end to the old practice of

official examiner
individual who is licensed to operate a business to conduct out-of-court examinations, such as cross-examinations on affidavits and discoveries

serving a responding affidavit after cross-examination, followed by a response to the responding affidavit, and so on, which caused both delay and confusion.

There are some additional burdens on a party who cross-examines. The party bears the expense of ordering a transcript of the cross-examination for the court and for other parties. The party must also pay partial indemnity costs of every adverse party on the motion unless the court orders otherwise (Rule 39.02(4)).

Parties may wish to file factums, which are statements of fact, law, and case references; they are not required on all motions, except in Toronto on lengthy, complex motions, but the practice is recommended and encouraged by the judiciary.

Hearings are **summary proceedings**. Oral evidence is usually not heard; instead, counsel make submissions, referring to affidavits and other documentary evidence, including cross-examination transcripts.

The successful party on the motion then drafts the order from the judge's or master's endorsement, obtains approval as to form from the unsuccessful party, and has the order issued and entered by the court.

summary proceedings
proceedings designed to be conducted quickly and with reduced formality

Motions Without Notice

There are certain types of motions that may be brought without notice. For example, if you have been unable to serve a defendant with a statement of claim, you may bring a motion for substituted service, as you saw in Chapter 8. The motion is brought in the court where the proceeding was commenced (Rule 37.03(1)), but no notice to the other side is required. You file the notice of motion and the affidavit or other evidence you will use, appear before the judge or master, or submit the motion in writing, and make submissions. A notice of motion should be filed to set out the issues in advance for the judge or master. Once an order is made, unless the court orders otherwise, any party affected by the order must be served with a copy of the order immediately, along with a copy of the motion, and all the documents used on it. In that way, the process is reasonably transparent because the party, though not present, gets to see what was before the court. If the moving party misled the court, the other party will become aware of that fact and can take action to set the order aside. Because a motion without notice is rather one-sided, an affidavit must give full and fair disclosure and must be more neutral in tone than it would be had the motion been made on notice (Rule 39.01(6)).

If the judge or master is of the opinion that the motion should not have been brought without first giving notice, he or she may dismiss the motion or adjourn it until the other party is served, and he or she may direct that any order made be served on the non-attending party (Rule 37.07(5)).

master
minor judicial official with limited jurisdiction to hear and decide specific legal issues identified by the Rules or a statute

Jurisdiction to Hear a Motion

In the Superior Court, there are two types of judicial officials who decide legal issues and who can decide contested motions: a **master** and a judge. Masters have a more limited jurisdiction than judges do, and they sit in courts where the volume of cases is high, such as in Toronto and Ottawa. In other judicial regions, judges hear all motions.

Where you have a choice as to whether the motion is heard by a judge or master, you must decide before whom it should come. As a general rule, a motion that can be heard by a master must be heard by a master if masters sit in the court where the motion is brought. If you schedule it before a judge in a place where it could come before a master, he or she will refuse to hear it, and you will have to appear again before a master, wasting both time and money.[3]

A master's jurisdiction is more circumscribed than a judge's. Rule 37.02(2)(a) to (g) lists those matters that a master *cannot* hear:

- A master cannot hear a matter that has been given exclusively to a judge by a statute or regulation.
- A master cannot change an order that was made by a judge.
- A master cannot shorten or lengthen the time for doing something in an order made by a judge.
- A master cannot give a consent judgment where there is a party under disability—such as a minor—involved.
- A master cannot make an order that affects the liberty of a person—for example, because an order for contempt of court may result in jail time, contempt motions must be brought before judges.
- A master cannot make orders under s. 4 or s. 5 of the *Judicial Review Procedure Act* such as interim orders or orders extending the time for filing applications for judicial review.
- A master cannot make orders on an appeal.

Subject to these restrictions, masters have jurisdiction to hear all other matters.

While masters and judges share jurisdiction over contested motions, the registrar has jurisdiction over some motions if all parties consent to the order being sought on the motion, and no party is under disability. Rule 37.02(3) provides that if all parties to the proceeding or affected by it consent, and the subject of the motion is one that is listed in the rule, then the motion documents may be submitted to the registrar, who will sign the order, if the documentation is in order. If the registrar has any doubts, he or she will not sign the order, and will return the documents to the moving party, who then has to bring the motion in the ordinary way. This is sensible and practical. Since the motion is being made on consent, there is no need to resort to a legally trained judge or master to make an order. Here, the making of an order is an administrative act that can be performed inexpensively and quickly by a registrar.

Obtaining a Hearing Date

In large regions such as Toronto, motions are heard every day. In small centres, there is often a "motion day,"[4] which is a day on which a judge usually hears all motions filed since the last motion day. Generally, the moving party may choose any date on which motions are heard without needing first to obtain a date from the court office. When choosing a date, however, it is a good idea to check with the responding parties to the motion to be sure that counsel will be available. This will avoid wasting time and money on adjournments and rescheduling. To some extent, the requirement under Rule 37.10.1 that parties confer and confirm with one another on the motion before the hearing date reinforces this action as a wise one to take.

However, if a lawyer estimates that the hearing is likely to take more than two hours, the moving party should confer with the other party, and then must obtain a fixed hearing date from the registrar (Rule 37.05(2)). In this case, the registrar will arrange a date where a judge is available, and this will prevent a long motion from keeping other motions from being heard in a busy motions court. It is not difficult to imagine how a two-hour motion could throw off a court schedule and cause delay and inconvenience to others requiring the court's attention that day.

In Toronto, the practice for obtaining a hearing date for nearly all motions is governed by the Toronto Practice Direction (*Practice Directions for Civil Applications, Motions and Other Matters in the Toronto Region* (amended January 20, 2012)). In Toronto you must schedule (reserve or book) a motion date before serving a motion. This is discussed in more detail in Appendix I to this chapter.

Generally, if you are involved with a motion that is to be heard in a court or region where you are not familiar with local scheduling and hearing practices, it is a good idea to call the court office to find out whether there are special requirements for hearing dates, service, or documents required on the motion.

Notice of Motion

The primary document you need to prepare is the notice of motion. This tells the other side the issue that you wish to have decided, the evidentiary materials you rely on, the remedy you seek, and the reason you believe you are entitled to the remedy. The prescribed form is Form 37A; an example of a completed notice of motion is set out in Figure 9.1 and the relevant rule is Rule 37.06, which sets out the information required:

1. *To whom the motion is made.* Is the motion made to a master or to a judge? Check Rule 37.02.

2. *Time, date, and place where the motion will be heard.* Remember that the best practice is to confer with the other side on the date so that all materials can be served and filed seven days prior to the hearing. Try to arrange a convenient time with the responding party, and file a confirmation of motion in Form 37B. Remember to reserve the date and time with the court if the motion is going to take more than two hours.

3. *Whether the motion is to be heard orally or in writing.* The lawyer will make oral or written submissions. Evidence, however, in either case, is by affidavit. You need permission from the court to proceed with oral evidence.

4. *Legal basis or grounds that support the remedy requested.* Briefly list a rule, statute, case, or legal principle, if relevant.

5. *Documentary evidence that will be relied on.* Affidavits and other documents listed on the notice of motion should be identified by the date the document was created and the maker of the document if this is not obvious.

6. *Name, address, and telephone number of the lawyer for the moving party.* Provide the same information for the lawyers who are being served on behalf of the responding party. Many lawyers also include their fax number and their Law Society registration number, although the motion form does not appear to require it.

Figure 9.1 sets out Abigail's motion for an order for inspection of the defendants' premises. The relevant rule for inspection of property is Rule 32. Read all of Rule 32 and notice that its language is incorporated into the statement of the grounds of the motion itself. Feel free to use the rule as an organizational guide for stating the grounds, and feel free to borrow from the language of the rule. Don't make it more complicated than it is.

Affidavits as Evidence on Motions and Applications

One of the ways in which hearings on motions and applications are speeded up is by using affidavit evidence instead of having witnesses give evidence orally. What a witness would have said in examination-in-chief is reduced to a sworn statement. If cross-examination is desired, arrangements need to be made to cross-examine the deponent on the contents of his or her affidavit. In that case the transcript of that cross-examination is used with the affidavit itself at the hearing. While affidavits are designed to be a faster and more efficient way of getting evidence before the court on a motion, the process of adjourning a motion or application to permit cross-examination and obtain transcripts may end up costing more and taking more time than using oral evidence on the motion or affidavit.

Drafting Affidavits

The basic requirements for affidavits are set out in Rule 4.06. Form 4D sets out a prescribed format.

Use the First Person Form When Writing Statements

The statements in affidavits are set out in the first person singular ("I"), although joint affidavits may be used where appropriate, in which case the first person plural ("we") must be used.

Figure 9.1 Motion for Order for Inspection of Premises (Form 37A)

Wed Afternoon 12 noon Start

Court file no. 01-CV-1234

ONTARIO
SUPERIOR COURT OF JUSTICE

BETWEEN:

ABIGAIL BOAR

Plaintiff

and

RATTLE MOTORS LTD. and FRED FLOGEM

Defendants

NOTICE OF MOTION

The plaintiff will make a motion to the court on Monday, October 16, year 1 at 10:00 a.m., or as soon after that time as the motion can be heard, at 393 University Avenue, Toronto, Ontario, M5G 1Y3.

PROPOSED METHOD OF HEARING: The motion is to be heard

- ❑ in writing under subrule 37.12.1 (1);
- ☒ in writing as an opposed motion under subrule 37.12.1 (4);
- ❑ orally.

THE MOTION IS FOR an order permitting Eldred Klump, consulting electrical engineer, to inspect the level of lighting in the automobile showroom operated by the corporate defendant at 1240 Bay Street in the City of Toronto, Province of Ontario, on such terms and at such times as the court considers just.

THE GROUNDS FOR THE MOTION ARE that there is an issue between the parties as to the adequacy of lighting in the corporate defendant's showroom, and it is necessary to determine that issue in this proceeding to carry out an inspection of the corporate defendant's premises to examine the lighting, pursuant to Rule 32 of the Rules of Civil Procedure.

Figure 9.1   Concluded

THE FOLLOWING DOCUMENTARY EVIDENCE will be used at the hearing of the motion:

1. Statement of claim filed January 4, year 1;

2. Statement of defence filed January 12, year 1; and

3. Affidavit of Eldred Klump sworn October 3, year 1.

October 16, year 1

Just & Coping
Barristers and Solicitors
365 Bay Street – 8701
Toronto, Ontario, M3J 4A9

I.M. Just
LSUC #12345R
tel. 416-762-1342
fax 416-762-2300

Lawyers for the Moving
Party (Plaintiff)

TO: Huey Sue
LSUC #23456T
Barrister and Solicitor
65 False Trail
Toronto, Ontario, M6Y 1Z6

tel. 416-485-6891
fax 416-485-6892

Lawyer for the Responding
Parties (Defendants)

RCP-E 37A (July 1, 2007)

Identify the Deponent

Before setting out the first numbered paragraph, give the deponent's full name, followed by the municipality and county or region where the deponent resides. In Toronto, however, the deponent's name is followed by the municipality (City of Toronto) and the province.[5] Set out the deponent's status—for example, as a party, lawyer for a party, or officer of a corporation—so that the testimony can be seen in context. Two examples of paragraphs identifying a deponent are set out below. The second example, although not in conformity with the directions in Form 4D, is often used.

> I, Eldred Klump, of the City of Brampton, in the Regional Municipality of Peel,[6] consulting electrical engineer, MAKE OATH AND SAY:

> I, Eldred Klump, of the City of Brampton, in the Regional Municipality of Peel, MAKE OATH AND SAY:
>
> 1. I am a consulting electrical engineer, retained by the plaintiff, and as such have knowledge of the matters sworn to in this affidavit.

Set Out the Statement in Consecutive Paragraphs

Much like a statement of claim or defence, the affidavit is divided into consecutively numbered paragraphs, with each paragraph confined as far as possible to a specific statement of fact. Again, this may mean that many paragraphs are just two or three sentences long. The writing should be concise and in the first person singular ("I"). However, it is not limited to material facts, and evidentiary material may be set out.

Sign and Swear the Affidavit

The deponent must sign the affidavit at the end, or foot, after he or she has been affirmed or sworn by a commissioner for taking oaths and affidavits. Every lawyer is a commissioner and is authorized to swear or affirm affidavits. Law clerks employed in law offices may apply through their offices to the provincial government to become commissioners while employed in that law office and doing work for it. A lawyer signs the **jurat** as commissioner when he or she has sworn or affirmed the deponent. A non-lawyer signs the jurat and also applies his or her commissioner's stamp, identifying the law office for which he or she works and the date of the expiry of the commission. A lawyer's commission does not require use of a stamp.

jurat
part of an affidavit that appears at the bottom on the left side of the page and begins with the words "Sworn (or affirmed) before me"

An affidavit is commissioned when it is being used in an Ontario proceeding. If it is being sworn for use in another province or in a foreign jurisdiction, it should be notarized instead, and the notary's seal should be affixed next to the notary's signature.

Where a lawyer commissions an affidavit without a seal and the signature is an illegible scrawl, the lawyer should print his or her name underneath the signature. The format of a standard jurat[7] is set out in Figure 9.2.

Determine Whether Hearsay Is Admissible

The content of an affidavit, like the evidence on a witness's oral examination-in-chief, is usually restricted to matters of which the deponent has personal knowledge.

Figure 9.2 Standard Jurat (Form 4D)

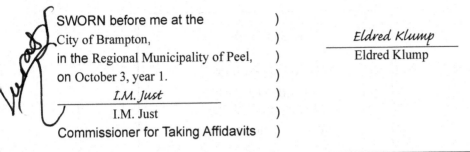

SWORN before me at the)	
City of Brampton,)	*Eldred Klump*
in the Regional Municipality of Peel,)	Eldred Klump
on October 3, year 1.)	
I.M. Just)	
I.M. Just)	
Commissioner for Taking Affidavits)	

Hearsay is not permitted unless it falls into one of the numerous exceptions to the hearsay rule. However, this requirement, set out in Rule 4.06(2), is subject to the qualifications set out in Rules 39.01(4) and (5).

If the affidavit is for use on a motion, it may contain statements of the deponent's information and belief, provided that the deponent identifies the source of the information and states that he or she believes the information to be true. In this instance, hearsay is admissible.

This rule also applies to affidavits used on applications, provided that the source of the information is revealed, the deponent states that he or she believes it to be true, and the *facts in question are not contentious.* Therefore hearsay is admissible, provided that it is not disputed. Where a contentious statement is included, the proper response is to move to strike out the objectionable part of the affidavit.

Using an example from Abigail Boar's case, the usual method for expressing information and belief is as follows: "I am informed by Abigail Boar, the plaintiff in this action, and I believe that she was unable to see the oil spill because of inadequate lighting at the site of her fall."

Follow the Rules Regarding Exhibits

Occasionally the deponent's statement refers to a document or other material. The document or other material should be clearly described and given an exhibit number (usually a letter), which is stamped on a copy of the document. If the exhibit to be attached or filed is a copy, the deponent should so state. Once it is made an exhibit, the document or other material should be made available to other parties and the court. This can be done in one of two ways: (1) it can be attached to the affidavit or (2) it can be referred to in the affidavit and filed in court. Rule 4.06(3) prescribes language for each of the two ways of dealing with exhibits, and you should take care to use the appropriate word formula. Examples from Abigail's case appear below.

- If the exhibit is attached, write "Now *shown to me,* marked exhibit A, *and attached to this affidavit* is a copy of the bar bill of Abigail Boar from Barbeerian's restaurant, dated September 14, year 0."

- If the exhibit is shown to the deponent and filed in court, write "*Now produced and shown to me,* and marked exhibit A is a copy of the bar bill of Abigail Boar from Barbeerian's restaurant, dated September 14, year 0."

Figure 9.3   Exhibit Stamp

```
┌─────────────────────────────────────┐
│  ┌───────────────────────────────┐  │
│  │        This is Exhibit        │  │
│  │              A                │  │
│  │       to the affidavit of     │  │
│  │        ELDRED KLUMP           │  │
│  │       sworn before me this    │  │
│  │    3rd day of October, year 1 │  │
│  │    ──────────────────────     │  │
│  │         I.M. Just             │  │
│  │  Commissioner for Taking Affidavits │
│  └───────────────────────────────┘  │
└─────────────────────────────────────┘
```

Law firms usually use an exhibit stamp with blank spaces to be filled in with the exhibit number or letter, the name of the deponent, and the date of the affidavit. The person who commissions the affidavit signs in the space provided. An exhibit stamp is reproduced in Figure 9.3.

Figure 9.4 shows what Eldred Klump's affidavit in the Abigail Boar case looks like. Figure 9.5 sets out the affidavit filed by Sunil Tharper on behalf of Rattle Motors Ltd.[8]

Motion Records

Assume for the moment that you have now obtained a date for the motion, determined who hears it, prepared a notice of motion and affidavit, and served this on the responding party. The responding party has served its documents on you. You are now ready to prepare a motion record. An example of a complete motion record is set out in Appendix III to this chapter.

Why Use a Motion Record?

Formerly when a motion was brought, the moving party served and filed a motion and affidavit, and the responding party served and filed an affidavit. On each filing, the court clerk stamped the incoming document and put it in the appropriate court file, noting the day of the motion. On the day before the motion, the clerk would bring the court file to the judge or master who was to hear the matter. The judicial official then found himself or herself with a court file full of documents in no particular order. If a matter were complex, there might be dozens of documents and hundreds of pages in the court file. The judge or master would go through the file, looking for the notice of motion and the appropriate affidavits, and reading what he or she hoped was the correct material. To introduce some order to this chaos, the Rules now require a motion record that contains all the material necessary for hearing and determining the motion to be filed. Only the motion record will be delivered to the judge or master unless a party separately requisitions the whole file. There is no longer any need for judges and masters to fumble around in a court file in search of the appropriate documents.

Figure 9.4   Affidavit of Eldred Klump (Form 4D)

Court file no. 01-CV-1234

2.

ONTARIO
SUPERIOR COURT OF JUSTICE

BETWEEN:

~~ABIGAIL BOAR~~ *Nathaniel Simmons*   Plaintiff

and

~~RATTLE MOTORS LTD. and FRED FLOGEM~~ *Ryan milloney.*

Defendants

AFFIDAVIT OF ~~ELDRED KLUMP~~ *Derek Ruscombe. Note Ryan milloney*

Ryan Derek Ruscombe milloney.

I, ~~Eldred Klump~~, of the City of Brampton, in the Regional Municipality of Peel, MAKE OATH AND SAY:

1. I am a consulting electrical engineer, retained by the plaintiff, and as such have knowledge of the matters sworn to in this affidavit.

2. I am advised by I.M. Just, lawyer for the plaintiff, and I believe that there is a disagreement between the parties as to whether or not there was adequate illumination in the area where the plaintiff allegedly fell in the showroom of Rattle Motors Ltd.

3. There are Building Code and other standards for safe and adequate lighting for various areas in buildings, including showrooms.

4. It is possible to measure the amount of light at the location in question and check the measurements against known standards.

5. The information obtained from these tests would be relevant in assisting the court in making findings as to the adequacy of the lighting in question.

6. In order to properly measure the light, it is necessary for me to enter the showroom of the corporate defendant, adjust the lights in the location where the plaintiff fell as they were on the day of the accident, and take measurements of the light available.

SWORN before me at the	)
City of Brampton,	)
in the Regional Municipality of Peel,	)
on October 3, year 1.	)
I.M. Just	)
I.M. Just	)
Commissioner for Taking Affidavits	)

Eldred Klump
Eldred Klump

RCP-E 4D (July 1, 2007)

Figure 9.5   Affidavit of Sunil Tharper (Form 4D)

Court file no. 01-CV-1234

ONTARIO
SUPERIOR COURT OF JUSTICE

BETWEEN:

ABIGAIL BOAR

Plaintiff

and

RATTLE MOTORS LTD. and FRED FLOGEM

Defendants

AFFIDAVIT OF SUNIL THARPER

I, Sunil Tharper, president and general manager of Rattle Motors Ltd., of the City of Toronto, in the Province of Ontario, AFFIRM:

1. I have read the affidavit of Eldred Klump, sworn October 3, year 1 and filed on behalf of the plaintiff in this proceeding.

2. On or about February 1, year 1, the corporate defendant's directors decided to renovate its automobile showroom to better display the automobiles that the company sells.

3. The renovations were extensive, involving a complete gutting of the interior and replacement of flooring, ceilings, showroom windows, and offices.

4. In the course of carrying out this renovation, all of the pre-renovation lighting, including spotlights or pot lights, was removed, and new lighting was installed.

5. The new lighting is of a different type from the old lighting and is placed differently. In particular, the spotlighting now used is of the halogen type, rather than the conventional incandescent floodlight type.

6. Since the lighting fixtures and the illumination they cast are completely different from the lighting that was used at the time the plaintiff fell, the inspection proposed by the plaintiff would serve no purpose.

7. The defendants have consulted a lighting expert, Elihu Dunck, who has prepared a report in which he advises that it would now be impossible to carry out the tests and inspections proposed by the plaintiff, and that the inspection would be of no assistance to the court. Now shown to me and attached hereto and marked exhibit A to this affidavit is a report dated October 5, year 1 from Elihu Dunck to the defendant's lawyer, which sets out Mr. Dunck's opinion.

Figure 9.5 Concluded

SWORN before me at the)	
City of Toronto,)	_Sunil Tharper_
in the Province of Ontario,)	Sunil Tharper
on October 6, year 1.)	
Huey Sue)	
Huey Sue)	
Commissioner for Taking Affidavits)	

RCP-E 4D (July 1, 2007)

Contents of a Motion Record

Rule 37.10(2) sets out what a motion record should contain, in consecutively numbered pages:

- an index (the motion record index), with a general heading and title of proceedings at the top, that describes each document, identified by its nature or date, including exhibits filed or attached to affidavits and identified by exhibit numbers (Figure 9.6 sets out a motion record index for the case of Abigail Boar)—it is a good idea to include the date on which the motion is returnable so that a judge or master can easily pluck it out of the court file;
- a copy of the notice of motion;
- a copy of all affidavits and other material served by any party;
- a list of all relevant transcripts (cross-examinations on affidavits, discoveries, or other evidence) in chronological order (if the transcript or the part relied on is short, it may be included in the motion record; if it is too long for that, be sure that it is in the court file, and requisition the court file for the motion); and
- a copy of any other material in the court file that might be relevant to the issues on the motion (lawyers often file copies of the pleadings to provide a context) or that may be required by the court.

Although it is not required, it is a good idea to use tabs to separate documents so that the judge or master can easily find what the lawyer is referring to in argument. Rule 4.07 requires that a motion record be bound with a light blue backsheet.

If, as it should, the motion record contains the notice of motion and supporting affidavits, these documents need not be filed separately with the court.

Note that there is no prescribed form for a motion record. Some firms will start with a first page that consists of the title of proceedings, the title of the document, the table of contents, and the names and contact information for the law firms that represent the moving and responding parties. Other firms may add a cover or title page

Figure 9.6 Motion Record Index

Court file no. 01-CV-1234

ONTARIO
SUPERIOR COURT OF JUSTICE

BETWEEN:

ABIGAIL BOAR

Plaintiff

and

RATTLE MOTORS LTD. and FRED FLOGEM

Defendants

MOTION RECORD INDEX
Motion Returnable October 16, year 1

Tab	Document	Page
1	Notice of motion brought by the plaintiff, returnable on October 16, year 1	2
2	Affidavit of Eldred Klump, sworn October 3, year 1	4
3	Affidavit of Sunil Tharper, sworn October 6, year 1	5
3a	Exhibit A to the affidavit of Sunil Tharper, sworn October 6, year 1: report from Elihu Dunck, dated October 5, year 1	7
4	Statement of claim, issued January 4, year 1	8
5	Statement of defence, dated January 12, year 1	13

that has the general heading, title of proceedings, title of the document, and contact information for the law firms that represent the parties. If a cover page is used, the following page with the motion record index on it will omit the contact information for the parties' law firms. An example of a cover sheet is included in Appendix III.

Responding Party's Motion Record

If enough time is allowed for both parties to serve each other with their motion material and there is cooperation, one motion record can be prepared for use by the parties and the court on the motion. This is the approach preferred by judges and masters, who dislike having to shuffle through several sets of documents. However, where the responding party is not satisfied that the record is complete, he or she may prepare a responding party's motion record that will include the additional documents. The responding party's motion record should have a table of contents that describes the included documents that were not presented in the moving party's motion record (Rule 37.10(3)). It must be served on all other parties and filed at least four days before the hearing. A responding party's motion record is required where the moving party refuses or neglects to include a court document that the responding party wishes to be included, or where the responding party decides that a document is required after the moving party's motion record has been filed.

Factums for Use on Motions

Factums are recommended and strongly encouraged for use on motions, particularly for "long," complex motions. Factums are required for opposed motions in writing (Rule 37.12.1(4)(b)). Factums are also required on certain types of motions in some regions—for example, on long motions in Toronto. A factum can set out in neutral terms the facts of the case, concise arguments on these facts, and statements of the principles of law relied on, including case references. A motion factum is simply a version of the type of factum that has long been filed on appeals (Rule 37.10(6)). If a factum is to be filed, the moving party's factum should be filed at least seven days prior to the hearing (Rule 37.10(7)) and the responding party's factum at least four days prior to the hearing (Rule 37.10(8)).

If a factum is to be filed, case citations may include citations from recognized electronic databases in addition to citations for traditional print versions of case reports. However, if you use a case reproduced from an electronic source, the paragraph numbering and content must correspond to that in the decision as it was originally released by the court; as well, care should be taken that the original electronic version of a case has not been subsequently edited.[9]

Service of Motions and Motion Records

The requirements for service of motion material are scattered through Rules 37 and 39. As noted earlier, you should confer with the other parties and pick a return date that is far enough in advance so that you will have time to serve your documents, receive the responding party's documents, and file a complete motion record on time. It is a good idea to consult the responding party when choosing a date. But where time is of the essence, here are the steps you must follow:

1. *Determine the location.* The place of hearing for the motion shall be the place where the proceeding was commenced or to which it was transferred (Rule 37.03).

2. *Serve the motion.* The notice of motion, supporting affidavit, and other documents must be served at least seven days before the hearing (Rules 37.07(6) and 39.01(2)).

3. *File the notice of motion.* The notice of motion with proof of service must be filed at least seven days before the day of the hearing (Rule 37.08(1)).

4. *File the motion record.* A motion record should be filed at least seven days before the date of hearing. If it contains all the documents necessary for the motion, there is no need to follow the separate rule for filing the notice of motion noted above.

5. *File the responding party's motion record.* If required, this should be served and filed at least four days before the hearing (Rule 37.10(3)). Everything that is going to be filed must be with the court four days before the hearing so that the judge or master can read the documents before the hearing.

If the matter is an emergency, both the notice and the service and filing rules may be suspended (Rules 2.03 and 37.07(2) to (4)). When proceeding this way, it is wise to ask in the notice of motion for "leave to dispense with service of this notice of motion" and "leave to abridge the time for serving and filing the notice of motion and supporting affidavits" on the grounds that the matter is urgent. If leave is granted, you can proceed with the substantive part of the motion.

Confirmation of Motions

Often, a motion is served on a party and there is no further discussion before the motion hearing. Ideally, however, parties should confer and discuss ways of resolving the issue. If the parties do resolve the issue, they should alert the court that the matter has been resolved and the motion will not proceed. Even if they cannot resolve the issues, they can and should agree on a sensible timetable to serve motion material on each other, so that they can file all material in the motion record seven days before the hearing. To encourage the resolution of issues arising on motions, Rule 37.10.1 requires parties to confer, or to attempt to confer. Then, not later than 2 p.m. two days before the hearing, the moving party is to file with the registrar a confirmation in Form 37B (see Figure 9.7) that the motion is confirmed to be heard on the date set by the court. If the nature of the confirmation changes, a corrected confirmation must be filed.

Figure 9.7 Confirmation of Motion (Form 37B)

ONTARIO
SUPERIOR COURT OF JUSTICE

BETWEEN:

ABIGAIL BOAR

Plaintiff

and

RATTLE MOTORS LTD. and FRED FLOGEM

Defendants

CONFIRMATION OF MOTION

I, I.M. Just, lawyer for the moving party, confirm that the moving party has conferred or attempted to confer with the other party and confirm that the motion to be heard on Monday, October 16, year 1 will proceed on the following basis:

[ ]   for an adjournment on consent to .... *(date)*

[ ]   for a contested adjournment to .... *(date)*, for the following reason: *(specify who is requesting the adjournment and why, and who is opposing it and why)*

[ ]   for a consent order

[x] for a hearing of all the issues

[ ]   for a hearing of the following issues only *(specify)*

The presiding judge will be referred to the following materials:

1. Statement of Claim, January 4, year 1

2. Statement of Defence, January 12, year 1

3. Affidavit of Eldred Klump, sworn October 3, year 1

4. Affidavit of Sunil Tharper, sworn October 6, year 1

I estimate that the time required for the motion, including costs submissions, will be 15 minutes for the moving party and 15 minutes for the responding party for a total of 30 minutes.

Figure 9.7   Concluded

October 6, year 1

Just & Coping
Barristers and Solicitors
365 Bay Street – 8701
Toronto, Ontario, M3J 4A9

I.M. Just
LSUC #12345R
tel. 416-762-1342
fax 416-762-2300

Lawyers for Plaintiff

TO: Huey Sue
LSUC #23456T
Barrister and Solicitor
65 False Trail
Toronto, Ontario, M6Y 1Z6

tel. 416-485-6891
fax 416-485-6892

Lawyer for the Defendants

RCP-E 37B (July 1, 2007)

Abandoned Motions

A party who has made a motion and has served but not filed it, or filed a motion but did not confirm it, and who does not appear in court is deemed to have abandoned the motion. However, a party who has made a motion may abandon it by delivering a notice of abandonment. In either case, the responding party is likely to have done some work and paid some legal fees in getting ready to respond. Provided that the moving party served the motion, the responding party is entitled to immediate costs of the motion unless the court specifically orders otherwise (Rule 37.09). This means that the responding party may move to fix or assess costs without waiting for the trial judgment. If the responding party appears on a motion that has been abandoned, he or she can ask the court to fix costs immediately, saving the need for a separate assessment of costs, and yet another court attendance. A notice of abandonment is set out in Figure 9.8.

Motions Made Without Oral Argument

The usual way to argue a motion is for counsel to appear at the hearing on the return date and to make submissions orally with references to the motion, affidavits, transcripts, or other documents. However, there are some circumstances where a motion does not require anyone to appear at a hearing.

Motion on Consent

If a motion has been made and the responding party consents to the order sought, the moving party needs to file a consent and a draft order along with the notice of motion (Rule 37.12.1(2)). A judge simply signs the order after reviewing the consent. You may wish to contact the court office to find out the procedure for filing a consent motion. Some regions ask moving parties to indicate on the motion that it is returnable during "the week of," which is followed by a date, for example, rather than on a specific day.

Unopposed Motion

If a motion has been served and the responding party signals that he or she does not oppose it, the moving party should file a notice from the responding party that the motion is unopposed, together with a draft order (Rule 37.12.1(3)). The notice should indicate that there is no opposition to the order sought. An example of the wording of such a notice is set out in Figure 9.9.

Motions Without Notice

Motions without notice may be made in writing. For example, a motion for substituted service may not require oral argument. The notice of motion should make it clear what the moving party requires, and the affidavit should provide all of the evidence and facts a master would need to grant the order.

Figure 9.8 Notice of Abandonment

Court file no. 01-CV-1234

ONTARIO
SUPERIOR COURT OF JUSTICE

BETWEEN:

ABIGAIL BOAR

Plaintiff

and

RATTLE MOTORS LTD. and FRED FLOGEM

Defendants

NOTICE OF ABANDONMENT

TAKE NOTICE that the moving party, Abigail Boar, wholly abandons the motion returnable on October 16, year 1.

October 10, year 1

Just & Coping
Barristers and Solicitors
365 Bay Street – 8701
Toronto, Ontario, M3J 4A9

I.M. Just
LSUC #12345R
tel. 416-762-1342
fax 416-762-2300

Lawyers for the Moving
Party (Plaintiff)

TO: Huey Sue
LSUC #23456T
Barrister and Solicitor
65 False Trail
Toronto, Ontario, M6Y 1Z6

tel. 416-485-6891
fax 416-485-6892

Lawyer for the Responding
Parties (Defendants)

Figure 9.9   Notice That Motion Is Unopposed

Court file no. 01-CV-1234

ONTARIO
SUPERIOR COURT OF JUSTICE

BETWEEN:

ABIGAIL BOAR

Plaintiff

and

RATTLE MOTORS LTD. and FRED FLOGEM

Defendants

NOTICE THAT MOTION IS UNOPPOSED

TAKE NOTICE that the defendant, Rattle Motors Ltd. (responding party), does not object to the order sought by the plaintiff (moving party) to permit an inspection by a lighting engineer of the defendant's premises at 1240 Bay Street, Toronto, Ontario, M4H 0K8.

October 1, year 1

Huey Sue
LSUC #23456T
Barrister and Solicitor
65 False Trail
Toronto, Ontario, M6Y 1Z6

tel. 416-485-6891
fax 416-485-6892

Lawyer for the Responding
Parties (Defendants)

TO: Just & Coping
Barristers and Solicitors
365 Bay Street – 8701
Toronto, Ontario, M3J 4A9

I.M. Just
LSUC #12345R
tel. 416-762-1342
fax 416-762-2300

Lawyers for the Moving
Party (Plaintiff)

Opposed Motions in Writing

Where a motion is opposed and the issues are not overly complicated, the moving party may propose in the notice of motion that there be no oral argument and that the documents on the motion be submitted to the court. This is attractive because it saves the cost of a hearing, but most lawyers are loath to give up the opportunity for oral argument because it gives them the chance to gauge the court's reaction to the arguments made by the opposing party, and respond to them. However, the elimination of oral argument is the way of the future for some procedures because it saves time and money. If the moving party wishes to take this route, the motion must be served 14 days before the return date. The moving party must serve a motion record *with* the notice of motion, a draft order, and a factum for a motion in writing, and at the same time file all of this with the court.

Within 10 days of being served, the responding party must serve and file a consent to the order, a notice that the order is not opposed, or a motion record with a notice that the responding party agrees to have the contested motion dealt with in writing without oral argument. In this case, the responding party must also file a factum.

If the responding party requires oral argument, he or she serves the moving party with notice that the responding party intends to make oral argument as well as file material. The moving party must then decide whether to appear and argue the motion or rely on his or her motion record and factum (Rule 37.12.1(4)).

CHAPTER SUMMARY

In this chapter, we examined the procedures for making motions, beginning with an overview of the procedure for a motion on notice. We then saw how motions without notice are dealt with, how to determine whether a motion should come before a master or a judge, and how to obtain a hearing date, noting the way in which practice directions in Toronto have complicated motion procedure there. We then examined the requirements for notices of

motion and affidavits, focusing on criteria and rules for drafting and preparing these documents. Following this discussion, we turned to the preparation of motion records and to the rules that govern time limits for serving motion materials. Finally, we examined the consequences of abandoning a motion and looked at the requirements and procedure for bringing a motion in writing without oral argument.

KEY TERMS

jurat, 208

master, 202

motion, 200

official examiner, 201

return of a motion, 200

summary proceedings, 202

NOTES

1. In a proper case, Rule 37.17 permits a motion to be brought before a proceeding has been commenced, provided that the moving party undertakes to commence proceedings promptly.

2. The confirmation report form used in Toronto is different from the Form 37A that is used in other courts in the province. See the Toronto Practice Direction.

3. A master's motion, as a matter of convention, may be brought before a judge in an emergency if no master is available.

4. In some courts this is a "motion morning" or a "motion afternoon." Once you have ascertained in which court the matter is to be heard, call the court office to find out when the motion time is.

5. When Toronto was reorganized and consolidated, the regional entity called the Municipality of Metropolitan Toronto disappeared, which left the city without a county or regional level of government.

6. While the form calls for the municipality and the county or region as a residential description, the City of Toronto, since the abolition of the former Municipality of Metropolitan Toronto, is no longer part of a county or region. The practice of describing a deponent who resides in Toronto as residing in the "City of Toronto, Province of Ontario" has developed.

7. The wording of the jurat changes slightly when it is sworn by two or more deponents, when it is sworn by a blind or illiterate person, or when it is sworn by a person who does not understand the language in which it is written. If the deponent is blind or illiterate, the jurat must indicate that the deponent had it read to him or her, that he or she understood it, and that he or she signed it or made his or her mark (usually an "X"). If the deponent does not understand the language, the jurat must indicate that a named person interpreted the affidavit and swore to translate it correctly.

8. Some practitioners include this wording as the last paragraph in affidavits used in support of a motion: "I make this affidavit in support of this motion and for no other or improper purpose."

9. *Practice Direction Regarding Filing of Judicial Decisions from Electronic Databases, and Regarding Citation of All Judicial Decisions*, October 1, 2011: http://www.ontariocourts.ca/scj/practice/practice-directions/filing. This practice direction provides detailed guidance on forming citations for electronic sources and gives direction on the use of electronic citations for all court documents.

REFERENCES

Carthy, James J., W.A. Derry Millar, and Jeff G. Cowan. *Ontario Annual Practice, 2013-2014*. Toronto: Canada Law Book, 2013.

Class Proceedings Act, 1992, SO 1992, c. 6.

Construction Lien Act, RSO 1990, c. C.30.

Courts of Justice Act, RSO 1990, c. C.43.

Judicial Review Procedure Act, RSO 1990, c. J.1.

Rules of Civil Procedure, RRO 1990, reg. 194.

Superior Court of Justice, *Practice Directions and Policies*: http://www.ontariocourts.ca/scj/practice/practice-directions.

Superior Court of Justice, *Practice Direction for Civil Applications, Motions and Other Matters in the Toronto Region* (consolidated), January 30, 2012, including links to forms: http://www.ontariocourts.ca/scj/practice/practice-directions/toronto/civil-applications.

Superior Court of Justice, *Practice Direction Regarding Filing of Judicial Decisions from Electronic Databases, and Regarding Citation of All Judicial Decisions*, September 1, 2011: http://www.ontariocourts.ca/scj/practice/practice-directions/filing.

REVIEW QUESTIONS

1. What is the purpose of motions?

2. What does the phrase "motioning the other side to death" mean, and how may the practice be prevented?

3. Explain to your client what happens when you bring a motion on his or her behalf.

4. Indicate whether a master can hear the following motions:

   a. a motion to strike out parts of a statement of claim

   b. a motion to commit a witness to jail for failure to appear at trial when summonsed

   c. a motion to vary an order made by Judge Jeffreys

   d. a motion to join parties to a lawsuit

   e. a motion for a judgment on consent where 16-year-old Rory is a party

5. Suppose Abigail's lawyer wishes to bring a "long motion" in Toronto. Is there anything special the law firm should do that it would not have to do in other courts in Ontario?

6. When can hearsay be used in an affidavit?

7. What is included in a motion record?

8. What is the purpose of a motion record?

9. a. Today is March 2. Your instructing lawyer wants to bring a motion on notice returnable March 5. Can she do it? Why?

   b. A motion is scheduled for March 16. When is the last day the lawyer could have filed a motion record?

   c. Using the date from your answer to question 9.b, when is the last day the responding party could have filed a responding party motion record?

10. Can a law firm bring a motion and then change its mind and abandon the motion without consequences?

11. Suppose your law firm wishes to make a motion in writing, rather than have an oral hearing. Can it?

DISCUSSION QUESTIONS

1. Read and respond to the following memorandum:

   To: E. Egregious, law clerk

   From: I.M. Just, lawyer

   Re: *Boar v. Rattle Motors Ltd. et al.*

   When, under Rule 32, we brought a motion for inspection of Rattle Motors' showroom, we were surprised to hear that the defendant had gutted the interior of the showroom and destroyed important evidence. I don't believe that this renovation had anything to do with marketing cars. I want to bring a motion to have the defendant found in contempt for the intentional destruction of evidence. But before I do that, I want to examine Sunil Tharper, the manager, on this issue. Write me a brief memo setting out what authority there is for doing this.

2. Read and respond to the following memorandum:

   To: E. Egregious, law clerk

   From: I.M. Just, lawyer

   Re: *Boar v. Rattle Motors Ltd. et al.*

   I have just received a report from Diedre Kuflesnout. She is an automobile engineer and a member of the Society of Automotive Engineers. She is a consultant and expert on assessing mechanical and design defects in cars. Her report indicates that leaking oil pans on new models, affecting about 12 cars in 1,000, have plagued the year 0 Super Coupe. If there were no defect, the expected rate of reported leaking oil pans would be about 1 in 2,000 cars. There is also information that the manufacturer was aware that there might be a problem and did nothing. Although we are about to start discoveries, I want to add Skunk Motorcar Company Ltd., the manufacturer of the Super Coupe, as a party defendant in this lawsuit. Find out what rule gives me the right to do this, and then draft the notice of motion and an affidavit in my name setting out the reasons why the proposed defendant should be added. Also research whether we would likely have to pay costs and what rights the other defendants might have.

Appendix I: Motion and Application Procedure in Toronto

Until recently, there was a confusing collection of practice directions for procedures on various types of motions in Toronto. All of these were designed to spread out the motion workload so that the Toronto judges and masters could handle it efficiently, but case-managed and non-case-managed motions were handled differently, as were motions before judges and masters. There were also other specialized procedures for other areas such as Estates List, Commercial List, and construction lien matters. Sifting through all this administrative chaos was an exercise in frustration for law clerks and lawyers alike.

As of January 2012, there is one procedural guide for scheduling and bringing motions and applications in Toronto, the *Practice Direction for Civil Applications, Motions and Other Matters in the Toronto Region*, which can be found online at http://www.ontariocourts.ca/scj/practice/practice-directions/toronto/civil-applications. If you are involved with Toronto motions, you should obtain a copy of this document, and any amendments, and read it carefully. You can get it from the Toronto Court Office at 393 University Avenue. You will also find this practice direction reproduced at the beginning of Rule 37 in the latest edition of the *Ontario Annual Practice*. Highlights are set out below.

1. Application of Practice Direction

The practice direction does not apply to motions or applications heard on the Commercial List, the Estates List, or under the *Class Proceedings Act*. This is consistent with those matters having a procedural system and rules that are largely separate from the rules of civil procedure that cover other proceedings.

The discussion of the practice direction that follows focuses on motions and applications. But note that it also deals with practice and procedure in respect of assignments to case management (Rule 77.05), mandatory mediation, certification of an action as ready for trial, materials for use of the court (factums), and where to get Toronto-based administrative forms relevant to the practice direction.

2. Applications and Motions—General Principles

a. A motion or application that can be argued in under two hours is considered to be "short." Anything that takes more than two hours is defined as "long." Each involves differences in procedure.

b. Whether long or short, motions before masters and before judges follow different procedures when being scheduled.

c. Short matters: Book short motions and applications before a judge or master through the Civil Scheduling Unit (except master's motions in *Construction Lien Act* cases, or within a reference).

d. Long matters before a judge: To schedule a long motion or application that must be heard by a judge rather than a master, the lawyer must appear before the Motion Scheduling Court to obtain a date. The reason for this is, as noted earlier in the chapter, that long motions would disrupt the usual motion list, and throw everything off schedule, so a special time slot with an assigned judge must be used. The lawyer must also appear before the Motion Scheduling Court to get a hearing date for the urgent hearing of a matter before a judge, motions for summary judgment before a judge, and contested requests for case management by a judge under Rule 77. These matters are by nature usually lengthy and are included on the list for that reason.

e. Long motions before a master: Most long motions are booked by filing a requisition in the Master's Administration Office. Other procedures are used for long motions in case-managed actions, *Construction Lien Act* motions, and long motions within a reference.

3. Short Motions or Applications Before a Judge or Master

a. Book these by phone, email, or delivery to:

Civil Scheduling Unit
393 University Avenue, 10th Floor
Toronto, ON M4G 1E6

Telephone: 416-327-5535

Email: jus.g.mag.csd.civilmotionsscheduling@ontario.ca

b. Exceptions: Summary judgment motions, *Construction Lien Act* motions, and motions within a reference.

c. Consult and confer: As noted earlier in the chapter, because all material must be filed well before the motion date, the parties need to know what the motion date is at the beginning of the process. So, when bringing a motion, confer with the other side to try to agree on a date. It is a good idea to have several alternative dates agreed to far enough in advance that each party can serve its material on the other, conduct cross-examinations on affidavits, and have some assurance that a hearing date set far enough in advance will be available. Parties are expected to give realistic estimates of the time required for oral argument.

d. Complete a Requisition to Schedule Short Motion or Application (before a Judge or Master) form. Send the requisition via email to the Civil Scheduling Unit. See Figure 9.10.

e. Construction lien and other special motions before masters: Short motions in construction lien cases are booked through the Masters Construction Lien and Reference Office in Toronto at 393 University Avenue on the 6th floor or by phone at 416-327-5481. Short motions and hearings for directions within a reference are booked with the registrar of the master assigned to conduct the reference.

Figure 9.10   Requisition to Schedule Short Motion or Application (Before a Judge or Master)

SUPERIOR COURT OF JUSTICE **CIVIL SCHEDULING UNIT** **REQUISITION TO SCHEDULE SHORT MOTION OR APPLICATION**	393 University Avenue, 10th Fl. Toronto ON M5G 1E6 Telephone: (416) 327-5535 Fax: (416) 327-9470 E-mail: jus.g.mag.csd.civilmotionsscheduling@ontario.ca

☒ **Requisition to Schedule Short Motion or Application (before a Judge or Master)**

** Please return this completed form to the civil scheduling unit, 10th floor, 393 University Avenue by fax or e-mail to: jus.g.mag.csd.civilmotionsscheduling@ontario.ca

Court File Number: 01-CV-1234

Short Title: Boar v. Rattle Motors et al.

Moving Party Is (Name): ☒ **Plaintiff** Abigail Boar ☐ **Defendant** _____ ☐ **Other** _____

This Case Is Under: ☐ **Case Management** ☐ **Simplified Procedure** ☒ **Ordinary Procedure**

Motion Manner: ☐ **On Consent** ☒ **Opposed** ☐ **Unopposed** ☐ **Exparte**

1. Estimated time for oral argument by all parties:	1.4 hours
2. Nature of the action or application (e.g., personal injury, specific tort, contract or other case type identified on Form 14F):	personal injury
3. Rule(s) or statutory provisions under which the motion / application is brought:	rule 32.01
4. May the motion be heard by a master or must it be heard by a judge?	master
5. Whether a particular judge or master is seized of all motions in the proceeding or of the particular motion?	n /a
6. If the proceeding is governed by the Simplified Procedure Rule (Rule 76), does the motion concern undertakings given or refusals made on examination for discovery?	n/a
7. Is the motion seeking summary judgment?	no
8. Is the application or motion urgent?	no
9. Is any party self-represented?	no
10. Is this proceeding under case management?	no
11. Does the motion or application require a bilingual Judge or Master?	no
12. What are the requested date(s) that you would like to schedule the motion on?	yr 1-03-12 yr 1-03-20 yr 1-04-17

Name of Party/Lawyer Scheduling the Motion: I.M. Just, Just & Coping, Barristers and Solicitors
_____
Name and Firm (please type or print clearly)

yr 1-01-15
_____   Tel. 416-762-1342, Fax 416-762-2300, imjust@isp.on.ca
Date   _____
                                                          Telephone Number, Fax Number and Email Address

Name of Party/Lawyer Responding to Motion: Huey Sue, Barrister and Solicitor
_____
Name and Firm (please type or print clearly)

Tel. 416-485-6891, Fax 416-485-6892, hsue@barsol.on.ca
_____
Telephone Number, Fax Number and Email Address

4. Matters Before a Judge—Motion Scheduling Court

If you have a long motion or application or an urgent motion or application or a motion for summary judgment before a judge, counsel must appear before the Motion Scheduling Court to obtain a motion date. To book an attendance date before Motion Scheduling Court you must email a completed Requisition to Attend Motion Scheduling Court Before a Judge form to motionsschedulingcourt@ontario.ca. See Figure 9.11.

Motion Scheduling Court information on location, start times, and contact information can be found in the table at the end of this appendix.

Prior to attending Motion Scheduling Court, the parties must confer and try to establish an agreed timetable to complete all necessary procedures prior to the hearing. The timetable must be presented to the judge for approval at the scheduling hearing. There is no special form for the timetable.

5. Matters Before Masters

a. Long motions: In order to schedule a long motion before a master you need to file a Requisition to Schedule Appearance Long Motion Dates in the Masters Administration Office in Toronto at 393 University Avenue on the 6th floor, or fax the form to 416-326-5416, or email it to Civil.Masters .Long.Motions@ontario.ca. A master will then be assigned to hear the motion.

The requisition form is set out in Figure 9.12.

b. Other master's motions: If the motion is in a case-managed proceeding, a request for a long motion may be sent directly to the registrar for the particular master assigned to the case-managed proceeding. A requisition form is not necessary. A request for a long motion in a construction lien proceeding should be sent to the Masters Construction Lien and Reference Office.

All long motions to be heard by a master require a telephone case conference via a telephone conference call with the master to be hearing the case in order to determine the length of the hearing, establish a timetable to complete remaining steps, and set a hearing date.

c. *Ex parte* motion before a master: A motion made without notice or on consent may be "walked in" to the Masters' *Ex-Parte* Motions Court any day that a master has been assigned to the court. No appointment is necessary. If the motion must be heard before the next *ex parte* master's court sitting, the Civil Scheduling Unit will send you before the Duty Master (a master who is not scheduled to hear matters that day, but who can be made available) who will determine whether the matter is urgent, and either hear the motion or send it to another master. *Ex parte* motions made without notice and consent motions in construction lien actions are heard daily from 9:30 to 10:00 a.m., prior to the start of the day for scheduled motions.

Note that there are special procedures for masters' motions in class proceedings and Commercial List and Estates List matters that are governed by other practice directions.

Figure 9.11   Requisition to Attend Motion Scheduling Court Before a Judge

SUPERIOR COURT OF JUSTICE **CIVIL SCHEDULING UNIT** **REQUISITION TO ATTEND MOTION SCHEDULING COURT**	393 University Avenue, 10th Fl. Toronto ON M5G 1E6 Telephone: (416) 327-5535 Fax: (416) 327-9470 E-mail: motionsschedulingcourt@ontario.ca

☒ **Requisition to Attend Motion Scheduling Court before a Judge to Schedule (select one of the following):**

☐ Urgent Hearing ☒ Long Motion or Application ☐ Summary Judgment Motion ☐ Request for Case Management

** To book a date through Motion Scheduling Court, please return this completed form by e-mail to:
motionsschedulingcourt@ontario.ca

Court File Number: 01-CV-1234

Short Title: Boar v. Rattle Motors et al.

Moving Party Is (Name): ☒ **Plaintiff** Abigail Boar ☐ **Defendant** _____ ☐ **Other** _____

This Case Is Under: ☐ **Case Management** ☐ **Simplified Procedure** ☒ **Ordinary Procedure**

1. Estimated time for oral argument by all parties:	2.5 hours
2. Nature of the action or application (e.g., personal injury, specific tort, contract or other case type identified on Form 14F):	personal injury
3. Rule(s) or statutory provisions under which the motion / application is brought:	rule 34.15(2)
4. May the motion be heard by a master or must it be heard by a judge?	judge
5. Whether a particular judge or master is seized of all motions in the proceeding or of the particular motion?	n/a
6. If the proceeding is governed by the Simplified Procedure Rule (Rule 76), does the motion concern undertakings given or refusals made on examination for discovery?	n/a
7. Is the motion seeking summary judgment?	no
8. Is the application or motion urgent?	no
9. Is any party self-represented?	no
10. Is this proceeding under case management?	no
11. Does the motion or application require a bilingual Judge or Master?	no

Name of Party/Lawyer Scheduling the Motion: I.M. Just, Just & Coping, Barristers and Solicitors

Name and Firm (please type or print clearly)

yr 1-01-02 _____   Tel. 416-762-1342, Fax 416-762-2300, imjust@isp.on.ca

Date   Telephone Number, Fax Number and Email Address

Name of Party/Lawyer Responding to Motion: Huey Sue, Barrister and Solicitor

Name and Firm (please type or print clearly)

Tel. 416-485-6891, Fax 416-485-6892, hsue@barsol.on.ca

Telephone Number, Fax Number and Email Address

Figure 9.12 Requisition to Schedule Appearance Long Motion Dates (Over 2 Hours Before a Master)

SUPERIOR COURT OF JUSTICE **MASTER'S ADMINISTRATION OFFICE** **REQUISITION TO SCHEDULE LONG MOTION**	393 University Avenue, 6th Fl. Toronto ON M5G 1E6 Telephone: (416) 327-0506 Fax: (416) 327-6405 E-mail: Masters.LongMotions@ontario.ca

Requisition to Schedule Appearance Long Motion Dates (Over 2 Hours Before A Master)

** Please fill in this form so that we may be better able to assist you with scheduling your motion or application date. Once completed, please fax the form to 416-327-6405 or hand deliver to the administrative master's secretary on the 6th floor at 393 University Avenue.

Court File Number: 01-CV-1234

Short Title: Boar v. Rattle Motors et al.

The Moving Party Is (Name): ☒ **Plaintiff** Abigail Boar ☐ **Defendant** _____ ☐ **Other** _____

This Case Is Under: ☐ **Case Management** ☐ **Simplified Rules** ☒ **Non-Case Management**

Jurisdiction of Motion: n/a
☒ Traditional Master ☐ Case Management Master   _____
                                              Name of Managing Master

Please Check If This is a: ☒ **New Motion**   ☐ **Return of Motion**

Estimated Duration (Including Reply): __2.3 hours_____
Motion Type: if more than one of the following sought, please indicate the most applicable.

☐ Amend Pleadings	☐ Set Aside Registrar's Dismissal
☐ Dismiss Action	☐ Extension of Time
☐ Judgment	☐ Particulars of Pleadings
☐ Stay of Proceedings	☐ Security for Costs
☐ Strike Pleadings	☐ Remove Solicitor of Record
☐ Set Aside Default Judgment	☐ Refuse/Undertake at Discovery
☐ Summary Judgment	☒ Motion Other inspection of property
	Describe briefly

***Once a Master has been assigned, you will be notified by fax. The moving party must obtain a case conference with a Master to establish a timetable and set a hearing date. If the matter is case managed and a managing Master has been assigned, please contact the Master's registrar to schedule a case conference to set the special appointment date.

Name of Party/Lawyer Scheduling the Motion: I.M. Just, Just & Coping, Barristers and Solicitors
                                        _____
                                        Name and Firm (please type or print clearly)

yr 1-01-03   **Tel. 416-762-1342, Fax 416-762-2300, imjust@isp.on.ca**
_____   _____
Date   Telephone Number, Fax Number and Email Address

Name of Party/Lawyer Responding to Motion: **Huey Sue, Barrister and Solicitor**
                                        _____
                                        Name and Firm (please type or print clearly)

                                        Tel. 416-485-6891, Fax 416-485-6892, hsue@barsol.on.ca
                                        _____
                                        Telephone Number, Fax Number and Email Address

6. Motions That Must Be Brought Before a Master

Except for special motions as noted above, all motions, except those directed to a judge under Rule 37.02(2), must be made to a master, and the notice of motion must be made to "the court" rather than to a judge. Judges may and probably will refuse to hear a master's motion.

7. Motions in Writing

Unless otherwise directed by a master or judge, motions in writing should be filed in the Civil Intake Office in Toronto at 393 University Avenue on the 10th floor. These need not be scheduled for a hearing as no lawyer appears on them to make oral submissions. If a motion in writing concerns a reference or construction lien matter, it should be filed at the Construction Lien and Reference Office on the 6th floor at 393 University Avenue.

8. Confirmation of Motions and Applications

As noted earlier in this chapter, under Rule 37.10.1, the moving party must consult with the responding party and determine the amount of time required by both sides to argue the motion and then file a confirmation report with the registrar no later than 2 p.m., three days prior to the hearing date. The Toronto version of the form is different from the confirmation report form filed in other counties on motions and applications. A copy of the form to be used in Toronto can be found in the *Ontario Annual Practice* table of cases and forms volume following the standard confirmation report, Form 37B. A sample is set out here in Figure 9.13.

9. Adjournments of Motions and Applications

Short motions and applications: Once a date has been set, you may adjourn a short motion or application on any two occasions by contacting the Civil Scheduling Unit or the Construction Lien and Reference Office, as the case may be.

Long motions and applications: To adjourn an application or a long motion before a judge, counsel must appear in Motion Scheduling Court. If a long motion is before a master, you must request a case conference before the master to adjourn the matter, well before the hearing date.

It is important to remember that if a matter has been adjourned and set down for a new date, the motion material may be returned to the court file or sent to storage. It is counsel's responsibility to ensure that motion materials returned to the court file are pulled and returned to staff in the court office at least one week prior to the new hearing date.

Figure 9.13   Confirmation Form for all Judges/Masters

SUPERIOR COURT OF JUSTICE **CIVIL SCHEDULING UNIT** **CONFIRMATION FORM**	393 University Avenue, 10th Fl. Toronto ON M5G 1E6 Telephone: (416) 327-5292 Fax: (416) 327-5484 Email: jus.g.mag.csd.civilmotionsconfirmation@ontario.ca

Confirmation Form for all Judges/Masters
Civil Motions/Applications

Court File Number: 01-CV-1234

Short Title: Boar v. Rattle Motors Ltd. et al.

Jurisdiction of Motion:

☐ Judge ☒ Traditional Master ☐ Case Management Master   _____
                                                                                Name of Managing Master

I, I.M. Just, counsel for the moving party/applicant confirm:

☒ I have discussed with Huey Sue, opposing counsel/party, the matter referred to above and confirm,

Or

☐ I have been unable to confirm with opposing counsel/party because _____,

that the motion/application listed to be heard on <u>Friday</u> the 4 day of <u>October</u>, 2013 is:

Tick One Box Only:

☐ Withdrawn on Consent   ☐ Consented to   ☐ Unopposed, All Other Issues   ☐ Opposed, Cost Issue Only

☐ Adjourned on Consent to: _____ (Date Booked With Scheduling Unit)

☐ Opposed Adjournment to be Requested By: _____

☒ Opposed on issues as set out in the Notice of Motion/Motion Form

☐ Opposed Only on the Following Issues: _____.

Time Estimate Required: 1 Hours 25 Minutes

Will any party be self-represented at the hearing?   ☐ Yes ☒ No

☒ **The following materials (moving and responding) have been filed and will be relied upon for the hearing of this matter:**

Or

☐ **Amended motion/application materials (please indicate which document has been amended from a previously filed one):**

☒ Applicant's Motion or Application Record	☐ Respondent's Motion or Application Record
☒ Applicant's Factum	☒ Respondent's Factum
☒ Applicant's Brief of Authorities	☒ Respondent's Brief of Authorities
☐ Other (Please specify): _____	☐ Other (Please specify): _____

I.M. Just, Just & Coping, Barristers and Solicitors
Solicitor for Moving Party (please type or print clearly)

<u>2013-09-06</u>   **Tel. 416-762-1342, Fax 416-762-2300, imjust@isp.on.ca**
Date   Telephone Number, Fax Number and Email Address

Note:

☐ Confirmation of motion must be faxed or e-mailed by 2:00 p.m. three days prior to the scheduled date of hearing.
☐ If confirmation is not received by the scheduling unit, the scheduled motion/application will be noted as abandoned.
☐ This form must be attached to the materials being filed and all materials to be relied on at hearing must be filed in one complete
   package within the required timelines.
☐ No late materials will be accepted by the court.
☐ This form should be copied to opposing counsel/party.

10. Factums and Books of Authorities

Factums are required for all applications and all long motions, except motions that concern undertakings and refusals on discovery, which turn usually on factual arguments where a factum would add little. Factums are highly recommended for all other motions, including short ones.

Unless the court has given leave to do so, a factum should not be more than 30 pages, and parties are encouraged to file electronic copies on a CD (there is no reference to the use of USB memory sticks—yet), along with hard copy. The CD should be labelled with the court name, file number, return date of the motion, and case name.

Cases in books of authorities should be copied on both sides of a page to reduce document volume, and electronic copies of books of authorities are encouraged.

Toronto Long and Short Motion and Application Information: Contacts and Checklist

Location	Days	Contact Name(s) and Number(s)	Long Motions	Short Motions	Other Information
361 University Ave., 330 University Ave., 393 University Ave., and 130 Queen St. West (Osgoode Hall)	Every day Start Time: 10:00 a.m.	Civil Scheduling Unit 393 University Avenue, 10th Fl. Toronto, Ontario, M5G 1E6 Tel: 416-327-5535 Fax: 416-327-9470 Email: jus.g.mag.csd .civilmotionsscheduling@ ontario.ca		Under 2 hours	No appearance in Motion Scheduling Court is required for short motions; parties may continue to book their short motion through the Civil Scheduling Unit. Practice Directions and Policies: http://www.ontariocourts.ca/scj/ practice/practice-directions
Motion Scheduling Court: 393 University Ave., 8th floor Court Room 801	Every day except Thursday Start Time: 9:30 a.m.	Civil Scheduling Unit 393 University Avenue, 10th Fl. Toronto, Ontario, M5G 1E6 Tel: 4160327-5535 Fax: 416-327-9470 Email: MotionsSchedulingCourt @ontario.ca	Urgent and long motions (except Summary Judgment), and contested requests for case management		Long Motions are considered anything over 2 hours to argue. Practice Directions and Administrative Advisories: http://www.ontario-courts.ca/scj/en/notices A requisition to attend Motion Scheduling Court must be completed. Download a Requisition to Attend Motion Scheduling Court before a Judge (Word): http://www .ontariocourts.ca/scj/practice/ practice-directions/toronto/ civil-applications
Motion Scheduling Court: 393 University Ave., 8th floor Court Room TBA	Tuesday and Friday Start Time: 9:30 a.m.	Civil Scheduling Unit 393 University Avenue, 10th Fl. Toronto, Ontario, M5G 1E6 Tel: 416-327-5535 Fax: 416-327-9470 Email: MotionsScheduling Court@ontario.ca	All summary judgment motions	All summary judgment motions	All summary judgment motions A Requisition to attend Motion Scheduling Court: Summary Judgment must be completed. Requisition to Attend Motion Scheduling Court before a Judge to Schedule (Word): http://www. ontariocourts.ca/scj/practice/ practice-directions/toronto/ civil-applications

Source: Adapted from Superior Court of Justice, Practice and Procedure, Practice Directions and Procedure, Practice Directions and Policies, Civil and Family Motions Procedures, Civil Motions Information— Toronto: http://www.ontariocourts.ca/scj/practice/practice-directions/civil-family/civil-t.

Appendix II: Special Motions

The following are some examples of special motions that are commonly encountered in a civil practice with special procedural or substantive requirements.

Interlocutory Injunctions and Mandatory Orders: Rule 40 and Section 101(2) of the Courts of Justice Act

Interlocutory injunctions and mandatory orders are used where the moving party wishes to stop the respondent from engaging in acts that continue to cause harm to the moving party that may not be adequately remedied by damages. The injunction prohibits or enjoins the respondent from continuing to persist in doing the acts complained of. A mandatory order is a positive injunction—it directs a party to perform specified actions. Often this motion, by stopping objectionable conduct, will bring the case to an end in a settlement—the real goal of the action.

The motion may be made only to a judge. The motion may be brought before a proceeding is commenced, provided that the proceeding is eventually commenced. The moving party must undertake to pay damages to the respondent for any unjustifiable harm done to the respondent as a result of the injunction. The order may be obtained without notice, but it is valid for only 10 days and may be renewed on notice to the respondent. A factum is required on this motion.

Appointment of a Receiver: Rule 41 and Section 101 of the Courts of Justice Act

A receiver is a person appointed by the court to exercise the powers granted in a receivership order to step in and stand in the shoes of the responding party in order to carry out the powers granted in the order. In commercial secured debt transactions, the creditor may apply to the court to have a receiver take over control of the debtor in order to liquidate it in an orderly way that will protect the creditor's investment where the debtor's finances and operations are in chaos. In some circumstances, a receiver-manager may also be appointed to take control of and run the debtor's business.

The motion may be brought prior to commencement of proceedings, and must be brought before a judge. The order must name the receiver and specify the security that the moving party is to provide for any damages that result from the receivership. If the receiver is also a manager, it must set out the management powers. The responding party or any party may require a reference to examine the conduct of the receiver, and a receiver may apply for direction from a judge on a motion.

Certificate of Pending Litigation: Rule 42 and Section 103 of the Courts of Justice Act

A certificate of pending litigation is available when the moving party claims an interest in land in a civil action. Once a certificate has been issued, it may be registered on title; this provides notice to others that the moving party has an interest in the land as a result of the litigation, which may cause others to exercise caution in dealing with the land's current owners.

Certificates of pending litigation may be found on title, for example, where there is litigation over the dissolution of a partnership (or other type of business) where the partners' interests in land are in dispute.

To bring this motion, you must claim leave to obtain a certificate of pending litigation in your action or application, and then bring the motion. Factums are required on any motion to discharge a certificate of pending litigation.

Interpleader Order: Rule 43

An interpleader order is one in which the court gives directions to a person in possession of personal property where others are making claims with respect to that property. A trustee, for example, may bring an interpleader motion where two beneficiaries are claiming competing interests in the same property under Rule 43.02(1). A sheriff or other person may also do so if holding property as a result of a seizure under a writ of execution where there are competing claims, usually between creditors and a debtor, under Rule 43.02(2). There are different requirements under each branch of Rule 43.02 for an order, and this should be reflected in the contents of the affidavit in support of the motion. The purpose of the motion is for the interpleading person to obtain court directions as to what should be done with the property that that person is holding and, by doing so, avoid being sued by one of the disputants for mishandling the property.

Where there are substantive issues of law involved, the motion should be brought before a judge. If the matter is under Rule 43.02(1), and no proceeding has been commenced, the person seeking an interpleader order shall commence an application. Otherwise, the person proceeds by motion.

Interim Recovery of Personal Property Order: Rule 44

An interim order for recovery of personal property directs the sheriff to seize and hold personal property until further order of the court where there is a dispute about property ownership. The court may direct that the property remain with one party or the other, subject to undertakings to pay damages or to post security for the prompt return of the property. The idea behind this order is that where there is a dispute over possession of the property, the property will be safe and secure until the court can hear and decide the issues.

The motion may be made without notice if a party is taking steps that will permanently prevent recovery of the property. In the action or proceeding there must be a claim to recover personal property before the motion may be brought. If an order is made without notice, the sheriff must hold the property for 10 days after service of the order so that the defendant may take steps to recover the property. Otherwise, the court may order the sheriff to take possession of the property, or leave it with the defendant, subject to posting of security and undertaking to immediately return the property if ordered to do so. If the defendant is blocking the sheriff in an attempt to seize the property, the sheriff may seize other property belonging to the defendant that is of equivalent value.

Interim Preservation Order: Rule 45

An interim preservation order may be given not only to secure disputed property, as in the case of an order to recover property under Rule 44, but to preserve personal property that may be evidence, or to recover personal property held by another who is not a party to the proceeding. This may include the sequestration or control of a specific fund. If the property is perishable, the court may order its sale or disposal. Conditions may be imposed on the order for preservation of property. If a debtor claims that security was wrongfully seized, he may recover the security, but will have to post other security until the matter has been adjudicated.

Motion for Security for Costs: Rule 56

In some situations, a plaintiff may be obliged to post security for costs in the event that the action is dismissed, and the defendant would be likely to have difficulty enforcing an order to pay costs against a plaintiff. Those plaintiffs who

- reside outside the jurisdiction and have no assets in Ontario,
- are nominal plaintiffs with no assets,
- have previously failed to pay a judgment owed to the defendant in an earlier proceeding, or
- appear to be vexatious litigants

may be compelled to post security for costs before they can proceed further with their lawsuits.

Security for costs can only be ordered on a motion after the defence has been served. Once an order is made, the court may entertain other motions to increase security as the proceeding progresses.

Appendix III: Complete Motion Record

This appendix contains the motion record for Abigail Boar and Rattle Motors Ltd. et al., which would be prepared and filed for use at the motion hearing by the judge (or master) and counsel. You will notice that it includes the documents that we have discussed in this chapter that comprise the documentation used on a motion that a judge or master will need.

We have also included an optional cover sheet, which is used by some law firms. If you do not use a cover sheet, remember to include the contact information for the parties' law firms on the motion record index page.

Court file no. 01-CV-1234

ONTARIO
SUPERIOR COURT OF JUSTICE

BETWEEN:

ABIGAIL BOAR

Plaintiff

and

RATTLE MOTORS LTD. and FRED FLOGEM

Defendants

MOTION RECORD
Motion Returnable October 16, year 1

Just & Coping
Barristers and Solicitors
365 Bay Street – 8701
Toronto, Ontario, M3J 4A9

I.M. Just
LSUC #12345R
tel. 416-762-1342
fax 416-762-2300

Lawyers for the Moving
Party (Plaintiff)

TO: Huey Sue
LSUC #23456T
Barrister and Solicitor
65 False Trail
Toronto, Ontario, M6Y 1Z6

tel. 416-485-6891
fax 416-485-6892

Lawyer for the Responding
Parties (Defendants)

NOTE: This is a cover sheet, which may or may not be included in a motion record.

1

Court file no. 01-CV-1234

ONTARIO
SUPERIOR COURT OF JUSTICE

BETWEEN:

ABIGAIL BOAR

Plaintiff

and

RATTLE MOTORS LTD. and FRED FLOGEM

Defendants

MOTION RECORD INDEX
Motion Returnable October 16, year 1

2

Court file no. 01-CV-1234

ONTARIO
SUPERIOR COURT OF JUSTICE

BETWEEN:

ABIGAIL BOAR

Plaintiff

and

RATTLE MOTORS LTD. and FRED FLOGEM

Defendants

NOTICE OF MOTION

The plaintiff will make a motion to the court on Monday, October 16, year 1 at 10:00 a.m., or as soon after that time as the motion can be heard, at 393 University Avenue, Toronto, Ontario, M5G 1Y3.

PROPOSED METHOD OF HEARING: The motion is to be heard

- ❑ in writing under subrule 37.12.1 (1);
- ☒ in writing as an opposed motion under subrule 37.12.1 (4);
- ❑ orally.

THE MOTION IS FOR an order permitting Eldred Klump, consulting electrical engineer, to inspect the level of lighting in the automobile showroom operated by the corporate defendant at 1240 Bay Street in the City of Toronto, Province of Ontario, on such terms and at such times as the court considers just.

THE GROUNDS FOR THE MOTION ARE that there is an issue between the parties as to the adequacy of lighting in the corporate defendant's showroom, and it is necessary to determine that issue in this proceeding to carry out an inspection of the corporate defendant's premises to examine the lighting, pursuant to Rule 32 of the Rules of Civil Procedure.

3

THE FOLLOWING DOCUMENTARY EVIDENCE will be used at the hearing of the motion:

1.   Statement of claim filed January 4, year 1;

2.   Statement of defence filed January 12, year 1; and

3.   Affidavit of Eldred Klump sworn October 3, year 1.

October 16, year 1

Just & Coping
Barristers and Solicitors
365 Bay Street – 8701
Toronto, Ontario, M3J 4A9

I.M. Just
LSUC #12345R
tel. 416-762-1342
fax 416-762-2300

Lawyers for the Moving
Party (Plaintiff)

TO: Huey Sue
      LSUC #23456T
      Barrister and Solicitor
      65 False Trail
      Toronto, Ontario, M6Y 1Z6

      tel. 416-485-6891
      fax 416-485-6892

      Lawyer for the Responding
      Parties (Defendants)

RCP-E 37A (July 1, 2007)

4

Court file no. 01-CV-1234

ONTARIO
SUPERIOR COURT OF JUSTICE

BETWEEN:

ABIGAIL BOAR

Plaintiff

and

RATTLE MOTORS LTD. and FRED FLOGEM

Defendants

AFFIDAVIT OF ELDRED KLUMP

I, Eldred Klump, of the City of Brampton, in the Regional Municipality of Peel, MAKE OATH AND SAY:

1. I am a consulting electrical engineer, retained by the plaintiff, and as such have knowledge of the matters sworn to in this affidavit.

2. I am advised by I.M. Just, lawyer for the plaintiff, and I believe that there is a disagreement between the parties as to whether or not there was adequate illumination in the area where the plaintiff allegedly fell in the showroom of Rattle Motors Ltd.

3. There are Building Code and other standards for safe and adequate lighting for various areas in buildings, including showrooms.

4. It is possible to measure the amount of light at the location in question and check the measurements against known standards.

5. The information obtained from these tests would be relevant in assisting the court in making findings as to the adequacy of the lighting in question.

6. In order to properly measure the light, it is necessary for me to enter the showroom of the corporate defendant, adjust the lights in the location where the plaintiff fell as they were on the day of the accident, and take measurements of the light available.

SWORN before me at the	)
City of Brampton,	)
in the Regional Municipality of Peel,	)
on October 3, year 1.	)
I.M. Just	)
I.M. Just	)
Commissioner for Taking Affidavits	)

Eldred Klump

Eldred Klump

5

Court file no. 01-CV-1234

ONTARIO
SUPERIOR COURT OF JUSTICE

BETWEEN:

ABIGAIL BOAR

Plaintiff

and

RATTLE MOTORS LTD. and FRED FLOGEM

Defendants

AFFIDAVIT OF SUNIL THARPER

I, Sunil Tharper, president and general manager of Rattle Motors Ltd., of the City of Toronto, in the Province of Ontario, AFFIRM:

1. I have read the affidavit of Eldred Klump, sworn October 3, year 1 and filed on behalf of the plaintiff in this proceeding.

2. On or about February 1, year 1, the corporate defendant's directors decided to renovate its automobile showroom to better display the automobiles that the company sells.

3. The renovations were extensive, involving a complete gutting of the interior and replacement of flooring, ceilings, showroom windows, and offices.

4. In the course of carrying out this renovation, all of the pre-renovation lighting, including spotlights or pot lights, was removed, and new lighting was installed.

5. The new lighting is of a different type from the old lighting and is placed differently. In particular, the spotlighting now used is of the halogen type, rather than the conventional incandescent floodlight type.

6. Since the lighting fixtures and the illumination they cast are completely different from the lighting that was used at the time the plaintiff fell, the inspection proposed by the plaintiff would serve no purpose.

7. The defendants have consulted a lighting expert, Elihu Dunck, who has prepared a report in which he advises that it would now be impossible to carry out the tests and

6

inspections proposed by the plaintiff, and that the inspection would be of no assistance to the court. Now shown to me and attached hereto and marked exhibit A to this affidavit is a report dated October 5, year 1 from Elihu Dunck to the defendant's lawyer, which sets out Mr. Dunck's opinion.

SWORN before me at the	)	
City of Toronto,	)	*Sunil Tharper*
in the Province of Ontario,	)	Sunil Tharper
on October 6, year 1.	)	
Huey Sue	)	
Huey Sue	)	
Commissioner for Taking Affidavits	)	

RCP-E 4D (July 1, 2007)

Attaching
an affidavit
to an exhibit 7

Elihu Dunck, B.Eng.
143 W. Dean St.
Brampton, Ontario L6P 0A1
Tel: 905-222-1234
Email: lightsrus@dmail.ca

October 5, year 1

Sunil Tharper, Manager
Rattle Motors Ltd.
1240 Bay Street
Toronto, Ontario, M5W 2Z4

Dear Sir,

RE: LIGHTING INSPECTION—PREMISES, RATTLE MOTORS LTD.

I am an electrical engineer with a specialty in determining the adequacy of lighting in and around commercial buildings. My qualifications and background are set out in the curriculum vitae attached to this letter.

My instructions were to attend at the premises of Rattle Motors, with light meters and other instruments, and to investigate the lighting in the showroom of Rattle Motors in order to furnish an opinion on the adequacy of lighting in the floor area of the showroom in and around the automobiles on display at or about the time the customer, Abigail Boar, was injured on the premises.

I am unable to furnish an opinion as to the state of the lighting and the amount of light provided in the showroom at the relevant time, because the showroom was subsequently completely renovated. All of the lighting at the time of the alleged injury has been removed and disposed of, and it is not possible to measure or determine the extent or degree of lighting that was provided on the premises at the relevant time. The new lighting fixtures are of a new halogen type and are not comparable to the previous lighting fixtures as they were described to me.

I am therefore unable to provide an opinion on the adequacy of the lighting in the showroom at the relevant time.

Sincerely,

Elihu Dunck

Elihu Dunck, B.Eng.

This is Exhibit
A
to the affidavit of
SUNIL THARPER
sworn before me this
6th day of October, year 1

Huey Sue

Commissioner for Taking Affidavits

8

Court file no. 01-CV-1234

ONTARIO
SUPERIOR COURT OF JUSTICE

BETWEEN:

ABIGAIL BOAR

Plaintiff

and

RATTLE MOTORS LTD. and FRED FLOGEM

Defendants

STATEMENT OF CLAIM

TO THE DEFENDANTS

A LEGAL PROCEEDING HAS BEEN COMMENCED AGAINST YOU by the plaintiff. The claim made against you is set out in the following pages.

IF YOU WISH TO DEFEND THIS PROCEEDING, you or an Ontario lawyer acting for you must prepare a statement of defence in Form 18A prescribed by the Rules of Civil Procedure, serve it on the plaintiff's lawyer or, where the plaintiff does not have a lawyer, serve it on the plaintiff, and file it, with proof of service, in this court office, WITHIN TWENTY DAYS after this statement of claim is served on you, if you are served in Ontario.

If you are served in another province or territory of Canada or in the United States of America, the period for serving and filing your statement of defence is forty days. If you are served outside Canada and the United States of America, the period is sixty days.

Instead of serving and filing a statement of defence, you may serve and file a notice of intent to defend in Form 18B prescribed by the Rules of Civil Procedure. This will entitle you to ten more days within which to serve and file your statement of defence.

IF YOU FAIL TO DEFEND THIS PROCEEDING, JUDGMENT MAY BE GIVEN AGAINST YOU IN YOUR ABSENCE AND WITHOUT FURTHER NOTICE TO YOU. IF YOU WISH TO DEFEND THIS PROCEEDING BUT ARE UNABLE TO PAY LEGAL FEES, LEGAL AID MAY BE AVAILABLE TO YOU BY CONTACTING A LOCAL LEGAL AID OFFICE.

9

IF YOU PAY THE PLAINTIFF'S CLAIM, and $500.00 for costs, within the time for serving and filing your statement of defence, you may move to have this proceeding dismissed by the court. If you believe the amount claimed for costs is excessive, you may pay the plaintiff's claim and $400.00 for costs and have the costs assessed by the court.

Date: January 4, year 1

Issued by: *A.B. Smith*
Local registrar

Address of
court office: Courthouse
393 University Avenue
Toronto, Ontario, M5G 1E6

TO: Rattle Motors Ltd.
1240 Bay Street
Toronto, Ontario, M8H 0K8

AND TO: Fred Flogem
21 Cypress Boulevard
Scarborough, Ontario, M8Q 1P3

CLAIM

1. The plaintiff claims, against both defendants:

    a. general damages in the amount of $200,000;

    b. special damages in the amount of $3,649 to the date of this pleading. The full extent of special damages is not yet known, but full particulars will be furnished before the date of trial.

    c. prejudgment interest from September 14, year 0 to the date of payment or judgment pursuant to the *Courts of Justice Act*, RSO 1990, c. C.43;

    d. postjudgment interest from the date of judgment to the date of payment pursuant to the *Courts of Justice Act*, RSO 1990, c. C.43;

    e. costs of this action; and

    f. such further relief as seems just to this court.

2. The plaintiff is an individual who resides in the City of Toronto, in the Province of Ontario, and at the relevant time was a customer lawfully on the premises of the corporate defendant.

corporate (handwritten margin note)

3. The defendant Fred Flogem is an individual who resides in the City of Toronto, in the Province of Ontario, and at the relevant time was an employee of the corporate defendant.

4. The defendant Rattle Motors Ltd. is a business corporation, incorporated under the laws of Ontario with business premises in the City of Toronto, in the Province of Ontario.

5. On September 14, year 0, at about 7:30 p.m., the plaintiff entered the retail automobile premises owned and operated by the defendant Rattle Motors Ltd. at 1240 Bay Street, in the City of Toronto, in the Province of Ontario, in order to view a Super Coupe, which she was thinking of purchasing, in the showroom.

6. She was met at the door by Linda Lucre, a salesperson employed by the corporate defendant, who showed her some of the automobiles displayed on the showroom floor.

7. The plaintiff saw a Super Coupe model on the showroom floor and walked over to have a better look at it.

P.o. the physical lig. fall before question start. (handwritten margin note)

8. The Super Coupe model was in an open area of the showroom, where two of the four spotlights trained on the car were off, so that one side of the car was well illuminated while the other was not well illuminated.

9. The plaintiff walked around to the side of the car near the wall, which was in relative darkness. She walked onto a part of the floor that was covered with oil. Because of the restricted lighting, she did not see the oil, slipped on it, lost her footing, and fell.

10. As a result of the fall, she struck her head, suffered a concussion, and lost consciousness. She also fractured her right wrist and several bones in her right arm.

injuries. (handwritten margin note)

11. Following the fall, the plaintiff was hospitalized for 4 days and the plaintiff's arm was in a cast for 6 weeks; she suffered much pain and discomfort. In addition, she was required to attend for physiotherapy for 10 weeks after her cast was removed.

12. As a result of these injuries, the plaintiff suffers from pain in her arm and head as well as chronic lower back pain, and is unable to walk long distances or sit at a desk for long periods. She has limited mobility in her right arm and is unable to work at a computer keyboard for more than 10 minutes without experiencing pain. The plaintiff is right-handed and severely disadvantaged by these injuries.

13. Since she sustained these injuries, and as a result of them, the plaintiff has become far less active physically than she had been before the accident, and she is far less cheerful and gregarious than she had been. She is now quieter, more withdrawn, and has difficulty sleeping. She also suffers from depression. Before being injured, the plaintiff was an avid tennis player and a competent amateur violinist. Since sustaining the injuries, and as a result of them, she is unable to engage in either activity. She also has suffered some memory loss. In particular, she has no memory of sustaining the injuries complained of.

14. Since the plaintiff sustained these injuries, she has been unable to return to her work as a securities analyst. She returned to work for the month of March, year 1, but because of chronic pain, and difficulty using a computer which is essential to her work, she was unable to continue. She has been off work since April 1, year 1, and on long-term disability, where she remains at the time of pleading.

15. The plaintiff has suffered catastrophic and permanent injuries, and it is unlikely that she will ever be able to return to work as a securities analyst. At the time of injury, she earned $80,000 per year in this occupation. She would likely have had a lengthy career with a high level of income, had she not been injured.

16. The defendant Fred Flogem, a salesperson employed by the corporate defendant, caused the plaintiff's injuries through his negligence, for which the corporate defendant is at law responsible. The particulars of negligence are as follows:

a. He was aware that there was oil on the floor and knew or ought to have known that the oil constituted a danger to the safety of persons such as the plaintiff.

b. He knew or ought to have known that he had a duty to see that persons such as the plaintiff did not come to harm while on the premises.

c. He failed to clean up or remove the spill expeditiously, although he had the opportunity and the means to do so.

d. He turned off lighting that illuminated the area where the plaintiff fell, with the intention of making the oil spill less visible or noticeable to persons such as the plaintiff. By so doing, he negligently, or in the alternative knowingly, created a situation of danger for the plaintiff.

12

[handwritten margin notes: Could the cap- bringing a reasonably foreseeable that the area of the floor was unsafe for the plaintiff. Put/plead a general standard of care]

e. He knowingly created a situation of danger for the plaintiff by deliberately not taking steps to clean up the spill so as to hide a defect in the automobile from the plaintiff and other customers.

17. The defendant Flogem was an employee of the corporate defendant, for whose acts of negligence the corporate defendant is vicariously liable.

18. The corporate defendant is also directly responsible for the injuries sustained by the plaintiff as a result of its negligence, the particulars of which are as follows:

a. It failed to take such care as was reasonable to see that the plaintiff entering the corporate defendant's showroom would be reasonably safe while on the property. The plaintiff pleads and relies on the *Occupiers' Liability Act,* RSO 1990, c. O.2.

b. It failed to instruct its employees, including the individual defendant, in maintaining safe premises.

c. It knew or ought to have known that the floor area where the plaintiff fell was unsafe for the plaintiff.

d. It failed to maintain a system of inspection to ensure that the showroom was safe for persons on the premises, including the plaintiff.

e. In the alternative, it knowingly permitted the area where the plaintiff fell to remain in an unsafe condition so as not to attract customer attention to a defect in the car it was selling.

Date of issue: January 4, year 1

Just & Coping
Barristers and Solicitors
365 Bay Street – 8701
Toronto, Ontario, M3J 4A9

I.M. Just
LSUC #12345R
tel. 416-762-1342
fax 416-762-2300

Lawyers for the Plaintiff

13

Court file no. 01-CV-1234

ONTARIO
SUPERIOR COURT OF JUSTICE

BETWEEN:

ABIGAIL BOAR

Plaintiff

and

RATTLE MOTORS LTD. and FRED FLOGEM

Defendants

STATEMENT OF DEFENCE

1. The defendants admit the allegations contained in paragraphs 1, 2, 3, and 4 of the statement of claim.

2. The defendants deny the allegations contained in paragraphs 5, 6, 7, 8, 9, 10, 11, 12, 13, 14, 15, 16, 17, and 18 of the statement of claim.

3. The plaintiff entered the corporate defendant's premises at about 7:30 p.m. on September 14, year 0. She indicated to Linda Lucre, a salesperson on the showroom floor at that time, that she was interested in purchasing a Super Coupe.

4. Lucre showed the plaintiff several automobile models. Then the plaintiff walked over, on her own, to look at another model. She walked around the car and fell.

5. The defendants admit that there was a small pool of oil on one side of the car but claim that it was easily visible to any reasonably prudent person who could have avoided it without difficulty.

6. The defendants admit that two of the four spotlights were off but deny that the area was not well illuminated. The defendants state that the area was well and clearly illuminated. Any hazard, if there was one, which is specifically denied, could easily be seen and avoided.

7. The defendants admit that the plaintiff fell and appeared to lose consciousness momentarily. She also appeared to injure her lower right arm in the fall.

8. The defendants state that the plaintiff, before coming to the corporate defendant's place of business, had consumed two glasses of wine and that she was intoxicated when she entered the defendant's premises.

14

[handwritten: intoxicatn]

9. The plaintiff fell solely as a result of her intoxication. Any injuries she sustained were solely the result of her own intoxicated state and not the result of any acts of the defendants.

10. With respect to paragraphs 10, 11, 12, 13, 14, and 15 of the statement of claim, the defendants deny that the plaintiff suffered such injuries as described. Further or in the alternative, the defendants state that the plaintiff has exaggerated both the extent of her injuries and the consequences of them.

11. With respect to the plaintiff's allegation that she cannot return to work, the defendants state that the plaintiff is exaggerating her injuries and that she is a malingerer. In the alternative, the defendants state that the plaintiff has failed to mitigate her damages.

[handwritten: reasonable in contravning p[ar]gr[aph] 11.]

12. With respect to the allegations of negligence in paragraph 16, the defendant Flogem states that he knew there was oil on the floor but that it was contained and did not constitute a danger to any reasonably prudent person. The defendant Flogem admits that he turned off two of the four spotlights, but he specifically denies that he created a situation of danger for the plaintiff because the area in question remained well illuminated and safe for a reasonably prudent person.

13. The defendants therefore request that this action be dismissed with costs.

January 12, year 1

Huey Sue
LSUC #23456T
Barrister and Solicitor
65 False Trail
Toronto, Ontario, M6Y 1Z6

tel. 416-485-6891
fax 416-485-6892

Lawyer for the Defendants

TO: Just & Coping
Barristers and Solicitors
365 Bay Street – 8701
Toronto, Ontario, M3J 4A9

I.M. Just
LSUC #12345R
tel. 416-762-1342
fax 416-762-2300

Lawyers for the Plaintiff

Default Judgment 10

Introduction

Once you have served the plaintiff's statement of claim, the defendant must serve you with a statement of defence within the time provided for in the Rules. If you receive no statement of defence, the defendant is deemed to have admitted the truth of the facts in the statement of claim and admitted liability. The plaintiff may then obtain a judgment against the defendant in default of a defence. The plaintiff may also obtain a default judgment if a defence was delivered but was struck out without leave to file another (Rule 19.01(2)). Where there are several defendants and one has not delivered a defence, and the plaintiff has not noted that defendant in default, a defendant who has delivered a defence can require the registrar to order the plaintiff to note the non-filing defendant in default (Rule 19.01(3)).

If a claim is a liquidated amount (an easily calculated amount that can be determined by using a simple, objective formula), there is a quick and straightforward administrative process for obtaining a judgment for the amount due—judgment may be signed before the registrar (in practice, a clerk in the court office) at the counter, without having to appear before a judge and without having to schedule a separate hearing, simply by filing the forms discussed in this chapter. Most debt collection cases are liquidated claims—for example, claims for payment for goods sold or services rendered, or claims for repayment of loans.

Signing default judgment before the registrar is also available under Rule 19.04(1) on a claim to recover possession of land or personal property, or on the foreclosure, sale, or redemption of a mortgage. In each of these cases, as with a liquidated claim, there is no real discretion to be exercised, no evidence of damages to assess, that would require a judge's attention.

Abigail's claim against Fred and Rattle Motors Ltd., however, is not liquidated. Her claim for general damages cannot be calculated by using a simple, objective formula. Even her special damages, which can be calculated that way, are still accruing, so we do not know what they will total. In this kind of case, even if the defendant is deemed to have admitted the truth of the facts in the statement of claim and to have admitted liability, the plaintiff is obliged to prove the monetary value of damages on a motion to a judge. Evidence may be given by affidavit or orally in a hearing if the court requires it. An affidavit, usually the plaintiff's, may detail injuries, pain, treatment, and post-injury disabilities by way of general damages; it can also provide details of special damages. Other witnesses' affidavits provide further evidence that supports the claim for damages.

In this chapter, we examine both the summary method of signing default judgment for liquidated damages before the registrar and the method whereby a judge assesses general damages.

Default Judgment for a Liquidated Demand

To obtain or sign default judgment on behalf of a plaintiff, you must prepare certain documents and file them with the registrar of the Superior Court (this person will be a clerk at the public counter in the court office of the region where the action is commenced). If the documents are properly prepared and in order, the clerk acts on the registrar's behalf to sign judgment for the full amount of the claim, prejudgment interest, and costs. Be sure that your claim is accurately stated and that your calculations are precise, because it is embarrassing and time-consuming to amend a judgment later to correct an error.

Consider another of Abigail's claims. Hieronymus Bloggs owes Abigail Boar $38,182.79 for financial analysis services provided by Abigail. Payment should have been made on July 28, year 0, and interest runs on overdue amounts at the rate of 12 percent per annum. On September 26, year 0, I.M. Just issued a claim on Abigail's behalf and served it on Hieronymus Bloggs. No statement of defence was received, and I.M. Just intends to sign default judgment on Abigail's behalf on October 17, year 0. The cost of issuing a claim is $181.00. You paid a process server $41.00 to serve the claim and provide you with an affidavit of service. You have receipts to attach to the bill of costs for all disbursements. HST is chargeable on all fees and on disbursements that are services, such as photocopies, fax, postage, and service of pleadings, at 13 percent. HST is not chargeable on government fees, such as the $181.00 paid to issue the statement of claim.

Forms Required to Sign Default Judgment

The following are the forms required to sign default judgment:

- an affidavit of service, proving service of the statement of claim, and the original statement of claim;
- a requisition for default judgment, noting the defendant in default;
- a bill of costs (the original and two copies) to provide a basis for fixing the amount of costs;[1]
- a draft judgment (the original and two copies);
- a cheque payable to the Minister of Finance for filing for default judgment;
- a requisition for a writ of seizure and sale (optional);
- a writ of seizure and sale (the original and two copies) (optional); and
- a cheque, payable to the Minister of Finance, to issue the writ of seizure and sale.

The procedure for signing default judgment is set out in Rule 19.04. The defendant may be noted in default separately by filing a requisition to note the defendant in default. But it saves some time and paper to note the defendant in default as part of the requisition for default judgment. The effect of noting the defendant in default is to note pleadings closed, which bars the late filing of a statement of defence.

The requisition for default judgment requires you to state that the claim is liquidated or otherwise comes within the class of claims for which you may sign default judgment. You also show on this form how much is owing, less payments made by the debtor, if any.

Procedure for Signing Judgment

Set out below is a step-by-step guide to signing default judgment.

Prepare a Requisition for Default Judgment

You will need the original statement of claim attached to the process server's affidavit of service so that the clerk can see when and where the claim was served, and satisfy himself or herself that the time for filing the defence has elapsed. Remember that the time runs from the time of service, not from the time the claim was issued. Figure 10.1 at the end of the chapter shows a completed requisition for a default judgment.

1. On the requisition itself, after the words "TO THE LOCAL REGISTRAR AT," type in the name of the municipality where the court office is located (in our example it is Toronto). Below this, type "I REQUIRE you to note the defendant (*name*) in default in this action and that pleadings be noted closed against the defendant on the ground that the defendant has failed to file a statement of defence within the time provided for in the *Rules of Civil Procedure*."

2. Check off the basis for signing default judgment.

3. Indicate whether any payments have been made on account with respect to the claim. If some payments have been made, complete part A; if none have been made, complete part B.

4. If some payments have been made, indicate the principal amount claimed, without interest. Then show the payment on account, and show how much of that payment is allocated to interest and how much to principal. At common law, amounts received are applied first to outstanding interest. If there is any amount remaining, it is applied to outstanding principal. After allocating the payment received, indicate the principal amount outstanding. This is "total A" on the form.

5. With respect to the calculation of prejudgment interest, indicate the date on which the claim was issued and the date on which the cause of action arose. This is the date from which prejudgment interest is claimed. This allows the clerk (and you) to determine how many days of interest your client is entitled to, and what the appropriate rate is if interest is calculated under the prejudgment interest provisions of the *Courts of Justice Act*. If you have not previously learned how to apply the prejudgment and postjudgment interest rules, see Chapter 17.

6. Show how the prejudgment interest is calculated. Calculate simple interest unless you have a contractual right to compound interest. Calculate interest on the principal amount outstanding from the date of the last payment previously identified in the form. To do this, count the number of days from the date of the last payment to the date on which judgment is to be signed (the last "end date" in the form). Then multiply that number by the annual rate of interest, multiply that result by the principal amount owing, and divide by 365. This is "total B" on the form.

7. From the calculations in 6 above, enter total B, and from the calculations in 4 above, enter total A in order to fill in the total amount for which to sign judgment.

8. If no payment was received, then complete part B, indicating amount A, the total amount of the claim less interest. Provide the interest data, including the date on which the claim arose and was issued. Then show your interest calculations, using simple interest unless you have a contractual right to compound interest and have claimed this in your statement of claim. Count the number of days from the date the cause of action arose to the date of judgment, and do the calculations as described previously for part A (part payments received). Add the sum claimed (total A) to the interest claimed (total B) to determine the amount for which the judgment is to be signed.

9. Complete part C, "Postjudgment interest and costs." Insert the rate of post-judgment interest that applies (this is either a rate contractually agreed on between the parties or the rate set by statute for the quarter in which the judgment is signed), and indicate the basis for claiming interest. Then check off whether you wish the registrar to fix costs or have the costs assessed later. The usual practice is to have the registrar fix the costs based on your bill of costs, which you prepare in accordance with the Rules. This is much quicker and less expensive than coming back at a later date to have the costs assessed. One might ask to have a bill of costs assessed if costs to the plain-tiff had been much higher than is usually the case in a default judgment sit-uation. In this situation, having costs assessed might be worth the time and expense because costs are fixed in accordance with flat rates based on a "normal" proceeding.

Prepare a Bill of Costs

See Figure 10.2 at the end of the chapter for Abigail's bill of costs (Form 57A). In 2005, amendments to the Rules established a procedure for fixing costs at the end of a hearing, rather than referring them for an assessment in a separate proceeding. These procedures are discussed in detail in Chapter 18, the chapter on costs. The general theory is that fixing costs is quicker and cheaper than assessing them, and Rule 19.04(2)(e) clearly permits a plaintiff to use either method.

Generally, however, plaintiffs signing default judgment opt to have the registrar fix costs when judgment is signed by the registrar. Normally this would require the plaintiff to file a costs outline to fix costs. But under Rule 58.13 the registrar may fix costs using a bill of costs with receipts for disbursements attached, if the overall costs are low: the lawyer's fees must be $2,000.00 or less, not including HST, for a costs award of no more than $750.00 plus disbursements and HST. For most default judgments, where the plaintiff has only served and filed a statement of claim, the legal fees will be low enough so that this process is available and worthwhile. But if the case is complex, with multiple parties and/or multiple causes of action, you may wish to ask the registrar to either fix costs, using the more detailed costs outline, or refer costs for assessment. In the example we are discussing here, we will assume that your instructions are to have the registrar fix costs, using a bill of costs under the process described in Rule 58.13.

partial indemnity
usual order for costs, based on a cost grid that establishes hourly rates for tariff items listed in the grid; provides less than full recovery for the client

As is usually the case, the defaulting defendant is obliged to pay costs on a **partial indemnity** scale. The basis for fixing a lawyer's fees is Rule 57.01(1), which creates broad discretion in determining the fee component of a costs award. Costs were subject to a notice from the Costs Subcommittee of the Civil Rules Committee, which established a costs grid. This grid was revoked in 2005, but in a document entitled "Information for the Profession" the Costs Subcommittee has retained the upper limits of the costs grid and in the absence of any other guidelines that can be used to interpret Rule 57.01(1), the grid figures continue to be used by judges, lawyers, and law clerks, and are included here. The costs grid sets out the following *maximum* rates (not adjusted for inflation) to be used:

- law clerk: $80.00 per hour;
- student-at-law (articling student): $60.00 per hour;
- lawyer with less than 10 years' experience: $225.00 per hour;
- lawyer with 10 or more but less than 20 years' experience: $300.00 per hour;
- lawyer with 20 or more years' experience: $350.00 per hour.

However, as we have noted, for simpler matters, including obtaining a default judgment, the rates should be well below the maximums, although there is no prescription or formula to tell you with precision what they should be. You should refer to the lawyer's actual rates and docketed time, and whatever instructions the lawyer gives you about the appropriate rates to use. This is not something you should be determining on your own, without instructions.

disbursements
out-of-pocket expenses incurred by a lawyer for fees and services paid to others as part of proceeding with a case

A lawyer's out-of-pocket expenses, or **disbursements**, are another story. These are covered in Tariff A, Part II, Disbursements, which can be found in the *Ontario Annual Practice*. Here, cost recovery is usually on a dollar-for-dollar basis. For example, if $41.00 is paid to a process server to serve a statement of claim, then that is the amount that will be recovered in costs, although there are limits on some Part II disbursements. Court fees[2] and sheriff costs[3] can be recovered in full. Always check the tariff and court fees before preparing a bill of costs because the allowable amounts change from year to year. The items usually included in the bill of costs on default judgment are as follows:

1. *Pleadings.* Hours spent multiplied by the appropriate hourly rate from the costs grid.

2. *Court fees paid to issue statement of claim.* Obtain fees from the schedule of fees that follows Tariffs A and C in commercial editions of rules of practice that include the *Rules of Civil Procedure*, such as the *Ontario Annual Practice*—note that these fees change from time to time. Retain your receipts for proof of expenditure.

3. *Fees paid to serve statement of claim.* See Tariff A, Part II—reasonable costs backed by receipt for payment to process server (this includes HST).

4. *Determination of costs and signing order for default judgment.* Hours spent multiplied by the appropriate, suitably reduced, hourly rate from the costs grid.

5. *Court fees paid to file requisition for default judgment.* As in item 2 above, see the schedule of fees.

In the bill of costs, fees and disbursements are recorded separately and totalled. Disbursements include Tariff A, Part II items, as well as court fees and sheriff fees. If for any reason you wish to recover costs on a **substantial indemnity** scale, this is a claim for a full recovery of costs and will have to be dealt with by being set down for hearing before an assessment officer. Recovery on this scale is unusual in default situations, because this scale is usually applied when a party misconducts himself or herself in the course of proceedings.

substantial indemnity costs scale, usually used as a punitive costs award, that results in near indemnity for the winner on a dollar-for-dollar basis

Draft a Judgment

Draft a judgment such as the one shown in Figure 10.3 (at the end of the chapter), and make two copies of it. A judgment is a one-paragraph document in which you must insert the sum claimed, composed of the principal amount and interest (taken from the requisition for default judgment), and the costs (taken from the bill of costs). Remember to include a sentence that says "This judgment bears interest at the rate of ___ percent per year from its date." If this statement is not present in the draft judgment, even though interest is claimed in the statement of claim and identified in the requisition for default judgment, the clerk might not insert the phrase for you, and you might not obtain postjudgment interest.

Prepare a Requisition for a Writ of Seizure and Sale

While a requisition for a writ of seizure and sale and a writ of seizure and sale are not required to obtain a default judgment, these documents are often prepared when obtaining default judgment because you may wish to file the writ of execution as quickly as possible in order to catch the debtor's assets before they are dissipated.[4]

The requisition for a writ of seizure and sale, which is set out in Figure 10.4 at the end of the chapter, is directed to the sheriff of each county, region, or district where you think the debtor has assets. If the debtor has assets in more than one area, you must refer in the requisition to each sheriff's office in which you intend to file a writ of seizure and sale. Be sure to set out the name of the debtor accurately. Include the amount to be seized, the amount of costs claimed, and the applicable postjudgment interest rate, all of which can be copied from the judgment.

Prepare a Writ of Seizure and Sale

This writ is set out in Figure 10.5 at the end of the chapter. You should prepare an original and one copy of it for each sheriff's office in which you plan to file it. When you obtain the default judgment and pay the fee to issue the writ, file the original and one copy with the sheriff's office, along with a covering letter instructing the sheriff to file the writ in the land registry and land titles system (if there is one). If the writ is not filed in the land titles system, the writ will not attach the execution debtor's land registered in the land titles system. Filing the writ with the sheriff is sufficient to attach an interest in land registered in the land registry system. Check with the sheriff's office to ascertain the fee for filing with the land registry system.

To complete each writ, fill in the blanks, using the judgment and the requisition for a writ of seizure and sale as sources of relevant information. Keep one copy of each writ for your office file. Remember to complete the backsheet by adding in the fee paid to the province to issue the writ, and the fee paid to the lawyer for doing the work. Note that Rule 60.19(2)(a) sets the lawyer's fee for the preparation of the writ at $50.00. The sheriff is entitled to add these costs to the amount on the face of the writ that may be collected from the debtor in the future.

Prepare a Cheque Payable to the Minister of Finance

To cover the cost of issuing each original writ of seizure and sale, check the current court and sheriffs' fees.[5]

Default Judgment for an Unliquidated Demand

Where a claim is not liquidated or does not fall into the other categories set out in Rule 19.04(1) and the defendant has defaulted on a defence, or where the registrar is uncertain about a liquidated claim and refuses to sign default judgment, the plaintiff must bring a motion for judgment before a judge against the defendant to claim judgment on the statement of claim.

Evidence of Damages

Where the claim is unliquidated, more detail is required than in the case of a liquidated claim. Initially, this detail is provided by way of affidavit evidence. If the judge is satisfied with the contents of the affidavit, he or she may grant judgment in accordance with the motion. But if there is any doubt, the judge can order that the matter proceed to trial for an assessment of damages. The judge may also decide that the claim is without merit—for example, if the claim concerns a breach of a right of the plaintiff that the law does not recognize. In that case, it does not matter whether the plaintiff can prove damages. If there is no right of action, the claim is dismissed even though the defendant has not put in a defence.

Contents of the Affidavit

Where the statement of claim discloses a breach of the plaintiff's rights, the affidavit need only focus on the damages, but should do so in considerable detail. Abigail's affidavit would describe the accident very briefly and focus on her injuries, convalescence, recovery, treatment, and the consequences of the injury on her social life, employment, and general enjoyment of life. An exhibit should be attached to the affidavit, listing the totals for special damages, such as medications, homecare assistance, and income loss. You may wish to have an affidavit from Abigail's doctor with medical reports about her prognosis attached as exhibits. You may want an affidavit from her employer or from the human resources person who has handled her work disability issues. You may also wish to have affidavits from one or two of her acquaintances who can describe the pre- and post-injury Abigail to show how the injuries have affected her daily life in a negative way and should result in compensation for her loss of quality of life.

If a judge decides that oral evidence should be heard, the witnesses who made the affidavits will testify, and the topics covered will be the same as those covered in the affidavits.

Figure 10.6 (at the end of the chapter) shows what Abigail's affidavit might look like. Because it includes both evidence from which factual conclusions can be drawn and the facts themselves, it appears to be like a detailed version of the paragraphs in Abigail's statement of claim that deal with damages. Since liability is deemed to be admitted, little space is devoted to facts about liability.

Setting Aside Default Judgment

Often a plaintiff will serve a defendant, and the defendant will not respond. While the plaintiff is entitled to assume that the defendant's lack of response is simply an admission of the plaintiff's case, this is not always so. Where, for example, the defendant was served by an alternative to personal service, the defendant may not be aware of the case against him or her because of ineffective service. For example, the plaintiff may have attempted personal service at the defendant's residence and followed up, under Rule 16.03(5), by delivering and then mailing the statement of claim to the defendant at his or her residence. Perhaps the defendant was out of town, and did not see the delivered letters. The defendant may return to find that there is a judgment against him or her. In other cases, the defendant is served and turns the claim over to a lawyer with instructions to defend; the lawyer then inadvertently misses the time limit. In these cases, Rule 19.08 provides that a judgment signed by the registrar or a judgment made after motion to a judge may be set aside or varied by the court. The noting of the defendant in default may also be set aside, which technically reopens pleadings and allows a statement of defence to be filed. Decided cases[6] have made it clear that the defendant must satisfy the court on three factors if the judgment is to be set aside:

1. the default must be adequately explained as the result of a mistake or error on the part of one or more of the parties,
2. the motion to set the judgment aside must be brought promptly, and
3. the defendant must disclose a plausible defence that cannot be decided without cross-examination or further judicial inquiry.

Figure 10.7 (at the end of the chapter) sets out the kind of affidavit that can be used to set aside a default judgment.

Table 10.1   Routes for Setting Aside an Order on Motion

Nature of original order	Before whom motion to set aside should be made
Order of a registrar	Judge or master in accordance with Rule 37.14(3).
Order of a judge	1. Judge who made the order in any place where the judge is sitting. 2. Any other judge in accordance with Rule 37.14(4).
Order of a master	1. Master who made the order in any place where the master is sitting. 2. Any other judge or master in accordance with Rule 37.14(5).
Order of a judge of Court of Appeal or Divisional Court	1. Judge who made the order. 2. If the order was made by a panel of judges, the panel that made it in accordance with Rule 37.14(6).

Setting Aside Orders on Motions

What Rule 19.08 does for default judgments, Rule 37.14 does for orders made on motions. Any order made by a judge or master on a motion, or made by a registrar, may be set aside by bringing a motion to set aside or vary the order in question.

When a Motion to Set Aside May Be Brought

Anyone who is affected by an order made on a motion without notice may move to set the order aside. The person need not be a party to the proceeding. The breadth of this rule demonstrates the safeguards that are built into the Rules where a motion is made without notice. Where a motion is made with notice and a responding party or other interested person fails to appear through inadvertence, mistake, or insufficient notice, that person may move to set the motion aside. Here, because of the short minimum period for serving and filing, a responding or interested party may not have enough time to prepare adequately. In a case like this, it is appropriate to tell the moving party that the time period is too short and ask for an adjournment. If the moving party refuses, Rule 37.14 provides an adequate, if cumbersome, remedy. If a person is affected by an order of a registrar, he or she may move to set the judgment aside.

Motion Procedure

The rule requires that a motion be brought immediately on finding out about the order. The motion is returnable on the first available day that is at least three days after the service of the motion (the minimum notice period under the Rules). Rule 37.14(3) to (6) tells you before whom a motion may be brought, depending on who made the original order. This is necessary because of jurisdictional issues. A master does not have the power to set aside a judge's order. Table 10.1 summarizes the routes to follow to set aside an order made on a motion.

CHAPTER SUMMARY

In this chapter we examined the procedure for obtaining a default judgment when the defendant fails to file a statement of defence. We noted the difference between a liquidated claim, where the registrar of the court signs judgment as an administrative act, and an unliquidated claim, where the plaintiff is obliged to present evidence to show what the quantum of damages should be. We noted how to prepare the necessary documentation for a default judgment (requisition, bill of costs, draft judgment, requisition for a writ of seizure and sale, and a writ of seizure and sale) with some of the optional procedures available, particularly with respect to assessing or fixing costs. We then examined what is required to set aside a default judgment both for judgments and for orders made on other kinds of motions.

KEY TERMS

disbursements, 260
partial indemnity, 260
substantial indemnity, 261

NOTES

1. Rule 57.01(3) indicates that costs are to be fixed using a costs outline instead of being assessed under Rule 58 using a bill of costs. However, Rule 58.13 permits a registrar to use a bill of costs to fix costs if the lawyer's fee, excluding disbursements, does not exceed $2,000.00, in which case the costs fixed shall not exceed $750.00 plus disbursements.

2. *Administration of Justice Act*, O. Reg. 293/92, as amended.

3. *Administration of Justice Act*, O. Reg. 294/92, as amended.

4. For more detailed information on issuing and filing writs of execution, see Olivo and Gonsalves, *Debtor–Creditor Law and Procedure*, 4th ed. (Toronto: Emond Montgomery, 2012).

5. Supra notes 2 and 3, respectively.

6. For example, see *Grieco v. Marquis* (1998), 38 OR (3d) 314 (Gen. Div.).

REFERENCES

Carthy, James J., W.A. Derry Millar, and Jeffrey G. Cowan. *Ontario Annual Practice* (Aurora, ON: Canada Law Book, published annually).

Courts of Justice Act, RSO 1990, c. C.43.

Grieco v. Marquis (1998), 38 OR (3d) 314 (Gen. Div.).

Rules of Civil Procedure, RRO 1990, reg. 194.

REVIEW QUESTIONS

1. Under what circumstances can a plaintiff apply to sign default judgment?

2. Explain the difference between a liquidated and an unliquidated claim.

3. What documents must you present to the court in order to sign a default judgment before the registrar?

4. What is the function of the requisition for default judgment?

5. Suppose the defendant defaults on his or her defence but pays some money on account of the amount claimed. How does this affect the process of signing default judgment?

6. What determines the prejudgment and postjudgment interest rate you ask for?

7. **a.** How do you determine the amounts that go into a bill of costs?

   b. May a registrar use a bill of costs when fixing costs on signing default judgment?

8. In what circumstances do you need to requisition more than one writ of seizure and sale?

9. If you wish to set aside a default judgment, what must you show to the court?

10. Explain how setting aside an order under Rule 37.14 differs from setting aside a judgment under Rule 19.

DISCUSSION QUESTIONS

1. Read and respond to the following memorandum:

   To: Law clerk

   From: Lawyer

   Re: *Ulock v. Foot*

   Date: April 26, year 1

   We issued a claim against Ophelia Foot on March 23, year 1. Foot had signed a promissory note to our client, Murgatroyd Ulock, for $30,000.00 on August 1, year 0. The note was due on December 1, year 0. It provided for interest at 11 percent per year from the time it was past due until payment. Interest has been claimed on this basis. The claim was thus for $30,000.00 plus interest on the overdue amount. On April 1, year 1, Foot paid $2,000.00 on account, but she has paid nothing since. Foot was served with the statement of claim on March 24, year 1. Because Foot has not defended, and the time for filing a defence has passed, please prepare the necessary documents to sign default judgment on April 28, year 1. The lawyer's fees are $250.00 per hour. The dockets show that lawyer Dewey Sue spent 1.2 hours on preparing the statement of claim, and 0.5 hours signing default judgment and fixing costs. The original statement of claim and affidavit of service is in the file, together with a receipt for $53.21, including HST, for service of the claim and a receipt for $181.00 for the court fee paid to issue the statement of claim. It is rumoured that Foot owns property in Toronto and Oshawa in the region of Durham.

2. Read and respond to the following memorandum:

   To: Law clerk

   From: Lawyer

   Re: *Foot ats Ulock*

   Date: April 30, year 1

   I have just learned that default judgment has been signed on April 28, year 1 against our client, Ophelia Foot, on a promissory note made to Murgatroyd Ulock. Foot brought the statement of claim in two weeks ago, and I meant to draft a defence. The defence is to be based on the fact that Ophelia does not speak or read English, she thought she was signing a lease rather than a promissory note, and Ulock misled her and intended to defraud her. Unfortunately, I spilled coffee all over the statement of defence, put it on the radiator in the copier room to dry out, and then forgot about it. I think the cleaners threw it out, so I do not have a copy, though I remember it was a simple claim on a promissory note. Draft a notice of motion and affidavit in support in my name so that we can move to set aside default judgment.

Figure 10.1   Requisition for Default Judgment (Form 19D)

Done

Court file no. 01-CV-7777

ONTARIO
SUPERIOR COURT OF JUSTICE

BETWEEN:

ABIGAIL BOAR

Plaintiff

and

HIERONYMUS BLOGGS

Defendant

REQUISITION FOR DEFAULT JUDGMENT

TO THE LOCAL REGISTRAR AT Toronto

I REQUIRE you to note the defendant, Hieronymus Bloggs, in default in this action and that pleadings be noted closed against the defendant on the ground that the defendant has failed to file a statement of defence within the time provided for in the *Rules of Civil Procedure.*

I REQUIRE default judgment to be signed against the defendant Hieronymus Bloggs.

Default judgment may properly be signed in this action because the claim is for

- [x] a debt or liquidated demand in money
- [   ] recovery of possession of land
- [   ] recovery of possession of personal property
- [   ] foreclosure, sale or redemption of a mortgage
- [x] There has been no payment on account of the claim since the statement of claim was issued. *(Complete Parts B & C.)*

OR

- [   ] The following payments have been made on account of the claim since the statement of claim was issued. *(Complete Parts A & C.)*

Figure 10.1   Continued

Part A — PAYMENT(S) RECEIVED BY PLAINTIFF

(Complete this part only where part payment of the claim has been received. Where no payment has been received on account of the claim, omit this part and complete Part B.)

1. Principal

Principal sum claimed in statement of claim (without interest) $ . . . .

Date of Payment	Amount of Payment	Payment Amount Principal	Applied to Interest	Principal Sum Owing
TOTAL	$	$	$	A $ . . . .

2. Prejudgment interest

(Under section 128 of the Courts of Justice Act, judgment may be obtained for prejudgment interest from the date the cause of action arose, if claimed in the statement of claim.)

Date on which statement of claim was issued . . . .

Date from which prejudgment interest is claimed . . . .

The plaintiff is entitled to prejudgment interest on the claim, calculated as follows:

(Calculate simple interest only unless an agreement relied on in the statement of claim specifies otherwise. Calculate interest on the principal sum owing from the date of the last payment. To calculate the interest amount, count the number of days since the last payment, multiply that number by the annual rate of interest, multiply the result by the principal sum owing and divide by 365.)

Principal Sum Owing	Start Date	End Date (Date of Payment)	Number of Days	Rate	Interest Amount

(The last End Date should be the date judgment is signed.)

	TOTAL B $ . . . .
Principal Sum Owing (Total A above)	$ . . . .
Total Interest Amount (Total B above)	$ . . . .
SIGN JUDGMENT FOR	$ . . . .

Figure 10.1   Continued

PART B — NO PAYMENT RECEIVED BY PLAINTIFF

(Complete this part only where no payment has been received on account of the claim.)

1. Principal

Principal sum claimed in statement of claim (without interest) A $ . . . . 38,182.79 ✓

2. Prejudgment interest

(Under section 128 of the Courts of Justice Act, judgment may be obtained for prejudgment interest from the date the cause of action arose, if claimed in the statement of claim.)

Date on which statement of claim was issued . . . . . September 26, year 0 . . . . .

Date from which prejudgment interest is claimed . . . July 29, year 0 . . . .

The plaintiff is entitled to prejudgment interest on the claim, calculated as follows:

(Calculate simple interest only unless an agreement relied on in the statement of claim specifies otherwise. To calculate the interest amount, count the number of days and multiply that number by the annual rate of interest, multiply the result by the principal sum owing and divide by 365.)

Principal Sum Owing	Start Date	End Date (Date of Payment)	Number of Days	Rate	Interest Amount
38,182.79	July 29, year 0	Oct. 17, year 0	81	12%*	1,016.81

TOTAL B	$ 1,016.81
Principal Sum Owing (Total A above)	$ . . 38,182.79
Total Interest Amount (Total B above)	$ 1,016.81
SIGN JUDGMENT FOR	$ . . 39,199.60

[Assume that the interest rate is based on the agreed term of a contract.]*

Figure 10.1   Concluded

PART C — POSTJUDGMENT INTEREST AND COSTS

1. Postjudgment interest

   The plaintiff is entitled to postjudgment interest at the rate of 12 percent per year

   [   ]   under the *Courts of Justice Act*, as claimed in the statement of claim.

OR

   [x]   in accordance with the claim made in the statement of claim.

2. Costs

   The plaintiff wishes costs to be

   [x]   fixed by the local registrar.

OR

   [   ]   assessed by an assessment officer.

Date   . . . . . . October 17, year 0 . . . . *I.M. Just* . . . .

Just & Coping
Barristers and Solicitors
365 Bay Street – 8701
Toronto, Ontario, M3J 4A9

I.M. Just
LSUC #12345R
tel. 416-762-1342
fax 416-762-2300

Lawyers for the Plaintiff

RCP-E 19D (July 1, 2007)

Figure 10.2   Bill of Costs (Form 57A)

DONE

Court file no. 01-CV-7777

ONTARIO
SUPERIOR COURT OF JUSTICE

BETWEEN:

ABIGAIL BOAR

Plaintiff

and

HIERONYMUS BLOGGS

Defendant

BILL OF COSTS

AMOUNTS CLAIMED FOR FEES AND DISBURSEMENTS

FEES OTHER THAN COUNSEL FEES

1. Preparing and drafting statement of claim, I.M. Just, October 16, year 1   1 hour
2. Signing default judgment and fixing costs   0.6 hour
   Fee for I.M. Just, Barrister and Solicitor,
   1.6 hours x $300 = $480.00

TOTAL FEE $480.00

HST* ON FEE $62.40

DISBURSEMENTS**

1. Paid to issue statement of claim $181.00
2. Paid to serve claim (includes HST) $41.00
3. Paid to file requisition for default judgment $127.00

TOTAL DISBURSEMENTS $349.00

HST RO12534

TOTAL FEES AND DISBURSEMENTS $891.40

---

*   HST of 13 percent. HST is applied to legal fees and disbursements paid out to third parties for services other than court fees and fixed government fees. Not all lawyers charge HST on bills of costs, although the better practice is to do so.

**   Court fees to issue a statement of claim and file a requisition for default judgment can be found under O. Reg. 293/92 of the *Administration of Justice Act*. Note that these fees change every few years.

Figure 10.2 Concluded

STATEMENT OF EXPERIENCE

A claim for fees is being made with respect to the following lawyers:

Name of lawyer	Years of experience
I.M. Just	12 years

TO: Huey Sue
LSUC #23456T
Barrister and Solicitor
65 False Trail
Toronto, Ontario, M6Y 1Z6

tel. 416-485-6891
fax 416-485-6892

Lawyer for the Defendants

THIS BILL assessed and allowed at $ this   day of

Registrar,
Ontario Superior Court of Justice

RCP-E 57A (November 1, 2005)

Figure 10.3   Default Judgment (Debt or Liquidated Demand) (Form 19A)

Court file no. 01-CV-7777

ONTARIO
SUPERIOR COURT OF JUSTICE

BETWEEN:

ABIGAIL BOAR

Plaintiff

and

HIERONYMUS BLOGGS

Defendant

JUDGMENT

On reading the statement of claim in this action and the proof of service of the statement of claim on the defendant, filed, and the defendant having been noted in default,

1. IT IS ORDERED AND ADJUDGED that the defendant pay to the plaintiff the sum of $39,199.60 and the sum of $891.40 for costs of this action.

This judgment bears interest at the rate of 12 percent per year from its date.

Date: October 17, year 0   Signed by: _____
                                                   Local registrar

                                     Address of
                                     court office: 393 University Avenue
                                                     Toronto, Ontario, M5G 1E6

RCP-E 19A (November 1, 2005)

Figure 10.4   Requisition for Writ of Seizure and Sale

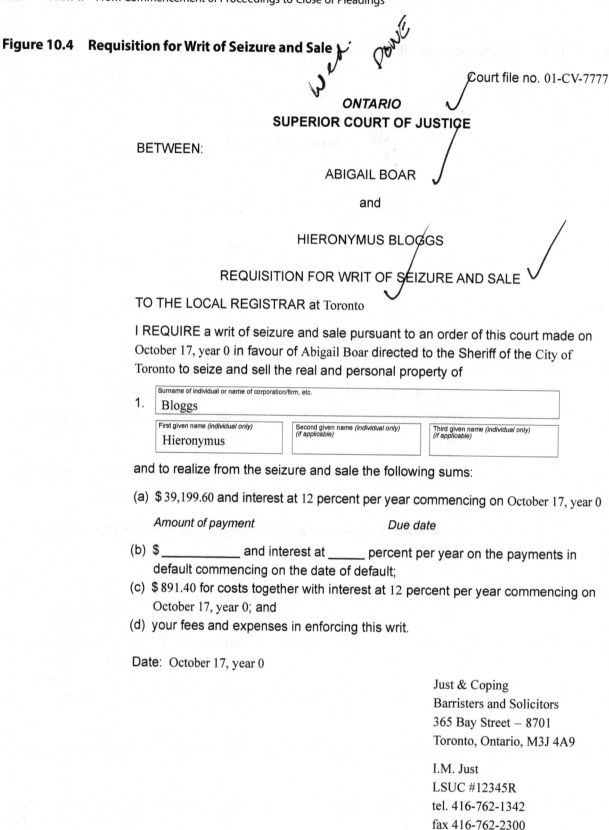

Court file no. 01-CV-7777

ONTARIO
SUPERIOR COURT OF JUSTICE

BETWEEN:

ABIGAIL BOAR

and

HIERONYMUS BLOGGS

REQUISITION FOR WRIT OF SEIZURE AND SALE

TO THE LOCAL REGISTRAR at Toronto

I REQUIRE a writ of seizure and sale pursuant to an order of this court made on October 17, year 0 in favour of Abigail Boar directed to the Sheriff of the City of Toronto to seize and sell the real and personal property of

Surname of individual or name of corporation/firm, etc.

1.   Bloggs

First given name *(individual only)*   Second given name *(individual only)* *(if applicable)*   Third given name *(individual only)* *(if applicable)*

Hieronymus

and to realize from the seizure and sale the following sums:

(a) $ 39,199.60 and interest at 12 percent per year commencing on October 17, year 0

      Amount of payment   *Due date*

(b) $ _____ and interest at _____ percent per year on the payments in default commencing on the date of default;

(c) $ 891.40 for costs together with interest at 12 percent per year commencing on October 17, year 0; and

(d) your fees and expenses in enforcing this writ.

Date: October 17, year 0

Just & Coping
Barristers and Solicitors
365 Bay Street – 8701
Toronto, Ontario, M3J 4A9

I.M. Just
LSUC #12345R
tel. 416-762-1342
fax 416-762-2300

Lawyers for the Plaintiff

Figure 10.5 Writ of Seizure and Sale (Form 60A)

Court file no. 01-CV-7777

ONTARIO
SUPERIOR COURT OF JUSTICE

BETWEEN:

ABIGAIL BOAR

and

HIERONYMUS BLOGGS

WRIT OF SEIZURE AND SALE

TO the Sheriff of the City of Toronto

Under an order of this court made on October 17, year 0, in favour of Abigail Boar, YOU ARE DIRECTED to seize and sell the real and personal property within the City of Toronto of

Surname of individual or name of corporation/firm, etc.

Bloggs

First given name *(individual only)*

Hieronymus

and to realize from the seizure and sale the following sums:

(a) $ 39,199.60 and interest at 12 percent per year commencing on October 17, year 0

Amount of payment   *Due date*

(b) $_____ and interest at _____ percent per year on the payments in default commencing on the date of default;

(c) $ 891.40 for costs together with interest at 12 percent per year commencing on October 17, year 0; and

(d) your fees and expenses in enforcing this writ.

YOU ARE DIRECTED to pay out the proceeds according to law and to report on the execution of this writ if required by the party or lawyer who filed it.

Dated at Toronto   Issued by _____

on October 17, year 0   Registrar

                                   Address of
                                   court office: Courthouse
                                                   393 University Avenue
                                                   Toronto, Ontario, M5G 1E6

RCP-E 60A (July 1, 2007)

Figure 10.5   Writ of Seizure and Sale — Backsheet (Form 60A)

HIERONYMUS BLOGGS

and

ABIGAIL BOAR

(Short title of proceeding)

Court file no. 01-CV-7777

ONTARIO
SUPERIOR COURT OF JUSTICE

Proceeding comment at Toronto

**WRIT OF
SEIZURE AND SALE**

Creditor's name: Abigail Boar
Creditor's address:
c/o Just & Coping
Barristers and Solicitors
Lawyer's name:
I.M. Just
LSUC #12345R
Lawyer's address:
Just & Coping
365 Bay Street – 8701
Toronto, Ontario, M3J 4A9
Tel. no.: 416-762-1342
Fax no.: 416-762-2300

Lawyer for the Plaintiff

FEES

Fee	Item	Officer
$100.00	Paid for this writ	
$15.00	Lawyer's fee for issuing writ	
	First renewal	
	Second renewal	
	Third renewal	

RENEWAL

Date	Officer				

Figure 10.6   Affidavit of Abigail Boar

Court file no. 01-CV-1234

ONTARIO
SUPERIOR COURT OF JUSTICE

BETWEEN:

ABIGAIL BOAR

Plaintiff

and

RATTLE MOTORS LTD. and FRED FLOGEM

Defendants

AFFIDAVIT OF ~~ABIGAIL BOAR~~ Nathaniel Simmons

I, ~~Abigail Boar~~ Nathaniel Simmons, of the City of Toronto, in the Province of Ontario, MAKE OATH AND SAY:

1. I am the plaintiff in this proceeding and as such have knowledge of the matters set out in this affidavit.

2. I slipped on oil on the floor of the showroom of the corporate defendant. My fall and subsequent injuries were solely the result of the negligent acts of the defendants.

3. As a result of the fall, I struck my head, suffered a concussion, and lost consciousness. I also fractured my right wrist and several other bones in my right arm. I was taken to the Toronto Hospital emergency room, where my fractures were set and my arm was put in a cast. I was hospitalized and also underwent neurological examination for my head injury.

4. My arm was in a cast for six weeks. I was in great pain for the first two weeks and was unable to sleep or rest without medication to mask the pain. I required homecare assistance. Because I am right-handed and my right arm was immobilized, I was unable to dress myself or look after myself.

5. I had to undergo 10 weeks of physiotherapy to help restore mobility to my right hand and arm.

6. Since the accident, I have also suffered from headaches and chronic lower back pain. I am unable to walk long distances or sit at a desk for long periods. I have not recovered mobility in my right arm, and I am unable to work at a computer keyboard for more than 10 minutes without great pain.

Figure 10.6 Concluded

7. As a result of these injuries, I have been far less active and less outgoing than I had been. I have become withdrawn and morose. I can easily become upset by little things that would not have bothered me in the past. I am often tired and have difficulty sleeping because of the chronic pain from my back and head injuries.

8. Before I was injured, I was outgoing and gregarious, an avid tennis player, and a competent amateur violinist. Since I was injured, I have become uninterested in maintaining my social life, and I am unable to engage in the sports and cultural activities from which I formerly derived much pleasure.

9. I have also suffered some memory loss, which has interfered with both my employment and my social life.

10. I have been unable to return to work as a result of my injuries. My work as a securities analyst requires me to sit at a desk and computer keyboard for lengthy periods of time. I also now have difficulty focusing and concentrating on my work because of memory loss and chronic pain. I tried to return to work but was able to work only for a month before my employer and I agreed that I was no longer able to perform my duties. I have been on long-term disability from April 1, year 1 and am unlikely to be able to return to my former employment.

11. At the time of the accident, I was earning $80,000 per year plus benefits worth another $20,000. My work performance was excellent. I expected to work another 25 years and retire early at age 51. I am advised by Eatom Shredlu, the vice-president of human resources at Megadoon Investments Ltd., and believe, that my salary would likely have increased on average about 6 percent per year during my career had I continued my work for this employer.

12. I am advised by Dr. Morris Furgazy, a neurologist, and I believe, that I am unlikely to be employable in any office position on a permanent basis because of my mental disabilities arising from my accident and my physical inability to perform office work.

SWORN before me at the	)	
City of Toronto,	)	_Abigail Boar_
in the Province of Ontario,	)	Abigail Boar
on February 18, year 1.	)	
I.M. Just	)	
I.M. Just	)	
Commissioner for Taking Affidavits	)	

RCP-E 4D (July 1, 2007)

Figure 10.7   Affidavit to Set Aside Default Judgment

4D

No word.

Court file no. 01-CV-1234

ONTARIO
SUPERIOR COURT OF JUSTICE

BETWEEN:

Nathaniel Simmns S.

~~ABIGAIL BOAR~~

Plaintiff

and

Ryan Mulluney

~~RATTLE MOTORS LTD. and FRED FLOGEM~~

Defendants

Jaspers

AFFIDAVIT OF HUEY SUE

I, ~~Huey Sue~~, of the City of Toronto, in the Province of Ontario, AFFIRM:

1. I am the lawyer for the defendants and as such have knowledge of the matters deposed to in this affidavit.

2. On January 4, year 1, the defendants were served with the statement of claim in this action.

3. On January 6, year 1, I met both defendants and arranged to file a statement of defence. Attached hereto and marked exhibit A to my affidavit is a copy of the proposed statement of defence in this proceeding.

4. The defendants have a good defence to the plaintiff's claim. It is the position of the defendants that the plaintiff was intoxicated at the time of the accident and that her injuries were wholly the result of her intoxicated condition, rather than the result of any alleged act of negligence by either defendant, which negligence, if any, is denied by the defendants.

5. Because of the pressures of practice, I overlooked the passage of the time for filing the statement of defence.

6. I discovered my oversight on January 28, year 1. I attempted immediately to file the statement of defence, but learned that the defendants had been noted in default and that a default judgment had been entered.

Figure 10.7 Concluded

7. On January 29, year 1, I served the plaintiff with a notice of motion to set aside the noting of pleadings closed and the default judgment in this action.

AFFIRMED before me at the	)	
City of Toronto,	)	*Huey Sue*
in the Province of Ontario,	)	Huey Sue
on January 30, year 1.	)	
Henry Hood	)	
Henry Hood	)	
Commissioner for Taking Affidavits	)	

RCP-E 4D (July 1, 2007)

Summary Judgment: Rule 20   11

Introduction

Once the pleadings have been delivered, one of the parties may take the position on all or some of the issues raised by the opposing party that there is no genuine issue that requires a trial. For example, Abigail Boar, the plaintiff, may believe that the defendants, Fred Flogem and Rattle Motors, have raised no defence known in law to her claim. On the other hand, the defendants may take the position that Abigail does not have sufficient evidence to make a case against them on the balance of probabilities.

In such circumstances, either the plaintiff or the defendant may bring a motion for summary judgment once a statement of defence or notice of motion has been delivered by the defendant. If the plaintiff brings the motion for summary judgment, she will ask the court to make a final judgment in her favour. If the defendants bring the motion for summary judgment, they will ask for a dismissal of all or part of the plaintiff's case. Rule 20 provides the procedure for summary judgments.

Summary judgment is a final decision about all or part of a case that is made by the court without a full trial. The parties may not rely only on their pleadings in trying to persuade the court that there is no genuine issue requiring a trial. They must provide the court with affidavits that set out the facts on which they are relying. The affidavits may be based on information supplied by others that the deponent believes to be true. However, basing a motion for summary judgment on affidavit evidence that is entirely based on matters outside the personal knowledge of the deponent may be risky. The court may **draw an adverse inference** if the affidavits contain material based solely on information and belief and not on the direct, personal knowledge of the deponents. For example, the court may take the view that the reason that no direct personal knowledge evidence has been presented is that there is none.

The affidavits of the party responding to the motion must do more than deny the allegations of the moving party or say that more evidence may be available at trial. The material must set out specific facts showing that there is a genuine issue that requires a trial (Rule 20.02(2)).

In addition to the affidavits they wish to rely on in the motion for summary judgment, each party must also serve and file a factum before the hearing of the motion (Rule 20.03). A factum is a document that gives a concise summary of the facts in the case and sets out the case law and statutes that the party is relying on to support its position. Factums are dealt with in more detail in Chapter 20. The moving party must serve and file its factum in the court office, with proof of service, at least seven days in advance of the date for hearing the motion. The responding party must serve and file, with proof of service, its factum at least four days before the hearing.

draw an adverse inference
make a factual determination that is contrary to the interests of a party

Test for Granting Summary Judgment

After hearing the motion, the court can order summary judgment in one of two situations. The first situation in which summary judgment must be granted is when the court is satisfied that there is no genuine issue requiring a trial. For instance, in

Abigail's negligence action, if the defendants can establish that the plaintiff's case is statute barred because it was commenced outside the time set in the *Limitations Act, 2002*, they will be able to satisfy the court that there is no genuine issue requiring a trial. In such a case, the court must grant summary judgment.

The second situation in which summary judgment must be granted is when the parties agree to have all or part of the case dealt with on a motion for summary judgment and the court agrees that it is an appropriate case for this treatment. A motion for summary judgment can be brought before a master or a judge. However, if a motion based on a question of law can only be heard by a judge and is brought before a master, it must be adjourned for hearing before a judge (Rule 20.04(4)).

In determining whether there is a genuine issue requiring trial, the court will consider the evidence and if the motion is heard by a judge, rather than a master, the judge (but not a master), unless it would be more in the interests of justice to do so at trial, may weigh the evidence, evaluate the credibility of the deponent, and draw any reasonable inference from the evidence (Rule 20.04(2.1)).

Although summary judgment motions are usually heard on affidavit evidence, a judge can conduct what amounts to a mini-trial by ordering oral evidence under Rule 20.04(2.2), to be presented by one or more parties, with or without time limits on its presentation. If the court decides that the only genuine issue requiring a trial is the amount of money to which the moving party is entitled, the court can order a trial limited to that issue or grant judgment in favour of the moving party and direct a **reference** to determine the exact amount (Rule 20.04(3)).

Summary judgments are often sought in cases involving debt issues because a plaintiff may obtain judgment for all or part of a debt claim at an early stage in the proceedings without the cost and delay of discovery and trial.

reference

judicial proceeding used when it is necessary to delve into an issue in detail before a decision can be reached

Where a Summary Judgment Is Not Ordered or Is Ordered Only in Part

If, after a motion for summary judgment, a judgment is refused or granted only in part, and a trial will therefore be necessary, a judge may, at his or her discretion, make an order specifying what material facts are not in dispute in the case and defining what issues are to go to trial in an expeditious manner. In the event that the court exercises this discretion, the trial will essentially be a summary trial in that it will be narrowed down to the central issues that require trial. Rule 20.05(2) sets out a non-exhaustive list of directions and terms that the court can make in relation to ordering a summary trial. For example:

- specified times might be set for any motions and the delivery of various documents;
- particular requirements could be directed for discovery;
- requests that trial dates be set might be given; and
- there could be a request that part or all of a claim be paid into court and that there be security for costs. If the payment or security for costs is ordered but

not complied with, the opposing party may bring a motion to dismiss the action, strike out the statement of defence, or ask for such other relief as is just.

Summary judgment can be a very effective litigation tool in that it can, in appropriate cases, avoid costly and time-consuming procedures. However, if a party improperly uses the rule, the court may apply cost sanctions. In determining whether to award costs, the court must consider whether a party acted unreasonably in bringing or responding to the motion or acted in bad faith in an attempt to cause delay. If so, it may fix and order the costs on a substantial indemnity basis (Rule 20.06).

Where there are many claims in an action, summary judgment may address only some of those claims, leaving others to be determined through the trial process. A plaintiff who obtains summary judgment may proceed against the defendant for any other relief that he or she is claiming. In an appropriate case, the court may order a stay of the summary judgment until the entire matter, including any crossclaim, counterclaim, or third-party claim, is dealt with.

Although the summary judgment procedure has been available in the Rules for quite some time, there has been some reluctance to use it. Judges, who are used to making final decisions after hearing evidence at a full trial, have shown some disinclination to make a final decision that there is no genuine issue for trial based on affidavit evidence alone. Motions for summary judgments regularly resulted in dismissal and a ruling that the matter proceed to trial. As a result, lawyers were not using the procedure as often as they might.

However, the early 2014 judgment by the Supreme Court of Canada in the case of *Hryniak v. Mauldin* will change the entire approach to summary judgment. In *Hryniak,* the court ruled that given the major financial and time implications of a full trial to most ordinary litigants, access to justice would best be served by more frequent and aggressive use of summary judgment. The Court set out very specific directions to judges in the lower courts that summary judgment should be viewed as the preferred method of resolving a civil case. This decision of the Supreme Court will greatly increase the use of summary judgments to resolve cases without a full-blown trial. The face of civil litigation may drastically change with the use of this much more streamlined and less complicated process.

CHAPTER SUMMARY

In this chapter, we have seen that summary judgment is a final decision that is made about a case by a court without a trial. Either the plaintiff or the defendant may bring a motion for summary judgment, which must be accompanied by affidavit evidence and factums. The test for granting a summary judgment is that there is no genuine issue requiring a trial. A summary judgment may be granted either in whole or in part.

The parties may agree to have the case determined in this manner; however, the court is not obligated to grant a summary judgment and may direct that the case proceed by way of a full trial. Debt cases are often dealt with by way of summary judgment. Summary judgment may prove to be an effective litigation tool to avoid costly and time-consuming trials, but there can be severe cost consequences for a party that behaves in an unreasonable manner in responding to or bringing a motion.

KEY TERMS

draw an adverse inference, 282

reference, 283

REFERENCES

Hryniak v. Mauldin, 2014 SCC 7 (CanLII).

Limitations Act, 2002, SO 2002, c. 24, sch. B.

Rules of Civil Procedure, RRO 1990, reg. 194.

REVIEW QUESTIONS

1. Set out the steps you would take and the documents you would prepare to bring a motion for summary judgment.

2. What must a party prove to obtain a summary judgment?

3. What sort of evidence should be used in support of the motion?

4. Are there costs consequences on a motion for summary judgment?

Counterclaims, Crosssclaims, and Third-Party Claims

12

Introduction

A simple proceeding involves only two parties: the plaintiff and the defendant. As you know, the plaintiff can sue more than one defendant in the proceeding, as Abigail Boar is doing. She believes both Fred Flogem and Rattle Motors Ltd. are responsible for her injuries, and she is suing them both. In Abigail's case, there are multiple defendants.

It is also possible to have multiple plaintiffs in a proceeding when several people claim that they suffered damages caused by the defendant or group of defendants. But a proceeding can become more complicated than this. The Rules provide for a number of different combinations of plaintiffs and defendants, and they outline the pleadings and the procedures for each. These pleadings are the counterclaim, the crossclaim, and the third-party claim.

When you first try to sort out the nature of these other pleadings, they may seem extremely complicated because of the additional parties and steps involved. However, when reviewing the procedures, keep in mind the basic principle that all parties should know the legal claim made against them and have the opportunity to answer the claim. Remember the basic pleadings in an action: the statement of claim, the statement of defence, and the reply. All other pleadings follow the same general principles.[1]

Counterclaims: Rule 27

The defendant may wish to sue the plaintiff in the proceeding. Maybe the defendant was seeking legal advice about suing the plaintiff, but the plaintiff was the one who issued the statement of claim first. The legal system and the Rules have an interest in resolving disputes between parties in the most cost-effective and efficient manner. To force the defendant who wants to sue the plaintiff to commence a proceeding separate from the one already commenced by the plaintiff would be more expensive and time-consuming than allowing the defendant to bring his or her action against the plaintiff at the same time.

counterclaim
claim made by the defendant in the main action against the plaintiff or against the plaintiff and other persons

When a defendant sues a plaintiff, this is called a "**counterclaim**." The proceeding in which the plaintiff is suing the defendant is then called the "**main action**."

In a counterclaim, the defendant in the main action must be suing the plaintiff in the main action. The defendant can also sue anyone else in his or her counterclaim, as long as the original plaintiff is one of the persons being sued.

main action
primary case brought by the plaintiff against the defendant

There is no restriction as to the basis for the defendant's counterclaim against the plaintiff. It may have the same subject matter as the claim in the main action, or it may have a completely different subject matter. Assume that Abigail Boar did not go to Rattle Motors Ltd. to buy a car on the day that she fell. Assume instead that she had already bought the car and went into the dealership that day to make a payment on the car she had purchased. After she slipped and fell, she refused to make additional payments on the car. Rattle Motors Ltd. wants to enforce its contract of sale against her. Therefore, when she starts her action against Rattle Motors Ltd., it counterclaims against her for the debt owing. Abigail is suing Rattle Motors Ltd. for the tort of negligence, and Rattle Motors Ltd. is suing Abigail on a contract.

Assume as well that Abigail's boyfriend purchased the car with her and also entered into a sales contract with Rattle Motors Ltd. He has made no further payments on the car either, and Rattle Motors Ltd. wants to sue him too, for breach of the loan contract. Rattle Motors Ltd. can add him to the counterclaim, even though he is not one of the parties in the main action. As long as Rattle Motors Ltd. is suing Abigail, the plaintiff in the main action, it may also include her boyfriend, or anyone else, in the counterclaim.

Pleadings in a Counterclaim

The possible pleadings in a counterclaim are:

1. statement of claim (Form 14A), delivered by the plaintiff in the main action;

2. statement of defence and counterclaim (Form 27A or 27B), delivered by a defendant in the main action who is making a counterclaim against the plaintiff in the main action (Form 27B is to be used by a person who is not already a party to the main action);

3. defence to counterclaim (Form 27C), delivered by the plaintiff in the main action who wishes to defend against the counterclaim; and

4. reply to defence to counterclaim (Form 27D), delivered by the plaintiff in the main action who wants to reply to the defendants' statement of defence in the main action and defend against the counterclaim.

Statement of Defence and Counterclaim

The defendants commence the counterclaim by including it in the same pleading as their defence to the main action. Instead of being called a "statement of defence," it is called a "statement of defence and counterclaim." There are two forms for this pleading: Form 27A and Form 27B. Form 27A is used when the defendant is suing only people who are parties to the main action. Form 27B is used if the defendant is adding someone to the counterclaim who is not a party to the main proceeding. If Rattle Motors Ltd. were suing only Abigail, it would use Form 27A. If it were also suing Abigail's boyfriend, because the boyfriend is not a party to the main action, it would use Form 27B. Figure 12.1 at the end of the chapter sets out a statement of defence and counterclaim.

There is a major distinction between the two forms. Because Form 27A is not an originating process, it does not need to be issued. However, because Form 27B brings in a new party to the proceeding, it is an originating process. It must therefore be issued within the time prescribed in Rule 18.01 for delivery of the statement of defence or any time before being noted in default—that is, within 20 days if the statement of claim was served in Ontario, 40 days if it was served elsewhere in Canada or in the United States, or 60 days if it was served anywhere else in the world.

Form 27B must also contain a second title of proceeding showing the plaintiff by counterclaim and the defendants to the counterclaim. In our example, Rattle Motors Ltd. is the plaintiff by counterclaim, and Abigail and her boyfriend are the defendants to the counterclaim (Rule 27.03).

The statement of defence and counterclaim (Form 27A or 27B) raises two separate issues for the plaintiff in the main action. She has been served with a defence to her claim in the main action and with a new claim against her by the defendant. In the main action, in which Abigail is suing Rattle Motors Ltd. in negligence, she may want to reply to any new issue that Rattle Motors Ltd. has raised in its defence. In addition, Abigail will want to raise her defence against Rattle Motors Ltd.'s claim for payment for the car. Her boyfriend will also want to raise his defence against Rattle Motors Ltd.

Defence to Counterclaim or Reply to Defence to Counterclaim

If Abigail has no reply to Rattle Motors Ltd.'s defence in the main action but wants to defend herself against Rattle Motors Ltd.'s counterclaim, she must file a defence to counterclaim, Form 27C, within 20 days after being served with the statement of defence and counterclaim. Figure 12.2 at the end of the chapter sets out a defence to the counterclaim. If Abigail's boyfriend or any other defendant who is not a party to the main action wishes to file a defence to the counterclaim, that person has 20 days, 40 days, or 60 days to file a statement of defence and counterclaim, depending on the place of service (Rule 27.05(3)).

If Abigail wants to file a reply to Rattle Motors Ltd.'s defence in the main action and raise a defence to the counterclaim, she must include the defence to the counterclaim in the reply. This means she first addresses all the issues she wishes to address in reply and follows those paragraphs with all the points she wishes to raise in the defence to the counterclaim.

If Rattle Motors Ltd. wants to reply to Abigail or to another defendant's defence and counterclaim, it may do so in Form 27D within 10 days after being served with the defence to the counterclaim (Rule 27.06).

Amending Defence to Add Counterclaim

If the defendants in the main action deliver a statement of defence and then decide that they want to bring a counterclaim, they may amend their statement of defence to add the counterclaim and deliver the amended pleading, as long as the counterclaim is against the plaintiff and someone else who is already a party to the main action. But if the counterclaim brings in a defendant who is not a party to the main action, the defendants may amend their pleading to add the counterclaim only with leave of the court (Rule 27.07).

Trial and Disposition of the Counterclaim

A counterclaim that goes to trial is usually heard at the end of the trial of the main action. However, if it appears that the counterclaim may delay, complicate, or prejudice a party, the court may order separate trials or may order that the counterclaim proceed as an action separate from the main action (Rules 27.08(1) and (2)).

In some cases the defendant may not dispute the plaintiff's claim in the main action but may want to assert a counterclaim. Conversely, the plaintiff may not dispute the counterclaim but may want to proceed with his or her claim in the main action. In such a situation, the court may either stay or grant a judgment in the undisputed part of the case and then hear the claims that are disputed. If the plaintiff is successful in the main action and the defendant is successful on the counterclaim—that is, if each party wins the part of the case it brought against the other—the court may dismiss the smaller claim and order that the difference between the two damage awards be paid (Rule 27.09).

For example, assume that Abigail Boar wins her negligence action against Rattle Motors Ltd., and Rattle is ordered to pay her $175,000. Rattle Motors Ltd., however, also wins its counterclaim for the money still owing on the car, which is $15,000. In this instance, the court may dismiss Rattle Motors Ltd.'s case and order Rattle to pay Abigail $160,000, the difference between the two claims.

Crossclaims: Rule 28

A **crossclaim** is a claim made by one defendant against another defendant in the main action. Rule 28 governs the procedure on a crossclaim. The rule provides that crossclaims may be brought only in certain limited circumstances. These circumstances exist if:

1. the **co-defendant** is or may be liable to the defendant for all or part of the plaintiff's claim;
2. the co-defendant is or may be liable to the defendant for an independent claim for damages or other relief, arising out of the same transaction or occurrence involved in, or related to, the main action;
3. the co-defendant should be bound by the determination of an issue arising between the plaintiff and the defendant; or
4. the defendant is claiming a contribution from a co-defendant under the *Negligence Act* (Rules 28.01(1) and (2)).

In short, the crossclaim must have a direct relationship to the main action in terms of subject matter and some level of joint liability to the plaintiff in the main action. For instance, Abigail is suing both Fred Flogem and Rattle Motors Ltd. for negligence. Fred and Rattle Motors Ltd. are therefore co-defendants. If Fred believes that he did nothing to cause Abigail's fall and that Rattle Motors Ltd. created an unsafe showroom and is totally responsible for Abigail's injuries, Fred can bring a crossclaim against Rattle Motors Ltd. However, if Fred wants to start an action against Rattle Motors Ltd. for unpaid wages, that issue has no connection to the main action and is not a proper subject for a crossclaim.

The defendant in the main action who brings the crossclaim is referred to in the Rules as the **crossclaiming defendant**. The defendant against whom the crossclaim

crossclaim
claim brought by one defendant whom the plaintiff is suing against another defendant whom the plaintiff is suing

co-defendant
one defendant in a multi-defendant proceeding

crossclaiming defendant
defendant in the main action who commences a crossclaim against one or more of the other defendants in that action

defendant on the crossclaim
defendant in the main action against whom a crossclaim is brought

is brought is called the **defendant on the crossclaim**. In our example, Fred is the crossclaiming defendant, and Rattle Motors Ltd. is the defendant on the crossclaim.

Until now, in our scenario involving Abigail, Fred, and Rattle Motors Ltd., Rattle and Fred have used the same lawyer. There was no conflict of interest for the lawyer because both Fred and Rattle were taking the same position against Abigail. Now, however, Fred is suing Rattle on the crossclaim and he cannot use the same law firm because of the conflict created by the crossclaim.

Pleadings in a Crossclaim

The following is a list of pleadings on a crossclaim:

1. statement of claim (Form 14A), delivered by the plaintiff in the main action against more than one defendant;

2. statement of defence (Form 18A), delivered by any defendant who is not crossclaiming;

3. reply (Form 25A), delivered by the plaintiff in the main action to answer any new issues raised in the statement of defence;

4. statement of defence and crossclaim (Form 28A), delivered by a defendant who wishes to answer the plaintiff's claim against him or her and bring a crossclaim against one of the other defendants being sued by the plaintiff in the main action;

5. defence to crossclaim (Form 28B), delivered by the co-defendant against whom the crossclaim has been commenced; and

6. reply to defence to crossclaim (Form 28C), delivered by the defendant who is bringing the crossclaim and who wants to reply to issues raised by the co-defendant he or she is suing on the crossclaim.

Statement of Defence and Crossclaim

A crossclaim is included in the same document as the statement of defence and is called a statement of defence and crossclaim (Form 28A). Figure 12.3 at the end of the chapter sets out a statement of defence and crossclaim. If the defendant has already filed a statement of defence in the main action and then decides he or she wants to bring a crossclaim, the defendant may simply amend the statement of defence under Rule 26 and include the crossclaim (Rule 28.03). No leave of the court is required.

The statement of defence and crossclaim must be served within the time limits for filing a statement of defence under Rule 18.01 or anytime before the defendant is noted in default. It may be served after a noting in default only with leave of the court (Rule 28.04(1)). There is no requirement for personal service of the statement of defence and crossclaim, unless the defendant in the crossclaim has failed to deliver a statement of defence or a notice of intent to defend in the main action.

Defence to the Crossclaim

The defence to the crossclaim, Form 28B, must be delivered within 20 days after service of the statement of defence and crossclaim. Figure 12.4 at the end of the chapter sets out a defence to a crossclaim. However, a defence to a crossclaim is not needed in the circumstances specified in Rule 28.05. When the crossclaim seeks only contribution or indemnity under the *Negligence Act* and the defendant to the crossclaim has delivered a defence in the main action that addresses the issues raised in the crossclaim, the defendant need not deliver a specific defence to the crossclaim. He or she can rely on the statement of defence delivered in the main action and is deemed to deny every allegation in the crossclaim.

In a crossclaim, the defendants are being sued by the plaintiff, and the crossclaim must have something to do with the plaintiff's claim in the main action. Very often the defendant on the crossclaim will be liable for damages on the crossclaim only if the plaintiff is successful in the main action. If the plaintiff loses his or her case, none of the defendants bears any liability.

Therefore, Rule 28.06 provides a procedure by which the defendant on the crossclaim may raise a defence to the plaintiff's claim against the other defendant—that is, the crossclaiming defendant. If the defendant wants to raise a defence to the plaintiff's claim against the crossclaiming defendant, he or she may do so in a separate part of the defence to the crossclaim. This part of the defence against the crossclaim must be headed with the wording "DEFENCE TO A PLAINTIFF'S CLAIM AGAINST CROSSCLAIMING DEFENDANT."

A defendant who does not defend against the crossclaiming defendant in this way is bound by any order made in the main action between the plaintiff and the crossclaiming defendant.

A defendant may be noted in default on a crossclaim just as a defendant can be noted in default in the main action. If the defendant on the crossclaim is noted in default on the crossclaim, judgment can be obtained against him or her only at the trial of the main action or on a motion to a judge. In other words, a default judgment cannot be obtained from the registrar in this circumstance.

Reply to the Defence to the Crossclaim

The reply to the defence to a crossclaim must be delivered within 10 days of the service of the defence to the crossclaim.

Trial of the Crossclaim

The crossclaim is usually heard at the trial of the main action or immediately thereafter. However, if the plaintiff believes that the crossclaim will prejudice or delay the trial of the main action, he or she may bring a motion seeking an order that the crossclaim proceed as a separate action. The court may order a separate trial on the crossclaim, or it may impose any terms necessary to ensure that the main action is not prejudiced or delayed.

Third-Party Claims: Rule 29

Introduction

One or more of the defendants to the main action may take the position that the plaintiff has not named all persons who are liable for his or her injuries. For instance, assume that unbeknownst to Abigail Boar, the car on display in the showroom had a manufacturer's defect in the oil pan that caused it to leak onto Rattle Motors Ltd.'s showroom floor. In its own investigation into Abigail's fall, Rattle Motors Ltd. discovers this defect and believes that Skunk Motorcar Company Ltd. is responsible for Abigail's injuries. But Abigail has not sued the car manufacturer. The Rules provide a procedure for Rattle Motors Ltd. to bring Skunk Motorcar Company Ltd. into the action. This is called a **third-party claim**, and it may be commenced by a defendant against any person who is not a party to the main action but who:

third-party claim
claim brought by a defendant in the main action against a person who is not already a party to the main action

- is or may be liable to the defendant for all or part of the plaintiff's claim,
- is or may be liable to the defendant for an independent claim for damages or other relief arising out of the same transaction or occurrence or series of transactions or occurrences involved in the main action, or
- should be bound by the determination of an issue arising between the plaintiff and the defendant (Rule 29.01).

Pleadings on a Third-Party Claim

A third-party claim is a new claim made against a person who is not a party to the main action. It is unlike a counterclaim and a crossclaim because these proceedings involve someone who is already a party to the existing proceeding. For instance, in a counterclaim, the defendant must make a claim against the plaintiff. A crossclaim involves defendants who are already parties by virtue of the fact that they are being sued by the same plaintiff or plaintiffs. There are therefore two sets of pleadings in a third-party proceeding: the pleadings in the main action and the pleadings in the third-party proceeding.

The pleadings in the main action are the regular pleadings: the statement of claim, the statement of defence, and the reply. The second set of pleadings between the defendant who is making the claim against the third party and the third party consists of:

- the third-party claim (Form 29A), delivered by the defendant asserting the claim and resembling a statement of claim in its form and content;
- the third-party defence (Form 29B), delivered by the third party to raise a defence to the claim being brought against him or her; and
- the reply to the third-party defence (Form 29C), delivered by the defendant asserting the third-party claim.

The Third-Party Claim

Because a third-party claim brings someone new into the proceeding and asserts a new claim, it is an originating process. It must be issued by the court within 10 days after the defendant delivers a statement of defence or anytime before the defendant is noted in default (Rule 29.02(1)). However, if the plaintiff replies to the statement of defence in the main action, the third-party claim may be issued within 10 days of the plaintiff's delivering his or her reply (Rule 29.02(1.1)).

There are exceptions to these time limits for commencing a third-party claim. A claim may be issued at any time if the plaintiff consents or if the court grants leave, and the court will grant leave unless the plaintiff will suffer prejudice (Rule 29.02(1.2)).

Like other originating processes, the third-party claim must be served on the third party personally or by an alternative to personal service under Rule 16.03. At the same time, the third party must also be served with all the pleadings previously delivered in the main action, any counterclaim, any crossclaim, and any other third-party claim. Service of the documents must take place within 30 days after the third-party claim is issued (Rule 29.02(2)).

The third-party claim must also be served on every other party to the main action within 30 days after it has been issued, but it need not be served personally on these parties (Rule 29.02(3)). Figure 12.5 at the end of the chapter sets out a third-party claim.

Third-Party Defence

The third-party defence must be delivered within 20, 40, or 60 days, depending on where the third-party claim is served (Rule 29.03).

Once the third party has delivered a third-party defence, there are several consequences that affect the third party:

- The third party must be served with any subsequent pleadings filed by any party to the main action.
- The plaintiff cannot obtain a consent judgment or note the defendant in default without notice to the third party.
- The third party has a right of discovery against any defendant to a crossclaim brought by the defendant who asserted the third-party claim (Rule 29.06).

Where a third party is noted in default for failing to file a third-party defence, judgment may be obtained against the third party only at trial of the main action or on a motion to a judge. The registrar cannot issue a default judgment against a third party. Figure 12.6 at the end of the chapter sets out a third-party defence.

Reply to Third-Party Defence

The defendant who commenced the third-party proceeding has a right to reply to a third-party defence within 10 days after being served with the defence.

Defence of the Main Action by the Third Party

A third party may defend against the plaintiff in the main action's claim against the defendant by delivering a statement of defence, and the third party may raise any defence open to the defendant. The reason for this rule is obvious: Since the defendant's third-party claim is based on the allegation that the third party is liable for the plaintiff's damages in whole or in part, if the plaintiff is unsuccessful in the main action, the defendant will have no need or interest in pursuing the third-party claim.

The statement of defence must be delivered within the standard time frames of 20, 40, or 60 days from the service of the third-party claim, depending on where the third party was served (Rule 29.03). The plaintiff may reply to that statement of defence within 10 days after being served (Rule 29.04).

Once the third party has delivered a statement of defence in the main action, he or she has the same rights and obligations in the main action as the defendant. The third party may seek discovery, participate in the trial of the main action, and appeal any decision made at the trial. In addition, he or she is bound by any order made in the main action between the plaintiff and the defendant who made the third-party claim. In the event that the third party does not deliver a statement of defence in the main action, he or she is still bound by any order made in that action between the plaintiff and the defendant who made the third-party claim.

Trial of the Third-Party Claim

After the close of pleadings in the third-party claim, the claim must be listed for trial without undue delay in accordance with Rule 48. It is to be placed on the trial list immediately after the main action, and it must be tried at the same time or immediately after the main action.

If the plaintiff is concerned that the third-party claim will delay or prejudice the main action, he or she may bring a motion. The court may order that the third-party claim be tried as a separate action or set terms for a trial of the action that will prevent delay or prejudice. However, the order or terms may not cause any injustice to the defendant or the third party.

Subsequent Party Claims

A third party may bring a fourth-party claim against a person who is not a party to the main action as long as it meets the criteria set out in Rule 29.01 for the commencement of a third-party action. A fourth party may then assert a fifth-party claim under the same criteria, and so on (Rules 29.11 and 29.12).

Rule 29.14 requires that all third-party and subsequent claims shall be given the same court file number as the main action, followed by a suffix letter. For example, in Abigail's case the court file number is 01-CV-1234. The court file number for any third-party claim would have a file number such as 01-CV-1234-A. Any fourth-party claim would have a court file number such as 01-CV-1234-B, and so on. However, each courthouse uses a different style of letter suffix. In Toronto, for example, the court may use a suffix for a third-party court file number that, in Abigail's case, would be 01-CV-1234-CP1. If it is not clear what type of suffix numbering the court in a particular region uses, it would be best to either call the court office for clarification or simply put in the file number for the main action and the court office will add the suffix during the filing process.

CHAPTER SUMMARY

In this chapter, we have explored counterclaims, crossclaims, and third-party claims.

Rule 27 governs counterclaims, a procedure in which the defendant is suing the plaintiff and any number of other persons along with the plaintiff. The basis for the counterclaim does not have to have the same subject matter as the main claim. Pleadings relating only to the counterclaim are the statement of defence and counterclaim, the defence to the counterclaim, or the reply to defence to the counterclaim. A counterclaim that goes to trial is usually heard at the completion of the trial of the main action. However, if it appears that the counterclaim may delay the main action, the court may order it to be tried separately.

Rule 28 governs crossclaims, a procedure that involves one defendant suing another defendant. The crossclaim must be directly related to the main action in terms of its content and the joint liability of the defendants to the plaintiff. Pleadings relating only to the crossclaim are the statement of defence and crossclaim, the defence to the crossclaim, or the reply to the defence to the crossclaim. The trial of the crossclaim is usually held at the same time as or immediately after the trial of the main action. However, the plaintiff may bring a motion to have the crossclaim tried separately if there is a possibility that the crossclaim could delay the main action.

Rule 29 governs third-party claims, a procedure in which the defendant commences an action against a person whom the plaintiff is not suing. It must be directly related to the main action respecting subject matter and liability of the parties. The pleadings related solely to a third-party claim are the third-party claim, the third-party defence, and the reply to the third-party defence. Since a third-party claim brings a new party into the proceeding, it is an originating process and must be issued by the court. The third-party action is usually tried at the same time as or immediately after the main action, although the plaintiff may move to have it tried as a separate matter if it will delay the main action. A third party may make a fourth-party claim and bring an additional party into the proceeding. A fourth party may bring in a fifth party, and so on. All third-party and subsequent claims shall be given the same court file number as the main action, followed by a suffix letter.

KEY TERMS

co-defendant, 291

counterclaim, 288

crossclaim, 291

crossclaiming defendant, 291

defendant on the crossclaim, 292

main action, 288

third-party claim, 294

NOTE

1. If you are using a publisher's version of the Rules, such as Carswell's *Ontario Annual Practice*, that contains procedural charts, you may find it helpful to locate in your rules book the chart that deals with the procedure in counterclaims, crossclaims, and third-party claims and follow it as you read through this chapter.

REFERENCES

Negligence Act, RSO 1990, c. N.1.

Rules of Civil Procedure, RRO 1990, reg. 194.

REVIEW QUESTIONS

1. John Smith is suing Big Bob's Building Emporium Ltd. Big Bob believes that Diddlehopper Cleaning Ltd. bears some of the liability for the claim. What can Big Bob do? What rule applies?

2. Draft the general heading for the pleading in question 1.

3. What is the document used to bring a counterclaim? What is this document's form number?

4. In a counterclaim, is the defendant limited to suing the plaintiff in the main action?

5. What are the pleadings used on a counterclaim?

6. In what circumstances is a crossclaim available and what rule applies?

7. The defendant has already filed a statement of defence. However, he now wants to commence a crossclaim against one of his co-defendants. Do the Rules permit him to do this?

8. Which of the proceedings you have studied in this chapter are originating processes?

9. John Green wishes to commence a crossclaim against his co-defendant George Black. What steps must be taken to commence the crossclaim?

10. At what stage of the proceedings may a third-party claim be issued?

11. If a third-party claim has been commenced, is there any step the plaintiff can take to have the third-party claim heard separately from the main action?

DISCUSSION QUESTIONS

1. Kule Kiddie Fashions Inc. is being sued by Mindy McGillicuddy for a breach of contract. Mindy is claiming that Kule Kiddie did not deliver her line of spring clothing to her boutique as required under her contract with it. Kule Kiddie claims that it did not deliver the spring line of clothing because Mindy still owes $40,000 on the winter line and must pay before there will be any more clothing deliveries. What can Kule Kiddie do to recover its money from Mindy? What rule applies?

2. Kule Kiddie Fashions Inc. is being sued by Mindy McGillicuddy for a breach of contract for its failure to deliver a clothing line to Mindy's boutique. Kule Kiddie has had many business dealings with Mindy. Last year, Mindy did some clothing design work for it but did not complete the job because she left to open her own boutique. Kule Kiddie was forced to retain another designer to finish the job. The second designer charged twice as much for the job. Because it was late, Kule Kiddie lost $100,000 in income. Can Kule Kiddie bring a counterclaim in this situation?

3. Kule Kiddie Fashions Inc. wants to sue Mindy's son, Boris, an electrician. When he did some work at its factory last year, he crossed the wires, causing its major knitting machine to blow up. While Kule Kiddie was awaiting a new machine, it lost $20,000 in business. Can Kule Kiddie bring a counterclaim against Boris in the main action that his mother has commenced against it?

Figure 12.1 Statement of Defence and Counterclaim (Form 27B)

Court file no. 01-CV-1234

ONTARIO
SUPERIOR COURT OF JUSTICE

BETWEEN:

ABIGAIL BOAR

Plaintiff

and

RATTLE MOTORS LTD. and FRED FLOGEM

Defendants

AND BETWEEN:

RATTLE MOTORS LTD.

Plaintiff by Counterclaim

and

ABIGAIL BOAR and JAMES JINGLEHIMER

Defendants to the Counterclaim

STATEMENT OF DEFENCE AND COUNTERCLAIM

TO THE DEFENDANTS TO THE COUNTERCLAIM

A LEGAL PROCEEDING has been commenced against you by way of a counterclaim in an action in this court. The claim made against you is set out in the following pages.

IF YOU WISH TO DEFEND THIS COUNTERCLAIM, you or an Ontario lawyer acting for you must prepare a defence to counterclaim in Form 27C prescribed by the Rules of Civil Procedure, serve it on the plaintiff by counterclaim's lawyer or, where the plaintiff by counterclaim does not have a lawyer, serve it on the plaintiff by counterclaim, and file it, with proof of service, in this court, WITHIN TWENTY DAYS after this statement of defence and counterclaim is served on you.

If you are not already a party to the main action and you are served in another province or territory of Canada or in the United States of America, the period for serving and filing your defence is forty days. If you are served outside Canada and the United States of America, the period is sixty days.

If you are not already a party to the main action, instead of serving and filing a defence to counterclaim, you may serve and file a notice of intent to defend in Form 18B prescribed by the Rules of Civil Procedure. This will entitle you to ten more days within which to serve and file your defence to counterclaim.

Figure 12.1   Continued

IF YOU FAIL TO DEFEND THIS COUNTERCLAIM, JUDGMENT MAY BE GIVEN AGAINST YOU IN YOUR ABSENCE AND WITHOUT FURTHER NOTICE TO YOU. IF YOU WISH TO DEFEND THIS PROCEEDING BUT ARE UNABLE TO PAY LEGAL FEES, LEGAL AID MAY BE AVAILABLE TO YOU BY CONTACTING A LOCAL LEGAL AID OFFICE.

IF YOU PAY THE AMOUNT OF THE COUNTERCLAIM AGAINST YOU, and $500.00 for costs, within the time for serving and filing your defence to counterclaim, you may move to have the counterclaim against you dismissed by the court. If you believe the amount claimed for costs is excessive, you may pay the amount of the counterclaim and $400.00 for costs and have the costs assessed by the court.

Date: January 12, year 1   Issued by: _____

                                                         Local registrar

                                         Address of
                                         court office: Courthouse

                                                         393 University Avenue

                                                         Toronto, Ontario, M5G 1E6

TO: James Jinglehimer

       4747 Memory Lane

       Toronto, Ontario, M7T 8U9

       Defendant to the counterclaim

TO: Just & Coping

       Barristers and Solicitors

       365 Bay Street – 8701

       Toronto, Ontario, M3J 4A9

       I.M. Just

       LSUC #12345R

       tel. 416-762-1342

       fax 416-762-2300

       Lawyer for the Defendant to the Counterclaim, Abigail Boar

1. The defendants admit the allegations contained in paragraphs 1, 2, 3, and 4 of the statement of claim.

2. The defendants deny the allegations contained in paragraphs 5, 6, 7, 8, 9, 10, 11, 12, 13, 14, 15, 16, 17, and 18 of the statement of claim.

Figure 12.1   Continued

3. The plaintiff entered the corporate defendant's premises at about 7:30 p.m. on September 14, year 0. She indicated to Linda Lucre, a salesperson on the showroom floor at that time, that she was interested in purchasing a Super Coupe.

4. Lucre showed the plaintiff several automobile models. Then the plaintiff walked over, on her own, to look at another model. She walked around the car and fell.

5. The defendants admit that there was a small pool of oil on one side of the car but claim that it was easily visible to any reasonably prudent person who could have avoided it without difficulty.

6. The defendants admit that two of the four spotlights were off but deny that the area was not well illuminated. The defendants state that the area was well and clearly illuminated. Any hazard, if there was one, which is specifically denied, could easily be seen and avoided.

7. The defendants admit that the plaintiff fell and appeared to lose consciousness momentarily. She also appeared to injure her lower right arm in the fall.

8. The defendants state that the plaintiff, before coming to the corporate defendant's place of business, had consumed two glasses of wine and that she was intoxicated when she entered the defendant's premises.

9. The plaintiff fell solely as a result of her intoxication. Any injuries she sustained were solely the result of her own intoxicated state and not any acts of the defendants.

10. With respect to paragraphs 10, 11, 12, 13, 14, and 15 of the statement of claim, the defendants deny that the plaintiff suffered such injuries as described. Further or in the alternative, the defendants state that the plaintiff has exaggerated both the extent of her injuries and the consequences of them.

11. With respect to the plaintiff's allegation that she cannot return to work, the defendants state that the plaintiff is exaggerating her injuries and that she is a malingerer. In the alternative, the defendants state that the plaintiff has failed to mitigate her damages.

12. With respect to the allegations of negligence in paragraph 16, the defendant Flogem states that he knew there was oil on the floor but that it was contained and did not constitute a danger to any reasonably prudent person. The defendant Flogem admits that he turned off two of the four spotlights, but he specifically denies that he created a situation of danger for the plaintiff because the area in question remained well illuminated and safe for a reasonably prudent person.

13. The defendants therefore request that this action be dismissed with costs.

Figure 12.1   Concluded

COUNTERCLAIM

14.   The plaintiff by way of counterclaim claims:

   a. the sum of $11,275.98;

   b. interest in the said amount of $11,275.98 at the rate of 5 percent per year from September 1, year 1 to the date of payment on the judgment;

   c. its costs of this counterclaim; and

   d. such further relief as seems just to this court.

15.   On November 15, year −1, the defendants to the counterclaim, Abigail Boar and James Jinglehimer, entered into a contract of purchase and sale with the plaintiff by counterclaim, Rattle Motors Ltd., for the purchase on credit of a Super Coupe, year 0 model. The full purchase price of the vehicle was $22,472.89. The price was to be paid in monthly installments of $329.47, commencing December 1, year −1.

16.   Between December 1, year −1 and September 1, year 0, the defendants to the counterclaim paid the requisite amount owing each month. No payment has been made pursuant to the agreement since September 1, year 0.

17.   The defendants to the counterclaim have made no payment since September 1, year 0 and are currently 4 months in arrears.

Date: January 12, year 1

Huey Sue
LSUC #23456T
Barrister and Solicitor
65 False Trail
Toronto, Ontario, M6Y 1Z6

tel. 416-485-6891
fax 416-485-6892

Lawyer for the Plaintiff by Counterclaim

Figure 12.2 Defence to Counterclaim (Form 27C)

Court file no. 01-CV-1234

ONTARIO
SUPERIOR COURT OF JUSTICE

BETWEEN:

ABIGAIL BOAR

Plaintiff

and

RATTLE MOTORS LTD. and FRED FLOGEM

Defendants

AND BETWEEN:

RATTLE MOTORS LTD.

Plaintiff by Counterclaim

and

ABIGAIL BOAR and JAMES JINGLEHIMER

Defendants to the Counterclaim

DEFENCE TO COUNTERCLAIM

1. The defendants to the counterclaim admit the allegations contained in paragraphs 15 and 16 of the counterclaim.

2. The defendants to the counterclaim deny the allegations contained in paragraph 17 of the counterclaim.

3. The defendants to the counterclaim have no knowledge in respect of the allegations contained in paragraph 14 of the counterclaim.

4. The automobile that was the subject of the contract of sale between the plaintiff by counterclaim and the defendants to the counterclaim has required 4 major motor repairs since purchase. For the 7 months that the defendants to the counterclaim have had possession of the vehicle, the vehicle has been inoperable for all or part of 5 of those months.

Figure 12.2   Concluded

5. On September 14, year 0, the defendants to the counterclaim attempted to return the vehicle to the plaintiff by counterclaim, but the sales manager refused to accept the return.

6. The defendants to the counterclaim allege that there has been a fundamental breach of the contract of sale by the plaintiff by counterclaim and that they are no longer liable for payments on the contract.

7. The defendants to the counterclaim therefore submit that the counterclaim in this action be dismissed.

February 1, year 1

> Just & Coping
> Barristers and Solicitors
> 365 Bay Street – 8701
> Toronto, Ontario, M3J 4A9
>
> I.M. Just
> LSUC #12345R
>
> tel. 416-762-1342
> fax 416-762-2300
>
> Lawyers for the Defendants to the Counterclaim

TO: Huey Sue
> LSUC #23456T
> Barrister and Solicitor
> 65 False Trail
> Toronto, Ontario, M6Y 1Z6
>
> tel. 416-485-6891
> fax 416-485-6892
>
> Lawyer for the Plaintiff by Counterclaim

RCP-E 27C (July 1, 2007)

Figure 12.3   Statement of Defence and Crossclaim (Form 28A)

Court file no. 01-CV-1234

ONTARIO
SUPERIOR COURT OF JUSTICE

BETWEEN:

ABIGAIL BOAR

Plaintiff

and

RATTLE MOTORS LTD. and FRED FLOGEM

Defendants

STATEMENT OF DEFENCE AND CROSSCLAIM OF THE DEFENDANT
FRED FLOGEM

1. The defendant Fred Flogem admits the allegations in paragraphs 1, 2, and 3 of the statement of claim.

2. The defendant denies the allegations contained in paragraphs 7, 8, 9, 10, 11, 12, 13, 14, 15, 16, and 17 of the statement of claim.

3. The plaintiff entered the defendant Rattle Motors Ltd.'s premises at about 7:30 p.m. on September 14, year 0. She indicated to Linda Lucre, a salesperson on the showroom floor at that time, that she was interested in purchasing a Super Coupe.

4. Lucre showed the plaintiff several automobile models. Then the plaintiff walked over, on her own, to look at another model. She walked around the car and fell.

5. The defendant Fred Flogem admits that there was a small pool of oil on the floor to one side of the car but claims that it was easily visible to any reasonably prudent person who could have avoided it without difficulty.

6. The defendant Fred Flogem admits that two of the four spotlights were off but denies that the area was not well illuminated. The defendant Fred Flogem states that the area was well and clearly illuminated. Any hazard, if there was one, which is specifically denied, could easily be seen and avoided.

7. The defendant Fred Flogem admits that the plaintiff fell and appeared to lose consciousness momentarily. She also appeared to injure her lower right arm in the fall.

Figure 12.3 Continued

8. The defendant Fred Flogem states that the plaintiff, before coming to the defendant Rattle Motors Ltd.'s place of business, had consumed two glasses of wine and that she was intoxicated when she entered the premises.

9. The plaintiff fell solely as a result of her intoxication. Any injuries she sustained were solely the result of her own intoxicated state and not any acts of the defendant Fred Flogem.

10. With respect to paragraphs 10, 11, 12, 13, 14, and 15 of the statement of claim, the defendant Fred Flogem denies that the plaintiff suffered such injuries as described. Further or in the alternative, the defendant Fred Flogem states that the plaintiff has exaggerated both the extent of her injuries and the consequences of them.

11. With respect to the plaintiff's allegation that she cannot return to work, the defendant Fred Flogem states that the plaintiff is exaggerating her injuries and that she is a malingerer. In the alternative, the defendant Fred Flogem states that the plaintiff has failed to mitigate her damages.

12. With respect to the allegations of negligence in paragraph 16, the defendant Fred Flogem states that he knew there was oil on the floor but that it was contained and did not constitute a danger to any reasonably prudent person. The defendant Fred Flogem admits that he turned off two of the four spotlights, but he specifically denies that he created a situation of danger for the plaintiff because the area in question remained well illuminated and safe for a reasonably prudent person.

13. The defendant Fred Flogem therefore requests that this action be dismissed with costs.

CROSSCLAIM

14. The defendant Fred Flogem claims against the defendant Rattle Motors Ltd.:

   a. contribution and indemnity for any and all claims of the plaintiff,

   b. costs of this action on a substantial indemnity basis, and

   c. such further relief as seems just to this court.

15. The defendant Fred Flogem is the employee of Rattle Motors Ltd.

16. The defendant Fred Flogem states that if the plaintiff has suffered damage, which is not admitted, such damage was caused by the negligence of the defendant Rattle

Figure 12.3   Concluded

Motors Ltd. and did not result from any act or omission of the defendant Fred
Flogem.

17.   *[Any additional facts on which the crossclaiming defendant relies are to be set out
here in paragraphs in the same manner as in a statement of claim.]*

January 12, year 1

> Brenda Brilliant
> LSUC #86421X
> Barrister & Solicitor
> 1400 Willsa Way
> Toronto, Ontario, M6V 9T7
>
> tel. 416-766-4321
> fax 416-766-9876
>
> Lawyer for the Crossclaiming Defendant

TO: Huey Sue
LSUC #23456T
Barrister and Solicitor
65 False Trail
Toronto, Ontario, M6Y 1Z6

tel. 416-485-6891
fax 416-485-6892

Lawyer for the Defendant to the Crossclaim

RCP-E 28A (July 1, 2007)

Figure 12.4   Defence to Crossclaim (Form 28B)

Court file no. 01-CV-1234

ONTARIO
SUPERIOR COURT OF JUSTICE

BETWEEN:

ABIGAIL BOAR

Plaintiff

and

RATTLE MOTORS LTD. and FRED FLOGEM

Defendants

DEFENCE TO CROSSCLAIM

1. The defendant Rattle Motors Ltd. admits the allegations contained in paragraph 15 of the crossclaim.

2. The defendant Rattle Motors Ltd. denies the allegations contained in paragraphs 16 and 17 of the crossclaim.

3. The defendant Rattle Motors Ltd. has no knowledge in respect of the allegations contained in paragraph 14 of the crossclaim.

4. *[Any facts relied on as a defence to the crossclaim must be laid out in consecutively numbered paragraphs, as they would be in a statement of defence.]*

DEFENCE TO A PLAINTIFF'S CLAIM AGAINST
CROSSCLAIMING DEFENDANT

7. *[If the defendant to the crossclaim wishes to defend against the plaintiff's claim against the crossclaiming defendant, pursuant to Rule 28.06, further consecutively numbered paragraphs are included here. If no such defence is being raised, this part of the document is not included.]*

Figure 12.4   Concluded

January 25, year 1

Huey Sue
LSUC #23456T
Barrister and Solicitor
65 False Trail
Toronto, Ontario, M6Y 1Z6

tel. 416-485-6891
fax 416-485-6892

Lawyer for the Defendant to the Crossclaim

TO: Brenda Brilliant
LSUC #86421X
Barrister & Solicitor
1400 Willsa Way
Toronto, Ontario, M6V 9T7

tel. 416-766-4321
fax 416-766-9876

Lawyer for the Crossclaiming Defendant

RCP-E 28B (July 1, 2007)

Figure 12.5   Third-Party Claim (Form 29A)

Court file no. 01-CV-1234-A

ONTARIO
SUPERIOR COURT OF JUSTICE

BETWEEN:

ABIGAIL BOAR

Plaintiff

and

RATTLE MOTORS LTD. and FRED FLOGEM

Defendants

and

SKUNK MOTORCAR COMPANY LTD.

Third Party

THIRD-PARTY CLAIM OF THE DEFENDANT
RATTLE MOTORS LTD.

TO THE THIRD PARTY

A LEGAL PROCEEDING HAS BEEN COMMENCED AGAINST YOU by way of a third-party claim in an action in this court.

The action was commenced by the plaintiff against the defendant for the relief claimed in the statement of claim served with this third-party claim. The defendant has defended the action on the grounds set out in the statement of defence served with this third-party claim. The defendant's claim against you is set out in the following pages.

IF YOU WISH TO DEFEND THIS THIRD-PARTY CLAIM, you or an Ontario lawyer acting for you must prepare a third-party defence in Form 29B prescribed by the Rules of Civil Procedure, serve it on the lawyers for the other parties or, where a party does not have a lawyer, serve it on the party, and file it, with proof of service, WITHIN TWENTY DAYS after this third-party claim is served on you, if you are served in Ontario.

If you are served in another province or territory of Canada or in the United States of America, the period for serving and filing your third-party defence is forty days. If you are served outside Canada and the United States of America, the period is sixty days.

Figure 12.5   Continued

Instead of serving and filing a third-party defence, you may serve and file a notice of intent to defend in Form 18B prescribed by the Rules of Civil Procedure. This will entitle you to ten more days within which to serve and file your third-party defence.

YOU MAY ALSO DEFEND the action by the plaintiff against the defendant by serving and filing a statement of defence within the time for serving and filing your third-party defence.

IF YOU FAIL TO DEFEND THIS THIRD-PARTY CLAIM, JUDGMENT MAY BE GIVEN AGAINST YOU IN YOUR ABSENCE AND WITHOUT FURTHER NOTICE TO YOU. IF YOU WISH TO DEFEND THIS PROCEEDING BUT ARE UNABLE TO PAY LEGAL FEES, LEGAL AID MAY BE AVAILABLE TO YOU BY CONTACTING A LOCAL LEGAL AID OFFICE.

IF YOU PAY THE AMOUNT OF THE THIRD-PARTY CLAIM AGAINST YOU, and $500.00 for costs, within the time for serving and filing your third-party defence, you may move to have the third-party claim dismissed by the court. If you believe the amount claimed for costs is excessive, you may pay the amount of the third-party claim and $400.00 for costs and have the costs assessed by the court.

Date: May 25, year 1   Issued by: _____

                                        Address of
                                        court office: Courthouse
                                                       393 University Avenue
                                                       Toronto, Ontario, M5G 1E6

TO: Skunk Motorcar Company Ltd.
     349 Losers' Lane
     Windsor, Ontario, J4T 6Y7

CLAIM

1. The defendant Rattle Motors Ltd. claims against the third party:

    a. a declaration that the third party is liable to the defendant for all or part of the plaintiff's claim that the defendant may be ordered by this court to satisfy;

    b. further, or in the alternative, contribution, indemnity, and relief in respect to any damages, interest, and costs awarded to the plaintiff as against the defendant;

Figure 12.5   Concluded

    c. costs of defending the main action and the third-party action on a substantial indemnity basis; and

    d. such further relief as seems just to this court.

2. The plaintiff in the main action alleges that as a result of the negligence of the defendants, she slipped and fell on a patch of oil while viewing automobiles for sale in the showroom of the defendant Rattle Motors Ltd.

3. The plaintiff in the main action alleges that as a result of her fall in the showroom of the defendant Rattle Motors Ltd., she suffered damages totalling $203,649.00, together with interest and costs.

4. The defendant Rattle Motors Ltd. denies that it is negligent and further denies any liability to the plaintiff.

5. *[Each allegation of a material fact relied on must be set out in consecutively numbered paragraphs. The form and content should resemble the form and content of a statement of claim.]*

6. If the defendant Rattle Motors Ltd. is found at trial to be liable for the plaintiff's claim, or any part of it, then the defendant Rattle Motors Ltd. is entitled to contribution, indemnification, or relief from the third party to the full extent of the damages found and the costs of the main and third-party actions on a substantial indemnity basis.

Date of issue: February 6, year 1

Huey Sue
LSUC #23456T
Barrister and Solicitor
65 False Trail
Toronto, Ontario, M6Y 1Z6

tel. 416-485-6891
fax 416-485-6892

Lawyer for the Defendants

RCP-E 29A (July 1, 2007)

Figure 12.6   Third-Party Defence (Form 29B)

Court file no. 01-CV-1234-A

ONTARIO
SUPERIOR COURT OF JUSTICE

BETWEEN:

ABIGAIL BOAR

Plaintiff

and

RATTLE MOTORS LTD. and FRED FLOGEM

Defendants

and

SKUNK MOTORCAR COMPANY LTD.

Third Party

THIRD-PARTY DEFENCE

1. The third party admits the allegations contained in paragraphs 2 and 3 of the third-party claim.

2. The third party denies the allegations contained in paragraphs 5 and 6 of the third-party claim.

3. The third party has no knowledge in respect of the allegations contained in paragraph 1 of the third-party claim.

4. *[Each allegation of a material fact must be set out in a consecutively numbered paragraph. The form and content should resemble the form and content of a statement of defence.]*

Figure 12.6 Concluded

February 16, year 1

U.R. Smart
LSUC #13579S
Barrister & Solicitor
4700 Bay Street
Toronto, Ontario, M4T 8V2

tel. 416-387-7882
fax 416-387-7883

Lawyer for the Third Party

TO: Huey Sue
LSUC #23456T
Barrister and Solicitor
65 False Trail
Toronto, Ontario, M6Y 1Z6

tel. 416-485-6891
fax 416-485-6892

Lawyer for the Defendants

RCP-E 29B (July 1, 2007)

Amending Pleadings 13

Introduction

Ideally, before issuing a pleading, you will have carefully investigated the facts, researched the law, and drafted the claim, defence, or crossclaim. All parties should expect to be able to rely on that pleading as an accurate statement of your case right through the pretrial and trial stages. However, after a pleading has been issued, often as the result of information obtained on discovery, or even at trial, new facts may emerge that expand or change a claim or defence, so that the pleading is no longer accurate. For example, if, on the eve of trial, further medical tests showed that Abigail had suffered more serious mental impairment than was evident from the description of her injuries when the claim issued and when she appeared for discovery, I.M. Just would need to amend the pleadings. He would do this by adding this information to a description of the consequences of her injuries. He would also have to amend paragraph 1 to increase the claim for general damages. If her claim was not amended and the evidence at trial showed more serious damages than had been pleaded, Abigail would be limited to judgment for the amount she had claimed in her pleadings. The reason for this is that the defendant expects to answer the case as pleaded. If a plaintiff changes his or her claim, the defendant is entitled to proper notice; if it is not given, the plaintiff is confined to the case as originally pleaded. The balance of this chapter concerns how a party goes about giving that notice.

Right to Amend

Rule 26.01 states that the court *shall* amend a pleading at *any stage* of the action, including trial, unless the prejudice to the other side cannot be compensated by costs or by an adjournment. There are relatively few cases where costs and an adjournment have been found to not compensate the opposite party when an amendment is sought, even at a late stage. While judges usually grant the request, given the language of the rule, they often remain skeptical of a defence or claim that arises late in a proceeding. If your law firm is going to amend, it should do so at the earliest opportunity. The longer it waits, the more expensive it will be. For example, if an amendment is sought and granted on the eve of trial, it will often be on terms that the case be adjourned and that the opposite party be given the opportunity to have discovery, both oral and documentary, on the issues covered by your amendment. In addition, your amendment may trigger an amendment to the opposite party's pleading as he or she pleads to your amendment. The costs of all the procedures spawned by the amendment will be borne by the party seeking the amendment.

When You Amend Makes a Difference

Before pleadings are noted closed, any party may amend his or her pleading without seeking leave of the court and without having terms imposed as a condition for making the amendment, provided that the amendment does not result in new parties being added or existing parties being deleted (Rule 26.02(a)). Once pleadings have closed, then you must bring a motion (Rule 26.02(c)), in which case the court follows the requirements of Rule 26.01, and permits the amendment on terms unless it is so prejudicial that costs and adjournment will not adequately compensate the other party. However, if all parties consent, the amendment may be made without the court's permission on filing the consent. Any new party being added as a result of the amendment must consent as well (Rule 26.02(b)).

How to Make an Amendment

Rule 26.03, which governs the making of amendments, predates the age of electronic document creation. It provides one of the few instances in the Rules where interlineations in pen seem to be required, although you should be able to use litigation software or ordinary word processing software to underline text in an existing pleading file—you should not necessarily need to get out a quill pen to do the job.

If the amendment is not extensive, consisting of a phrase or a sentence or two, it can simply be written in the appropriate place on the face of the document and underlined. If the amendment is so extensive that interlineations would make the document difficult to read, the party should file a fresh copy of the original pleading as amended, bearing the date of the original pleading, with the title preceded by the word "amended" (AMENDED STATEMENT OF DEFENCE, for example). The amended parts of the fresh pleading must be underlined.

In each case, the registrar must note on the pleading the date on which the amendment was made and the authority for it: (a) the order of the judge or master who permitted it, (b) Rule 26.02(a) if leave was not required because pleadings were not noted closed, or (c) the filed consent of all parties.

If the pleading is amended more than once, each subsequent amendment is underlined an additional time. The text of the second amendment made is underlined twice to distinguish it from the previous amendment, and so on. So, for example, in Figure 13.1, Abigail's claim for relief in her statement of claim set out her damages at $200,000 in paragraph 1a. It was then amended to $250,000 (and underlined once), then later amended to $400,000 (and underlined twice).

Figure 13.1   Amended Pleading

1. The plaintiff claims, against the defendant:

$250,000 $400,000
    ↑   ↑

a. general damages in the amount of $200,000; ...

Amended Pleadings Must Be Served

Every party to the proceeding, including any party added by the amendment, is to be served with the amended pleading. This includes not only the opposite party but also those added by counterclaim, crossclaim, and third-party claim. Proof of service of the amended pleading must be filed "forthwith."[1] If the amended pleading is an originating process, such as a statement of claim, it need not be served personally on a party that was served with and responded to the original pleading. However, if the party had previously defaulted or is added as a result of the amendment, he or she must be served personally (Rule 26.04). The defaulting party's opportunity to plead and rejoin the proceeding is revived by being served with the amended pleading. The reason for this is that a defaulter with no defence to the original claim might have defence to the amended claim and may now wish to defend.

A party served with an amended pleading has 10 days to respond. If the amendment is made at an early date, while the time to respond to the original pleading is still running, then the party has the balance of the time remaining, if it is greater than 10 days (Rule 26.05(1)).

If a pleading is amended and served on another party and that party responded to the original pleading but not to the amended version, that party is deemed to be relying on its original pre-amended pleading (Rule 26.05(2)). Interestingly, the Rules do not specify what form this "response" should take. Refer back to Rule 1.04(2), which states that where the Rules do not provide for a situation, you should proceed by analogy to the Rules—in other words, find a similar process in the Rules and adapt it. You might use a reply and modify it to respond to the amended pleading. Alternatively, you could develop a document called a "response to the amended statement of claim," or other amended document, with the usual general heading and title of proceedings. Then set out your response in consecutively numbered paragraphs, following the usual rules for pleadings. However, if your response also requires you to amend your pleadings, you must bring a motion to do so if pleadings are closed or the 10 days permitted for responding to amended pleadings under Rule 25.06(1) has passed.

If an amendment is made at trial and is recorded on the trial record by the court reporter, no formal written order need be drafted, issued, or entered. It is likewise unnecessary to formally amend the pleading (Rule 26.06).

CHAPTER SUMMARY

This chapter reviewed the process of amending pleadings, and it noted the general rule that amendments are to be permitted unless they are so prejudicial that the other side cannot be compensated in costs or by an adjournment. We then noted how amendments are made technically on the face of the pleadings by underlining and, in some cases, by issuing a fresh copy of the original pleadings as amended. Once an amendment is made, the pleading must be served on all parties, who then have the opportunity to respond to the amended pleadings and to amend their own pleadings.

NOTE

1. "Forthwith" is not defined as a specific time period, but it means "as soon as possible."

REFERENCE

Rules of Civil Procedure, RRO 1990, reg. 194.

REVIEW QUESTIONS

1. Amir claims that you can amend pleadings at any time. Is he correct?

2. What constitutes prejudice in the context of amending pleadings?

3. When do you need leave to amend and when do you not need it?

4. How do you make amendments?

5. What happens after a pleading is formally amended?

DISCUSSION QUESTION

1. Read and respond to the following memorandum:

To: E. Egregious, law clerk

From: I.M. Just, lawyer

Re: *Boar v. Rattle Motors Ltd. et al.*, amending claim

Although trial is only three weeks away, I have just had a supplementary report and updated prognosis from Ms. Boar's neurologist, Dr. Morris Furgazy. In his report, dated May 30, year 2, Dr. Furgazy says that as a result of recent neurological tests, he has found that there is much more brain damage than he originally thought. Specifically, there are neurological lesions present, which cause impaired cognitive function. Originally, these looked to be transient or relatively minor, but it now appears that they are permanent and will result in much-reduced abilities to reason and to remember information. This changes the nature of the injury sustained and increases the damages that we should be claiming. I called Huey Sue to see if he would consent to the amendments. He refused, saying that we should have had this information much earlier. We will need to move to amend.

a. What do you think the likely outcome of a motion to amend will be?

b. Please draft a motion and an affidavit in the lawyer's name.

PART III

From Discovery to Trial

Discovery

14

Introduction

In terms of time, and therefore cost, **discovery** takes up a large part of the proceedings prior to trial. The purposes of discovery are:

- to discover the evidence on which the opponent relies to establish the facts of his or her case,
- to obtain admissions that will help prove your case,
- to obtain admissions that will assist you in weakening the opponent's case,
- to narrow issues for trial by requiring disclosure,
- to assess the credibility of the opposing party and your client as witnesses, and
- to determine whether there is a basis for settlement before trial.

While the purposes of discovery outlined here have not changed, we will see in this chapter that the process has changed dramatically because much of what used to be printed documentary evidence, or hard copy, is now in digital format, and that has had a dramatic effect on the way in which discovery must now be approached.

Overview of the Discovery Process and e-Discovery

No discussion of the discovery process in Ontario would be complete without recognition of the impact that electronic documents and e-data have had on it. Data sources and volumes have expanded exponentially, and this has, since the beginning of the century, forced drastic changes in the way discovery is conducted.

The greatest impact has been on discovery of documents, but the potential expansion of electronic documentary evidence has also affected oral examination for discovery of a party: it is possible that a party will be questioned about the nature or content of a potentially vast pool of e-documents. This has resulted not only in changes to the *Rules of Civil Procedure*, but also in changes to discovery "best practices." As the legal profession comes to grips with these changes, you can expect that what is described here as "best practices" will evolve and change further as the legal profession discovers what works well and what does not.

Air Canada v. WestJet Airlines

We can better understand some e-data issues by looking at how they arose and were handled in *Air Canada v. WestJet Airlines Ltd.*[1]

Air Canada sued WestJet, alleging that WestJet had illegally obtained access to Air Canada's computers and a variety of databases in order to get inside information about Air Canada's operations so that WestJet could gain a competitive edge. Air Canada alleged that WestJet had misused confidential data that primarily pertained to passenger loads and flight scheduling. There were a variety of databases and massive volumes of data, including deleted material, and material that had been altered or had gone through various versions. Some of the data were numeric and some were text, and various types of software had been used to produce usable, current copies of data, as well as earlier versions. Buried in the data were various documents that were privileged and confidential. There was no cooperation between the parties in arranging discovery; there were attempts to strike out pleadings, and motions alleging abuse of process were served.

Air Canada refused to produce e-data or documents regarding routes, fares, or scheduling until WestJet had completed its examination for discovery and it was clear how Air Canada's confidential information had been used to benefit WestJet. Air Canada also disputed expert opinion obtained by WestJet on the extent of information from Air Canada's data used to determine the scale of losses that Air Canada claimed it had suffered. Air Canada claimed that WestJet had not told its experts how it had used Air Canada's confidential data, and that Westjet was asking for too much data. What WestJet had asked for was baseline data for two years covering a number of categories relating to scheduling, fares, passenger loads, etc. WestJet also asked for further data obtained by an investigator for Air Canada. WestJet claimed privilege for some of its documents that the investigator had examined.

Air Canada was ordered to produce further documents that were relevant to the proceeding. Air Canada was not permitted to refuse to provide documentary discovery until WestJet had finished its examination for discovery. Of particular importance, Air Canada was required to produce two years' worth of data in various categories as requested by WestJet—a very large pool of data. Further, Air Canada was not entitled to determine what data WestJet's experts required.

Nor was that the end of the matter. In a further motion to the court,[2] Air Canada requested that if there were any privileged documents buried in the mass of e-data it was producing on discovery, such document production would not be deemed to be a waiver of privilege over those documents. Air Canada had already produced 10,000 documents, with potentially 70,000 to come depending on the outcome of this motion. The parties had agreed on the search terms to be used by software experts when searching Air Canada's databases, but Air Canada proposed to produce the documents from the search without further vetting or review, arguing that further review would be too costly.

The court refused Air Canada's request. The concept of solicitor–client privilege was too important and a manual search of privileged documents was required; the principle of privilege was "too important … to [sacrifice] to … expediency or economics."

There are a number of issues in *Air Canada v. WestJet* that are particular to cases where e-data is an issue:

- Searching very large volumes of data for subsets that are relevant to the issues in the action, and that are not privileged.
- Reaching an agreement on search parameters.
- Deciding on appropriate search software.
- Retaining experts.
- Deciding whether **active data** is required, or whether one must also produce **residual data**, **metadata**, or **archival data**.

active data
data currently in use in the database

residual data
previous versions of data not currently in use including deleted data

metadata
information about how data was routed, stored, or transmitted—its "travel" history

archival data
older versions of data that have been stored or archived on a database system

- Apportioning the costs of e-data searches, including the retention of experts, and the purchase of software to sort and categorize data.
- Preventing inadvertent or intentional deletion or destruction of data.
- Instructing employees involved in data search and retention.
- Producing data in usable format for the parties and the courts.

The Sedona Principles

There have been a number of efforts made to address problems that arise in e-discovery, some of which resolve some of the issues that arose in *Air Canada v. WestJet*. First, civil litigation practitioners in the United States and Canada have developed a set of principles to guide e-discovery, *The Sedona Principles*. Second, the Rules have been changed to encourage discussion, cooperation, and planning by the parties well in advance of the commencement of the discovery process, subject to the concept of proportionality—that is, that the cost and labour involved in discovery should be proportional to what is at stake in the action. Third, as we shall see in the discussion of documentary discovery later in this chapter, various practices are beginning to emerge that deal with e-discovery in practical ways.

Rules That Relate to Discovery

Rules 29.1 and 29.2 focus on requirements that are now mandatory: parties must jointly plan and organize the discovery process and take into account the principle of proportionality that weighs the time and expense involved in answering questions or producing documents against what is at stake in the action for the parties. Rules 30 to 33 include the basic forms of discovery that can be used. Rules 34 and 35 cover discovery procedures. An overview of these rules is set out in Table 14.1.

Table 14.1   Overview of Discovery Rules

Regulation of the Forms of Discovery: Rules 29 to 33	Regulation of the Procedure for Conducting Discovery: Rules 34 and 35
Rule 29.1: Discovery Plan	Rule 34: Procedure on Oral Examinations
Rule 29.2: Proportionality in Discovery	Rule 35: Procedure on Examination for Discovery by Written Questions
Rule 30: Discovery of Documents	
Rule 30.1: Deemed Undertaking	
Rule 31: Examination for Discovery	
Rule 32: Inspection of Property	
Rule 33: Medical Examination of Parties	

The Sedona Canada Principles Addressing Electronic Discovery—At a Glance

1. Electronically stored information is discoverable.

2. In any proceeding, the parties should ensure that steps taken in the discovery process are proportionate, taking into account

    (i)   the nature and scope of the litigation, including the importance and complexity of the issues, interest and amounts at stake;

    (ii) the relevance of the available electronically stored information;

    (iii) its importance to the court's adjudication in a given case; and

    (iv) the costs, burden and delay that may be imposed on the parties to deal with electronically stored information.

3. As soon as litigation is reasonably anticipated, parties must consider their obligation to take reasonable and good faith steps to preserve potentially relevant electronically stored information.

4. Counsel and parties should meet and confer as soon as practicable, and on an ongoing basis, regarding the identification, preservation, collection, review and production of electronically stored information.

5. The parties should be prepared to produce relevant electronically stored information that is reasonably accessible in terms of cost and burden.

6. A party should not be required, absent agreement or a court order based on demonstrated need and relevance, to search for or collect deleted or residual electronically stored information.

7. A party may satisfy its obligation to preserve, collect, review and produce electronically stored information in good faith by using electronic tools and processes such as data sampling, searching or by using selection criteria to collect potentially relevant electronically stored information.

8. Parties should agree as early as possible in the litigation process on the format in which electronically stored information will be produced. Parties should also agree on the format, content and organization of information to be exchanged in any required list of documents as part of the discovery process.

9. During the discovery process, parties should agree to or, if necessary, seek judicial direction on measures to protect privileges, privacy, trade secrets and other confidential information relating to the production of electronic documents and data.

10. During the discovery process, parties should anticipate and respect the rules of the forum in which the litigation takes place, while appreciating the impact any decisions may have in related actions in other forums.

11. Sanctions should be considered by the court where a party will be materially prejudiced by another party's failure to meet any obligation to preserve, collect, review or produce electronically stored information. The party in default may avoid sanctions if it demonstrates the failure was not intentional or reckless.

12. The reasonable costs of preserving, collecting and reviewing electronically stored information will generally be borne by the party producing it. In limited circumstances, it may be appropriate for the parties to arrive at a different allocation of costs on an interim basis, by either agreement or court order.

Source: The Sedona Conference, *The Sedona Canada Principles Addressing Electronic Discovery—At a Glance* (2008). Copyright 2000-2013 The Sedona Conference. https://thesedonaconference.org/node/4412.

In addition to the discovery procedures covered by Rules 30 to 35, there are three other discovery-like provisions in the Rules.

1. The pretrial conference covered by Rule 50 creates a forum that enhances settlement and allows for narrowing of the issues if the case proceeds to trial.

2. Rule 51 facilitates a process in which the parties ask each other to admit the authenticity of a document or the truth of a fact, which narrows issues by reducing matters that must be formally proved at trial.

3. Rule 53 requires the disclosure of experts' reports before trial to reduce surprise and narrow issues.

These discovery-like procedures are discussed later in the text. In this chapter, after briefly discussing the creation of a discovery plan (Rule 29.1) and proportionality in discovery (Rule 29.2), the deemed undertaking rule (Rule 30.1), property inspections (Rule 32), and medical examinations (Rule 33), we focus on discovery of documents (paper and electronic), oral discovery, and following up on **undertakings** because these procedures are featured in almost every civil action.

undertaking
when you cannot answer right now but will undertake to check on a matter and give an answer later

Discovery Plans: Rule 29.1

As a result of the increasing complexity of discovery, when parties intend to obtain evidence by way of discovery under Rules 30 to 33 and 35 they must agree to a discovery plan within 60 days of the close of pleadings—that is the default time period, but the parties may, and often will, extend that period (Rule 29.1.03(2)). This rule is based on an assumption that the parties will be cooperating in the production of evidence for discovery, and working together in creative ways to facilitate the discovery process. A party who chooses to approach the creation of a discovery plan by engaging in adversarial obstructionist tactics will likely end up as a respondent on a motion, where the court may step in and take control of the discovery plan process and will impose penalties on uncooperative parties in appropriate cases.[3]

Deciding on the range of documents to be subjected to discovery, protocols for how they are to be produced, how large data pools are to be managed, and how privileged material hidden in data pools may be protected will involve research, planning, and discussion between the parties that may well take longer than the 60-day default period provided for in the rule. In particular, the complexities involved in managing electronic documents require a great deal of flexibility, planning, and cooperation.

There is some variation in the format of a discovery plan and, if the parties agree, the plan may be customized and depart from the elements set out for plans in Rule 29.1.03(3). The elements that should be included are described in broad and general terms, leaving a lot of scope for creative and customized plans:

- The plan shall be in writing and shall determine the intended scope of documentary discovery, in some cases describing the type or nature of the documents to be produced, sometimes in detail, following guidelines for what must be disclosed and produced. These guidelines are set out in Rule 30.02. In the plan, parties may set out principles or guidelines that they have agreed to follow based on the importance and complexity of the issues in the action, and the relevance of documents to those issues, together with the costs of production. As we will see later in the chapter, producing electronic documents that fit these criteria can be very difficult and very costly in some cases, so cost may be as much a consideration as relevance to the issues.

- The plan shall set out the dates on which affidavits of documents under Rule 30.03 will be produced. These dates will depend on the time involved in producing the documents, because they cannot be listed in the affidavit of documents until they have been found, disclosed, and produced. The old rule that the affidavit of documents had to be delivered within 10 days of the close of pleadings is now restricted to actions under the simplified procedure where the issues are not complex, where relatively small amounts of money are at stake (Rule 76.03), and where discovery plans are not required.

- The plan should set out a schedule that respects the timing, costs (cost limits and who pays production costs), and manner in which documents are produced by a party or by other persons (electronically, on a CD or USB flash drive, or as hard copy). The plan should indicate the names of persons to be produced for oral examination for discovery, and should set out information about the timing and length of the examination as the parties may agree.

- The plan shall include any other information that could reduce cost and delay in conducting discovery in a way that is proportional to what is at stake in the action for the parties.

- Where an action involves electronic discoveries, the parties are expected to develop the discovery plan by paying attention to the principles for electronic discovery set out in "The Sedona Canada Principles Addressing Electronic Discovery." These principles are discussed above as well as in the footnotes to Figure 14.2, Discovery Checklist, below. The parties will find this Ontario Bar Association checklist to be very useful in preparing a discovery plan as a guide to organizing the discovery process.

You will note that there is no prescribed form for discovery plans; they are customized for each case, and the content and format is left to the parties. A sample short form plan for Abigail's case is set out in Figure 14.1, together with the discovery checklist (Figure 14.2).

Figure 14.1   Sample Discovery Plan

Court file no. 01-CV-1234

ONTARIO
SUPERIOR COURT OF JUSTICE

BETWEEN:

ABIGAIL BOAR

Plaintiff

and

RATTLE MOTORS LTD. and FRED FLOGEM

Defendants

DISCOVERY PLAN
(Dated as of January 1, year 1)

*[NOTE TO USER OF THIS DOCUMENT: Read Model Document #9: Checklist
for Preparing a Discovery Plan for important information on factors to consider
in preparing a discovery plan. Refer also to Model Document #8: Annotated
E-Discovery Checklist for detailed suggestions on the preservation, review, and
production of relevant records. These model documents may be found at: http://
www.oba.org/Advocacy/E-Discovery/Model-Precedents.]*

**1. Applicable
   Procedural
   Regime:**

[ ]	Commercial List
[ ]	*Construction Lien Act*
[ ]	*Class Proceedings Act, 1992*
[ ]	Estates List
[ ]	Simplified Procedure (Rule 76)
[ ]	Civil Case Management (Rule 77)
[x]	Superior Court of Justice — ordinary regime

Figure 14.1 Continued

| 2. Legal Issues For Determination at Trial:

Use numbered paragraphs. Include specific references to pleadings. | *For each party, identify:*

Name of Party: Abigail Boar, Plaintiff

Causes of Action/Defences as against Rattle Motors Ltd.: Breach of *Occupiers' Liability Act* knowingly permitting a public area to remain unsafe. Failure to train and instruct employees, failure to carry out safety inspections (paragraph 18 statement of claim).

Causes of Action/Defences as against Fred Flogem: Negligence in knowingly creating a dangerous situation for the plaintiff and failing to remediate the dangers (paragraph 16 statement of claim).

Legal Issues Raised by Each Cause of Action or Defence: For both defendants,
1. whether their actions created an unsafe public area amounting to negligence and/or breach of *Occupiers' Liability Act*,
2. whether the corporate defendant is responsible in law for the acts of the individual defendant.

Heads of Damages Claimed as against both defendants jointly and severally:
General damages for pain and suffering as a result of injuries sustained.
General damages for loss of enjoyment of the quality of life.
General damages for loss of future income.
Special damages for loss of wages and salary.
Special damages for expenses and costs arising from the injury.

Name of Party: Rattle Motors Ltd.

Defences as Against Plaintiff: Premises were safe for reasonable user, plaintiff is the author of her own misfortune by reason that she was intoxicated (paragraphs 5-9 in the statement of defence). Damages are exaggerated (paragraph 11 of the statement of defence).

Name of Party: Fred Flogem

Defences as Against Plaintiff: Premises were safe for reasonable user, plaintiff is the author of her own misfortune by reason that she was intoxicated (paragraphs 5-9 in the statement of defence). Defendant denies that any act of his created a situation of danger (paragraph 12 in the statement of defence). Damages are exaggerated (paragraph 11 in the statement of defence).

Legal Issues Raised by Defence:
For both defendants,
1. whether they took necessary steps to keep the premises safe for such persons as the plaintiff.
2. whether the plaintiff was intoxicated to the extent that she was the author of her own injuries. |

Figure 14.1 Continued

3. Scope of Documentary Discovery: *Identify and prioritize key authors and custodians, record types, relevant time frames, locations, and other parameters within which search will be conducted for relevant records.* *Consider anticipated volume of records, cost and resources required to search for and review records for relevance, and the importance and complexity of the issues.* *Prioritize steps to be taken and consider whether a phased approach is appropriate. If so, set out protocol for phased search.*	*For each party, identify:* **Name of Party: Abigail Boar, Plaintiff** Scope of Documents to Be Disclosed and Produced: Receipt for dinner at Barbeerian's: September 14, year 0, paper receipt in possession of counsel Toronto Hospital Records, September 16, year 0, electronic records in possession of Toronto Hospital to be transferred to USB and produced in MS Word format and produced on USB Prescriptions for medications September 14 to November 10, year 0 scanned to MS Word format and produced on USB Wage and Salary statement search to be conducted for weekly wage amounts, less deductions from records of Megadoon Investments Ltd. for period September 1, year –1 to December 1, year 0. Search of records request made as of December 31, year 0. Information not yet received as of this date, but expected. **Name of Parties: Rattle Motors Ltd. and Fred Flogem** Scope of Documents to be Disclosed and Produced: Insurance policy as requested by plaintiff, currently in possession of corporate defendant and produced on request. Floor plan of Rattle Motors Ltd. showroom Building inspection and maintenance records January 1, year 0 to December 31, year 0 in various formats to be scanned to USB in PDF format and made available when completed—completion date expected January 10, year 1
4. Affidavits of Documents: *Establish common format for the schedules to the affidavits.*	**Format for the schedules:**[1] Schedule, date, type, format, no. of pages, description, location **Delivery deadline:** March 1, year 1
5. Timing/ Format of Production of Records:[2] *Use common protocol.*	**Format for Exchange of Paper Records:**[3] *[Original format, if commonly accessible. Otherwise, black and white single page TIF images with resolution of 300 dpi (dots per inch) with OCR generated text]* **Deadline for production:** March 1, year 1 **Format for Exchange of Electronic Records:**[4] *[Original format, if commonly accessible. Otherwise, black and white single page TIF images with resolution of 300 dpi (dots per inch) with OCR generated text]* **Deadline for production:** March 1, year 1

Figure 14.1   Continued

6. Oral Discovery: *Limited to 7 hours per examining party unless parties consent or leave of court is obtained.[5]* *For simplified procedure actions, oral discovery is limited to 2 hours.[6]*	*For each party that is to be examined, identify:* **Name of Party: Abigail Boar** Employer: Megadoon Investments—currently on sick leave Dates for Discovery: April 3, year 1 Agreed Length of Discovery: 5 hours Agreed Number of Hours of Discovery for Each Examining Party: N/A **Name of Party: Sunil Tharper, Manager, Rattle Motors Ltd.** Dates for Discovery: April 4, year 1 Agreed Length of Discovery: 4 hours Agreed Number of Hours of Discovery for Each Examining Party: N/A **Name of Party: Fred Flogem** Dates for Discovery: April 5, year 1 Agreed Length of Discovery: 4 hours Agreed Number of Hours of Discovery for Each Examining Party: N/A
7. Other Discovery: *Consider whether an inspection of property (Rule 32) or a medical examination (Rule 33) is appropriate.*	*For each party that is to conduct an inspection or medical examination, identify:* **Name of Party Inspecting or Examining: Abigail Boar, Plaintiff** **A. Inspection of Property** Property to Be Inspected: Premises and showroom of Rattle Motors Ltd. Location of Property: 1240 Bay Street, Toronto, Ontario M8H 0K8 Agreed Date of Inspection: March 15, year 1 Other Agreed Terms: Plaintiff's counsel lighting engineer of plaintiff's choosing and building inspector from City of Toronto may attend and examine premises and carry out lighting tests in showroom area. **B. Medical Examination** Person to Be Examined: Abigail Boar Physician or other Person Conducting Examination: Dr. Quack Location of Examination: Quack U Wellness Centre Agreed Date of Examination: March 20, year 0 Other Agreed Terms: Examinee to be subject to MRI, general physical examination, stress test

Prepared and agreed upon by:

I.M. Just on behalf of the Plaintiff, Abigail Boar

Huey Sue on behalf of the Defendants, Rattle Motors Ltd. and Fred Flogem

Figure 14.1 Concluded

---

1. A recommended format would include: unique document ID number (Alpha/numeric); date of document; (YYYY/MM/DD); document type (e.g., memorandum, letter, contract, etc.); author, author organization; recipient, recipient organization; and type of privilege claimed (where applicable). If parties do not agree on a common format, set out an alternative format/process to be used.

2. Consider also what measures are to be taken to prevent inadvertent disclosure of confidential or privileged material or how such disclosure is to be handled in the event that it occurs. See the EIC's Checklist for Preparing a Discovery Plan (Model Document #9) [this can be seen below in Figure 14.2].

3. See the EIC's Checklist for Preparing a Discovery Plan (Model Document #9) [this can be seen below in Figure 14.2]. Consider the following, for example:

   a. Are records to be provided as paper copies or scanned?

   b. If scanned, what format? (Suggested default: Black and white, single-page TIF images with a resolution of 300 dpi (dots per inch) with OCR generated text.)

   c. Common coding protocol for scanned documents? Production of records in a common format is important to facilitate the exchange of productions between parties.

   d. Should a third-party service provider be engaged to facilitate production? Can one provider be agreed upon for both parties?

4. Electronic records should, whenever possible, be produced in electronic form. See the EIC's Checklist for Preparing a Discovery Plan (Model Document #9) [this can be seen below in Figure 14.2]. Consider the following, for example:

   a. Will electronic records be produced in common format? (Suggested default: Original format, if commonly accessible. Otherwise, black and white, single-page TIF images with a resolution of 300 dpi (dots per inch) with OCR generated text.)

   b. Are there exceptions to the agreement to produce electronic records in this common format? Production of records in a common format is important to facilitate the exchange of productions between parties.

   c. Is production of metadata required? Can production of metadata be limited to date, author, recipients, and/or other specified fields?

   d. Is specific software or hardware required to permit electronically stored information to be inspected?

   e. What, if any, queries or other steps may be required to interact with electronic data in order to create producible electronically stored information?

   f. Should a third-party service provider be engaged to facilitate production? Can one provider be agreed upon for both parties?

   g. Is there a liaison person who can be contacted regarding technical issues?

5. See Rule 31.05.1.

6. See Rule 76.04(2).

Source: Ontario Bar Association, Model Document #9B: Discovery Plan (Short Form); http://www.oba.org/Advocacy/E-Discovery/Model-Precedents.

Figure 14.2   Discovery Checklist

ONTARIO E-DISCOVERY IMPLEMENTATION COMMITTEE
CHECKLIST FOR PREPARING A DISCOVERY PLAN

PHASE I.   ISSUE IDENTIFICATION AND SCOPE OF DISCOVERY

1. **Identify the issues in the litigation.**
   - The parties should begin by identifying each cause of action and each defence raised in the action and the heads of damages. (The objective of the discovery plan is to assist parties in identifying and focusing on the important issues in the litigation in order to promote fair, expeditious, and efficient results.)
   - It will be helpful for the parties to prepare, exchange and attempt to agree on outlines of the causes of action, defences and heads of damages in advance of the discovery plan negotiations.

2. **Identify the applicable legal tests.**
   - For each cause of action, each defence and each head of damages, identify the specific legal test to be met or responded to (in order to articulate reasons why particular evidence may be relevant).
   - Again, this is best accomplished by agreement in advance of the discovery plan negotiations.

3. **Consider, for each legal issue, the type of evidence required by each party.**
   - For each cause of action, each defence and each head of damages, identify the type of evidence required to prove or defend that element of the case (e.g., testimony, documents, other evidence), as part of the analysis as to the nature and scope of potentially relevant records.

PHASE II.   IDENTIFICATION OF RELEVANT RECORDS

4. **Identify, for each issue, the location of relevant records held by each party.**
   - The purpose is to identify the location of all potentially relevant documents[1] in both paper and electronic formats.
   - In respect of each cause of action, defence and head of damages, consider and identify:
     a. the individuals who had a role in the relevant events on behalf of the party, whether as a decision-maker, implementer, observer, or otherwise;
     b. other individuals who had a role in the events, as a decision-maker, implementer, observer, or otherwise, including agents of the party, consultants, or unrelated third parties and others; and
     c. other potential sources of records (including banks, accountants, lawyers, insurers, third-party service providers, affiliated companies or internet service providers, for example).

Figure 14.2   Continued

- In identifying sources of documentary evidence, consideration must be given to how a party creates, stores, and maintains electronic records generally.[2]

5. **Identify the types of potentially relevant records held by each party.**

   - Consider with respect to each party and individual/organization identified above as an anticipated source of evidence:

     a. what types of documents it is anticipated that those individuals/organizations created or obtained that may be "relevant to an issue in the action";[3]

     b. during what time period is it anticipated that such records would have been created, obtained, archived, backed up and/or destroyed; and

     c. where these records may be located, if they still exist.[4]

   - Prioritize who the most important records custodians are likely to be, the key time frames, and the most important and easily accessible locations where records are likely held.

   - Where there are multiple copies of certain types of information, identify the sources that are the most readily available and easiest to preserve and retrieve.

PHASE III.   PRESERVATION AND RETRIEVAL OF POTENTIALLY RELEVANT RECORDS

6. **Agree what is to be preserved by each party**[5] **and how urgently the preservation measures must be taken.**[6]

   - For each party, consider and determine:

     a. whether an e-discovery consultant or computer forensics specialist is needed in order to preserve and collect relevant records;

     b. whether to preserve more broadly (such as by making forensic/bitmap copies of hard drives and servers, with culling for relevance to occur later) or more narrowly based on specific relevance parameters;[7]

     c. whether forensic/bitmap copies of hard drives, servers or portable devices are needed for other reasons, such as in order to preserve the machine or device or for other evidentiary reasons;[8]

     d. what methods are to be used to search for the client's records, including the possible use of indexing software and other search tools;

     e. whether and to what extent to preserve metadata;[9]

     f. whether to preserve archival and backup media and, if so, whether to seek to retrieve specific records from the archival and backup media;[10]

     g. whether and how to seek to preserve deleted or residual data or records that use obsolete hardware or software;[11]

     h. the cost associated with all contemplated preservation steps and resources required;

     i. the cost associated with retrieval of all preserved records;

Figure 14.2   Continued

  j. what constitutes a proportionate preservation response,[12] taking into account the amounts at issue, the importance of the case, the importance of various types of files, the total volume of material to be preserved and retrieved, and other factors;[13]

  k. the risks associated with not undertaking the contemplated preservation steps; and

  l. what steps will not be undertaken due to the cost, burden or delay associated with doing so.

- Consider what documentation shall be maintained to demonstrate compliance with the preservation measures agreed upon.

- Record the basis for decisions. Such a record may be important if parties are required to later defend a decision as having been reasonable, particularly where parties have (unilaterally or jointly) decided not to take a particular step or not to preserve or retrieve particular types or categories of records.

- Consider whether amendments to the pleadings are likely to be made and consider whether or how to preserve other records that may become relevant and the cost/benefit of taking such steps at the outset or in the future.

- Reference to the EIC's Model Document #8 (Annotated E-Discovery Checklist) is encouraged for further information regarding considerations relating to the preservation, review and production of electronic records in particular. [This model document is available as a download from http://www.oba.org/ Advocacy/E-Discovery/Model-Precedents.]

PHASE IV.   SEARCHING AND FILTERING RECORDS

7. **Agree upon the parameters to be used in isolating records to be produced from within the records that have been preserved.**

  - Within the subset of materials to be preserved, consider and discuss how to identify the relevant records for production and, if appropriate, use electronic tools and processes to assist in doing so.[14]

  - Consider a phased approach to identifying relevant documents, based on the key custodians, record types or locations, or other factors identified above.[15]

  - Relevant electronic records may be identified using:

    a. Keyword search terms (such as employee names, key words in the litigation, names of persons on the other side, etc.) using Boolean, whole language and fuzzy electronic searching tools;[16]

    b. date range; and

    c. file type.[17]

  - Consider also using electronic analytic tools for clustering records, for concept mapping, for de-duplicating records and for identifying email strings.

Figure 14.2   Continued

- Relevant records may also be sought in some or all specific physical locations, whether in hard-copy record storage or on servers, desktop computers, laptops, home computers, PDAs such as BlackBerrys or Palm Pilots, floppy disks, CDs, DVDs, zip drives, backup media, external hard drives and USB ("thumb" [or "flash"]) drives.

- Conduct a cost/benefit analysis. For all contemplated steps, evaluate what constitutes a proportionate response, taking into account: the amounts at issue; the importance of the case; the importance of various types of files;[18] the total volume of records that may be generated;[19] the cost and resources required in undertaking particular steps; and other factors.[20]

- Record the basis for the decisions made, particularly decisions made not to take a particular step. Consider whether there are any variables the full scope or impact of which cannot be assessed that may impact timing or cost.[21]

PHASE V.   REVIEW OF RECORDS

8. **Agree upon a protocol for reviewing and refining the records identified in any initial search as potentially relevant.**

- Consider again whether a phased approach to reviewing records may be appropriate, based on the same cost/benefit considerations as outlined in Step #7 above.

- Identify what measures can be taken to eliminate duplicate records.[22]

- Identify what measures are to be taken with respect to private, personal or commercially sensitive information identified in the course of the search and review.[23]

- Consider how processing and review of the records will be managed to ensure completeness, to track information as it is collected, and to avoid delays. Identify whether the use of specific software or specialist services are appropriate.

- Record the basis for the decisions made, particularly decisions made not to pursue a particular step.

PHASE VI.   EXCHANGING RECORDS

9. **Establish a protocol for the exchange of relevant records.**

- Consider and, if possible, agree upon:
  a. the format for exchange of electronic and paper records (whether in paper, native file formats or .tif format, for example).[24] The production of electronic records in electronic form is to be preferred;[25]
  b. whether specific software or hardware must be made available in order to allow electronically stored information to be inspected;

Figure 14.2 Continued

---

    c. whether to use a common third-party litigation support service provider to scan and/or code or process producible records;

    d. whether to use a common protocol for coding records to be produced (which is important to facilitate the exchange of records between parties) and for preparing affidavits of documents;

    e. measures to be taken to redact documents;[26]

    f. other measures to be taken to protect privilege, privacy, trade secrets or other confidential information (including measures to address inadvertent production of privileged documents);[27]

    g. whether a cost sharing/allocation agreement is desirable; and

    h. a time frame for complying with obligations agreed upon.

- Consider again whether a phased approach to producing records may be appropriate, based on the same cost/benefit considerations as outlined in Step #7 above.

10. **Consider whether agreement can be reached or procedures are required to ensure the authenticity and integrity of records.**

- Identify specific procedures to be implemented to ensure the authenticity and integrity of producible electronically stored information.[28]

PHASE VII. EXAMINATIONS FOR DISCOVERY

11. **Agree whether to exchange "contextual facts" in advance of oral discovery.**

- Contextual facts are the facts required in order to place other facts in their appropriate context. Examples of contextual facts that parties might wish to exchange in advance of oral discovery, in order to streamline the discovery process and reduce cost and delay, include: casts of characters, organizational charts, corporate structure charts, chronologies of events, IT infrastructure maps, information regarding the source of documentary productions, and the parties' records retention policies, among others.

12. **Identify who is to be produced for discovery as the representatives of each party.**

- Consider whether it would facilitate the discovery process to produce more than one representative per party, with each representative to be examined on a limited range of topics within their personal knowledge (with one representative to answer any other proper questions).

13. **Establish dates when oral examinations for discovery are to be conducted, and confirm the number of hours of discovery to be conducted by each examining party.**

- Rule 31.05.1 limits the duration of oral examinations conducted by any one party to seven hours, regardless of the number of parties or persons to be examined, unless the parties consent or leave of the court is obtained.

Figure 14.2   Continued

- If an increase in the number of hours for the conduct of examinations for discovery is to be negotiated, identify the considerations militating in favour of such an increase of time, and how much additional time is to be allocated.
- For simplified procedure actions, oral discovery is limited to 2 hours. A longer period of oral discovery is not permitted: Rule 76.04(2).

PHASE VIII.   OTHER FORMS OF DISCOVERY

14. **Agree whether part or all of the discovery is to be conducted through written questions and answers.**
    - Consider and, if appropriate, agree whether some questions may be asked in written form in advance of oral discovery so as to make the oral discovery more efficient.
    - Review Rule 35 regarding the procedure for written discoveries.
    - Note that a party does not have the right to conduct both written and oral discovery except with leave of the court: Rule 31.02. However, the parties may consent to conduct both written and oral discovery.
    - Written discovery is prohibited in simplified procedure actions: Rule 76.04(1).

15. **Consider whether the inspection of property is required.**
    - Under Rule 32, the court may make an order for the inspection of real or personal property where it appears to be necessary for the proper determination of an issue in a proceeding. In cases where an inspection of property is appropriate, the parties should seek to agree in the discovery plan on the terms under which the inspection will occur.

16. **Consider whether a physical or mental examination of a party is required.**
    - Under Rule 33, a party may bring a motion for an order for the physical or mental examination of a party whose physical or mental condition is in question. In cases where a physical or mental examination is appropriate, the parties should seek to agree in the discovery plan on the terms under which the examination will occur.

PHASE IX.   OTHER ISSUES

17. **Address the possibility of changes to the discovery plan.**
    - Parties should agree that, as additional information becomes available throughout the action, it may become apparent that: (a) it is impracticable or impossible for a party to complete all of the steps contemplated by the discovery plan or to do so in a cost- and time-efficient manner, or (b) further steps, beyond those set out in the discovery plan, are required in order for a party to obtain access to relevant documents in the action.

Figure 14.2   **Continued**

- Parties should agree to notify each other promptly of such changes in circumstances and agree to negotiate in good faith with respect to any potential changes or, in appropriate cases, seek the assistance of the court.
- Note that Rule 29.1.04 requires that the parties ensure that the discovery plan is updated to reflect any changes in the information listed in Rule 29.1.03(3).

18. **Consider whether it is appropriate to share the reasonable costs required to comply with this discovery plan.**

- In general, parties may claim the reasonable costs incurred in complying with the discovery plan as "costs of and incidental to a proceeding or a step in a proceeding" for purposes of s. 131 of the *Courts of Justice Act*. Parties should consider whether it is appropriate to agree upon a different allocation or sharing of costs.

---

1. The word "document" is used in this Model Document in its broadest sense, as meaning "information recorded in any form, including electronically stored information." The word "document" is used interchangeably with the word "record."

2. Comment 4.c of the *Sedona Canada Principles* recommends that counsel be prepared in a substantive way to discuss their client's documentary discovery and production obligations with opposing counsel by gaining "a thorough understanding of how electronically stored information is created, used and maintained by or for the client." To this end, it is useful for counsel to ask the client and its IT representative to complete an IT questionnaire, or to provide information orally in advance of the discovery plan negotiations, regarding:

   a. system architecture (network structure, geographic location of hardware, etc.);

   b. types of hardware and software used by the client;

   c. what forms of potentially relevant electronically stored information exist, such as emails, word processing documents, databases, Excel documents, voice mail records, web-based files or metadata;

   d. methods of data storage, such as on servers, desktop computers, laptops, home computers, PDAs such as BlackBerrys or Palm Pilots, floppy disks, CDs, DVDs, zip drives, backup media, external hard drives and USB ("thumb" [or "flash"]) drives;

   e. data storage by third parties such as banks, accountants, lawyers, insurers, third-party service providers, affiliated companies or internet service providers;

   f. the client's backup protocol, including types of backups performed and their schedule;

   g. the physical location of backup media;

   h. procedures for retrieving data from backup media;

   i. the client's archiving protocol, if applicable, and procedures for retrieving data from archives;

   j. costs and resources required to retrieve information from backup and other storage media; and

   k. any retention policies and/or schedules for the systematic destruction of paper and electronic records.

   For sample IT questionnaires, see *The Electronic Evidence and Discovery Handbook* (Chicago: ABA Law Practice Management, 2006) at pp. 3 and following.

3. Rule 30.02 and 30.03 are amended effective January 1, 2010 to require that every document "relevant to any matter in issue" be produced. The broader language of "relating to any matter in issue" is repealed effective January 1, 2010.

Figure 14.2   Continued

4. Review the party's record retention policy, if one exists. Consider providing written litigation hold notices to all employees, contract workers and third parties who may be custodians of potentially relevant documents to inform them of the need to preserve these documents in their original format without modification. Consider involving the client's IT department in the litigation hold process. A description of the litigation hold obligation, and a sample litigation hold notice, are found in the EIC's model memorandum to a corporate client regarding documentary discovery (Model Document #3). [This and other model documents mentioned in these footnotes are available as downloads from http://www.oba.org/Advocacy/E-Discovery/Model-Precedents.]

5. Principle #3 of the *Sedona Canada Principles* states that "As soon as litigation is reasonably anticipated, parties must consider their obligation to take reasonable and good faith steps to preserve potentially relevant electronically stored information." The *Sedona Canada Principles* also recognize, however, that "it is unreasonable to expect organizations to take every conceivable step to preserve all electronically stored information that may be potentially relevant" and a "reasonable inquiry based on good faith to identify and preserve active and archival data should be sufficient."

6. Determine immediately whether there are urgent preservation issues because relevant records may be destroyed, altered or removed in the short term, whether by your party/client, other parties, or non-parties. For example, consider: whether the litigation is concerned with very recent or ongoing events, such that there is a risk of destruction of relevant records in "real time"; the frequency with [which] backup media may be recycled; whether there is any email deletion policy; the possibility of alteration to electronic records that are in continuing use, such as databases or portable devices, including smart phones; destruction of potentially relevant records in the ordinary course pursuant to a records retention policy; and the possibility of a relevant hard drive, portable device, etc. being scrubbed or otherwise rendered inaccessible (e.g., the personal computer of a departing employee). Refer to the EIC's Annotated E-Discovery Checklist (Model Document #8).

    In addition, consideration should be given to sending a preservation letter to the opposing parties or their counsel as soon as litigation is commenced, and sometimes before. Consider that several preservation letters may be useful as the action proceeds and parties are able to better define the scope of preservation in terms of date range, record types, custodians, search terms, etc. See the EIC's model preservation letters (Model Documents #5 and #6) and the model preservation order (Model Document #7).

7. Preserving broadly and then using culling software to identify relevant records will in some cases be quicker and more efficient than seeking to identify relevant records on an individualized basis. Consider what volume of information will have to be stored outside of the day-to-day business environment and the costs for any additional hardware or software or services that may be required.

8. Comment 4.c of the *Sedona Canada Principles* suggests that "[w]hile the making of bit-level images of hard drives is useful in selective cases for the preservation phase, the further processing of the total contents of the drive should not be required unless the nature of the matter warrants the cost and burden. Making forensic image backups of computers is only the first step in a potentially expensive, complex, and difficult process of data analysis. It can divert litigation into side issues involving the interpretation of ambiguous forensic evidence." Note that it is difficult in practice to make a forensic copy of a server, as servers are typically not able to be brought out of service for copying. However, in a smaller organization, the simplest and most effective way to preserve electronic evidence may be simply to make a forensic copy of the drives.

9. Metadata is information about a particular data set or document which describes how, when and by whom it was collected, created, accessed, [and] modified and how it is formatted. Metadata can be altered intentionally or inadvertently. It can be extracted when native files are converted to image. Some metadata, such as file dates and sizes, can easily be seen by users; other metadata can be hidden or embedded and unavailable to computer users who are not technically adept.

Figure 14.2   **Continued**

Metadata is generally not reproduced in full form when a document is printed. Counsel are encouraged to refer to the EIC's Annotated E-Discovery Checklist (Model Document #8) for additional information regarding metadata.

10. Relying upon backup media in order to locate relevant records is generally costly and inefficient. Backup media should be preserved only where they contain unique information that cannot otherwise be obtained, or where other special circumstances apply.

11. Principle #6 of the *Sedona Canada Principles* states that "A party should not be required, absent agreement or a court order based on demonstrated need and relevance, to search for or collect deleted or residual electronically stored information." Comment 6.a suggests that deleted or residual data that can only be accessed through forensic means should not be presumed to be discoverable and ordinarily, searches for electronically sorted information will be restricted to a search of active data and reasonably accessible online sources. The "evaluation of the need for and relevance of such discovery should be analyzed on a case by case basis" as "only exceptional cases will turn on 'deleted' or 'discarded' information."

12. Rule 1.04(1.1) states that, in applying the Rules, the court shall make orders and give directions that are proportionate to the importance and complexity of the issues, and to the amount involved, in the proceeding.

13. In considering the proportionality principle, note that extreme preservation efforts should not be requested except in unusual circumstances: Comment 3.f, *Sedona Canada Principles*. Consider also the party's own ability and willingness to undertake the same preservation steps, since any preservation demand made of opposing parties may be reciprocated. Also, make sure to maintain careful records of the preservation and retrieval plan as it is implemented. Counsel should consider whether to send written confirmation to the client, documenting the preservation plan.

14. Principle #7 of the *Sedona Canada Principles* states that parties may satisfy their obligations "by using electronic tools and processes such as data sampling, searching or by using selection criteria to collect potentially relevant electronically stored information." Comment 7.a indicates that, as it may be impractical or prohibitively expensive to review all information manually, parties and counsel should where possible agree in advance on targeted selection criteria. Comment 7.b suggests various processing techniques to use in searches including filtering, de-duplication, and sampling.

15. Consider which custodians, time frame, and/or locations are likely to produce the most significant information. Also evaluate whether there are alternate sources for information that may no longer be available or may be burdensome (whether due to cost or time) to retrieve, process, review, and/or produce. In a phased approach, the parties may agree, for example, that the records of specific custodians or found in specific locations are to be searched for relevance as part of a first phase, and then, after a review of those results, parties may consider whether or what additional steps are required in a second phase to search for and/or produce additional records.

16. Obviously, narrow search terms will yield a more manageable volume of records, but parties face the risk of inadvertent omission of relevant records. The selection of appropriate search terms requires legal judgment, and the search results should be tested to evaluate whether relevant records are being caught. Consider collaborating with counsel for the other parties regarding appropriate search terms and developing search terms with advice from key individuals involved or from a review of the key documents identified (to identify commonly used terms or names, for example). Keep careful records of the search terms and tools used and techniques employed.

    The search tools used can also affect the reliability of the searches conducted. Determine whether your search tool permits only keyword searching, or also permits Boolean, whole language and fuzzy searching. Some tools permit concept mapping or clustering of related records using algorithms which analyze the records and look for patterns in the words used within the record.

17. In most cases, the vast majority of electronic records will consist of email, word processing documents and data within databases.

Figure 14.2 Continued

18. Electronic searches for relevant records may omit nested emails, attachments, or compressed, encrypted or corrupted files, depending upon the process and software used. Address whether this is a concern.

19. Pursuant to Rule 29.2.03, the court will consider the overall volume of documents that may be produced in response to a request before granting an order for production.

20. Principle #5 of the *Sedona Canada Principles* states that "The parties should be prepared to produce relevant electronically stored information that is reasonably accessible in terms of cost and burden." Comment 5.a suggests that, given the volume and technical challenges associated with the discovery of electronically stored information, the parties engage in a cost benefit analysis, weighing the "cost of identifying and retrieving the information from each potential source against the likelihood that the source will yield unique, necessary and relevant information." Counsel are encouraged to exercise judgment based on a reasonable good faith inquiry having regard to the location and cost of recovery or preservation. The more costly and burdensome the effort that will be required to access a particular source "the more certain the parties need to be that the source will yield responsive information." Comment 5.a suggests that, if potentially relevant documents exist in a format that is not "readily usable," cost-shifting may be appropriate. Refer to the EIC's Annotated E-Discovery Checklist (Model Document #8), which provides more detailed suggestions regarding steps to be considered in preserving, collecting, processing, and reviewing records.

21. Parties should advise each other forthwith if, at any stage of the process, information becomes known that will impact on their ability to comply with their discovery plan obligations—for example, if records are discovered to be corrupt or inaccessible for a reason unknown at the time that the discovery plan was agreed upon.

22. Consider, for example, whether there are types of emails, office documents or file types that can be automatically removed from collection (such as social notices, marketing, emails from lists, and news sources). Consider the use of technology to remove duplicate copies of records, facilitate identification and tracking of email chains, etc. Refer to the EIC's Annotated E-Discovery Checklist (Model Document #8) for additional suggestions and information.

23. For example, counsel may consider employing a combination of electronic search techniques and manual review to identify private, personal or commercial sensitive information.

24. Principle #8 of the *Sedona Canada Principles* states that "[p]arties should agree as early as possible in the litigation process on the format in which electronically stored information will be produced. Parties should also agree on the format, content and organization of information to be exchanged in any required list of documents as part of the discovery process." See the EIC's Annotated E-Discovery Checklist (Model Document #8) and the model Discovery Agreement (Model Document #1) for an annotated and expanded list of topics to consider. Also, it may be necessary to deal with certain issues in successive meetings during the proceedings; Principle 4 of the *Sedona Canada Principles* recommends that counsel and parties meet and confer on an ongoing basis.

25. Comment 8.a of the *Sedona Canada Principles* states that "production of electronic documents and data should be made only in electronic format, unless the recipient is somehow disadvantaged and cannot effectively make use of a computer, or the volume of the documents to be produced is minimal and metadata is known (and agreed by all parties) to be irrelevant." Comment 8.a suggests that the practice of producing electronically stored information in paper form should be discouraged in most circumstances. Comments 8.b and 8.c suggest that parties attempt to agree on a "methodology of production that (a) preserves metadata and allows it to be produced when relevant; (b) communicates accurately the content; (c) protects the integrity of the information; (d) allows for the creation of a version that can be redacted; (e) assigns a unique production identification number to each data item, and (f) can be readily imported into any industry-standard litigation review application." Recommended default standards for the format of exchange of electronic records are set out in the model Discovery Agreement prepared by the EIC (Model Document #1), at sections 6 and 10.

Figure 14.2   Concluded

26. Do not redact documents using white, as it may not be clear whether redaction has occurred or the extent of the redaction. Use black.

    Also, if redacting electronically, ensure that the method of redacting images of electronic records also removes the associated text. Otherwise, the text will remain searchable even if the text is not visible within the image.

27. Principle #9 of the *Sedona Canada Principles* states that "[d]uring the discovery process parties should agree to or, if necessary, seek judicial direction on measures to protect privileges, privacy, trade secrets and other confidential information relating to the production of electronic documents and data." Consider, for example, entering into a "clawback" agreement with opposing parties, under which the parties agree to permit one another to retrieve inadvertently produced privileged records. To mitigate the risk of inadvertent disclosure of privileged documents, conduct searches for the names of counsel, for example, during the search and review phase to identify potentially privileged documents. Consider how metadata and embedded data will be reviewed when native production is required.

28. Section 12 of the EIC's model Discovery Agreement (Model Document #1) contains suggested provisions regarding authenticity and reliability.

Source: Ontario Bar Association, Model Document #9: Checklist for Preparing a Discovery Plan; http://www.oba.org/Advocacy/E-Discovery/Model-Precedents.

Deemed Undertaking Rule: Rule 30.1

Rule 30.1 codifies a rule, which developed at common law, that parties give an implied undertaking not to use the fruits of discovery other than in the proceeding in which the information was obtained.[4]

The purpose of the rule is to protect the privacy of parties because discovery requires them to disclose information that they might not otherwise need or want to disclose publicly. Remember that court proceedings and the content of this court file are public. Anyone may look at the discovery transcripts and filed documents.

This common law rule has now been incorporated into Rule 30.1. All parties and counsel are governed by this rule with respect to any information obtained from any form of discovery under the Rules (oral, written, and documentary discovery, medical examinations, and property inspections). The information obtained may be used only in the proceeding in which it was obtained (Rules 30.1.01(1) and (3)). However, if a party uses other investigative techniques to discover information in the course of a proceeding, Rule 30.1 does not cover that kind of information—it covers only information obtained through the discovery process (Rule 30.1.01(2)). There are some exceptions: If a party consents to the use of evidence, it may be filed in another proceeding (Rule 30.1.01(4)). If evidence is filed in court or given or referred to in a hearing, or if information is obtained from evidence given at a hearing, either orally or as a document, it may be disclosed. This exception is based on the notion that court proceedings are open, and the information given in court is public and may be disseminated generally (Rule 30.1.01(5)(a) to (c)). Evidence obtained in one proceeding through discovery may be used against a witness to impeach that witness's credibility in another proceeding (Rule 30.1.01(6)). If, for example, Fred gave evidence on discovery in one proceeding and in a separate proceeding gave evidence that contradicted his previous discovery evidence, counsel in the second proceeding is entitled to introduce the discovery evidence in the first proceeding to challenge Fred's credibility. The undertaking rule may be waived by the court where the interest of justice demands it (Rule 30.1.01(8)).

Inspection of Property: Rule 32

Rule 32 sets out a procedure for the inspection of property as part of the discovery process. It may be used in conjunction with Rule 45, which gives the court the authority to order the preservation of property for inspection and for other purposes in connection with a proceeding. Rule 32.01(1) permits the inspection of real or personal property. The rule is broad and permissive. It allows the court to authorize the entry onto property of any person and may allow the property to be taken out of the possession of its owner, whether the owner is a party to the proceeding or not. The court may permit all kinds of tests and inspections to be carried out, though notice must be given to the party who owns or has possession of the property unless there are good reasons not to give notice (Rules 32.01(3) and (4)).

Medical Examinations of Parties: Rule 33

This form of discovery usually occurs in cases involving claims for damages for personal injury where the plaintiff's own doctors have furnished expert medical evidence. With difficult-to-diagnose injuries, such as back problems or neurological problems, the defendants may wish to have their own expert conduct an examination. Where a party raises his or her own health or medical state as an issue, an opponent can test the allegations. Where an opponent raises the other party's medical condition as an issue, the court is more reluctant to order the party to submit to an examination. However, where the parties cannot agree on an examination, s. 105 of the *Courts of Justice Act* permits a medical examination. Rule 33 governs the procedure to be followed after an order for an examination has been made under s. 105.

Medical Examination Procedure

Where one party wishes to subject an opponent to an examination, he or she must bring a motion, serving all parties, not just the party who is the focus of the inquiry (Rule 33.01). An order under s. 105 of the *Courts of Justice Act* may name the practitioner to conduct the examination and set the terms and limits on the examination. If the circumstances warrant, subsequent examinations may be ordered (Rules 33.02(1) and (2)). Within seven days of the examination, the party to be examined must provide the party requesting the examination with a copy of relevant medical reports and hospital or other records. However, records that were prepared in contemplation of litigation, and for no other purpose, and that will not be used at trial may be withheld. This may include, for example, preliminary examinations conducted at the behest of the injured party's lawyers to advise the lawyers of the nature of the injury or its cause, where the report is used to guide the lawyer to other experts whose reports eventually will be used (Rule 33.04). The medical examination ordered under s. 105 is not a three-ring circus. Unless the court orders otherwise, only the person to be examined, the medical practitioner, and assistants may attend the examination (Rule 33.05).

Once an examination has been conducted, its results cannot be swept under the carpet. The practitioner is required to prepare a written report of observations, test results, diagnosis, and prognosis, and deliver it to the party who requested the order for an examination. That party is then obliged to serve the report on every other party to the proceeding (Rule 33.06). For a party who does not cooperate with an order under s. 105, there are the usual remedies of striking out pleadings, dismissing the action, or making "such further order as is just."

Discovery of Documents

In this part of the chapter we will examine the procedural and substantive requirements for documentary discovery. Many of the procedures and presumptions that were made under Rule 30 were developed when cases rested primarily on a finite number of paper documents. In a case such as *Air Canada v. WestJet*, which involves thousands of electronic documents, the parties may follow other practices, some of which are described in earlier parts of this chapter. For example:

- The parties may dispense with the use of an affidavit of documents altogether, and simply produce electronic documents.
- No hardcopies of anything will be introduced; instead the parties will provide all relevant documents on a USB flash drive or CD.
- Parties may not conduct searches to segregate privileged documents, and instead rely on "clawback agreements" where they undertake not to look at documents that are privileged, and agree to return privileged documents or permit them to be returned.
- The parties may share the costs of producing documents, hiring experts, and developing plans to sort through active and residual data.

But the ensuing discussion of discovery of documents is still important because it sets out the base rules that govern all documentary discovery, as well as the principles that underlie discovery of documents, whether the documents are electronic or hard-copy versions.

Discovery of Documents: When and What

In every action, every party must serve on every other party an affidavit of documents (Rule 30.03(1)). The time for doing this is as agreed to in the discovery plan. The scope of what must be included is broad. The affidavit must list and disclose every document relating to any matter in issue in an action. As a general rule, when in doubt as to its relevance, include it (Rule 30.02(1)).

To be disclosed, the document must be or have been in the possession, control, or power of the party. This means that the party has the document, or has the power or right to obtain it, where the other party does not (Rule 30.01(1)(b)). If the other party has the document or can get it, you need not list it and can take the position that the other party can satisfy itself by obtaining the document itself (Rule 30.01(1)(b)).

Once listed in the affidavit of documents, every document must be produced for inspection if requested unless privilege is claimed for it. If the other party wishes to challenge a claim of privilege, it may do so by bringing a motion (Rule 30.02(2)). Whether privilege may be claimed depends on what kind of document is being considered. There are three categories you need to consider.

1. *Lawyer–client communications to get and receive advice on issues relevant to the action.* This category is covered by lawyer–client privilege and probably includes most of the lawyer's correspondence on the file with the client and with others on the client's behalf.

2. ***Without prejudice** documents.* Typical of this category is settlement correspondence where offers are made on a without prejudice basis. These documents are privileged and may be described as correspondence regarding settlement between the parties.

3. *Documents for which the dominant purpose is litigation.* A document may have been created for several purposes, but if the dominant purpose was litigation, then it may be privileged.[5] For example, in one case, the lawyers for the defendant obtained a police officer's summary report of his investigation of an accident for the dominant purpose of litigation. Although the document had other purposes, such as data for traffic accident statistics, its primary purpose conferred a privilege on it.[6]

There is a special rule about insurance policies. Where there is an insurance policy that may cover a claim in all or part of a lawsuit, or may cover a settlement of a claim, the insured party, whether plaintiff or defendant, must disclose and produce the insurance policy if requested. However, no evidence about the insurance policy can be admitted into evidence unless it is relevant to an issue in the action. Its purpose is to let other parties know that the judgment can be satisfied from the insurance and to permit other parties to notify the insurer if the insured party has not done so so that the insurer is not able to deny coverage because there was a failure to give timely notice of a claim (Rule 30.02(3)). Insurance companies are entitled to use technical defences to deny coverage, and they are not shy about doing so.

Subsidiary corporations, affiliated corporations, and corporations controlled by a party may be forced to produce documents in a lawsuit to which they are not parties. In this situation, the court may order a party to disclose documents in the power, possession, or control of a subsidiary, affiliate, or wholly controlled corporation. The key here is that the party controls these corporations, or at least has a right of access to information from them because of the relationship (Rule 30.02(4)). The nature of the corporate relationship that ties a corporation to a party is further spelled out:

without prejudice term used, usually in correspondence, to indicate that an offer or admission cannot be used against its maker, admitted in evidence, or disclosed to the court

1. A subsidiary corporation is one that is directly or indirectly controlled by another. This means that the controlling corporation has a majority of voting shares or at least a large enough minority to give it *de facto* control in alliance with others.

2. A corporation is affiliated if:

   a. one corporation is a subsidiary of another;

   b. both corporations are subsidiaries of another so that they are linked; or

   c. the same person, where one corporation is a party and the other is not, controls both corporations directly or indirectly (Rule 30.01(2)).

A "document" can be of the usual paper type, but it also includes all kinds of information that is stored electronically, as well as maps, videos, and films.

Electronic Discovery

The document discovery procedures in Rule 30 were developed at a time when documents were mostly paper records that were created by hand. A physical record search of hard copy was involved in finding them, and the result was usually a finite number of identifiable documents.

The use of office and personal computers, as well as various handheld data-generating and data-gathering devices since the mid-1990s, has resulted in a growing awareness of the impact of these technological changes on the discovery process, and practitioners have started to talk about electronic discovery or "**e-discovery**." They recognize that e-discovery is different from "paper" discovery in a variety of ways:

e-discovery
a term used to describe discovery of documents where the discovery procedures primarily involve the collection and production of information that is stored electronically

1. The sheer volume of electronic information (emails, documents, databases, etc.) that is potentially relevant for discovery purposes is beyond the comprehension of many lawyers and clients.

2. Electronic documents and information can easily be deleted, either intentionally or inadvertently, and data thought to be destroyed in the ordinary course of business can sometimes be recovered, but often at considerable cost.

3. Collections of electronic data will often contain a mixture of business and private communications.

4. The preservation, review, and production of large volumes of electronic data can be time-consuming, costly, and difficult when there are no standard formats or protocols.

5. Protection of privacy and privileged information is much more difficult in the electronic realm.[7]

Rather than amend Rule 30 to create new e-discovery rules, the response in Ontario so far has been to rely on the broad definition of "document" in Rule 30.01(1)(a), which clearly includes information in electronic form, and to use case law[8] and practice directions to the profession to guide the development of e-discovery procedures. In this regard, the Ontario Bar Association has set out principles that are designed to alert you to problems and issues with e-discovery and that can also serve as a guide for use in a case where discovery of documents is primarily e-discovery:

1. Electronic documents containing relevant data are discoverable under Rule 30 (as is clear from Rule 30.01(1)(a)).

2. The obligations of the parties with respect to e-discovery are subject to balancing and may vary with

   - the cost, burden, and delay that may be imposed on parties;

   - the nature and scope of the litigation, the importance of the issues, and the amounts at stake; and

   - the relevance of the available electronic documents, and their importance to the court's adjudication in a given case.[9]

3. In most cases, the primary source of electronic documents should be the parties' active data, and any other information that was stored in a manner that anticipated future business use and that still permits efficient search and retrieval. (This principle may relieve parties of having to search every nook and cranny in a party's computer system when it is not practical to do so.)

4. Absent an agreement or a court order based on demonstrated need or relevance, a responding party should not be required to search for, review, or produce documents that are deleted or hidden, nor should they have to do this with residual data such as fragmented or overwritten files. (This means that backup data and data that has become corrupted or that is no longer readable because the hardware to read it is obsolete and no longer available do not have to be made available unless there is a clear case for relevance or need, due to the effort and expense required to produce it.)

5. As soon as litigation is contemplated or threatened, parties should immediately take reasonable and good-faith steps to preserve relevant electronic documents. However, it is unreasonable to expect parties to take every conceivable step to preserve all documents that may be potentially relevant. (This may require collecting client archives, creating backup and deletion policies, and instructing client's staff to conform to policies of backup and preservation of relevant data, including metadata, and the cessation of overwriting disks and tapes.)

6. Parties should place each other on notice with respect to preserving electronic documents as early in the process as possible because electronic documents may be lost in the ordinary course of business.

7. Parties should discuss the need to preserve or produce metadata as early as possible. If a party considers metadata relevant, it should notify the other party immediately.

8. Counsel should meet and confer as soon as practicable, on an ongoing basis, regarding the location, preservation, review, and production of elec-

tronic documents. They should seek to agree on the scope of each party's rights and obligations with respect to e-discovery, and create a process for dealing with them.

9. The scope of e-discovery should be defined by parties and their counsel before commencing oral examination for discovery. This can best be achieved if parties' requests for preservation of electronic documents and pre-discovery meetings between counsel are as specific as possible in identifying what is being requested, what is being produced and what is not being produced, and the reasons for any **refusals**.

10. A party may satisfy its obligation to produce relevant electronic documents in good faith by using electronic tools and processes such as data sampling, searching, or selection criteria to identify the documents that are most likely to contain relevant data or information. (This means that a party may not have to review every bit of data in an e-file in some circumstances; for example, where the relevance of the data lies in its indicating a trend or direction.)

11. Parties should agree early in the litigation process on the format in which electronic documents will be produced. Such documents may be produced in electronic form where this would

    - provide more complete and relevant information;
    - facilitate access to the information in the document by means of electronic techniques to review, search, or otherwise use the documents in the litigation process;
    - minimize costs to the producing party; and/or
    - preserve the integrity and security of the data.

12. During the discovery process, where appropriate, parties should agree to measures to protect privileged information and other objections to the production of electronic documents. (Where databases are large, inadvertent disclosure of privileged information may be a significant problem.)

13. In general, consistent with the rules regarding production of paper documents, pending any final disposition of the proceeding, the interim costs of preservation, retrieval, review, and production of electronic documents will be borne by the party producing them. The other party will, similarly, be required to incur the cost of making a copy of the resulting productions for its own use. However, in special circumstances, it may be appropriate for the parties to arrive at a different allocation of costs on an informal basis, by agreement, or by court order.[10]

refusal
the refusal to answer a question at all; when a party refuses to answer a question, a reason should be given for not answering

Affidavit of Documents

The affidavit of documents has a prescribed format (Form 30A for individuals and Form 30B for corporations or partnerships). The difference is that an officer or director of a corporation or a partner on behalf of a partnership completes Form 30B, whereas an individual party completes his or her own affidavit using Form 30A. The deponent must not only search his or her own records but also take steps to inquire about the kinds of documents that might be relevant and inquire of others who may have control of various types of classes of relevant documents. After a thorough inquiry and search, the deponent swears that he or she has disclosed all documents that are relevant and in his or her power, possession, or control.

The documents are then divided into three schedules:

1. Schedule A documents are those that the deponent has or can get and that he or she will produce if asked.

2. Schedule B documents are those that the deponent has or once had but that he or she objects to producing on the ground of privilege. The basis for privilege must be stated: correspondence subject to lawyer–client privilege, documents for which the dominant purpose is litigation, or correspondence related to settlement made on a without prejudice basis.

3. Schedule C documents are those that were once in the possession, power, or control of the deponent but no longer are. It is necessary to state how control was lost and to give the present location of the documents if known.

There is also a fourth schedule, schedule D, but it is used only in cases brought under Rule 76, the simplified procedure rule. Here, in addition to disclosing documents, a party also discloses the names and addresses of persons who might reasonably be expected to have knowledge of transactions or occurrences in issue. Some of these persons may be called as witnesses, and some may not, but those who eventually become witnesses should be on this list. Once the names are known, lawyers for any party may approach the potential witnesses to ask them questions. It is then up to the person contacted to decide whether he or she wishes to talk to the lawyer. There is no obligation to do so. The only obligation is to attend court and give evidence if summonsed to do so. In a proceeding that is *not* conducted under Rule 76, names of persons with information can be obtained on oral discovery.

The deponent's signature must appear on the affidavit of documents. A lawyer must also sign the certificate on the form, stating that he or she informed the deponent of the requirement that full disclosure of all documents be made.

Clerk's Role in the Discovery of Documents

Now that we have examined the basic document disclosure and production rules, and the contents of the affidavit of documents, we can turn to your role in the document discovery process.

The law clerk needs to understand both the issues involved in the action and the individual lawyer's approach to the issues in the file. This means that you need to understand the theory of the case, and how that might affect the organization of documents. The theory for Abigail's allegation of negligence, for example, is that she fell because Fred left the oil on the floor and hid it by turning down the lights so that one would notice it.

The clerk needs to find out how the lawyer prefers information to be presented in the affidavit. The main variation is in how documents are described, for example: "letter from Dr. Morris Furgazy, neurologist, to Dr. Edwina Dhrool, family physician for Abigail Boar, regarding results of PET scan taken June 13, year 1" or "letter from Dr. Morris Furgazy to Dr. Edwina Dhrool, Abigail Boar's family physician." Either version is acceptable. The shorter version will force the opponent's lawyer to review the document and determine its relevance.

The next step is to review the client's documents. If they are numerous, and are composed of ordinary business records, it may be necessary to conduct your review on the client's premises. Otherwise, the documents can be taken to the lawyer's office. Whichever approach is taken, it is important not to disturb the way in which the client arranged the material. If a client keeps account records in a particular sequence in a shoebox, then they should remain in that sequence in that shoebox. Each document should be located, copied, identified, and put back in its original location. With many documents now available electronically, whole folders and files may be downloaded onto CDs, flash drives, or other electronic storage devices. If this is done, all material should be downloaded in the order and format in which it is found, insofar as this is possible.

The management of the documents by the law firm may be accomplished using a variety of specialized software programs, or it may be done using a standard word-processing program, making use of the table and sort functions. What follows is an overview of how to prepare an affidavit of documents from client files.

Preparing an Affidavit of Documents from Client Files

Go through the client's documents in the exact order that you find them, without disturbing that order, and review them for relevance and privilege, using the guidelines discussed earlier. Number each document in each file in sequence, as it appears. This includes every phone message, invoice, memorandum, letter, videotape, and so on.

Each file can be labelled as a subfile and given a sequential number. The documents in all subfiles can then be numbered in sequence as well, starting with the first document in the first subfile and ending with the last document in the last subfile. This means that the first document in subfile 4 is not F4/D1 but may be F4/D632. In this way, each document has a unique number, allowing you to easily find a document to be produced, or one that is privileged or irrelevant, and to know how many documents there are in total.

When numbering documents, do not write on originals; instead, use small coloured stickers, writing the document number and the subfile number on the sticker.

As you assign document and file numbers, you prepare a table in which a complete list of all documents in all files can be entered. This is a master list for office use, although by using the sort function of your software later, you will be able to select documents for the schedule A list, with all necessary location details. Table 14.2 provides a format for a document table.

Table 14.2   Document Table

Schedule	Date	Type	Pages	Description	Location

- In the schedule column, insert A, B, or C for the relevant schedule on the affidavit of documents.

- In the date column, insert the date of the document; leave it blank if the document is undated.

- In the type column, indicate whether the document is an original, photocopy, video, or fax copy.

- In the pages column, indicate the length of the document in pages.

- In the description column, bearing in mind your lawyer's approach, enter a description of the document.

- In the location column, indicate the document's location by subfile number and individual document number—for example, F3/D67.

List each document, starting with the first document in the first subfile and going to the last document in the last subfile. Then sort the list chronologically. Undated items appear at the head or foot of the list, depending on your preference and the capabilities of your software.

Using this chronological list, you can now prepare the list for schedule A in the affidavit. From the chronological list, sort for all schedule A documents and list them in a separate table in chronological order, undated items first. The schedule A documents should now be listed in sequence (1, 2, 3) on the affidavit, and the document identifier numbers (F1/D3) previously used to locate them can be deleted from the affidavit. Most lawyers do not give individualized lists of documents for which privilege is claimed in schedule B. Rather, they identify and describe a class of documents, as the following examples illustrate:

- "all notes prepared by or on behalf of Abigail Boar in anticipation of litigation or for use in instructing counsel and prosecuting this action,"

- "all correspondence passing between the plaintiff and her lawyers," and

- "narrative prepared by Abigail Boar of events following her fall, prepared for her lawyers."

Abigail Boar's Affidavit of Documents

In a case such as Abigail's, most of the documentation concerns her injuries and their consequences. But to keep matters simple, let us assume that we have looked through Abigail's files and found the following documents:

1. a receipt for dinner at Barbeerian's, September 14, year 0 [D1];
2. a written narrative prepared by Abigail for I.M. Just describing events after the accident, January 21, year 1 [D2];
3. a daily "pain diary" prepared by Abigail and kept on a daily basis, from November 10, year 0, recording pain and other effects of the injuries sustained [D3];
4. Toronto Hospital records from September 14 to 16, year 0 [D4];
5. a letter from Dr. Furgazy to Dr. Dhrool, January 10, year 1, advising on treatment for Abigail [D5];
6. a prescription, October 14, year 0 [D6];
7. a prescription, October 21, year 0 [D7];
8. a prescription, November 3, year 0 [D8]; and
9. a birthday card from Aunt Emma, August 31, year 0 [D9].

Because there are not many documents, and the client hasn't created subfiles, you would not necessarily arrange them in subfiles; but if you did, you could create the following subfiles and place the documents in them:

- F1 receipts: D1, D6, D7, D8;
- F2 medical records: D4; and
- F3 correspondence and memoranda: D2, D3, D5, D9.

D2 is privileged because it was prepared for use by her lawyer in this litigation. You can eliminate D9 from the affidavit because Abigail's birthday is not relevant to the issues in the action. It is included in the office list but will not appear in the affidavit. The rest are clearly relevant to the issues and belong in schedule A.

Figure 14.3 shows Abigail Boar's affidavit of documents.

Figure 14.3   Affidavit of Documents (Form 30A)

Court file no. 01-CV-1234

ONTARIO
SUPERIOR COURT OF JUSTICE

BETWEEN:

ABIGAIL BOAR

Plaintiff

and

RATTLE MOTORS LTD. and FRED FLOGEM

Defendants

AFFIDAVIT OF DOCUMENTS

I, Abigail Boar, of the City of Toronto, in the Province of Ontario, the plaintiff in this action, MAKE OATH AND SAY:

1. I have conducted a diligent search of my records and have made appropriate enquiries of others to inform myself in order to make this affidavit. This affidavit discloses, to the full extent of my knowledge, information and belief, all documents relevant to any matter in issue in this action that are or have been in my possession, control or power.

2. I have listed in Schedule A those documents that are in my possession, control or power and that I do not object to producing for inspection.

3. I have listed in Schedule B those documents that are or were in my possession, control or power and that I object to producing because I claim they are privileged, and I have stated in Schedule B the grounds for each such claim.

4. I have listed in Schedule C those documents that were formerly in my possession, control or power but are no longer in my possession, control or power, and I have stated in Schedule C when and how I lost possession or control of or power over them and their present location.

5. I have never had in my possession, control or power any document relevant to any matter in issue in this action other than those listed in Schedules A, B and C.

SWORN before me at the)	
City of Toronto,)	*Abigail Boar*
in the Province of Ontario,)	Abigail Boar
on February 10, year 1.)	
I.M. Just)	
I.M. Just)	
Commissioner for Taking Affidavits)	

Figure 14.3   Concluded

LAWYER'S CERTIFICATE

I CERTIFY that I have explained to the deponent,

(a) the necessity of making full disclosure of all documents relevant to any matter in issue in the action;

(b) what kinds of documents are likely to be relevant to the allegations made in the pleadings; and

(c) if the action is brought under the simplified procedure, the necessity of providing the list required under rule 76.03.

Date January 14, year 1

I.M. Just
_____
I.M. Just

Schedule A

Documents in my possession, control or power that I do not object to producing for inspection.

1. Receipt for dinner from Barbeerian's: September 14, year 0
2. Toronto Hospital records: September 14–16, year 0
3. Prescription: October 14, year 0
4. Prescription: October 21, year 0
5. Prescription: November 3, year 0
6. Pain diary: November 10, year 0 to date of this affidavit
7. Letter from Dr. Furgazy to Dr. Dhrool: January 10, year 1

Schedule B

Documents that are or were in my possession, control or power that I object to producing on the grounds of privilege.

1. Written narrative describing post-accident events, prepared for counsel for the purpose of conducting litigation: January 21, year 1.
2. All correspondence passing between the plaintiff and her lawyer.
3. All notes, reports, and memoranda prepared by or on behalf of the plaintiff in anticipation of litigation or for use in instructing counsel and conducting this litigation.

Privilege is claimed on the basis that these documents were prepared in contemplation of or for the purpose of litigation or are the subject of lawyer–client privilege.

Schedule C

Documents that were formerly in my possession, control or power but are no longer in my possession, control or power.

There are no such documents.

RCP-E 30A (November 1, 2008)

Inspection of Documents

Once the other parties have received an affidavit of documents, they have a right to inspect any of the documents in schedule A. They may do this by serving a request to inspect documents (Form 30C). An example of a request to inspect documents is set out in Figure 14.4.

Most lawyers do not bother with the request to inspect; instead, they usually cooperate by producing and providing to the other side copies of their client's documents in schedule A, often bound and tabbed in a binder. With e-discovery, the parties may supply each other with CDs that contain relevant documents. The affidavit of documents is not usually filed in court unless it is relevant to an issue on a motion or at trial. Its primary function is to serve as an index to the productions themselves.

However, where a party does not produce documents voluntarily, Rule 30.04 sets out a procedure for obtaining them for inspection. If there are further difficulties, a court on a motion may order production. In considering an order for production, a court may order "divided production" (Rule 30.04(8)). Such an order may be made where a document that is prejudicial to a party becomes relevant only after an issue in the action has been decided. The court may allow disclosure to be withheld until the issue is decided. If the decision on the issue results in the second issue becoming relevant, then discovery may be had on the other documents.

Without further notice or summons, documents in schedule A are to be produced at discovery of the party who swore the affidavit of documents and at trial (Rule 30.04(4)).

Incomplete Affidavits of Documents

A party may find relevant documents after completing the affidavit of documents and producing documents. In this case, the party must make a supplementary affidavit of documents, indicating which further documents have been discovered and take the necessary steps to produce the documents (Rule 30.07). Where the affidavit is incomplete or privilege is improperly claimed, the court may order cross-examination on the affidavit of documents, service of a revised and amended affidavit of documents, and disclosure and production of omitted documents. If a claim of privilege is in issue, the court may inspect the document to determine whether the claim of privilege is improper (Rule 30.06). Where a party fails to disclose a document or produce it for inspection on the issue whether or not it is privileged, the court may, if the document is favourable to the party withholding it, prohibit its use in evidence in the action. If the document is not favourable, the court may make any order as is just (Rule 30.08). There are similar rules with respect to documents for which privilege is improperly claimed. Once a document is privileged, the other side does not get to see it or refer to it in evidence. It would be unfair to allow the party claiming privilege to take the other side by surprise by suddenly waiving privilege and introducing the document in evidence at trial. If a party does wish to waive privilege, it must do so by notice in writing at least 90 days before the commencement of trial. There is one exception to this rule: A party may, without giving

Figure 14.4   Request to Inspect Documents (Form 30C)

Court file no. 01-CV-1234

ONTARIO
SUPERIOR COURT OF JUSTICE

BETWEEN:

ABIGAIL BOAR

Plaintiff

and

RATTLE MOTORS LTD. and FRED FLOGEM

Defendants

REQUEST TO INSPECT DOCUMENTS

You are requested to produce for inspection all the documents listed in Schedule A of your affidavit of documents.

Date: January 23, year 1

Huey Sue
LSUC #23456T
Barrister and Solicitor
65 False Trail
Toronto, Ontario, M6Y 1Z6

tel. 416-485-6891
fax 416-485-6892

Lawyer for the Defendants

TO: Just & Coping
Barristers and Solicitors
365 Bay Street – 8701
Toronto, Ontario, M3J 4A9

I.M. Just
LSUC #12345R
tel. 416-762-1342
fax 416-762-2300

Lawyers for the Plaintiff

RCP-E 30C (July 1, 2007)

advance notice, use the privileged document to challenge the credibility of a witness (Rule 30.09).

Production from Non-Parties

The rules governing discovery of documents apply only to parties. What happens if a non-party has a relevant document that is not privileged and is legally beyond the reach of any party? Rule 30.10 provides an answer by permitting any party to bring a motion for the inspection (as to relevance and privilege, if claimed) and production of a document. The moving party must show that the document is relevant and that it would be unfair to require the party to proceed to trial without it. Because the motion involves someone who is not a party to the proceeding, the non-party must be served with the motion personally or by an alternative to personal service.

Oral Examination for Discovery

Introduction

Examination for discovery is probably the most important procedure prior to trial in a civil action. It permits a lawyer to obtain admissions to prove his or her case and to undermine the other party's case. It narrows the issues that must be proved at trial and identifies evidence on which the other party relies. It may also reveal the opponent's theory and strategy for proof of the case.

Thorough preparation is extremely important. The client must understand the theory of his or her case and be **wood-shedded** so that he or she is prepared to answer questions on cross-examination and deal with various cross-examination styles. The client must review the pleadings, witness statements, documents, and relevant memoranda. The client should also review with counsel the issues to be canvassed and the questions to be asked in examining the opposing party.

Opposing counsel will try to obtain answers that help his or her case and hurt yours. A witness who answers a question without thinking has lost many a case. David Stockwood, an experienced civil litigator, has the following suggestions[11] to aid a witness on examination for discovery or any examination:

1. If the lawyer objects to a question, the client should not answer it unless he or she is told to do so. Objections are used sparingly because they may be seen as an attempt to hide evidence.

2. The client should listen to the question and be sure he or she understands it before answering.

3. If the client does not understand the question, he or she should say so.

4. If the client does not know the answer to a question or does not remember the answer, he or she should say so. This information can be supplied after discovery.

5. Unless the client has clear and accurate figures in writing, he or she should give an estimate.

---

wood-shedded
prepared for later cross-examination by an opposing lawyer

6. The client should not rush to answer and should take time to think, if it is needed.

7. The client should be concise and should not ramble.

8. The client should not argue with opposing counsel.

The client also needs to know how oral discovery works and what the physical layout is in the place where the examination will occur. Discovery is an out-of-court examination that is arranged and supervised by the lawyers. The lawyer conducting the examination, usually after consultation with opposing counsel, determines the date and time for the examination and reserves space with one of the private reporting services or, in smaller centres, with the official examiner. If a reporting service or an official examiner is used, the service or the official examiner supplies a meeting room with a long table, exhibit stamps, a Bible, and a court reporter who takes down the evidence on tape and later transcribes it. There is no judicial official present. The party being examined and his or her lawyer sit on one side of the table. The lawyer conducting the examination sits on the other side, together with his or her client, who is allowed to be present. The witness is then sworn and questioned by the opposing counsel. If the witness's lawyer believes a question is irrelevant, abusive, or otherwise improper, he or she may object to the question and tell the witness not to answer it. In this case, the lawyer states the basis of the objection for the record. The lawyer may then permit the party to answer, subject to the objection. In this case, the answer cannot be used in court later unless on a motion the court determines that the question was proper. Alternatively, the lawyer may tell the client not to answer, in which case a motion is necessary to compel the answer. Because there is no judge present to rule on an objection, if the examining lawyer wants the question answered, he or she must bring a motion to compel re-attendance to answer the question, provided, of course, that the court finds the objection improper. When the witness does not know an answer or does not have information, he or she may be asked to give an undertaking to provide the answer or information. The witness should wait for his or her lawyer to agree or not. A lawyer who is not sure "takes it under **advisement**." This means that the lawyer will consult with the client and provide an answer later, either refusing to give an undertaking or providing what is required. If a lawyer cuts off his or her client and answers the question, the client is deemed to have adopted the lawyer's answer as his or her own if the client does not object or correct the lawyer's answer (Rule 31.08).

> **advisement**
> "taking it under advisement" means to not answer the question now, but to think about whether you will answer the question later

Questioning styles vary. Some lawyers hop around from issue to issue, often returning to a specific issue several times. This may result in a witness's being caught off guard and contradicting himself or herself. But the transcript from this kind of examination is often hard to follow. Other lawyers take a more chronological or sequential approach. Often the lawyer doing the discovery is a junior associate. One purpose here is to save the client from the senior counsel's higher fees. The other purpose is strategic, so that the party being examined is not exposed to and therefore is not ready for the style of questioning of senior counsel at trial.

estoppel
term indicating that a
witness is bound by his or
her original position and
evidence and cannot later
take a contrary position

Lawyers often agree to certain ground rules to save time. Often counsel adopts an **estoppel** technique in conducting the examination. For example, in Abigail Boar's case, counsel might ask Fred Flogem, "Can you show me anything in the correspondence with Skunk Motorcar Company Ltd. that indicates that the problem with the leaking oil pan had been fixed?" This may produce a lengthy wait, while Fred goes through the exhibits to inform himself. Instead, counsel can state, "Unless I hear from you to the contrary, may I take it that there is nothing in the correspondence with Skunk Motorcar Company Ltd. to suggest that the problem with the leaking oil pan had been fixed?" In the latter case, no undertaking need be given. Fred can look at the correspondence and report back if he finds something relevant. If he is silent, Fred is estopped, or barred, from taking the position at trial that there is something relevant in the correspondence.

More time is saved when both lawyers consult at the beginning of the examination and come to an agreement about the facts that are not in dispute. The witness can then be asked to adopt the position that certain facts have been agreed to. The facts in question can be set out in writing and made an exhibit to the discovery, so the witness does not have to be taken through each one. If the discussion about which facts might be agreed to takes place in the examination, the lawyer who initiates the discussion may ask to go "off the record." This means that the reporter will not record the discussion. This cuts the length of the transcript and its cost. Not every discussion should be off the record, however. Discussions about the basis for an objection should be on the record, as the transcript of that discussion may be evidence or an exhibit in a motion to compel a party to answer the question objected to.

In dealing with documents on discovery, much time can be wasted making each document a separate exhibit. Each party usually has a pile of documents that are in schedule A of the affidavit of documents. If there are 40 documents in schedule A, the easiest thing to do is to produce copies in a tabbed binder and agree to enter them as exhibits 1 to 40 on discovery and later at trial. Any other documents that emerge can be entered separately as exhibits 41, 42, and so on after a witness has identified them and testified as to their authenticity.

Cross-examination is permitted at discovery, except on issues of credibility, which are explored at trial. This allows a lawyer to lead a witness with simple questions that can be answered "yes" or "no." This saves time and transcript space. It is permissible to ask about evidence that lies behind a statement of fact and to ask for the names and addresses of persons who have knowledge of matters in the action, whether these people become witnesses or not. Because insurance policies must be produced if they cover the liabilities raised by the lawsuit, they can be the subject of questions on discovery. A party may also be asked to disclose findings, opinions, and conclusions of experts who will give evidence, though the report does not have to be produced unless the party intends to rely on it at trial (Rule 31.06). Parties who subsequently learn the answer to a question they were asked on discovery are obliged to disclose it.

Once the examination is completed, a lawyer does not terminate it but adjourns it, subject to the fulfillment of undertakings and the bringing of motions on disputed questions.

The lawyer for the party who has been examined may, at the conclusion of the examination, re-examine the party to clarify an answer, or the answer may be clarified by letter later.

In the event that information is obtained that requires the correction of an answer given on discovery, there is a duty to provide the correct information forthwith in writing. The writing can be treated as evidence, but an adverse party may insist that it be given in affidavit form to have the same weight as the sworn evidence given on discovery (Rules 31.09(1) and (2)). If a party fails to disclose new information as required by Rule 31.09, if it is favourable, he or she cannot use it at trial. If it is not favourable, the court has broad discretion to do what is just (Rule 31.09(3)).

Arranging Discoveries

A party to an action may examine every other party who is adverse in interest. The examination may be oral or written, but not both. If a corporation or partnership is a party, get directions from your supervising lawyer before arranging for a particular representative to be examined. Counsel may examine any party once. If the corporation's counsel gets to choose who represents the company, the examination may be very uninformative. If counsel has a person in mind to question, that person should be summonsed to the examination (Rule 31.03). If a person under disability is a party, the litigation guardian may be discovered, but if the disabled party is competent to give evidence, the disabled party may be examined (Rule 31.03(5)).[12]

There is some debate over whether it is advantageous to be examined first or to examine first.[13] Some think that it is an advantage to examine first because the examining lawyer gets a chance to assess the credibility and demeanour of the opponent and take him or her by surprise. Others think that by going last, you will know more about your opponent's theory of his or her case and be able to shape your own examination accordingly. Where credibility is an issue, however, whoever goes first, the time between examinations of the plaintiff and defendant should be short, so that a dishonest party does not have the opportunity to tailor evidence. If the examinations are to last a half day each, scheduling back to back is one solution to this problem. Another solution is to have both examinations well under way before transcripts are available.

The governing rules for arranging discoveries are Rules 31.04 and 34. A defendant who wishes to examine a plaintiff must have served a statement of defence and an affidavit of documents. A plaintiff who wishes to examine a defendant may do so after the defendant has served a statement of defence and affidavit of documents, or the defendant has been noted in default. The parties may also agree to other arrangements regarding timing. In any event, the person who first serves a notice of examination may examine first and complete his or her examination before being examined by the other party (Rule 34.01).

Rule 34.04 sets out the procedure for compelling attendance. A notice of examination, Form 34A, must be served on the lawyer of record, if there is one, or on the party personally or by an alternative to personal service. The alternative service procedure may not be used if the person is appearing as a representative of a company or other non-individual. An example of the notice of examination is set out in Figure 14.5.

Figure 14.5   Notice of Examination (Form 34A)

Court file no. 01-CV-1234

ONTARIO
SUPERIOR COURT OF JUSTICE

BETWEEN:

ABIGAIL BOAR

Plaintiff

and

RATTLE MOTORS LTD. and FRED FLOGEM

Defendants

NOTICE OF EXAMINATION

TO: Abigail Boar

YOU ARE REQUIRED TO ATTEND, on Tuesday, September 14, year 1, at 10:00 a.m. at the office of Victory Verbatim Reporting Services, Toronto Dominion Centre, 66 Wellington Street West, Suite 3320, PO Box 182, Toronto, Ontario, M5K 1H6 for:

[   ]   Cross-examination on your affidavit dated (*date*)
[x]   Examination for discovery
[   ]   Examination for discovery on behalf of or in place of (*identify party*)
[   ]   Examination in aid of execution
[   ]   Examination in aid of execution on behalf of or in place of (*identify party*)

YOU ARE REQUIRED TO BRING WITH YOU and produce at the examination the documents mentioned in subrule 30.04(4) of the Rules of Civil Procedure, and the following documents and things:

All documents, as defined in the Rules of Civil Procedure, relating to any matter in this action within your possession, power, or control.

Figure 14.5   Concluded

August 23, year 1

Huey Sue
LSUC #23456T
Barrister and Solicitor
65 False Trail
Toronto, Ontario, M6Y 1Z6

tel. 416-485-6891
fax 416-485-6892

Lawyer for the Defendants

TO: Just & Coping
Barristers and Solicitors
365 Bay Street – 8701
Toronto, Ontario, M3J 4A9

I.M. Just
LSUC #12345R
tel. 416-762-1342
fax 416-762-2300

Lawyers for the Plaintiff

RCP-E 34A (July 1, 2007)

If a lawyer expects that the party being summonsed for examination will not appear, it may be wise to serve the party personally as well as by his or her lawyer. Then if the lawyer brings a motion for contempt, the party can be jailed if he or she has been served personally with the notice (and later with the motion). Usually, however, service on the lawyer of record will suffice.

If the person being examined resides in Ontario, he or she must be given at least two days' notice of the examination (Rule 34.05). The person is entitled to be examined in the county where the person resides (Rule 34.03). If the person resides outside Ontario, the terms and conditions of the examination, whether it is held in Ontario or elsewhere, are set by the court (Rule 34.07). Examinations outside Ontario, which are governed by Rules 34.07 and 36.01, are beyond the scope of this text.

All of this rigmarole can be avoided, and sensible lawyers usually do avoid it, by agreeing to the time, place, and order of the examinations and to the furnishing of documents. Taking the sensible approach can save much time and money, and there is little to be gained by being unnecessarily adversarial in making these procedural arrangements.

Examination of Non-Parties

An analogy to Rule 30.10, which covers requiring production of documents from non-parties in certain circumstances, is found in Rules 31.10 and 34.04(4) and (5), governing the examination of non-parties. The test for bringing such a motion is set out in Rule 31.10(2), and it is a stringent one. Non-parties are strangers to the lawsuit, at least technically, and they ought not to be inconvenienced by being made to participate in it. If non-parties are required for examination, the moving party must show that:

- he or she could not obtain the information from a party on discovery, or from the person who has possession, power, or control of the information or document in question;

- it would be unfair to require the moving party to proceed to trial without the opportunity of examining the person; and

- the examination will not unduly delay the trial, create unreasonable expense for the person, or be unfair to the non-party.

If the moving party is successful, he or she must provide transcripts free of charge to the other parties. The costs of the examination cannot be recovered from other parties as part of a general costs award at trial unless the court expressly permits it. Evidence of a non-party, unlike the evidence of parties, cannot be read into evidence under Rule 31.11(1).

If you are examining a non-party for discovery, see Rules 34.04(4) and (5). You will use a summons to witness (Form 34B) and pay the witness **attendance money** under Tariff A, Part II, item 21, as you would when serving a summons on a witness at trial.[14] Summons procedure is discussed in Chapter 16, Trial Preparation and Trial.

attendance money
formerly called conduct money, composed of the *per diem* witness fee and an amount for transportation and lodging in accordance with Tariff A

Controlling Disruptive and Uncooperative Behaviour

Although lawyers should know better, there are some who cannot resist engaging in improper or disruptive behaviour, or who do not take steps to prevent their clients from behaving improperly and disruptively. Some members of the legal profession who think this is a growing problem look back to a "golden age," when lawyers behaved with civility toward other counsel and their clients. Whether the problem is or is not on the increase, the Law Society of Upper Canada, in August 2001, mailed a pamphlet on civility to all lawyers in the province, a sort of lawyer etiquette manual. With respect to discovery, and out-of-court examinations generally, the kinds of questionable conduct one might expect to encounter are set out in Rule 34.14(1):

- an excessive number of improper questions, interruptions, or objections designed to wear down or distract the person being examined or to disrupt the examination completely;

- an examination conducted in bad faith (for a purpose other than that intended by the Rules) or in an unreasonable manner so as to embarrass, intimidate, or oppress the person being examined (examples include using a loud, angry, or sarcastic voice, asking irrelevant or embarrassing questions, and/or making personal remarks—in one extreme case, coffee was poured on opposing counsel's notes and later on his lap);

- answers from a party that are evasive, unresponsive, or unduly lengthy (examples include answering questions with questions, giving irrelevant answers that do not respond to the question asked, and going on at great length about irrelevant matters); and

- neglect or refusal of a party to produce relevant documents on the examination.

A lawyer faced with this kind of behaviour has several choices. If it is only moderately disruptive, so that he or she is still getting information, it may be best to ignore it. Let the examination transcript speak for itself at trial if the issue of bad faith, non-responsiveness, or credibility arises, or when addressing costs at trial. An examination for discovery is not a chat among friends. Some friction, though it should be avoided, may have to be tolerated. There may come a time, however, when it is clear that a lawyer is simply being stonewalled or a client is being subjected to stressful and/or intimidating tactics. At that point, it is appropriate to break off the examination and state that you are adjourning the examination in order to seek directions from the court for the continuation of the examination, or for an order terminating the examination or limiting its scope. If the court finds that there was improper conduct, the court may levy costs against the person who engaged in improper conduct, especially if it was wilful or in bad faith. Costs may be levied personally against a lawyer in this regard (Rule 34.14(2)). The same cost penalties may be levied against a moving party who improperly adjourned an examination to bring a motion for directions.

While the motion under Rule 34.14 for directions focuses on improper conduct of an examination, Rule 34.15 is directed at default or misconduct by a witness on an examination including:

- failure to attend at the time and place fixed for examination,

- refusal to take an oath or make an affirmation,

- refusal to answer a proper question,

- refusal to produce a document or thing that he or she is required to produce, or

- refusal to comply with an order made under Rule 34.14 to correct previously noted improper behaviour.

The remedy granted depends on the nature of the default or misconduct. If counsel considers a question to be improper, he or she can state the objection on the record and direct the client not to answer the question. If opposing counsel wishes to challenge the objection, a Rule 34.15 motion is the way to do it. If the moving party is successful, the court will order the party to re-attend at his or her own expense and answer the question, and any proper questions that flow from that answer. This is not uncommon. Reasonable lawyers may honestly disagree about whether a question is proper or not. But the other kinds of misconduct identified in Rule 34.15 are more likely to be unreasonable and wilful. For this misconduct, a plaintiff's action may be dismissed, or a defendant's defence may be struck out. Lesser penalties include striking out the person's evidence recorded on the transcript or in an affidavit.

The ultimate penalty, where someone refuses to attend or be sworn or continues to obstruct an examination after a Rule 34.14 order has been made, is committal to jail for contempt. If a lawyer is seeking committal for contempt, the Rule 34.15 motion must be served personally, and the motion must be brought before a judge because a master has no authority to make an order depriving someone of his or her liberty.

Ordering and Using Transcripts

Check with the lawyer responsible for the file before ordering transcripts of an examination for discovery. Depending on the issues and the complexity of the case, and whether settlement is imminent, the lawyer may not wish to go to the expense of ordering transcripts. On the other hand, it may be important to obtain transcripts quickly, in which case counsel may wish to have the transcripts expedited. This means that instead of taking several weeks, copies will be available in a few days, but the cost is high. The lawyer who conducts an examination usually orders a copy, and a copy is also to be sent to and filed in court (Rule 34.17). A party who intends to use a transcript on a motion or at trial is responsible for seeing that the transcript is filed with the appropriate court office (Rule 34.18).

The transcript may be used in a variety of ways. At trial, counsel may read into the record, as part of his or her own case, all or part of the discovery transcript of an adverse party or a non-party. Counsel may later call other evidence at trial to rebut the answers given on discovery. This procedure of "reading in" is usually done by referring to the questions and answers by the question numbers. At that point, and not before, the transcript or the relevant parts should be filed with the court (Rule 31.11(1)). The opposing party may ask that other parts of the transcript also be included because they qualify the answers or give them a proper context.

The transcript may be used to impeach the credibility of the deponent as a witness at trial when he or she gives an answer that contradicts the answer given on discovery. Counsel puts the discovery question and answer to the witness and asks if he or she gave that answer then. The assumption is that the discovery answer, earlier in time, is more likely to be accurate.

The transcript of any party may be read into evidence if that party has died, is unable to attend the trial, refuses to attend the trial, refuses to be sworn, or stands mute and refuses to answer questions.

If discovery is held in an action, the action is discontinued or dismissed, and a new action dealing with the same subject matter is commenced, the discovery in the first proceeding may be used in the second proceeding as if it had been the discovery transcript in the second proceeding (Rule 31.11(2) to (8)).

Examination for Discovery by Written Questions

Written questions and answers as a form of discovery have long been in use in England, where they are called interrogatories, and in the United States, where they supplement oral discovery. Although available here under Rule 35, they are rarely used. Most lawyers are not familiar with the format and find it inflexible. Most lawyers prefer the fluidity of an oral examination, where a question may be inspired by the answer to the previous question. An oral examination is especially desirable when the person being examined is uncooperative or evasive, credibility is in issue, or a lawyer needs to get a sense of what the party being examined is like. However, a written examination for discovery is much cheaper because it does not involve court reporters, rental of meeting rooms, out-of-office attendances, or the cost of transcripts. Where credibility is not an issue and the fact situation is simple, a Rule 35 written discovery may be more appropriate.

Serving a list of questions in Form 35A on the person to be examined and on every other party commences a written examination. Once the list is served, the party waives a right to oral discovery. Answers are given by affidavit in Form 35B within 15 days after being served with the list of questions. If the party objects to a question that has been asked, he or she must state the objection in the affidavit and give reasons for refusing to answer. The examining party, after receiving the affidavit, has 10 days to serve a further list of supplementary questions, which must be answered in 15 days from the date of service of the supplementary questions. Where there is an unresolved dispute about an unanswered question, the court may order the question answered by affidavit or by oral examination. Similarly, if the answers are evasive, the court may order attendance for a complete oral examination, thereby abandoning the Rule 35 process. The questions and the answers given under Rule 35 may be filed and treated as transcripts at trial under Rule 31.11. Figure 14.6 provides an example of questions on a written examination for discovery, and Figure 14.7 provides an example of answers on such an examination.

Figure 14.6   Questions on Written Examination for Discovery (Form 35A)

Court file no. 01-CV-1234

ONTARIO
SUPERIOR COURT OF JUSTICE

BETWEEN:

ABIGAIL BOAR

Plaintiff

and

RATTLE MOTORS LTD. and FRED FLOGEM

Defendants

QUESTIONS ON WRITTEN EXAMINATION FOR DISCOVERY

The plaintiff has chosen to examine the defendant Fred Flogem for discovery by written questions and requires that the following questions be answered by affidavit in Form 35B prescribed by the Rules of Civil Procedure, served within fifteen days after service of these questions.

1.   On what date and at what time did you notice an oil leak on the showroom floor?
2.   What steps did you take upon discovering the oil leak?

• • •

Date: May 15, year 1

Just & Coping
Barristers and Solicitors
365 Bay Street – 8701
Toronto, Ontario, M3J 4A9

I.M. Just
LSUC #12345R
tel. 416-762-1342
fax 416-762-2300

Lawyers for the Plaintiff

TO: Huey Sue
       LSUC #23456T
       Barrister and Solicitor
       65 False Trail
       Toronto, Ontario, M6Y 1Z6

       tel. 416-485-6891
       fax 416-485-6892

       Lawyer for the Defendants

RCP-E 35A (July 1, 2007)

Figure 14.7   Answers on Written Examination for Discovery (Form 35B)

Court file no. 01-CV-1234

ONTARIO
SUPERIOR COURT OF JUSTICE

BETWEEN:

ABIGAIL BOAR

Plaintiff

and

RATTLE MOTORS LTD. and FRED FLOGEM

Defendants

ANSWERS ON WRITTEN EXAMINATION FOR DISCOVERY

I, Fred Flogem, of the City of Toronto, in the Province of Ontario, one of the defendants in this action, AFFIRM that the following answers to the questions dated May 15, year 1 submitted by the plaintiff are true, to the best of my knowledge, information and belief:

1. I first became aware of some fluid on the floor of the showroom at about 6:30 p.m. on September 14, year 0.
2. The fluid did not seem to be an urgent problem, so I left it until later to clean up and turned off the lights to discourage customers from wandering into the area.

• • •

AFFIRMED before me at the) City of Toronto,) in the Province of Ontario,) on May 20, year 1.) *Huey Sue*) Huey Sue) Commissioner for Taking Affidavits)	*Fred Flogem* Fred Flogem

RCP-E 35B (November 1, 2005)

Undertakings and Follow-up on Discovery

When a discovery transcript has been prepared, it is often the duty of a law clerk to go through the transcript and do the following:

- prepare a summary of the transcript, noting key points; and
- prepare a list of undertakings to provide information, refusals to provide information or answer a question, and requests taken under advisement.

Many reporters list undertakings, objections, and refusals at the front of the transcript, but you would be wise to scan it yourself to be sure nothing was missed. You will also wish to note questions taken under advisement—that is, questions that the opposing lawyer wishes to think about and advise you on later.

Once you have recorded the necessary material, write to the lawyer for the other party, asking him or her to honour the undertakings and answer the questions objected to or taken under advisement. You probably will not get a positive response on the questions objected to or taken under advisement, but there is no harm in asking. If the information is not provided and the lawyer feels it is necessary for the case, you will have to bring a motion to compel the party to re-attend and answer the questions at his or her own expense.

When you have received the answers, they should be bound together and added as an appendix to the discovery transcript.

Your law firm will be asked to provide answers to undertakings on behalf of your client. If the letter is a general request, you will have to go through your client's transcript and find the undertakings, prepare a list, and ask the client to provide answers, including answers to disputed questions if nothing much turns on them. The letter to the client should request that the answers be in writing, and you should note the question number and page of the transcript on which the question appears. The lawyer should review the client's answers and forward them in a letter to opposing counsel.

In your review of the transcript, if you note any errors in the answers or any answers that are not complete, you have an obligation to provide corrections as soon as possible. Your instructing lawyer should be notified of errors immediately.

Summaries and Undertaking Lists Prepared from Transcripts

To demonstrate how an undertaking list and summary are prepared, Figure 14.8 sets out an excerpt of the transcript of Abigail Boar's evidence.

Figure 14.8   Examination for Discovery of Abigail Boar

EXAMINATION FOR DISCOVERY OF ABIGAIL BOAR ON BEHALF OF FRED FLOGEM AND RATTLE MOTORS LTD., HELD SEPTEMBER 14, YEAR 1

1		Abigail Boar, sworn
2	By Mr. Sue:	
3	Q1:	Madam, please state your name for the record.
4	A:	Abigail Boar.
5	Q2:	Ms. Boar, I understand that on September 14, year 0
6		you entered the showroom of Rattle Motors Ltd. to look
7		at new cars.
8	A:	Yes.
9	Q3:	What time did you arrive there?
10	A:	About 7:30 p.m.
11	Q4:	What time did you leave work?
12	A:	About 5:30.
13	Q5:	How did you spend the time between leaving work and
14		arriving at the car showroom?
15	A:	I walked to a restaurant, Barbeerian's, had dinner with a
16		friend, and then I walked on alone to Rattle Motors.
17	Q6:	Ms. Boar, I am producing and showing to you a restaurant
18		receipt from Barbeerian's, dated September 14, year 0.
19		Can you identify this receipt?
20	A:	Yes, it is mine for my dinner that evening. I had dinner with
21		a friend.
22	Q7:	I notice that the bill includes two glasses of wine. Did you
23		drink both glasses?
24	A:	Yes, it was a fine Bordeaux. When I drank the first glass, it
25		was very fine, and not the plonk it often is, so I had another,
26		to savour it. And very nice it was, raspberry overtones with
27		a hint of oak. Yes, very fine indeed.
28	Q8:	You mentioned a friend. Please tell me the name and
29		address of that friend.
30	Mr. JUST:	Just a moment. Who that person is is entirely irrelevant to
31		the issues; Ms. Boar will not provide that information.
32	Mr. SUE:	I am entitled to the names and addresses of anyone with
33		knowledge of the matters in issue in this litigation.
34	Mr. JUST:	I don't have the address; we will undertake to provide that
35		information.

Figure 14.8   Concluded

1	Q9:	Now, Ms. Boar, you claim that the lighting on the premises
2		was inadequate for you to see the oil on the floor. Aside
3		from your own inability to see the oil, do you have any expert
4		evidence or reports that indicate the lighting was not
5		adequate?
6	Mr. JUST:	Just a moment, counsel. You have no right at this time to
7		any experts' reports we might have on hand, and we are
8		refusing to produce any such report at this time.
9	Q10:	Well, Ms. Boar, can you summarize what the findings are
10		in any report on the adequacy of lighting that you may
11		have?
12	A:	Well, we have one, but I only glanced at it, and I don't
13		remember what it actually said.
14	Q11:	Will you undertake to review the report and provide me
15		with a summary of its findings and conclusions?
16	Mr. JUST:	No, because the report's dominant purpose was litigation
17		and you therefore have no right to production.
18	Q12:	What kind of shoes were you wearing when you got to the
19		showroom?
20	A:	Swamp green dress shoes with a narrow 4-inch heel.
21	Q13:	Would you describe your footwear as giving you good foot
22		and ankle support when you are walking?
23	A:	Well, they are really for office wear. I wouldn't go rock
24		climbing in them.
25	Q14:	Ms. Boar, do you have any accident insurance that covers
26		the personal injuries you sustained?
27	A:	Yes, I think Mr. Just gave you the particulars of it.
28	Q15:	Will you please provide me with a copy of the policy?
29	Mr. JUST:	No, we will not give you that undertaking. You have all
30		of the information that you require.

Preparation of a Transcript Summary

Create a two-column table. In the left-hand column, note the question number or numbers and the page number. In the right-hand column, write a brief summary of the point or issue covered. Your table should look like the one set out in Table 14.3.

List of Undertakings

You also need to prepare a list of undertakings to provide information later where the information was not available to answer a question on discovery. The list also includes refusals or objections to answering questions or providing documents or further information, as well as a list of questions taken under advisement. To record this information, set out a six-column table, such as the one in Table 14.4. The last two columns, designed for the date you receive an answer and the substance of the answer/disposition by the court, are left blank for now. They will be filled in later when and if you get answers to the undertakings, or when a court deals with a refusal to answer. The table can also be used for motions to compel a party to answer an undertaking; it meets the format requirement for Form 37C.

Table 14.3   Summary of Transcript of Examination of Abigail Boar

Q1-2, p. 1	introduction of Boar, setting context
Q3-8, p. 1	Boar accounts for time after work, dinner with friend with two drinks before going on to Rattle
Q9-11, p. 2	Boar is asked for lighting expert's report and her recollection of what it said: didn't recall what it said; counsel refused to produce report
Q12-13, p. 2	Boar describes her footwear at time of accident, and whether it was safe or suitable
Q14-15, p. 2	Boar acknowledges she had accident insurance, refusal to provide copy of policy

Table 14.4   Summary of Undertakings, Objections, and Advisements (Form 37C)

REFUSALS AND UNDERTAKINGS CHART

REFUSALS					
Refusals to answer questions on the examination of Abigail Boar, dated September 14, year 1					
Issue and relation-ship to pleadings or affidavit	**Question no.**	**Page no.**	**Specific question**	**Answer or precise basis for refusal**	**Disposition by the court**
1. Provision of expert lighting report	9	2	Now, Ms. Boar, you claim that the lighting on the premises was inadequate for you to see the oil on the floor. Aside from your own inability to see the oil, do you have any expert evidence or reports that indicate the lighting was not adequate?	Refused on the basis that the report is privileged and prepared for use by counsel	
2. Whether to provide name and address of dinner companion (defence, paras. 8 and 9; reply para. 3)	8	1	You mentioned a friend. Please tell me the name and address of that friend.	Name of individual is not relevant.	
3. Provision of accident insur-ance policy	15	2	Will you please provide me with a copy of the policy?	Refused on the basis that the policy is not relevant.	

UNDERTAKINGS					
Outstanding undertakings given on the examination of Abigail Boar, dated September 14, year 1					
Issue and relation-ship to pleadings or affidavit	**Question no.**	**Page no.**	**Specific undertaking**	**Date answered or precise reason for not doing so**	**Disposition by court**
Provision of summary of lighting expert report	8	1	Mr. JUST: I don't have the address; we will undertake to provide that information.		

RCP-E 37C (November 1, 2005)

CHAPTER SUMMARY

This chapter introduced you to various discovery procedures. We began with an overview of the general purposes of discovery and discussed the deemed undertaking rule, which prevents you from using information obtained on discovery in other proceedings. We then identified and described the various forms that discovery takes: discovery of documents, including e-documents, oral examination for discovery, inspection of property, medical examinations, and written discovery. Our primary focus in this chapter was on documentary discovery and oral discovery because these are used in practically all cases, whereas other forms of discovery are narrower and more specialized in their usage. We then examined the rules for discovery of documents, noting the obligations on a party to identify and produce all non-privileged documents that are relevant. We discussed how to assist clients in collecting documentary material and how to organize it both for office use and for the preparation of an affidavit of documents. We then turned to how to set up an oral examination for discovery and described its scope and how it is conducted. Then, through the use of sample transcripts, we saw how a summary and a list of undertakings are prepared by a clerk for use by a lawyer.

KEY TERMS

active data, 325

advisement, 361

archival data, 325

attendance money, 366

discovery, 324

e-discovery, 349

estoppel, 362

metadata, 325

refusal, 351

residual data, 325

undertaking, 328

without prejudice, 348

wood-shedded, 360

NOTES

1. *Air Canada v. WestJet Airlines Ltd.*, 2006 CanLII 14966 (ON SC), (2006) 267 DLR (4th) 483, 81 OR (3d) 48, 30 CPC (6th) 321.

2. Ibid.

3. *TELUS Communications Co. v. Sharp* (2010), 102 OR (3d) 93, 97 CPC (6th) 148, 2010 ONSC 2878.

4. *Goodman v. Rossi*, 1995 CanLII 1888 (ON CA), 24 OR (3d) 359, 125 DLR (4th) 613.

5. *General Accident Assurance Co. v. Chrusz* (1997), 34 OR (3d) 354 (Gen. Div.); var'd. 37 OR (3d) 790 (Div. Ct.); rev'd. 45 OR (3d) 321 (CA).

6. *Ferber v. The Gore Mutual Insurance Co.* (1991), 3 CPC (3d) 41 (Ont. Gen. Div.).

7. For an introduction to issues and problems involved in e-discovery, and relevant links to other material and resources, see the Ontario Bar Association's E-Discovery Guidelines and Resources on its website at http://www.oba.org/Advocacy/E-Discovery.

8. See in particular *Air Canada v. WestJet Airlines Ltd.*, supra note 1.

9. Ibid. The balance of obligations was the issue in *WestJet* where counsel argued, unsuccessfully in this case, that review for relevant material in the vast volumes of data in various databases would be unduly time-consuming and expensive.

10. The Discovery Task Force, *Guidelines for the Discovery of Electronic Documents in Ontario* (Toronto: Ontario Bar Association) can be found at http://www.oba.org/CBAMediaLibrary/cba_on/pdf/E-Discovery/E-DiscoveryGuidelines.pdf.

11. See, generally, David Stockwood, *Civil Litigation*, 4th ed. (Toronto: Carswell, 2004).

12. Rule 31.03(5); see also Rules 31.03(6), (7), and (8) with respect to assignees, trustees in bankruptcy, and nominal parties.

13. Supra note 10.

14. Always consult the current tariff before issuing a cheque because the tariffs change from time to time.

REFERENCES

Air Canada v. WestJet Airlines Ltd. (2006), 267 DLR (4th) 483, 81 OR (3d) 48 (SCJ).

Courts of Justice Act, RSO 1990, c. C.43.

Ferber v. The Gore Mutual Insurance Co. (1991), 3 CPC (3d) 41 (Gen. Div.).

General Accident Assurance Co. v. Chrusz (1997), 34 OR (3d) 354 (Gen. Div.); var'd. 37 OR (3d) 790 (Div. Ct.); rev'd. 45 OR (3d) 321 (CA).

Goodman v. Rossi (1995), 125 DLR (4th) 613 (Ont. CA).

Ontario Bar Association, Discovery Task Force, *Guidelines for the Discovery of Electronic Documents in Ontario* (Toronto: Ontario Bar Association, 2003): http://www .oba.org/CBAMediaLibrary/cba_on/pdf/E-Discovery/ E-DiscoveryGuidelines.pdf.

Ontario Bar Association, The Discovery Task Force E-Discovery Guidelines and Resources Page: http:// www.oba.org/Advocacy/E-Discovery.

Ontario Bar Association, Model Document #9: Checklist for Preparing a Discovery Plan: http://www.oba.org/ Advocacy/E-Discovery/Model-Precedents.

Ontario Bar Association, Model Document #9B: Discovery Plan (Short Form): http://www.oba.org/Advocacy/E- Discovery/Model-Precedents.

Rules of Civil Procedure, RRO 1990, reg. 194.

The Sedona Conference, *The Sedona Canada Principles Addressing Electronic Discovery—At a Glance.* Copyright 2000-2013 The Sedona Conference: https:// thesedonaconference.org/node/4412.

Stockwood, David, *Civil Litigation*, 5th ed. (Toronto: Cars- well, 2004).

REVIEW QUESTIONS

1. What are the purposes of discovery?

2. What forms of discovery are available in a civil action?

3. What is the deemed undertaking rule?

4. Can you run tests on property during an inspection under Rule 32?

5. Under what circumstances will a medical examination be ordered as a form of discovery?

6. What documents must be disclosed during discovery?

7. What determines whether a document is privileged?

8. The plaintiff's lawyer would like to see the defendant's insurance policies. Can she?

9. Company A is a defendant in a lawsuit. A minority of company A's and company B's shares are held by company C, but the minority is large enough to give company C total control because the rest of the shares in companies A and B are widely dispersed. Company B has some documents that are relevant to the plaintiff's claim against company A. Can the plaintiff demand these documents from company B?

10. Consider the principles that guide e-discovery when answering the following questions.

    a. What should you do if you consider the information about who created a document and when it was created to be as important as the content of the document itself?

    b. What should you do if your opponent insists that you review every bit of data in your client's databases?

    c. What should you do if some of your client's relevant data appears to have been deleted or to be in formats that are no longer readable with the use of available software?

11. How does a law clerk organize client materials for an affidavit of documents?

12. How do lawyers obtain the schedule A documents in order to inspect them?

13. What should you do if you notice that a document was omitted from the affidavit of documents or that an answer given in oral discovery was in error?

14. Can a lawyer obtain production from a non-party?

15. How should you prepare a witness for an examination for discovery?

16. Describe for the client the physical environment where discovery takes place.

17. How do lawyers control the discovery process?

18. How can lawyers shorten the process of entering exhibits?

19. How do you arrange discoveries?

20. Can a lawyer examine a non-party for discovery?

21. What kinds of misconduct at discovery do the Rules contemplate and how is it controlled?

22. How do you obtain transcripts of the examination?

23. When would you be likely to use a written question-and-answer discovery format?

24. What do you need to do with a transcript when it comes back from the reporter?

DISCUSSION QUESTIONS

1. Read and respond to the following memorandum:

To: Law Clerk

From: Lawyer

Re: Examination of Phineas Whipsnade

We act for Henry in a family law dispute. Wendy claims that the property she owns in which Henry claims a half interest is heavily mortgaged to her father, Phineas Whipsnade. If this is so, Henry's share is likely peanuts. If this is a load of codswallop, as I suspect it is, then Henry may well get a bundle. On discovery, Wendy claimed she had no mortgage documents in her possession, power, or control. She said it was an unregistered equitable mortgage, based on a promissory note giving the property as security. She said she didn't have a copy of the note and claimed her father had the original. I wrote to Phineas requesting that he provide me with a copy and let me examine the original. That was two weeks ago, and I have had no answer.

Please write a short memorandum telling me what our options are.

2. Read and respond to the following memorandum:

To: E. Egregious, law clerk

From: I.M. Just

Re: *Boar v. Rattle Motors Ltd. et al.*

Attached is a copy of a transcript of the examination of Fred Flogem for discovery. Please prepare a summary and a list of undertakings, objections/refusals, and questions taken under advisement. Also prepare a draft notice of motion to compel Fred to re-attend at his own expense to answer unanswered questions and provide documents. Assume that Fred will not respond to the refusals, objections, or advisements.

EXAMINATION FOR DISCOVERY OF FRED FLOGEM ON BEHALF OF ABIGAIL BOAR,
HELD October 21, year 1

1	Fred Flogem, affirmed	
2	By Mr. Just:	
3	Q1:	Sir, will you please state your name for the record.
4	A:	Fred Flogem.
5	Q2:	I understand that you are employed as a salesperson for
6		Rattle Motors Ltd. and that you were present on the
7		premises on September 14, year 0.
8	A:	Yes.
9	Q3:	I understand at about 6:30 p.m. you spotted an oil leak on
10		the floor by the Super Coupe.
11	A:	Well, there was some fluid on the floor, but I didn't know
12		for sure it was oil, or that it came from a leak.
13	Q4:	Well, Freddie boy, did you think the spirits of the air
14		suddenly dropped this stuff out of the sky?
15	Mr. SUE:	I object to that question, and Mr. Flogem will not answer it.
16		It is not necessary to use that sarcastic and flippant tone,
17		calculated as it is to intimidate and harass the witness.
18	Q5:	Well, Mr. Flogem, where did you think this stuff came
19		from?
20	Mr. SUE:	I object to the question. It is not relevant where it came
21		from. He has already acknowledged in his answers that it
22		was there, and that is sufficient.
23	Q6:	Mr. Flogem, do you have an insurance policy covering the
24		damages claimed in this action?
25	A:	Me? Not personally, but I believe Rattle Motors has a
26		policy, or at least so I have been told.
27	Q7:	Can you furnish me with the particulars of the policy?
28	A:	Well, not offhand. Sunil, the manager, has a copy, I think,
29		but I have never seen it, and I have no idea where it is.
30	Q8:	Will you undertake to find out what the particulars are?
31	A:	Well, Sunil has it with him, and he is out of town, so I don't
32		know.
33	Mr. SUE:	We will take it under advisement.

1	Q9:	After you saw the fluid on the floor, what did you do?
2	A:	Well, I thought I would clean it up later, and to discourage
3		anyone from going into the area, I turned off two of the
4		four spotlights in that part of the room.
5	Q10:	Why did you put off cleaning this up?
6	A:	Well, it wasn't much of a spill, it was mostly under the car,
7		and it didn't seem urgent.
8	Q11:	Did you have any information before September 14, year 0
9		that Skunk Motorcar had issued an alert about leaking
10		oil pans on the Super Coupe model?
11	A:	Well, I think there were some letters, but I haven't read
12		them.
13	Q12:	Can you provide me with copies of those letters?
14	A:	Well—
15	Mr. SUE:	No, he cannot because he does not have them or have
16		access to them.

Pretrial Procedures 15

Introduction

Once the parties have completed the discovery process, it is time to think about going to trial. As we have discussed, the discovery process gives both sides a good opportunity to examine the case of the opposite party and determine whether or not they have a chance of winning their case at trial. During discovery, the parties often decide to settle the case.

In the *Rules of Civil Procedure*, Rules 46, 47, 48, 50, and 51 are the major rules that deal with pretrial procedures. The various procedural steps are as follows:

1. determining the place of trial: Rule 46;
2. deciding whether the case will be tried with a jury and issuing a jury notice if so: Rule 47;
3. listing the case for trial: Rule 48;
4. pretrial conference: Rule 50; and
5. dealing with admissions: Rule 51.

Place of Trial: Rules 13.1 and 46

Usually, the plaintiff may choose where to commence the proceeding. The general rule set out in Rule 46.01 is that a trial shall be held in the place where the proceeding was commenced. For example, if a plaintiff chose to issue a statement of claim in the court office in Newmarket, that is where the trial will be held.

However, where a statute or another rule specifies the place of trial, then Rule 13.1.01 makes it clear that the plaintiff cannot choose any location to start proceedings. The proceeding must start and the trial must be held where the statute or rule requires.

The court always has the power to change the place of trial on its own initiative or on the motion of any party. The change of place of trial is called a "change of venue." Under Rule 13.1.02(1) the court may change the venue or place of trial if the plaintiff has not complied with a statute or rule requiring that a matter be commenced in a specific location. However, this is not the only reason the court might order a change of venue. Rule 13.1.02(2) provides a set of factors to be considered on a request to change the place of trial. First, the court must be satisfied that

- it is likely that a fair hearing cannot be held in the place where proceedings were commenced, or
- a transfer is desirable in the "interest of justice."

The second branch of the rule focuses on a number of factors for the court to consider, such as where most of the events in issue occurred; where damages were sustained; where the subject matter of the proceeding is located; and the convenience of the parties, witnesses, and the court (the core of the old balance-of-convenience test). In addition, whether court facilities and judges are available to try the matter is explicitly a factor to consider, as is the local community's interest in the subject matter of the proceeding. The court may also consider any other relevant matter, indicating that the factors to be considered "in the interest of justice" are not limited to the specific ones referred to in the rule.

Despite Rules 37.03(1) and 76.05(2), a motion for a change of venue may be brought and heard in a court of the county to which the transfer is sought. It does not have to be brought in the court where the action was commenced.

Even if no one moves to change the place of trial, Rule 13.1.02(4) gives the regional senior judge the power to move on his or her own initiative to order a change of venue, subject to the rights of interested parties to be heard.

Once a change of venue order has been made, the registrar shall transfer the file to the appropriate court office named in the order, and all subsequent filings shall be made in the named court office.

Jury Notice: Rule 47

Right to a Jury Trial

Section 108 of the *Courts of Justice Act* gives any party in a proceeding in the Superior Court of Justice the right to a jury trial. Whether or not a party wants a jury trial will depend on a number of factors, including the complexity of a case, the amount of sympathy or hostility the party believes that it may receive from a jury, and the length of the trial list for jury trials. The role of a jury is to determine the facts of the case. If there is no jury, the judge determines the facts.

If a jury trial is chosen, the jury can hear the entire case and make a determination about whether or not the defendant is liable for damages, or it can be called in to hear only the damages part of the case. In the latter instance, the trial proceeds from the beginning without a jury. The judge makes all the determinations of facts in the case and decides whether or not the defendant is liable to the plaintiff. Then, once the liability issue has been decided, the jury is called in to determine the amount of damages that the plaintiff will receive.

There is no absolute right to a jury trial. Section 108(2) of the *Courts of Justice Act* lists the types of cases in which a jury trial is never permitted. The list includes most family law matters, cases involving equitable remedies, partition or sale of real property, requests for injunctions, and a number of other matters. Even if the case is one where a jury trial is not prohibited under s. 108(2), a judge has the discretion to decide that a jury trial is not appropriate in a particular case.

Procedure for Obtaining a Jury Trial

Either party can decide that it wants to have a jury trial. It then must prepare and serve a jury notice on all the other parties. The jury notice is in Form 47A. It may be served any time before the close of pleadings (Rule 47.01). Once served, the notice is then filed with the court. A jury notice in Abigail Boar's case is set out in Figure 15.1 (at the end of the chapter).

Striking Out a Jury Notice

If any other party does not wish to have a jury trial, that party can bring a motion asking that the jury notice be struck out. If the notice is struck out, the trial proceeds without a jury. There are two grounds under Rule 47.02 for striking out a jury notice:

1. the jury notice is not in accordance with a statute or the Rules, or
2. it is inappropriate to have a jury trial in a particular case.

Not in Accordance with a Statute or the Rules

If there is a statute that governs a particular type of case and the statute prohibits a trial by jury, a party's attempt to have a trial by jury is not "in accordance" with a statute and the jury notice must be struck out. For example, in a case involving the partition or sale of real property, if one of the parties served a jury notice, this notice would not be in accordance with a statute because s. 108(2) of the *Courts of Justice Act* prohibits jury trials in all cases of this nature. The other party would bring a motion to strike the jury notice out and the court would grant that motion (Rule 47.02(1)(a)).

Likewise, a jury notice would not be in accordance with the Rules if it were served after the close of pleadings. Rule 47.01 requires that the jury notice be served *before* the close of pleadings. If served after pleadings have closed, it is out of time, and it may be challenged on that basis. A motion to strike out a jury notice on the grounds that it is not in accordance with a statute or the Rules may be brought before a master.

Jury Trial Would Be Inappropriate

If a jury notice cannot be struck out on the basis that it is not in accordance with the Rules or a statute, it is still possible to bring a motion under Rule 47.02(2) asking that it be struck out on the grounds that it is not appropriate to have a jury hear a particular case. This motion, unlike a motion to strike on the basis of not according with a statute or the Rules, must be brought before a judge. A master has no jurisdiction to hear this type of motion.

When deciding whether or not a jury trial is appropriate, the judge will look at a number of issues, including the complexity of the case. If a case involves difficult questions of law, a judge may decide that it is best to proceed without a jury. It is the jury's role in a trial to determine which version of the facts is the most plausible. In a jury trial, it is the role of the judge to decide the legal issues. We call the jury "the finder of fact" for this reason. Sometimes the parties are not in a major dispute about the facts of a case: The source of their disagreement is how the law should be applied to those facts. In a case like this, there is no role for a jury, and a judge would likely decide that the case should proceed without one.

Even if the party wanting to have the jury notice struck is not successful on a motion, that party may try again to have the jury notice struck by the trial judge (Rule 47.02(3)).

Listing the Case for Trial: Rule 48

Setting the Action Down for Trial: Rules 48.01 and 48.02

The court does not automatically schedule a trial once a lawsuit has been started. The parties must first let the court know that they are ready to proceed to trial. The process of letting the other side and the court know that your side is ready for trial is called **setting an action down for trial**.

Any party who has not been noted in default can set the case down for trial after the close of pleadings, but usually the plaintiff takes this step. The plaintiff is the party who has the most interest in having the case decided. For example, Abigail Boar wants to have the court decide that she is entitled to be compensated by the defendants for her injuries. It is likely that she would be the party to set the matter down for trial.

In order to set her matter down for trial, Abigail must serve and file a **trial record** (Rule 48.02(1)). The trial record must be served and filed on all the parties to the action, including the parties to a counterclaim, a crossclaim, or a third-party claim. Once this has been done, the trial record is filed with the court along with proof of service. The court is now aware that this case is ready for trial.

If there is a third-party claim in your action, the third party must be served along with all the other parties, but there are additional procedural requirements. A party that wants to have the third-party claim set down for trial must prepare a separate trial record. This third-party trial record must be served on all the parties to the third-party claim. Therefore, if an action has a third-party claim, there are two trial records: one for the main action and one for the third-party claim.

When an action is undefended—that is, when the defendant does not file a statement of defence—the plaintiff has the defendant noted in default, and the case does not proceed to trial. However, in rare instances, a judge can order that an **undefended action** proceed to trial. In that case, Rule 48.03(2) requires that a trial record be prepared in the usual way, but there is no requirement that it be served on any other party. If you are setting an undefended action down for trial, you file the trial record with the court without serving anyone.

Once again, there are slightly different rules for third-party claims. If a third-party claim is undefended, a party that wants to set it down for trial must prepare a separate trial record for the third-party claim. Rule 48.02(4) requires that the trial record for the undefended third-party claim be served on the plaintiff in the main action, but no other party in the main action needs to be served. After service on the plaintiff in the main action, the trial record in the undefended third-party claim can be filed with the court.

For example, suppose that Abigail Boar, the plaintiff in the main action, is suing Rattle Motors Ltd. and its employee Fred Flogem. Both Rattle Motors Ltd. and Fred Flogem have served and filed statements of defence in the main action. The main action is therefore a defended action. Both Rattle Motors Ltd. and Fred Flogem are planning to defend against Abigail's claim that they are liable to pay her damages because they caused her injuries. Rattle Motors Ltd. has commenced a third-party

setting an action down for trial
procedure that a party must follow in order to have its case placed on the trial list

trial record
bound set of documents prepared by the party setting the action down for trial and containing the pleadings of all parties, any relevant orders, all notices, and certificates

undefended action
an action in which no statement of defence is delivered

claim against Skunk Motorcar Company Ltd., the manufacturer of the Super Coupe, claiming that the oil pan on the car was defective and that it caused the leak that resulted in Abigail's fall. Because Skunk Motorcar Company Ltd. has also filed a statement of defence in the third-party claim, the third-party claim is also defended.

Abigail wants to set the main action involving herself, Rattle Motors Ltd., and Fred Flogem down for trial. I.M. Just prepares the trial record for the main action and it is served on Fred Flogem, Rattle Motors Ltd., and the third party, Skunk Motorcar Company Ltd. Abigail really does not care whether Rattle Motors Ltd.'s third-party claim against the car manufacturer comes to trial or not. She intends to get all compensation for her injuries from Fred Flogem and Rattle Motors Ltd.

Rattle Motors Ltd., however, cares that the third-party claim comes to trial because it thinks Skunk Motorcar Company Ltd. caused Abigail's injuries. Rattle Motors Ltd.'s lawyer, Huey Sue, would prepare the trial record in the third-party claim, serve it on all the other parties, and file it with the court. There would then be two trial records: one for the main action involving Abigail, Rattle Motors Ltd., and Fred Flogem and the other for Rattle's third-party claim against Skunk Motorcar Company Ltd.

Let's change the facts. Assume that Rattle Motors Ltd. and Fred Flogem have not filed a statement of defence. There is now no third-party claim because Rattle Motors Ltd. never brought one. In this example, there is only one action, the main action, and it is undefended. Nevertheless, a judge has ordered that this undefended action proceed to trial. I.M. Just would prepare the trial record and file it with the court immediately without serving it on Rattle Motors Ltd. and Fred Flogem.

Now let's say that the main action between Abigail, Rattle Motors Ltd., and Fred Flogem is a defended action. In this situation, Rattle Motors Ltd. has brought a third-party claim, but Skunk Motorcar Company Ltd. has not filed a statement of defence. The third-party claim is now undefended. If this undefended third-party claim is to be set down for trial, Huey Sue must prepare a third-party trial record. He does not need to serve the third party or Fred Flogem, but he must serve Abigail, the plaintiff in the main action.

Consequences of Setting an Action Down for Trial: Rule 48.04

trial list
list kept by the registrar in each courthouse of cases that are ready for trial

There can be a very long wait for cases to come to trial. Therefore, a party may be anxious to set the action down as soon as possible, but there are consequences of setting the action down that a party will want to consider before moving too quickly. By setting an action down for trial or consenting to an action's being placed on the **trial list**, a party is advising the court that it is ready for trial. Therefore, Rule 48.04(1) prohibits parties from bringing any motions or conducting any further discoveries without leave of the court once they have set the action down. The other parties can bring motions and continue with discoveries if they wish. Only the party that sets the action down is prohibited from continuing these procedures. A party will want to make sure that it has brought all the necessary motions and conducted all the discoveries it will need before setting the action down.

The rule prohibiting discoveries for the party setting down the action does not mean that the other parties are not obligated to follow through on their undertakings or their other obligations listed in Rule 48.04(2)(b). Leave of the court is not required to bring a motion to request an order compelling compliance for any obligation listed in Rule 48.04(2)(b).

The party that sets an action down for trial may seek permission from the court to bring further motions, but the court will be reluctant to grant permission to do so unless the proposed motion concerns a serious issue that could not have been brought before the action was set down. It is rare that the court will give leave to a party to initiate or continue with discoveries after the party has set the action down. It should be noted, however, that leave of the court is not required to bring a motion to request an order compelling compliance for any obligation listed in Rule 48.04(2)(b).

Placing the Action on the Trial List: Rules 48.05 to 48.13

Once the trial record is filed, the action must be placed on the trial list 60 days later by the registrar of the court (Rules 48.05 to 48.09). The parties can agree that the action be listed for trial before the 60-day period has passed, but a party who consents to putting the case on the trial list loses the right to bring any further motions or to initiate or continue discoveries without leave of the court.

In larger cities, the court sits all year long, so it does not matter when the trial record is filed. Once it is filed, the registrar adds the name of the action to the bottom of the list of cases that are ready for trial. However, outside major centres, the judges may not hear civil litigation matters throughout the year. These cases are heard at certain designated periods called **sittings**. For instance, the Superior Court in Milton might have a sitting scheduled from October 15 to December 14. There is a trial list prepared for each sitting of the court. If you want your action added to the list for a particular sitting, you must file the trial record at least 10 days before the start of that sitting (Rules 48.05(2) and 48.06(2)). After that time, any new cases are added to the trial list for the next scheduled sitting. The only way a case that is filed less than 10 days before the start of the sitting can go on the list for that sitting is if a motion is brought and the judge orders that the action be placed on that list.

sittings
a time period during which a specific court may hear cases

A place on the trial list does not guarantee that the case will be heard right away. The trial lists are long, and a case is not heard until it reaches the top of the list. Usually the court notifies the lawyers as the case gets close to the top, but it is the responsibility of the parties' lawyers to keep track of where they are on the list. When the case reaches the top, the parties must be ready to go to trial. There are separate trial lists for jury and non-jury trials. Usually the jury trial list is shorter.

Rule 48.12 requires the lawyers for the parties to let the registrar's office know immediately if a case has been settled. Usually you call the registrar's office first, but the rule also requires that the settlement be confirmed in writing. If a case is settled, it is taken off the trial list. This is one of the reasons why the trial list must be monitored closely when your case gets near the top. Your case may be number 10 on the list, but if all the cases in front of you are settled and removed from the list, you will move to the top very quickly.

Status Notice

Sometimes, an action is commenced and a court file is opened, but nothing much happens on it. A statement of claim and a statement of defence may be filed. Maybe the parties are taking their time negotiating a settlement, or maybe they have settled and have forgotten to terminate the action.

The registrar is responsible for making sure that there are not a lot of these cases cluttering up the court files. Rule 48.14 requires the registrar to send a notification to the parties if an action has not been terminated or placed on a trial list within two years after a statement of defence, a notice of intent to defend, or a motion in response to an action (other than a motion challenging the court's jurisdiction) has been filed in the case. To notify the parties, the registrar sends them a status notice in Form 48C.1. Figure 15.2 (at the end of the chapter) sets out a status notice for an action not on a trial list in Form 48C.1.

In the event that an action is placed on the trial list but subsequently struck off the list and not reinstated within 180 days, the registrar will send out a slightly different status notice in Form 48C.2.

Both status notices advise the parties that an action will be dismissed for delay unless it is set down for trial, terminated, or documents are filed in accordance with Rule 48.14(10) within 90 days after service of the status notice. Rule 48.14(10) requires the filing of a timetable, signed by all the parties, that sets out all the steps that must be completed before the action may be set down for trial, gives dates for completion of those steps, and indicates a date no more than 12 months in advance of when the action will be set down for trial or restored to the trial list. Therefore, a case may be saved from being dismissed not only by setting it down for trial or restoring it to the trial list, but also by filing the timetable.

A lawyer who receives a status notice from the registrar is required to give a copy of the notice to his client right away.

If the action is not set down for trial, is not terminated, a timetable is not filed, or if a judge or case management master does not order an extension of time, the registrar makes an order dismissing the action with costs 90 days after the status notice is served. This order must also be given to the client immediately after it is served on the lawyer.

Sometimes there is a legitimate reason why the action has not been set down for trial. If this is the case, the lawyer for a party served with a status notice may request a status hearing before a judge (Rule 48.14(8)). The status hearing will be heard in writing without any of the parties attending if a party files a timetable, signed by all the parties, that sets out all the steps that must be completed before the action may be set down for trial, gives dates for completion of those steps, and indicates a date no more than 12 months in advance of when the action will be set down for trial or restored to the trial list (Rules 48.14(10) and (11)). The timetable must be filed at least seven days before the hearing along with a draft order establishing the timetable. If a hearing is not to be dealt with in writing, the parties must attend in person.

At this hearing, whether it is dealt with in writing or in person, the plaintiff must satisfy the court that the action should not be dismissed for delay. If the judge or case management master decides not to dismiss the action for delay, he or she may set time limits for the completion of steps to place the matter on or restore it to the trial list. If the judge or case master is not satisfied that the matter should proceed, the action may be dismissed.

Contents of a Trial Record

Rule 48.03 specifies the contents of a trial record. The record must include a table of contents, all pleadings, any orders made on motion relating to how the trial is conducted, all notices, and a certificate from the lawyer of record who is setting the action down for trial. The certificate must state, among other things, that the record contains all the required documents and that pleadings have closed. Only one of the parties serves and files the trial record, and it therefore must contain the pleadings of all the parties. It is like a short history of the proceedings.

The following shows I.M. Just's certificate:

CERTIFICATE

I, I.M. Just, lawyer for the Plaintiff in this action, certify as follows:

1. this trial record contains all the relevant documents required by Rule 48.03(1)(a) to (g); and
2. the time for delivery of pleadings has expired.

I.M. Just
_____
I.M. Just

A trial record is put together in the same way as a motion record. It is bound with a light blue backsheet (Rule 4.07(1)), and the pages should be numbered consecutively. The various documents should be separated by tabs to make the trial record easy to read. An example of a trial record is set out in Figure 15.3 (at the end of the chapter).

Note that the party that filed the trial record will also have to file copies of orders, notices, and other documents filed or delivered after the pretrial conference.[1]

Action Abandoned: Rule 48.15

Rule 48.15 authorizes the dismissal of an action by the registrar, unless the court orders otherwise, if the following conditions are satisfied:

1. More than 180 days have passed since the date the originating process was issued.
2. None of the following has been filed:
    a. a statement of defence,
    b. a notice of intent to defend,

   c. a notice of motion in response to an action, other than a motion challenging the court's jurisdiction.

3. The action has not been disposed of by final order or judgment.

4. The action has not been set down for trial.

5. The registrar has given 45 days' notice in Form 48E that the action will be dismissed as abandoned.

The parties may avoid the dismissal by the registrar if, within the 45-day notice period, they file a defence, have the matter disposed of by a final order or judgment, or set the action down for trial. If they do none of these things, the registrar will dismiss the matter as abandoned and serve the order in Form 48F on the parties.

An order of the registrar dismissing an action as abandoned may be set aside in accordance with Rule 37.14.

The Pretrial Conference: Rule 50

The court has a major interest in seeing that matters settle before they come to trial. Litigation is expensive and time-consuming for the parties, but it is costly and time-consuming from the court's perspective as well. There must be courtrooms, court staff, and judges available to accommodate the trial procedure. The courts therefore want to see that as many matters as possible are resolved before they require trial time. The pretrial conference is one of the procedural mechanisms used to try to achieve settlement.

In addition, even if a complete settlement without trial is not possible, it may be possible to narrow the issues at a pretrial conference. That means that the issues that can be settled are settled at pretrial and the pretrial judge will then give orders or directives on how to best handle the trial of the outstanding issues in the most expeditious and least expensive manner that is just. Rule 50.01 sets out the purpose of a pretrial conference.

The pretrial conference is an informal meeting between the lawyers for each party and a judge or case management master. The lawyers must attend the conference and, unless the judge or master orders otherwise, all parties are to attend. Parties can attend in person, but if cost and travel time would be problematic to personal attendance, they may attend by telephone or video conference. The reason for having the parties available is so that they will be able to give instructions to their lawyers about settlement proposals. If a party needs further approval from another person before agreeing to a settlement, that person must be available by telephone during the conference, no matter what time the conference occurs, even outside regular business hours.

The pretrial conference in actions is mandatory in every case. Within 180 days after the action is set down for trial, the parties must schedule with the registrar, on a mutually agreeable date, a pretrial conference to be held before a judge or case management master.

In the event that the parties fail to schedule a conference within the 180-day time requirement, the registrar will schedule a conference and give all the parties notice.

Pretrial conferences are not mandatory for applications, but a judge may order one in appropriate cases under Rule 50.03.

The matters to be considered at a pretrial conference are set out in Rule 50.06. They are:

- The possibility of settlement of any or all of the issues in the proceeding.
- Simplification of the issues.
- The possibility of obtaining admissions that may facilitate the hearing.
- The question of liability.
- The amount of damages, if damages are claimed.
- The estimated duration of the trial or hearing.
- The advisability of having the court appoint an expert.
- In the case of an action, the number of expert witnesses and other witnesses that may be called by each party, and dates for the service of any outstanding or supplementary experts' reports.
- The advisability of fixing a date for the trial or hearing.
- The advisability of directing a reference.
- Any other matter that may assist in the just, most expeditious, and least expensive disposition of the proceeding.

Settlement of the Case

During the pretrial conference, the lawyers each outline to the pretrial judge the case they intend to present at trial. They tell the judge what evidence they will call and how they intend to present the party's interests. Once the judge has heard the two sides of the case, he or she usually states how he or she would decide the case on the basis of this evidence. The lawyers then discuss the pretrial judge's decision with their client. The pretrial judge is not making the final decision but is merely advising the parties what he or she thinks of their likelihood of success. However, a judge's opinion can be helpful in encouraging a party to accept a reasonable settlement offer if the party thinks there is a possibility that they may lose the case at trial.

Rule 50.04 sets out the material that must be provided before the pretrial conference. Each party is required to file, with proof of service, a pretrial conference brief, containing concise statements, without legal argument, of the following matters:

1. The nature of the proceeding.
2. The issues raised and the party's position on those issues.
3. In the case of an action, the names of the witnesses that the party is likely to call at trial and the length of time the evidence of each witness is likely to take.

4. The steps that need to be completed before the action is ready for trial or the application is ready to be heard, and the estimated length of time it will take to complete those steps.

This rule should be read in conjunction with Rule 50.06, which we looked at above. Rule 50.06 sets out the matters that must be considered at a pretrial conference. In order to make the most effective use of a pretrial conference, the required conference brief should address all of the matters listed in Rule 50.06. In addition, all documents and expert reports should be provided if they may be of assistance to the judge or master conducting the pretrial conference.

A great deal of thought and organization must go into preparing a pretrial conference brief, because a well-prepared brief can lead to either a settlement of the case or a narrowing of the issues should the case require a trial. Either of these pretrial results are likely to save the client money and time. An example of a pretrial conference brief can be found in Figure 15.4 in this chapter. The example shows Abigail Boar's plaintiff's pretrial conference brief.

Sometimes, despite the parties' efforts to settle, the case is not settled and must proceed to trial. The judge who presided at the pretrial conference may not hear the case at trial unless the parties agree in writing. The parties may not be willing to consent due to concern that the judge may have already heard too much informally about the case to render a decision on the evidence presented at the trial alone (Rule 50.10). Moreover, Rule 50.09 prohibits providing information about pretrial statements to the judge at a trial, motion, or reference unless they are statements that are disclosed in the pretrial conference brief or an order made under Rule 50.07.

Narrowing the Issues at Trial

In many cases, it is not possible for the parties to settle all the issues between them, but it is possible to agree that certain facts are not in dispute. Although the case must go to trial, it can be significantly shorter and less costly when the parties spend time dealing only with the issues that are contested. For instance, in Abigail's case, none of the parties disputes the fact that Abigail fell while at Rattle Motors Ltd.'s showroom. What they do disagree on is the cause of the fall. Abigail alleges that she fell because the defendants negligently left oil on the floor, and Rattle Motors Ltd. claims she fell because she was intoxicated. If the defendants are prepared to admit that the plaintiff fell on their premises, the plaintiff need not call witnesses to prove that she fell.

It is important to determine exactly what the other side admits is true and what is not in dispute in a case. To do this, the parties can use Rule 51, which governs admissions.

Admissions: Rule 51

Under Rule 51, a party can formally request that any other party admit the authenticity of certain documents or the truth of certain facts. If a party makes an admission about a document or a fact, the party intending to rely on the document or the fact need not prove that the document is genuine and authentic or that the fact is true.

Every document relied on by a party at trial must usually be proven to be authentic. The person who wrote the letter or took the photograph or prepared the report must give evidence that the document is genuine or is a true copy of the original document. This can be very time-consuming, particularly in a trial where a lot of documents are being relied on. Likewise, every fact that a party relies on must also be proved in court. Admissions remove the need for proving every element that is not in dispute.

Rule 51.02 provides that a party may serve a request to admit (Form 51A) on the opposite party at any time during a proceeding. The request to admit may ask the other side to admit either a fact or a document. Any document for which a party is seeking an admission of authenticity must be attached to the request to admit unless the other side already has a copy. An example of a request to admit is provided in Figure 15.5 (at the end of the chapter).

The party that receives the request to admit must respond within 20 days after the request is served. A party responds to the request to admit by preparing and serving a response to request to admit, which is in Form 51B. An example of a response to a request to admit is set out in Figure 15.6 (at the end of the chapter). Parties must answer each request to admit a fact or document by stating that they admit or deny the fact or document. If they fail to respond to any part of the request to admit or fail to respond to the entire request, they are deemed to have admitted all the facts and documents contained in the request (Rules 51.03(2) and (3)).

An admission, either in a pleading or in a response to a request to admit, and all deemed admissions can be withdrawn only with the consent of all the other parties or with leave of the court. The court only grants leave to withdraw if the party asking to withdraw can show that there is something about the fact or document that is an issue between the parties, that the admission was made through inadvertence, and that there will be no injustice to the opposite party that cannot be made up in costs. Therefore, it is important to ensure that no admissions are made without major consideration.

If an admission is significant enough, a party to whom the admission is made can seek an order in the case based on that admission by bringing a motion to a judge. An admission made under oath or affirmation—in an affidavit, in examinations for discovery, or orally in court—can be used by another party to obtain an order in an entirely different proceeding (Rule 51.06).

CHAPTER SUMMARY

This chapter dealt with the decisions and the steps that must be taken to get ready for a trial. We noted that Rules 46, 47, 48, 50, and 51 are the major rules that deal with pretrial procedures.

The first decision that needs to be made is where the trial is to take place, and we noted the requirements of Rule 46 in this regard. The second decision is whether or not the trial should be held before a jury or a judge alone. We noted the procedural requirements for serving and filing a jury notice and for bringing a motion to strike the jury notice under Rule 47. Any party can decide to have a jury trial, but jury trials are not available in every type of proceeding.

We then covered the procedure for setting a case down for trial and examined the consequences of failing to set a matter down for trial within two years of its commencement under Rule 48.

We then considered the pretrial conference, an informal hearing before a judge that attempts to effect a settlement between the parties or, at the least, achieve a narrowing of the issues for trial under Rule 50.

Finally, we examined the matter of admissions and the procedures involved in the request to admit under Rule 51.

KEY TERMS

setting an action down for trial, 387

sittings, 389

trial list, 388

trial record, 387

undefended action, 387

NOTE

1. See Rule 48.03(2) of the *Rules of Civil Procedure*, which states:

   (2) It is the responsibility of the party who filed the trial record to place with the record, before the trial, a copy of,

   (a) any notice of amounts and particulars of special damages delivered after the filing of the trial record;

   (b) any order respecting the trial made after the filing of the trial record;

   (c) any order under rule 50.07 or pre-trial conference report under rule 50.08; and

   (d) in an undefended action, any affidavit to be used in evidence.

REFERENCES

Courts of Justice Act, RSO 1990, c. C.43.

Evidence Act, RSO 1990, c. E.23.

Rules of Civil Procedure, RRO 1990, reg. 194.

REVIEW QUESTIONS

1. If Abigail wants to have her trial held in Toronto, when must she decide this and how must she let the defendants know?

2. Are there any limitations on Abigail's choice of place of trial?

3. If Fred does not want the trial to be held in Toronto, what must he do?

4. If the parties agree that the place for trial should be changed to London, is the court obligated to change the location?

5. Who is most likely to want to set this case down for trial, and how must that party do it?

6. What are the consequences of a party's setting a matter down for trial?

7. What is a status notice, and who sends it?

8. What is the purpose of a pretrial conference?

DISCUSSION QUESTIONS

1. Abigail does not want to have a jury trial. However, Fred believes he will do better with a jury than without one. He thinks the jury will not be sympathetic to Abigail if he can show that she was drunk. Can Fred ask for a jury trial even though he is a defendant?

2. If Rattle Motors Ltd. has brought Skunk Motorcar Company Ltd. into the action, what must be done to set the matter down for trial?

3. If Rattle Motors Ltd. has made an admission in its statement of claim that Abigail fell on its premises, what would Rattle have to do to withdraw it? What criteria would determine whether a withdrawal could be made?

Figure 15.1   Jury Notice (Form 47A)

Court file no. 01-CV-1234

ONTARIO
SUPERIOR COURT OF JUSTICE

BETWEEN:

ABIGAIL BOAR

Plaintiff

and

RATTLE MOTORS LTD. and FRED FLOGEM

Defendants

JURY NOTICE

THE PLAINTIFF REQUIRES that this action be tried by a jury.

Date: May 3, year 3

Just & Coping
Barristers and Solicitors
365 Bay Street – 8701
Toronto, Ontario, M3J 4A9

I.M. Just
LSUC #12345R
tel. 416-762-1342
fax 416-762-2300

Lawyers for the Plaintiff

TO: Huey Sue
LSUC #23456T
Barrister and Solicitor
65 False Trail
Toronto, Ontario, M6Y 1Z6

tel. 416-485-6891
fax 416-485-6892

Lawyer for the Defendants

RCP-E 47A (July 1, 2007)

Figure 15.2   Status Notice (Form 48C.1)

Court file no. 01-CV-1234

ONTARIO
SUPERIOR COURT OF JUSTICE

BETWEEN:

ABIGAIL BOAR

Plaintiff

and

RATTLE MOTORS LTD. and FRED FLOGEM

Defendants

STATUS NOTICE: ACTION NOT ON A TRIAL LIST

TO THE PARTIES AND THEIR LAWYERS

1. According to the records in the court office:

    (a) more than 2 years have passed since a defence in this action was filed;

    (b) this action has not been placed on a trial list; and

    (c) this action has not been terminated by any means.

2. AS A RESULT, THIS ACTION SHALL BE DISMISSED FOR DELAY, with costs, unless within 90 days of service of this Notice,

    (a) the action is set down for trial;

    (b) the action is terminated by any means;

    (c) documents have been filed in accordance with subrule 48.14(10); or

    (d) a judge or case management master orders otherwise.

NOTE: A "defence" means a statement of defence, a notice of intent to defend, or a notice of motion in response to a proceeding, other than a motion challenging the court's jurisdiction.

NOTE: You may request that the registrar arrange a status hearing to show cause why the action should not be dismissed. Unless the presiding judge or case management master orders otherwise, a status hearing may be held in writing by filing, at least 7 days before the day of the hearing, a timetable signed by all the parties to the action that contains the information set out in subrule 48.14(11) and a draft order establishing the timetable.

Figure 15.2   Concluded

NOTE: Unless the court orders otherwise, where the plaintiff is a party under a disability, an action may not be dismissed for delay under rule 48.14 unless the defendant gives notice to the Children's Lawyer or, if the Public Guardian and Trustee is litigation guardian of the plaintiff, to the Public Guardian and Trustee.

Date: February 26, year 3   Signed by   _[signed by local registrar]_
                                                          Local registrar

Address of
court office: Courthouse
                393 University Avenue
                Toronto, Ontario, M5G 1E6

TO: Just & Coping
       Barristers and Solicitors
       365 Bay Street – 8701
       Toronto, Ontario, M3J 4A9

       I.M. Just
       LSUC #12345R
       tel. 416-762-1342
       fax 416-762-2300

       Lawyers for the Plaintiff

AND TO: Huey Sue
          LSUC #23456T
          Barrister and Solicitor
          65 False Trail
          Toronto, Ontario, M6Y 1Z6

          tel. 416-485-6891
          fax 416-485-6892

          Lawyer for the Defendants

RCP-E 48C.1 (July 30, 2009)

Figure 15.3 Trial Record

ONTARIO
SUPERIOR COURT OF JUSTICE

BETWEEN:

ABIGAIL BOAR

Plaintiff

and

RATTLE MOTORS LTD. and FRED FLOGEM

Defendants

TRIAL RECORD

Just & Coping
Barristers and Solicitors
365 Bay Street – 8701
Toronto, Ontario, M3J 4A9

I.M. Just
LSUC #12345R
tel. 416-762-1342
fax 416-762-2300

Lawyers for the Plaintiff

TO: Huey Sue
      LSUC #23456T
      Barrister and Solicitor
      65 False Trail
      Toronto, Ontario, M6Y 1Z6

      tel. 416-485-6891
      fax 416-485-6892

      Lawyer for the Defendants

Figure 15.3   Concluded

TRIAL RECORD TABLE OF CONTENTS

Tab	Document	Page
1	Statement of claim, dated January 4, year 1	1
2	Statement of defence, dated January 12, year 1	5
3	Reply, dated February 2, year 1	9
4	Jury notice, dated May 3, year 3	12
5	Certificate of I.M. Just	13

Figure 15.4   Pretrial Conference Brief

Boar v. Rattle Motors Ltd. and Flogem   Date: May 20, year 3

PLAINTIFF'S PRETRIAL CONFERENCE BRIEF

Just & Coping
Barristers and Solicitors
365 Bay Street – 8701
Toronto, Ontario, M3J 4A9

I.M. Just
LSUC #12345R
tel. 416-762-1342
fax 416-762-2300

Lawyers for the Plaintiff

TO: Huey Sue
     LSUC #23456T
     Barrister and Solicitor
     65 False Trail
     Toronto, Ontario, M6Y 1Z6

     tel. 416-485-6891
     fax 416-485-6892

     Lawyer for the Defendants

NATURE OF THE PLAINTIFF'S CASE

The plaintiff was a customer of the defendant corporation, Rattle Motors Ltd., an automobile dealership. The defendant Fred Flogem is an automobile salesperson for Rattle Motors Ltd. The plaintiff slipped and fell while in the corporate defendant's showroom, sustaining considerable physical and psychological damage. The plaintiff alleges that Rattle Motors Ltd. was negligent in permitting an oil spill to remain on the showroom floor and that Fred Flogem was negligent in lowering the showroom lighting so that the spill could not be detected.

LEGAL ISSUES RAISED IN THE PLEADINGS AND TO BE DETERMINED AT TRIAL

1. Was the defendant Rattle Motors Ltd. negligent?
   It is the position of the plaintiff that the defendant was negligent both personally and vicariously.

Figure 15.4   Continued

2. Was the defendant Fred Flogem negligent?
   It is the position of the plaintiff that the defendant was negligent.
3. Was there contributory negligence on the part of the plaintiff?
   It is the position of the plaintiff that she did not contribute to her injuries in any manner and that liability rests solely with the defendants.
4. What general damages were suffered by the plaintiff?
   It is the position of the plaintiff that she suffered general damages of $200,000.

LIST OF WITNESSES TO BE CALLED BY PLAINTIFF

1. Abigail Boar
   1425 Down Home Lane
   Toronto ON M6Y 4G8

   Estimated time for examination-in-chief: 2 hours

2. James Jinglehimer
   1425 Down Home Lane
   Toronto ON M6Y 4G8

   Estimated time for examination-in-chief: 1 hour

3. Beverly Benga
   23 Vast Gap Blvd.
   Toronto ON M8T 9H3

   Estimated time for examination-in-chief: 1 hour

4. Dr. Morris Furgazy
   13 Jolly Good Lane
   Toronto ON M9P 5G3

   Estimated time for examination-in-chief: 2 hours

PLEADINGS AND RELEVANT MATTERS

1. Are the pleadings in order or do they require amendments?
   The pleadings are in order and do not require further amendments.
2. Are there any contemplated or outstanding motions?
   No.
3. Are productions complete?
   Yes.
4. Are all the transcripts available?
   Yes.

Figure 15.4   Continued

MOTIONS

Will there be any motions at trial?
No.

ADMISSIONS

The defendants admit that the plaintiff slipped and fell while on the premises of the corporate defendant and momentarily lost consciousness, but they allege that the fall was the result of the plaintiff's intoxicated state and not of any negligence of the defendants.

BUSINESS RECORDS

Will any business records be entered under the *Evidence Act*, and has the appropriate notice been given?
No business records will be produced.

EXPERT EVIDENCE

1. Will any be called?
   Yes, if required by defendant.
2. On what issues?
   The long-term neurological effects of the injuries that the plaintiff suffered.
3. Identity of Experts
   The plaintiff will call her neurologist, Dr. Morris Furgazy.
4. There are no outstanding reports.
5. The medical report of Dr. Furgazy is attached.

TRIAL DATE

1. Are the parties ready for trial?
   Yes.
2. Are there times when the trial cannot proceed because of witness or other matters?
   No.
3. How long will the trial last?
   It is estimated that it will last three days.

SETTLEMENT

What are the prospects of settlement?
Settlement is not likely in this case.

Figure 15.4   Concluded

DAMAGES

The plaintiff claims:

1. general damages in the amount of $200,000; and
2. special damages in the amount of $20,769.

IS THIS A CASE WHERE IT MAY BE ADVISABLE TO DIRECT A REFERENCE?

No.

WHAT PRETRIAL ORDERS ARE REQUESTED?

None.

Figure 15.5 Request to Admit (Form 51A)

Court file no. 01-CV-1234

ONTARIO
SUPERIOR COURT OF JUSTICE

BETWEEN:

ABIGAIL BOAR

Plaintiff

and

RATTLE MOTORS LTD. and FRED FLOGEM

Defendants

REQUEST TO ADMIT

YOU ARE REQUESTED TO ADMIT, for the purposes of this proceeding only, the truth of the following facts:

1. The plaintiff drank two glasses of wine at Barbeerian's before arriving at the corporate defendant's place of business on September 14, year 0.

2. The plaintiff was intoxicated at the time that she entered the corporate defendant's place of business.

YOU ARE REQUESTED TO ADMIT, for the purposes of this proceeding only, the authenticity (see rule 51.01 of the Rules of Civil Procedure) of the following documents:

1. Receipt for dinner from Barbeerian's, dated September 14, year 0.

Attached to this request is a copy of each of the documents referred to above.

The above document has not been attached because the plaintiff has copies.

YOU MUST RESPOND TO THIS REQUEST by serving a response to request to admit in Form 51B prescribed by the Rules of Civil Procedure WITHIN TWENTY DAYS after this request is served on you. If you fail to do so, you will be deemed to admit, for the purposes of this proceeding only, the truth of the facts and the authenticity of the documents set out above.

Figure 15.5   Concluded

Date: March 15, year 3

Huey Sue
LSUC #23456T
Barrister and Solicitor
65 False Trail
Toronto, Ontario, M6Y 1Z6

tel. 416-485-6891
fax 416-485-6892

Lawyer for the Defendants

TO: Just & Coping
      Barristers and Solicitors
      365 Bay Street – 8701
      Toronto, Ontario, M3J 4A9

      I.M. Just
      LSUC #12345R
      tel. 416-762-1342
      fax 416-762-2300

      Lawyers for the Plaintiff

RCP-E 51A (July 1, 2007)

Figure 15.6   Response to Request to Admit (Form 51B)

Court file no. 01-CV-1234

ONTARIO
SUPERIOR COURT OF JUSTICE

BETWEEN:

ABIGAIL BOAR

Plaintiff

and

RATTLE MOTORS LTD. and FRED FLOGEM

Defendants

RESPONSE TO REQUEST TO ADMIT

In response to your request to admit, dated March 15, year 3, the plaintiff:

1. Admits the truth of fact number 1.

2. Admits the authenticity of document number 1.

3. Denies the truth of fact number 2.

4. Denies the authenticity of documents numbers: N/A.

5. Refuses to admit the truth of fact number 2 for the following reasons:

   There is no truth in the allegation that the plaintiff was, in fact, intoxicated when she entered the place of business of the corporate defendant.

6. Refuses to admit the authenticity of documents numbers for the following reasons: N/A.

Date: March 22, year 3

Just & Coping
Barristers and Solicitors
365 Bay Street – 8701
Toronto, Ontario, M3J 4A9

I.M. Just
LSUC #12345R
tel. 416-762-1342
fax 416-762-2300

Lawyers for the Plaintiff

Figure 15.6 Concluded

TO: Huey Sue
LSUC #23456T
Barrister and Solicitor
65 False Trail
Toronto, Ontario, M6Y 1Z6

tel. 416-485-6891
fax 416-485-6892

Lawyer for the Defendants

RCP-E 51B (July 1, 2007)

Trial Preparation and Trial

16

16 B3 Affidavits + 40's backshots

Introduction

If the parties do not settle at the pretrial conference, it is important to start preparing for an eventual trial as soon as possible. If the evidence has not been prepared and the work not done well in advance, parties can find themselves pressed for time when they suddenly realize that their action is near the top of the trial list. In order to prepare the evidence for trial, it is important to understand some very basic principles of the law of evidence.

Procedures for Using Expert Evidence

- In an adversarial proceeding, each party calls its own witnesses, whose evidence is expected to be favourable to that party's case. Expert witnesses are, in theory, expected to be objective, dispassionate, and not partisan, but in practice that is not always the case. To reinforce that expert witnesses are intended to assist the court with a neutral evaluation of the issues, they are required to certify in writing their duty to the court to be fair, objective, and non-partisan.

- Expert reports must contain certain specific details and be served no later than 90 days before the pretrial conference. The reports are considered to be part of the pretrial process. Also, a party filing a responding expert's report shall file that report 60 days before the pretrial conference. Experts are not free to determine the format of a report because that is determined by the Rules.[1]

Some Basic Principles of Evidence

Relevant and Material

To be admissible into evidence, a fact must be both relevant and material. To be relevant, a fact must logically lead to something that is important to prove in the case. For example, in Abigail's case, it would be relevant that she had been drinking just before she fell in the Rattle Motors Ltd. showroom because the defendant is claiming that she fell down due to being drunk, rather than because of any danger in its showroom. However, the fact that she may have had wine with dinner two days before the fall would likely be irrelevant.

In order to be material, a fact must relate to the matter in dispute between the parties. In Abigail's case, the issue between the parties is what caused Abigail's injuries or, in other words, who is at fault in causing her injuries. The fact that Abigail graduated from her law clerk course five years ago is not material because it has absolutely nothing to do with who is at fault in causing her injuries.

Reliability

Even though a fact may be relevant and material, it may not be entered into evidence if it is not reliable. Most of the rules of evidence deal with ensuring that evidence is as reliable as possible. The primary way that evidence is tested for reliability is through the process of cross-examination of witnesses. Cross-examination of a witness is done by a lawyer for a party that is adverse in interest to the party that called the witness.

Hearsay

Hearsay is an out-of-court statement being admitted in court for the truth of its contents. For example, Tom, a friend of Abigail's boyfriend, would not be permitted to give evidence in court that Abigail's boyfriend told him that he saw Abigail drink six glasses of wine just before she fell in the automobile showroom. That would be hearsay. It cannot be tested on cross-examination for its truth. Tom was not present when Abigail was drinking and has no personal knowledge of how much she did or did not drink. All Tom could be cross-examined on is whether Abigail's boyfriend actually told him this. Hearsay is not admissible into evidence unless it fits within one of the exceptions to the hearsay rule.

The exceptions to the rule about the inadmissibility of hearsay are numerous and have developed over many centuries of the common law. These exceptions have grown up primarily because the law recognizes that there are circumstances in which a statement made out of court is likely reliable even though it cannot be tested by cross-examination. One example of an exception to the hearsay rule is that most statements made by a party to a proceeding are admissible. If Abigail herself had told Tom that she had drunk six glasses of wine before her fall, that would be an exception to the hearsay rule. Since her own statement about how much she had to drink weakens her claim that the fall was completely the fault of the defendants, it is regarded as having some intrinsic reliability even though Tom cannot be cross-examined on whether or not the statement is true. The principle underlying this exception to the hearsay rule is that, in accordance with human nature, Abigail is more likely to lie about a fact that would hurt her case and more likely to tell the truth about something that would help her.

However, not only oral evidence or testimony can involve hearsay. In an affidavit, which is evidence in written form, if the deponent states that another person told him or her something, then that too is hearsay. That is why Rule 4.06(2) generally restricts an affidavit to matters of which the deponent has personal knowledge. Hearsay is not permitted, but there are some exceptions provided by Rules 39.01(4) and (5). These exceptions as they relate to affidavits in support of motions are discussed in Chapter 9.

Organizing the Evidence

There are three types of evidence used at trial: documentary evidence, physical evidence, and the testimony of witnesses. We will examine each type in turn.

Documentary Evidence

Documentary evidence consists of all written documents, such as letters and contracts, that a party wants to rely on to prove the facts of the case. Documents also include all the things that are mentioned in Rule 30.01(1)(a), such as, among other things, sound recordings, videotapes, film, and charts.

Most of the work done in relation to documentary evidence is done during discoveries and the preparation of the affidavit of documents. Not all the documents listed in the affidavit of documents will be used at trial. In fact, only a small portion of the existing documentary evidence will be so used. This is because the material often addresses a matter that is not at issue between the parties.

After the completion of discoveries, check with the lawyer who is handling the case to see what documents he or she expects will be needed should the case go to trial. Keep note of these documents, and once the matter has passed the pretrial stage without settling, copies of the identified documents should also be made. You will need enough copies of the documents to provide them to the other side, to the court, and to any witness who will be asked to validate or otherwise give evidence related to that document. Many lawyers tend to make notes on copies of the documents they are using in the case. Make sure that you make copies from clean documents—that is, make sure that they do not have a lawyer's notes all over them.

Lawyers are urged by the court to submit joint **document books**. This cuts down on duplication and provides more manageable material for the judge to review. If you are using a joint document book, you will have to contact the law clerk or lawyer for the other side to determine which documents will go into the joint document book.

The rules of evidence do not commonly permit a document to be introduced into evidence without a witness to authenticate it. For instance, if a lawyer wants to introduce a letter into evidence, the lawyer has the writer of the letter come to court to give oral evidence that the letter was indeed written by him or her and that his or her signature appears on the document. However, calling a witness for every single piece of material introduced at trial could add a significant amount of time to a trial. In an effort to keep a trial as short as possible, some documents are treated in a particular manner that does not require their identification by a witness.

Business Records

If a party wants to introduce records that are kept by a business in the ordinary course of its operation and the records were made at or near the time of the incident that they record, the records may be admitted without calling the person who made them. For instance, if Abigail were taken to the emergency department after her fall at Rattle Motors Ltd., her lawyer could use the emergency room admission records

document book
a bound book of all the documents that a party intends to introduce into evidence at trial; it is sometimes referred to as a book of documents

at the trial as business records. Many people may have seen Abigail at the emergency room: the admission clerk, a series of nurses, a medical intern, a resident doctor, the emergency physician, and perhaps a specialist. All of these people would have written things in Abigail's chart. Without the special provisions in the *Canada Evidence Act* and the Ontario *Evidence Act*, in order to admit these records, the lawyer would need to call all these people to verify the records.

The evidence statutes, however, provide that if at least seven days' notice is given to all other parties, the court may admit a record without having a person in court to verify it. The other parties are given an opportunity to object to the admission of the record, and an objection is argued before the court. If business records are involved in your case, you must ensure that notice of intention to introduce them as evidence at trial is served on all the other parties at least seven days before trial.

The other parties have a right to inspect the documents and may give notice to the party introducing the records that they wish to examine them. The introducing party must then produce the records within five days after receiving the notice.

Medical Reports

Section 52 of the Ontario *Evidence Act* provides a procedure whereby medical evidence may be presented through a written report without the presence of the medical practitioner. To comply with the statute, you must give 10 days' notice that you intend to introduce the report at trial to all the other parties. The other parties have a right to review the report before trial, and a copy of the report should therefore be included with the notice.

Even if the intention is to call the medical practitioner to give evidence, if the lawyer wishes to introduce the report itself, the other side should be given 10 days' notice.

It is important to remember that "medical practitioner" refers not only to a medical doctor. Section 52 also relates to reports prepared by a chiropodist, a physiotherapist, a registered psychologist, a denture therapist, a dentist, a nurse practitioner, and many other types of health care providers covered by the *Regulated Health Professions Act, 1991* and the *Drugless Practitioners Act*.

Using a Copy of an Original Document

An original document is usually used at trial. If, for any reason, it is necessary to use a copy of the original at trial, the Ontario *Evidence Act* requires that notice be given to all the other parties at least 10 days before the trial. The notice should also provide an appropriate date and time when the other parties may come to inspect the document.

Sometimes a statute may allow for the admission of a certified copy of the original. A certified copy is a copy that the person certifying the document compares to the original and swears to be a true copy.

In title documents pertaining to a real estate transaction, the land registrar certifies the copy to be a true copy of the original. The party wishing to introduce the document must give at least 10 days' notice to all the other parties that he or she intends to introduce the certified copy. Any other party may challenge the document within four days of being served with the notice.

Under s. 29 of the Ontario *Evidence Act*, public or official documents may also be certified by the person who has custody or control of the document. They then may be admitted into evidence without further verification.

Physical Evidence

Physical evidence consists of an actual object relating to an issue in the action between the parties. It may be brought into court and introduced into evidence. For instance, if a party were suing a manufacturer for damages caused by a faulty or unsafe product, the product might be brought into the court. In our case, Rattle Motors Ltd. may want to claim that the oil spill in its showroom resulted from a faulty oil pan made by Skunk Motorcar Company Ltd. and might wish to bring the oil pan into the courtroom.

Sometimes, if the object is too large to be brought into the courtroom, the Rules provide a method whereby the judge, jury, and other trial participants can go to a site outside the courtroom to look at the object or the property. This is called a "view," and it is governed by Rule 52.05.

Testimony of Witnesses

testimony
oral evidence given by a witness

The usual way to introduce evidence to be given by a person is to summon that person to court to give oral evidence called "**testimony**." The witnesses are asked questions by the lawyers for the parties. The judge and the jury, if there is a jury, listen to the answers. The testimony is recorded by a court reporter or a recording device that takes down every word said in the courtroom.

It is unusual for evidence at a trial to be given in affidavit form. Affidavits may be used at a trial under the ordinary procedure only with special leave of the court, although they are used in the simplified procedure.

When a witness comes to give evidence at trial, the lawyer for the party who has asked the witness to give evidence asks questions first. This is called **examination-in-chief**.

examination-in-chief
series of questions asked of a witness by the lawyer for the party who called the witness

Any party who is adverse in interest to the party that called the witness then gets to ask questions. This is called **cross-examination**. The purpose of cross-examination is for the opposing side to try to shake the credibility of that witness. Cross-examination can be gruelling, and sometimes witnesses are reluctant to attend voluntarily to give evidence. Witnesses should also be prepared for the fact that the judge may ask some questions. Judges usually only ask questions if they need clarification of some point that a witness has made, but if a witness is unprepared for the situation, it may intimidate and fluster him or her.

cross-examination
series of questions asked of a witness by a lawyer for a party adverse in interest to the party that called the witness

During the course of a witness's testimony, counsel for an opposing party may make an objection to the question being asked. The objection is often based on a rule of evidence such as relevance or hearsay. As witnesses are being prepared to give their evidence, they should be told to not answer or stop answering a question in the face of an objection until the judge makes a ruling on the objection and instructs them as to whether or not they may give their answer.

In rare cases, a witness's testimony may be essential to a party's case, but the witness may not want to give evidence. Such a situation might arise when the witness is a friend or family member of an adverse party, or when the witness is afraid. In such instances, counsel for the party calling the witness, who would normally only be entitled to ask non-leading questions in examination-in-chief, may seek leave of the judge to cross-examine their own witness.

Summons to a Witness

Witnesses can be compelled to attend trial. They can be served with a summons in Form 53A if they are in Ontario or in Form 53C if they are outside Ontario. An example of a summons in Form 53A is provided in Figure 16.1. A summons is a court order to a person to attend a court hearing at a certain date and time. It can also direct a person to bring certain documents with him or her. A person who does not appear can suffer severe legal consequences. A warrant may be issued for his or her arrest, and he or she can then physically be brought to court.

It is important to serve each witness with a summons even if the witness is your client's best friend and says he or she is more than willing to attend to give evidence. If witnesses have not been served with a summons and they do not appear, it is much more difficult to convince the judge to adjourn the matter until they do. If witnesses are important to your client's case and they come down with the flu or are in a car accident on their way to the courthouse, and you have not served them with a summons, it is possible that their evidence will never be heard and your client's case will be irreparably damaged.

The summons to a witness must be issued by the court. You may request a blank summons from the court office, and it will be signed by the registrar and sealed. You can then fill in the rest of the form later, at your office.

The summons must be served personally on the witness, and a cheque for the full amount of the attendance allowance and any travel allowance must accompany the summons. Attendance money is a small allowance that is set by Tariff A, Part II—Disbursements.

Witnesses are entitled to a payment of $50.00 for each day they are expected to attend a trial and give evidence. In addition, if they live in the same city or town as the courthouse, they are entitled to $3.00 per day travel allowance. If they live within 300 km of the courthouse, they are entitled to a travel allowance of $0.24 per km. If they live farther away than 300 km, they are entitled to return airfare, $0.24 per km to and from their residence to the airport and from the airport to the place of hearing or examination, and an overnight accommodation and meal allowance of $75.00 per night.

If a witness requires an interpreter in a language other than French, the person calling the witness must provide the interpreter. In larger centres, the court usually keeps lists of interpreters who have been approved to interpret in various languages, including sign language. French interpreters are usually provided by the court.

Figure 16.1   Summons to Witness (at Hearing) (Form 53A)

Court file no. 01-CV-1234

ONTARIO
SUPERIOR COURT OF JUSTICE

BETWEEN:

ABIGAIL BOAR

Plaintiff

and

RATTLE MOTORS LTD. and FRED FLOGEM

Defendants

SUMMONS TO WITNESS

TO: Donny Dilhouse
1700 Bloor Street East
Toronto, Ontario, M6Y 3K9

YOU ARE REQUIRED TO ATTEND TO GIVE EVIDENCE IN COURT at the hearing of this proceeding on July 10, year 3, at 10:00 a.m., at the Courthouse at 393 University Avenue, Toronto, and to remain until your attendance is no longer required.

YOU ARE REQUIRED TO BRING WITH YOU and produce at the hearing the following documents and things: N/A

ATTENDANCE MONEY for one day of attendance is served with this summons, calculated in accordance with Tariff A of the Rules of Civil Procedure, as follows:

Attendance allowance of $50.00 daily	$50.00
Travel allowance	$ 3.00
Overnight accommodation and meal allowance	$ Nil
TOTAL	$53.00

If further attendance is required, you will be entitled to additional attendance money.

IF YOU FAIL TO ATTEND OR REMAIN IN ATTENDANCE AS REQUIRED BY THIS SUMMONS, A WARRANT MAY BE ISSUED FOR YOUR ARREST.

Figure 16.1 Concluded

Date June 1, year 3

Issued by: _____

Local Registrar

Address of
court office: Courthouse

393 University Avenue

Toronto, Ontario, M5G 1E6

This summons was issued at the request of, and inquiries may be directed to:

Huey Sue

LSUC #23456T

Barrister and Solicitor

65 False Trail

Toronto, Ontario, M6Y 1Z6

tel. 416-485-6891

fax 416-485-6892

Lawyer for the Defendants

RCP-E 53A (July 1, 2007)

Expert Witnesses

An expert witness is permitted to give opinion evidence. An ordinary witness must stick strictly to what they saw, heard, or otherwise perceived. For instance, Fred Flogem can say that he saw oil under the car directly beneath the oil pan. He can describe the oil pan and the car, but he cannot say that, in his opinion, a defective oil pan in the car caused the leak onto the floor of the showroom. However, an engineer, qualified to design and examine cars, can give his or her opinion about what caused the leak. The purpose of expert evidence is to provide the court with assistance in an area of expertise with which the court is not familiar.

Before being classified as experts, witnesses must satisfy the court that they have the necessary qualifications and experience. They must also be experts in some area that the court recognizes as a valid area of study. For instance, a person may have studied UFOs for years, but the court may not find that to be a legitimate area of study.

A party who intends to call an expert must follow the requirements for expert witnesses as set out in Rule 53.03. The party must serve all the other parties with a report, signed by the expert, setting out his or her name, address, area of expertise, qualifications, and employment history and educational experience in his or her area of expertise. In addition, the report must state the instructions provided to the expert by the party calling him or her, and the nature of the expert's opinion respecting each issue. If there is a range of opinions given in the report, a summary of the range and reasons for the expert's own opinion within that range must be given, along with reasons for the expert's opinion, including any factual assumptions relied on; a description of any research conducted; and a list of every document relied upon to form the opinion. Finally, the expert must acknowledge, in writing, his or her duty under Rule 4.1.01 to provide assistance if the court requires it and to provide opinion evidence that is fair, objective, and non-partisan, and that is related only to matters within his or her area of expertise. This acknowledgment of expert's duty is in Form 53 and can be found in Figure 16.2. The expert's report, with the acknowledgment of expert's duty attached, must be served at least 90 days before the commencement of the pretrial conference.

If any of the other parties wishes to call another expert to challenge the testimony of the first expert, the party must serve a similar report containing the same information pertaining to the expert. This report must be served on all the other parties at least 90 days before the start of the pretrial conference (Rule 53.03).

If these timelines are not met, the expert cannot testify at the trial without the court's permission.

Preparation of Witnesses

A law clerk may be asked to help prepare witnesses for trial. Most witnesses are not accustomed to being in a courtroom and will need some help and reassurance in getting ready to give evidence.

Most lawyers run their witnesses through the proposed examination-in-chief and may rehearse a possible cross-examination to give them experience in answering difficult questions asked by a lawyer who is challenging their testimony. Witnesses should be told some basic things about giving evidence, such as the fact that in examination-in-chief, the lawyer asking the questions is not able to help the witness find the answer. This technique is called "**leading a witness**," and it violates the rules of evidence if used during examination-in-chief. However, the opposing counsel might lead the witness in cross-examination, and witnesses must be aware that an opposing lawyer could attempt to lead them into giving answers that they do not wish to give.

leading a witness
asking a witness a question that suggests the answer

Witnesses should be told that they can ask the lawyer to repeat a question. They do not need to rush their answer, but if they are too slow, they might appear to be avoiding the question. If they do not understand the question or do not recall something, they should say so.

Finally, witnesses should understand that they must, for the most part, rely on their recollections of the event or incident. If they use notes that were made at the time of the incident, they must be prepared to show their notes to the other party's counsel. They can only use notes that were made at the same time or almost immediately after the incident at issue. They cannot write down what they want to say

Figure 16.2   Acknowledgment of Expert's Duty (Form 53)

Court file no. 01-CV-1234

ONTARIO
SUPERIOR COURT OF JUSTICE

BETWEEN:

ABIGAIL BOAR

Plaintiff

and

RATTLE MOTORS LTD. and FRED FLOGEM

Defendants

ACKNOWLEDGMENT OF EXPERT'S DUTY

1. My name is Dr. Morris Furgazy. I live at 13 Jolly Good Lane, Toronto, in the Province of Ontario.
2. I have been engaged by or on behalf of Abigail Boar, the plaintiff, to provide evidence in relation to the above-noted court proceeding.
3. I acknowledge that it is my duty to provide evidence in relation to this proceeding as follows:
    (a) to provide opinion evidence that is fair, objective and non-partisan;
    (b) to provide opinion evidence that is related only to matters that are within my area of expertise; and
    (c) to provide such additional assistance as the court may reasonably require, to determine a matter in issue.
4. I acknowledge that the duty referred to above prevails over any obligation which I may owe to any party by whom or on whose behalf I am engaged.

Date February, 14, year 3   *Morris Furgazy*
                                         _____
                                                Morris Furgazy

NOTE: This form must be attached to any report signed by the expert and provided for the purpose of subrule 53.03(1) or (2) of the Rules of Civil Procedure.

RCP-E 53 (November 1, 2008)

just before they are called to give evidence and then use those notes to jog their memories while they are in the witness box.

In the event that the trial lasts more than one day, the witnesses may be released by the court and called back to give their evidence as the proceedings progress. Often, if an expert witness is to give testimony in a case, the court will permit them not to be at court but to be available by telephone so they can be called when they are needed.

Trial Brief

Once all the material is organized, it is time to prepare a trial brief. A trial brief is not the same as a trial record. A trial record is for the use of the court. A trial brief is for a lawyer's use at trial. It helps the lawyer keep his or her material organized as he or she is presenting the case.

Lawyers have their own preferences for the organization of a trial brief, but it must be composed in such a way that lawyers are able to find things easily while they are on their feet and making their case in the courtroom.

Unlike the documents filed with the court, which are usually spiral-bound, the trial brief is usually in a three-ring binder so that the material can be moved around freely. A trial does not always follow a straight path, particularly if something unexpected arises, and a lawyer must be able to adapt the organization of the material to the flow of the trial.

Most lawyers will want the material organized by type and placed in the binder in chronological order. For instance, the opening and closing arguments will be in one binder, the pretrial motions in another, the witness statements and summaries of evidence in another, and the discoveries in yet another. If the material is not voluminous, some of these binders may be combined in a single binder.

The binders should be different colours so that they can easily be distinguished from one another when they are sitting on the counsel table in a courtroom. There should be clearly marked tabs separating the material.

Once the trial brief has been prepared, it is time to go back and ensure that sufficient copies of proposed exhibits and transcripts have been made.

Book of Authorities

A book of authorities puts together all the legal cases, statutes, and regulations that support your client's action. It should be organized with an index, listing the cases and the legislation. The cases and legislation must be properly cited. Tabs should be used to separate the material, and the index should identify the tab at which the material can be found. A book of authorities is usually spiral-bound. The judge is given a copy of the book of authorities, as are counsel for the other side. Remember that if a lawyer is referring a judge to an authority, the judge must be able to find it easily. If the lawyer wishes to rely on a particular portion of a case or legislation, it is helpful to highlight the portion that will be relied upon.

In many court proceedings, lawyers are relying upon the same leading cases. In the Divisional Court, the court itself has a Judges' Book of Authorities. This book contains cases that are commonly referred to by lawyers appearing in that court. In an effort to avoid repetition and huge amounts of paper waste, there is a practice direction for the Divisional Court that advises lawyers not to include cases in their own book of authorities that are already included in the Judges' Book of Authorities. Both the practice direction and the list of cases in the book can be found on the court's website. Because the list changes from time to time, it should be checked for every book of authorities prepared for Divisional Court.

Trial Procedure

Trial by Judge and Jury, or Judge Alone

As we learned in Chapter 15, in accordance with s. 108 of the *Courts of Justice Act*, a trial may be conducted with or without a jury. If the party has an option under the statute for a jury trial, the decision to try the matter before a jury or by judge alone will be made on the basis of a number of factors that include the complexity of the case, the amount of sympathy or hostility the party believes that it may receive from a jury, and the length of the trial list for jury trials.

If the trial is conducted before a jury, it is the role of the jury to be the "trier of fact." That is, the jury must decide which of the facts presented in evidence they will accept as the truth. The judge in a jury trial ensures that the law is properly applied and the jury is properly instructed on the law. In a jury trial, the judge is the "trier of law."

In a trial by judge alone, the judge is both the trier of fact and the trier of law. In other words, the judge both applies the law and determines the facts that are accepted as true.

Overview of a Trial

Generally, a trial proceeds as outlined below.

1. Preliminary motions are dealt with. This includes any motions dealing with the amendment of pleadings, adjournment of trial, and striking out of the jury notice.

2. Jury selection takes place, when there is to be a jury.

3. Order excluding witnesses. Rule 52.06 provides that the judge may, at the request of a party, exclude a witness from the courtroom until the witness is called to give evidence. It is a common practice for parties to ask for such an order so that a witness cannot hear other witnesses testifying and have what they hear influence their own testimony. There can be no communication with an excluded witness until the witness has been called to give evidence. An exclusion order does not apply to a party to the proceeding or to a witness who is necessary to instruct counsel; however, such an instructing witness may be required to give evidence first.

4. Opening statement of the plaintiff in which counsel for the plaintiff presents an overview of the case to be presented. The defendant's counsel may make an opening statement at this time (leave of the judge will be required to do so at this time in a jury trial), or he or she may wait until the start of the presentation of the defence. Any document briefs or agreed statements of facts are presented to the court at this time.

5. Presentation of the plaintiff's evidence by calling witnesses and reading into the record any admissions from examinations for discoveries or requests to admit. The plaintiff's witnesses are examined in-chief by the plaintiff's counsel and cross-examined by counsel for any party that is adverse in interest to the plaintiff.

6. Presentation of the defendant's case. Counsel for the defendant will examine the witnesses in-chief and then the adverse parties will cross-examine.

7. Reply evidence may be called.

8. Closing arguments take place. In a trial by judge alone, the plaintiff's closing argument is presented first, followed by the defendant's closing argument. In a jury trial, the defendant closes first, unless the defendant has called no evidence.

CHAPTER SUMMARY

In this chapter, we discussed the two steps involved in getting ready for a trial: (1) organizing the evidence and (2) assembling the materials that will be needed in the courtroom for the presentation of the case. We also discussed three general types of evidence: (1) documents, (2) physical evidence, and (3) testimony.

We observed that much of the documentary evidence in a trial is identified through discoveries. The rules of evidence require most documents to be verified in the course of the trial by calling the person who made the documents as a witness. However, there are special rules of evidence permitting business records and medical reports to be entered into evidence without calling the person who made them. In connection with testimony, we discussed summons and the need to summons even witnesses who agree to appear voluntarily.

Finally, we covered the drafting of a trial brief and the compilation of a book of authorities, and provided an overview of how a trial proceeds.

KEY TERMS

cross-examination, 416

document book, 414

examination-in-chief, 416

leading a witness, 420

testimony, 416

NOTE

1. O. Reg. 438/08, s. 48, amending Rules 53.03(1) and (2).

REFERENCES

Canada Evidence Act, RSC 1985, c. C-5.

Courts of Justice Act, RSO 1990, c. C.43.

Drugless Practitioners Act, RSO 1990, c. D.18.

Evidence Act, RSO 1990, c. E.23.

Regulated Health Professions Act, 1991, SO 1991, c. 18.

Rules of Civil Procedure, RRO 1990, reg. 194.

REVIEW QUESTIONS

1. What is a trial brief, and who uses it? How does it differ from a trial record?

2. What are the three types of evidence that may be introduced in a trial?

3. How is evidence usually admitted at a trial?

DISCUSSION QUESTIONS

1. Your instructing lawyer is calling Dr. Hardy Ames as an expert witness. Dr. Ames is an engineering professor at Trent University. He has a PhD in chemical engineering. What must the lawyer do to ensure that Hardy's evidence will be heard?

2. John Doe is suing Mary Smith. Draft a summons in the case for the plaintiff's witness Dan Doe. Dan lives at 1400 Winding Lane, Peterborough, Ontario, L4T 7Y6. The trial is to take place in Newmarket. There is a distance of about 120 km between Peterborough and Newmarket. The trial starts on March 15, year 1, and the witness will be needed for one day of testimony.

Judgments

17

Procedure for Drafting, Issuing, and Entering Judgments and Orders

Introduction

When a court makes a decision, that decision is a command to one or more of the parties to do something: to pay money or to cease doing something in the case of an injunction, for example. These commands from the court are referred to as orders. They take three forms under the Rules:

1. an order in Form 59A, called an "order" and used for a decision on motions and applications;
2. an order in Form 59B, called a "judgment" and used for a final decision in actions; and
3. an order in Form 59C, called an "order on appeal" and used for a decision by an appellate court (the Court of Appeal and the Superior Court when it acts in an appellate capacity).

Make sure to determine the type of order you are drafting so that you use the correct form.

Drafting Orders and Judgments

Order-Drafting Process

There are several steps to the creation of a final order or judgment:

1. obtaining the judge's or master's endorsement of the record,
2. drafting a formal order from the endorsement,
3. approving and signing the order, and
4. entering the order.

Obtaining the Judge's or Master's Endorsement

In any proceeding, whether it is a motion or a trial, when a judge makes a decision, he or she writes or endorses the decision on the back of a trial or motion record, notice of motion, or other court document. If you were wondering why the back-sheet on these documents is printed in landscape format (rather than portrait) with a large blank space, it is to give a judge room to write an endorsement. If a judge or master wishes to give reasons for the decision, he or she may write them as part of the endorsement, if that is practical, or may state "reasons to follow" (Rule 59.02). (In an appellate court, if reasons are given, an endorsement is not required.) In the rare cases where written reasons are given, they are usually written separately from the judgment, typed by the judge's secretary, released to the parties, and filed in the court file. Since January 2010, if counsel provide an email address, the court will send an electronic copy of the reasons for judgment as a PDF so that going to pick up a paper copy from the court is no longer necessary. But for those who prefer it, paper copies will still be available. As well, reasons for judgment are posted shortly after release at http://www.ontariocourts.on.ca/decisions_index/en so that others who are not parties may obtain copies of the reasons for judgment without paying the fee otherwise charged to non-parties for a paper copy of the reasons.[1]

Figure 17.1 shows what an endorsement in Abigail Boar's case might look like.

Drafting a Formal Order

The court does not create the final order for you. It is the responsibility of the parties to prepare the order. One of the parties, usually the one who has been successful and has a real interest in completing the process, prepares the order. You begin by going to the court file, finding, and photocopying or writing out the endorsement. Using the appropriate version of Form 59, you then prepare a draft order.

Before you draft, it is a good idea to use as a drafting guide the appropriate version of Form 59A, 59B, or 59C as found in the *Ontario Annual Practice* online at http://www.ontariocourtforms.on.ca/english/civil. The reason for this is that embedded in these "official" versions of the forms will be instructions on how to handle variations in the language you need to use in drafting an order. These instructions are in italics and they tell you when you may have to vary or change language. They may provide a suggested format or phrasing you can use. These instructions can also provide a checklist for you when you are drafting.

For example, perhaps the defendants in Abigail's case are self-represented at trial. The embedded instructions in Form 59B (judgment after trial) will remind you that this may change the language used in the recital. Instead of writing "in the presence of lawyers for all parties" the language would be altered to "in the presence of lawyers for the Plaintiff, and for the Defendants, Rattle Motors Ltd. and Fred Flogem, appearing in person."

An order must contain the following:

- the name of the judge or officer who made it;
- the date on which it was made (not necessarily the date or dates on which the matter was heard, because judgment may have been reserved);
- the recital, which gives a context for the order and may include the date(s) of the hearing and whether parties or counsel or both were present or failed to appear; and
- the operative parts of the order—the commands from the court.

Each command is set out in a separately numbered paragraph. The paragraphs usually begin with "THIS COURT ORDERS AND ADJUDGES" or some variation of this phrase, depending on the court and the type of order (Rules 59.03(1) to (4)). Damages are usually expressed as a total consisting of general and special damages together with prejudgment interest, if awarded, calculated to the date of the order.[2] Costs are listed in a separate paragraph.

Figure 17.1   Endorsement (Form 4C)

ABIGAIL BOAR

Plaintiff(s)

and

RATTLE MOTORS LTD. ET AL.

Defendant(s)

Court file no. 01-CV-1234

(Short title of proceeding)

ONTARIO

SUPERIOR COURT OF JUSTICE

Proceeding commenced at Toronto

TRIAL RECORD

Name, address and telephone number of plaintiff's lawyer or plaintiff:

I.M. Just

LSUC #12345R

Just & Coping

Barristers and Solicitors

365 Bay Street – 8701

Toronto, Ontario, M3J 4A9

tel. 416-762-1342

fax 416-762-2300

Lawyers for the Plaintiff

July 12, year 3:

Judgment for the plaintiff in the amount of $53,000 with interest thereon at the rate of 3.8 percent from August 13, year -1. Costs fixed at $8,000.

Snork, J

If the order requires payments to a minor directly or through a trustee, the order must show the minor's date of birth and address, and it must contain a direction that it be served on the Children's Lawyer. This ensures that an independent public agency has notice of the minor's interest, and that there is an indication of when the minority status ends (Rule 59.03(5)). At that point, the minor, on becoming an adult, has the right to take charge of funds held on his or her behalf under the terms of the order.

An order for the payment of costs must direct that the costs be paid to the party, and not to the lawyer for the party. This prevents the lawyer from obtaining the funds for his or her own use. It is permissible for the payer to pay the costs to the lawyer in trust for the client, however. In this way the lawyer has to account for what is held in trust (Rule 59.03(6)).

Where postjudgment interest is payable, you draft the order with a provision for the payment of postjudgment interest, setting out the rate at which it is payable and the date from which it begins to run. Sometimes the rate and date are left blank and filled out by the court clerk when the order is signed.

Support orders must set out the last known addresses of the support creditor and support debtor.

Figure 17.2 sets out what a draft judgment in Form 59B might look like if Abigail Boar succeeded in getting judgment for $200,000 for general damages, $25,000 for special damages, and costs.

An order in Form 59A has a somewhat different format. Set out in Figure 17.3 is an order on a motion to compel Fred Flogem to re-attend and answer questions on his examination for discovery.

Approving and Signing the Order

Once you have drafted the judgment or order from an endorsement, you must obtain approval as to the form of the order from the other parties who are affected by it and who were present and participated in the proceeding. The lawyer for the other party checks the draft against the endorsement to see that your draft is fair and accurate. If it is, the lawyer writes on the face of the order "approved as to form" and signs his or her name and capacity as lawyer for a party in the proceeding. Then he or she returns the signed copy to you. Approval can also be given over the phone, by email, or by faxing a copy that has been marked "approved." The rule is not restrictive here with respect to how a copy may be marked as approved.

You then take the approved copy and an original to the office of the local registrar. If all parties who were present at the hearing have approved the order, the registrar examines the order and, if satisfied with the form, signs the order on behalf of the court.[3] If the registrar is not satisfied, he or she rejects the order and returns it unsigned. In this case, the party can either make the required corrections or, if he or she believes the registrar is in error, obtain an appointment before the judge or master who made the order to settle the terms of the order (Rules 59.04(5), (8), and (9)).

Where the parties cannot agree on the form of the order and a party has withheld approval, the other party may obtain an order to settle the terms of the order before

Figure 17.2 Judgment (Form 59B)

Court file no. 01-CV-1234

ONTARIO
SUPERIOR COURT OF JUSTICE

THE HONOURABLE
MADAM JUSTICE SNORK

Friday, the 12th day
of July, year 3

BETWEEN:

ABIGAIL BOAR

Plaintiff

and

RATTLE MOTORS LTD. and FRED FLOGEM

Defendants

JUDGMENT

THIS ACTION was heard on July 10, 11, and 12, year 3, without a jury at Toronto, in the presence of the lawyers for all parties,

ON READING THE PLEADINGS AND HEARING THE EVIDENCE and the submissions of lawyers for the parties,

1. THIS COURT ORDERS AND ADJUDGES that the plaintiff recover from the defendants the sum of $200,000.00 for general damages.
2. THIS COURT ORDERS AND ADJUDGES that the plaintiff recover from the defendants the sum of $25,000.00 for special damages.
3. THIS COURT ORDERS AND ADJUDGES that the plaintiff recover prejudgment interest at the rate of 4 percent from July 3, year 0 to the date of judgment.
4. THIS COURT ORDERS AND ADJUDGES that the defendants pay to the plaintiff her partial indemnity costs of this action forthwith after assessment.

THIS JUDGMENT BEARS INTEREST at the rate of _____ percent per year commencing on _____.

_____
Registrar, Superior Court of Justice

RCP-E 59B (July 1, 2007)

Figure 17.3   Order (Form 59A)

Court file no. 01-CV-1234

ONTARIO
SUPERIOR COURT OF JUSTICE

MASTER BELLWETHER

Friday, the 3rd day
of June, year 2

BETWEEN:

ABIGAIL BOAR

Plaintiff

and

RATTLE MOTORS LTD. and FRED FLOGEM

Defendants

ORDER

THIS MOTION, made by the plaintiff for an order that the defendant Fred Flogem re-attend at his own expense to answer questions 4, 5, and 7 on his examination for discovery was heard this day at Toronto.

ON READING the affidavit of Dianne Swan, sworn and filed, and on reading the transcript of the examination for discovery of the defendant Fred Flogem and on hearing the submissions of the lawyers for both parties,

1.   THIS COURT ORDERS that the plaintiff's motion be dismissed.

2.   THIS COURT ORDERS that costs be in the cause.

_____
Registrar, Superior Court of Justice

the registrar. The registrar examines the draft order and the endorsement and, if satisfied, signs the order. If the registrar is uncertain, he or she refers the order to the judge or master who made the order to determine whether or not it should be signed (Rule 59.04(10)). If a party disagrees with the registrar's decision, he or she may obtain an appointment with the judge or master to settle the terms of the order (Rule 59.04(12)).

If the referral is to a court consisting of more than one judge, the application to settle the terms of an order should be brought before the presiding judge in that court. Once the order has finally been settled, the registrar signs it (Rules 59.04(12) to (16)). If a case is urgent, a lawyer can ask the judge who issued the order to sign it. In this case, the judge may do so without approval if he or she is persuaded that the matter is urgent. The judge will then sign a draft order, which you need to prepare beforehand, and write on the face of the order: "let this judgment issue and enter."

Entering the Order

Once the order has been signed, it must be officially recorded and filed by the court. The court's seal is applied in the upper left-hand part of the order, just below the name of the judge or master who made the order. At the bottom, a note is affixed identifying the entry book in which the order is inserted. If the order is entered in the court records electronically or is microfilmed or photocopied, the note on the order will provide appropriate information to retrieve the order. This is done in the office of the court where the proceeding commenced. If an order is amended or varied by a subsequent order, the subsequent order is entered in the same court office as the original order, as well as in the office where the subsequent order was made. If the order is made in the Court of Appeal, it is entered both in the Court of Appeal office and in the office of the court where the action commenced (Rule 59.05).

An order found to contain an inadvertent error resulting from an accidental slip or omission may be corrected on motion to the court that made the order (Rule 59.06).

Where an outstanding judgment has been paid to the judgment creditor's satisfaction (even if not paid in full), it can no longer be enforced. A document attesting to the satisfaction of the judgment creditor, called a "satisfaction piece," may be filed and entered in the office of the court where the order was entered (Rule 59.07).

Prejudgment Interest

Introduction

When a party obtains judgment in a lawsuit for money to which he or she is entitled, the party is also entitled to interest because he or she has been deprived of the use of the money or its value from the time it was owing. Interest is paid on the amount owing to compensate the party for what he or she might have earned as profit on that money or to compensate the party for the loss of the use of it. Another reason for awarding interest is to make it less attractive for the defendant to stall proceedings in the hope that the plaintiff will run out of money or the will to pursue the case. A defendant who knows that interest is running on the amount of the claim may be more inclined not to waste time and to settle the claim.

Sections 127 to 129 of the *Courts of Justice Act* set out the rules for calculating prejudgment interest. Section 127 sets out definitions of relevant terms and the formula for determining prejudgment and postjudgment interest. The person designated by the deputy attorney general calculates the basic interest rate for each quarter of the year. The rate for each quarter is available on the Attorney General's website at http://www.attorneygeneral.jus.gov.on.ca/english/courts/interestrates .asp. The rates are also posted at court offices, but are no longer published in the *Ontario Gazette*. There is also a computerized source of rate information that even does the calculations: http://www.judgmentcalc.com. Whatever source you use, all you need to do is determine what the relevant quarter is and look up the interest rate for that quarter in the given year. The rates are set out in table form, using two tables. The first table covers rates for prejudgment interest for causes of action that arose before October 23, 1989 and for postjudgment interest in all cases, both before and after 1989. The second table sets out the rates for prejudgment interest for all causes of action that arose after October 23, 1989. Prejudgment interest is calculated differently before and after that date as a result of an amendment to the *Courts of Justice Act*, which is why we need the second table for post-1989 prejudgment interest.

Step-by-Step Calculation Instructions

1. *Determine whether you should claim interest under the prejudgment interest rules or whether you have an alternative right to interest.* Contracts often provide an interest rate and method of calculation for any amount that may be payable under the contract, including when there is a default in payment. A contract for a loan will certainly contain an interest rate. A penalty clause may also provide for interest. Sections 128(4)(g) and 129(5) of the *Courts of Justice Act* state that neither prejudgment nor postjudgment interest is payable under ss. 127 to 129 if there is a right to interest that arises other than under these sections. If you have a right to interest that arises outside the Act, it is still a good idea to claim prejudgment interest under the Act in the alternative in the statement of claim. If your claim to a right to interest arising outside the Act is unsuccessful, you can then fall back on the Act's provisions for prejudgment and postjudgment interest, calculated on the basis of the rates set out under the *Courts of Justice Act*. The clause in the claim for relief might read: "prejudgment and postjudgment interest at the rate of 14 percent in accordance with the provisions of s. 3 of the contract between the parties or, in the alternative, prejudgment and postjudgment interest in accordance with the provisions of the *Courts of Justice Act*."

2. *If you have a right to claim interest under the Act, you must classify the damages on which interest may be charged because this may determine what the rate of interest is and how interest is calculated.* There are three types of damages for the purpose of s. 128:

a. *General rule: Section 128(1).* Money awarded under an order is generally subject to interest at the appropriate quarterly rate for the quarter when the proceeding was commenced from the date the cause of action arose until the date of the order.

b. *First exception: Section 128(2) damages for non-pecuniary loss for personal injury.* The rate of interest on damages for **non-pecuniary** loss (for personal injuries) does not use the quarterly rates, but instead uses the rate determined under Rule 53.10, which is still 5 percent. The type of damages you are looking for is a non-monetary loss in a personal injury action. This means the amount of general damages awarded by the court for pain and suffering or the emotional shock that results from a personal injury. Because no money was actually lost, the s. 128(2) rule was meant to limit interest to 5 percent, which was lower than the usual quarterly rates at the time the rule was made. If Abigail is awarded $100,000 in general damages for pain and suffering, use 5 percent as the interest rate for this head of damages.

c. *Second exception: Section 128(3) special damages accruing over time.* Special damages are liquidated damages. These include out-of-pocket expenses and other sums that can be determined with precision by using a simple formula. They may occur all at once at the time the cause of action arises, or you may have continuing out-of-pocket expenses from the time the cause of action arose—if this is the case, you must calculate interest every six months on these damages as they accrue. If Abigail had continuing out-of-pocket expenses for medications, you would add up her expenditures for each six-month period. Beginning with the date the action arose, you would calculate interest using the quarterly rate on the day the action was commenced on the total for the first six-month period and do the same for any other six-month period, and for any part period up to the date of the order. You may not calculate interest on interest from any previous six-month period. Total the interest separately from the special damages for each six-month or part period to determine interest under this head of damage. This interest is added to any other interest arising under other heads of damage and added to the amount of the total judgment.

3. *Identify amounts on which no interest may be charged.* Section 128(4) identifies amounts that are not subject to interest calculation. They are listed below.

a. *Exemplary or punitive damages.* **Exemplary damages** (also called aggravated damages) are awarded to compensate a plaintiff for emotional harm when a defendant's conduct has been particularly outrageous. **Punitive damages** are also awarded when a defendant's behaviour is particularly outrageous, but the purpose here is to punish the defendant to deter him or her from behaving in the impugned way again. Because these damages are penalties, interest on these amounts as a further penalty could be said to be overly harsh.

non-pecuniary
non-monetary

exemplary damages
damages over and above the plaintiff's actual loss, paid to compensate the plaintiff for hurt feelings or mental stress caused by the defendant's particularly outrageous behaviour

punitive damages
damages in the nature of a fine paid to the plaintiff when the defendant's behaviour has been particularly outrageous

b. *Interest under s. 128.* Interest is not compounded and generally there is no interest charged on accrued interest. It is calculated separately and then added in with the other damages. However, when postjudgment interest is calculated, it is calculated on the entire judgment, including the component that is prejudgment interest.

c. *Award of costs.* The costs awarded at the time of judgment, whether fixed or to be assessed, are not subject to prejudgment interest, although they are subject to postjudgment interest.

d. *Pecuniary loss that is identified as occurring after the date of the judgment.* Sometimes a judge can identify a plaintiff's loss that is connected to the cause of action but that has not yet accrued. For example, in Abigail's personal injury action, a judge may be able to determine an amount for her future loss of income because she will continue to be unable to work. On this amount, no interest may be charged.

e. *Advance payment of the amount to settle a claim before judgment after the payment was made.* Suppose you owe $100 as of January 1, and you pay $75 as an advance payment to settle the claim on February 1. If the plaintiff continues to go after you for the balance, prejudgment interest on the $75 will run only from January 1, when the cause of action arose, to February 1, when that amount was paid. But interest will run on the balance, $25, for the whole period from the time the cause of action arose until judgment: from January 1 until the date of the judgment.

f. *Where the order is made on consent.* There is no prejudgment interest on an order made on consent unless the debtor agrees.

g. *Where interest is payable by a right other than under s. 128.* As noted earlier, if you have a right of interest arising, for example, under a contract, you must claim interest under the contract and not under the Act.

4. *Establish the prejudgment interest rate that applies to your damages claim.* Except for damages for non-pecuniary loss on personal injuries, where the interest rate is 5 percent, the applicable rate of interest is the rate for the quarter in which the action was commenced. Do not confuse this with the quarter in which the cause of action arose. The right to sue always arises earlier than the day on which you commence proceedings, and it may well be in a different quarter. You do not have to do the calculations in s. 127 to determine the rate. This is done for you in the table that is updated quarterly by the Ministry of the Attorney General. Remember, as noted earlier, that there are two tables. Use the first table (beginning with 1985) for prejudgment interest on cases where the cause of action arose before October 23, 1989 and for postjudgment interest in all cases. Use the second table (beginning with October 23, 1989) for prejudgment interest in cases where the cause of action arose *after* October 23, 1989.

5. *Having established the rate, calculate the prejudgment interest.* You will need to determine the following dates: (a) the date on which the cause of action arose (interest is calculated from this date); (b) the date on which proceedings commenced (the interest rate is the rate for the quarter in which proceedings commenced); and (c) the date on which the order or judgment was made (interest runs to this date). The prejudgment interest calculation formula for simple interest is:

$$I = P \times R \times T$$

where

I = interest,
P = amount for the head of damage on which the claim is made,
R = rate of interest from the rate for the quarter when the action was commenced, and
T = number of days from the day the cause of action arose to the day of judgment, which is expressed as a fraction of a year—for example, 40 days is expressed as $40/365$.

Suppose Abigail Boar sues her employer for wrongful dismissal when her employer terminates her employment without notice on August 12, year 0. She sues the employer on October 1, year 0 and recovers judgment with general damages of $80,000 on November 15, year 1.

1. *Determine whether you have a right to interest under the Act.* In this case, there is no rate set out in a contract and no other right to interest. Therefore prejudgment interest can be claimed under the Act.

2. *Classify the damages to determine the rate and calculation mode.* The damages are general damages and come within neither exception to the general rule: They are not damages for personal injuries and they are not special damages accruing over time before judgment.

3. *Identify the amount on which no interest may be charged.* Interest may be charged on the general damages claimed; there are no claims that are exempt from prejudgment interest on these facts.

4. *Establish the prejudgment interest rate for this claim.* The rate is the rate for the quarter in which the cause of action arose. August 12, year 0 is in the third quarter of year 0, and the rate must be taken from the second table for proceedings where the cause of action arose after 1989. Assume that the rate is 5.3 percent.

5. *Calculate the prejudgment interest:*

$$I = P \times R \times T$$

August 12, year 0 to August 11, year 1 (one year):

$80,000 \times 0.053 = $4,240

August 12, year 1 to November 14, year 1 (95 days, not including the day on which judgment is given):

$$\$80{,}000 \times 0.053 \times {}^{95}\!/_{365} = \$1{,}103.56$$

[handwritten: turn into decimal]

$$I = \$5{,}343.36$$

Postjudgment Interest

Introduction

Postjudgment interest is also available. If a party has a right to interest from the time the cause of action arose, a party has that right after judgment until he or she is paid. Postjudgment interest therefore compensates a party for the loss of the use of money that he or she should have had. It also encourages a judgment debtor to pay what he or she owes. The longer the delay, the greater the amount that must be paid.

The general principles are the same as for prejudgment interest but the calculation rules are slightly different. If an order awards periodic payments, such as in a divorce support order, postjudgment interest runs from the date each payment becomes due.

As noted in note 2 to this chapter, some court offices start postjudgment interest running from the date after the order is made. In the text, postjudgment interest runs from the date of the order.

Step-by-Step Calculation Instructions

1. *Determine the amount of the judgment.* This includes the amount of the damages, the interest on that amount, and the costs awarded.

2. *Determine the postjudgment interest rate.* This requires you to use the rate in the first table for the quarter in which judgment was given.

3. *Calculate the postjudgment interest.*

   a. Determine the day of judgment, when the interest begins to run.

   b. Count the days from the day the order is made to the day on which payment is received. Since prejudgment interest stopped on the day *before* the order was given, postjudgment interest begins on the day the order was given.

   c. Calculate the postjudgment interest using the formula: $I = P \times R \times T$.

4. *Calculate the amount due on the date of payment.* Add the postjudgment interest just calculated to the amount of the outstanding judgment.

Let's assume Abigail Boar had her costs assessed at $2,000 and that she was paid on November 30, year 1.

1. *Determine the amount of the judgment.*

   Judgment was for $80,000 + costs of $2,000 + prejudgment interest of $5,343.36 = $87,343.36.

2. *Determine the postjudgment interest rate.*

   The day of judgment is November 15 in the fourth quarter of year 1, and assume that the rate in table 1 is 7 percent.

3. *Calculate the postjudgment interest.*

   Interest runs from the day of judgment to the date of payment:

   November 15, year 1 to November 30, year 1 = 16 days
   $87,343.36 \times 0.07 \times {}^{16}/_{365} = \$268.01$

4. *Calculate the amount due on November 30, year 1.*

   $87,343.36 + $268.01 = $87,611.37

CHAPTER SUMMARY

In this chapter, we examined the procedural requirements involved in drafting, approving, signing, and entering orders, including challenging and varying orders that are not in accordance with a judge's endorsement. We distinguished between orders generally and orders on applications, motions, and from the Court of Appeal. We also distinguished orders generally from judgments after trial, noting the differences in form. We then turned to prejudgment and postjudgment interest, noting that pre-judgment interest runs from the time the cause of action arises to the day of judgment, and is calculated on the amount of the judgment at an interest rate determined by a formula and set out in a table. We also made note of exclusions and types of damages using special calculation methods and special rates. We then turned to the calculation of postjudgment interest from the date of the order to payment, noting how the rate is established and the amount of the judgment on which it is calculated.

KEY TERMS

exemplary damages, 436

non-pecuniary, 436

punitive damages, 436

NOTES

1. See Court of Appeal for Ontario, Notice to the Profession, "Electronic Delivery of Copies of Reasons for Judgment," November 2009 at http://www .ontariocourts.ca/coa/en/notices/adminadv/ electronicdelivery.htm.

2. There is some variation from one court to another on how this is done. Some courts calculate prejudgment interest up until the day *before* the order is made, with postjudgment interest running from the date of judgment. In some other courts, prejudgment interest is calculated *up to and including* the date the order is made, with postjudgment interest running from *the day after* the judgment. It is advisable to check with the court clerk where you are filing an order to see how they calculate prejudgment and postjudgment interest. In this text, prejudgment interest runs to the date *before* judgment.

3. The procedure varies. In some places, a court clerk signs the order on behalf of the registrar. Judges can sign their own orders but rarely do so.

REFERENCES

Courts of Justice Act, RSO 1990, c. C.43.

Carthy, James J., W.A. Derry Millar, and Jeffrey G. Cowan, *Ontario Annual Practice* (Aurora, ON: Canada Law Book, published annually).

Rules of Civil Procedure, RRO 1990, reg. 194.

REVIEW QUESTIONS

1. What is the difference between a judgment and an order?

2. What is an endorsement?

3. What does it mean to "approve the order as to form"?

4. Describe the process of signing an order.

5. What happens if the order is not approved as to form?

6. What happens if the registrar refuses to sign an order because he or she is not satisfied that it is in proper form or that it correctly reflects the contents of the endorsement?

7. Where are orders entered?

8. What should you do if you pay the amount due on an order or an amount that satisfies the judgment creditor?

9. What happens if there is an inadvertent error in the judgment?

10. On what can you obtain prejudgment and postjudgment interest?

11. How do you determine the appropriate interest rate to calculate prejudgment interest?

12. How do you determine the interest rate for calculating postjudgment interest?

13. How do you calculate the interest for special damages where they continue to accrue after the cause of action arose?

DISCUSSION QUESTIONS

1. Suppose Abigail is not successful at trial. You are asked to draft the judgment. You get the court file and find this endorsement on the back of the trial record: "September 27, year 1. Action dismissed with costs. Palardeau J." The trial took place in Toronto on September 10, 12, 13, 14, 26, and 27. Counsel and parties were all present and evidence was given orally. Draft the judgment.

2. Assume the same trial dates as in question 1, but suppose that Abigail is successful. The endorsement reads: "Judgment for the plaintiff. General damages $225,000. Special damages $87,242.03. Partial indemnity costs for the plaintiff together with prejudgment interest in the amount of $12,098.21."

3. Determine how much is owing to Abigail. Assume that Abigail obtained judgment for $100,000 for general damages for pain and suffering and $50,000 for out-of-pocket expenses or special damages, which accrued as follows: September 14, year 0 to March 13, year 1: $22,000; March 14, year 1 to September 13, year 1: $23,000; September 14 to 28, year 1: $5,000. The accident occurred on September 14, year 0. The action commenced on October 23, year 0, and judgment was granted on September 28, year 1.

4. Assume that Abigail obtained judgment on June 5, year 0 for $150,000, her costs were assessed at $10,000, and prejudgment interest was $3,000. Assume also that she was paid on October 15, year 0. Determine the amount of postjudgment interest and the total amount payable on October 15, year 0.

Costs

18

Introduction

Although there are exceptions, a judge usually orders that the losing side pay part of the legal costs of the winning side. When speakers of legalese say "the costs are in the cause" or "the costs follow the event," this is what they mean: the winning side recovers some of its legal expenses from the losing side.

The jurisdiction of the court to award costs is provided in s. 131 of the *Courts of Justice Act*. The amount of costs or whether costs are awarded at all are matters totally in the discretion of the court. Although costs usually "follow the event" (that is, are awarded to the winner), the court sometimes awards costs or denies costs to express its disapproval of the way that one of the parties has conducted itself during the proceeding (Rule 57.01(2)). For instance, if a party has prolonged the proceedings unnecessarily, the court may refuse to award costs to the party, even if the party wins the case. Moreover, depending on the inappropriateness of the conduct during the litigation, the court may even order the winning party to pay costs to the losing side.

How Costs Are Determined

In determining whether costs are to be awarded, the court uses the factors set out in Rule 57.01(1). These factors include such things as the amount of money the winning party recovered in the proceeding; the complexity of the proceeding; the importance of the issues; and the conduct of any party, including conduct resulting from negligence, mistake, or excessive caution. These factors now also include consideration of the experience of the lawyer for the party awarded costs, the rates charged, and the time spent. (The implication here is that the costs awarded bear some resemblance to what the client is actually paying for legal services.) Also to be considered is the amount of costs the party paying those costs might reasonably be expected to pay in the circumstances of the case.[1]

Rule 57.01(4)(e) now permits costs to be awarded to a party who represented himself or herself. Formerly, because the party did not pay fees to a lawyer, no costs were awarded in respect of fees. The court may now recognize the time and trouble spent by an unrepresented party on his or her own case and award an amount for expenses incurred by the unrepresented party, such as the loss of a day's pay. In addition, Rule 57.05 provides costs sanctions if the case was brought improperly in the Superior Court rather than in the Small Claims Court. As you can see, in providing for the awarding of costs, the Rules encourage parties to move their cases speedily and efficiently through the litigation process.

Although Rule 57.01(4)(d) now explicitly permits the court to fully indemnify a costs recipient, costs in Ontario courts are rarely awarded on that basis. Rather, they usually cover only a portion of the actual legal costs of the party. The portion of the real legal costs covered depends on what scale is used to calculate the costs awarded. The court determines which scale is to be used when it awards costs. The two usual scales used are the partial indemnity scale and the substantial indemnity scale. In most cases, the partial indemnity scale is used. The court usually orders that the substantial indemnity scale be used only if the party who must pay costs has done something blameworthy during the litigation. Substantial indemnity costs, if awarded, are 1.5 times what they would have been if they had been awarded on a partial indemnity basis. On very rare occasions of particularly obnoxious conduct by a party, the court may order full indemnification.

Before January 1, 2002, when the rules relating to costs went through substantial change, the trial judge could determine both which party would be awarded costs and the actual monetary amount of the costs. Alternatively, the judge might make an order determining which party was to be awarded costs and leave the actual calculation of the amount of those costs to a court official called an assessment officer. When the judge determines not only who receives costs but also how much that person receives, this is called **fixing costs**. When the judge decides which party receives costs but leaves the assessment officer to decide the amount, this is called making an **assessment of costs**.

When is it appropriate to follow the procedure for fixing costs rather than assessing them? Rules 57.01(3) and (3.1) indicate that when the court awards costs, it shall fix them unless the case is "exceptional." This clearly indicates a default rule that costs should be fixed rather than assessed whenever costs are ordered. It is not entirely clear what makes a case exceptional, so that an assessment should be ordered. If "it is likely that the assessment process is more suited to effect procedural and substantive justice," it should be used.[2] The fact that the case is complex or involves great expense will not make it exceptional. Rather, "there must be some element ... that is out of the ordinary or unusual that would warrant deviating from the presumption that costs are to be fixed."[3]

Whether costs are to be fixed or assessed, Rules 57.01(5) and (6) indicate that after a trial, or on an application or a motion that finally disposes of an issue, it is appropriate to serve and file a **bill of costs** in Form 57A and, presumably, have the costs assessed, provided the judge has so ordered. If costs have been awarded on a step in a proceeding, for example, after a motion, it is usual to fix costs at the end of the hearing rather than leave the costs of the motion to be dealt with by the trial judge at the end of the entire case. In this case, where costs are ordered to be fixed, unless the parties have agreed on costs for that step, each side is expected to come to the hearing with a copy of a costs outline in Form 57B, and give a copy to every other party. The costs outline is not to exceed three pages and it should summarize the disbursements and the basis for the claim for partial indemnity fees to be requested, focusing on the discretionary factors used to determine costs in Rule 57.01.

Bills of costs, which look a lot like a client's account in terms of detail, are used on an assessment, often with additional written submissions that may mirror some of the submissions in the costs outline, touching on relevant Rule 57.01(1) factors. The costs outline is usually used on motions or other steps in a proceeding where costs are ordered to be fixed.[4]

Prior to 2002, Rule 57.01 set out the general factors that judges and assessment officers were to use in exercising their discretion in fixing or assessing costs. Rule 57.01 was substantially amended in 2002 and again in 2005. The purpose of the changes was:

fixing costs
making an order that a specific party pay a specific amount of costs

assessment of costs
a costs order made by a judge where the actual amount of the costs is determined at a separate hearing by an assessment officer

bill of costs
list of allowable fees and disbursements that is used by an assessment officer to assess a litigant's costs after the litigant is successful in obtaining judgment; differs from an account because it does not include all fees charged to a client

- to encourage judges to fix costs in the quickest and least formal way possible, rather than to leave the determination of amounts to the more formal, expensive, and cumbersome assessment process;
- to make costs awards more predictable, uniform, and consistent; and
- to ensure that all relevant factors affecting costs are considered in making an award.

A costs grid that created a formula for determining hourly rates for fees for lawyers based on years of practice experience was introduced into Tariff A, Part I in 2002. Rates were also set for law clerks and students-at-law (articling students). The grid did create a more uniform and consistent pattern of awards, but it was perceived by the lawyers for clients who had to pay costs as being overly generous. The judges and masters began to treat the grid as a ceiling for fees and exercised their discretion to award less than the ceiling in most cases, thereby reducing consistency and predictability.

In 2005, the costs grid was repealed, and Tariff A, Part I—Fees now directs a judge, master, or assessment officer to set fees for lawyers, clerks, and students-at-law for any step or steps in the judicial process in accordance with the discretionary factors set out in Rule 57.01(1). While primary reliance in determining costs is placed on the factors in Rule 57.01(1), the Civil Rules Committee has attempted to resurrect the costs grid in a simplified form. In an undated "Information for the Profession,"[5] it proposed an abbreviated version of the repealed costs grid, with suggested maximum rates for clerks, articling students, and lawyers at three experience levels to be used in determining partial indemnity and substantial indemnity costs. The Information for the Profession referred to above that contains this "baby costs grid" is not part of the Rules, nor is it a practice direction. Consequently, it has no legal force and, considering the criticism levelled at the old costs grid, it might be thought that the courts would ignore the old grid as well as the baby costs grid. It is clear, however, that that is not what is happening. In *Magnussen Furniture Inc. v. Mylex Ltd.*, decided in March 2008, the Court of Appeal held that a trial judge was entitled to use the old costs grid as a reference or guide in considering costs, particularly in assessing counsel fees at trial.

The mixed messages on factors to be considered to determine costs have created some confusion. However, to help guide the exercise of discretion to fix costs and to assist parties in focusing on those factors, Form 57B, costs outline, has been introduced. Figure 18.1 shows the costs outline for the Boar–Rattle proceeding. Unless the parties have agreed on costs for a proceeding or a step in it, each party must give a copy of the costs outline to other parties involved, and bring a copy to any hearing to fix costs.

In the costs outline, each party seeking costs sets out the fees for services at each step of the proceeding other than appearing in court, an estimated counsel fee for each day or part of a day spent in court, and all disbursements, which should be set out as an appendix to Form 57B. The form sets out Rule 57.01 costs factors, where parties can indicate information relevant to each factor. For example, for "the amount claimed and the amount recovered in the proceeding," a party may indicate that he or she claimed $100,000 in damages but obtained judgment for $60,000.

Figure 18.1 Costs Outline (Form 57B)

Court file no. 01-CV-1234

ONTARIO
SUPERIOR COURT OF JUSTICE

BETWEEN:

ABIGAIL BOAR

Plaintiff

and

RATTLE MOTORS LTD. and FRED FLOGEM

Defendants

COSTS OUTLINE

The plaintiff provides the following outline of the submissions to be made at the hearing in support of the costs the party will seek if successful:

Fees (as detailed below)	$ 1,712.50
Estimated counsel fee for appearance	3,750.00
HST on fees	710.13
Disbursements (as detailed in the attached appendix)	813.49*
Total	$6,986.12

The following points are made in support of the costs sought with reference to the factors set out in subrule 57.01(1):

- the amount claimed and the amount recovered in the proceeding

$203,649.00 was claimed, and the amount recovered was $190,000.00

- the complexity of the proceeding

personal injury action, made more complicated factually by corporate defendant's destruction of lighting system prior to discovery; inadequate lighting was central to the plaintiff's allegation of negligence

- the importance of the issues

injury to plaintiff was severe, causing her serious financial loss

- the conduct of any party that tended to shorten or to lengthen unnecessarily the duration of the proceeding

the corporate defendant unnecessarily resisted inspections of premises under Rule 32

---

* Fees are calculated at the partial indemnity rate claimed. In this case, 50 percent of the rate is charged to the client. The partial indemnity rate is subjective and could be between 40 and 60 percent of the rate charged to the client.

Figure 18.1   Continued

- whether any step in the proceeding was improper, vexatious or unnecessary or taken through negligence, mistake or excessive caution

not applicable

- a party's denial of or refusal to admit anything that should have been admitted

the defendants refused to cooperate on admissions under Rule 51

- the experience of the party's lawyer

I.M. Just, 9 years' experience

- the hours spent, the rates sought for costs and the rate actually charged by the party's lawyer

FEE ITEMS (e.g., pleadings, affidavits, cross-examinations, preparation, hearing, etc.)	PERSONS (identify the lawyers, students, and law clerks who provided services in connection with each item together with their year of call, if applicable)	HOURS (specify the hours claimed for each person identified in column 2)	PARTIAL INDEMNITY RATE (specify the rate being sought for each person identified in column 2)	ACTUAL RATE*
Drafting statement of claim	I.M. Just, year of call year −9	1.5 hrs	150.00	300.00
Drafting reply to statement of defence	I.M. Just	0.75 hrs	150.00	300.00
Drafting affidavit of service	Edward Egregious, Law Clerk	0.5 hrs	50.00	80.00
Drafting affidavit of documents	Edward Egregious, Law Clerk	4.5 hrs	50.00	80.00
	I.M. Just	0.5 hrs	150.00	300.00
Attendance at discovery	I.M. Just	5.0 hrs	150.00	300.00
Attendance at pretrial	I.M. Just	2.0 hrs	150.00	300.00

- any other matter relevant to the question of costs

not applicable

---

*   Specify the rate being charged to the client for each person identified in column 2. If there is a contingency fee arrangement, state the rate that would have been charged absent such arrangement.

Figure 18.1   Concluded

LAWYER'S CERTIFICATE

I CERTIFY that the hours claimed have been spent, that the rates shown are correct and that each disbursement has been incurred as claimed.

Date: September 5, year 3   _____   _I.M. Just_ _____

Signature of lawyer

APPENDIX A: DISBURSEMENTS

DISBURSEMENTS SUBJECT TO HST

Paid to process server to serve statement of claim	$ 60.00
Paid to official examiner	200.00
	$260.00
HST	35.49*
Total disbursements subject to HST	$295.49

DISBURSEMENTS NOT SUBJECT TO HST

Paid to issue statement of claim	$181.00
Paid to set matter down for trial	337.00
Total disbursements not subject to HST	$518.00
TOTAL DISBURSEMENTS	$813.49

RCP-E 57B (July 1, 2007)

---

*   HST calculated at 13 percent.

HST and Costs

Charging Clients HST on Legal Fees and Disbursements

Fees charged by lawyers and paralegals for legal services are subject to HST, and some, but not all, disbursements are also subject to HST. When preparing bills of costs, costs outlines, and client accounts, HST, where appropriate, should be included. Below is a list of disbursements that are subject to HST and a list of those that are not. Generally, fees paid to the court to issue or file documents are exempt from HST. Services paid for, such as expert reports and transcript preparation, are subject to HST.

NOTE: When making claims for costs, you should always ask for costs inclusive of HST to maximize the costs award.

COMMON DISBURSEMENTS EXEMPT FROM HST

Court fees paid to file claims, defences, motions, and pleadings, or to set a matter down for trial, file a trial record, obtain an order, obtain a summons or subpoena, or file an enforcement document are not subject to HST. Generally, any fee paid to a court to file a document or take a step in a proceeding is not subject to HST.

COMMON DISBURSEMENTS SUBJECT TO HST

- Witness fee, whether set by legislation or agreed to by the parties; this includes witnesses' travel and accommodation expenses.
- Fees for recording services, transcript production, and special examiner fees, whether prescribed by statute or not.
- Fees to serve documents.
- Fees for expert report/attendance, including the costs of preparing a report.
- Fee to obtain a court transcript.

For further information about HST on legal fees and disbursements, including information on various practice areas, see Canada Revenue Agency Policy Statement P-209R, available on the CRA website at http://www.cra-arc.gc.ca. Search for P-209R.

Because the party did not obtain full recovery, this factor might be given a lower weight than it otherwise would have been and could reduce the costs awarded.

Specifically, the form requires that the hours docketed for each step be given, along with the hourly rate charged to the client for the lawyer, clerk, or student-at-law doing it. The form then requires the partial indemnity rate sought for each person providing service. This rate should clearly be below the rate actually charged, although how much lower is difficult to determine. Prior to the introduction of the costs grid, the costs awards varied from one-third to two-thirds of the fees actually charged based on fees for each step in the proceeding, set out in Tariff A. The amounts in Tariff A prior to 2002 had not changed in years and were unrealistically low, given the actual costs of litigation. But, as deficient as the old tariff was, it at least provided monetary amounts for each step. Now, with no objective means of determining the appropriate fee, outcomes will, at least initially, be hard to predict. One thing is clear: if substantial indemnity costs are ordered, they will be 1.5 times what the partial indemnity costs would have been. As substantial indemnity costs should be somewhat less than the costs charged to the client, a "cap" of sorts is created for partial indemnity costs; because the scales are still subjective, it is hard to be more precise than this in stating what proportion partial indemnity costs should be to costs charged to the client. After determining the fee to be claimed, the lawyer completing Form 57B must then also complete the certificate indicating that the hours claimed, rates for fees, and disbursements incurred are correctly stated.

Rule 57.01(7) indicates that the court shall keep cost and delay to a minimum when fixing costs by keeping the process as simple as possible. In particular, the court may require written submissions, including copies of the costs outline, without holding oral hearings.

Costs may be fixed after a trial, and also in other proceedings, including contested motions. Rule 57.03 requires judges and masters to fix costs on contested motions, rather than refer them to the trial judge, unless there is a good reason for doing otherwise. The costs outline is clearly designed for use here.

After a trial, the party that has been awarded costs must prepare a bill of costs in Form 57A. The amounts in the bill of costs for fees are based on Tariff A, as with the costs outline. The disbursements are found in Tariff A, Part II. If the costs are fixed after a trial, a party prepares and files a bill of costs with the court and, if there is a dispute, a copy of the costs outline as well. If costs have been ordered to be assessed under Rule 58 by an assessment officer, the parties must follow the procedures in Rule 58.

Preparation of a Bill of Costs

A bill of costs is Form 57A and appears as Figure 18.2. In order to complete the form, you need the time dockets for the client's files, showing specific work that has been done on the file and the amount of time it took to accomplish each task.

You must then sort the time dockets into tasks that involve procedures authorized by the Rules, such as drafting of pleadings or attendance at a mandatory mediation session, and tasks that are services provided to the client but that are not covered by the Rules, such as meetings with clients for the purpose of taking instruction.

A step-by-step guide for calculating costs is provided below.

1. *Determine the scale that the costs are to be calculated under.* This can be determined from the order or judgment.

2. *Divide the time dockets for the file into items that cannot be included in the bill of costs, items to be included as non-counsel fees, and items to be included as counsel fees.* Counsel fees are those fees directly related to the lawyer's appearance in court and are flat amounts per day or, if for less than a full day, for a half day. It is up to the lawyer to determine his or her counsel fees, usually based on years of experience.

Figure 18.2 Bill of Costs (Form 57A)

Court file no. 01-CV-1234

ONTARIO

SUPERIOR COURT OF JUSTICE

BETWEEN:

ABIGAIL BOAR

Plaintiff

and

RATTLE MOTORS LTD. and FRED FLOGEM

Defendants

BILL OF COSTS

AMOUNTS CLAIMED FOR FEES AND DISBURSEMENTS

FEES OTHER THAN COUNSEL FEES

1.	Drafting and issuing statement of claim	1.5 hours
	I.M. Just, January 3, year 1	
2.	Receiving and drafting reply to statement of defence	0.75 hours
	I.M. Just, February 5, year 1	
3.	Drafting affidavit of service	0.5 hours
	Edward Egregious, law clerk, January 5, year 1	
4.	Drafting affidavit of documents	
	Edward Egregious, February 7, year 1	4.5 hours
	I.M. Just, February 9, year 1	0.5 hours
5.	Attendance at examination for discovery	5.0 hours
	I.M. Just, February 10, year 1	
6.	Attendance at pretrial conference	2.0 hours
	I.M. Just, May 20, year 3	

FEES OTHER THAN COUNSEL FEES	1,712.50
COUNSEL FEE	
7. Attendance at trial of the matter	
I.M. Just, July 10, 11, 12, year 3	
3 days x $1,250	
COUNSEL FEE	3,750.00
TOTAL FEES (BEFORE HST)	$5,462.50
HST FEES	710.13
TOTAL FEES	$6,172.63

Figure 18.2 Concluded

DISBURSEMENTS SUBJECT TO HST

Paid to process server to serve statement of claim	$ 60.00
Paid to official examiner	200.00
	$260.00
HST	35.49*
Total disbursements subject to HST	$295.49

DISBURSEMENTS NOT SUBJECT TO HST

Paid to issue statement of claim	$181.00
Paid to set matter down for trial	337.00
Total disbursements not subject to HST	$518.00
TOTAL DISBURSEMENTS	$813.49
TOTAL FEES AND DISBURSEMENTS	$6,986.12

STATEMENT OF EXPERIENCE

A claim for fees is being made with respect to the following lawyers:

Name of lawyer	Years of experience
I.M. Just	9 years

TO: Huey Sue
     LSUC #23456T
     Barrister and Solicitor
     65 False Trail
     Toronto, Ontario, M6Y 1Z6

     tel. 416-485-6891
     fax 416-485-6892

     Lawyer for the Defendants

RCP-E Form 57A (November 1, 2005)

---

* HST calculated at 13 percent.

3. *Determine the years of experience for each lawyer involved in the file, and the actual rate charged the client, as well as the partial indemnity rate your firm wishes to claim.*

4. *Determine whether any procedure to be included in the bill of costs was performed by a law clerk or a student-at-law and determine the rate to be charged to the client, as well as the partial indemnity rate your firm wishes to claim.*

5. *Calculate allowable disbursements.* Look at Part II of Tariff A to determine whether a particular type of disbursement is an allowable item in the bill of costs, and ascertain how much can be billed for each type.

6. *Attach time dockets.* You must attach the actual time dockets for the fees claimed to the bill of costs.

7. *Attach evidence of disbursements.* For disbursements claimed, you must attach copies of invoices, cancelled cheques for payment of issuing fees, and any other evidence that proves the disbursements were incurred.

Assessment of Costs

If the court does not fix costs at the completion of the motion or trial, the court awards costs to a particular party and refers the matter to an assessment officer for an assessment of costs. The assessment officer is a court official who has the responsibility of determining the exact monetary amount to be awarded to that party. In assessing the costs, the assessment officer looks to Rule 58, which determines the assessment procedure.

A party entitled to costs files a bill of costs, including supporting documents (such as receipts and docket sheets), and a copy of the order awarding costs (Rule 58.03(1)). Once these documents are filed, the entitled party can then obtain a notice of appointment for assessment of costs, Form 58A, from the office of the assessment officer. The notice of appointment for assessment and the bill of costs must be served on all parties who have an interest in the assessment at least seven days before the date of the assessment (Rule 58.03(2)). A sample notice of appointment for assessment of costs appears as Figure 18.3.

If the party entitled to costs does not serve the bill of costs for assessment within a reasonable time, the party who has been ordered to pay the costs may obtain a notice to deliver a bill of costs for assessment, Form 58B, from the assessment officer and serve it on every party who has an interest in the costs issue at least 21 days before the date set for the assessment. A sample notice to deliver a bill of costs for assessment appears as Figure 18.4.

Once the party entitled to costs is served with the notice to deliver a bill of costs for assessment, the entitled party must file and serve a bill of costs on every interested party at least seven days before the date set for the assessment. If the entitled party does not serve a bill of costs as required, then the assessment officer may proceed to fix the costs, without the bill of costs.

Figure 18.3   Notice of Appointment for Assessment of Costs (Form 58A)

Court file no. 01-CV-1234

ONTARIO
SUPERIOR COURT OF JUSTICE

BETWEEN:

ABIGAIL BOAR

Plaintiff

and

RATTLE MOTORS LTD. and FRED FLOGEM

Defendants

NOTICE OF APPOINTMENT FOR ASSESSMENT OF COSTS

TO THE PARTIES

I HAVE MADE AN APPOINTMENT to assess the costs of the plaintiff, a copy of whose bill of costs is attached to this notice, on Tuesday, July 30, year 3 at 2:00 p.m., at the Courthouse, 393 University Avenue, Toronto, Ontario, M5G 1E6.

Date: July 20, year 3

_____
Assessment officer

TO: Huey Sue
      LSUC #23456T
      Barrister and Solicitor
      65 False Trail
      Toronto, Ontario, M6Y 1Z6

      tel. 416-485-6891
      fax 416-485-6892

      Lawyer for the Defendants

RCP-E Form 58A (July 1, 2007)

Figure 18.4   Notice to Deliver a Bill of Costs for Assessment (Form 58B)

Court file no. 01-CV-1234

ONTARIO
SUPERIOR COURT OF JUSTICE

BETWEEN:

ABIGAIL BOAR

Plaintiff

and

RATTLE MOTORS LTD. and FRED FLOGEM

Defendants

NOTICE TO DELIVER A BILL OF COSTS FOR ASSESSMENT

TO THE PARTIES

I HAVE MADE AN APPOINTMENT, at the request of the defendant, Rattle Motors Ltd., to assess the costs of the plaintiff on Tuesday, July 30, year 3, at 2:00 p.m., at the Courthouse, 393 University Avenue, Toronto, Ontario, M5G 1E6.

TO: Just & Coping
     Barristers and Solicitors
     365 Bay Street – 8701
     Toronto, Ontario, M3J 4A9

     I.M. Just
     LSUC #12345R
     tel. 416-762-1342
     fax 416-762-2300

     Lawyers for the Plaintiff

YOU ARE REQUIRED to file your bill of costs with me and serve your bill of costs on every party interested in the assessment at least seven days before the above date.

Date: July 21, year 3

_____
Assessment officer

RCP-E 58B (July 1, 2007)

On the date of the assessment, the interested parties appear before the assessment officer. The items in the bill of costs are examined, and the parties make submissions orally and in writing on any items that they wish to challenge or defend. The assessment officer then reviews the items and determines whether they reflect a reasonable amount of time spent on a particular step. For instance, the assessment officer might not allow a party to claim 3.5 hours for drafting a simple notice of motion. That amount of time is excessive for a routine matter. In deciding whether the expenditure of time or any other item in the bill of costs is reasonable, the assessment officer may take into consideration the factors listed in Rule 58.06(1).

The assessment officer must apply Tariff A, Parts I and II with respect to fees and disbursements. Part I, fees, directs the officer to the factors in Rule 57.01. Part II lists the disbursements that are allowable. These include court fees and necessary expenses incurred by or on behalf of a party, such as the costs of serving documents. Sometimes, with an unusual disbursement, it may be necessary to prepare an affidavit to prove the disbursement. The assessment officer also has the authority under the Rules to require a party to produce books and records for the purpose of the assessment.

In addition, the assessment officer is bound to follow any direction given by the court that made the order for costs. Pursuant to Rule 57.02, the court that awards costs may provide specific directions to the assessment officer as to how the costs are to be assessed. If there is such a direction on any item, the assessment officer must follow it. For example, the court may order that an item that is not included in Part II of Tariff A be assessed as a legitimate disbursement.

As you can see, an assessment hearing requires the lawyers to provide ample documentary evidence to support claimed fees and disbursements, and each side can cross-examine the other on any of the material presented. The process is, in effect, an accounting, which is by its nature a time-consuming process. In a complex matter, an assessment hearing could take days. It is no wonder that Rules 57.01(3) and (3.1) direct that costs be fixed rather than assessed unless the case is exceptional.

Following the assessment, the assessment officer must provide a certificate of assessment of costs, Form 58C, that sets out the amount of the costs allowed. Once the certificate is completed, it has the same effect as an order of the court and may be enforced in the same way as a court order. A sample of a certificate of assessment of costs appears as Figure 18.5.

If, at the completion of the assessment, any of the parties is unhappy with the assessment officer's decision, he or she may ask the assessment officer to withhold the certificate for seven days. During the period that the certificate is withheld, the objecting party must serve a written copy of his or her objections on every other interested party and file them with the assessment officer. Any party served with the objections may prepare a reply to the objections, serve them on the other parties, and file the reply with the assessment officer. The assessment officer, on receiving an objection, must reconsider the initial assessment and then complete the certificate of assessment, which may be amended as a result of the reconsideration. A party that is still not satisfied may appeal the assessment officer's decision to the court that made the original costs order.

Figure 18.5   Certificate of Assessment of Costs (Form 58C)

Court file no. 01-CV-1234

ONTARIO
SUPERIOR COURT OF JUSTICE

BETWEEN:

ABIGAIL BOAR

Plaintiff

and

RATTLE MOTORS LTD. and FRED FLOGEM

Defendants

CERTIFICATE OF ASSESSMENT OF COSTS

I CERTIFY that I have assessed the costs of the plaintiff in this proceeding under the authority of the order of the Honourable Madam Justice Snork, dated July 12, year 3, and I ALLOW THE SUM OF $12,000.

THE COSTS ALLOWED IN THIS ASSESSMENT BEAR INTEREST at the rate of 6.75 percent per year commencing on July 12, year 3.

Date: July 12, year 3

_____
Assessment officer

Assessment of Costs on Settlements and Abandoned Cases

It is usually costs that have been awarded by the court at the completion of a trial or a motion that are referred to assessment. However, sometimes a case settles or is abandoned before it gets to trial. In such cases, the parties may agree that costs are appropriate. Especially where a case is abandoned, one party may believe it is entitled to costs.

It is often a condition of the settlement of a proceeding that one party pay costs. Parties that agree to costs being a condition of settling a case usually draft minutes of settlement that contain the specific amount of costs to be paid. However, where the payment of costs is a condition of settlement and the amount is not included in the settlement, the costs may be assessed pursuant to Rule 57.04 by one of the parties filing a copy of the minutes of settlement in the office of the assessment officer.

Likewise, the costs on an abandoned motion, application, or appeal may also be assessed if one of the parties files

- the served notice of motion or application and an affidavit stating that the document was not filed within the time prescribed by the Rules or that the initiator of the proceeding did not appear on the court date;
- a served notice of abandonment; or
- a copy of any order dismissing the case as abandoned.

Cost Implications of Offers to Settle

The legal system has a major interest in having matters settle without trial. The Rules provide many methods of encouraging parties to settle their disputes. One of these rules is Rule 49, which deals with offers to settle. An offer to settle is a proposal made by a party to the litigation that attempts to resolve one or more of the issues between the parties. For example, the defendant may offer the plaintiff a portion of the damages being sought.

Rule 49 provides procedures for making and withdrawing offers. Rule 49.10 deals with the cost consequences when reasonable offers to settle are made by one party but not accepted by the party to whom they are made. The rule sets out three criteria regarding the offer to settle and its acceptance:

1. the offer to settle must have been made at least seven days before the commencement of the hearing;
2. the offer to settle must not be withdrawn and must not expire before the commencement of the hearing; and
3. the offer must not be accepted by the opposite party.

The consequences that flow from meeting these criteria are set out below.

Offer to Settle Made by Plaintiff

If all three of these criteria are met and the offer to settle is made by a plaintiff who obtains an order at the end of the proceeding that is *as good as, or better than, the offer made*, the plaintiff is entitled to partial indemnity costs to the date the offer to settle was served and substantial indemnity costs from that date onward unless the court orders otherwise.

Stated another way, the plaintiff makes an offer to the defendant to settle the case for less money than the plaintiff is suing for. The defendant does not accept the plaintiff's offer, and the case goes to trial. At the end of the trial, the plaintiff wins the case, and the court awards the plaintiff the same amount of money or more than the amount that the plaintiff offered to settle the case for. The defendant may be ordered to pay higher costs than he or she would usually have to pay because the costs are based on the substantial indemnity scale from the date that the offer was made until the end of the trial. The higher costs for the defendant are ordered because the defendant, by refusing a "good" offer, was the cause of an unnecessary trial.

Offer to Settle Made by Defendant

If all three of the criteria are met and the offer to settle is made by a defendant and the plaintiff obtains an order at trial that is *only as good as, or is worse than, the offer made*, the plaintiff is entitled to partial indemnity costs to the date the offer was served, and the defendant is entitled to partial indemnity costs from that date onward, unless the court orders otherwise.

In this situation, the defendant has made an offer to settle the case for less money than the plaintiff is seeking from the court. The plaintiff does not accept the offer and ultimately wins the case. However, the court does not accept the plaintiff's claim for damages and instead orders the defendant to pay damages to the plaintiff in an amount that is equal to, or lower than, the amount contained in the defendant's offer to settle. Because the plaintiff could have saved the time and expense of the trial by accepting an offer that was as good as, or better than, the one he or she ultimately received in the judgment, the plaintiff is entitled to costs on a partial indemnity scale only to the time the offer was made. After that date, the plaintiff must pay partial indemnity costs to the defendant.

The obvious intention of this rule is to ensure that parties think carefully about rejecting any reasonable offer to settle. If they reject an offer that turns out to be either as good as, or better than, the order eventually made by the court, the rejecting party suffers cost consequences.

Because of this rule, it is wise to structure all offers to settle a case in such a way that they automatically expire either within a specified period or at the commencement of the trial. If the offer to settle does not contain an automatic expiry period, it is important to withdraw it before the commencement of a trial, unless it is intended as a Rule 49 offer.

Offer Made in a Case with Multiple Defendants

In many cases, the plaintiff names more than one defendant and claims they are jointly and severally liable for damages. Rule 49.10 does not apply to the situation of multiple defendants unless the plaintiff makes an offer to settle that includes all the defendants. If the offer is made by the defendants to the plaintiff, Rule 49.10 does not apply unless the offer includes all the defendants or the defendants making the offer also agree to pay the costs of any defendant not joining in the offer (Rule 49.11). An offer to settle in the Boar case, which involves more than one defendant, appears at Figure 18.6. Much the same wording would be used in a case involving a single defendant but, of course, there would be no mention of being "jointly and severally" liable. The basic form used for an offer to settle is 49A.

Offer to Contribute

If the plaintiff is suing more than one defendant and claiming that the defendants are jointly and severally responsible for the damages, one defendant can make an offer to another defendant under Rule 49.12. The offer would be to contribute to the plaintiff's claimed damages in a specific amount.

A plaintiff who is suing more than one defendant, claiming that they are jointly and severally liable, is saying that they each are totally liable for all the damages. A plaintiff who wins such a case can go after any of the defendants for all the money. He or she need not take a specific portion from each of them unless the court orders otherwise. The plaintiff obviously wants to go after the defendant with the most money to collect the amount owing with the least trouble. For instance, if Abigail is successful against both the defendants Fred Flogem and Rattle Motors Ltd., unless the court orders otherwise, she is likely to seek all the money from Rattle Motors Ltd. Rattle Motors Ltd. is more likely to have the money available because Rattle Motors Ltd. is a business, whereas Fred, who is an individual employed as a car salesman, may or may not have the funds available.

Rule 49.12 provides that Fred Flogem can offer to split Abigail's claim with Rattle Motors Ltd., on a percentage basis. If this offer is accepted, Fred will pay that percentage of Abigail's total damages, and Rattle Motors Ltd. will pay the remaining percentage of the total. Fred initiates this by serving Rattle Motors Ltd. with an offer to contribute in Form 49D.

If Rattle Motors Ltd. rejects Fred's offer and Abigail eventually wins her case against both of them, the court can take Rattle Motors Ltd.'s rejection of Fred's offer to contribute into account when awarding costs. The court may require Rattle Motors Ltd. to pay Fred's costs, and it may require Rattle Motors to pay not only its own share of the costs to Abigail, but Fred's share as well.

On the facts of the Boar case, there is not likely to be an offer to contribute because Fred is an employee of Rattle Motors. Under tort law, the employer may be liable for its own negligent actions as well as vicariously liable for the negligence of its employee. Abigail is suing both defendants for their own alleged negligence and Rattle Motors for vicarious liability for Fred's alleged negligent actions. Since Rattle

Figure 18.6   Offer to Settle (Form 49A)

Court file no. 01-CV-1234

ONTARIO
SUPERIOR COURT OF JUSTICE

BETWEEN:

ABIGAIL BOAR

Plaintiff

and

FRED FLOGEM and RATTLE MOTORS LTD.

Defendants

OFFER TO SETTLE

The defendants jointly and severally offer to settle the plaintiff's claims in this proceeding on the following terms:

1. The defendants, or any or all of them, shall pay to the plaintiff the following amounts:
   (a) the sum of $100,000 for damages,
   (b) interest on that sum to the date of payment at the rate pursuant to the *Courts of Justice Act*, RSO 1990, c. C.43.

2. The plaintiff shall execute and deliver a release of all claims in favour of all defendants in a form acceptable to counsel for the defendants acting reasonably.

3. Upon payment of these amounts and delivery of the release, the plaintiff's claim shall be dismissed on a without costs basis.

4. This offer remains open for acceptance until the commencement of the trial in this proceeding at which time it shall expire unless it has been withdrawn earlier or amended.

Figure 18.6   Concluded

March 10, year 3

Huey Sue
LSUC #23456T
Barrister and Solicitor
65 False Trail
Toronto, Ontario, M6Y 1Z6

tel. 416-485-6891
fax 416-485-6892

Lawyer for the Defendants

TO: Just & Coping
Barristers and Solicitors
365 Bay Street – 8701
Toronto, Ontario, M3J 4A9

I.M. Just
LSUC #12345R
tel. 416-762-1342
fax 416-762-2300

Lawyers for the Plaintiff

RCP-E 49A (July 1, 2007)

Motors Ltd. is likely to be on the hook for any damages awarded to Abigail, neither Fred nor Rattle Motors Ltd. is likely to make an offer to contribute to the other.

In addition, Abigail is much less likely to accept the offer to settle the entire case if the defendants agree to split the damages. As noted, Rattle Motors Ltd. will be in a much better financial position to pay the damages than Fred, an employee. Abigail is not going to want to diminish her chances of collecting all the moneys owed to her.

Withdrawal or Acceptance

An offer to settle may be withdrawn at any time before it is accepted by serving a notice of withdrawal on the party to whom the offer was made. An offer not accepted by any expiry date set out in the offer is deemed to have been withdrawn if it has not been accepted by the specified date. Form 49B is used to make notice of withdrawal.

The acceptance of an offer to settle may be made by serving written acceptance on the party that made the offer (in Form 49C, acceptance of offer), any time before the offer expires, is withdrawn, or the court disposes of the case. Even if the offer is initially rejected, as long as the offer is not withdrawn and the court has not disposed of the matter, the party who rejected it may still change its mind and accept it.

Discretion of the Court to Consider Any Offer to Settle

Rule 49.13 gives the court discretion to consider any offer to settle when making an order as to costs. This means that the court is not restricted to addressing cost issues in the manner set out in the Rules.

Security for Costs

If a plaintiff is unsuccessful, the defendant is usually entitled to costs. Collecting costs from a plaintiff who does not have sufficient assets in Ontario is difficult. Rule 56 therefore provides a method for a defendant to bring a motion to the court asking that a plaintiff be required to pay money into court to be held for the duration of the proceeding. If the plaintiff is the successful party, the money is returned at the conclusion of the case. However, if the plaintiff is unsuccessful and the defendant is awarded costs, the costs are paid out of the money held by the court. The money held in the court is called "security for costs."

Rule 56.01(1) lists the circumstances in which security for costs is available. Security is most commonly sought and granted when plaintiffs reside outside the jurisdiction and may not have sufficient assets in Ontario to satisfy an order for costs made against them.

A defendant who is not certain where a plaintiff normally resides can demand in writing that the plaintiff's lawyer declare in writing whether the plaintiff is a resident of Ontario (Rule 56.02). Failure of the plaintiff's lawyer to answer the demand may result in the court dismissing or staying the case. Staying a case means suspending it.

When the case is brought by way of an action, the motion for security for costs can be brought only after the defendant has delivered a defence. Notice of the motion must be served on the plaintiff and on every defendant who has delivered a defence or a notice of intent to defend.

When the case is brought by way of application, the motion for security can be brought only after the respondent has delivered a notice of appearance. Notice of the motion must be served on the applicant and every other respondent who has delivered a notice of appearance.

Once security for costs has been ordered, the plaintiff cannot take any further steps in the proceeding until the security has been paid into court. If the plaintiff does not comply with the order for security, the court may dismiss or stay the case.

When the plaintiff has posted the security, he or she must immediately give notice to every other party that he or she has complied with the order.

CHAPTER SUMMARY

In this chapter, we saw that s. 131 of the *Courts of Justice Act* gives the court jurisdiction to award costs and that Rules 57 and 58 deal with the procedure for awarding costs and the assessment of costs. Generally, the losing party must pay costs to the successful party, but we have noted exceptions to this. The Rules require that the court fix costs in all but exceptional cases, where the court may refer the case for an assessment of costs.

We observed that costs may be awarded on either a partial indemnity scale, a substantial indemnity scale, or a full indemnity scale. The ordinary scale is partial indemnity. Tariff A, Part I refers to the factors in Rule 57.01 that guide discretion in determining costs. Part II of the tariff deals with the disbursements that may be included in an award of costs.

At the end of the proceeding, we saw that the party who is awarded costs must prepare, serve, and file a bill of costs or a costs outline, depending on the costs order and the nature of the proceedings. A guide was provided for preparing a costs outline and a bill of costs.

Since the court wants to encourage litigants to settle cases wherever possible, there are cost penalties for rejecting a reasonable offer to settle made by the opposite party pursuant to the Rules. We reviewed Rule 49 in this regard. Finally, we examined Rule 56, which provides a procedure for requiring a plaintiff to post security for costs.

KEY TERMS

assessment of costs, 445
bill of costs, 445
fixing costs, 445

NOTES

1. See Rule 57.01(1) for a complete list of the factors to be considered in the awarding of costs.
2. *Boucher v. Public Accountants Council for the Province of Ontario* (2002), 166 OAC 281, 28 CPC (5th) 25 (SCJ).
3. Ibid.
4. The authors wish to thank Toronto litigators D. Barry Prentice, Austin Riley, and Gregory W.M. Cooper for sharing their experience with the costs fixing and assessment process in Toronto.
5. See Rule 57 in James J. Carthy, W.A. Derry Millar, and Jeffrey G. Cowan, *Ontario Annual Practice* (Aurora, ON: Canada Law Book, 2013-2014), 1234.

REFERENCES

Carthy, James J., W.A. Derry Millar, and Jeffrey G. Cowan, *Ontario Annual Practice* (Aurora, ON: Canada Law Book, published annually).

Courts of Justice Act, RSO 1990, c. C.43.

Magnussen Furniture Inc. v. Mylex Ltd. (2008), 89 OR (3d) 401 (CA).

Rules of Civil Procedure, RRO 1990, reg. 194.

REVIEW QUESTIONS

1. The plaintiff in the case of *Smith v. Jones* sued for $150,000 in damages and was successful. No offer to settle was made. What costs is a court likely to award?

2. The plaintiff in the case of *Mahoud v. Balucci* sued for $25,000. She won the case, but the court awarded her only $7,000 in damages. How might the court approach a cost award in this case? What rule would apply? Why do you think this rule exists?

3. Explain the difference between the fixing of costs and the assessment of costs.

4. Your law firm acted for an unsuccessful plaintiff in a proceeding. The court awarded costs to the defendant. Two months have passed since the making of the order, and the defendant has not yet served and filed a bill of costs. How should your firm proceed? What rule or rules should it look to for guidance?

5. Your client is a defendant being sued by a plaintiff who lives in New York State. What are the cost implications? What must be done to protect your client? What rule applies?

6. The plaintiff is suing the defendant for damages in the amount of $300,000. Following the examinations for discovery, the defendant makes an offer to settle for $200,000. The plaintiff rejects

the offer. A trial takes place. The plaintiff is successful and is awarded $200,000 in damages by the court. What are the cost implications? What rule applies?

DISCUSSION QUESTIONS

1. You are the law clerk for B.A. Doowright and Associates, the lawyers for the plaintiff in the case of *Sam Sunshine v. Fast and Loose Delivery Services Ltd.* Sam has won his case against the defendant, and you must now draft a bill of costs. The court has ordered that the plaintiff shall have costs on a partial indemnity scale up to January 10, year 1 and substantial indemnity scale after that date. This order was made because the defendant had rejected an offer to settle made by the plaintiff. However, at the end of the case, the court awarded the plaintiff larger damages than those he proposed in the rejected offer. The various members of the firm who worked on this file are:

   B.A. Doowright, lawyer: 21 years' experience

   M.A. Blitz, lawyer: 2 years' experience

   Sally Smart, law clerk

   The file shows the following time docket items:

   a. institution of action, including drafting pleadings: July 10, year 0
      i. Doowright: 0.5 hours
      ii. Blitz: 3.0 hours
      iii. Smart: 2.0 hours
   b. discovery of documents, including drafting affidavit of documents: September 16, year 0
      i. Smart: 1.5 hours
      ii. Blitz: 1.0 hours
   c. examination for discovery: October 11 and 12, year 0
      i. Doowright: 1.5 hours
      ii. Smart: 1.0 hours
   d. counsel fee at trial: February 1, 2, and 3, year 1
      i. Doowright: 3 days
   e. drafting judgment: February 6, year 1
      i. Smart: 0.5 hours

The disbursements on the file are as follows:

a. paid court $181 for issuing of statement of claim
b. paid $40 for service of statement of claim
c. paid $40 for service of affidavit of documents
d. paid $250 to expert witness at trial
e. paid $337 to file the record

Draft a bill of costs.

2. Your law firm represents the plaintiff. The defendant brought a motion to dismiss your client's action. Your law firm spent a great deal of time preparing the necessary documents, serving and filing them, and taking other necessary steps to deal with the defendant's motion, including appearing in court to argue it. Neither the defendant nor his counsel appeared on the motion. You telephoned the office of the defendant's counsel and were told that the client no longer intends to ask for a dismissal of the case. Your client asks if there is anything you can do to force the defendant to pay some of her legal expenses. Is there something you can do? What is it? What rule applies?

Statement of Accounts

19

Introduction

You may have learned about procedures for preparing client accounts in courses dealing with other legal subjects, or in a legal office systems course, so much of what you read here may be familiar. Some of the procedures you may have learned about previously are common to the preparation of all client accounts, but in this chapter we will examine the process with particular attention to the accounts of clients in civil litigation matters. If you have not previously encountered client accounts, this chapter should provide the necessary background information needed to prepare them.

If Abigail Boar wins at trial and there is no appeal, the work on her case is done, and I.M. Just will send out her final account. If the law practice is managed well, Just & Coping will have sent her interim accounts at the end of various stages in the proceeding. In most civil litigation cases, interim accounts are sent out at the close of pleadings, at the conclusion of discoveries, and near the beginning of trial when pretrial preparation gets under way. Just & Coping may also have asked Abigail to **refresh the retainer** by making further deposits on account of fees when each interim account is rendered. If Just & Coping had taken Abigail on as a client on a contingency-fee basis, she would not have paid them anything prior to trial. But her lawyers will be able to take between 15 and 30 percent of a judgment as their fee (and will get nothing if Abigail loses the case). Before reading this chapter, review the section of Chapter 2 that deals with client accounts, particularly docketing and disbursements.

refresh the retainer
make a further deposit against future fees as a case progresses

Gathering Information to Prepare the Client's Account

The following is a step-by-step guide to gathering the relevant information.

1. *Collect all docketing data on the file.* You may recall that we discussed how to docket (record the work done on a client's file) in Chapter 2. If a file has been well managed, this information will have been entered periodically on docketing software by the lawyers and law clerks who worked on the file. Lawyers who are not partners (as well as those who are) and law clerks have their salaries tied directly or indirectly to their billings. It is important for their hours to be properly billed.

   If, in reviewing a file, you see that there has been work done for which there is no corresponding docketing data, you should alert the lawyer with **carriage** of the file. Do not try to solve this problem yourself, and do not feed docketing data into the docketing software after the fact, even if you think they are likely to be accurate, because the Law Society considers this to be unprofessional conduct.

carriage
responsibility for a file or a case

2. *Check billable disbursements.* Disbursements are expenses paid by the law firm out of the firm's general account. These include charges for photocopying, long-distance calls, courier services, fees paid to witnesses, fees paid for expert reports, and filing fees. Some expenses that generate receipts (for example, courier services) will probably be properly entered on the client file in the accounting system, with receipts saved as hard copy or scanned into accounting software. In many offices, account data involving long-distance charges and photocopying may be easily retrieved and listed electronically as disbursements, but some may not be, and you may need to search out this information.

3. *Check credits to the client's account.*[1] Credits include any retainer/deposits not yet billed or accounted for, and any amounts received by the lawyer in trust for the client—for example, payment of a judgment. You should be able to use this information to summarize trust account transfers in a trust statement at the end of the account.

You should now be ready to prepare the draft account.

Components of a Client Account

An account is usually prepared on the firm's letterhead or on special account letterhead and addressed to the client, to be sent as hard copy or by email. The format may vary. Some lawyers favour sending out a brief account, which simply says "for professional services rendered," followed by the total fees and disbursements. This is accompanied by a reporting letter from the lawyer, describing the work done, giving further advice if required, and informing the client that details of the account will be furnished on request. Other lawyers favour a more detailed account with a reporting letter. What follows is a description of what goes into a detailed account.

Description of Fees

The description of fees is almost always presented in chronological order. It tells the story of what work the lawyer and law clerk did on a case. It may be in one long narrative paragraph, setting out the date of an activity, its description, and the time taken to do it, in 10ths of an hour—for example, .1 hour or .2 hour. If the account covers several months, it may list all activities for each month under a subheading for each month. Whatever variation is used, you should describe the activity, the date(s) on which it occurred, the person who did it, and the amount of time taken to do it.

For example:

September 18, year 0, Drafting statement of claim (I.M. Just) 1.3 hrs.

Totalling of Fees

When you have finished describing the work done on the file, add up the work done by each lawyer or law clerk and multiply the hours by the appropriate rate.

For example:

I.M. Just, lawyer: 18.3 hours × $250 per hour = $4,575

Edward Egregious, law clerk: 10 hours × $75 per hour = $750

Total the fees. To the total of $5,325 from the above example you must add 13 percent HST ($5,325 × 0.13 = $692.25), for a grand total of $6,017.25.

HST

HST is the harmonized provincial sales tax and federal goods and services tax. It applies to some, but not all, of the items that are billed by lawyers in an account. There is room for interpretation as to how the tax applies to specific items, but you should note that HST is chargeable on fees charged by lawyers for their professional services, including the services of clerks, articling students, and associates, as well as disbursements where a service is provided. Court fees are not subject to HST. See the note on HST and legal services in Chapter 18 on page 450.

Adjusting the Fee

In preparing a draft account, multiply the hourly rate by the hours of work done; the lawyer may adjust the fee, usually by discounting it. Lawyers often adjust the fee based on the results for the client, the benefit to the client from those results, the complexity or difficulty of the work undertaken, and other subjective factors. For example, where the unadjusted fee is high in comparison to the benefit to the client, the lawyer may lower the fee. This reflects what an assessment officer might do if a client moves to assess the account because he or she thinks it too high.

Disbursements

After identifying all of the disbursements charged to the client's ledger, and any others not yet posted to the ledger, divide them into disbursements subject to HST and disbursements not subject to HST. Then you can add each subset of disbursements, and calculate and add in the HST.

Total Fees and Disbursements

You are now ready to total all fees and disbursements, including the HST. The total HST on fees and disbursements should be set out on a separate line below the total, along with the firm's HST number so that commercial clients can include this amount in any tax credits available to them.

Deduct Credit Balance in Trust from Total

If the client has a retainer/deposit held in trust, it should be credited against the amount due on the account, thereby reducing the amount owing from the client.

Balance Now Due

On this line, you can now record the net amount due after deducting credits from the client funds held in trust.

Signature Line

Only a lawyer can sign an account. This job should not be delegated to a law clerk or other office staff.

E&OE

This initialism is a standard business account notation and means "errors and omissions excepted." This means that the lawyer is not bound by the account if the lawyer finds that he or she made a mistake in preparing the account. The lawyer can still subsequently bill for an amount that was overlooked.

Interest on Overdue Accounts

At one time, lawyers could not charge interest on overdue accounts because it was considered improper for professionals to do so. Times change. Interest can now be charged at up to 1.5 percent per month or 18 percent per year, putting lawyers in the same league as bank credit cards. There should be a statement just below the signature that says interest will be charged at a specified rate on accounts that remain unpaid for more than 30 days after they are rendered.

Trust Statement

A trust or ledger statement that shows a record of transfers of money held in trust by the lawyer, including the purpose of each transfer, should appear at the end of the account. The trust statement underlies the lawyer's right to transfer money from the lawyer's trust account to his or her general account when an account is rendered to the client. And to be clear, a lawyer may not transfer client funds from a client trust to the lawyer's own account unless the lawyer sends an account to the client, showing the transfer.

Abigail Boar's Final Account

Account Information and Data

Let's suppose that Abigail's case went to trial on some of the issues raised in the pleadings, that the trial lasted three days (July 10, 11, and 12, year 3), and that Abigail obtained judgment for $100,000. On July 14, year 3, I.M. Just rendered his final account, covering the period from July 1, year 3, after completion of some of the pretrial work, through to the end of trial. Abigail's previous account was rendered on June 30, and was paid for by an amount on deposit in her trust account. She has refreshed the retainer with a cheque for $10,000, deposited to I.M. Just's trust account on July 2. I.M. Just's hourly rate is $250. When attending court, litigation lawyers often charge a flat counsel fee for each day or half day in court. I.M. Just's counsel fee is $2,500 per day and $1,200 per half day. The rate charged by the firm for Edward Egregious, the law clerk, is $75 per hour.

Edward's work on the file entered on the docketing software is as follows:

- July 6: arranging for issuing and serving summonses to witnesses: 0.5 hours
- July 8: meeting with witnesses: 1.0 hours
- July 10: organizing files and documents for trial: 1.0 hours
- July 10–12: attending court to assist I.M. Just, 6 hours per day for 3 days: 18 hours
- July 14: preparing account and telephone calls arranging for payment of judgment by defendants: 0.6 hours

I.M. Just's dockets are as follows:

- July 2: reading law and preparing trial brief: 8.0 hours
- July 3: reading law and preparing trial brief: 6.0 hours
- July 5: interviewing witnesses: 4.0 hours
- July 6: meeting client and preparing client for trial: 3.0 hours
- July 10, 11, 12: attending trial: 3 full days
- July 13: reporting to client: 1.0 hours

The client's file on the accounting software shows the following entries:

- July 2, year 3: received from client further retainer of $10,000
- July 5, year 3: paid witness fees, 3 summons at $53 each per court-prescribed fee ($159)
- July 6, year 3: paid to serve summonses: $45.00
- July 8, year 3: photocopying: $73.20

Draft Account

Figure 19.1 shows what the draft account in Abigail's case might look like.

Figure 19.1   Draft Account

JUST & COPING
Barristers and Solicitors
365 Bay Street – 8701
Toronto, Ontario, M3J 4A9

July 14, year 3

TO:
Abigail Boar
72 Sumach Street
Toronto, Ontario, M4R 1Z5

RE: BOAR v. RATTLE MOTORS LTD. AND FLOGEM
FOR ALL PROFESSIONAL SERVICES from and after July 1, year 3,
including:

I.M. Just, July 2-3, reading law and preparing trial brief: 14 hours; I.M. Just,
July 5, interviewing witnesses: 4 hours; I.M. Just, July 6, meeting client and
preparing client for trial: 3 hours; E. Egregious, July 6, arranging for issuing
and serving witness summonses: 0.5 hours; E. Egregious, July 8, meeting
witnesses: 1 hour; E. Egregious, July 10, organizing files and documents for
trial: 1 hour; E. Egregious, July 10, 11, 12, attending court to assist counsel: 6
hours per day for 3 days: 18 hours; I.M. Just, July 13, reporting to client: 1
hour; E. Egregious, telephone calls arranging for payment of judgment: 0.6
hours

OUR FEE:	$7,082.50
COUNSEL FEE: I.M. Just, 3 days at trial at $2,500 per day	$7,500.00
TOTAL FEE:	$14,582.50
*HST:	$1,895.73
TOTAL FEES INCLUDING HST:	$16,478.23
DISBURSEMENTS SUBJECT TO HST:	
Photocopies	$73.20
Service of summonses	$45.00
TOTAL SUBJECT TO HST:	$118.20
HST:	$15.37
TOTAL DISBURSEMENTS AND HST	$133.57

---

* HST calculated at 13 percent.

Figure 19.1 Concluded

DISBURSEMENTS NOT SUBJECT TO HST:

Court prescribed witness fee,

  3 summonses at $53.00 per summons $159.00

LawPro surcharge $50.00

TOTAL NOT SUBJECT TO HST: $209.00

TOTAL FEES AND DISBURSEMENTS: $16,820.80

(TOTAL HST IS $1,911.10 — HST # RO12534)

LESS TRANSFERRED FROM TRUST: −$10,000

BALANCE NOW DUE AND OWING: $6,820.80

THIS IS OUR ACCOUNT HEREIN

JUST & COPING

Per: _____

Interest will be charged at the rate of 18 percent per annum on all accounts outstanding for over 30 days.

E&OE

TRUST STATEMENT

Date	Transaction	Disbursement	Receipt
July 2, year 3	Received from client in trust		10,000.00
July 14, year 3	Paid to Just & Coping, transfer of funds for fees and disbursements, invoice # year 3-1298	10,000.00	
	TOTAL TRUST	10,000.00	10,000.00
	TRUST BALANCE	NIL	NIL

CHAPTER SUMMARY

In this chapter, we continued to explore the docketing of hours and the recording of disbursements on the client's account, and we used this information to render an account to a client. From assembled docket sheets and disbursements recorded from the client's ledger card, we created a draft account. The account described the work done and the time taken to do it. It established the fee and total disbursements and recorded the HST charged on all fees and disbursements that are subject to HST. We also accounted for any moneys received from the client in trust, using these funds to reduce the balance owing.

KEY TERMS

carriage, 470

refresh the retainer, 470

NOTE

1. The client billing account is usually a client file on accounting software. It is also called a client ledger or client ledger card, an older name used when client accounting information with debits and credits was recorded on a large file card, or ledger card.

REVIEW QUESTIONS

1. In a well-managed law practice, does the lawyer in a civil litigation matter usually wait until the trial is over before billing the client?

2. Does a client usually make a single deposit payment when he or she retains a lawyer?

3. What must you do before drafting an account?

4. What should you do if dockets are missing for work you know has been done?

5. What is subject to HST?

6. Does a lawyer always establish a fee by adding up all of his or her billable hours?

7. What does "E&OE" mean?

8. May a lawyer charge interest on overdue accounts?

DISCUSSION QUESTION

1. Read and respond to the following memorandum:

> To: Law clerk
>
> From: Lawyer
>
> Re: Farthbottle v. Blob
>
> We opened this file on September 16, year 0, and it has just settled. Please draft an account to Fabian Farthbottle for the end of November of this year. My hourly rate is $250. Charge $50 per hour for your time on the file.

An examination of docket sheets reveals the following:

Law clerk's dockets:

- September 16: attending meeting with client: 1.0 hours
- October 25: meeting client to review documents: 3.0 hours
- October 26: organizing documents and drafting affidavits of documents: 3.5 hours

Lawyer's dockets:

- September 16: initial meeting with client: 1.0 hours
- September 25: drafting statement of claim: 0.5 hours
- September 26: telephone conversation with client concerning amendments to statement of claim: 1.0 hours
- October 5: reviewing statement of claim and defence: 2.0 hours

- October 10: drafting reply and defence to counterclaim: 0.5 hours
- November 21: meeting to prepare a discovery plan and preparing for examination for discovery: 3.0 hours
- November 21: preparing client for discovery by telephone: 2.0 hours
- November 22: attending examination for discovery: 5.0 hours
- November 24: negotiating on telephone with defendant's lawyer: 2.0 hours
- November 24: discussing offer to settle with client on telephone: 0.2 hours
- November 25: discussion with defendant's lawyer accepting offer: 0.1 hours

Client's ledger card shows the following:

• September 16: received in trust	$2,000.00
• September 16–November 25: photocopies	$25.00
• September 26: fee to issue statement of claim	$181.00
• September 26: service of statement of claim by process server	$41.00
• October 1: postage	$6.00
• October 26: fax charges	$3.00
• October 30: examiner's fee for notice of examination	$9.50
• November 24: discovery transcript	$16.00
• November 24: court reporter's fees	$100.00
• November 24: examination facilities	$80.00

Appeals

20

Introduction

An appeal is not a retrying of a case. Many clients misunderstand this. They think an appeal is a redetermination of the case by a higher court that will hear all the evidence presented to the **court of first instance**. This is not the function of the higher court hearing the appeal.

court of first instance
court that made a decision
that is under appeal

The client must be helped to understand that an appeal can be commenced only if the court of first instance made a legal error. It is not the role of the appeal court to hear new evidence, make new determinations of facts, or reassess the credibility of witnesses. In fact, the appeal court does not hear any witnesses. An appeal is conducted by way of written documentation and submissions of the lawyers for the parties. The submissions centre on the legal error that the appealing party claims the court of first instance made. The party commencing the appeal is called the **appellant** and the party responding to the appeal is called the **respondent**.

appellant
party that commences
an appeal

respondent
party that answers or
defends against an appeal

Rules 61, 62, and 63 deal with procedure on appeals. You also must look to the *Courts of Justice Act* to determine which level of court has jurisdiction to hear an appeal. In addition, there is a lengthy practice direction that governs civil appeals in the Court of Appeal that must be followed when bringing an appeal to that court, as well as several notices to the profession. As with all practice directions (see Chapter 4), this one can be found on the court's website, or if you are using *Ontario Annual Practice*, in the grey-shaded pages that precede the specific rule to which it refers. It can also be found online at http://www.ontariocourts.ca/coa/en/notices/pd/civil2003.htm.

Nature of the Order Appealed From

Once it has been decided that there are arguable legal grounds for an appeal, the next step in determining which procedure to follow is to establish whether the order appealed from is final or interlocutory in nature.

final order
order that resolves all of
the outstanding issues
between the parties

All orders can be classified as either final or interlocutory. A **final order** is one that determines all the outstanding issues in the proceeding. An **interlocutory order** is one that resolves only a particular issue in the proceeding on a temporary basis. It is not a complete determination of all the issues between the parties.

interlocutory order
order that resolves only
a particular issue in the
proceeding; it does not
resolve all the issues
between the parties

Many, but not all, motions lead to interlocutory orders. Similarly, most orders made at a trial of an issue are final. However, it is important to look at the content of the order, not the proceeding in which it was granted, to determine whether it is final or interlocutory in nature. For instance, a successful motion for summary judgment results in a final order. The order is final because all the issues in the proceeding are dealt with on the basis of summary judgment.

When trying to decide whether a particular order is final or interlocutory, it is a good idea to ask whether the order resolves all the outstanding issues between the parties or whether there are still issues to be litigated. The issue is not always cut and dried, and there are many cases in which the courts have been asked to determine whether a particular order is final or interlocutory in nature.

There are different routes through the court system for appeals of final orders and interlocutory orders. Therefore, determining whether a particular order is final or interlocutory is the first step in establishing the procedure to be followed on an appeal.

Right to Appeal

There is not always an automatic right to appeal an order of the court. In many instances, permission or **leave of the court** must be sought in order to commence an appeal. If the Rules require that leave must be granted before an appeal can be commenced, the party wishing to appeal must bring a motion to the court that is to hear the appeal, asking for permission or leave. If leave to appeal is required under any statute, leave to cross-appeal must also be sought. A cross-appeal would mean that both parties are appealing the order on different grounds. However, if there is a right to appeal, that is, of the court is not required, or leave to appeal has already been granted, the respondent wishing to cross-appeal need not seek leave and may just serve a notice of cross-appeal.

leave of the court
permission of the court to take a procedural step

Which Court Hears the Appeal?

After establishing whether the order is interlocutory or final, the next step is deciding which court has the jurisdiction to hear the appeal. There are three courts that can hear appeals:

1. the Ontario Superior Court of Justice,
2. the Divisional Court, and
3. the Court of Appeal.

To determine which court has jurisdiction in each particular appeal, you must look at the *Courts of Justice Act*. Section 17 of the Act provides that a judge of the Superior Court of Justice has jurisdiction to hear appeals from the following orders:

(a) an interlocutory order of a master or case management master;

(b) a certificate of assessment of costs issued in a proceeding in the Superior Court of Justice, on an issue in respect of which an objection was served under the rules of court.[1]

Section 19 of the *Courts of Justice Act* provides the types of orders that the Divisional Court may hear appeals from:

19(1) An appeal lies to the Divisional Court from,

(a) a final order of a judge of the Superior Court of Justice as described in subsections (1.1) and (1.2);[2]

(b) an interlocutory order of a judge of the Superior Court of Justice, with leave as provided in the rules of court;

(c) a final order of a master or case management master.

...

(1.2) If the notice of appeal is filed on or after October 1, 2007, clause (1)(a) applies in respect of a final order,

   (a) for a single payment of not more than $50,000, exclusive of costs;

   (b) for periodic payments that amount to not more than $50,000, exclusive of costs, in the 12 months commencing on the date the first payment is due under the order;

   (c) dismissing a claim for an amount that is not more than the amount set out in clause (a) or (b); or

   (d) dismissing a claim for an amount that is more than the amount set out in clause (a) or (b) and in respect of which the judge or jury indicates that if the claim had been allowed the amount awarded would have been not more than the amount set out in clause (a) or (b).

The Divisional Court, pursuant to s. 31 of the *Courts of Justice Act*, also has jurisdiction to hear appeals from Small Claims Court matters in which the amount of the claim exceeds the prescribed amount. The regulation sets the amount at $2,500, excluding costs.

Sections 6(1)(a) through (c) of the *Courts of Justice Act* provide that the Court of Appeal has jurisdiction to hear an appeal of the following orders:

6(1)(a) an order of the Divisional Court, on a question that is not a question of fact alone, with leave of the Court of Appeal as provided in the rules of court;

   (b) a final order of a judge of the Superior Court of Justice, except an order referred to in clause 19(1)(a) [an order that should be appealed to the Divisional Court] or an order from which an appeal lies to the Divisional Court under another Act;

   (c) a certificate of assessment of costs issued in a proceeding in the Court of Appeal, on an issue in respect of which an objection was served under the rules of court.[3]

In summary, a final order of a judge of the Superior Court of Justice may be appealed to the Divisional Court if the monetary value of the order is $50,000 or less. A final order for more than $50,000 from a judge of the Superior Court goes to the Court of Appeal. An interlocutory order of a master goes to the Superior Court of Justice on appeal, but a final order of a master goes to the Divisional Court. Table 20.1 sets out the various routes of appeal.

Appeal to the Divisional Court or the Court of Appeal

Rule 61 applies to appeals to the Divisional Court or the Court of Appeal, except for an appeal of a certificate of assessment of costs issued in a Court of Appeal proceeding. Rule 62 governs that type of appeal. In addition, on appeals to the Court of Appeal, the practice direction relating to those appeals must also be followed.

Section 20(1) of the *Courts of Justice Act* requires that an appeal to the Divisional Court be brought in the region where the proceeding is commenced unless the parties agree otherwise or the Chief Justice of the Superior Court orders otherwise.

Table 20.1 Appeal Routes

Nature of the Order Made	Court to Which the Appeal Goes
Final order of a judge of the Superior Court of Justice in an amount over $50,000 (exclusive of costs)	Court of Appeal
Final order of a judge of the Superior Court of Justice in an amount of $50,000 or less (exclusive of costs)	Divisional Court
Interlocutory order of a judge of the Superior Court of Justice (with leave)	Divisional Court
Final order of a master	Divisional Court
Interlocutory order of a master	Judge of the Superior Court of Justice
Certificate of assessment of costs issued in a proceeding in the Court of Appeal	Court of Appeal
Certificate of assessment of costs (where objection served) in a proceeding in the Superior Court of Justice for an amount of $50,000 or less	Superior Court of Justice
Certificate of assessment of costs (where objection served) in a proceeding in the Superior Court of Justice for an amount over $50,000	Court of Appeal
Small Claims Court order for an amount over $2,500	Divisional Court

Since there is only one Court of Appeal in Ontario, at Osgoode Hall in Toronto, an appeal to that court is commenced through the court office there.

Title of Proceeding on Appeals

In an appeal, the parties are identified as the appellant and the respondent. Rule 61.04(2) requires that the title of the proceeding be in accordance with Form 61B. This means that the plaintiff and defendant are still identified as such, and remain in the same order in the general heading as they were in the original proceeding, but for the appeal documents, under the words "Plaintiff" and "Defendant" in the general heading, the nature of the parties' roles in the appeal should be identified. For instance, if Abigail Boar is appealing, the word "Appellant" should appear under the word "Plaintiff" in the general heading. Rattle Motors Ltd. and Fred Flogem would still be identified as the defendants, but the word "Respondents" should appear under the word "Defendants." See Figure 20.3.

Motions for Leave to Appeal

There is not always a right to appeal a decision. Sometimes it is necessary to seek leave or permission from the appellate court to appeal a judgment of a lower court. The procedure on motions for leave to appeal to the Divisional Court is similar to the procedure on motions for leave to appeal to the Court of Appeal. Because there are some procedural differences, however, we will deal with these appeals separately.

Motion for Leave to Appeal to the Divisional Court: Rule 61.03

A motion for leave to appeal to the Divisional Court must be served within 15 days of the making of the order or the decision being appealed unless the matter is governed by a statute that provides a different time limit. If the court reserves a decision, the 15-day period starts to run on the day the decision is released.

The notice of motion, along with proof of service, must then be filed within 5 days of service in the office of the registrar of the Divisional Court in the region where the proceeding resulting in the appeal was commenced. A notice of motion for leave to appeal, which appears as Figure 20.1, is generally in the same format as a regular motion. (See Chapter 9 on motions.) However, in the portion of the form that requires a date, instead of including a date, you write "on a date to be fixed by the Registrar" (Rule 61.03(1)(a)).

In addition, the questions that the Divisional Court is being asked to answer, should leave be granted, must be included in the notice of motion.

On the motion for leave, you need a motion record. A motion record on an application for leave to appeal is similar to a regular motion record. The pages must be consecutively numbered, and the contents must be arranged in the following order:

1. a table of contents, describing each document, including each exhibit, by its nature and date and, in the case of an exhibit, by its exhibit number or letter;

2. a copy of the notice of motion;

3. a copy of the order or decision from which leave to appeal is sought as signed and entered;

4. a copy of the reasons of the court or tribunal from which leave to appeal is sought with a further typed or printed copy if the reasons are handwritten;

5. a copy of any order or decision that was the subject of the hearing before the court or tribunal from which leave to appeal is sought;

6. a copy of any reasons for the order or decision with a further typed or printed copy if the reasons are handwritten;

7. a copy of all affidavits and other material used before the court or tribunal from which leave to appeal is sought;

transcript
written record of proceedings transcribed word for word

8. a list containing each relevant **transcript** of evidence in chronological order, but not necessarily the transcripts themselves; and

9. a copy of any other material in the court file that is necessary for the hearing of the motion.

In addition to the motion record, the factum and the transcripts of the proceeding must be provided. A factum is a statement of the facts and the law on which the moving party is relying. Facts are determined by going through the transcripts of the trial and listing each fact, as found by the court at the trial.

Figure 20.1 Notice of Motion for Leave to Appeal

Court file no. 03-DC-5678

ONTARIO
SUPERIOR COURT OF JUSTICE
DIVISIONAL COURT

BETWEEN:

ABIGAIL BOAR

Plaintiff

and

RATTLE MOTORS LTD. and FRED FLOGEM

Defendants

NOTICE OF MOTION FOR LEAVE TO APPEAL

THE DEFENDANT Rattle Motors Ltd. will make a motion to the court on a date to be fixed by the Registrar.

PROPOSED METHOD OF HEARING: The motion is to be heard orally.

THE MOTION IS FOR leave to appeal the order of the Honourable Madam Justice Snork, made July 12, year 3.

THE GROUNDS FOR THE MOTION ARE:

1. Should leave to appeal be granted, the questions the court will be asked to address on the appeal are:
   a. Did the trial judge err in finding that the defendant Rattle owed a duty of care to the plaintiff?
   b. ...
2. *(List all further grounds for the motion.)*
3. ...

THE FOLLOWING DOCUMENTARY EVIDENCE will be used at the hearing of the motion:

1. The order of the Honourable Madam Justice Snork made July 12, year 3.
2. *(List the affidavits or other documentary evidence to be relied on in the motion.)*

Figure 20.1   Concluded

July 30, year 3

Huey Sue
LSUC #23456T
Barrister and Solicitor
65 False Trail
Toronto, Ontario, M6Y 1Z6

tel. 416-485-6891
fax 416-485-6892

Lawyer for the Defendants

TO: Just & Coping
Barristers and Solicitors
365 Bay Street – 8701
Toronto, Ontario, M3J 4A9

I.M. Just
LSUC #12345R
tel. 416-762-1342
fax 416-762-2300

Lawyers for the Plaintiff

The facts and law are to be set out in the document. They are to be presented in the form of a concise argument. For an overview of the contents of a factum on appeal, see the next section in this chapter, which deals with motions for leave to appeal to the Court of Appeal.

Three copies of the motion record, factum, and transcripts must be filed with the court, along with proof of service, within 30 days after filing of the notice of motion for leave. Three copies are required because the Divisional Court usually sits as a panel of three judges, but one judge alone may hear a motion for leave. In addition to the copies for the court, you will need copies for each of the other parties, as well as a copy for your own lawyer.

The responding party may file a motion record if he or she believes that the moving party's record is not complete. It must be filed with proof of service within 15 days after the responding party is served with the moving party's record. The responding party's motion record must have a table of contents, followed by any additional material that the respondent believes should be before the court on the motion for leave. Responding parties may also file a factum, and in most cases they do.

Once all the documents are filed, the registrar fixes a date for the hearing of the motion. The Divisional Court is made up of judges from the Superior Court of

Justice, but since the motion for leave cannot come before the same judge that made the order or judgment being appealed, the motion cannot be scheduled for any date that the judge will be sitting as a member of the Divisional Court.

Should the moving party be granted leave to appeal, the party must file a notice of appeal within seven days after leave to appeal has been granted.

One of the orders or judgments that cannot be appealed without leave is an order for costs. If only costs are being appealed, then a motion for leave must be brought in the usual way. But often costs are appealed along with another issue that does not require leave. An appeal that does not require leave of the court is called an **appeal as of right**. If the costs appeal or cross-appeal is brought along with an appeal as of right, or cross-appeal as of right, the leave to appeal costs is included in the notice of appeal as part of the relief sought. The motion for leave to appeal is then heard at the start of the appeal on the other issues and not on a separate date.

> **appeal as of right**
> appeal that a party has a legal right to bring and for which leave to appeal is not required

Motion for Leave to Appeal to the Court of Appeal: Rule 61.03.1

Rule 61.03.1 provides the procedure for bringing a motion for leave to appeal to the Court of Appeal. The rule must be read in conjunction with the practice direction that governs appeals to the Court of Appeal. In many ways, the procedure mirrors that of a similar motion to the Divisional Court, but there are some major differences prescribed by both the Rules and the practice direction.

Most motions in the Court of Appeal are heard by one judge of the court, but a motion for leave to appeal, a motion to quash an appeal, or any other motion specified in the Rules is heard by a panel of at least three judges of the court.

A motion for leave to appeal to the Court of Appeal is usually considered based on the appeal documents submitted without any of the parties or their counsel attending before the court. However, once all the necessary documents have been filed on the motion, the court may decide to order that the motion be heard orally. If that is the case, the registrar will fix a date for the hearing and advise the parties.

The Court of Appeal is now equipped to conduct motions and appeals by way of video conference. If parties wish to have a motion conducted by way of video conference, they should contact the registrar for the Court of Appeal at 416-326-1029 when a date has been set for the motion, or is about to be set, and make appropriate arrangements.

The notice of motion must state that the court will hear the motion in writing 36 days after service of the moving party's motion record, factum, and transcripts, or on the filing of the moving party's reply factum, whichever is earlier. Since the Court of Appeal has its own filing system, do not put the court file number of the lower court on the notice of appeal. The registrar's office will assign a new file number to the case.

The notice of motion must be served within 15 days after the date of the order or decision that the party wants to appeal. It must then be filed, along with proof of service, with the Court of Appeal within five days of service. A motion record, factum, and transcripts must also be served on the respondent and filed with the court along with proof of service.

Although the factum and transcripts for the motion may be filed in person at the court, the practice direction regarding appeals to the Court of Appeal encourages parties to file the factum and transcripts electronically by email. See the notice to the profession on the Court of Appeal website and the information that follows in this chapter regarding the formatting of electronically filed documents on appeals to the Court of Appeal.

Unlike the rule regarding motions for leave to appeal to the Divisional Court, Rule 61.03.1(4) spells out exactly what is to be put into a factum used on a motion for leave to appeal. It should contain the following sections:

1. Part I, which identifies the moving party, the order or decision they want to appeal, and the content of the order.

2. Part II, containing a concise statement of the facts with any references to the transcripts given by page and line.

3. Part III, outlining any specific questions that would be put to the Court of Appeal if the motion for leave is granted.

4. Part IV, containing a concise statement of each issue raised, immediately followed by a statement of the law and the citation for the authorities supporting that legal point.

5. Schedule A, containing a list of all the authorities used in part IV.

6. Schedule B, containing the text of all relevant provisions of statutes, regulations, and bylaws upon which the moving party will be relying.

All the paragraphs in the factum should be numbered consecutively from start to finish. This means that if the last paragraph in part I is number 5, the first paragraph in part II should be number 6.

As with all documents that are prepared for court, the presentation of a factum is important. You should use tabs if it will help make the document more accessible. You should always put tabs in for the schedules in all cases, even if you do not use them in any other part of the factum. If there are only a few authorities being used, you can put them right in the back of the factum. However, if there are a lot of authorities, prepare a separate book called a "book of authorities" and put all cases and any other authorities being relied upon in it.

There should be a list of the cases at the front of the book of authorities, and each case should be separated by a tab. Number all the pages in the book of authorities. The court must be provided with three copies, and the opposite parties should each be served with one. It is also necessary to prepare a book for the lawyer from your firm who is arguing the motion. Books of authorities may also be used on motions for leave to appeal to the Divisional Court, and they are always used on the appeal itself.

Three copies of the moving party's motion record, factum, transcripts, and book of authorities must be filed, with proof of service, within 30 days after the notice of motion has been filed. In addition to the filing of the hard copy of the factum and transcript, the practice direction requests that counsel also file an electronic copy of the factum or transcript. More details on the specifics of electronic filing are provided later in this chatper.

The responding party may serve a motion record as well, if it is his opinion that the moving party's motion record is incomplete. In any event, the responding party must file a factum organized as follows:

1. Part I, containing a statement of the facts that identifies those facts given by the moving party that he accepts and those with which he disagrees. In addition, the responding party must incorporate a summary of any facts that he believes the moving party has not included in her factum, along with reference to the evidence in the transcripts that supports these facts.

2. Part II, containing the responding party's position with respect to each issue raised by the moving party, immediately followed by a concise statement of the law and the citations for the authorities related to the issue in question.

3. Part III, containing a statement of any additional issues raised by the responding party, followed by a concise statement of the law on the issue and citations for the relevant authorities.

4. Schedule A, containing a list of the citations for the authorities referred to in the factum.

5. Schedule B, with photocopies of the portions of any relevant statutes, regulations, and bylaws upon which the responding party is relying.

The factum must be laid out in the same fashion as the moving party's factum, with all paragraphs numbered consecutively throughout the parts.

The three copies of the factum, any book of authorities, and the motion record of the respondent (if any), must be filed with the court, along with proof of service, within 25 days of the service of the moving party's factum and other documents. This means that you will need to prepare at least five copies of the documents, one for your lawyer, three for the court, and at least one for the opposite party. Of course, if there is more than one opposite party, you must prepare a separate set of documents for service on each of them. In addition, the responding party must also file an electronic copy of his or her factum with the court.

In the event that the responding party has raised some new issue that is not addressed by the moving party in his factum, the moving party is entitled to serve and file a reply factum, including an electronic copy, within 10 days after service of the responding party's factum.

As with a motion in Divisional Court for leave to appeal costs, which is joined to another issue that can be appealed as of right, the request for leave to appeal must be included in the notice of appeal as part of the relief sought. The panel of the Court of Appeal that hears the appeal as of right decides whether or not to grant leave on the costs appeal.

Practice Direction Requirements for Motions to the Court of Appeal

First, the practice direction requires that all parties include their telephone number, fax number, email address, and, in the case of counsel, Law Society number on the documents filed with the court.

The registrar will not set a date on a motion for leave to appeal until the moving party has filed the motion record, factum, and transcript (if any). All motions before a panel of judges, such as a motion for leave to appeal, will be limited to 15 minutes for the moving party, 10 minutes for the responding party, and 5 minutes for reply. If the motion is expected to take more time than this, a special request must be made to the List Judge. This can be arranged through the Appeal Scheduling Unit by fax at 416-327-6256.

Once the hearing date is set, the moving party must attempt to confer with the responding party and then, not later than 2 p.m., two days before the hearing, give the registrar of the Court of Appeal a confirmation of motion in Form 37B. The confirmation can be sent by fax to 416-327-5032. If the confirmation is not given, the motion will not be heard unless the court orders otherwise. If there are any changes to the confirmation once it has been given to the registrar, the moving party must send a corrected copy of the confirmation.

Commencement of Appeals: Rule 61.04

The document that commences an appeal is a notice of appeal to an appellate court in Form 61A, which is set out in Figure 20.2. If leave to appeal is sought and granted, the moving party has 7 days to file the notice of appeal after leave is granted. On an appeal as of right, the notice of appeal must be served on every party whose interest may be affected and on every person entitled by statute to be heard within 30 days of the granting of the order or decision that is being appealed. The only exception to the 30-day rule comes into play if a statute or the Rules prescribe another time limit for filing of the notice.

As with all court documents, there is no need to serve the notice of appeal on a party to an action who has been noted in default or a respondent in an application who has failed to file a notice of appearance unless that respondent was given permission by the court to participate in the hearing in which the order being appealed was made.

The notice of appeal must set out the relief sought by the appellant, the grounds for the appeal, and the basis for the appellate court's jurisdiction. In some cases, the notice of appeal is filed to protect the party's right to appeal. After the transcripts have been ordered, the appellant may wish to make some changes to the grounds or the relief sought. The notice of appeal may be amended without leave of the court at any time before the appeal is perfected. **Perfecting an appeal** means completing the procedural steps to ensure that the appeal is ready to be heard by the court. Perfecting an appeal is discussed in more detail later in this chapter.

In order to amend the notice of appeal, the appellant must serve a supplementary notice of appeal in Form 61F and file it with the registrar, along with proof of service.

perfecting an appeal
taking all the necessary procedural steps to ensure that an appeal is ready to be heard

Figure 20.2 Notice of Appeal to an Appellate Court (Form 61A)

Court file no. 03-CA-1234

COURT OF APPEAL FOR ONTARIO

BETWEEN:

ABIGAIL BOAR

Plaintiff
(Appellant)

and

RATTLE MOTORS LTD. and FRED FLOGEM

Defendants
(Respondents)

NOTICE OF APPEAL

THE PLAINTIFF APPEALS to the Court of Appeal from the judgment of the Honourable Justice Snork, dated July 12, year 3, made at Toronto.

THE APPELLANT ASKS that the judgment be set aside and judgment be granted as follows:

1. the respondent Rattle Motors Ltd. be found jointly and severally liable for the appellant's injuries along with the respondent Fred Flogem;

2. damages be awarded to the appellant in the full amount of her claim; and

3. the appellant be awarded costs of this appeal.

THE GROUNDS OF APPEAL are as follows:

1. the learned trial judge erred in finding that the defendant Rattle Motors Ltd. did not owe a duty of care to the plaintiff;

2. the learned trial judge erred in finding that the defendant did not breach the standard of care owed to the plaintiff; and

3. such further and other grounds as counsel may advise and this court permit.

THE BASIS OF THE APPELLATE COURT'S JURISDICTION IS:

1. the appellant relies on s. 6(1)(b) of the *Courts of Justice Act*;

2. the order appealed from is a final order of a judge of the Superior Court of Justice for an amount of damage exceeding $50,000; and

3. no leave to appeal is necessary.

Figure 20.2   Concluded

July 30, year 3

Just & Coping
Barristers and Solicitors
365 Bay Street – 8701
Toronto, Ontario, M3J 4A9

I.M. Just
LSUC #12345R
tel. 416-762-1342
fax 416-762-2300
email imjust@isp.on.ca

Lawyers for the Appellant

TO: Huey Sue
LSUC #23456T
Barrister and Solicitor
65 False Trail
Toronto, Ontario, M6Y 1Z6

tel. 416-485-6891
fax 416-485-6892

Lawyer for the Respondents

Figure 20.3   General Heading for Appeal (Form 61B)

Court file no. 03-CA-1234

COURT OF APPEAL FOR ONTARIO

BETWEEN:

ABIGAIL BOAR

Plaintiff
(Appellant)

and

RATTLE MOTORS LTD. and FRED FLOGEM

Defendants
(Respondents)

The appellant must obtain leave of the court to rely on grounds or seek relief not specified in the original or supplementary notice of appeal.

The precedent for the general heading on an appeal is in Form 61B. The court file number on the appeal is not the same as the file number in the lower court. The Divisional Court and the Court of Appeal both have their own filing systems and will issue their own file numbers. Therefore, initially leave the court file number blank when you prepare the notice of appeal, unless you have previously brought a motion for leave to appeal and have been given a file number by the court. The file number will be given to you by the court office.

Along with the notice of appeal, the appellant must also serve a certificate in which he or she sets out the portion of the evidence that he or she believes to be required for the appeal. The precedent for this document is Form 61C. Within 15 days of service of the appellant's certificate, the respondent must serve a responding certificate on the appellant in which he or she either confirms the appellant's certificate or sets out any additions or deletions that he or she wants to make. If the respondent fails to serve and file a certificate within the required time, the respondent is deemed to have accepted the appellant's certificate.

Instead of complying with the Rules about the certificate of evidence, the parties may choose to consult each other and come to an agreement respecting the evidence to be used on the appeal and included in the appeal book and compendium. If they choose this option, within 30 days of service of the notice of appeal they must make a decision about which documents and portions of the transcripts will be needed for the court on the appeal. If the appellant has already placed an order for portions of the transcript that both parties agree will not be needed, the appellant may provide the court reporter with an amended order for the transcripts.

The purpose of the certificate of evidence or the agreement respecting the evidence is to cut down on the amount of documentation that the Court of Appeal must deal with. Not all of the evidence given at a trial is required on the appeal because much of it covers issues that are not being appealed. These two procedures ensure that only the necessary evidence is filed with the court and that only one copy of each document is filed. Without the rule, both parties might file all the transcripts and copies of identical documents.

During a trial, a court reporter or a recording device takes down every word said in the courtroom. The written version of a trial is called a transcript. The appellant must order the transcript of the trial within 30 days of filing the notice of appeal and must file proof that he or she has ordered them. However, the appellant need only order copies of the transcript of the evidence that the parties have agreed should be admitted on the appeal. It is important to keep the quantity of transcript to a minimum because transcripts are expensive and take a great deal of time to read. If the respondent has not agreed to the appellant's certificate of evidence and has required unnecessary additional parts of the transcript to be prepared, the court may impose costs against the respondent.

In any event, the transcript must not include:

- any challenge of the jury;
- the opening address of the judge;

- the opening and closing addresses of counsel;
- any part of the proceeding that took place in the absence of the jury, except an objection to the charge to the jury by the judge; or
- any objections to the admissibility of evidence, but the ruling of the judge on the objection is to be included.[4]

The court reporter should be aware of these automatic exclusions and not include them unless there is a court order requiring a normally excluded part of the transcript to be included. Therefore, if there is an order for inclusion, you should provide the court reporter with a copy when you order the transcript or as soon as possible after the order is made.

Transcripts are ordered through the court reporter who recorded the oral proceedings in the court of first instance. If more than one reporter was involved in recording the proceeding, transcripts may be ordered through the coordinator for reporters. The reporter will provide a confirmation to you and to the court that the transcripts have been ordered. You must order five copies for the court, a copy for yourself, and one for each of the other parties. Transcripts being prepared for the Court of Appeal are expected to be completed within 90 days of being ordered. If they are not, the court will look into the delay to see whether preparation can be facilitated. Once the transcripts are ready, the reporter will notify all the parties and the registrar in writing.

Where it appears that the appeal is frivolous and vexatious, and the appellant does not have sufficient assets to pay costs, or if an order for security for costs could be made under Rule 56.01, or for any other good reason, the respondent may bring a motion asking that the appellant be required to provide security for costs and the court may order the appellant to do so. If the appellant fails to comply with the order for security, the court may dismiss the appeal.

Court reporters have been instructed that once a transcript has been ordered for an appeal in the Court of Appeal, they may not suspend completion of the transcript on the request of a party. A court order is required to suspend completion except in legal aid cases.

On some appeals to the Court of Appeal, the parties do not have a different version of the facts. Instead, they are appealing the manner in which the trial judge applied the law to these facts. If there is no dispute as to the facts, the parties may file an agreed statement of facts rather than a transcript. This saves money and time in bringing the appeal before the court.

Cross-Appeals: Rule 61.07

In some cases, the respondent may also want to appeal the same judgment that the appellant is setting out to overturn, or the respondent may be satisfied with that judgment but wish to seek different or additional relief in the event that the appellant is successful on the appeal. The respondent's appeal is a cross-appeal. A respondent wishing to cross-appeal must, within 15 days after service of the notice of appeal, serve a notice of cross-appeal on all parties whose interests may be affected or who are entitled to be heard.

No leave to appeal is required on a cross-appeal if there is an appeal as of right or if leave to appeal has already been granted. If the respondent requires leave to bring the cross-appeal, he or she may bring a motion for leave pursuant to the same rules that the appellant would rely on in seeking leave: Rule 61.03(8) if the appeal is to the Divisional Court, and Rule 61.03.1(18) if it is to the Court of Appeal.

A notice of cross-appeal is in Form 61E. It must state the relief sought and the grounds for the cross-appeal and must be filed, along with proof of service, in the office of the registrar within 10 days of service. If the respondent does not deliver a cross-appeal, no cross-appeal may be heard, except with leave of the court.

Perfecting an Appeal: Rule 61.09

Perfecting an appeal means to complete all the necessary legal steps that ensure the appeal is ready to be heard by the court. There are different time limits for perfecting an appeal, depending on whether or not transcripts need to be ordered. If the appeal does not require transcripts, it must be perfected within 30 days after the notice of appeal was filed. If transcripts are required, the appeal must be perfected within 60 days of the court reporter's giving notice that the transcripts are available.

In addition to the oral evidence set out in the transcripts, the appellant or cross-appellant may require for the appeal any or all of the exhibits presented in the court of first instance. To obtain these exhibits for the appeal, the party must bring a motion before a judge of the appellate court seeking an order that they be sent to the registrar of the court hearing the appeal.

In order to perfect the appeal, the appellant must

61.09(3)(a) serve on every other party to the appeal and any other person entitled ... to be heard on the appeal,

(i) the appeal book ... referred to in Rule 61.10,

(ii) the exhibit book [if any] referred to in Rule 61.10.1,

(iii) a typed or printed copy of the transcript of evidence,

(iv) an electronic version of the transcript of evidence, unless the court reporter did not prepare an electronic version, and

(v) a typed or printed copy of the appellant's factum referred to in Rule 61.11;

(b) file with the Registrar, with proof of service,

(i) three copies of the appeal book ... and where the appeal is to be heard by five judges, two additional copies,

(ii) one copy of the exhibit book,

(iii) a typed or printed copy of the transcript of evidence,

(iv) an electronic version of the transcript of evidence, unless the court reporter did not prepare an electronic version,

(v) three typed or printed copies of the appellant's factum, and where the appeal is to be heard by five judges, two additional copies, and

(vi) an electronic version of the appellant's factum; and

    (c) file with the Registrar a certificate of perfection,

        (i) stating that the appeal book and compendium, exhibit book, transcripts, if any, and appellant's factum have been filed, and

        (ii) setting out, with respect to every party to the appeal and any person entitled ... to be heard on the appeal,

            (A) the name, address and telephone number of the party's or other person's lawyer, or

            (B) the name, address for service and telephone number of the party or other person, if acting in person.

Preparation of all the documentation on an appeal may cost a great deal and take a long time to prepare. Where compliance with the Rules for perfecting an appeal would cause undue expense or delay, on motion a judge of the appellate court may make an order giving special instructions and direction.

When all of the above steps have been taken, the appeal is perfected. Once it has been perfected, the registrar sends both counsel a notice of listing for hearing in Form 61G. This notice does not contain the date set for the appeal. Counsel are notified of the date at a later point.

Appeal Book and Compendium: Rule 61.10

Rule 61.10 sets out in detail the required content and organization of the appeal book and compendium. The registrar may refuse to accept any appeal book and compendium that does not comply with the Rules or is not legible. The appeal book must contain, in consecutively numbered pages arranged in the following order:

1. a table of contents describing each document by its nature and date;

2. a copy of the notice of appeal and any notice of cross-appeal or supplementary notice of appeal or cross-appeal;

3. a copy of the order or decision appealed from, as signed and entered;

4. a copy of the reasons of the court or tribunal appealed from with a further typed or printed copy if the reasons are handwritten;

5. a copy of any earlier order or decision that was the subject of the hearing before the court or tribunal appealed from, as signed and entered, and a copy of any reasons for it, with a further typed or printed copy if the reasons are handwritten;

6. a copy of the pleadings or notice of application or any other document that initiated the proceeding or defines the issues in it;

7. a copy of any excerpts from a transcript of the evidence referred to in the appellant's factum;

8. a copy of any exhibits that are referred to in the appellant's factum;

9. a copy of any other documents relevant to the appeal that are referred to in the appellant's factum;

10. a copy of the certificates of agreements respecting evidence referred to in Rule 61.05;

11. a copy of any order made in respect to the conduct of the appeal; and

12. a certificate (Form 61H) signed by the appellant's lawyer, or on the lawyer's behalf by someone he or she has specifically authorized, stating that the contents of the appeal book and compendium are complete and legible.

In addition to the requirements in Rule 61.10, the practice direction also stipulates that the appeal book and compendium for the Court of Appeal be indexed in such a way that the court can easily locate documents referred to in the appellant's factum. For example, number 7 above requires that if the appellant has referred to an excerpt from a transcript, copies of the excerpts must be included in the appeal book and compendium. This means that each excerpt included should indicate the tab number (if tabs are used in the factum), page number, and line number where the reference to the excerpt is made in the factum. Sample wording might be: "This is the excerpt from the transcript of evidence referred to at tab 3, page 7, line 35 of the appellant's factum." If no tabs were used in the factum, then reference would only be made to the page and line numbers; the judge and lawyers would then have to flip through pages of material to find the reference instead of just opening the tab.

If the evidence in the court of first instance is presented, in whole or in part, by affidavit, then relevant extracts and exhibits from the affidavit must also be included in the compendium. Do not include the entire affidavit or all of the exhibits unless they are relevant to the appeal. It is important to remember that the appeal book and compendium is an important working document for the members of the court in preparing for and conducting the appeal. It is essential that it be as easy to read and accessible as possible, and not cluttered up or made unwieldy by the inclusion of material that is not needed for the appeal. The respondent must also serve and file a compendium indexed in the same manner as the appellant's to make it easy to locate documents referred to in the respondent's factum.

Although the practice direction applies only to the Court of Appeal and not to the Divisional Court, it would be a good idea to prepare your materials for both courts with the practice direction in mind.

Appellant's Factum: Rule 61.11

An appellant's factum, which is set out in Figure 20.4, is laid out in essentially the same form as the factum on a motion for leave to appeal, described earlier in this chapter. However, in addition to the four parts and the two schedules required on motions for leave to appeal, the factum for the appeal must contain a fifth part, stating the precise order that the appellate court will be asked to make, including any order for costs. The factum must also be signed by the appellant's lawyer or someone the lawyer has specifically authorized to sign in his or her place. In addition, the factum must contain a certificate that states

- that an order requiring the forwarding of the original record and exhibits has been obtained or is not needed, and

- how long the party will require for his or her oral argument on the appeal to the closest quarter hour.

Figure 20.4 Appellant's Factum

COURT OF APPEAL FOR ONTARIO

BETWEEN:

ABIGAIL BOAR

Plaintiff
(Appellant)

and

RATTLE MOTORS LTD. and FRED FLOGEM

Defendants
(Respondents)

APPELLANT'S FACTUM

Just & Coping
Barristers and Solicitors
365 Bay Street – 8701
Toronto, Ontario M3J 4A9

I.M. Just
LSUC #12345R
tel. 416-762-1342
fax 416-762-2300
email imjust@isp.on.ca

Lawyers for the Appellant

TO: Huey Sue
LSUC #23456T
Barrister and Solicitor
65 False Trail
Toronto, Ontario, M6Y 1Z6

tel. 416-485-6891
fax 416-485-6892

Lawyer for the Respondents

Part I: Statement identifying the appellant, the court appealed from, and the judgment appealed from

1. The appellant, Abigail Boar, is the plaintiff in a negligence action brought in the Superior Court of Justice. She appeals from the judgment of the Honourable Justice Snork, dated October 15, 2008, wherein the learned trial judge dismissed the plaintiff's action and awarded costs to the defendants, Fred Flogem and Rattle Motors Ltd., in the amount of $72,000.00.

Figure 20.4   Continued

Part II: Overview statement describing the nature of the case and the issues on appeal

2.   The plaintiff brought an action in negligence in the Superior Court of Justice against the defendants after she was injured in a slip and fall at the place of business of the corporate defendant, Rattle Motors Ltd., a motor vehicle dealership. At the time of the injury, the plaintiff was a customer of Rattle Motors Ltd. and was being escorted through the property by the defendant Fred Flogem, an employee of Rattle Motors Ltd.

3.   The plaintiff alleges
     a. that the defendants owed a duty of care to the plaintiff as a customer at their place of business,
     b. that they breached the required standard of care by failing to safely maintain the property, and by failing to warn the plaintiff of a known dangerous condition, and
     c. that the injuries suffered by the plaintiff were reasonably foreseeable given the state of repair and the failure of the defendants to warn the plaintiff.

4.   The plaintiff says that the learned trial judge erred in
     a. finding that the defendants did not owe a duty of care to the plaintiff, and
     b. finding that the defendants did not breach the standard of care owed to the plaintiff in the maintenance of their property.

Part III: Statement of the facts relevant to the appeal

5.   On September 14, 2006, the appellant, while a customer at Rattle Motors Ltd., slipped and fell on a patch of oil leaking from a vehicle in the showroom.

6.   The respondent, Rattle Motors Ltd., is a corporation in the business of selling automobiles to the public.

7.   The respondent, Fred Flogem, is an employee of the respondent corporation, Rattle Motors Ltd.

8.   … [etc.]

Part IV: Statement of each issue raised

9.   The two issues on this appeal are:
     a. Did the learned trial judge err in finding that the defendants did not owe a duty of care to the plaintiff?
     b. Did the learned trial judge err in finding that the defendants did not breach the standard of care owed to the plaintiff in the maintenance of their property?

Issue 1: Did the trial judge err in finding that the defendants did not owe a duty of care to the plaintiff?

10.   It is respectfully submitted that the appellant was a customer at the respondent Rattle Motors Ltd.'s place of business and as such was owed a duty of care by the respondent. *M'Alister (or Donoghue) v. Stevenson*, [1932] AC 562 (HL).
Hercules Managements Ltd. v. Ernst & Young, [1997] 2 SCR 165.

Figure 20.4   Concluded

Issue 2: Did the learned trial judge err in finding that the defendants did not breach the standard of care owed to the plaintiff in the maintenance of their property?

11.   It is further respectfully submitted that the respondent Rattle Motors Ltd. breached the standard of care when its employee, Fred Flogem, dimmed the lights in the automobile showroom to hide the spillage of oil underneath one of the vehicles. *LeBlanc v. Marson Canada Inc.* (1995), 139 NSR (2d) 309 at 312 (CA).

12.   It is further respectfully submitted … [etc.]

Part V: Order requested

14.   It is therefore respectfully submitted that the appeal should be allowed, with costs, and that

   a.   the respondent Rattle Motors Ltd. be found jointly and severally liable with the respondent Fred Flogem,

   b.   the appellant be awarded the full amount of her claim,

   c.   the appellant be awarded costs of this appeal and the trial below,

   d.   such further relief as counsel may advise and this honourable court deem just.

ALL OF WHICH IS RESPECTULLY SUBMITTED.

Date March 12, year 3   _I.M. Just_

                                          I.M. Just
                                          Lawyer for the Appellant

LAWYER'S CERTIFICATE

I, I.M. Just, lawyer for the appellent, CERTIFY that:

1.   The record and original exhibits from the court or tribunal from which the appeal is taken are not required.

2.   The estimated time for my oral argument is 3 hours, not including reply.

March 12, year 3   I.M. Just
                                          LSUC #12345R

                                          Just & Coping, Barristers and Solicitors
                                          365 Bay Street – 8701
                                          Toronto, Ontario, M3J 4A9
                                          tel. 416-762-1342   fax 416-762-2300

                                          Lawyers for the Appellant

[*You must also include two schedules:*
• *Schedule A, containing a list of the authorities referred to, and*
• *Schedule B, containing a list of all relevant provisions of statutes, regulations, and bylaws, followed by the text of those provisions.*]

Remember, the factum, the appeal book and compendium, and the exhibit book must all be cross-referenced so that the court may easily locate the various documents referred to. In the factum, when references are made to the transcript, it must be done by tab, page number, and line number in the appeal book and compendium. References to exhibits must be by page number in the exhibit book and by tab and page number in the appeal book and compendium.

The practice direction for the Court of Appeal requires that a motion be brought to the chambers judge for leave to file a factum that is more than 30 pages long. The proposed factum must be included in the motion record.

Respondent's Factum and Compendium: Rule 61.12

The respondent must prepare, serve, and file the requisite copies of a factum and compendium as well. It must be delivered within 60 days after the service of the appeal book and compendium, transcripts, exhibit book, if any, and appellant's factum. In addition to the hard copies that must be delivered, the respondent must also file an electronic version of the factum with the court within that time period. The factum must be signed by the respondent's lawyer or someone specifically authorized by the lawyer to sign the document in his or her place. It is laid out in the same general manner as other factums,[5] and it must also contain a certificate that states

- that an order requiring the forwarding of the original record and exhibits has been obtained or is not needed, and
- how long the party will require for his or her oral argument on the appeal to the closest quarter hour.

A respondent who is cross-appealing must deliver an appellant's factum in the cross-appeal. It can be a separate factum from the respondent's factum or can be incorporated into the respondent's factum, and it must be delivered within the allowable times for delivery of the respondent's factum.

The appellant on the main appeal, who is also the respondent on the cross-appeal, may file a respondent's factum on the cross-appeal within 10 days after service of the respondent's factum.

Restrictions on the Length of Factums

The Rules require that the factum contain a "concise" summary of the facts and the applicable law. Although there is no limit on the length of a factum in the Rules, a practice direction of the Court of Appeal states that factums usually should be no more than 30 pages unless the case is exceptional. A lawyer who believes that the case is exceptional and that the factum will exceed 30 pages must bring a motion seeking leave to file a longer factum from a judge of the Court of Appeal.

Exhibit Book: Rule 61.10.1

This book is a collection of the documentary evidence, filed as exhibits, in the trial that the parties intend to rely on in the appeal. The parties can agree that certain exhibits from the trial may be omitted; however, unless both parties consent to the omission, the exhibit must be included.

The exhibit book is to be bound and laid out in consecutively numbered pages. There is to be a table of contents describing each exhibit by its nature, date, and exhibit number or letter. A copy of each exhibit must follow. The exhibits can be arranged in order of their date, or they can be arranged in groups, with similar documents sharing common characteristics grouped together. Do not arrange the exhibits by their trial exhibit numbers.

Book of Authorities

Although there is no specific requirement for a book of authorities in the Rules, it is helpful to both the court and the lawyers to prepare bound books containing copies of all the case law that a party will rely on in the appeal. The practice direction, which can be found on the court's website, provides guidelines for preparing these books. They should:

- include only the cases that have been referred to in the factum—passages that are specifically referred to should be highlighted;
- indicate whether the appellant or the respondent filed them (lawyers for the parties should consult each other beforehand to ensure that they are not filing duplicate copies of cases)—a joint case book is acceptable if the parties can agree on what is to be included in it;
- have a tab for each case with either a number or a letter on the tab;
- have an index of the cases and indicate the number or letter of the tab where the case can be found;
- have consecutively numbered pages unless the actual page number of each case is clear on the photocopy; and
- be filed, if possible, with the factum, but if this is not possible, then not later than the Monday of the week preceding the hearing of the appeal so that the judges on the panel have an opportunity to read them before the appeal.

Copies of case law in a book of authorities may be either photocopies from law reports or cases obtained from Internet legal reporting services or other electronic databases, but if an Internet or electronic database is used, the case must have the same paragraph numbers as the judgment released by the court. The citation from the law report should be given as well as the electronic citation, and the date the copy was obtained from the Internet or electronic source should be included. It is important to ensure that the copy submitted to the court is the most current one available from the electronic source.

You must prepare three or five copies of the book of authorities to be filed with the court, depending on how many judges will be sitting on the panel. There must also be a copy for the lawyer for each of the parties.

Dismissal for Delay: Rule 61.13

A notice of appeal must be filed within a specifically limited time period after the order being appealed has been made. Sometimes a lawyer for a party files the notice to protect the party's right to appeal, but the party may decide not to proceed. In other cases, a party may file a notice of appeal as a tactical matter in order to create a delay; for example, the party might not order the transcript as required and may delay in perfecting the appeal.

In such instances, either the respondent or the registrar may take procedural steps to dismiss the appeal for delay. The respondent may make a motion to the registrar to dismiss the appeal with 10 days' notice to the appellant.

However, the registrar does not need to wait for the respondent to take action. Where the appellant has not

- filed a transcript within 60 days after the court reporter has provided written notice that it is ready,
- perfected the appeal within one year of filing the notice of appeal, or
- perfected the appeal within 30 days of filing the notice of appeal where no transcript is needed for the appeal,

the registrar may serve notice on the appellant to correct the default within 10 days, or the appeal will be dismissed.

Within the 10 days following the service of the respondent's motion or the registrar's notice, the appellant must perfect the appeal and order the transcript or obtain an order from the court providing him or her with an extension of time in which to take these steps. If the appellant does nothing, the registrar will dismiss the appeal for delay and award costs to the respondent fixed in the amount of $750 and serve the order on the respondent.

It is not only the appellant who must act in a timely fashion on the appeal. If the respondent has brought a cross-appeal and has not delivered a factum on the cross-appeal within 60 days after he or she has been served with the appeal book and compendium, the appellant may make a motion on 5 days' notice to the respondent to have the cross-appeal dismissed for delay. The respondent has 5 days in which to file the factum or obtain an order for an extension of time. If the respondent does neither, the registrar will dismiss the cross-appeal with costs fixed at $750.

Similar consequences apply to a party who does not act in a timely fashion on a motion seeking leave to appeal. If the moving party has not served and filed a motion record and other documents within 60 days of filing the notice of motion, the registrar may give notice to the moving party to file the record and documents within 10 days. If the defect has not been cured within 10 days, the registrar will dismiss the motion for leave with costs fixed at $750.

The responding party on the motion for leave need not wait the 60 days for the registrar to take action. If the motion record and other documentation has not been filed within 30 days of the notice of motion being filed, the responding party may bring a motion, on 10 days' notice, to dismiss the motion for leave (Rules 61.03(2) and 61.03.1(4) to (6)). Once again, the appellant has 10 days to correct the defect or obtain an order for an extension of time. If he or she does neither, the registrar will dismiss the motion for leave to appeal with costs fixed at $750.

Abandoned Appeals: Rules 61.14 and 61.15

After filing the notice of appeal, if the appellant decides to not continue with it, the proper thing to do is to file a notice of abandonment in Form 61K. A party who serves a notice of appeal but does not file it with the court within 10 days of service is deemed to have abandoned the appeal. A party who abandons an appeal or a cross-appeal may be liable for costs to the opposite party or parties.

If the main appeal has been dismissed for delay or abandoned, and a cross-appeal has been commenced, the respondent on the main appeal must deliver a notice of election to proceed with the cross-appeal in Form 61L or bring a motion to the court for directions. Otherwise, the cross-appeal will be deemed to be abandoned without costs.

Motions in Appellate Court: Rule 61.16

In the event that a party finds it necessary to bring a motion relating to the appeal to the appellate court, parts of Rule 37,[6] the general rule for motions, and Rule 61.16 govern. The two rules must be read together.

There are a number of different types of motions that may be made in an appeal. Some of the motions are heard by only one judge of the appellate court. Others are heard by a panel of judges.[7] Motions in appellate courts are commenced in the same manner as other motions—that is, with a notice of motion. The notice of motion for an appellate court must, however, include a certificate stating how long the party estimates the motion will take. The notice of motion must be served and filed at least seven days in advance of the motion being heard.

If a motion is to be heard by more than one judge, the notice of motion should not set a date but should rather state that the motion is to be heard on a date to be fixed by the registrar. The registrar then arranges for a date when a panel of judges is sitting and notifies the parties. A motion record must also be served and filed along with a factum. The moving party must file three copies of the motion record, along with proof of service, with the court within 30 days of the filing of the notice of motion. If the respondent believes that the appellant's motion record is incomplete, he or she may also file a motion record and factum, along with proof of service, with the court within 25 days of service of the moving party's motion record.

In addition to Rule 61.16, there is a practice direction that pertains to motions in the Court of Appeal. This practice direction provides specific, additional requirements to the rule, depending on whether the motion is being brought before a single judge or a panel of judges. Both the rule and the practice direction must be followed for motions in this court.

Appeals from Interlocutory Orders and Other Non-Appellate Court Appeals

Rule 62 deals with the procedure on appeals of interlocutory orders. The procedure is different from the appeals of a final order, which we discussed above. Appeals of this type of order lie either with a judge of the Superior Court of Justice or with the Divisional Court.

If the order being appealed is an interlocutory order of a master, a certificate of assessment of costs, or an appeal under any statute that does not specifically require another procedure for appeal, then the appeal will proceed to a single judge of the Superior Court of Justice. Unlike an appeal of a final order, it will not proceed to an **appellate court**. Interlocutory orders that fall within any of these three categories may be appealed without leave.

If the order being appealed is an interlocutory order of a judge of the Superior Court of Justice, the appeal must be heard by the Divisional Court unless it is to be heard in Toronto, where it will be heard by a judge of the Divisional Court who is sitting as a judge of the Superior Court of Justice. However, there is no automatic right to appeal an interlocutory order of a judge. A party that wants to appeal this type of order must bring a motion seeking leave to the Divisional Court. Since Divisional Court judges are the same as those who sit in the Superior Court of Justice, the judge hearing the motion for leave must be different from the judge who made the order being appealed.

As mentioned above, the procedure on these appeals is different from the procedure on appeals of final orders, which we looked at earlier under Rule 61. Rule 62.01 deals with the procedure on the appeal of interlocutory orders that do not require leave. Rule 62.02 sets out the procedure on seeking leave for appeal, when leave is required on an interlocutory order.

appellate court
the Court of Appeal or the Divisional Court

Commencement of the Appeal When No Leave Is Required

If the appeal does not require leave, it is commenced by serving and filing a notice of appeal on all parties whose interests may be affected by the appeal. The prescribed form is Form 62A. The notice of appeal must be served within seven days of the making of the order being appealed. The notice must then be filed with the court, along with proof of service, no later than seven days before the appeal is to be heard.

The notice of appeal must set out the relief sought and the grounds of the appeal. The grounds must be specific and only those grounds stated in the notice may be relied on at the hearing unless the presiding judge orders otherwise. Therefore, the grounds must be carefully drafted and be as comprehensive as possible.

Rule 37.03 governs the place of hearing of motions. The appeal must be commenced in the same place where the original proceeding was commenced.

Material for Use on the Motion

The appellant must prepare, serve, and file both an appeal record and a factum. These must be filed in the court office, along with proof of service, at least four days before the hearing of the appeal.

Rule 62.01(7) sets out the required contents of an appeal record. It must contain, in consecutively numbered pages,

- a table of contents that describes each document, including each exhibit, by its nature, date, and exhibit number or letter, if there is one;

- a copy of the notice of appeal;

- a copy of the signed and entered order or certificate of costs appealed from, along with a copy of any reasons for judgment relating to the order or certificate; and

- any other material used at the hearing at which the order being appealed was made that is necessary for the hearing of the appeal.

The contents of the appeal record must be set out exactly in the order listed above. The appeal record must also have a light blue backsheet, not the buff-coloured back cover required for appeals to appellate courts.

The title of proceedings does not change for this type of appeal, except that the appellant and respondent must be identified by placing "(Appellant)" and "(Respondent)" below the words "Plaintiff" and "Defendant," as appropriate. If there is more than one defendant and the appeal does not involve all of them, the names of those involved must be underlined in the title of proceedings.

The respondent must also prepare a factum and any other material that was before the judge who made the order being appealed, which is necessary for the hearing of the appeal and which has not been provided by the appellant in his or her appeal record. The factum and the additional material must be served and filed with the court at least two days before the hearing of the appeal.

The judge hearing the appeal may dispense with the requirements of the parties to file any or all of this material.

If the appellant commences the appeal by serving and filing the notice of appeal and then decides not to proceed with it, he or she should serve and file a notice of abandonment. If the appellant does not file the necessary documentation on the appeal at least three days before the hearing date, he or she will be deemed to have abandoned the appeal.

Motions for Leave to Appeal

If the order being appealed is an interlocutory order of a judge of the Superior Court of Justice, leave is required to bring the appeal and the prospective appellant must serve a notice of motion for leave within seven days after the order to be appealed was made. Rule 62.02 sets out the procedure on the motion for leave to appeal.

It is usually quite difficult to obtain leave to appeal. Leave will not be granted unless one of the tests in Rule 62.02(4) is met.

In preparing a motion record for leave to appeal, it is not necessary to reproduce an entirely new motion record. Remember that what is being appealed here is likely an order made on a motion. The original motion record may be requisitioned for the motion for leave. A supplementary motion record should then be prepared, and it should contain the notice of appeal, a copy of the order being appealed, and any reasons given by the judge for making the order.

Both parties must serve and file factums on the motion. The moving party's factum must be served and filed with proof of service at least seven days before the hearing. The responding party must file his or her factum, along with proof of service, at least four days before the hearing. The factums are to be filed in the office of the court that is hearing the motion.

If the motion is successful and leave to appeal is granted, the moving party, who now becomes the appellant, must serve and file a notice of appeal as required by Rule 61.04, along with the appellant's certificate of evidence required by Rule 61.05(1). This must be done within seven days after the order granting leave to appeal is made (Rule 62.02(8)).

Stays Pending Appeal: Rule 63

During the appeal process, both final and interlocutory orders for the payment of money, other than orders for family support, are usually stayed or suspended. Only a judge of the appellate court can order that the judgment remain in effect while it is being appealed. Without such an order, the order appealed from is automatically stayed, and it cannot be enforced.

Note that the appeal of an order refusing to set aside a default judgment does not automatically stay the judgment, but the judgment may be stayed under Rule 63.02. Likewise, the filing of a notice of appeal does not automatically stay orders made under the *Residential Tenancies Act, 2006* and the *Co-operative Corporations Act*.

A party may bring a motion to have an automatic stay lifted while the appeal is winding its way through the system. The court may lift the stay totally or partially on terms that are just.

If the order being appealed is an order for relief other than the payment of money, the order is not automatically stayed when the appeal commences. However, a party may apply to the appellate court or to the court that made the order being appealed to request a stay during the appeal. If a stay is ordered, it may be varied or set aside later through the bringing of a motion. An order for a stay that was made by the same court that made the order expires if a notice of appeal or a motion for leave to appeal is not commenced within the time required under the Rules.

The automatic stay comes into effect when the notice of appeal is filed or, in the case of a stay granted by an order, on the day the order granting the stay is made. Once the stay takes effect, no enforcement action can be taken on the order that is being appealed. In order to ensure that the sheriff's office does not commence enforcement on a stayed order, a party may requisition a certificate of stay from the registrar of the court that granted the stay or the court to which the appeal was taken. This certificate can then be filed with the sheriff's office to notify the sheriff that he or she may not take any further enforcement action until the stay is lifted. If the stay is granted by an order, particulars of the order must be included in the certificate. A certificate of stay is in Form 63A.

CHAPTER SUMMARY

This chapter has dealt with appeals and Rules 61, 62, and 63, which govern the procedure for appeals. We have seen that Rule 61 governs appeals of final orders, Rule 62 governs appeals of interlocutory orders, and Rule 63 governs stays on both types of orders, pending an appeal. We have noted that there are three courts that may hear appeals in Ontario: the Superior Court of Justice, the Divisional Court, and the Court of Appeal. The *Courts of Justice Act* sets out the types of appeal that each court may hear, and we have provided an overview of the courts' jurisdiction.

We have addressed the matter of commencing an appeal, with or without the necessity of seeking leave. We have noted the various time limits and procedures in this regard. An appeal must be perfected before it is ready to be heard. An appeal is perfected when the appellant has taken all the procedural steps, including the service and filing of such material as an appeal book, an exhibit book, the transcript, and a factum. Finally, we examined automatic stays of orders under appeal and the lifting of such stays by means of motion.

KEY TERMS

appeal as of right, 487

appellant, 480

appellate court, 505

court of first instance, 480

final order, 480

interlocutory order, 480

leave of the court, 481

perfecting an appeal, 490

respondent, 480

transcript, 484

NOTES

1. An objection to an assessment may be made pursuant to Rule 58.10.

2. The section refers to s. 19(1.1), but because s. 19(1.1) deals with appeals filed before October 1, 2007, it is no longer relevant and has therefore been eliminated from our discussion.

3. Supra note 1.

4. Practice direction of the Chief Justice of Ontario, January 1, 2004.

5. See Rule 61.12 for specific details of the content of the respondent's factum on an appeal.

6. Rules 37.02 to 37.05, 37.07(6), 37.08, 37.10, and 37.17 do not apply to motions to an appellate court.

7. See Rules 61.16(2), (2.1), and (2.2).

REFERENCES

Co-operative Corporations Act, RSO 1990, c. C. 35.

Courts of Justice Act, RSO 1990, c. C.43.

Rules of Civil Procedure, RRO 1990, reg. 194.

Residential Tenancies Act, 2006, SO 2006, c. 17.

REVIEW QUESTIONS

1. What is the difference between a final and an interlocutory order?

2. What factors determine which court will hear an appeal?

3. What three courts hear appeals?

4. What types of appeals are heard in the Superior Court of Justice?

5. What types of appeals are heard in Divisional Court?

6. What types of appeals are heard in the Court of Appeal?

7. Identify the court to which the following judgment or orders should be appealed:

   a. a decision by a judge that Widgets Inc. has breached its contract with John Doe and that John should be awarded $60,000, exclusive of costs;

   b. a decision by a master to permit an amendment of a pleading after pleadings have closed;

   c. a decision by a Small Claims Court judge to award the plaintiff $3,500 in damages caused by his neighbour's negligence;

   d. a decision by a judge at the end of trial that the defendant is not liable for the plaintiff's claim of $100,000;

   e. a decision by a judge at the end of trial that the defendant is liable for the plaintiff's claim but awarding the plaintiff only $30,000; and

   f. a decision by a judge of the Superior Court to strike out a jury notice after hearing the motion brought by the defendant.

8. Where does the Ontario Court of Appeal sit?

9. How much time do you have to serve a motion for leave to appeal to the Divisional Court? What rule applies?

10. How is a factum for leave to appeal to the Court of Appeal arranged? What rule applies?

11. What document commences an appeal?

12. How long does an appellant have to order the transcript for an appeal?

13. Your law firm is appealing a matter to the Court of Appeal and needs some of the exhibits from the trial. How do you obtain them?

14. In an appeal to the Divisional Court, must the respondent file a factum?

15. A party does not wish to continue with an appeal after filing a notice of appeal. How does the party terminate the appeal process?

DISCUSSION QUESTION

1. The defendant, Global Steel Works Inc., wishes to appeal a decision of the Superior Court of Justice. The decision ordered it to pay its former employee, Romeo Capulet, $250,000 for wrongful dismissal. Draft a general heading for the notice of appeal.

Case Management

21

Introduction

What Is Case Management?

Case management is a system designed to give the courts control over the pace at which a case moves to trial. Before the introduction of case management, lawyers, and to some extent their clients, determined the pace at which a case moved forward. Once an originating process was issued, lawyers could waive many of the time limits imposed by the Rules. For example, the statement of defence is due 20 days from the time the statement of claim is served in most cases. Defence counsel would often ask for, and get, an extension of time, simply as a matter of courtesy. And so the case would progress, at a stately and leisurely pace. The court was passive, waiting for lawyers and litigants to take the next step.

The result was that cases could take a long time to get to trial, particularly if one of the litigants decided to employ delaying strategies, or one of the lawyers had many files on the go. Lawyers used to joke about files so old that they had moss growing on their north side.[1] In addition, there was the natural tendency among many lawyers to procrastinate about getting things done. As a student, you may be familiar with this tendency and will appreciate how it could prevent a case from moving forward quickly to trial.

These kinds of delays did not matter all that much in judicial regions where the volume of cases was low. But in larger centres, such as Toronto, it created problems. Because lawyers controlled the pace that a case took getting to trial, individual decisions about when a case was to move forward at various stages of the proceeding resulted in uneven flows of cases through the court system. This created backlogs at points where court time was needed: at motions, at discovery, and at trial. In Toronto, a case could take two years or more to get to trial. In addition, because the court was not proactive in assisting the parties to explore settlement in a rational way, settlement was often left to the last minute, with a deal being struck at the courtroom door. This approach to settlement was wasteful for both the court system and the litigants. If a deal had been explored earlier in the process, much time and money might have been saved for the litigants. For the courts, a last-minute settlement often meant collapse of the trial list because the next cases on the list were not necessarily ready to start immediately. This sometimes resulted in empty courtrooms and judges with nothing on their schedule for the day—hardly a good use of public funds.

Case management was an attempt to solve problems of cost and delay and to promote settlement at an early stage by having the court intervene and oversee a case as it moved along, making procedural decisions and ensuring that the case adhered to a timetable so that it either settled or came to trial within a reasonable time. You could look at this as a sort of judicial version of an automobile assembly line—but instead of producing cars, the desired outcome was to produce finished cases on schedule. The trick to an assembly line is to have the object assembled in predetermined steps on a time schedule in order to predict how quickly and in what quantities the finished product will emerge at the end of the assembly line process.

Judges and case management masters, in theory, would function like assembly line foremen, making sure that the product was being produced on time, that it was going down the assembly line in a predictable way, and that procedures were being used efficiently. By contrast, so the theory went, without case management, lawyers looking solely at their own cases and their own needs might delay matters and create bottlenecks and inefficiency, which would result in unpredictable times for case completion.

The Retreat from Mandatory Case Management to Case Management When Necessary

Case management was first introduced as an experiment for randomly selected cases and then made mandatory in the cities of Toronto, Ottawa, and the County of Essex (which in practical terms means the City of Windsor). When case management was made mandatory in Toronto in July 2001, the view was that a case timetable that was strictly enforced and controlled by the court would bring an end to high costs and lengthy delays in the Superior Court. By 2004, however, it was apparent that case management was not working the way the rules committee thought it would. There were continued and increasing delays in getting motions heard and actions tried. It was also clear that rather than cutting costs, case management was increasing them by requiring extra appearances at mandatory case conferences and through an increased number of formal steps that had to be taken. The case timetables, with their insistence that a case be ready for a settlement conference 240 days after the first defence was filed, were often too rigid for cases with complex issues or many parties. It was, in fact, taking longer to get to trial where case management was in operation, particularly in Toronto, than it had taken prior to case management being introduced, although this was less of a problem in the County of Essex (Windsor) and Ottawa, where case management was also in place.

The rules committee responded by issuing a practice direction for civil cases in Toronto, which took effect on December 31, 2004. In the words of the practice direction itself, it could be summed up as case management as necessary, but not necessarily case management. In 2007 and 2010, there were further changes, so that currently:

- Case management is no longer automatic, but is available in Toronto, Ottawa, and the County of Essex (Windsor) under Rule 77, to be used as and when required.
- Parties are given greater responsibility for managing actions and moving them quickly to trial or other resolution. It is where parties do not exercise this responsibility, or are having difficulty exercising it, that case management may be invoked either at the request of a party or by a judge on his or her own motion.

- Case management is not the only procedure available that can be used to control cost and delay. It is now also supplemented by the proportionality rule for cases generally, and for discovery in particular; as well, a discovery plan, in theory, should help to keep discovery, which is potentially a complex and time-eating procedure, under control. Further, the registrar now has the power under Rules 48.14 and 48.15 to dismiss cases, both defended and undefended, that have not proceeded in a timely fashion.[2]

In this context we can now turn to case management in its current form in Toronto, Ottawa, and the County of Essex (Windsor).

Rule 77.01 now makes it quite clear that case management will be used only where management by a judge or case management master is required, and intervention is to be restricted to the minimum necessary to achieve the goal of case management: to move a case quickly to trial where the parties are unable to do this without the court's intervention. Rule 77.02 makes it clear that parties should not drag their feet until a **case management judge or master** "cracks the whip." Instead, parties have the primary responsibility to be proactive and take the initiative in managing a case and moving it along as quickly as possible to resolution and conclusion.

case management judge or master
court official assigned to each case-managed case to ensure court control over the case on its way to trial

What's In ...

Rule 77.02 stipulates that all actions and applications begun in or transferred to the cities of Toronto, Ottawa, and the County of Essex (Windsor) are eligible to be case managed under Rule 77.

These locations were chosen in 2001 as part of the original case management pilot project. They remain eligible for case management in part because it appears to work well in Ottawa and the County of Essex (Windsor), both busy courts in major centres; Toronto, with the highest case loads, many complex cases, and a history of system delays, obviously will also benefit from continued access to case management. At the same time, as we shall see later in this chapter, a case commenced somewhere other than Toronto, Ottawa, or the County of Essex (Windsor) that needs to be case managed, can be: the rule appears to permit the transfer of cases, under certain circumstances, to any of these courts so that they can be case managed.

Case Management and Mandatory Mediation

mandatory mediation
process in which disputants are required to allow a neutral third party to facilitate their communication and assist them in negotiating a settlement

While Rule 77 does not explicitly link itself to **mandatory mediation**, Rule 24.1 makes mandatory mediation a requirement for all actions commenced in Toronto, Ottawa, and the County of Essex (Windsor), whether they are case managed or not. It therefore follows that if a case is case managed, it will also be subject to mandatory mediation, unless the court has ordered otherwise (Rule 24.1.09(1)). When case management was first introduced, mandatory mediation was considered to be an integral part of the case management process, on the theory that early compulsory mediation might result in early settlement and less waste of time and money in lengthy pretrial proceedings. That view has prevailed, although many practitioners think that mandatory mediation comes too early in the process to be useful. Mandatory mediation is discussed in greater depth in Chapter 22.

What's Out ...

There are some types of cases that are excluded altogether from case management under Rule 77. But if you look at the list of cases excluded, you will note that many of them either use a procedure imposed by statute or operate under other procedural rules that effectively allow the courts to manage cases without having to resort to Rule 77.

- *Commercial List cases in Toronto.* These cases are overseen and managed by a judge with expertise in commercial law matters who deals with all matters in a case; this indirectly results in effective case management, even when these cases are very complex (Rule 77.02(a)). Commercial List cases have simplified systems for motions and other procedures that potentially reduce costs and delay.
- *Estate and trust matters:*
  - Cases under Rule 74 or 75 dealing with estate litigation (Rule 77.02(2)(b)).
  - Applications to remove or replace a trustee under the *Trustees Act* (Rule 77.02(2)(c)).
  - Application under part V of the *Succession Law Reform Act* for support for the dependant of a deceased person (Rule 77.02(2)(d)).

In these cases, there are statutory procedural provisions, some of which are focused on expediting matters, so as to reduce the need for case management under Rule 77. For estate litigation in Toronto, there is also a practice direction that contains a number of procedural controls:

- *Guardianship applications under the Substitute Decisions Act, 1992.* The statute sets out an expedited procedure involving a fairly narrow set of issues in most cases (Rule 77.02(2)(e)).
- *Mortgage actions.* Summary foreclosure procedures are set out in part under the *Mortgages Act* so that intervention under Rule 77 should not be necessary (Rule 77.02(2)(f)).
- *Simplified procedure actions.* Rule 76 sets out a procedure for these cases that is simplified so that opportunities for delay are reduced and intervention under Rule 77 is irrelevant (Rule 77.02(2)(g)).
- *Construction lien proceedings under the Construction Lien Act.* This act sets out a summary procedure for trying construction lien actions so that further controls under Rule 77 should be unnecessary (Rule 77.02(2)(h)).

- *Proceedings under the Bankruptcy and Insolvency Act.* The statute sets out procedural codes that provide a summary procedure, with much of the bankruptcy process occurring outside the court and in the hands of a bankruptcy trustee or the Superintendent of Bankruptcy. But even where court proceedings are involved, the statute provides a procedural framework, and in Toronto proceedings are run under the streamlined procedures of the Commercial List so that resort to Rule 77 should not be necessary (Rule 77.02(2)(i)).
- *Class proceedings under the Class Proceedings Act.* If a plaintiff applies to certify a proceeding as a class proceeding under the Act, and the proceeding is certified, Rule 77 does not apply. However, if certification is refused, the result is a case that potentially has a very large number of plaintiffs suing for relatively small amounts and great opportunities for procedural mayhem, not to mention delay, so in these circumstances a proceeding may be subject to case management (Rules 77.02(3)(a) and (b)).

Authority to Assign a Case to Case Management

When case management was first introduced in 2001, all cases in Toronto, Ottawa, and the County of Essex (Windsor) that were not exempt under Rule 77 were case managed, whether they needed it or not. Under the current rule, only cases that need management are sent to case management—either because the parties agree, or because one party brings a motion to assign a case to case management, or because a judge on his or her own motion thinks a case is in need of case management. In deciding whether or not a case should come into case management, the rule sets out criteria that must be considered.

Rule 77.05(1) makes it clear that a regional senior judge in every instance has the power to assign a case to case management on consent of the parties at any time, including at the time a proceeding is commenced. The regional senior judge may also direct any judge or a case management master to assign cases to case management. The effect is that parties do not have to make special application to the regional senior judge, who presumably has lots of other things to do, and can apply to other judges or, if a motion is appropriately to be made before a master, to case management masters.

A regional senior judge may also transfer a case to case management on his or her own initiative or at the request of a party with or without a motion, but only *after* the first defence has issued (Rules 77.05(1)(a) and (b)). The rationale for this may be that if the case is not being defended, there is no real basis for the judge to assign it to case management.

The language of Rules 77.05(1) and (2) also makes it clear that the power to assign cases to case management exercised by a regional senior judge may be delegated by him or her to another judge or a case management master.

Can You Move a Case from Anywhere in Ontario to a Rule 77 Region?

If case management under Rule 77 is in fact a tool that is well suited to procedurally problematic cases, is there a way to get cases that require case management to one of the regions where Rule 77 is in force?

There is an argument that it could be done under Rule 13.1.02. Unless a statute requires a trial in a particular county, a judge in another region could consider or make an order on a motion to transfer a case to a county where Rule 77 is available, where the transfer would secure the "just, most expeditious and least expensive determination of the proceeding on its merits" or on the basis of "any other relevant matter" (Rules 13.1.02(2)(vii) and (ix)).

Criteria for Assigning a Case to Case Management

Guidelines for exercising discretion are set out in Rule 77.05(4). The guidelines are general, which indicates that the judge must consider all relevant factors. And if you were wondering what kinds of situations or procedural mayhem might be appropriate for assignment to case management, the guidelines provide some examples of situations where case management is likely to be required. The discretion to decide on case management is broad but may include any or all of the following, although the language of the rule suggests that the exercise of discretion is not solely dependent on the 10 types of criteria set out in Rule 77.05(4).

1. The purpose set out in Rule 77.01(1): where intervention is warranted and only to the degree required when parties are not taking responsibility for properly managing the progress of an action.

2. The complexity of the facts or issues of law both as to their number and nature is a factor to be considered. Greater complexity is a basis for assigning case management to a proceeding.

3. If there are important public issues, case management may be required to, for example, grant intervenor status to other parties when procedural direction might be useful.

4. The number or type of parties and whether they are represented may require case management. Numerous unrepresented parties can easily result in procedural chaos if there is no firm judicial hand to direct proceedings. When numerous parties with different causes of action are involved in the same transactions, events, or series of transactions or events, they can be linked together in one proceeding under Rule 6; in situations of this type, Rule 77 can be very helpful in sorting things out. Note that in areas where Rule 77 does not operate, it is possible in these circumstances to bring a motion for directions to a judge, who can do many of the things that would be done under case management in order to help move a complex case along.

5. The number of proceedings involving similar parties and causes of action. Where parties and actions should be consolidated under Rule 6, or at least tried together, Rule 77 provides procedural solutions up to and including consolidation of cases, and coordination of them through case conferences and the subsequent use of case timetables.

6. The amount of intervention by the court that the proceeding is likely to require. In a complex case with multiple parties, or where there are unruly or unrepresented parties who are creating procedural chaos, court intervention via case conferences or the assignment of a single judge for all pretrial motions under Rule 77 may be necessary.

7. The time required for discovery or preparation for trial. While the discovery plan required under Rule 29.1 should prevent discoveries from careening out of control, if the parties cannot create an agreed-upon plan, or won't adhere to it, case management may be a solution; case management will give a judge control over the process. Similarly, if there are endless delays or non-cooperation in the trial preparation process following the pretrial conference under Rule 50, case management can be used to direct the process with judicial oversight via case conferences or the appointment of a single judge under Rule 77. In areas where Rule 77 is not available, if a case is not settled at the pretrial conference under Rule 50, at that stage the judge can establish a timetable under Rule 50.07(1).

8. In the case of an action, the number of expert and other witnesses to be called at trial. Here, case management can be used to control the number of witnesses, the scheduling of their appearances, and the timing of production of related documentary evidence prior to trial and during the trial preparation period.

9. The time required for a trial or hearing. Excessively long trials are expensive for clients, but also for the public because judges and court staff can be tied up for prolonged periods with the result of increased delay for other cases waiting for judges and courtrooms to become available. To some extent, case conferences can be used to control delay in the trial process under Rule 77.

10. Whether there has been substantial delay in the conduct of a proceeding. This ground overlaps with many others, because delay (and its attendant costs) is a primary focus of Rule 77. As previously noted, case conferences can be used to set schedules and ensure that parties adhere to them.

Several outcomes emerge from consideration of the 10 factors used to decide whether case management should be employed:

- control of foot dragging, ineptness, and bad behaviour by parties and/or counsel, and
- control of factually or legally complicated cases.

While Rule 77 can provide ways to deal with these issues, it is not the only rule available. In regions where case management does not apply, as well as in regions where it applies, other rules can be used to deal with these issues. For example, under Rule 37.15 a motion for directions may be brought for procedural intervention by any party to sort out procedural issues at any stage in a proceeding. Where parties are not cooperating under Rule 29.1, the court can create and enforce a discovery plan that meets the proportionality principles in Rule 29.2. After a pretrial conference, Rule 50 grants a judge broad powers to make binding orders to facilitate the trial of an action and the preparation for it, including the establishment of a timetable.

Why Is Rule 77 Necessary?

If these other rules can do much of what Rule 77 can do, then why do we need Rule 77? There are several reasons. One reason is that some of these other procedural control mechanisms can be employed only at certain stages: at discovery or at the pretrial conference. They do not really provide a solution for procedural issues that affect the case throughout the pretrial process where continuous oversight may be required and can be provided with case conferences under Rule 77. Another reason is that typically these other procedural tools require a motion before a judge or master. The judge or master can make an order, but there is no judicial oversight to ensure compliance. Another motion might follow before a different judge or master who may not know or focus on the history or context of the case. Rule 77 allows for the appointment of a single judge to oversee the process; this appointed judge will get to know the parties and issues, and become highly aware of whatever procedural problems or pathologies affect the case, with the result that this judge can then more effectively, efficiently, and quickly control them.

To better see how the Rule 77 process works, we now turn to the powers available under case management once a case is assigned to it.

Case Management Powers

Judicial Powers

Rule 77.04 grants broad powers to a judge or case management master, allowing him or her to extend or abridge not only a time prescribed by the Rules, but also a time that was set out in an order previously made by another judge or master. A judge or master can also set aside any order previously made by a registrar, such as a default judgment or an order dismissing an action for abandonment under Rule 48. And if a case conference is called, they can adjourn it. Lastly, they have the very broad power to "make orders, impose terms, give directions and award costs as necessary" to carry out the purpose of Rule 77. This power is important because it gives a judge or case management master real control over the parties and the proceeding—with the power to give precise directions, and the power to award costs, including punitive costs that are not based solely on a wronged party's actual costs, which is a useful way of controlling counsel and parties who abuse the process.

Rule 77.04(2) grants an additional power to a judge or case management master to require parties to appear before him or her, or to participate in a conference call to deal with any matter related to the management of the proceeding, including a failure to comply with an order or the Rules. This is in addition to the power to call a case conference (case conferences are discussed later in this chapter). Importantly, the judge or case management master does not have to wait for a party to ask him or her to exercise these powers—he or she can act on his or her own initiative.

All of this is in addition to any other powers set out in Rule 77. There are two other powers set out in Rule 77 that are more specifically defined judicial tools, to which the powers in Rule 77.04 can be harnessed: assignment of a case to an individual judge and the calling of a case conference.

Appointment of a Single Case Management Judge

There are certain advantages to having a single judge oversee all procedural steps in a proceeding (and, in particular, hear all motions) and call a case conference, or summon the parties to appear even without a case conference. A judge gets to know the parties, counsel, and issues in the proceeding and, as with the conductor of an orchestra, he or she can make the parties work together efficiently and effectively. By contrast, as noted previously, where different judges or masters hear motions as a matter proceeds, they will have only a glimpse of what might be going on, and will not have the knowledge, or perhaps the interest, to follow up and keep the parties and counsel in line in the same way that a single judge might be able to.

Rule 77.06 clearly recognizes that the appointment of a single judge to oversee all aspects of a proceeding is an efficient means of effective judicial control. The power to appoint a single judge to oversee any case put into case management rests with the Chief Justice of the Superior Court, or the Associate Chief Justice or any judge designated by them. A single judge appointed to hear all steps in a proceeding may, however, under Rule 77.07, delegate some of his or her powers. The judge may refer a motion within a master's jurisdiction to a case management master, or the single judge may hear those motions—the choice is that of the appointed case management judge, unless the judge who appointed the single case management judge has specified that the judge is to hear all motions. If the appointing judge is concerned about overuse of motions or attempts to create confusion by involving more than one adjudicator, the appointed judge may well be directed to hear all motions whether they are in a master's jurisdiction or not.

Note that where a single judge is appointed to oversee pretrial proceedings, that judge shall not preside at trial. As with a judge at a pretrial conference under Rule 50, the pretrial judge will have heard far too much to necessarily be as open-minded about the case and the parties as a judge with no previous involvement in the matter would be.

Case Management Motions

Rule 77 mimics Rule 76 in that it zeroes in on ways to reduce cost and delay on motions made under case management. Where appropriate, a motion can be made without written supporting material or a motion record. Nor is a formal order required to be prepared if the order is taken down in writing by whoever is hearing it, if a judge or case management master so orders, unless it is to be appealed. If this is the case, a written record will be required for the appeal. A motion can be made by attendance, but to save time it may also be made in writing or by fax, or by conference call or video conference under Rule 1.08. Costs on a motion may be fixed at the end of the motion, whether it is contested or not, under Rule 57.03. That rule also provides that if the costs are not paid within 30 days, a claim may be dismissed or a defence struck out. This rule gives a case management judge the power to prevent one party from "motioning to death" the other party with unnecessary, costly, and complex motions. While there are no longer any prescribed forms for Rule 77, an adaptation of a motion form used for Rule 77 motions prior to 2010 is set out here in Figure 21.1. You can also use an adaptation of Form 76B, the simplified procedure motion form.

Case Conferences

If a case is in case management, a **case conference** under Rule 77.08(1) can be convened at any time by a judge or case management master, either at a party's request or at the judge's or master's own initiative, if this is thought to be necessary—there is no need to wait for a party to ask when a case might be going off the rails and is in need of firm control. There is no specific form for this, and a letter setting out the request, with a brief statement of the reasons for it, should suffice. In addition to summoning counsel to appear at a case conference, a judge or case management master may, under Rule 77.08(2), also require the client or the person instructing the lawyer to be present in person, or be available by phone, in the same way as in a pretrial conference under Rule 50. This authority is recognition that many of the problems arising in case-managed proceedings stem from a client who may be beyond the control of counsel. Also, decisions may be taken that require a client's consent or instructions to counsel.

case conference
conference managed by the case management judge or master, who controls timetables and settles all procedural matters

Once everyone who is required is in attendance, what can be done at a case conference? The powers of a case management judge or master in a case conference, in addition to any powers previously discussed, are set out in Rule 77.08(3). The judge or master can identify the issues in the case, note which are contested or not, and explore ways to resolve contested issues. In this case, "issues" may refer to substantive factual and legal matters in the case, or procedural issues—any problem, in effect, that is holding matters up, increasing cost, and causing delay. The judge or master also has the power to put the parties on a timetable that requires steps to be completed on set dates, or can alter an existing timetable (while there is no prescribed form for timetables, an example is included here in Figure 21.2). Where appropriate, Rule 77.08(5) indicates that at a case conference a judge or case management master may make a procedural order without a formal motion having being made and can convene a pretrial conference without the usual conditions precedent for doing so under Rule 50. And, of course, a judge or case management master can also give directions with respect to procedural next steps, using or amending an existing timetable, or in the absence of a timetable. A judge, in addi-

Figure 21.1 Case Management Motion Form

Court file no. 01-CV-1234

ONTARIO
SUPERIOR COURT OF JUSTICE

BETWEEN:

ABIGAIL BOAR

Plaintiff

and

RATTLE MOTORS LTD. and FRED FLOGEM

Defendants

CASE MANAGEMENT MOTION FORM

JURISDICTION [ ] Case management judge
     [x] Case management master

THIS FORM FILED BY *(Check appropriate boxes to identify the party filing this form as a moving/responding party on this motion AND to identify this party as plaintiff, defendant, etc. in the action)*

[x] moving party
[ ] Plaintiff _____
[ ] responding party
[ ] defendant/respondent name _____
[ ] other — specify kind of party and name _____

MOTION MADE
[ ] on consent of all parties   [ ] on notice to all parties and unopposed
[ ] without notice   [x] on notice to all parties and expected to be opposed

Notice of this motion was served on: October 6, year 2
by means of: service on the lawyer for the defendants by courier.

METHOD OF HEARING REQUESTED
[x] by attendance
[ ] in writing only, no appearance
[ ] by fax
[ ] by telephone conference under rule 1.08
[ ] by video conference under rule 1.08

Date, time and place for attendance or for telephone or video conference

September 16, year 1, at 10:00 a.m.,
Courthouse, 393 University Avenue, Toronto, Ontario, M5G 1E6

Figure 21.1 Continued

ORDER SOUGHT BY THIS PARTY *(Responding party is presumed to request dismissal of motion and costs)*

[   ] Extension of time — until *(give specific date)*: _____

[   ] serve claim/application   [   ] file or deliver defence

[   ] complete discoveries

[   ] other _____

[   ] Assignment of proceeding (and related proceedings if applicable) to judge(s) for case management.

[x] Other relief — be specific

1. The plaintiff seeks an order permitting Eldred Klump, lighting engineer, to inspect the level of lighting in the automobile showroom operated by the corporate defendant at 1240 Bay Street, Toronto, Ontario, M8H 0K8 on such terms and times as the court considers just.

2. The costs of this motion.

MATERIAL RELIED ON BY THIS PARTY

[x] this form   [x] pleadings   [x] affidavits — specify

[   ] transcript — specify   [   ] other — specify

Affidavit of Eldred Klump, sworn October 3, year 1

GROUNDS IN SUPPORT OF/IN OPPOSITION TO MOTION (INCLUDING RULE AND STATUTORY PROVISIONS RELIED ON)

There is an issue between the parties as to the adequacy of lighting in the corporate defendant's showroom, and it is necessary to carry out an inspection of the corporate defendant's premises to examine the lighting, pursuant to Rule 32 of the *Rules of Civil Procedure*, in order to determine that issue.

CERTIFICATION BY LAWYER

I certify that the above information is correct, to the best of my knowledge.

Signature of lawyer *(If no lawyer, party must sign)*

I.M. Just   *LSUC #12345R*

Date: September 4, year 1

Figure 21.1   Concluded

THIS PARTY'S LAWYER *(if no lawyer, give party's address for service, telephone and fax number)*	OTHER LAWYER *(if no lawyer, give other party's name, address for service, telephone and fax number)*
Name and firm	Name and firm
I.M. Just, Just & Coping	Huey Sue
LSUC #12345R	LSUC #23456T
Address	Address
365 Bay Street – 8701	65 False Trail
Toronto, Ontario, M3J 4A9	Toronto, Ontario, M6Y 1Z6
Telephone 416-762-1342	Telephone 416-485-6891
Fax 416-762-2300	Fax 416-485-6892

DISPOSITION BY CASE MANAGEMENT JUDGE/MASTER

[   ] order to go as asked   [   ] adjourned to

[   ] order refused   [   ] order to go as follows:

_____

_____

_____

_____

Hearing method _____   Hearing duration _____ min.

Heard in: [   ] courtroom   [   ] office

[   ] Successful party MUST prepare formal order for signature

[   ] No copy of disposition to be sent to parties

[   ] Other directions — specify

_____

_____

Date _____ Name _____ Signature _____

Judge's/Master's   Judge's/Master's

Figure 21.2   Case Timetable

Court file no. 01-CV-1234/year 1

ONTARIO
SUPERIOR COURT OF JUSTICE

BETWEEN:

ABIGAIL BOAR

Plaintiff

and

RATTLE MOTORS LTD. and FRED FLOGEM

Defendants

CASE TIMETABLE

[x] **AGREED**

[   ] **DATES TO BE RESOLVED**

DATE ACTION COMMENCED: July 10, year 1

1. Mediator Selected By (within 30 days of first defence):   Date: October 1, year 1

2. Affidavits of Documents Exchanged By: Date: November 15, year 1

3. **Mediation Completed By:**   Date: **November 30, year 1**

4. Discoveries Completed By: Date: February 5, year 2

5. Undertakings/Refusals Completed By: Date: April 4, year 2

6. Discovery Motions Completed By: Date: April 29, year 2

7. Other: PLAINTIFF'S EXPERT REPORT   Date: January 15, year 2

8. **Settlement Conference Completed By: (Max. 180**   Date: **April 25, year 2**
    days from date action set down for trial)

TIMETABLE DATE: September 9, year 2

Figure 21.2   Concluded

ACTION NO: 3, year 1

1) Is this action settled?   YES [ ]   NO [x]

   If the action is settled, **ALL** counsel and self-represented parties must confirm this in writing and return the consent with this form. Otherwise, personal attendance is required. Counsel are not required to gown.

2) If not settled—what is the status of this action and any other related proceeding?

   Comment _____

   ACTION NO. OF ALL RELATED PROCEEDINGS: _____ N/A _____

   a) Pleadings completed?   YES [x]   NO [ ]

   b) Affidavits of documents completed?   YES [x]   NO [ ]

   c) Discovery completed?   YES [ ]   NO [x]

   d) Experts reports available?   YES [ ]   NO [x]

3) Any Motions intended to be brought?   YES [x]   NO [ ]

   If yes —   What Motions?   Motion to inspect premises

              Under which rules?   Under Rule 32

4. Is this action ready for a pretrial conference?   YES [ ]   NO [x]

5. Is this action ready for a trial?   YES [ ]   NO [x]

6. Have the parties attended mediation?   YES [x]   NO [ ]

7. Approximately how long will the trial take?   3   Days

8. JURY [ ]   NON-JURY [x]

9. Has the action been affected by bankruptcy or other transmission of interest?

                                                YES [ ]   NO [x]

tion, may make a substantive interlocutory order (an order that deals with the rights of parties, but does not finally dispose of the issues or matter before the court) without any party having made a motion, and he or she may also convene a hearing on an issue or matter.

It is quite clear from Rule 77.08(4) that a case conference is not some kind of pro forma step in proceedings to which a junior lawyer or articling student can be sent. To do this would risk judicial wrath. The rule makes it clear that the lawyer who appears is to be fully briefed on the issues in the case, and is to have full authority to act on any matter that may arise at a case conference.

Making Effective Use of Case Conferences

Missing a time limit or failing to complete a procedural step can often trigger an application to assign a case to case management and then trigger a case conference, at the request of a party, or a judge or case management master, particularly where a judge or master has already been assigned to handle all pretrial matters under Rule 77. This in turn can lead to the imposition of timetables or sanctions, which will raise costs for your client. Rule 77 procedures and time limits should cause lawyers to introduce a form of case management to their office operations in order to control their practice. Gone are the days when lawyers take on all files that come in the door. It will be much more important to manage the flow of cases in the office so that the lawyer is able to meet all deadlines and does not end up, for example, with two cases being tried back to back, while he or she is trying to complete discoveries in a third case and schedule mediation in a fourth. This will be particularly problematic for sole practitioners, who do not have a stable of associates or articling students to assign work to.

A case conference is designed to make the litigation process more efficient, and less expensive. To make good use of a case conference, lawyers and legal staff need to prepare for it. An early meeting of counsel may avoid the need to convene a case conference. When a case conference is called, counsel with carriage of the file in your office should attend. Alternatively, another lawyer who has been thoroughly briefed on the case so that the conference time is not wasted may attend. The lawyer should bring his or her calendar or scheduler so that conflicts can be avoided. A calendar is also necessary if you are seeking to extend time or amend the timetable or if another party is doing so. Lawyers may wish to consider holding the case conference by conference telephone call. This may be done by pre-arrangement with the judge or case management master under Rule 77.04(2).

If a case conference is scheduled, consider the following specific suggestions from Case Management Master MacLeod, who has set out nine ideas[3] to help make case management work more efficiently:

1. *Complete all research and investigation before you commence proceedings.* In doing this, also pay careful attention to the proportionality principle in Rule 1.04(1.1) generally and in Rule 29.2 for discovery in determining what steps you intend to take, and how you intend to take them.

2. *Meet and discuss procedural steps prior to commencement of proceedings where possible.* Increasingly, litigation "best practices" focus on early collaborative efforts to help the case proceed quickly and efficiently, particularly with pretrial matters that tend to consume time and money, such as discovery.

3. *Once the claim issues, serve it immediately because time limits start running.* The Rules require certain things to happen within certain time periods based on when a claim issues. For example, defences are due within a fixed number of days after service of a claim. The filing of a defence may then trigger other time limits—for example, mandatory mediation should commence within 180 days after the first defence is filed. So, getting a claim issued and served is key in moving a proceeding along quickly.

4. *Once all parties have appointed counsel, try to get agreement on a discovery plan and, if necessary, a timetable for other pretrial steps.* If extensions of times beyond the limits set in the Rules or in what was previously agreed to are required, be ready to apply for an order. Be willing to consult on the creation of a timetable, and be realistic about the amount of time required to complete steps.

5. *Watch your time limits.* Use ticklers with multiple time warnings—for example, set them at one month, two weeks, five days, two days, and one day before a deadline.

6. *Consider the timing of mediation.* Mediation must take place within 180 days of the filing of the first defence. This may be too soon in some cases—for example, where there are multiple defendants or third parties, or both. In this type of case, consider applying for an order to extend time, and be careful to extend other times that will be affected by the extension of mediation.

7. *Consider using requests to admit facts and documents to narrow issues before trial.* Consider also whether you can proceed by stated case, with an agreed statement of facts, in whole or in part.

8. *Continue to watch time limits.* If the case timetable is becoming unrealistic, consider obtaining the consent of all parties to schedule a case conference and revise it, or revise it on a consent motion.

9. *Focus on results.* Avoid useless procedural wrangling. The court is likely to be far less tolerant of delay tactics than it was before mandatory case management was put in effect.

CHAPTER SUMMARY

This chapter introduced you to the optional case management procedure that is available for proceedings in Toronto, Ottawa, and the County of Essex (Windsor). Certain types of cases are exempt from case management under Rule 77, largely because they operate under a statutory scheme that allows a case to be managed without resort to Rule 77. Case management was introduced to help reduce cost and delay in civil litigation where cost or delay had become a noticeable problem, as would be the case in factually or legally complex proceedings, or where parties are being uncooperative or disruptive. The rule sets out criteria that help to determine whether a proceeding should be assigned to case management and to what extent it should be subject to case management. Case management is an option that may be tailored to the needs of a particular case—it is not based on a "one size fits all" model. In addition to greater judicial powers, including the right of a judge to intervene without waiting for a party to request intervention, the rule permits a single judge to oversee all pretrial steps in proceedings. It also permits the parties, or a judge or case management master, to call a case conference in a case where there are broad powers available for use in gaining control over cost and delay issues, and in bringing a case forward to trial with power to compel cooperation by parties.

KEY TERMS

case conference, 521

case management judge or master, 514

mandatory mediation, 514

NOTES

1. Delay in the courts is nothing new. Charles Dickens's novel *Bleak House* involves an estate litigation case, *Jarndyce v. Jarndyce*, that went on for more than a generation, with lawyers dying or retiring and being replaced by others, until most of the beneficiaries were dead, and the estate had been consumed by legal fees. This is a fictional and extreme example, but it shows that problems with cost and delay have been a constant concern, historically. A large part of the cause is attributed to delay tactics and procrastination by the legal profession. The 19th-century reform that attacked this problem was the abolition of the Court of Chancery, which combined law and equity in one superior court. The late 20th-century solution has been case management, which transfers control of how a case progresses from the lawyers to the courts.

2. The civil justice reforms that took effect on January 1, 2010 brought the Toronto case management system under Rule 78 to an end, with a single, flexible, case management system for Toronto, Ottawa, and the County of Essex (Windsor) that is now reflected in Rule 77. The current practice direction can be found at http://www.ontariocourts.ca/scj/practice/practice-directions/toronto/civil-applications.

3. Originally there were 10 suggestions, but the one referring to timing of discovery is no longer applicable and has not been included. Discovery is scheduled flexibly through a discovery plan under Rule 29.1.

REFERENCES

Air Canada v. WestJet Airlines Ltd. (2006), 267 DLR (4th) 483, 81 OR (3d) 48 (SCJ).

Bankruptcy and Insolvency Act, RSC 1985, c. B-3, as amended.

Class Proceedings Act, 1992, SO 1992, c. 6.

Construction Lien Act, RSO 1990, c. C.30.

Evidence Act, RSO 1990, c. E.23.

MacLeod, C., "Commencing an Action and the Key New Concept: The Early Timetable," in *Civil Litigation—100% Case Management Alert*, Advocates' Society conference, held in Toronto, May 31, 2001.

Mortgages Act, RSO 1990, c. M.40.

Rules of Civil Procedure, RRO 1990, reg. 194.

Substitute Decisions Act, 1992, SO 1992, c. 30.

Succession Law Reform Act, RSO 1990, c. S.26.

Trustees Act, RSO 1990, c. T.23.

REVIEW QUESTIONS

1. Why was case management introduced in Toronto, Ottawa, and the County of Essex (Windsor)?

2. What are the key features of case management?

3. What cases does case management cover?

4. What specific procedures must you follow when commencing a proceeding?

5. Is there any rationale that might explain the exceptions to case management in Rule 77.02?

6. Can the time for taking steps under the Rules be changed in case management?

7. What is included in a case timetable?

8. What is the procedure for bringing motions in case management?

9. For what purposes is a case conference convened and by whom?

10. How and when is a case conference convened?

11. What powers can case management judges and masters exercise in a case conference?

DISCUSSION QUESTION

1. A made a deal with B to import raisins from Turkey. B had the contacts, and A put up the cash. The time for payment arrived, but B kept putting off paying A. A finally sued B for the agreed payment in Toronto. B had sold the raisins to Bakecorp to use to make raisin cookies, but the raisins turned out to have pebbles and sand mixed in with them. Bakecorp then sued B for breach of contract for delivering raisins that did not meet the requirements of the contract. B defended the action against Bakecorp, and also filed a defence to A's action against him. In addition, B also filed a third-party claim against A in the Bakecorp action claiming that if he, B, were liable to Bakecorp, then A, as his partner in the raisin venture, was jointly liable to Bakecorp. A filed a defence to that stating that he had only put up capital and had no idea who the raisins were to be sold to, and had no knowledge of the transaction. When A's lawyer inquired, Bakecorp indicated that it had no interest that was adverse to A, and that it held B solely responsible.

A now discovered that B and his counsel were not cooperating on a discovery plan, were demanding to see all kinds of documents of questionable relevance, wanted an interpreter for B, who claims not to understand English very well, and wanted the other parties to contribute to the cost of the interpreter, to be chosen by B. A and Bakecorp are not keen on this course of action and want an independent interpreter, with B paying the whole cost. B has already brought several motions, which have been refused by the court.

Explain how A might use case management to assist the parties in getting this case tried with minimal cost and delay.

Mandatory Mediation

22

What Is Mediation?

Mediation is a form of **alternative dispute resolution** (ADR). It is one way for people to settle disputes or lawsuits without going to court. When a dispute is mediated, a neutral third party—the mediator—assists the parties in identifying their chief concerns and interests and helps them to negotiate a settlement that they can each live with. Mediators do not impose settlements by deciding disputes the way judges or arbitrators do. The mediator's job is to facilitate communication between the parties in a constructive way so that the parties can find their way to a satisfactory agreement. In mediation, the aim is not to identify winners or losers but to solve a problem that has led to a dispute or disagreement. The solution the parties fashion with a mediator's help may be based on factors other than the parties' legal rights.

Mandatory Mediation in Ontario

In the last decade of the 20th century, the civil courts began to come to grips with problems of cost and delay in the civil court system by looking for new ways of doing things. The court system was overhauled, and the civil court rules were amended to introduce procedures, such as case management, to cut cost and delay. Another approach was to divert some cases out of the civil courts to be dealt with under various alternatives to dispute settlement in court. This approach has a history going back to the mid-20th century, when courts were divested of jurisdiction over various types of disputes. Labour relations disputes, for example, began to be dealt with by arbitrators or in some cases by labour relations boards, but not by courts. Boards and tribunals often deal with disputes where parties are unable to use the court. The court's role in these situations is restricted, ensuring that the boards, arbitrators, or mediators provide a basically fair system when arriving at decisions. If a board or an arbitrator makes an error, the matter is usually sent back to the board or arbitrator to come to a decision properly. The court does not usually substitute its decision for that of the board or arbitrator.

The Ministry of the Attorney General introduced mandatory mediation in the superior court system in 1999 in the form of selected pilot projects. The original intention was to have mediation apply across the province as part of the civil litigation process. However, it is currently mandatory under Rule 24.1 only in certain types of actions (Rule 24.1.04(1)).

Does Mandatory Mediation Work?

That was the question the pilot project had to answer. The answer was that mandatory mediation was generally successful.[1] It resulted in significant reductions in the time taken to dispose of cases—a plus for clients and the courts, which can deal with the remaining cases more easily when the case load is reduced. Not surprisingly, the costs for litigants were also reduced when mediation was wholly or partially successful.[2] A high proportion of cases, over 40 percent in both Toronto and Ottawa, were settled at or within seven days of the completion of mediation. An additional 13 percent of cases in Ottawa and 21 percent of cases in Toronto were partially settled, with some issues being taken from the table, speeding up the proceedings and reducing costs. However, there were concerns voiced by some members of the bar, particularly in Toronto. One was that mediation came too early in the proceeding under Rule 24.1, before the parties were ready to consider it. Generally, the Toronto bar was more critical of the mandatory mediation process than the Ottawa and County of Essex (Windsor) bars were.

Mandatory Mediation—What's In and What's Out

After the initial experiments with mandatory mediation, the rules committee decided to continue it under Rule 24.1, with some modifications, in Toronto, Ottawa, and the County of Essex (Windsor).

What's In ...

- Actions governed by Rule 24.1 prior to January 1, 2010—in effect, if a proceeding was subject to mandatory mediation on that date, it continues to be until it is finished;
- case-managed actions under Rule 77 in Ottawa and the County of Essex (Windsor);
- actions governed by now-revoked Rule 78 (the predecessor to the current Rule 77) in Toronto where, under Rule 78.12, an action was moved into case management under Rule 77; and
- simplified procedure actions under Rule 76, when ordered by a judge.

After January 1, 2010, mandatory mediation under Rule 24.1 applies as follows:

- Actions commenced in Toronto, Ottawa, or the County of Essex (Windsor). Because mandatory mediation was originally conceived of as part of the case management process, it is not surprising to see that it continues to operate where case management is available and is in fact mandatory in those cases. However, it is also mandatory in all other cases, whether case managed or not, in Toronto, Ottawa, and the County of Essex (Windsor), unless a party applies for an exemption. Rule 24.1 does not operate in other parts of Ontario, although it may be extended to other judicial regions in the future.

What's Out ...

Rule 24.1 does not apply to certain types of actions in Toronto, Ottawa, or the County of Essex (Windsor) as noted in Rules 24.1.04(2), (2.1), and (3):

- Actions under Rule 75.1. This rule governs estate litigation and has its own form of mandatory mediation. There is a brief discussion of estate mediation at the end of this chapter.

- Actions involving death or serious injury arising from an automobile accident are exempt from mediation under Rule 24.1 *if* the parties resorted to mediation under s. 258.6 of the *Insurance Act* and provided that the mediation was conducted and presumably ended unsuccessfully less than a year before the delivery of the first defence in the action. If mediation occurred more than a year before that date, it is apparently considered to be "stale" and Rule 24.1 requires the parties to mediate again, on the off chance that things may have changed over time. But even if things haven't changed, if it has been more than a year since the first defence was filed, they are required to spend time and money on mediation once again.

- Commercial List cases. These cases are closely supervised by Commercial List judges, who are presumably alert to opportunities for mediation and can pressure the parties to mediate.

- Mortgage actions, as with case management, follow their own statutory procedures under the *Mortgages Act*.

- Actions under the *Construction Lien Act* follow their own summary procedures. However, under the Act, whether a lien has been registered or not, where a payer receives money earmarked for a construction lien holdback (to make sure there is a fund to pay those entitled to payment) or for direct payment to others, a payer's failure to set aside funds may result in a trust action. In this case, Rule 24.1 applies and the parties must engage in mandatory mediation.

- Actions under the *Bankruptcy and Insolvency Act* follow their own summary procedures.

- Under the *Class Proceedings Act, 1992*, as in case management, Rule 24.1 does not apply to a class action that is certified, but does apply to one in which certification has been denied where mediation may help to work out a protocol to settle a large number of small claims.

- Under the *Proceedings Against the Crown Act* in certain circumstances. Before a plaintiff issues a statement of claim, s. 7 of the Act requires the plaintiff to serve on the Crown a notice of intended action. If the notice has not been served, the Crown at its option may participate in mediation under Rule 24.1, but it is not required to do so.

Exemption from Mediation

Note that while mediation is mandatory, it may not be possible to apply it to certain cases. Arguably, if the parties are so antagonistic toward one another that there is no reasonable prospect for a successful mediation, then mediation should not be attempted. Indeed, Rule 24.1.05 permits a party to bring a motion for an order for exemption of a particular case from mandatory mediation. However, the bar for an exemption has been set very high. In at least two actions for sexual assault, the plaintiff in each case sought an exemption on the basis of fear of the defendant being in the same room with him, and the psychological trauma that would be caused. In both cases the court held that mediation still had to be attempted, and that the answer was to select a mediator with skills to address issues of violence and set up a protocol that would allow mediation as a process.[3] As well, Rule 24.1.11 permits a party to apply to the court for permission not to attend a mediation session in person—an order that might be appropriate in this type of case, and would make an exemption unnecessary.

Who Conducts the Mediation?

Because there is a high volume of mediation cases, it is necessary to have a great many mediators, and some administrative coordination of them. Rule 24.1.07 provides for the establishment of a mediation committee in each county where mandatory mediation is required, with the responsibility of developing criteria for appointing mediators, screening them, and approving them to be included on a list or roster of mediators. The committee also has the authority to monitor the performance of mediators, and respond to complaints about mediators named on the list. However, the rule does not set out any kind of specific procedure for dealing with complaints. The committee may also add and remove mediators from the list.

Under Rule 24.1.06, for each county or region where mandatory mediation has been imposed, a mediation coordinator appointed by the attorney general or his or her delegate administers the list. There are a variety of certificate and diploma courses where one may train to become a mediator. Given the high volume of actions where it is required, mediation is, if nothing else, a charter of full employment for lawyers and anyone who has taken an ADR course. There are no clear professional standards that all mediators must adhere to, and there is no single body that certifies mediators as professionals in the way that doctors and lawyers are certified. The mediation committee has broad discretion in appointing individuals to the list of mediators, although the Ministry of the Attorney General has provided some guidelines for exercising that discretion.

In any case, the litigants have some choice in who their mediator will be (Rule 24.1.08(2)). The mediation may be conducted by:

- a person the parties agree to, chosen from the list;
- a person assigned by the mediation coordinator from the list where the parties have not chosen a mediator in the time provided for under Rules 24.1.09(6) and (6.1); or
- a person the parties agree to who is not on the list.

When the parties have chosen a mediator, before the action is set down for trial, one of them, although it is usually the plaintiff, shall file with the mediation coordinator a notice in Form 24.1A, setting out the name of the mediator and the date of the mediation session if it has not concluded, or a copy of the mediator's report indicating that mediation has been completed. Figure 22.1 shows a sample notice in Form 24.1A.

Figure 22.1   Notice of Name of Mediator and Date of Session (Form 24.1A)

Court file no. 01-CV-1234

ONTARIO
SUPERIOR COURT OF JUSTICE

BETWEEN:

ABIGAIL BOAR

Plaintiff

and

RATTLE MOTORS LTD. and FRED FLOGEM

Defendants

NOTICE OF NAME OF MEDIATOR AND DATE OF SESSION

TO: MEDIATION CO-ORDINATOR

1. I certify that I have consulted with the parties and that the parties have chosen the following mediator for the mediation session required by Rule 24.1: Marielle Moosetrap.
2. The mediator is named in the list of mediators for the City of Toronto.
3. The mediation session will take place on December 13, year 1.

November 17, year 1

Just & Coping
Barristers and Solicitors
365 Bay Street – 8701
Toronto, Ontario, M3J 4A9

I.M. Just
LSUC #12345R
tel. 416-762-1342
fax 416-762-2300

Lawyers for the Plaintiff

RCP-E 24.1A (April 11, 2012)

Choosing a Mediator: Some Matters to Consider

Counsel is entitled to information from any mediator, on the list or off it, and there are questions a lawyer or client should ask before a mediator is selected.

- Where did the mediator train?
- What kind of mediation experience does he or she have?
- Is the mediator familiar with Rule 24.1, the court processes, and the role of mediation in a civil proceeding?
- What references can the mediator provide?
- Will the mediator agree to the fee schedule established under the rule?
- What are the mediator's fees for services above and beyond the fee schedule for the first three hours of mediation?

When Does Mediation Occur? The "180-Day Rule" and Its Exceptions

One of the complaints of counsel about the pre-2010 version of Rule 24.1 was that it occurred way too early in the proceedings. The rule is now more flexible in that regard, requiring that a mediation session be held within 180 days after the first defence is filed. This means that the parties must have met or talked to choose a mediator, and have that mediator schedule a session well before the 180-day period has expired; the process of finding a mediator should begin at the time the claim issues, if not earlier. As you will have noted in earlier chapters, there is increasing emphasis on counsel meeting relatively early, even before a claim is issued, to identify issues and make procedural decisions. This is most obvious with respect to discovery, but has become a "best practice" among civil litigators.

However, the "180-day rule" in Rule 24.1.09(1) is not rigid; the court has authority to alter the time requirement under the considerations set out in Rule 24.1.09(2). In permitting this flexibility, the rule spells out the criteria for the court to consider, and this provides a context in which to consider delaying mediation. Generally, the theme here is that if mediation delayed beyond the 180-day period is likely to be more successful, then delay mediation. The considerations under Rule 24.1.09(2) are:

- If a proceeding deals with a large number of parties, arranging mediation may be complicated because of the parties' scheduling needs. The same is true if the issues are legally or factually complex—it may take time to find a suitable mediator with the experience to take on a complicated case. Further, if there are multiple parties, the time limit starts running when the first defence issues, but parties added later may not have had sufficient opportunity to prepare for mediation or even to file a defence, in which case their position as set out in a statement of defence would not be available to the mediator, making mediation at that stage of little use.

- If a party expects to move for summary judgment under Rule 20, determination of an issue before trial under Rule 21, or statement of a special case for decision under Rule 22 on an issue, it may be wiser to wait for these early motions to narrow, eliminate, or redefine an issue before mediation. A decision on these matters will redefine the case that the mediator will work with, so there is no point in mediating prematurely. As well, looking at this strategically, a party is unlikely to engage seriously in mediation if it thinks it has a shot at obtaining summary judgment. Once that matter is disposed of, the parties may be more serious about mediation on the outstanding issues.

- The court may extend the 180-day time limit if a party can show that its attempts to complete various forms of discovery will provide information and evidence that will allow mediation to succeed because the parties have a fuller, more nuanced view of the case after discovery, and will engage more seriously in mediation once the picture is clearer.

- Lastly, there is a very broad and general provision that, given the nature of the case or circumstances of the parties, mediation is more likely to succeed if the 180-day time period is extended.

The discussion above is based on the idea that one party is in favour of delay and the other is not, so a court needs to sort matters out. However, Rule 24.1.09(3) permits the parties on consent to postpone the session to a later date provided that they do so in writing and file the written consent or agreement with the mediation coordinator. With a complex case, this may well make sense, and if the parties agree to delay they may do so at their option, so long as they inform the mediation coordinator.

What Happens When the Parties Do Not Proceed with Mediation as Required Under Rule 24.1?

One might well ask how the mediation coordinator knows whether the parties to an action have engaged in mediation. While the default rule is "180 days after the first defence," the mediator has no notice that a claim has been issued or when a first defence is filed, let alone whether mediation has occurred within 180 days of the first defence. But Rule 24.1.09 ensures that the mediation coordinator eventually finds out whether mediation has occurred:

- The mediation coordinator may receive a copy of an order from the court permitting mediation to be delayed beyond 180 days after the first defence is filed (Rule 24.1.09(1)).

- The mediation coordinator receives a consent from the parties to postpone mediation to a later date (Rule 24.1.09(3)).

- The mediation coordinator receives a notice that the action has settled.

- In any event, at the time the action is set down for trial, the parties *must* file with the mediation coordinator a notice in Form 24.1A that identifies the mediator and the date of the mediation session, or, if the mediation has been completed, a copy of the mediator's report.

If the mediation coordinator has not received notice as described above, there is a presumption that the parties have not selected a mediator, or otherwise addressed the requirement that they at least go through the motions and engage in the process. The mediation coordinator, who can presume that a mediator has not been chosen, may now, under Rule 24.1.09(6), assign a mediator from the list. If there is a consent, or an order delaying the mediation session to a later date, and Form 24.1A (notice of mediation session and date of session) has not been filed when the action is set down for trial, that too will result in a mediator being appointed from the list (Rule 24.1.09(6.1)).

At this point, the mediation process ceases to be controlled by the parties. The appointed mediator is directed to immediately fix a date for mediation, and on 20 days' notice, serve every party with a notice by assigned mediator (Form 24.1B), setting out the date, time, and place of the session, with the further information that attendance is compulsory. The date and time of the mediation session shall be no later than 90 days after the mediator is appointed by the mediation coordinator. A copy of the notice must also be sent to the mediation coordinator. Figure 22.2 shows a sample notice by assigned mediator in Form 24.1B.

If the parties are having difficulty in agreeing to mediate, it seems unlikely that forcing them to the table will result in anything more than additional delay and expense. You can lead a horse to water, but you can't make it drink—the same may be said about dragging unwilling parties to a process where voluntary participation is a fundamental feature. In this kind of situation, applying to delay mediation or obtain an exemption is advisable. Similarly, even where the delay arises because the case is complex but the parties are not unwilling to mediate, it is important to diarize taking steps under Rule 24.1.09(1) or (3) to obtain an order or file a consent; otherwise the mediation coordinator, hearing nothing from them, may appoint a mediator, which will result in the parties incurring unnecessary mediation fees for an unnecessarily appointed mediator.

Mediation Procedure and Attendance

Whether the parties have agreed to appoint a mediator, delayed the date of the session, or not agreed to anything and had a mediator appointed from the list by the mediation coordinator, the day of the mediation session will inevitably arise. A mediator is not expected to hear about the case for the first time at the mediation session—a good deal of time would be wasted with the parties having to inform the mediator as to what the case is about. Rule 24.1.10 solves this problem by requiring each party to prepare a statement of issues in Form 24.1C that identifies the factual and legal issues in dispute from the party's perspective. The plaintiff must attach a copy of the pleadings. All parties must attach a copy of any document they consider to be relevant. This does not mean you attach all of the documents from discovery, but you do attach key documents on the issues referred to in the statement of issues. If, for example, the case is about a dispute over the interpretation of a contract, it would be a good idea to attach a copy of the contract. If it is a personal injury case

Figure 22.2   Notice by Assigned Mediator (Form 24.1B)

Court file no. 01-CV-1234

ONTARIO
SUPERIOR COURT OF JUSTICE

BETWEEN:

ABIGAIL BOAR

Plaintiff

and

RATTLE MOTORS LTD. and FRED FLOGEM

Defendants

NOTICE BY ASSIGNED MEDIATOR

TO: Abigail Boar

AND TO: Rattle Motors Ltd. and Fred Flogem

The notice of name of mediator and date of session (Form 24.1A) required by Rule 24.1.09 of the Rules of Civil Procedure has not been filed in this action. Accordingly, the mediation coordinator has assigned me to conduct the mediation session under Rule 24.1. I am a mediator named in the list of mediators for the City of Toronto.

The mediation session will take place on December 13, year 1 from 10:00 a.m. to 1:00 p.m., at JPR Arbitration and Mediation Services, 390 Bay Street – 400, Toronto, Ontario, M5H 2Y2.

Unless the court orders otherwise, you are required to attend this mediation session. If you have a lawyer representing you in this action, he or she is also required to attend.

You are required to file a statement of issues (Form 24.1C) by December 6, year 1 (seven days before the mediation session). A blank copy of the form is attached.

When you attend the mediation session, you should bring with you any documents that you consider of central importance in the action. You should plan to remain throughout the scheduled time. If you need another person's approval before agreeing to a settlement, you should make arrangements before the mediation session to ensure that you have ready telephone access to that person throughout the session, even outside regular business hours.

YOU MAY BE PENALIZED UNDER RULE 24.1.13 IF YOU FAIL TO FILE A STATEMENT OF ISSUES OR FAIL TO ATTEND THE MEDIATION SESSION.

November 20, year 1

Marielle Moosetrap
1200 Yonge Street
Toronto, Ontario, M5R 1Z6
tel. 416-490-8765
fax 416-490-8766

cc. Mediation coordinator

RCP-E 24.1B (November 1, 2005)

where the extent of the injury is in dispute, the attachment of medical reports and documents might be advisable.

A copy of your report should be provided to the mediator and to all other parties, at least seven days prior to the date set for mediation. Figure 22.3 shows a sample statement of issues in Form 24.1C. While the rule does not specifically require you to serve the document, service may be a good idea, as failure to provide copies could derail mediation and proof of service might help you avoid being saddled with the cost of an aborted mediation.

The rule also contemplates the uncooperative party, who, now forced to mediate, refuses to serve the party's statement of issues. Failure to cooperate does not automatically cancel the session, but if the mediator thinks it is not practical to conduct a mediation session without a party's completed statement of issues, he or she may cancel the session and file a notice of non-compliance with the mediation coordinator. The consequences of non-compliance are discussed later in this chapter. Note that the wording of Rule 24.1.10(5) does not require a mediator to cancel a session if one party fails to provide a statement of issues. Other parties may have issues that they can settle between themselves even where another party is non-compliant. For example, where there are multiple defendants with crossclaims, they may be able to mediate and settle issues between themselves even though the plaintiff is non-compliant.

When the mediation session is held, parties and lawyers are expected to be present unless the court orders otherwise—for example, in a case where one party is terrorized by the other party, or where one party is incapacitated. The key is being able to give instructions to counsel who are participating in the mediation session (Rule 24.1.11(1)).

There is a special rule for cases where an insurer may be liable to indemnify one of the parties. In this type of case, the insurer is not a party, but obviously has a big stake in the outcome, as the insurer is the one who will have to pay whatever damages are ordered. For example, in the Boar case, Rattle Motors will have liability insurance and its insurers may be liable to pay damages to Abigail. Although the insurers are not a named party to the action, they certainly have a stake in mediation. Consequently, because the insurer has an interest in the outcome, Rule 24.1.11(1.1) provides that the insurer's representative (usually a claims agent) may be present rather than the party, who may attend, but is not required to if the insurer's representative is present; and it is the latter who will work with counsel in the mediation process (the insurer is generally responsible for the defence, and retains and instructs counsel).

Where a party requires approval by another person to settle a case at mediation, the party is responsible for telephone access throughout the mediation process, so that the other party is fully informed and can give informed instructions. In many respects the principles here are similar to those in other procedures focused on settlement, such as the pretrial conference under Rule 50.

What happens if a party fails to attend a mediation session? As with failure to provide an issues statement, the mediator has some discretion under Rule 24.1.12. He or she may cancel the session if a party fails to attend the first 30 minutes of the scheduled session, and file a certificate of non-compliance. There is no requirement

Figure 22.3   Statement of Issues (Form 24.1C)

Court file no. 01-CV-1234

ONTARIO
SUPERIOR COURT OF JUSTICE

BETWEEN:

ABIGAIL BOAR

Plaintiff

and

RATTLE MOTORS LTD. and FRED FLOGEM

Defendants

STATEMENT OF ISSUES

<u>1. Factual and legal issues in dispute</u>

The plaintiff states that the following factual and legal issues are in dispute and remain to be resolved:

1. whether oil leaking from an automobile in the corporate defendant's showroom caused the plaintiff to fall and be seriously injured;
2. whether the defendant Fred Flogem failed in his duty to the plaintiff by not cleaning up the oil spill when he became aware of it; and
3. whether the damages sustained by the plaintiff were solely the result of the defendants' negligence.

<u>2. Party's position and interests (what the party hopes to achieve)</u>

1. The plaintiff's position is that all of her injuries and subsequent losses and damages resulted from the negligent acts of the defendants.
2. The plaintiff hopes to receive adequate compensation for both special and general damages arising from her injuries.

<u>3. Attached documents</u>

Attached to this form are the following documents that the plaintiff considers of central importance in the action:

1. Statements of claim and defence
2. List of general damages sustained by the plaintiff
3. List of special damages sustained by the plaintiff

December 1, year 1

Abigail Boar
Abigail Boar

Figure 22.3   Concluded

Just & Coping
Barristers and Solicitors
365 Bay Street – 8701
Toronto, Ontario, M3J 4A9

I.M. Just
LSUC #12345R
tel. 416-762-1342
fax 416-762-2300

Lawyers for the Plaintiff

NOTE: When the plaintiff provides a copy of this form to the mediator, a copy of the pleadings shall also be included.

NOTE: Rule 24.1.14 provides as follows:

All communications at a mediation session and the mediator's notes and records shall be deemed to be without prejudice settlement discussions.

RCP-E 24.1C (November 1, 2005)

---

here to wait out the full three-hour period of the mandatory session. But if some of the parties who are prepared to mediate issues between themselves do attend, there is no reason for them to be deprived of the opportunity to mediate on their issues in the absence of a party who has not attended. Interestingly, where one party does not attend, but other parties do, and the mediator thinks it is practical to continue, the rule does not seem to contemplate the use of a certificate of non-compliance directed at the non-attending party. The language of the Rules suggests that this applies only if the mediator finds that it is impractical to conduct the session in the missing party's absence.

Consequences of Non-Compliance: A Good Way to Get into Case Management

Failure of any party to file an issues statement, or attend a scheduled mediation session within the first 30 minutes, or failure of the plaintiff to provide a copy of the pleadings to a mediator, may result in a certificate of non-compliance in Form 24.1D, a sample of which can be seen in Figure 22.4. The mediator sends the certificate of non-compliance to the mediation coordinator, who refers the matter to a

Figure 22.4   Certificate of Non-Compliance (Form 24.1D)

Court file no. 01-CV-1234

ONTARIO
SUPERIOR COURT OF JUSTICE

BETWEEN:

ABIGAIL BOAR

Plaintiff

and

RATTLE MOTORS LTD. and FRED FLOGEM

Defendants

CERTIFICATE OF NON-COMPLIANCE

TO: MEDIATION CO-ORDINATOR

I, Marielle Moosetrap, mediator, certify that this certificate of non-compliance is filed because:

(   )   (*Identify party(ies)*) failed to provide a copy of a statement of issues to the mediator and the other parties (*or* to the mediator *or* to *party(ies)*).

(   )   (*Identify party(ies)*) failed to provide a copy of the pleadings to the mediator.

(x)   The defendant Fred Flogem failed to attend within the first 30 minutes of a scheduled mediation session.

December 13, year 1

Marielle Moosetrap
1200 Yonge Street
Toronto, Ontario, M5R 1Z6
tel. 416-490-8765
fax 416-490-8766

RCP-E 24.1D (November 1, 2005)

judge or case management master. It is not an accident that mediation is mandatory in the same counties in which case management is available.

Rule 24.1.13 provides that a judge or case management master may convene a case conference under Rule 77.08. This should come as no surprise, because non-compliance with mandatory mediation is often a symptom of greater procedural dysfunction—a case may be complex as to issues or the number of parties involved, and therefore hard to coordinate, or the parties in a case may be diligently non-cooperative and obstructive—these are just the sorts of cases that will require judicial oversight and a firm hand under Rule 77. A case management judge will have broad discretion, as follows:

- A timetable can be established, including one for further mediation as well as for other steps in the proceeding.
- A party's documents may be struck out, including the statement of defence of a defendant, which will result in a default judgment for the plaintiff.
- A non-compliant plaintiff may have his or her action struck out and dismissed.
- A non-compliant party may be ordered to pay costs.
- The court may make any other order that is just.

Unless the behaviour is blatantly outrageous, a likely order is for costs to be paid by the non-compliant party for the cancelled mediation, the rescheduled mediation (including the mediator's fee), and the case conferences.

The Mediation Session and Its Results

The parties and their lawyers must attend the mediation session unless the court orders otherwise. Since the session is confidential and things said in it are said without prejudice, the sessions are not public. The three-hour mediation session usually opens with the mediator explaining the mediation process to the parties and reviewing the terms of the mediation and the issues set out in the statements of issues. The mediator usually then initiates the discussion and structures it. Each party gives his or her side of the story, sets out what is important, and asks questions. Once the mediator has a sense of the parties' status, he or she helps them to develop solutions to their problems. The mediator may meet the parties while they are face-to-face or may shuttle back and forth between them while the parties remain in separate rooms. The lawyer, sitting with the client, can determine when the client needs additional advice or a break. During the break, the client can get advice from the lawyer about how to negotiate and about possible solutions.

Preparing the Client for the Scheduled Mediation Session

If you are compelled to participate in mediation, you might as well make the best of it, so it is important to prepare your client. Unlike in a pretrial conference or settlement conference, where the client says little and the lawyer does most of the talking, a client may be expected to be an active participant in mediation, depending on the client's wishes and the mediator's style. This means that an intelligent and articulate client may have an advantage, which is something a lawyer with a less articulate client may have to counter by participating more actively. But a client will require careful preparation. In particular, the lawyer must

- give the client an overview of the mediation strategies and goals;
- explain to the client what the client's role is;
- remind the client that the goal is to find a mutually acceptable solution, not to beat the other side;
- discuss particular strategies with the client;
- be sure the client or the client's representative has authority to settle the lawsuit, and establish settlement ceilings;
- discuss with the client the cost, risks, and benefits of not settling during mediation;
- ensure that the client understands the theory of his or her own case, and its strengths and weaknesses;
- ensure that the client understands the theory of the other party's case, and its strengths and weaknesses;
- advise the client on how to present his or her position in the most positive and persuasive way;
- advise the client about any confidential information that should not be disclosed; and
- work with the client to develop an opening statement.

Rule 24.1 contemplates a single mediation session of up to three hours; if the parties agree, the session can be extended and other sessions scheduled. The three-hour limit is designed to control costs for litigants compelled to engage in mediation, although three hours is considered to be a relatively short period of time for mediation, generally. Rule 24.1.16 permits the court, with consent of the parties, to order continued mediation, including the provision of any directions to the parties and the mediator that the court considers to be appropriate. For example, the court may restrict further mediation to a particular issue or set of issues. Once mediation is concluded, whether it was extended beyond the three-hour standard session or not, the mediator shall give a report on the mediation to the parties and the mediation coordinator within 10 days after completion of the mediation. A mediator who is sluggish with paperwork and fails to do this risks being struck off the list of mediators by the mediation coordinator. There is no prescribed form for the report. If the mediation was not successful, then the report should simply state that. The purpose here is to show that mediation occurred and that Rule 24.1 was complied with so that the case can move on. Who said what to whom or who made what admissions is irrelevant at this stage and not reportable, because all statements made during mediation are privileged as a without prejudice settlement discussion so that nothing said at mediation is admissible in court. If the parties reached an agreement on any facts, issues, or remedies, the terms should be recorded and should be signed by the parties or by counsel, who presumably have instructions to sign. This is information the trial judge will need to have at trial. If the agreement settles the action with conditions to be fulfilled, such as the payment of damages, it shall be filed by the defendant in court within 10 days after the conditions are fulfilled. If the settlement is unconditional, it shall be filed by the defendant 10 days after it is signed. Once filed in court, it can become the basis for further action if a party fails to comply with its terms—a party may make a motion for judgment in terms of the agreement, or ask for an order that nullifies the agreement and permits the party seeking the order to continue with the action.

Who Pays for Mediation?

The maximum fees that a mediator can charge for a mandatory three-hour mediation session are set by regulation.[4] These fees were developed in response to charges from critics who say that mediation is an added, open-ended expense for clients. The mediator's fee covers one hour of preparation time for the mediator as well as the three-hour session. The client must pay lawyer's fees connected to the mediation process in addition to the mediator's fee. The fee rises along with the number of parties involved and is shared by the parties. The current schedule is set out in Table 22.1.

Table 22.1   Mediator Fees

Number of Parties	Maximum Fees for Mandatory Session
2	$600 plus GST
3	$675 plus GST
4	$750 plus GST
5 or more	$825 plus GST

If the client has a legal aid certificate, or is of modest means and meets the Ministry of the Attorney General's financial eligibility requirements, mediation is provided at no cost to the client. The ministry's eligibility form is set out in Figure 22.5.

Over and above the fees set out in Table 22.1, if mediation goes past three hours, the mediation may continue if the parties and the mediator agree, and agree on the mediator's fees for the additional time.[5]

Figure 22.5   Financial Eligibility Form

FINANCIAL ELIGIBILITY FORM*
ONTARIO MANDATORY MEDIATION PROGRAM

To be completed by litigants seeking pro bono mediation services under the MMP Access Plan.

Date: _____   Location (county): _____

        yy   mm   dd

Name: _____

          First   Last

1. How many people are in your family unit, including you, your spouse and any dependent children?

        1 2 3 4 5+

2. What is the total gross income of your family unit annually (or monthly)?

[ ] No income   [ ] Under $18,000 ($1,500)   [ ] $18,000-26,999 ($1,500-2,249)
[ ] $27,000-30,999 ($2,250-2,582)   [ ] $31,000-36,999 ($2,582-3,082)
[ ] $37,000-43,000 ($3,083-3,583)   [ ] Over $43,000 ($3,583)

3. Does the total amount of your liquid assets exceed $1,500 including all bank accounts, bonds, stocks, RRSPs, GICs, mutual funds and similar assets? (Do not include vehicles, real property, and household effects.)

    [ ] yes [ ] no

4. Does your net worth exceed $6,000?

    [ ] yes [ ] no

Declaration:

I, _____, of the _____ of _____, declare that the above information is true and correct and I make this statement conscientiously believing it to be true and knowing that it is of the same force and effect as if made under oath.

Declare before me at the _____ of _____ in the province of Ontario this _____ day of _____ 20 ___.

_____   _____   _____
Local Mediation Coordinator Signature   Litigant Signature / Counsel Signature
                                                (if applicable)

---

* The financial eligibility form can be found at http://www.attorneygeneral.jus.gov.on.ca/english/courts/manmed/accessplan.asp.

Mandatory Mediation in Estate, Trust, and Substitute Decision Proceedings: Rule 75.1

Introduction

This section provides an overview of mandatory mediation as it applies to what is generally called estates litigation, which concerns litigation about estates, trusts, and substitute decisions under Rule 75.[6] A related rule, Rule 75.1, requires that a form of mandatory mediation be applied to estates cases under Rule 75. Mandatory mediation under Rule 75.1 closely parallels Rule 24 but is adapted to suit the procedures in estates litigation. Mandatory mediation under Rule 75.1 applies to cases in Toronto, Ottawa, and the County of Essex (Windsor) in disputed matters that are related to estates, trusts, and substitute decisions (Rule 75.1.02(1)(a)). Not every type of estate litigation requires mediation, and you should refer to Rule 75.1.02(1)(b) for the kinds of estate cases to which mandatory mediation applies.

How Rule 75.1 Works

There are reasons for the differences between mandatory mediation under Rule 24.1 and mandatory mediation under Rule 75.1. Cases under Rule 75 are not exempt from case management under Rule 77. Cases under Rule 75 are usually brought by notice of application, which sets out a different and shorter pretrial procedure. Procedure is further complicated by rules in statutes that govern Rule 75 matters. It is usual in estate cases to have a great number of parties, consisting of estate beneficiaries and classes of estate beneficiaries, not all of whom are interested in all of the issues. A mechanism is needed to avoid dragging all parties into mediation that does not concern them.

When a Rule 75 proceeding has been commenced, an applicant on a notice of application is required to bring a motion for directions relating to the conduct of the mediation within 30 days of the last day on which the respondents may serve a notice of appearance. The rule does not specify a time limit for when the motion must be heard (Rule 75.1.05).

On the return of the motion for directions, the order may be a formality and a foregone conclusion, or it may be lengthy and customized. Estate litigation that involves a challenge to a will or raises issues interpreting a will can be very complex. There may be many beneficiaries, some of whom will be affected by the order but some of whom may not be. Some may be affected in different ways, or some may have one position on the outcome, and others may have another. In a complex estate case, the court may have to:

- identify the issues to be mediated and the order in which they are mediated,
- determine who has carriage of the mediation (usually the estate administrator or trustee),

- set the timetable for conducting the mediation when there are many parties with different interests, and
- decide which parties may attend the mediation and how the cost is to be shared among the parties or classes of parties.

Once an order for directions is made, the parties must select a mediator within 30 days (Rule 75.1.07). The parties may choose their own mediator or select one from the roster. Care should be taken to select a mediator who has some general knowledge of substantive and procedural estate law. Once the parties have agreed to a mediator, the party with carriage of the mediation is required to give the mediator a copy of the order for directions. If the parties fail to select a mediator within 30 days, the party with carriage of the mediation is responsible for filing a request to assign a mediator with the local mediation coordinator.

When the mediator is selected (or assigned), he or she must immediately fix a date for the mediation and, at least 20 days before that, must serve on every party designated by the order for directions notice of the place, date, and time of the mediation (Rule 75.1.07). At least seven days before the mediation, designated parties must provide the mediator and the other designated parties with a statement of issues. The statement of issues, in Form 75.1C, must identify the factual and legal issues in dispute and briefly set out the position and interest of the party making the statement. The party should also attach any documents that that party considers to be of relevance to its position (Rule 75.1.08). Form 75.1C is set out in Figure 22.6. It is completed in much the same way as is the statement of issues in Form 24.1C under Rule 24.1.

The mediator is obliged to give a copy of his or her report on the mediation to every party and to the mediation coordinator within 10 days of the conclusion of the mediation (Rule 75.1.12). An agreement is to be reported, and a breach of an agreement by any party can be enforced. If the standard three-hour mediation is not enough, and with many parties or issues it is likely not to be, the parties may consent to an order for further sessions. The fees are then to be negotiated between the parties and the mediator.

Figure 22.6   Statement of Issues (Form 75.1C)

Court file no. E-1111-01

ONTARIO
SUPERIOR COURT OF JUSTICE

IN THE ESTATE OF   Abigail Boar,   deceased,
late of   the City of Toronto, in the Province of Ontario,
occupation   investment analyst,
who died on   October 21, year 4.

STATEMENT OF ISSUES

1. Factual and legal issues in dispute

The undersigned designated party states that the following factual and legal issues are in dispute and remain to be resolved.

Whether or not there is a last will and testament of Abigail Boar, subsequent to that which is dated April 4, year −4, for which an application for probate has been made in this court.

2. Party's position and interests (what the party hopes to achieve)

This party is the brother of Abigail Boar, who is excluded from the beneficiaries mentioned in the Last Will and Testament of Abigail Boar, dated April 4, year −4. This party believes there is a subsequent will dated April 9, year −4, and that this will includes this party as a beneficiary of the estate of Abigail Boar.

3. Attached documents

Attached to this form are the following documents that the designated party considers of central importance in the proceeding:

1. Affidavit of Bill Boar, sworn November 5, year 1 and filed in this proceeding.
2. Photocopy of a Last Will and Testament of Abigail Boar, executed by her on April 9, year −4.

October 23, year 4

Bill Boar
_____
Bill Boar
2311 Baybottom Crescent
Toronto, Ontario, M5R 8X3
416-481-0003

NOTE: Rule 75.1.11 provides as follows:

All communications at a mediation session and the mediator's notes and records shall be deemed to be without prejudice settlement discussions.

RCP-E 75.1C (November 1, 2005)

CHAPTER SUMMARY

This chapter briefly explained the purpose of mediation and its role in diverting civil cases from the court system by promoting settlement at an early date. The encouraging results of the mediation pilot project have resulted in mediation becoming mandatory for all proceedings that are case managed under Rule 77 as well as other actions in Toronto, Ottawa, and the County of Essex (Windsor), even if they are not under case management. We discussed the lawyer's role in the mediation process and his or her duty in explaining to the client how mediation works.

Once a proceeding is commenced, we noted that the parties have 180 days after the first defence is filed to hold a mediation session, which means that a mediator must be selected well in advance of that date. We also noted that appropriate cases may be exempted from mediation, and on consent or on order the time for mediation may be extended. Mediation is conceived as a session of up to three hours' duration, but it may extend to more than three hours if the circumstances warrant and the parties consent. At least seven days before the mediation session, the parties must provide the mediator with an issues statement. On completion of the mediation, the mediator must, within 10 days, report to the mediation coordinator on the outcome of the mediation. The costs of mediation are borne by the parties, and the fees are fixed for the first three hours. The parties may, on consent, go on to further sessions, but the mediator's fees are no longer fixed. If a party does not cooperate with the process, the court may impose penalties. However, in appropriate cases, the court may order that the case proceed without mediation.

We also briefly discussed mandatory mediation under Rule 75.1 for contentious and disputed estate, trust, and substitute decision cases, noting differences from mandatory mediation under Rule 24.1.

KEY TERMS

alternative dispute resolution, 532
mediation, 532

NOTES

1. The description here of the results of the evaluation of mandatory mediation is adopted from R.G. Hann and Carl Baar et al., *Evaluation of the Ontario Mandatory Mediation Program: Executive Summary and Recommendations* (Toronto: Queen's Printer, March 2001). See also "Report of the Evaluation Committee of the Ontario Civil Rules Committee for the Mandatory Mediation Rule Pilot Project," in *Civil Litigation—100% Case Management Alert*, Advocates' Society conference, held in Toronto on May 31, 2001.

2. But costs increase where mediation fails because the parties must pay the mediator, and there are the additional costs of lawyers preparing for mediation.

3. *Owen v. Hiebert* (2000), 11 CPC (5th) 121 (SCJ, Master); *O (G.) v. H (C.D.)* (2000), 50 OR (3d) 82 (CA).

4. *Administration of Justice Act*, O. Reg. 451/98, as amended by O. Reg. 241/01.

5. Ibid., at s. 4(3).

6. The discussion is brief. Estate, trust, and substitute decisions litigation, known collectively as "estate litigation," is specialized and based on several statutes and a vast amount of case law.

REFERENCES

Administration of Justice Act, O. Reg. 241/01, Mediators' Fees (Rule 24.1, Rules of Civil Procedure).

Administration of Justice Act, O. Reg. 451/98, Mediators' Fees (Rule 24.1, Rules of Civil Procedure).

Bankruptcy and Insolvency Act, RSC 1985, c. B-3, as amended.

Class Proceedings Act, 1992, SO 1992, c. 6.

Construction Lien Act, RSO 1990, c. C.30.

Hann, R.G. and Carl Baar et al., *Evaluation of the Ontario Mandatory Mediation Program: Executive Summary and Recommendations* (Toronto: Queen's Printer, March 2001).

Insurance Act, RSO 1990, c. I.8.

Mortgages Act, RSO 1990, c. M.40.

Proceedings Against the Crown Act, RSO 1990, c. P.27.

"Report of the Evaluation Committee of the Ontario Civil Rules Committee for the Mandatory Mediation Rule

Pilot Project," in *Civil Litigation—100% Case Management Alert*, Advocates' Society conference, held in Toronto, May 31, 2001.

Rules of Civil Procedure, RRO 1990, reg. 194.

Substitute Decisions Act, 1992, SO 1992, c. 30.

Succession Law Reform Act, RSO 1990, c. S.26.

REVIEW QUESTIONS

1. What is mediation?

2. What are the advantages and disadvantages of mediation?

3. What cases are subject to mandatory mediation?

4. Must every case-managed proceeding go through mediation?

5. How are mediators selected?

6. What must be done to prepare for mediation?

7. Who must attend the mediation?

8. How long is a mediation session?

9. What are the costs of mediation?

10. What happens if a party is not cooperative in the mediation process?

11. What happens when mediation is complete?

12. How does mandatory mediation under Rule 24.1 differ from mediation under Rule 75.1?

DISCUSSION QUESTION

1. Draft a statement of issues to be filed on behalf of Fred Flogem and Rattle Motors Ltd. You will want to review Figures 7.2 (statement of claim), 7.3 (statement of defence), and 22.3 (Abigail Boar's statement of issues).

Simplified Procedure: Rule 76

23

Introduction

As we saw in our look at the *Rules of Civil Procedure*, litigation in the Ontario Superior Court of Justice can be a complicated, expensive, and time-consuming process. A party who is suing for $25,000 or less can take their case to Small Claims Court with its straightforward and relatively fast procedure. However, if a party wants to sue for more than $25,000, there is no option but to use the Superior Court, unless the plaintiff is willing to abandon any part of the claim that is in excess of the monetary limit for the Small Claims Court.

Not all actions in the Superior Court warrant the use of the usual lengthy procedure. Therefore, the Rules provide a manner of proceeding that falls somewhere between the Small Claims Court and the regular Superior Court process. This manner of proceeding is called the simplified procedure, and it is contained in Rule 76. This procedure reduces the time and expense associated with litigation.

Application of the Simplified Procedure

The simplified procedure *must* be used in all cases in the Superior Court in which a party is claiming $100,000 or less, exclusive of interest and costs. It may also be used for claims over $100,000, provided that the defendant does not object. The limit does not apply only to claims for money. It also applies to claims for real and personal property valued at $100,000 or less. The assessment of the value of the property is its fair market value at the time the action is commenced.

The simplified procedure is not available for actions brought under the *Class Proceedings Act, 1992* or the *Construction Lien Act*, except for trust claims. Actions following the simplified procedure are not subject to Rule 77 and are therefore not case managed. It is also not available for cases that proceed by application or in family law matters.

If there is more than one plaintiff in the action, each plaintiff's claim must independently meet the requirements for application of Rule 76; that is, the monetary amount must be within the limits and the type of action must be one to which the rule applies. If there is more than one defendant, the claim against each defendant must also fall within the requirements of the rule.

For example, if Abigail Boar sued Rattle Motors Ltd. and Fred Flogem for $100,000, and her boyfriend also decided to sue the defendants for the loss of Abigail's companionship as a result of her injuries, his claim would have to be for $100,000 or less and satisfy the other criteria as well.

If the plaintiff is suing more than one defendant in the same action, she must use the simplified procedure if each claim is for $100,000 or less. For instance, if Abigail sues Rattle Motors Ltd. for $100,000 and Fred Flogem for $80,000, she must use the simplified procedure. However, if she sues Rattle Motors Ltd. for $100,000 and Fred Flogem for $140,000, it is not mandatory for her to use the simplified procedure; however, she could use it if the defendant does not object.

All the other rules apply to actions brought under the simplified procedure unless Rule 76 specifically provides that another procedure applies. For example, the statement of claim or notice of action must be issued, served, and filed with the court in the same way as with any other action, and the statement of defence must be served and filed within the same time frame as any other action, as required under Rule 18.

Commencement of an Action

Since it is the plaintiff who commences the action, it is also the plaintiff who must use the simplified procedure if the amount claimed is $100,000 or less. It is also the plaintiff who may elect to use the simplified procedure for claims of more than $100,000. The statement of claim must indicate that the action is being brought under the simplified procedure. The proper wording is: "This action is brought against you under the simplified procedure provided in Rule 76 of the *Rules of Civil Procedure*." This wording is added at the top of the page on which the claim is commenced. It precedes the title "Claim" on the document.

Rule 76.02(5) provides that an action commenced under the simplified procedure will proceed under Rule 76 unless the defendant objects. The objection is made in the statement of defence. The basis for the objection would be one of the following:

1. the claim does not fit within the monetary requirements of the rule;
2. the claim is not of the type to which the simplified procedure applies; or
3. the defendant makes a counterclaim, crossclaim, or third-party claim in which he or she is claiming more than $100,000 and states in his or her statement of defence that the matter is to proceed under the ordinary procedure.

Once the defendant objects to the matter proceeding under Rule 76, the plaintiff, in his or her reply to the statement of defence, may state that he or she is abandoning forever the portion of the claim that is above $100,000 and the proceeding will continue under the simplified procedure. If he or she does not take the option to abandon the excess amount, the action will then continue under the ordinary procedure.

In the same way, an action that has been commenced under the ordinary procedure may continue under the simplified procedure if

- all the parties consent and a consent is filed with the court, or
- no consent is filed, but
  - the plaintiff has followed Rule 26 to amend the claim so that it falls within the requirements for use of the simplified procedure, and
  - all the other claims, counterclaims, crossclaims, or third-party claims meet the requirements to proceed under Rule 76.

Any counterclaim, crossclaim, or third-party claim attached to the main action may also proceed by way of the simplified procedure even if it does not meet the requirements, unless

- the defendant, by crossclaim, counterclaim, or third-party claim, objects in the statement of defence to the use of the simplified procedure and the claim is not amended so that it falls within the requirements of the Rules, or
- the defendant brings a crossclaim, counterclaim, or third-party claim that does not meet the requirements of Rule 76 and states in the pleading that the crossclaim, counterclaim, or third-party claim is to proceed under the ordinary procedure.

In either of these cases, the ordinary procedure will then apply.

If an action changes stream, from simplified to ordinary procedure or vice versa, the plaintiff must serve and file Form 76A, which states what change has been made. A portion of Form 76A is shown in Figure 23.1.

Affidavit of Documents

As in any action, parties must disclose and produce copies of documents relevant to the case. The manner of doing this is through the preparation of an affidavit of documents. See Figure 14.3 in Chapter 14 for a sample of an affidavit of documents.

Rule 76.03 requires that within 10 days after the close of pleadings, a party in a simplified procedure action must serve each of the other parties with an affidavit of documents in which they disclose all documents within their knowledge, information, and belief that are relevant to any matter at issue in the action. Only those documents that have been in the party's possession, control, or power need be disclosed and produced. In addition, copies of the documents referred to in schedule A of the affidavit of documents must also be served on all the other parties. The affidavit must also contain a list of potential witnesses, along with their addresses. If a party fails to disclose the name of a potential witness, the party may not call that witness to give evidence without the court's permission.

Finally, the affidavit must contain a lawyer's certificate under Rule 30.03(4), stating that the lawyer has explained to the person making the affidavit the necessity of disclosing and producing the required documents.

Differences Between the Simplified and the Ordinary Procedure

The major differences between the ordinary and simplified procedures are set out below.

1. *Discovery.* Until 2010, no discovery under Rule 31.03 or 31.10 was permitted at all under the simplified procedure, but this was changed (Rule

Figure 23.1   Notice Whether Action Under Rule 76 (Form 76A)

NOTICE WHETHER ACTION UNDER RULE 76

The plaintiff states that this action and any related proceedings are:

(   ) continuing under Rule 76

(   ) continuing as an ordinary procedure.

RCP-E 76A (November 1, 2008)

76.04(1)) to allow for a limited form of discovery. Rule 76.04(2) permits each party to conduct oral examinations for up to two hours, regardless of the number of parties. However, examination for discovery by written questions and answers under Rule 35 is not allowed.

2. *Cross-examination.* No cross-examination of a deponent on an affidavit on a motion under Rule 39.02 is permitted under the simplified procedure.

3. *Examination of a witnesses.* No examination of a witness on a motion under Rule 39.03 is permitted under the simplified procedure.

4. *Motions.* Motions under the simplified procedure are significantly different from those under the ordinary procedure. These differences are discussed below.

Motions

Rule 76.05 deals with simplified procedure motions. A motion is commenced with a simplified procedure motion form, Form 76B, rather than with a notice of motion. Reflecting the less complicated process under the simplified procedure, this form, for the most part, involves filling in the blanks and requires little drafting. Form 76B is set out in Figure 23.2. A motion must be served according to Rule 37.07 and then submitted to the court before it is brought and heard.

The motion is to be heard in the same court where the action was commenced or transferred unless the parties consent or the court orders that it be heard in another location. In many instances, the motion may be heard without a motion record and other supporting documents. This means that for simple motions, extensive paperwork is not required. Depending on the practical requirements of the situation, a motion may also be made in writing, by fax, or by telephone or video conference.

Many motions can be dealt with by the registrar pursuant to Rules 76.05(4) to (7) and do not require a hearing before a judge. For example, the registrar may deal with the following types of motions if they are on consent, a consent is filed, no party is under a disability, and no responding material is filed:

Figure 23.2   Simplified Procedure Motion Form (Form 76B)

SIMPLIFIED PROCEDURE MOTION FORM

JURISDICTION   ❑ Judge
                ❑ Master
                ❑ Registrar

THIS FORM FILED BY (*Check appropriate boxes to identify the party filing this form as a moving/responding party on this motion AND to identify this party as plaintiff, defendant, etc. in the action*)

❑ moving party
❑ plaintiff

_____

❑ responding party
❑ defendant

_____

❑ other — specify kind of party and name

_____

_____

MOTION MADE

❑ on consent of all parties   ❑ on notice to all parties and
                                        unopposed

❑ without notice   ❑ on notice to all parties and
                                        expected to be opposed

Notice of this motion was served on (date):

_____

by means of:

_____

_____

METHOD OF HEARING REQUESTED

❑ by attendance
❑ in writing only, no attendance
❑ by fax
❑ by telephone conference under rule 1.08
❑ by video conference under rule 1.08

Date, time and place for conference call, telephone call or appearances

_____   _____   _____
(date)   *(time)*   *(place)*

Figure 23.2 Continued

ORDER SOUGHT BY THIS PARTY *(Responding party is presumed to request dismissal of motion and costs)*

❑ extension of time — until (give specific date): _____
❑ serve claim
❑ file or deliver statement of defence
❑ other relief — be specific

_____

_____

MATERIAL RELIED ON BY THIS PARTY

❑ this form
❑ pleadings
❑ affidavits — specify
❑ other — specify

_____

_____

GROUNDS IN SUPPORT OF/IN OPPOSITION TO MOTION (INCLUDING RULE AND STATUTORY PROVISIONS RELIED ON)

_____

_____

CERTIFICATION BY LAWYER

I certify that the above information is correct, to the best of my knowledge. Signature of lawyer *(if no lawyer, party must sign)*

_____

Date _____

THIS PARTY'S LAWYER *(if no lawyer, give party's name, address for service, telephone and fax number)*

Name and firm:

Address:

Telephone:

Fax:

OTHER PARTY'S LAWYER *(if no lawyer, give party's name, address for service, telephone and fax number)*

Name and firm:

Address:

Telephone:

Fax:

Figure 23.2 Concluded

DISPOSITION

❏ order to go as asked

❏ adjourned to

❏ order refused

❏ order to go as follows:

_____

_____

Hearing Method: _____ Hearing duration: _____ minutes

Heard in: ❏ courtroom ❏ office

❏ Successful party MUST prepare formal order for signature

❏ No copy of disposition to be sent to parties

❏ Other directions — specify

_____

_____

Date _____ Name _____ Signature _____

Judge/Master/Registrar

RCP-E 76B (November 1, 2005)

- an amendment of a pleading or a notice of motion;
- an addition, deletion, or substitution of a party whose consent is filed;
- the removal of a lawyer of record;
- setting aside a noting in default;
- setting aside a default judgment;
- discharge of a certificate of pending litigation;
- security for costs in a specified amount; and
- dismissal of a proceeding with or without costs.

There is no need to take out a formal order unless the court or registrar specifically orders that it be taken out or the order is being appealed. The endorsement on the motion form is all that is necessary to establish that an order was made.

Dismissal by the Registrar

Until January 1, 2010, under Rule 76.06, the registrar had the power to dismiss a simplified procedure action that was deemed abandoned under specified criteria. Rule 76.06 has been revoked and is now dealt with under new Rules 48.14 and 48.15, which apply to all actions, including those brought under the simplified procedure.

Summary Judgment

A motion for summary judgment may be brought in relation to simplified procedure actions on the basis that there is no genuine issue requiring a trial or on consent of the parties. Rule 20 applies to summary judgment, which is dealt with in detail in Chapter 11.

Settlement Discussions, Setting the Matter Down for Trial, and the Pretrial Conference

Within 60 days after the first statement of defence or notice of intent to defend has been filed, the parties are required to have a meeting or a telephone discussion to determine whether all the documents relating to the case have been disclosed and whether settlement of any or all of the issues is possible. Within 180 days after the first statement of defence or the notice of intention to defend has been filed, the plaintiff must serve a notice of readiness for pretrial conference, Form 76C, on all the parties and file it with the court, along with proof of service. A sample Form 76C is shown in Figure 23.3. If the plaintiff does not take this step, any other party may do it. The party that sets the matter down for trial must certify in the notice of readiness for pretrial conference that a settlement discussion took place. The filing of the notice of readiness for pretrial conference sets the case down for trial. Following the filing of the notice of readiness, the registrar schedules a pretrial conference and gives the parties at least 45 days' notice.

At least five days before the pretrial conference, each party must file:

- a copy of the party's affidavit of documents and copies of the documents relied on for the party's claim or defence,
- a copy of any expert's report, and
- any other material necessary for the conference.

It is not necessary to serve this material on the other parties because they will already have copies. In addition, the parties must *serve* and file:

- a two-page statement setting out the issues and the party's position with respect to them, and
- a trial management checklist (Form 76D).

Form 76D, showing the trial management checklist, is provided in Figure 23.4.

Figure 23.3   Notice of Readiness for Pretrial Conference (Form 76C)

Court file no. 01-CV-6789

ONTARIO
SUPERIOR COURT OF JUSTICE

BETWEEN:

MABEL MADDENLY

Plaintiff

and

JIMMY JINGLE

Defendant

NOTICE OF READINESS FOR PRETRIAL CONFERENCE

The plaintiff, Mabel Maddenly, is ready for a pretrial conference and is setting this action down for trial. A pretrial conference in the action will proceed as scheduled and the trial will proceed when the action is reached on the trial list, unless the court orders otherwise.

CERTIFICATE

I CERTIFY that there was a settlement discussion under rule 76.08.

Date: January 10, year 2

Belinda Smart

Belinda Smart, Barrister & Solicitor
LSUC #13579C
47 Tempest Road
Toronto, Ontario, M6Y 5R7

tel. 416-555-1234
fax 416-555-1235

Lawyer for the Plaintiff

TO: George Fandoddle, Barrister & Solicitor
LSUC #24681B
2001 Space Lane
Toronto, Ontario, M8U 9I4

tel. 416-666-8910
fax 416-666-8911

Lawyer for the Defendant

RCP-E 76C (November 1, 2005)

Figure 23.4   Trial Management Checklist (Form 76D)

TRIAL MANAGEMENT CHECKLIST

Trial Lawyer — Plaintiff(s):

Trial Lawyer — Defendant(s):

Filed by Plaintiff
Filed by Defendant
Filed by Subsequent Party

1. Issues Outstanding
    (a) liability:
    (b) damages:
    (c) other:

2. Names of Plaintiff's Witnesses

3. Names of Defendant's Witnesses

4. Admissions

    Are the parties prepared to admit any facts for
    the purposes of the trial or summary trial?   ❑ yes   ❑ no

5. Document Brief
    Will there be a document brief?   ❑ yes   ❑ no

6. Request to Admit
    Will there be a request to admit?   ❑ yes   ❑ no
    If so, have the parties agreed to a timetable?   ❑ yes   ❑ no

7. Expert's Reports
    Are any expert's reports anticipated?   ❑ yes   ❑ no

8. Amendments to Pleadings
    Are any amendments likely to be sought?   ❑ yes   ❑ no

9. Mode of Trial
    Have the parties agreed to a summary trial?   ❑ yes   ❑ no
    Have the parties agreed to an ordinary trial?   ❑ yes   ❑ no
    If the parties have not agreed about the mode of
    trial, what mode of trial is being requested by
    the party filing this checklist?

10. Factum of Law
    Will the parties be submitting factums of law?   ❑ yes   ❑ no

RCP-E 76D (November 1, 2005)

The pretrial judge or master sets the trial date. The trial may be an ordinary trial or a summary trial under Rule 76.12. If the parties cannot agree about the type of trial, the pretrial judge or master will determine which type of trial is most appropriate for the case.

If the case is to proceed as a summary trial, the pretrial conference judge or the case management master shall fix a date for the delivery of all the parties' affidavits and may vary the order and time of presentation.

Immediately after the pretrial conference, the registrar will place the action on the appropriate trial list. At least 10 days before the trial, the party that set the matter down for trial by filing the notice of readiness for the pretrial conference must serve a trial record and file it with the court with proof of service. All the parties to the main action, counterclaim, crossclaim, or third-party claim must be served with the trial record.

If the trial is proceeding as an ordinary trial, the trial record is prepared in exactly the same way as the trial record for an action under the ordinary procedure (Rule 48.03). See Chapter 15 for information about trial records; Figure 15.3 shows a sample ordinary trial record.

If the trial is proceeding as a summary trial, Rule 76.11(4) requires that the trial record must contain, in consecutively numbered pages arranged in the following order:

1. a table of contents that describes each document, including each exhibit, by its nature and date and, in the case of an exhibit, by its exhibit number or letter;

2. a copy of the pleadings, including those relating to any counterclaim, crossclaim, or third-party claim;

3. a copy of any demand or order for particulars of a pleading and the particulars delivered in response;

4. a copy of any order respecting the trial;

5. a copy of all the affidavits served by all the parties for use in the summary trial; and

6. a certificate signed by the lawyer of the party filing the trial record, stating that it contains the documents listed above.

Summary Trial

In an ordinary trial, each party calls its witnesses into the courtroom, and each witness is first questioned by the lawyer for the party who called the witness. This is called examination-in-chief. The lawyers for the other parties who are adverse in interest are then entitled to ask the witness questions on cross-examination in order to question the witness's credibility. The plaintiff and defendants are adverse in interest to each other, but in some cases with more than one defendant, the defendants may blame each other for the plaintiff's injuries and are therefore adverse in interest to each other, as well as to the plaintiff.

Rule 76.12 sets out the order for presenting the evidence and examining witnesses at a summary trial. In a summary trial, parties present their evidence by affidavit rather than orally in the courtroom, and witnesses may be examined in-chief or cross-examined by adverse parties, but, unlike in an ordinary trial, the Rules place strict time limits on both types of examination. Examination-in-chief of each deponent on his or her affidavit is limited to 10 minutes and cross-examinations cannot extend beyond 50 minutes in total for all examinations. There are also limits placed on re-examination.

A party who wants a witness presented at trial for examination-in-chief or cross-examination on affidavit must give 10 days' notice to the party who presented the affidavit. The notice is to allow the party presenting the affidavit to arrange for the deponent's attendance at trial for cross-examination.

After all the evidence has been presented and all the examinations completed, each party is allowed to make an oral argument for no more than 45 minutes. All of the time limits for examinations and oral argument set out in Rule 76.12(1) may be extended by the trial judge.

Costs Consequences

Since the purpose of the simplified procedure is to reduce both expense and delay of litigation involving smaller amounts, there are severe costs consequences for failure to use the simplified procedure in appropriate actions. For instance, if the plaintiff proceeds to trial under the ordinary procedure seeking more than $100,000 in relief but at the end of the trial is awarded only $100,000 or less, the court will deny the plaintiff costs unless it is satisfied that it was reasonable for the plaintiff to proceed under the ordinary procedure. This ensures that plaintiffs will put appropriate thought into correctly valuing their claim before they begin the litigation.

Defendants may also face potential costs consequences if they object to the action proceeding under the simplified procedure because they say the property at issue is worth more than $100,000 and, as a result of their objection, the matter is continued under the ordinary procedure. If the court finds that the property is in fact worth $100,000 or less, the defendant will be ordered to pay the extra costs of the plaintiff that were incurred because he or she could not proceed under the simplified procedure. Any such costs will be awarded based on the substantial indemnity scale.

Any party who amends a pleading so that the action is changed from the ordinary procedure to the simplified procedure is liable for the other party's costs that were incurred because the action was originally commenced under the ordinary procedure. These costs will be awarded on a substantial indemnity basis.

CHAPTER SUMMARY

In this chapter, we saw that the simplified procedure is a process that is used for dealing with actions that involve claims of $100,000 or less. It is not available for class actions, construction liens, proceedings commenced by way of application, or family law matters. Cases involving a claim of $100,000 or less must use the simplified procedure, but cases involving a claim of more than that amount may also use this route if the parties consent. The plaintiff elects to proceed under the simplified procedure but the defendants, a third party, or a party in a crossclaim or counterclaim may object.

We have noted that the major differences between the simplified procedure and ordinary procedure are that in the simplified procedure, discovery is much more limited, no examination or cross-examination of deponents on affidavits for motions is permitted, and motions are commenced and conducted in a different manner. Motion records are not required, and the registrar has the power to deal with most simple or uncontested motions.

We also examined the various time limits in the simplified procedure. Within 60 days of the first defence being filed, the parties must hold a settlement conference to decide whether all the necessary documents have been produced and whether settlement is possible. Within 180 days, the plaintiff must set the action down for trial. The registrar will then give notice of a pretrial conference date to the parties. At the pretrial conference, and if no settlement can be reached, the judge or master will set a trial date.

The trial may be a regular trial, but the matter may also proceed to a summary trial, if appropriate. In a summary trial, the parties present their evidence in affidavits and the deponents may be examined or cross-examined under strict time limitations.

There are severe costs consequences for failing to use the simplified procedure in an appropriate case.

REFERENCES

Class Proceedings Act, 1992, SO 1992, c. 6.

Construction Lien Act, RSO 1990, c. C.30.

Rules of Civil Procedure, RRO 1990, reg. 194.

REVIEW QUESTIONS

1. Consider whether the simplified procedure is available in the following situations:

   a. a claim for damages in the amount of $100,000;

   b. a construction lien in the amount of $55,000;

   c. a divorce action in which the total value of the net family property is $45,000;

   d. a claim for damages in the amount of $175,000; and

   e. a damages claim for $80,000 each by Melinda March and her daughter against George Speedy whose snowmobile ran into their toboggan.

2. What is the purpose of the simplified procedure?

3. What is the difference between the statement of claim in an ordinary action and the statement of claim in an action under the simplified procedure?

4. What are the major differences between the regular procedure and the simplified procedure?

5. How is an action under the simplified procedure set down for trial?

6. What is the difference between a summary trial and an ordinary trial?

7. Why is it important to use the simplified procedure in the appropriate cases?

DISCUSSION QUESTION

1. Read and respond to the following memorandum:

   To: Law clerk

   From: I.M. Smug, lawyer

   Re: Tome Inc. v. Joseph Apostiledes

   Our client, Joe Apostiledes, was sued by Tome Inc. for non-payment of a debt of $85,000. We have filed a statement of defence in the case, but Mr. Apostiledes has now decided he does not want legal representation and he is going to represent himself in the action. Counsel for Tome is not objecting to this motion and will not be filing any material in response.

   Please prepare a motion having me removed as lawyer of record on the case.

   You look in the file and see that Tome Inc. is located at 1300 Winding Lane, Toronto, Ontario, M8U 5Y7. It is represented by the firm of Tilley and Tidy, 400 Bay Street, Suite 2200, Toronto, Ontario, M7K 2Y6. Howie Tilley is the lawyer with carriage of the case. The firm's telephone number is 416-878-0000 and their fax is 416-878-0001.

   Joe lives at 14 Foolhardy Way, Windsor, Ontario, N0P 4T8, and his telephone number is 613-555-1222.

   Your firm is located at 1750 Cornucopia Crescent, London, Ontario, L7T 8P4. The telephone number is 613-566-6666 and the fax is 613-566-6667.

   Prepare the necessary form to commence the motion.

The Commercial List 24

Introduction

The Commercial List was established in the Superior Court of Justice in Toronto for the hearing of actions, applications, and motions related to most types of corporate and commercial matters. Except for bankruptcy matters, it is a completely voluntary method of proceeding; however, lawyers usually want to use the Commercial List procedure when they have a case that is eligible to be placed on the list because it expedites court proceedings and allows them to appear before a specific group of Superior Court justices who have some expertise in commercial matters. The Commercial List, Toronto Practice Direction applies here; it can be found at http://www.ontariocourts.ca/scj/practice/practice-directions/toronto/commercial-list. Cases that may be placed on the list are those dealing with or related to

- the *Bankruptcy and Insolvency Act*;
- the *Bank Act* (in relation to realizations and priority disputes);
- the Ontario *Business Corporations Act*;
- the *Canada Business Corporations Act*;
- the *Companies' Creditors Arrangement Act*;
- the *Limited Partnerships Act*;
- the *Pension Benefits Act*;
- the *Personal Property Security Act*;
- receivership applications and all interlocutory motions to appoint, or give directions to, receivers;
- the *Securities Act*;
- the *Winding-up and Restructuring Act*;
- the *Credit Unions and Caisses Populaires Act, 1994*, with regard to credit unions and caisses populaires under administration or that are being wound up or liquidated; and
- any other commercial matters that a judge presiding over the Commercial List may direct be placed on the list. An inclusive list of the types of matters that may fall within this discretionary addition to the list is given in the practice direction itself. In applying discretion to add a matter to the Commercial List, the judge will take into account the current and expected caseload of the list.

The list was initially established in 1991 by a practice direction of the Chief Justice. In June 2010 the then existing practice direction was amended to take into account the changes to the *Rules of Civil Procedure* that took effect on January 1, 2010. While the formatting and filing of documents and the time limits for issuing and serving specific documents are generally the same as those set out in the Rules, many, if not most, of the other procedures for the Commercial List are governed by the practice direction. The practice direction stipulates that "[c]o-operation, communication and common sense" are to be the operating principles of the Commercial List.

The list is administered through the Commercial List Office, 7th Floor, 330 University Avenue, Toronto, ON M5G 1R7. Cases are usually heard in the courtrooms at that courthouse. Only matters originating in and having a material connection to the Toronto judicial region can be heard on the list unless the supervising judge orders otherwise. The fact that the lawyers for the parties are located in Toronto does not on its own qualify a matter to be placed on the list.

If a case is started in the usual manner in the Superior Court of Justice and one of the parties wishes to transfer it to the Commercial List for hearing, or it is on the Commercial List and a party wishes to have it removed from the list and put back into the regular procedure, a motion may be brought before a Commercial List judge for a transfer to or from the list. However, if all of the parties consent to a transfer of their case to the list, court staff in the Commercial List Office will transfer it without a motion being necessary if all the proper documents (that is, a request form and case timetable form) are completed and submitted, the case is a Toronto Regional case, and it clearly involves one of the statutes or matters listed above as eligible for a case to be placed on the Commercial List. These forms are not forms created by the Rules and they change often. Copies of the current forms may be obtained from the Commercial List Office.

Court Documents

For the most part, documents for the Commercial List are identical to the documents required in any Superior Court proceeding except that the name of the court in the title of proceeding for cases on the list is "Superior Court of Justice—Commercial List." In addition, all notices of application or notices of motion involving the Commercial List must state that the application or motion will be made to "a judge presiding over the Commercial List at 330 University Avenue, Toronto."

Originating process for either an action or an application may be issued in the Commercial List Office. Otherwise, the originating process must be issued in accordance with Rule 14.07 in the appropriate office of the Superior Court of Justice. In addition to the court documents required by the *Rules of Civil Procedure* for all actions or applications, cases to be heard on the Commercial List must be accompanied by a fully completed request form and a case timetable form.

All parts of the request form must be completed for every proceeding before the court and signed by all counsel. It is preferable for all counsel to sign the same form, but if this is not possible, each lawyer may sign an individual copy of the form. For any case schedule to take one day or longer to be heard, the form must set out an estimate of how long it will take for the judge to read the materials before the hearing date. The form is to be faxed to the court office.

A case timetable, setting out the schedule for all the steps in the proceeding, must be prepared. It must be agreed to by all counsel and sent to the Commercial List Office before the matter is first spoken to or as soon after as possible. If the lawyers cannot agree on the schedule, they must appear in chambers before the supervising judge of the Commercial List. The schedule is to be met and if, for some reason, a step cannot be completed by the date set, the lawyers are expected to get the matter back on track as soon as possible.

Documents are normally not filed in an electronic format, but many judges will ask lawyers to provide e-delivery of their documents. It is not helpful to the judge if these e-documents are delivered in differing formats, so as of June 2012, there is a pilot project operating in the court for the uniform formatting of all e-delivery documents. The guidelines for the format can be found at http://www.ontariocourts.ca/ scj/practice/practice-directions/toronto/electronic-documents.

Dates for Applications, Motions, and Trials

The Commercial List Office staff, acting under the direction of the supervising judge, may set dates for all matters other than trials. But it should be noted that there are special requirements for summary judgment motions and applications that must be met before the staff will set a date. These are discussed later in this chapter.

If dates are required for trial, only a judge may set those dates, and if parties are seeking to schedule trial dates, a motion must be brought. A trial requirements memorandum that includes a brief outline of the case and its issues, as well as time estimates for any witnesses to be called at trial, must accompany the motion documents. This form, like the request form and the case timetable form, can be obtained from the Commercial List Office.

Each day, a judge who hears Commercial List matters will be in chambers at 9:30 a.m. to deal with urgent matters, matters without notice, consent matters, and scheduling matters. No matter to be heard in chambers can take more than 10 minutes. These motions will be scheduled in such manner that all matters on the chambers list will be completed by 10 a.m. Materials to be used at a chambers appointment must be filed with the court office the day before the hearing.

For scheduling motions, the lawyers must try to provide three mutually agreeable dates for the judge to choose from. This means that when preparing the materials to bring such a motion, you must be in close contact with the lawyers for the other party. If a mutually agreed-upon return date cannot be found among the lawyers, it should be specified that the matter will return "on a date to be established by the Commercial List Office."

Counsel are expected to have discussed beforehand the matter that is going to be heard in chambers. A draft resolution for consideration by the judge should be prepared and it must be filed the day before the matter is to be heard so that the judge may consider it.

Sometimes a motion is brought to transfer a case that was started on the regular Superior Court of Justice list to the Commercial List. For such a motion, the consent of other counsel or a completed request form must be filed so that the judge can make an order that grants or refuses the motion.

By 4:00 p.m. each day, a list of matters scheduled to be heard the following day will be posted on the bulletin board at the Commercial List Office, and you can call the court after 4.00 p.m. to obtain information. Also, the Toronto Lawyers Association posts the court list for the following day on its website at http://www.tlaonline .ca. Reasonable estimates of the time required for the court to deal with the matter are crucial to the expeditious functioning of the Commercial List. These time estimates must be provided in the request form and signed by all the lawyers. If the lawyers do not all sign, the matter will be set down for only 10 minutes. If such an estimate cannot be made at the time, the form must be amended when the matter is rescheduled. In addition, the time estimate must be divided in relation to how long each lawyer will require. If no such division is provided, it will be assumed that the time is to be divided equally. Lawyers are expected to comply with the time estimates that they provide.

Commercial List Motions Before a Master

A Commercial List motion is not normally heard by a master unless a Commercial List judge refers it in writing to a master. If such an order is made, a motion to a master may be scheduled through the scheduling unit at the courthouse at 393 University Avenue. However, if the motion is going to be more than two hours long or will require a master to hear a series of motions on the issues, the motion will not be booked until a master has assigned a team leader. In such a case, the assigned master's registrar will contact the lawyers' offices to arrange scheduling.

Motions for Summary Judgment and Applications

Summary judgment motions under Rule 20 may be dealt with for cases on the Commercial List, but such a motion will not be booked until:

1. the parties have exchanged all motion materials on an agreed-upon schedule or one fixed at a 9:30 a.m. chambers appointment, and are sufficiently advanced in the preparation of the motion to crystallize the issues and the evidence relating to them;

2. a case conference has been booked at which counsel must be prepared to address whether oral evidence should be heard on the motion in accordance with Rule 20.04(2.2), the length of time necessary for the hearing of the motion, judicial preparation time necessary, and any other directions that may be required; and

3. the judge hearing the case conference has directed that a motion date be booked, bearing in mind that it is expected that the case conference judge will hear the motion.

Applications that require some oral evidence are handled in the same manner as motions for summary judgment.

Adjournments and Settlements

Once a date has been set, the matter is expected to go ahead. Adjournments are granted in only the most exceptional circumstances. If an adjournment cannot be avoided, you must advise the Commercial List Office at the earliest opportunity in order to permit staff to reschedule the list so that time is not wasted. Counsel waiting on standby can be alerted that their matter may be scheduled, on short notice, in the vacated time slot resulting from the adjournment.

If a case has been adjourned so that settlement discussions can continue and the case is not settled within a reasonable time, a report must be made to advise the court of the status of the discussions. The report must be made within 30 days after the adjournment and may be made in court, in chambers, or by letter, depending on which method is most appropriate in the circumstances.

Cases may be scheduled to be heard on a standby basis for a particular date. When a case is listed in this way, the parties should be prepared to proceed on short notice because they may get a call from the court office telling them to appear if their matter is next on the list for that day.

Case Management and Case Settlement

Case management under Rule 77 does not apply to matters on the Commercial List. However, the operation of the list is akin to informal case management. It is expected that the same judge will hear the matter through to completion. This means that if there is to be a motion on an important matter, the continuing judge must be contacted in writing by counsel in advance so that the matter can be scheduled before that judge wherever possible. The letter advising the judge of the need for a hearing on a particular issue in the case must contain a list of times when the lawyers are available to deal with the issue.

Sometimes a case-managed matter on the regular list is transferred to the Commercial List, or a party may want a Commercial List matter to be case managed and will bring a motion requesting that direction from the judge. In such instances, the matter will be case managed, and there is a provision in the practice direction for a scheduling conference. The conference is held in order to develop a plan for the timely processing of the case through the list.

A case conference is also held no later than a month after discoveries are completed. The purpose of the conference is to monitor the progress of the case and make efforts to settle it before trial. The plaintiff or the applicant has the responsibility of arranging the conference. The plaintiff then confers with the other parties and the court to determine a mutually agreeable date.

There is no mandatory mediation on the Commercial List. However, at any time the case management judge, on the consent of the parties, may refer any issue for alternative dispute resolution. If alternative dispute resolution is ordered on a particular case, the parties must keep the case management judge apprised of the progress of the matter while it is in such resolution.

Pretrial conferences may be scheduled for entire cases or for particular issues within a case. At least five days before the conference, each party must deliver a pretrial brief to all the other parties. The brief must contain the following:

- a concise statement of facts, including the agreed facts and admissions;
- a concise summary of the issues where necessary;

- any outstanding procedural issues;
- the current settlement position of each party; and
- an estimate of the trial time, including a list of witnesses with a time estimate for the oral testimony of each witness.

A time-management conference must be arranged by the lawyers at least two months before trial to deal with making arrangements for the trial or hearing.

Materials for Use of the Court at the Hearing

All materials that are required by the court must be filed within the times prescribed by the Rules for your particular type of hearing. However, the court encourages filing of documents as early as possible. The moving party's material must be filed seven days (excluding holidays) before the hearing, and the responding party's material must be filed four days (excluding holidays) before the hearing.

In addition to our discussion below about the nature of the contents of the various materials, a detailed list of the guidelines for the materials to be filed for the use of the courts can be found in the practice direction at paragraphs 50 to 58. You should refer to this list in conjunction with this portion of the text.

Commercial cases can be voluminous, and in order to avoid huge files being carted around from the filing office to the courtroom, parties are expected to notify court staff of the specific materials they want to use at hearings. In addition, in an effort to maintain huge files in an easily accessible manner, the court suggests that counsel coordinate a common numbering scheme for the various records, transcripts, factums, authorities, and other materials intended for use by the judge. Usually, the law clerks to counsel for the parties go to the court office before the hearing to ensure that the correct materials are available to the judge.

In addition to the documents and records used for matters on the regular list (for example, records, factums, transcripts, and so on), a Commercial List case may require a **compendium**. A compendium is a type of record that gives an overview of a complex case and organizes the documents to be referred to at the hearing in a way that makes it as easy as possible for the judge to locate them. A compendium usually contains a statement of the relief sought by the party and a copy of any pages from motion records, applications, or other documents that a party intends to rely on. The portions to be referred to should be highlighted. There should be a cover sheet that identifies the documents from which a page or pages have been extracted. The cover sheet should also summarize the general content of the document from which pages have been extracted. If a document is only a few pages long, the entire document may be included in the compendium, but if a document is lengthy and the party wishes to refer to only a portion of it, only the portion to be referred to should be included.

The compendium should also contain the headnotes and the pages of any case authorities on which a party is relying. There is no need to include the entire case in

compendium
summary of material to be referred to at a hearing, designed for easy access by the judge

the compendium, although it should be in the book of authorities. However, it should be noted that there is no need to include some often-argued cases in the book of authorities presented by the parties. The court has prepared a standing book of authorities that contains these commonly-referred-to cases. If a case that a party wants to rely on is in the court's book of authorities, the case does not need to be put into the parties' own book of authorities. A list of the cases included in the court's book of authorities can be found on the website of the Ontario Superior Court of Justice. It is important to check the site for any additions or deletions because it is subject to change as new cases are decided and older cases overturned.

All of these materials should be placed in a loose-leaf binder. All of the photocopies must be clear. The binder contents should be kept to a minimum, and wherever possible the parties should prepare a joint compendium.

If the evidence is complex or technical, the court encourages the use of diagrams, charts, lists of persons involved, point-form chronologies, and other summaries to assist in clarifying the issues and the parties. For trials, the court asks that sworn witness statements be used to replace examination-in-chief, in whole or in part, where appropriate. Statements must be exchanged with all parties well in advance of the hearing. The maker of a statement must be available at the trial for cross-examination on the statement unless the court has ordered otherwise.

In addition, draft orders should be prepared and presented by counsel for signing at the end of the hearing. Counsel for the moving party, or counsel for the plaintiff, must assist court staff in preparing the order by presenting a draft for the judge to edit. In order to facilitate the judge's editing, an electronic version of the draft order, should be presented to the court office along with hard copy of the draft, any handwritten endorsement of the judge, or a copy of the dictation media. Sometimes judges' handwritten endorsements can be difficult to read. If the person drafting the order has difficulty reading the endorsement, any illegible parts should be highlighted on the copy of the endorsement so that the judge can clarify the wording of the decision.

There are several model orders or templates related to matters that are heard on the Commercial List that may be found on the website of the Superior Court of Justice at http://www.ontariocourts.ca/scj/practice/practice-directions/toronto/#Commercial_List_Forms. These include a standard template receivership order, a model receiver discharge order form, and an approval and vesting order form. Other model orders or templates may be added from time to time, so it is a good idea to check this site regularly for updated information and guidelines related to the Commercial List.

In addition to the above, if a party wishes to rely on the evidence of an expert witness, they must comply with Rule 53.03. They must also advise the witness of the duty of an expert set out in Rule 4.1. A more detailed discussion of these rules may be found in Chapter 16.

Reasons for Decision

Once the judge has made an order or decision on a matter before the court, the lawyers must prepare a typed draft of the order for editing by the judge, along with an electronic version of the draft and a copy of the judge's endorsement or written version of the order. The copy of the endorsement must highlight any portion of the judge's endorsement that was difficult to read so that the judge can clarify and ensure that there is no problem with the final version of the order. For information on how to prepare an order, refer to Chapter 17.

Costs

The court will likely award and fix costs at the end of the hearing of a matter. Therefore, you must prepare a costs outline according to Rule 57.01(6) for the lawyer to bring with him or her to the hearing. Preparation of a costs outline is dealt with in Chapter 18.

Protocol Concerning Court-to-Court Communications in Cross-Border Cases

The Commercial List has seen a proliferation of cross-border proceedings, particularly in relation to insolvency and corporate restructuring. As a result, a set of guidelines called "Guidelines Applicable to Court-to-Court Communications in Cross-Border Cases," drawn up by the American Law Institute, has been approved for use in cross-border matters on the Commercial List. The guidelines provide cooperative procedures for insolvency proceedings and other types of commercial disputes involving cross-border proceedings where communications between the courts in the different jurisdictions might facilitate in harmonizing proceedings to help ensure consistent results and increase efficiency. They are not automatically applied, but will be used in specific cases and notice will be given to the parties.

Although the guidelines were prepared for court-to-court communications between courts in Canada and the United States, the Commercial List has also endorsed their application in court-to-court communications between Canada and other countries, and between Ontario and the other provinces and territories. They are to apply only in a manner that is consistent with the *Rules of Civil Procedure* and the practice in Ontario.

The guidelines are not meant to be static, but are meant to be adapted and modified to fit the circumstances of individual cases, and to change and evolve as experience is gained from working with them.

The guidelines may be viewed and downloaded at http://www.iiiglobal.org/component/jdownloads/?task=view.download&cid=1506 or http://www.ali.org/doc/Guidelines.pdf.

CHAPTER SUMMARY

This chapter provided an overview of the practice direction that outlines the procedure followed for cases on the Commercial List. The Commercial List is a specialized list of corporate and commercial cases that are dealt with through an informal case management process that allows for a speedy and efficient flow of cases through the court. Except for bankruptcy cases, which must go on the Commercial List, the use of the list is voluntary.

The practice direction works with the *Rules of Civil Procedure* and adds to the regular procedure for cases on the Commercial List. Pleadings are prepared in the same manner as regular pleadings, but the title of proceedings must appear as follows: "The Superior Court of Justice— Commercial List."

KEY TERM

compendium, 577

REFERENCES

American Law Institute, *Guidelines Applicable to Court-to-Court Communications in Cross-Border Cases* (Philadelphia: American Law Institute, 2003), http://www.ali.org/doc/Guidelines.pdf.

Bank Act, SC 1991, c. 46, as amended.

Bankruptcy and Insolvency Act, RSC 1985, c. B-3.

Business Corporations Act, RSO 1990, c. B.16.

Canada Business Corporations Act, RSC 1985, c. C-44.

Companies' Creditors Arrangement Act, RSC 1985, c. C-36.

Credit Unions and Caisses Populaires Act, 1994, SO 1994, c. 11.

Limited Partnerships Act, RSO 1990, c. L.16.

Pension Benefits Act, RSO 1990, c. P.8.

Personal Property Security Act, RSO 1990, c. P.10.

Rules of Civil Procedure, RRO 1990, reg. 194.

Securities Act, RSO 1990, c. S.5.

Winding-up and Restructuring Act, RSC 1985, c. W-11.

REVIEW QUESTIONS

1. What matters may be heard on the Commercial List?

2. Where are Commercial List matters issued?

3. If a matter is placed on the regular list and a party wants to have it transferred to the Commercial List, what is the procedure?

4. How do you obtain a hearing date for a Commercial List matter?

5. When you are preparing a motion for hearing on the Commercial List and no date has yet been set, what date do you put on the notice of motion?

6. What is the proper procedure for adjourning a matter on the Commercial List?

7. What material is required for a pretrial hearing?

8. What is the purpose of a compendium?

Glossary

A

absentee person whose rights or interests are being determined in a proceeding and whose whereabouts are unknown

action one of the two procedures by which a civil matter is commenced in the Superior Court; the other such procedure is an application

active data data currently in use in the database

advisement "taking it under advisement" means to not answer the question now, but to think about whether you will answer the question later

affiant person who swears an affidavit

affidavit written statement setting out the evidence of the person who swears or affirms its contents are true

alternative dispute resolution term used to describe various ways of settling disputes without going to court, including arbitration, mediation, and conciliation

appeal as of right appeal that a party has a legal right to bring and for which leave to appeal is not required

appellant party that commences an appeal

appellate court the Court of Appeal or the Divisional Court

application one of the two procedures by which a civil matter is commenced in the Superior Court; the other such procedure is an action

archival data older versions of data that have been stored or archived on a database system

assessment of costs a costs order made by a judge where the actual amount of the costs is determined at a separate hearing by an assessment officer

assignee person to whom rights, usually contract benefits, are granted by an assignor

assignor person who grants contract rights to an assignee

attendance money formerly called conduct money, composed of the *per diem* witness fee and an amount for transportation and lodging in accordance with Tariff A

B

backsheet part of every court document, it contains the name, LSUC number, address, and telephone and fax numbers of the lawyer who prepared the document, the short title of proceedings, the court and court file number, the fax number of the person to be served (if known), and a large space reserved for court officials to make entries on

bill of costs list of allowable fees and disbursements that is used by an assessment officer to assess a litigant's costs after the litigant is successful in obtaining judgment; differs from an account because it does not include all fees charged to a client

boilerplate standard wording that is part of every copy of a particular type of document

C

carriage responsibility for a file or a case

case conference conference managed by the case management judge or master, who controls timetables and settles all procedural matters

case management judge or master court official assigned to each case-managed case to ensure court control over the case on its way to trial

cause of action legal right to sue to obtain a legal remedy

Children's Lawyer official of the Ontario Ministry of the Attorney General whose office oversees the rights of some minors involved in civil litigation and custody disputes

chose in action intangible personal property whose value lies in what it represents

class proceedings fund public fund of the Law Foundation of Ontario, administered by the Law Society of Upper Canada, to provide funding for the costs of class actions that otherwise might be beyond the financial reach of the parties

co-defendant one defendant in a multi-defendant proceeding

common law law that is made by judges following precedents set by higher courts; often called "case law"

compendium summary of material to be referred to at a hearing, designed for easy access by the judge

contingency fee fee payable to a lawyer only if he or she wins the case for a client

contracting state country that is a signatory to a contract or convention

counterclaim claim made by the defendant in the main action against the plaintiff or against the plaintiff and other persons

court of first instance court that made a decision that is under appeal

cross-examination series of questions asked of a witness by a lawyer for a party adverse in interest to the party that called the witness

crossclaim claim brought by one defendant whom the plaintiff is suing against another defendant whom the plaintiff is suing

crossclaiming defendant defendant in the main action who commences a crossclaim against one or more of the other defendants in that action

D

damages compensation awarded by a court for harm done

defendant on the crossclaim defendant in the main action against whom a crossclaim is brought

deponent person who makes an affidavit

disbursements amounts lawyers pay on behalf of clients to third parties that lawyers can recover from clients

disbursements out-of-pocket expenses incurred by a lawyer for fees and services paid to others as part of proceeding with a case

discovery process that occurs after close of pleadings in which parties obtain more information about each other's cases before trial

document book a bound book of all the documents that a party intends to introduce into evidence at trial; it is sometimes referred to as a book of documents

draw an adverse inference make a factual determination that is contrary to the interests of a party

E

e-discovery a term used to describe discovery of documents where the discovery procedures primarily involve the collection and production of information that is stored electronically

endorsement judge's handwritten order or judgment from which a successful party is expected to prepare a formal draft of the order or judgment

estate administrator person appointed by a court to administer an estate where there is no will or where the appointment of an executor is ineffective

estoppel term indicating that a witness is bound by his or her original position and evidence and cannot later take a contrary position

examination-in-chief series of questions asked of a witness by the lawyer for the party who called the witness

executor person appointed by the maker of a will to administer an estate under the provisions of the will; a female executor is sometimes called an executrix

exemplary damages damages over and above the plaintiff's actual loss, paid to compensate the plaintiff for hurt feelings or mental stress caused by the defendant's particularly outrageous behaviour

F

factum document that sets out the facts, statutes, and cases that a party relies on to obtain a favourable decision

fees payment to lawyers for services rendered

fiduciary relationship one-sided relationship where one party relies on the other party's honesty and advice given in the reliant party's best interests

final order order that resolves all of the outstanding issues between the parties

fixing costs making an order that a specific party pay a specific amount of costs

G

garnishment notice directed to a third party who owes money to a defendant as a means of enforcing a judgment

general damages monetary damages for pain and suffering that cannot be determined on the basis of a formula

general heading heading on all court documents that identifies the court, the parties, and the status of the parties

I

impecunious insolvent

interlocutory order order that resolves only a particular issue in the proceeding; it does not resolve all the issues between the parties

issuing official commencement of court proceedings whereby documents that are originating processes are signed by the registrar, dated, sealed with a court seal, and given a file number

J

join (a party or claim) add a party to an existing proceeding

joinder describes the process of adding a party or claim to an existing proceeding

judgment *in personam* judgment that is binding only on the parties to the proceeding

judgment *in rem* judgment that is binding on everyone, whether a party to the proceeding in which the judgment is pronounced or not

judgment-proof unlikely to be able to pay any amount of a judgment

jurat part of an affidavit that appears at the bottom on the left side of the page and begins with the words "Sworn (or affirmed) before me"

L

law of equity a type of law developed several hundred years ago in England wherein judges, rather than following precedents, look at the issues in a case and apply certain principles to ensure a fair outcome

lawyer of record lawyer recognized by the court as the legal representative of a party in a proceeding

leading a witness asking a witness a question that suggests the answer

leave of the court permission of the court to take a procedural step

limitation period specified time within which court proceedings must be commenced

limited scope retainer a retainer where a lawyer performs some but not all legal services for a client

litigation guardian competent adult who directs and takes responsibility for the litigation of a legally disabled party, such as a minor, an absentee, or a mentally disabled person

M

main action primary case brought by the plaintiff against the defendant

mandatory mediation process in which disputants are required to allow a neutral third party to facilitate their communication and assist them in negotiating a settlement

master minor judicial official with limited jurisdiction to hear and decide specific legal issues identified by the Rules or a statute

mediation process whereby a neutral third party facilitates communication between disputants and assists them in negotiating a solution

metadata information about how data was routed, stored, or transmitted—its "travel" history

motion proceeding within the main proceeding to settle an issue, usually procedural and usually one that has arisen prior to trial

N

narrow questions questions in which the interviewer tries to elicit specific information

non-pecuniary non-monetary

notice of action document informing defendants that they have been sued

O

official examiner individual who is licensed to operate a business to conduct out-of-court examinations, such as cross-examinations on affidavits and discoveries

open-ended questions questions that allow the persons interviewed to choose what they want to talk about to the interviewer

order generic term used in the *Rules of Civil Procedure* to describe commands issued by courts on motions and at trials

originating process first document in a lawsuit that tells parties that they are being sued

P

partial indemnity usual order for costs, based on a cost grid that establishes hourly rates for tariff items listed in the grid; provides less than full recovery for the client

pecuniary of monetary value

perfecting an appeal taking all the necessary procedural steps to ensure that an appeal is ready to be heard

practice direction instructions set out by a chief justice to inform lawyers about special procedures that must be followed in particular courts as a result of administrative needs

principle of proportionality requires that the time spent on and the expense of a lawsuit be in proportion to the value of the case that is at stake for the parties

pro bono abbreviation of the Latin term *pro bono publico*, meaning "for the public good," used where a lawyer takes on a case without charging a fee as part of a duty to see that justice is done

punitive damages damages in the nature of a fine paid to the plaintiff when the defendant's behaviour has been particularly outrageous

R

reference judicial proceeding used when it is necessary to delve into an issue in detail before a decision can be reached

refresh the retainer make a further deposit against future fees as a case progresses

refusal the refusal to answer a question at all; when a party refuses to answer a question, a reason should be given for not answering

request to admit document in which one party requires the other to admit the truth of a fact or the authenticity of a document

res judicata Latin phrase meaning that a matter decided by a court is final and incapable of being relitigated in a subsequent proceeding

residual data previous versions of data not currently in use including deleted data

respondent party that answers or defends against an appeal

retainer contract between a lawyer and client describing the services to be provided by the lawyer and the terms of payment by the client; also refers to a cash deposit to be used by a lawyer to pay future fees and disbursements as they are incurred

return date the date on which the motion will be heard by the court

return of a motion day on which a motion is "returned" to court for a hearing; the hearing date is also referred to as "the return date"

reverse search a reverse search allows you to submit an address, telephone number, or email address to obtain the name of a resident or subscriber

S

service process by which documents are brought to the attention of a party in accordance with the Rules or a court order

setting an action down for trial procedure that a party must follow in order to have its case placed on the trial list

sheriff official appointed by the provincial government to assist in various court-related functions, such as the enforcement of orders and judgments

sittings a time period during which a specific court may hear cases

special damages monetary damages that are specific, ascertainable, and measured on an objective basis; sometimes referred to as out-of-pocket expenses

stay proceedings stop proceedings for a given or indefinite period, pending the fulfillment of a condition, without dismissing the proceedings

stayed a legal proceeding may be stopped from proceeding further, or stayed by a judge, until one of the parties does something they are obliged to do; for example, a plaintiff who is suing using an unregistered business name will have the proceeding stayed until he or she proves that the name has been registered as legally required

subrogated right the legal right that a person (or corporation) has when he or she pays someone's debt to recover that money from the debtor

substantial indemnity costs scale, usually used as a punitive costs award, that results in near indemnity for the winner on a dollar-for-dollar basis

summary proceedings proceedings designed to be conducted quickly and with reduced formality

summons to a witness order of a court telling the person named on the summons to attend a trial and give evidence

T

testimony oral evidence given by a witness

third-party claim claim brought by a defendant in the main action against a person who is not already a party to the main action

title of proceedings part of the general heading that identifies the parties and their status in a lawsuit

transcript written record of proceedings transcribed word for word

trial list list kept by the registrar in each courthouse of cases that are ready for trial

trial record bound set of documents prepared by the party setting the action down for trial and containing the pleadings of all parties, any relevant orders, all notices, and certificates

trier of fact judge or jury whose job is to determine the facts of the case from the evidence

true copy copy of an original document that is like the original in every particular, including copies of alterations, signatures, and court file numbers; signatures or other handwritten parts of the original are usually inside quotation marks on the copy

truing up making a handmade copy of a document at the court counter, usually by adding a seal and the registrar's signature inside quotation marks, by hand, to a photocopy of the original document

U

undefended action an action in which no statement of defence is delivered

undertaking when you cannot answer right now but will undertake to check on a matter and give an answer later

unincorporated association association of persons formed to carry out a specific purpose and not formally incorporated

V

***viva voce* evidence** oral evidence

W

without prejudice term used, usually in correspondence, to indicate that an offer or admission cannot be used against its maker, admitted in evidence, or disclosed to the court

wood-shedded prepared for later cross-examination by an opposing lawyer

writ of seizure and sale order from a court to a sheriff to enforce the court's order by seizing and selling the defendant's property and holding the proceeds to satisfy the judgment debt to the plaintiff; also known as a writ of execution

Index